Lecture Notes in Artificial Intelligence 1328

Subseries of Lecture Notes in Computer Science
Edited by J. G. Carbonell and J. Siekmann

Lecture Notes in Computer Science
Edited by G. Goos, J. Hartmanis and J. van Leeuwen

Springer
Berlin
Heidelberg
New York
Barcelona
Budapest
Hong Kong
London
Milan
Paris
Santa Clara
Singapore
Tokyo

Christian Retoré (Ed.)

Logical Aspects of Computational Linguistics

First International Conference, LACL '96
Nancy, France, September 23-25, 1996
Selected Papers

Springer

Series Editors
Jaime G. Carbonell, Carnegie Mellon University, Pittsburgh, PA, USA
Jörg Siekmann, University of Saarland, Saarbrücken, Germany

Volume Editor

Christian Retoré
INRIA Lorraine & CRIN-C.N.R.S.
615 rue du jardin botanique, BP 101
F-54602 Villers lès Nancy cedex, France
E-mail: retore@loria.fr

Cataloging-in-Publication Data applied for

Die Deutsche Bibliothek - CIP-Einheitsaufnahme

Logical aspects of computational linguistics : first international conference ; selected papers / LACL '96, Nancy, France, April 23 - 25, 1996. Christian Retore (ed.). - Berlin ; Heidelberg ; New York ; Barcelona ; Budapest ; Hong Kong ; London ; Milan ; Paris ; Santa Clara ; Singapore ; Tokyo : Springer, 1997
(Lecture notes in computer science ; Vol. 1328 : Lecture notes in artificial intelligence)
ISBN 3-540-63700-1

CR Subject Classification (1991): F.4, F.3, I.2.7, I.2.3, J.5

ISBN 3-540-63700-1 Springer-Verlag Berlin Heidelberg New York

Typesetting: Camera ready by author
SPIN 10645624 06/3142 – 5 4 3 2 1 0 Printed on acid-free paper

Preface

This volume contains selected papers of the first international conference on Logical Aspects of Computational Linguistics, held in Nancy, France, from September 23 to 25, 1996.[1] A general introduction by some members of the committee explains the relevance of developing a conference on this topic, situates the papers, and provides an account of the discussions, namely, *New syntaxes for linguistic theories*, *Logical aspects of the minimalist program*, and *Logical semantics*.

The volume contains eighteen selected papers and four invited papers. There were forty-four submissions, their overall quality was high, and selection was difficult. The programme committee is very grateful to everyone who submitted a paper and to all the referees listed overleaf for their essential assistance and generously given time. Let us also thank the participants for the pleasant and stimulating atmosphere during the meeting.

The committee is especially grateful to the invited speakers, namely, Jean-Yves GIRARD,[2] Aravind K. JOSHI, Marcus KRACHT, Dale MILLER, and Edward STABLER (respectively from Marseilles, Philadelphia, Berlin, Philadelphia, and Los Angeles). Indeed, not only did they accept our invitation and give their lectures, but they also substantially contributed to the conference, in particular to the discussions.

Finally we wish to thank the two institutions under one roof that co-organized this event, namely INRIA-Lorraine and CRIN-C.N.R.S., as well as the sponsors of this event: *France-Télécom CNET*, *Rank Xerox Research Center*, *l'Institut National Polytechnique de Lorraine*, *l'Université Henri Poincaré*, *La Région Lorraine*, and *La Communauté Urbaine du Grand Nancy*.

More personally, I wish to thank the members of the programme committee and the organizing committee, listed overleaf, for their hard work and support, as well as Roger Hindley, Claude Kirchner, and Pierre Lescanne, who gave me precious advice, not to forget my research project without whom nothing would have happened, CALLIGRAMME (INRIA-Lorraine & CRIN-C.N.R.S.).[3]

Nancy, July 1997 Christian Retoré

[1] The idea of this conference germinated during a workshop we organized in September 1995 on the same topic, whose selected papers are to be published in the January 1998 isssue of the *Journal of Logic, Language and Information*.

[2] His contribution, *Introduction to linear logic*, is not included in this volume, but Jean-Yves Girard recently published an introduction to linear logic: *Linear logic: its syntax and semantics*. In J.-Y. Girard, Y. Lafont and L. Regnier (Eds.) *Advances in Linear Logic*, volume 222 of *London Mathematical Society Lecture Notes*. Cambridge University Press, 1995. pp. 1–42

[3] CALLIGRAMME, *Logique linéaire, réseaux de démonstration et grammaires catégorielles*: D. Bechet, Ph. de Groote (group leader), F. Lamarche, A. Lecomte, S. Malecki, J.-Y. Marion, G. Perrier, N. Pierre (secretary), C. Retoré.

Programme Committee

V. Michele Abrusci	Università di Roma tre
Patrick Blackburn	Universität des Saarlandes, Saarbrücken
Marc Dymetman	Rank Xerox Research Center, Grenoble
Mark Johnson	Brown University, Providence
Alain Lecomte	Université Grenoble 2 & INRIA-Lorraine
Michael Moortgat	OTS, Universiteit Utrecht
Glyn V. Morrill	Universitat Politècnica de Catalunya, Barcelona
Aarne Ranta	Helsingin Yliopisto
Christian Retoré (Chair)	INRIA-Lorraine & CRIN-CNRS, Nancy
Eric Villemonte de la Clergerie	INRIA-Rocquencourt

Additional Reviewers

José L. Balcázar
François Barthélémy
Kalyan Basu
Denis Bechet
Francine Blanchet-Sadri
Joachim Gabarró
Bertrand Gaiffe
Philippe de Groote
Herman Hendriks
Miki Hermann
Barbara Heyd
Hélène Kirchner
François Lamarche
Bernard Lang
Denis Lugiez
Sophie Malecki
Richard Oehrle
Guy Perrier
Anne Reboul
Laurent Romary
Michael Rusinowitch
Klaus Schulz
Pascale Sébillot

Organizing Committee

Denis Bechet, **Anne-Lise Charbonnier**, **Philippe de Groote**, **François Lamarche**, **Bernard Lang** *, **Guy Perrier**, **Nathalie Pierre**, **Christian Retoré** (Chair), **Armelle Savary**
INRIA-Lorraine & CRIN-CNRS, Nancy — * : INRIA, Rocquencourt

Table of Contents

Invited papers

Selected papers

Logical Aspects of Computational Linguistics: An Introduction

Patrick Blackburn	(Universität des Saarlandes, Saarbrücken)
Marc Dymetman	(Rank-Xerox Research Center, Grenoble)
Alain Lecomte	(Université Grenoble 2)
Aarne Ranta	(Helsingin Yliopisto)
Christian Retoré	(INRIA-Lorraine, Nancy)
Eric Villemonte de la Clergerie	(INRIA-Rocquencourt)

Abstract. The papers in this collection are all devoted to single theme: logic and its applications in computational linguistics. They share many themes, goals and techniques, and any editorial classification is bound to highlight some connections at the expense of other. Nonetheless, we have found it useful to divide these papers (somewhat arbitrarily) into the following four categories: **logical semantics of natural language**, **grammar and logic**, **mathematics with linguistic motivations**, and **computational perspectives**. In this introduction, we use this four-way classification as a guide to the papers, and, more generally, to the research agenda that underlies them. We hope that the reader will find it a useful starting point to the collection.

1 Logical semantics of natural language

Logical semantics of natural language is a diverse field that draws on many disciplines, including philosophical and mathematical logic, linguistics, computer science, and artificial intelligence. Probably the best way to get a detailed overview is to consult the many excellent survey articles in [19]; this Handbook is likely to be the standard reference for work on logic in linguistics for some time to come. In the space of a short introduction like this, it is difficult to give an accurate impression of such a diverse area; nonetheless, by approaching the subject historically, we can at least hope to give a sense of the general direction the field is taking, and indicate how the articles on logical semantics to be found in this collection fit in with recent developments.

Modern logic begins with the work of Frege, and so does logical semantics. His celebrated Begriffsschrift [50] was not only one of the first formal treatments of quantified logic, it also discussed the structure of natural language quite explicitly. Moreover, Frege's work inspired others to attempt explicit logical treatments of natural language semantics: Carnap [25] and Reichenbach [98] are important (and still widely referenced) examples. Nonetheless, in spite of such impressive precedents, it is usual to regard the work of Montague as the starting point of the truly modern phase of formal semantics. Why is this?

Montague was a highly original thinker, and his three seminal articles on natural language semantics (*English as a formal language*, *The proper treatment of quantification in ordinary English*, and *Universal Grammar*, all in [116]) synthesise the best of what had gone before (namely, the possible worlds semantics of Carnap [25] and Kripke [72], together with the higher order logic of Church [41]) with a potent new idea: semantic construction need not be a hit-or-miss affair that relies on intuition. Precise — and indeed, reasonably straightforward — algorithms can be given which translate interesting chunks of natural language into logical formalisms. Moreover (as Montague proved in a very general way in *Universal Grammar*) if the translation procedure obeys certain natural rules, the semantics of the logical formalism induces the desired semantics on the natural language input. From the perspective of the 1990s it can be difficult to appreciate how revolutionary Montague's vision was — but this is largely because his insights are now a standard part of every working semanticist's toolkit. To be sure, semanticists rarely work with Montague's type theory any more, and Montague himself might well have been surprised by the wide range of semantic issues now addressed using logical methods. Nonetheless, the vision that drives modern logical semantics is essentially Montague's: it is possible to model an important part of natural language semantics using logical tools, and the construction of semantic representations is algorithmic.

Montague's work appeared in the late 1960s and the early 1970s. The 1970s were, by and large, a period during which his ideas were assimilated by the linguistic community. Thanks largely to the efforts of Partee (like [92]), Montague's logical methods (which linguists found strange and new, and often intimidating) slowly gained acceptance. During this period, Montague's ideas were extended to cover a wider range of linguistic phenomena; the investigations into the temporal semantics of natural language recorded in [45] by Dowty are a nice example of such work.

If the key themes of the 1970s were "assimilation" and "development" the key theme of the 1980s was "diversity". For a start, two new approaches to logical semantics were developed: Situation Semantics of Barwise and others [15] and Discourse Representation Theory of Kamp and others [68,60,69]. Like Montague semantics, Situation Semantics offered a model theoretic perspective on natural language semantics, but it changed the ground rules in seemingly radical ways. For a start, whereas Montague's logic was *total* (that is, every statement had to be either true or false, and not both, at every possible pair of possible worlds and times), Barwise and Perry took seriously the idea that real situations were often "small", partially specified, chunks of reality. Accordingly, it seemed appropriate to drop the assumption that every sentence had to be either true or false in every situation — hence situation semantics naturally leads to the use of *partial* logics. Furthermore, stipulating the conditions under which sentences were true was no longer to be the central explanatory idea in semantics. Rather, meaning was to be viewed as a relation between situations, a relation that emerged from the interplay of complex constraints.

The agenda set by Discourse Representation Theory (DRT) seemed, at first, less revolutionary. Essentially, DRT proposed using an intermediate level of representation in a more essential way than Montague's work did. Although Montague made use of translations into an intermediate level of logical representation, in his work this level is a convenience that is, in principle, eliminable. Kamp and Heim showed that by making heavier — indeed, intrinsic — use of this intermediate level, interesting treatments could be given of temporal phenomena, and a number of troublesome problems involving quantifier scopes could be resolved. This may sound reasonably innocuous — but actually DRT has proved to be far more genuinely subversive to received semantic ideas than Situation Semantics. For a start, the idea that an intermediate level of representation is intrinsic to meaning is both interesting and highly controversial philosophically. Moreover, from DRT stems one of key words of modern semantics: *dynamics*. Thinking of semantics in terms of DRT leads fairly directly to an interesting — and very different — conception of meaning: *meanings as functions which update contexts with new information*. This essentially computational metaphor has developed into an important perspective for looking at semantics; [58] by Groenendijk and Stokhof is a prominent example of such work.

While DRT and Situation Semantics are perhaps the two key new ideas that emerged in the 1980s, a number of other themes emerged then that continue to play an important role. For a start, linguists slowly became aware of other traditions in logical semantics (the game theoretic approach instigated by Hintikka is perhaps the most important example, see [105]). Moreover, perhaps for the first time, semantic investigations began feeding important ideas and questions back into logic itself; the development of generalised quantifier theory by Barwise and Cooper or van Benthem [14,16] is an important example of this.

So where do we stand in the 1990s? Here the key theme seems to be "integration". At the logical level, there seems to be an emerging consensus that what is needed are frameworks in which the insights gathered in previous work can be combined in a revealing way. For example, work in Situation Semantics and DRT has made clear that ideas such as partiality and dynamism are important — but are there well-behaved logical systems which capture such ideas? Some interesting answers are emerging here: for example, Muskens in [90] shows how the insights concerning partiality and situations can be integrated into classical type theories that are simpler (and far more elegant) than Montague's, while Ranta in [97] shows that constructive type theory offer a uniform logical setting for exploring many current problems in logical semantics, including those raised by DRT. A second theme that is emerging is the use of inference as a tool for solving semantic puzzles. This is a natural step to take: one of the advantage of doing semantics in well understood formalisms (such as various kinds of type theory) is that the inference mechanisms these formalisms possess offer plausible mechanisms for modeling further phenomena. A third — and crucial — theme is how best to link all this semantical and logical work with the new and sophisticated approaches to syntax (and phonology) that have been developed over the fifteen or so years. The syntax-semantics interface is likely to be a focus of research in coming years.

Bearing these general remarks in mind, let's consider the individual contributions.

Sloppy identity by Claire GARDENT, exploits for semantic purposes the existence of Higher Order Unification (HOU) algorithms for classical type theory. The key linguistic idea is that a wide variety of sloppy interpretation phenomena can be seen as arising from a semantic constraint on parallel structures. As the author shows, by making use of HOU — essentially a powerful pattern-matching mechanism — a precise theory of sloppy interpretation can be given for such parallel constructions. Among other things, this theory captures the interaction of sloppy/strict ambiguity with quantification and binding.

The papers *Vagueness and type theory*, by Pascal BOLDINI, and *A natural language explanation for formal proofs*, by Yann COSCOY, are both based on constructive type theory, but they use it for very different purposes. Boldini's paper gives an analysis of certain so-called vague predicates, such as "small", which, in addition to creating a problem for logical semantics, have played a role in the philosophical controversy between constructive and classical logic. Coscoy's paper is associated with one of the major computer applications of constructive type theory, proof editors. It explains an algorithm that produces natural language texts to express formal proofs, and discusses some stylistic principles to improve the texts. Coscoy's algorithm is actually available as a part of the latest release of the proof editor Coq [12].

The paper *A belief-centered treatment of pragmatic presupposition*, by Lucia MANARA and Anne DE ROECK, addresses the problem of linguistic presupposition — the phenomenon that the meaningfulness of a sentence may demand the truth of some proposition. For instance, "John's wife is away" presupposes that John has a wife. This problem is approached in terms of the logical calculus of property theory, which provides new ideas for the interference of beliefs with the phenomenon of presupposition.

Whereas the previous four papers essentially exploit in various ways the fact that formal semantics can be done in standard logical systems (be it classical type theory, constructive type theory, or property theory) *Language understanding: a procedural perspective*, Ruth KEMPSON, Wilfried MEYER VIOL and Dov GABBAY is an attempt to view the syntax-semantics interface from a logical perspective. In particular, the authors show how an incremental parser can be formulated using the idea of labeled deductions, aided by a modal logic of finite trees. They argue that this blend of ideas can deal with crossover phenomena in a way that eludes other frameworks.

2 Grammar and logic

The history of the relations between Grammar and Logic is as old as these two fields: we say they descend from the Ancient Greeks or the first grammar of sanskrit by Pāṇini. It is worth noticing in particular that Ancient Indian linguists around the 4th century B.C. had the idea of a concise system of rules (or *sutras*) for describing the formation of words and sentences. Some commentators [108] have argued that such a requirement of economy in the description is the departure point for a scientific study of language. In modern times, we can also refer to the Port-Royal School (17th century) for which it was natural to put a bridge between Grammar and Logic just because the language was supposed to express the logical thought. The reader interested in these aspects of the history of linguistics is referred to, for instance [89,102].

The generativism of the 20th century often compares itself to these traditions, and indeed many features of the Chomskyan program were already met in the ideas of 17th century philosophers as well as those of Indian grammarians, as explained by Chomsky in [35]. The most important similarity is definitely the concept of a finite device for generating an infinite set of sentences and the notion of an explicit procedure for generating grammatical strings. The main difference lies in the tools existing for expressing such ideas at different times. When Chomsky began his research on natural language in the fifties, mathematical logic was sufficiently developed to provide the concepts of *automaton* and *formal grammar* — see e.g. [83] for a survey. As firstly a logician, Chomsky himself helped to develop these concepts and we are indebted to him for a hierarchy of formal languages [30,31] and the relationship between linguistic theory and formal language theory [32,33,40]. Of course the notion of *rule* had no logical status by itself, even if it was possible to make a link with the notion of *sequent* in the Gentzen style presentation of logic, and grammatical symbols were conceived as atomic symbols. So, the link with traditional logic was rather poor.

But some decades before, Polish logicians, the first being Lesniewski, inspired by Husserl's philosophy, had explored the theory of *semantic categories* — see for instance [29] for an history. This had led Ajduckiewicz [8] to the idea of a very simple algorithm to check well-formedness. This algorithm for what Ajduckiewicz called "syntactic connectivity" was based on a "quasi-arithmetic notation for categories". For instance, an intransitive verb was represented by the fractional notation $\frac{s}{n}$ which expresses that in presence of a word of category n, trivial rules of simplification lead to an expression of category s. This was the starting point for *categorial grammar.*

After that, Bar-Hillel added the notion of directionality [10,11], thus making a distinction between s/n and $n\backslash s$ and considered that an expression could belong to several categories as explained in [29]. In 1958, Lambek [74] published his seminal *Mathematics of Sentence Structure*, that presents for the first time an authentic calculus of syntactic categories, defined by a system of axioms and rules and in which it was possible to deduce the set of categories to which an expression belonged. This *calculus of syntactic types* was presented as a sequent calculus and this logical formulation helped in clearly establishing important properties, and in particular the cut-elimination and sub-formula property (see next section).

In the eighties, while logicians studied the mathematical properties of the Lambek calculus (see next section), linguists became interested in categorial systems. Bach [9], Ades and Steedman [7], Dowty [46] recognized their expressive power for linguistic description essentially because of their direct account of the notion of *valency*. Steedman [112], Szabolcsi [114] and Desclés [43] (the latter influenced by a neighbouring school born in the former USSR and led by Shaumyan, that gave rise to the so-called Applicative Grammar [107]) used the relations existing between categorial grammars and *combinators* for expressing *reflexivisation*, *binding*, *gapping*, *coordination of non constituents* and *long-distance dependencies*.

Moortgat thoroughly explored the linguistic description capacities of the Lambek calculus in his book [85] and in [86], resetting in a proper way Montagovian semantics by means of the *Curry-Howard isomorphism* and also giving a description of the relation between the prosodic and the syntactic algebras. From then on, linguistic entities have been considered as triples $< Syn : Phon : Sem >$ where *Syn* is the syntactic part, *Phon* the phonetic part and *Sem* the semantic part of the sign.

At the end of the eighties Girard introduced Linear Logic [53], and the Lambek calculus was recognised as a fragment of non-commutative linear logic [2,103], thus putting a strong connection between syntax (categorial grammar) and logic (proof theory). Indeed Linear Logic provides a neat logical system to describe resource consumption, and, through the unary connectives called "exponentials" or "modalities", neatly relates the Lambek calculus to the classical and intuitionistic logics which are used for semantical descriptions.

But the pure Lambek calculus has many limitations, and several investigations were made in the direction of an enrichment with new connectives. These new connectives, which are different ways of combining grammatical resources, are mainly *modalities*, called "structural", and they have the same rules as those we can find in Modal Logic, or they behave like exponentials in Linear Logic [3]. These modalities were originally introduced by the Edinburgh School [13] and strongly used by Hepple [62] (island constraints) and by Morrill. The latter in [88] gives an impressive account of linguistic phenomena, including *extraction*, *coordination*, *pied-piping*, *prosodic phrasing*... in a grammar expressed in purely logical types.

During the same time, Ranta [97] gave another viewpoint on grammar and semantics based on the Constructive Type Theory of Martin-Löf [82]. Regarding the syntax, this approach is in certain respects more traditional than the afore mentioned advances because it relies on [30]; but is very powerful on the semantic (and even pragmatic) side because of its use of *dependent types*, allowing a proper treatment of dynamic binding (e.g. Geach sentences) and thus going beyond Montague semantics.

Finally, Moortgat in [87] provides the widest survey of *Categorial Type Logics*, including the syntax-semantics interface, multimodality, polymorphism, hybrid architectures and categorial parsing.

Chomsky's program was continued in parallel but we have no room here to trace back the long history of Generativism — one should refer to the main books by Chomsky [30,34–39] or to the introductive textbook [96]. What appears as a curious fact in the end of the nineties is a real convergence between the generativist trend and the categorial one (see below). Of course, on the theoretical side, Pentus [93] demonstrated that Lambek grammars have the same generative power as Context-Free grammars, and this is an important link. But it is only a formal result. From a historical point of view, we are presently witnessing a deep change in Generative Grammar: in the recent minimalist program [39], traditional levels (the deep level and the surface level) and even the X-bar theory are abandoned in favour of a unique system of Generalized Transformations very similar in their spirit to the reduction rules of Categorial Grammar.

Two main points concerning the so-called *Minimalist Program* [39] will be stressed here: one concerning the derivational conception advocated by Chomsky himself and the other the notion of Resource Consumption as it appears in the operations of Feature Checking for which the Generalized Transformation *Move* is required. The notion of a derivational theory is preferred to that of a representational one for many reasons and notably because it allows a better characterization of local phenomena like the satisfaction of the HMC constraint cf. [39, pp. 49–50]. Moreover, it is coherent with the general conception of Minimalism for which it is necessary to avoid all syntactic entities (like *rules*, *representations*, *representation-levels* and so on) which are not absolutely necessary for linguistic description and explanation. In a derivational perspective, only the derivation itself counts as a "representation" for an analysis of a sentence.

In this volume, *Derivational minimalism* by Edward STABLER proposes an attractive formalism to take such a view into account. His formalism provides a formulation for structure-building operations like *Merge* and *Move*, and he shows how to express the fact that such operations are "feature-driven". That means that *Move*, for instance, is applied only when necessary in order to check a feature, weak or strong. The weak/strong distinction is used to describe an opposition between *overt* and *covert* movements in syntax and it provides a parameter for distinguishing various families of natural languages (like SVO, VSO...). This paper also provides formal examples which are of great interest if we wish to compare this formalism to others like for instance *Tree Adjoining Grammars*.

Tree Adjoining Grammars (TAGs), introduced in [65] are present among the papers published here, and for a recent survey on TAGs one should refer to [67,1] for example. They, too, provide an appealing formalism, firstly because it is mathematically a very elegant one and secondly because it has often been explored and its properties regarding complexity and generative power are well-known [66]. One point is mainly dealt with in this volume: its connection with the derivational paradigm. As we said previously, there is a strong connection between Chomsky's Minimalism and Categorial Grammar, and Categorial Grammar could be a good candidate as a framework for Minimalism: for instance, a Generalized Transformation like *Merge* is very close to Cancellation Schemes, so familiar to the categorial grammarian. Nevertheless categorial grammar lacks some important notions which are easily described in (Lexicalized) TAGs like "the notion of an extended domain of locality (EDL)" and the consequent "factoring of recursion from the domain of dependencies (FRD)". Thus, exploring the link between the derivational paradigm (expressed by Linear Logic or Lambek calculus) and TAGs, is also useful for bringing together, as intuition suggests, the derivational paradigm and the minimalist program.

The paper *Tree adjoining grammars in non-commutative linear logic* by V. Michele ABRUSCI, Christophe FOUQUERÉ and Jacqueline VAUZEILLES presents a derivational conception of TAGs. It uses the concept of *proof net* which is an essential ingredient of the proof theory of linear logic. The encoding of substitution and adjunction, mainly uses the *cut-rule* restricted to atomic formulae. Let us recall that the cut-rule is a very particular rule in every logical system with "good properties": it does not provide more theorems than the system does without it, but is a simple way to combine two proofs into one. When using the cut-rule for the TAG purpose, trees are considered as provable sequents in the Non-Commutative Intuitionistic Linear Logic (N-ILL or Lambek calculus) and adjunction as two occurrences of the cut-rule. They thus obtain a complete translation of TAG-grammars into the Lambek calculus — but the notion of grammar they use is not the one defined by Lambek.

The paper *Partial proof trees, resource sensitive logics and syntactic constraints* by Aravind K. JOSHI and Seth KULICK tries to incorporate LTAG notions like ELD and FRD into the categorial framework, thus attempting to produce a new synthesis between LTAG and Categorial Grammar. By doing so, they switch from a notion where lexical entries are *formulae* (as in all the traditions of Categorial Grammar) towards a conception according to which they are pieces of *proofs* (so-called "Partial Proof-Trees"). The standard operations of *substitution* and *adjoining* in TAG are therefore replaced by operations on Partial Proofs, namely: *application*, *stretching* and *interpolation*. As its name indicates, *stretching* consists in duplicating a node in a Partial Proof Tree and inserting a new proof between the two instances. In *interpolation*, the place is reserved for a proof insertion between two nodes generated at the lexical stage. Exactly as in TAG-trees, dependencies can be registered as local relations in initial Proof-Trees. The authors also discuss the differences and proximities between their approach in the setting of Partial Proof Trees and the Proof Net approach, as they call the formalisms advocated in the paper by Abrusci et al., as well as by Lecomte and Retoré [78,79].

The latter viewpoint is reflected in another paper *Pomset logic and variants in natural languages* by Irene SCHENA. The author proposes another view on combining proofs by means of Pomset Logic, an extension of Linear Logic made by Retoré [99,101]. The main difference with Abrusci et al. resides in the fact that the cut-rule is used between general formulae, and also in the essential use of the cut-elimination algorithm. This formalism is particularly relevant for word-order phenomena: when *Cuts* are eliminated, new proof nets are produced, which can be read as giving the correct order of words in a sentence. The author goes deeper in the description of linguistic phenomena by means of this logic: she proposes analysis for topicalized sentences. According to her views, there are initial proof nets which are not associated with lexical entries but used in order to properly connect these entries. We can compare these modules to non-lexical signs (functional ones, associated with I and C) in the Chomskyan theory.

As we can see, these grammatical formalisms share many features: they all try to combine, in a way or another, elementary trees or their representations in some logic. Here Linear Logic is very often referred to because it gives the best account of Resource Consumption. When a feature, or a node, is used for some purpose (like checking agreement or case) it can no longer be used. The interest of Linear Logic is to keep encapsulated such "economy principles" so that we do not have to formulate them separately.

The paper *Inessential features* by Marcus KRACHT present another way, mainly model theoretical, of formulating trees in Logic. Indeed, the first order theory of trees may be axiomatised in Modal Logic. This is what this paper does, in a way similar to [20] or [57]. But Kracht's objective is not only to provide the best way for "talking about trees", it is to go very deep into the key insights of the Minimalist approach, asking when a feature is eliminable from a grammar. This is a way of taking very seriously the intentions of the Chomskyan program. If Chomsky abandons the levels of X-bar theory, it is because he intuitively thinks that such distinctions can be recovered if necessary from the remaining parts of the description. Moreover, another important point shared by all these approaches is *lexicalism*. The question arises of determining exactly what is the price to pay for reaching radical lexicalism. A true lexical theory is one where the computational system only treats features which are introduced at the lexical stage and need no other feature (like BAR, SLASH...). This is the objective that researchers like Stabler and others pursue, but a theoretical study is needed for defining in a precise way the conditions in which some "syntactic" features can be eliminated. Kracht's paper is an answer to this question.

3 Mathematics with linguistic motivations

As often the interplay between two areas of research open new research directions for both. Let us quote here a few interesting purely mathematical/logical questions motivated by linguistic considerations, related to the articles in this volume.

3.1 Formal language theory

The best known connection is certainly Formal Language Theory[1] which as stated above was initiated in the late fifties with the works of Chomsky [31,32] for natural language syntax.

Firstly this was considered as a part of logic, because of its relation to the theory of computability. Nevertheless it soon developed as an extended independent theory, with its own techniques, the major reason being its success for the study of programming languages and compilation. Therefore it is impossible to give a short account of such a wide research field; however the basic notions are by now part of the standard curriculum in computer science. For more advanced notions, the reader is referred to, for instance [104], which is a collection of comprehensive survey papers, the first one being quite introductive and general [83]. Now, let us just select a few topics relevant to this volume.

The classical grammars of Chomsky have been extended to grammars for trees. From a linguistic point of view this clearly makes sense: one is not only interested in the sentences, but also in their analysis into constituents or phrases. Thus tree grammars have been developed, in several ways: for instance one can consider regular trees, the ones generated by a tree automaton (see [52] for a survey), or the trees generated by substitution and adjunction from a finite set of trees (Tree Adjoining Grammars) (see [67] for a survey).

Formal grammars, either for strings or trees, describe a language, by means of a finite set of rules, and are especially useful from an algorithmic perspective. Indeed, a natural aim is to use them to actually parse a sentence. This leads to two mathematical questions. Can we decide whether a sentence is generated by a grammar of a given kind? If so, what is the complexity of the algorithm? For instance, one may decide in less than $O(n^3)$ whether an n-word sentence of n words is generated by a context free grammars.

Unfortunately, this kind of grammar is not sufficient for some syntactical phenomena, and does not handle non purely syntactic information, like morphology (for agreement), semantics etc. Therefore in the eighties, inspired by the Logic Programming formulation of standard grammars, unification grammars have been introduced: LFG [70,106,1], GPSG [51,106,117,1] and HPSG [95,1]. One mathematical problem put forward by these formalisms is the question of the decidability: in general it is undecidable

[1] Given that this conference took place in 1996 in France, let us seize the opportunity to salute the memory of Marcel-Paul Schützenberger (1920-1996). He had been a pioneer in formal language theory, not to mention his other numerous scientific interests. As an example of his work in Formal Language theory, let us just mention the famous paper he wrote with N. Chomsky on context-free languages [40]. He undoubtedly is one of the founders of the French school of Theoretical Computer Science, with M. Nivat and L. Nolin.

whether a sentence may be generated from such a grammar, and this is rather worrying from a computational point of view. Therefore, their logical counterpart, namely feature logics, have been studied [63,28,71] and tools for handling them have been developed like ALE [26], CUF [44], and TFS [119], a major challenge being to isolate a family of logics which would be sufficient for natural language purposes but, nevertheless decidable — and in polynomial time if possible!

But one can also consider less computational descriptions of the set of all languages generated by a particular kind of grammar, to prove properties of families of languages. These declarative descriptions may be either algebraic or model theoretic. The most familiar examples of algebraic description certainly are the regular expressions written with concatenation, union and the Kleene star operation, which describe regular languages. Model theoretic description are probably less well-known, and for a survey the reader is referred to [115]. As an example, a regular language may be viewed as the models of a formula of weak second order logic with a single successor symbol. These descriptive formulations, and the mathematical properties they allow to prove, are especially useful for characterising the expressiveness of the grammars, that is to say the set of languages they correspond to. This has an underlying theoretical linguistic motivation: which class of languages is actually needed for natural language syntax?

Let us give a famous example which stresses the linguistic relevance of non-algorithmic results in formal language theory. It has been *formally* shown that Swiss German is not context-free [109] not by the use of parsing considerations but by the use of algebraic results: the closure of context-free languages under homomorphisms and intersection with regular languages. [2]

In this volume several papers address the aforementioned questions:

Strict LT2 : Regular :: Local : Recognizable by James ROGERS is devoted to tree languages as models of second order formulae. It defines a class of logic formulae such that the tree analyses of context free grammars are exactly the sets definable in this class. Furthermore, this formula explicitly expresses how much smaller this class is than the class of trees generated by tree automata. Incidentally, the research agenda underlying this paper has much in common with that of *Inessential features* by Marcus Kracht. Roger's LT2 is yet another paper for "talking about trees". However, like Kracht, Rogers is interested in far more than simply developing a good descriptive format. The links this papers forges with formal language theory means that his language can be used to analyse the strength of various linguistic theories such as Government and Binding theory or Generalised Phrase Structure Grammar.

Semilinearity as a syntactic invariant by Jens MICHAELIS and Marcus KRACHT shows that actually some natural language, namely Old Georgian is not mildly context sensitive, because of its very particular genitive construction. The argument consists in showing that it is not semi-linear, a property which mildly context sensitive languages have.

A family of decidable logics which supports HPSG-style set and list constructions by Stephen J. HEGNER addresses the important topic of how to define a family of *decidable* feature logics which could support at least some of the key constructs of HPSG. In

[2] This is a strictly stronger result than showing that there is no *sensible* (when correctly bracketing the constituents) context-free grammar generating this language.

HPSG, sets and lists occur in fundamental ways, for example in filler-gap constructions or in the value of the feature COMP-DTRS (*subcategorization principle*). Hegner's paper brings "the only work to treat multisets and lists uniformly within a decidable feature-structure framework". Decidability is proven by mapping the logic into a sorted first-order logic, and then using variants of decidability results in that context.

3.2 Lambek calculus and non-commutative (linear) logic

Even if we take into account all the strange formal systems that have been proposed as "logics", one observes that logics are rarely non-commutative. The calculus introduced by Lambek in the late fifties [74–76] is the notable exception which undoubtedly deserves to be called a logic. It was introduced as a logical formalisation of the categorial grammars of Adjukiewicz and Bar-Hillel [10,11] together with the related calculi. Indeed, this calculus, a plain propositional logic defined by a sequent calculus à la Gentzen, admits cut-elimination and the subformula property, truth value semantics, denotational semantics, and is fairly simple: seven rules, one non-commutative conjunction and two implications (because of the non-commutativity).

The properties of this calculus, once rather isolated from other calculi, are now easily observed and formulated in the linear logic framework. Linear logic was introduced ten years ago by Girard [53] — see [54] for a recent survey and [118] for a textbook. Although it was conceived rather as a logic of computation and communication than for linguistic purposes, it explains the various aspects of logical calculi with restricted structural rules and their relations to the standard intuitionistic or classical logic, via the unary connectives called "exponentials" or "modalities". In this setting one observes the following properties of the Lambek calculus:

- There are no rules of contraction or weakening (aka thinning). This is responsible for the logic to be linear, in other words: the formulae may be viewed as resources, that may not be duplicated or erased. This property of linearity seems actually necessary to have a non-commutative logic, although this probably cannot be proved, because determining what a logic is certainly leads to Byzantine discussions.
- It is a multiplicative calculus, that is to say: in each rule with two premises, the context of the conclusion sequent is obtained by adding the contexts of the two premise sequents. This means that the calculus describes how the resources are combined. The other possibility would be to ask for both contexts to be equal, so the introduced connective would correspond to choice operators, called additive connectives.
- It is an intuitionistic calculus, that is to say there is a single formula on the right hand side. Intuitively, this means that a proof of a sequent may be viewed as a function that takes resources of the types/formulae of the left hand side and returns an object of the type of the conclusion.
- It is a non-commutative calculus. That is to say there is no exchange rule and thus no way to prove the commutativity of the product. This intuitively correspond to the fact that we handle an ordered list of resources.
- Finally, a proof should not contain any sequent without hypothesis. This is a linguistic requirement rather than a logical one: without this extra requirement, the

types of the empty sequence would be all Lambek tautologies, and thus one would not be able to specify that a word requires on its left or right a constituent whose type is a tautology. Fundamentally, it does not affect the logical properties of the calculus, except that, as shown by Zielonka in [120], the Lambek calculus is not finitely axiomatisable (in a Hilbert-style formulation) — see also [80].

This is a typical example of an elegant mathematical structure introduced for linguistic motivations. Indeed, this calculus was introduced as a lexicalised grammar, which logically formalises the Adjuckiewicz Bar-Hillel categorial grammars. The lexicon assigns a formula or type to each word; then analysing a phrase of type T consists in proving T from the lists of the types of the words in the phrase. In this parsing-as-deduction perspective, the subformula property, deduced from the cut-elimination theorem [74–76] is then highly important: it restricts the search space to a finite number of formulae, so this property makes the parsing obviously decidable and guides each step. Another important proof theoretical property of the Lambek calculus is interpolation, established by Roorda in [103], which states that whenever an implication holds there always exists an intermediate formula, whose only atomic formulae are common to the antecedent and consequent. This enables, as shown in this volume, a transformation from one bracketing of a sentence to another, e.g. from the syntagmatic one to the intonational one.

Now how does it relates to linear logic? What is the benefit of such a connection? What mathematical properties, preferably with a linguistic meaning, does it enable us to prove? The basic relation between the Lambek calculus and linear logic is that the Lambek calculus is exactly the multiplicative fragment of non-commutative linear logic. From this fact, the study of the Lambek calculus can benefit from the richer framework of linear logic — see e.g. [100] for a survey.

One of the advantages of linear logic is that it makes explicit the relationship of this calculus to intuitionistic and classical logics. Thus, the simply typed lambda calculus is easily viewed as an extension of the Lambek calculus. This way the semantical representation à la Montague, that is to say a simply typed lambda term, i.e. a proof in intuitionistic logic, has the same structure as a syntactical analysis, i.e. a proof in the Lambek calculus. This enables a particularly simple interface between syntax and semantics [85,88,27], which is especially clear in the proof net syntax [59].

This proof net syntax is precisely another convenient tool provided by linear logic [53,118,54,73]. It is a very compact and elegant notation for proofs in these logical calculi, which avoids, for instance, the so-called spurious ambiguities of categorial grammar analyses [100]. The structure of a proof net is very much like a family of trees, and thus one is able to picture in this setting numerous phenomena studied in the standard linguistic formalisms, usually described by trees; on the logical side they allow easy proofs, of cut-elimination, interpolation etc. As an example of a linguistic outcome, a recent paper [64] shows that using this kind of syntax allows one to measure the understanding complexity of center-embedded relatives. Finally, proof nets also enable the definition of efficient heuristics for parsing. This is especially useful because one exciting open question is the complexity of the parsing, or provability in the Lambek calculus.

Another advantage of having a purely logical calculus is that one may use semantics to prove properties of the calculus. Actually, there are basically two kinds of semantics that may be used: the usual truth valued semantics, for which the completeness theorem holds, and the denotational semantics, i.e., the semantics of proofs.

Denotational semantics was introduced by Scott for the semantics of programming languages and lambda calculus, see e.g. [113], and applies to typed lambda calculus and linear logic see e.g. [56,53,118]. Such a semantics associates a "space" $||F||$ to each formula F, and an object of the space $||F||$ correspond to a proof *up to cut-elimination*. The linguistic meaning of this kind of semantics is yet unclear. Nevertheless in [4] it is used to show the difference between the two analyses of the classical example "every man loves a woman". It should be observed that, as opposed to the general case, the multiplicative fragment of linear logic, quite sufficient for syntactic analysis, admits a complete denotational semantics [81]; this should help in finding a linguistic meaning for denotational semantics.

Truth value semantics, for which logic completeness results usually hold, have been substantially studied in categorial grammar, mainly by Buskowski and van Benthem, [22,23,16–18,24]. For instance, they established completeness with regards to *relational* interpretations and with regards to *monoidal* interpretations see e.g. the section 1 of Martin Emms'paper in this volume. These latter models are very similar to the so-called "phase semantics" of linear logic [53,2,118]. Roughly speaking, these models interpret a formula A as the sets of all phrases of type A, i.e. as a part of a monoid. Somehow these structures formalise the philosophical notion of a category and, technically, they lead to substantial results. The most famous concerns the relation between Lambek grammars and formal language theory. Given a context-free grammar, it is a simple exercise to find a Lambek grammar, even in a small fragment of the Lambek calculus, that generates the same language. Nevertheless it was conjectured by Chomsky in 1963 [33, p. 413] that Lambek grammars defined by the whole Lambek calculus should not go beyond context free languages. After several unsuccessful attempts, this was indeed proved by Pentus in 1993 [93], and the argument extensively uses this kind of models, together with a refinement of the interpolation theorem for the Lambek calculus established in [103].

This result confirmed the intuition: Lambek calculus is too restrictive to describe a linguistically sensible class of formal languages, as also shown in [77] and one should look for extensions of the Lambek calculus — still in a neat logical framework, if possible. A first direction, quite standard from a logical point of view, is to consider fragments of the second order Lambek calculus, i.e. to allow type variable and quantification over them, as developed by Emms [47–49]. For instance the conjunction "and" should received the type $\forall X.\ X\backslash X/X$. This way one goes beyond context-free languages [47], but still can remain within a decidable fragment of second order Lambek calculus [48] — indeed, unrestricted second order Lambek calculus is undecidable [49].

Linear logic provides newer ways to extend the Lambek calculus. Indeed, linear logic allows for several conceptions of a non-commutative logic. One way is to extend the Lambek calculus to the corresponding classical calculus defined by Abrusci [2,5]. This leads, in particular, to a mathematical definition for the philosophical notion of a syntactic category [6]. Another way, introduced by Retoré [99,101], is to enrich the commutative calculus with a non-commutative self-dual connective. Then one has to generalise slightly the notion of a Lambek grammar: the lexicon should associate partial proofs (partial proof nets in fact) to the words, and parsing consists in combining them into a complete proof — as done by Lecomte and Retoré in [78,79] and pursued by Schena in this volume.

Models for polymorphic Lambek calculus by Martin EMMS reviews truth value models for Lambek calculus, and then defines a notion of model for the second order Lambek calculus. Then the author establishes that this semantics is complete with respect to second order Lambek calculus.

Representation theorems for residuated groupoids by Marek SZCZERBA shows that every residuated groupoid — this is a rather general notion of model for the non-associative Lambek calculus — is isomorphic to a submodel of a residuated groupoid of a particular shape, namely the ones defined, as in phase semantics, by the powerset of a groupoid (groupoids are also known as "magmas").

Connected set of types and categorial consequence by Jacek MARCINIEC studies how one can infer from parsing data the type of each word, i.e. define a categorial grammar which generates these sentences and which is as simple as possible. This is done by studying unification over sets of types.

Constructing different phonological bracketings from a proof net by Denis BECHET and Philippe DE GROOTE gives a nice proof of the interpolation lemma for the Lambek calculus in the proof net syntax. This enables to move from a proof net of the Lambek calculus corresponding to one bracketing (e.g. the syntagmatic one) to another (e.g. the intonational one).

Generation as deduction on labelled proof nets by Josep M. MERENCIANO and Glyn V. MORRILL is devoted to generation in the framework of the Lambek calculus. It provides an algorithm for reconstructing the syntactic analysis of a sentence out of a Montague-like semantics — in the restricted case where there is no logical constant. The algorithm consists in constructing a proof net, i.e. a syntactic analysis in the Lambek calculus; the construction is guided by lambda terms which label the proof net: lambda terms must unify when they are "linked" by axioms of the proof net.

4 Computational perspectives

There is now a long tradition of using Logic Programming for implementing parsers (and generators) for natural language. In fact, Logic Programming itself originates in Natural Language Processing considerations. Prolog was created in 1972 by Colmerauer and Kowalski by merging Robinson's notion of unification in Automated Theorem Proving with the insights provided by Colmerauer's previous Q-systems, a programming language which he had designed for use in Machine Translation [42].

At the beginning of the eighties, the Unification Grammar paradigm [110,106,84], strongly connected to Logic Programming [94], gained more and more popularity in Computational Linguistics circles. One of the key advantages of such formalisms was their ability to free the grammar writer from an explicit management of many cases of "transversal information flow", that is, correlations between different points of analysis (the best known instance being agreement handling).

Since then, the fields of Computational Linguistics and Logic Programming have continued to gain insights from each other, in developments such as feature logics [71], resource accounting, constraint processing [61], concurrency, higher-order constructs (functionals).

Constraint logic programming for computational linguistics by Frieder STOLZENBURG, Stephan HÖHNE, Ulrich KOCH and Martin VOLK describes a system that uses Constraint Logic Programming to deal efficiently with typed feature-structures, with applications to finite set operations, variable-free negation and linear precedence constraints.

Quantitative constraint logic programming for weighted grammar applications by Stefan RIEZLER explains how a system of weights can be combined with a certain class of constraint languages and provides a formal semantics for the resulting programs. They show how the use of weights permits the parser to select the most "plausible" analysis in case of ambiguity, using a fuzzy logic notion of plausibility, rather than a probabilistic one.

The development of realistic parsers involves specific needs such as the efficient management of large sets of complex linguistic objects (for instance a lexicon). *The automatic deduction of classificatory systems from linguistic theories* by Paul John KING and Kirl Ivanov SIMOV explains how a classification system for typed feature structures may be derived automatically from a set of linguistic constraints about these structures (in a formalism related to HPSG). The resulting classification system is implemented as a tree whose each branch may be seen as a sequence of elementary queries and expected answers that are used to discriminate the objects to be classified.

In the continuation of his previous works to enrich Logic Programming, the extended abstract *Linear logic as logic programming* by Dale MILLER shows that the whole of linear logic can be considered as a logic programming language, which enables both high-order programming (functionals) and concurrency primitives. The author mentions several existing applications of this language in Computer Science and indicates its applicability to Filler-Gap Dependency Parsers, illustrating once more the practical relevance of linear logic to Computational Linguistics.

References

1. Anne Abeillé. *Les nouvelles syntaxes*. Armand Colin, Paris, 1993.
2. V. Michele Abrusci. Phase semantics and sequent calculus for pure non-commutative classical linear logic. *Journal of Symbolic Logic*, 56(4):1403–1451, December 1991.
3. V. Michele Abrusci. Exchange connectives for non commutative classical linear propositional logic. In V. Michele Abrusci, Claudia Casadio, and Michael Moortgat, editors, *Linear Logic and Lambek Calculus*. DYANA Occasional Publications, Institute for Logic, Language and Information, Amsterdam,1993.
4. V. Michele Abrusci. Coherence semantics for non-commutative linear logic and ambiguity in natural language. Technical report, Università di Roma tre, 1997. Talk at the ATALA meeting, Paris, December 94.
5. V. Michele Abrusci. Non-commutative proof nets. In Girard et al. [55], pages 271–296.
6. V. Michele Abrusci. Syntactical categories of a natural language as facts of a cyclic phase space. Technical report, Universita di Roma tre, 1997.

7. Anthony E. Ades and Mark J. Steedman. On the order of words. *Linguistics and Philosophy*, 4:517–558, 1982.
8. Kasimierz Adjuckiewicz. Die syntaktische konnexität. *Studia Philosophica*, 1:1–27, 1935.
9. Emmon Bach. Some generalizations of categorial grammars. In Fred Landman and Frank Veltman, editors, *Varieties of Formal Semantics*, pages 1–23. Foris, Dordrecht, 1984.
10. Yehoshua Bar-Hillel. A quasi-arithmetical notation for syntactic description. *Language*, 29:47–58, 1953.
11. Yehoshua Bar-Hillel. *Language and information*. Addison Wesley, Reading MA, 1964.
12. Bruno Barras, Samuel Boutin, Cristina Cornes, Judicael Courant, Jean-Christophe Filliatre, Eduardo Gimenez, Hugo Herbelin, Gerard Huet, Cesar Munoz, Chetan Murthy, Catherine Parent, Christine Paulin-Mohring, Amokrane Saibi, Benjamin Werner The Coq Proof Assistant Reference Manual : Version 6.1 Technical Report RT-203, INRIA, Rocquencourt, May 1997.
13. Guy Barry and Glyn V. Morrill, editors. *Studies in Categorial Grammar*. Edinburgh Working Papers in Cognitive Science, Edinburgh, 1990.
14. Jon Barwise and Robin Cooper. Generalised quantifiers and natural language. *Linguistics and Philosophy*, 4:159–219, 1981.
15. Jon Barwise and John Perry. *Situations and Attitudes*. MIT Press, Cambridge MA, 1983.
16. Johan van Benthem. *Essays in logical semantics*. D. Reidel, Dordrecht, 1986.
17. Johan van Benthem. The lambek calculus. In Oehrle et al. [91], pages 35–68.
18. Johan van Benthem. *Language in action: Categories, Lambdas and Dynamic Logic*, Number 130 of *Sudies in Logic and the foundation of mathematics*. North-Holland, Amsterdam, 1991.
19. Johan van Benthem and Alice ter Meulen, editors. *Handbook of Logic and Language*. North-Holland, Amsterdam, 1997.
20. Patrick Blackburn, Wilfried Meyer-Viol, and Maarten de Rijke. A proof system for finite trees. In Hans Kleine Büning, editor, *Computer Science Logic '95*, Volume 1092 of *Lecture Notes in Computer Science*, pages 86–105. Springer, Heidelberg, 1996.
21. Joan Bresnan, editor. *The mental representation of grammatical relations*. MIT Press, Cambridge MA, 1982.
22. Wojciech Buszkowski. Completeness results for lambek syntactic calculus. *Zeitschrift für mathematische Logik und Grundlagen der Mathematik*, 32:13–28, 1986.
23. Wojciech Buszkowski. Generative power of categorial grammar. In Oehrle et al. [91], pages 69–94.
24. Wojciech Buszkowski. Mathematical linguistics and proof theory. In van Benthem and ter Meulen [19], pages 683–736.
25. Rudolf Carnap. *Meaning and Necessity: A Study in Semantics and Modal Logic*. University of Chicago Press, 1946.
26. Bob Carpenter. ALE: The Attribute Logic Engine user's guide. Technical report, Carnegie Mellon University, Laboratory for Computational Linguistics, 1992.
27. Bob Carpenter. *Lectures on Type-Logical Semantics*. MIT Press, Cambridge MA, 1996.
28. Bob Carpenter. *The Logic of Typed Feature Structures: With Applications to Unification Grammars, Logic Programs and Constraint Resolution* Number 32 of Cambridge Tracts in Theoretical Computer Science. Cambridge University Press, 1992.
29. Claudia Casadio. Semantic categories and the development of categorial grammars. In Oehrle et al. [91], pages 95–124.
30. Noam Chomsky. *The logical structure of linguistic theory*. Plenum, New York, 1955.
31. Noam Chomsky. Three models for the description of language. *IRE Transactions on Information Theory*, 2(3):113–124, 1956.
32. Noam Chomsky. On certain formal properties of grammars. *Information and control*, 2:137–167, 1959.

33. Noam Chomsky. Formal properties of grammars. In *Handbook of Mathematical Psychology*, volume 2, pages 323 – 418. John Wiley and sons, New York, 1963.
34. Noam Chomsky. *Aspects of the Theory of Syntax*. MIT Press, Cambridge MA, 1965.
35. Noam Chomsky. *Cartesian Linguistics*. MIT Press, Cambridge MA,1966.
36. Noam Chomsky. *Reflections on language*. Pantheon, New York, 1975.
37. Noam Chomsky. *Some concepts and consequences of the theory of government and binding*. MIT Press, Cambridge MA, 1982.
38. Noam Chomsky. *Barriers*. MIT Press, Cambridge MA, 1987.
39. Noam Chomsky. *The Minimalist Program*. MIT Press, Cambridge MA, 1996.
40. Noam Chomsky and Marcel-Paul Schützenberger. The algebraic theory of context-free languages. In P. Bradford and D. Hirschberg, editors, *Computer programming and formal systems*, pages 118–161. North-Holland, Amsterdam, 1963.
41. Alonzo Church. A formulation of the logic of sense and denotation. In P. Henle, H. Kallen and H. Langer editors, *Structure, Method and Meaning: Essays in honor of Henry M. Sheffer*. Liberal Arts Press, New York, 1951.
42. Jacques Cohen. A view of the origins and development of Prolog. *Communications of the ACM*, 31(1):26–37, January 1988.
43. Jean-Pierre Desclés. *Langages applicatifs, langues naturelles et cognition*. Hermès, Paris, 1990.
44. Michael Dorna. The Comprehensive Unification Formalism user's manual. Technical report, Institut für maschinelle Sprachverarbeitung, Universität Stuttgart, 1994.
45. David Dowty. *Word Meaning and Montague Grammar*. D. Reidel, Dordrecht, 1979.
46. David Dowty. Type-raising, functional composition, and non-constituent coordination. In Oehrle et al. [91], pages 153–198.
47. Martin Emms. Extraction covering of the Lambek calculus are not context free. In *9th Amsterdam Colloquium*, pages 268–286, 1993.
48. Martin Emms. Parsing with polymorphism. In *6th Annual Conference of the European Chapter of the Association for Computational Linguistics*, 1993.
49. Martin Emms. Undecidability result for polymorphic Lambek calculus. In *10th Amsterdam Colloquium*, 1995.
50. Gottlob Frege. *Begriffsschrift*. Louis Nerbert, Halle A/S, 1879. English translation in: "From Frege to Gödel", edited by van Heijenoort, Harvard University Press, Cambridge MA, 1967.
51. Gerald Gazdar, Ewan Klein, Geoffrey Pullum, and Ivan Sag. *Generalized Phrase Structure Grammar*. Harvard University Press, Cambridge MA, 1985.
52. Ferenc Gécseg and Magnus Steinby. *Tree Languages*, chapter 1, pages 1–68. Volume 3 of Rozenberg and Salomaa [104], 1996.
53. Jean-Yves Girard. Linear logic. *Theoretical Computer Science*, 50(1):1–102, 1987.
54. Jean-Yves Girard. Linear logic: its syntax and semantics. In Girard et al. [55], pages 1–42.
55. Jean-Yves Girard, Yves Lafont, and Laurent Regnier, editors. *Advances in Linear Logic*, Volume 222 of *London Mathematical Society Lecture Notes*. Cambridge University Press, 1995.
56. Jean-Yves Girard, Yves Lafont, and Paul Taylor. *Proofs and Types*. Number 7 in Cambridge Tracts in Theoretical Computer Science. Cambridge University Press, 1988.
57. Valentin Goranko and Solomon Passy. Using the universal modality: Gains and questions. *Journal of Logic and Computation*, 2:5–30, 1992.
58. Jeroen Groenendijk and Martin Stokhof. Dynamic predicate logic. *Linguistics and Philosophy*, 14:39–100, 1991.
59. Philippe de Groote and Christian Retoré. Semantic readings of proof nets. In Geert-Jan Kruijff, Glyn V. Morrill, and Richard T. Oehrle, editors, *Formal Grammar*, Proceedings

of the Conference of the European Summer School in Logic, Language and Information, Prague, August 1996. pages 57–70.

60. Irene Heim. *The Semantics of Definite and Indefinite Noun Phrases*. PhD thesis, University of Massachusetts, Amherst, 1982.
61. Pascal van Hentenryck. *Constraint Satisfaction in Logic Programming*. MIT Press, Cambridge MA, 1989.
62. Mark Hepple. *The Grammar and Processing of Order and Dependency, a categorial approach*. PhD thesis, Centre of Cognitive Sciences, Edinburgh, 1990.
63. Mark Johnson. *Attribute-Value Logic and the Theory of Grammar*. Number 16 in CSLI Lecture Notes. Center for the Study of Language and Information, Stanford CA, 1989. (distributed by Cambridge University Press)
64. Mark Johnson. Proof nets and the complexity of processing center-embedded constructions. Technical report, Brown University, Providence RI, 1997.
65. Aravind K. Joshi, Leon Levy, and Masako Takahashi. Tree adjunct grammar. *Journal of Computer and System Sciences*, 10:136–163, 1975.
66. Aravind K. Joshi. Tree adjoining grammars : How much context-sensitivity is required to provide reasonable structural descriptions? In David Dowty, Lauri Kartunen, and Arnold M. Zwicky, editors, *Natural Language Parsing*, pages 206–250. Cambridge University Press, 1988.
67. Aravind K. Joshi and Yves Schabes. *Tree-Adjoining Grammars*, chapter 2, pages 69–124. Volume 3 of Rozenberg and Salomaa [104], 1996.
68. Hans Kamp. A theory of truth and semantic representation. In Janssen, Groenendijk and Stokhof, editors, *Proceedings of the Third Amsterdam Colloquium*, Foris, Dordrecht, 1981.
69. Hans Kamp and Uwe Reyle. *From Discourse to Logic*. Kluwer, Dordrecht, 1993.
70. Ronald Kaplan and Joan Bresnan. *Lexical functional grammar: a formal system for grammatical representation*, chapter 4, pages 173–281. In Bresnan [21], 1982.
71. Bill Keller. *Feature Logics, Infinitary Descriptions, and Grammar*, volume 44 of *CSLI Lecture Notes*. Center for the Study of Language and Information, Stanford CA, 1989. (distributed by Cambridge University Press)
72. Saul Kripke. A completeness theorem in modal logic. *Journal of Symbolic Logic*, 24:1–14, 1959.
73. François Lamarche and Christian Retoré Proof nets for the Lambek calculus – an overview. In Abrusci and Casadio, editors, *Proofs and linguistic categories, proceedings of 1996 Roma Workshop*, pages 241–262. CLUEB, Bologna, 1996.
74. Joachim Lambek. The mathematics of sentence structure. *American mathematical monthly*, pages 154–170, 1958.
75. Joachim Lambek. On the calculus of syntactic types. In Roman Jakobson, editor, *Structure of language and its mathematical aspects*, pages 166–178. American Mathematical Society, Providence RI, 1961.
76. Joachim Lambek. Categorial and categorical grammars. In Oehrle et al. [91], pages 297–318.
77. Alain Lecomte. Proof nets and dependencies. In *COLING-92*, pages 394–401. Nantes, August 1992.
78. Alain Lecomte and Christian Retoré. Pomset logic as an alternative categorial grammar. In Glyn V. Morrill and Richard T. Oehrle, editors, *Formal Grammar*, Proceedings of the Conference of the European Summer School in Logic, Language and Information, Barcelona, 1995. pages 181–196.
79. Alain Lecomte and Christian Retoré. Words as modules: a lexicalised grammar in the framework of linear logic proof nets. In Carlos Martin-Vide, editor, *International Conference on Mathematical Linguistics II*. John Benjamins, Amsterdam, 1997.

80. Marie-Ange Légeret. *Algèbres de démonstrations en grammaires catégorielles*. Thèse de Doctorat, spécialité Mathématiques, Université Blaise Pascal, Clermont-Ferrand, janvier 1996.
81. Ralph Loader. Linear logic, totality and full completeness. In *LICS'94*, pages 292–298. IEEE computer society, Washington, 1994.
82. Per Martin-Löf. *Intuitionistic Type Theory*. Bibliopolis, Napoli, 1984. (Notes by Giovani Sambin of a series of lectures given in Padua, June 1980)
83. Alexandru Mateescu and Arto Salomaa. *Formal Languages: an Introduction and a Synopsis*, chapter 1, pages 1–40. Volume 1 of Rozenberg and Salomaa [104], 1996.
84. Philip Miller and Thérèse Torris, editors. *Formalismes syntaxiques pour le traitement automatique du langage naturel*. Hermès, Paris, 1990.
85. Michael Moortgat. *Categorial Investigations. Logical and Linguistic Aspects of the Lambek Calculus*. Foris, Dordrecht, 1988.
86. Michael Moortgat. *La grammaire catégorielle généralisée – le calcul de Lambek-Gentzen*, chapter 3, pages 127–182. In Miller and Torris [84], 1990.
87. Michael Moortgat. Categorial type logics. In van Benthem and ter Meulen [19], pages 93–177.
88. Glyn V. Morrill. *Type Logical Grammar*. Kluwer, Dordrecht, 1994.
89. Georges Mounin. *Histoire de la linguistique – des origines au XXe siècle*. Presses Universitaires de France, Paris, 1967.
90. Reinhard Muskens. *Meaning and Partiality*. CSLI, 1996.
91. Richard T. Oehrle, Emmon Bach, and Deirde Wheeler, editors. *Categorial Grammars and Natural Languages Structures*. D. Reidel, Dordrecht, 1988.
92. Barbara Partee. Montague grammar and transformational grammar. *Linguistic Inquiry*, VI(2):203–300, 1975.
93. Matti Pentus. Lambek grammars are context free. In *LICS'93*, pages 371–373. IEEE computer society, Washington, 1993.
94. Fernando C. N. Pereira and Stuart M. Shieber. *Prolog and Natural Language Analysis*, volume 10 of *CSLI Lecture Notes*. Center for the Study of Language and Information, Stanford CA, 1987. (distributed by Cambridge University Press)
95. Carl Pollard and Ivan A. Sag. *Head-Driven Phrase Structure Grammars*. Chicago University Press, 1994.
96. Jean-Yves Pollock. *Langage et cognition – Une introduction au programme minimaliste de la grammaire générative*. Presses Universitaires de France, Paris, 1997.
97. Aarne Ranta. *Type-Theoretical Grammar*. Oxford University Press, 1994.
98. Hans Reichenbach. *Elements of Symbolic Logic*. The MacMillan Company, New York, 1948.
99. Christian Retoré. *Réseaux et Séquents Ordonnés*. Thèse de Doctorat, spécialité Mathématiques, Université Paris 7, février 1993.
100. Christian Retoré. Calcul de lambek et logique linéaire. *Traitement Automatique des Langues*, 37(2):39–70, 1996.
101. Christian Retoré. Pomset logic: a non-commutative extension of classical linear logic. In J. R. Hindley and Ph. de Groote, editors, *TLCA'97*, volume 1210 of *LNCS*, pages 300–319, 1997.
102. Robert H. Robins. *A short history of linguistics*. Longmans, Green, and Co., London, 1967.
103. Dirk Roorda. *Resource logic: proof theoretical investigations*. PhD thesis, FWI, Universiteit van Amsterdam, 1991.
104. Grzegorz Rozenberg and Arto Salomaa, editors. *Handbook of Formal Languages*. Springer, Heidelberg, 1996. (3 volumes)
105. Esa Saarinen, editor. *Game-Theoretical Semantics: Essays on Semantics by Hintikka, Carlson, Peacocke, Rantala, and Saarinen*. D. Reidel, Dordrecht, 1979.

106. Peter Sells. *An introduction to Government-Binding Theory, Generalised Phrase Structure Grammar, and Lexical-Functional Grammar*, volume 3 of *CSLI Lecture Notes*. Center for the Study of Language and Information, Stanford CA, 1985. (distributed by Cambridge University Press)
107. Sebastian Shaumyan. *Applicational grammar as a semantic theory of natural language*. Edinburgh University Press, 1977.
108. Betty Shefts. *Grammatical Method in Pāṇini*. American Oriental Society, New Haven CO, 1961.
109. Stuart M. Shieber. Evidence against the context-freeness of natural language. *Linguistics and Philosophy*, 8:333–343, 1985.
110. Stuart M. Shieber. *An Introduction to Unification-Based Approaches to Grammar*, volume 4 of *CSLI Lecture Notes*. Center for the Study of Language and Information, Stanford CA, 1986. (distributed by Cambridge University Press)
111. Stuart M. Shieber. *Les grammaires basées sur l'unification*, chapter 1, pages 27–86. In Miller and Torris [84], 1990.
112. Mark J. Steedman. *Surface Structure and Interpretation*. Center for the Study of Language and Information, Stanford CA, 1996. (distributed by Cambridge University Press)
113. Joseph E. Stoy. *Denotational Semantics: The Scott-Strachey Approach to Programming Language Theory*. MIT Press, Cambridge MA, 1977.
114. Anna Szabolcsi. Bound variables in syntax. In *Proceedings of the 6th Amsterdam Colloquium*, pages 331–351, Amsterdam, 1987. Institute for Language, Logic and Information.
115. Wolfgang Thomas. *Languages, Automata and Logic*, chapter 7, pages 389–456. Volume 3 of Rozenberg and Salomaa [104], 1996.
116. Richmond H. Thomason, editor. *Formal Philosophy: Selected Papers of Richard Montague*. Yale University Press, New Haven CO, 1974.
117. Thérèse Torris. *La grammaire syntagmatique généralisée*, chapter 2, pages 87–126. In Miller and Torris [84], 1990.
118. Anne Sjerp Troelstra. *Lectures on Linear Logic*, volume 29 of *CSLI Lecture Notes*. Center for the Study of Language and Information, Stanford CA, 1992. (distributed by Cambridge University Press)
119. Rémi Zajac. Notes on the Typed Feature System, version 4. Technical report, Institut für Informatik, Project Polygloss, Universität Stuttgart, 1991.
120. Wojciech Zielonka. Axiomatizability of Adjukiewicz-Lambek calculus by means of cancellation schemes. *Zeitschrift für mathematische Logik und Grundlagen der Mathematik*, 27:215–224, 1981.

Partial Proof Trees, Resource Sensitive Logics and Syntactic Constraints *

Aravind K. Joshi and Seth Kulick

Department of Computer and Information Science
and
Institute for Research in Cognitive Science
University of Pennsylvania
Philadelphia, PA 19104, USA
{joshi,skulick}@linc.cis.upenn.edu

Abstract. We discuss the relationship between a categorial system (PPTS) based on partial proof trees (PPTs) as the building blocks of the system, resource sensitive logics and the nature of syntactic constraints. PPTS incorporates some of the key insights of lexicalized tree adjoining grammar, namely the notion of an extended domain of locality and the consequent factoring of recursion from the domain of dependencies. PPTS therefore inherits the linguistic and computational properties of that system. We discuss the relationship between PPTS, natural deduction, and linear logic proof-nets, and argue that a natural deduction system rather than a proof-net system is more appropriate for the construction of the PPTs. We also show how the use of PPTs allows us to 'localize' the management of resources, thereby freeing us from this management as the PPTs are combined.

1 Introduction

A categorial system (PPTS) based on partial proof trees (PPTs) as the building blocks of the system has been investigated by Joshi and Kulick [8,9]. The main idea is to associate with each lexical item one or more PPTs, obtained by unfolding the arguments of the type that would be associated with that lexical item in a simple categorial grammar such as the Ajdukiewicz and Bar-Hillel grammar (AB). The basic PPTs (a finite set) then serve as the building blocks of the grammar. Complex proof trees are obtained by 'combining' these PPTs by a uniform set of inference rules that manipulate the PPTs.

The main motivation of this approach is to incorporate into the categorial framework the key insights from a tree rewriting system such as the lexicalized

* We would like to thank the following people for their valuable comments that helped us improve our paper both in its content and presentation: Christophe Fouqueré, Mark Johnson, Alain Lecomte, Dale Miller, Michael Moortgat, Glyn Morrill, Richard Oehrle, Christian Retoré, Ed Stabler and Mark Steedman. This work was partially supported by NSF grant SBR8920230 and ARO grant DAAH04-94-G-0426.

tree adjoining grammar (LTAG), namely the notion of an extended domain of locality (EDL) and the consequent factoring of recursion from the domain of dependencies (FRD). Roughly speaking, EDL allows one to deal with structural adjacency rather than the strict string adjacency in a traditional context-free grammar (CFG) or categorial grammar. This in turn permits the encapsulation of syntactic and associated semantic dependencies. All dependencies are local to the elementary trees of LTAG and long distance dependencies also become 'local' to the elementary trees. This is the property FRD. In LTAG this approach provides more formal power (both strong and weak generative power) without increasing the computational complexity too much beyond that of CFGs, while still achieving polynomial parsability (i.e., the class of mildly context-sensitive grammar formalisms [7]). Thus, EDL and FRD together lead from CFGs to LTAGs, with significant formal, linguistic, and computational properties. In this paper we want to examine the consequences of incorporating these notions into a categorial grammar, leading to the system based on PPTs. This work is also related to the work on description trees by [19] and HPSG compilation into LTAGs by [11].

In Section 2, we will give a brief introduction to LTAG by means of a few examples. Then in Section 3 we will present an overview of the partial proof tree system (PPTS) and the associated inference rules. In Section 4 we will discuss the relationship between PPTS, natural deduction and proof-nets, followed by a summary of our conclusions in Section 5.

2 A brief introduction to LTAG

LTAG is a tree rewriting system. It consists of a finite set of elementary trees. Each elementary tree is associated with a lexical item called the *anchor* of the tree. The anchors are sometimes 'heads' but not always. They are more like the 'functors' in a categorial grammar. Elementary trees are either INITIAL trees or AUXILIARY trees (see Figures 1 and 2 for some examples). An initial tree has at the frontier a lexical anchor and the other nodes (if any) are 'substitution' sites marked with $\downarrow$. An auxiliary tree is like the initial tree except that at the frontier, in addition to the lexical anchor and possible substitution sites, there is special node called the footnode marked with *, which has the same label as the label of the root of the tree.

There are two operations that combine trees of LTAG. The first operation is 'substitution' which is similar to tree substitution. The adjunction operation takes an auxiliary tree with the root and the footnodes labeled by a node X and splices (or inserts) it at the label X in another tree (elementary or derived). The tree language of an LTAG is the set of all trees derived from initial trees rooted in S and the string language is the set of all strings associated with the trees in the tree language (for a formal definition of LTAG and the associated mathematical and computational properties see [10]).

We will now illustrate LTAGs by some simple examples. In these examples we have omitted the feature structures associated with the nodes of the elementary trees. There are two sets of feature structures - top and bottom - for the interior nodes of a tree. Substitution and adjoining can then be defined in terms of unification of feature structures. Figure 3 shows a derivation consisting of three initial trees and one auxiliary tree and how they are put together. Figure 4 shows the resulting derived tree. Figure 5 and 6 illustrate how long distance dependencies are handled in LTAG. Figures 7 and 8 illustrate the treatment of raising and PRO control in LTAG. For details of a large wide coverage English grammar in the LTAG framework, see [20].

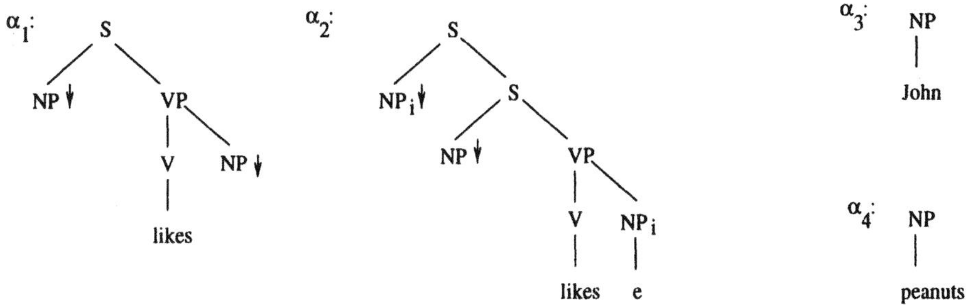

Fig. 1. LTAG initial trees

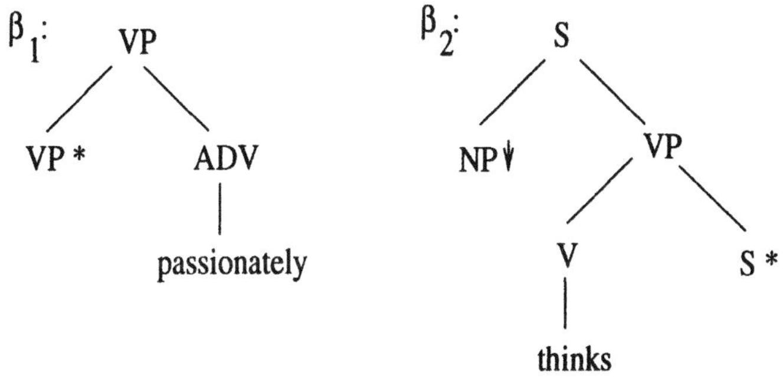

Fig. 2. LTAG auxiliary trees

From these few examples, it is easily seen that LTAG localizes dependencies such as agreement, subcategorization and filler-gap. It can also localize dependencies associated with flexible idioms and represent their semantic non-compositionality (these trees, not shown here, may have multiple anchors). Appropriate extensions of LTAG can localize word order phenomena such as local and long-distance scrambling.

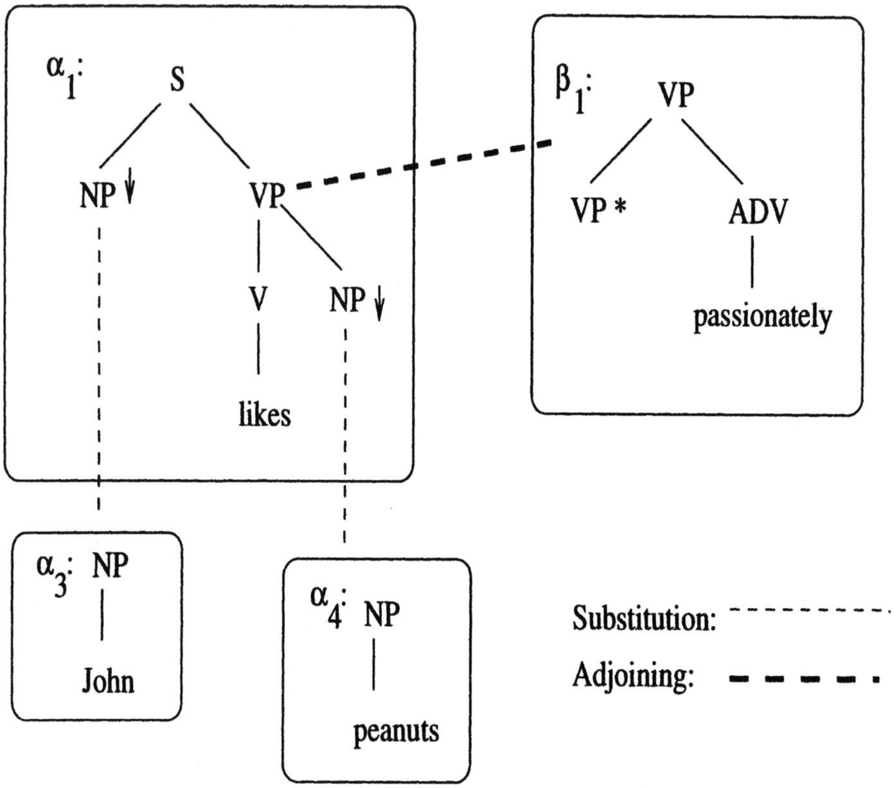

Fig. 3. Substitution and adjoining in LTAG

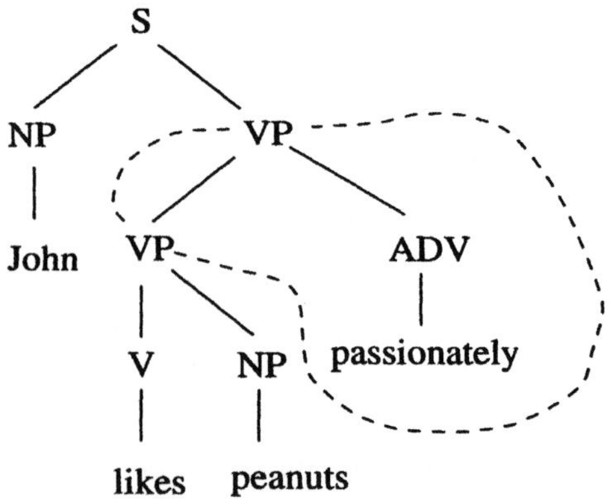

Fig. 4. Result of Figure 3

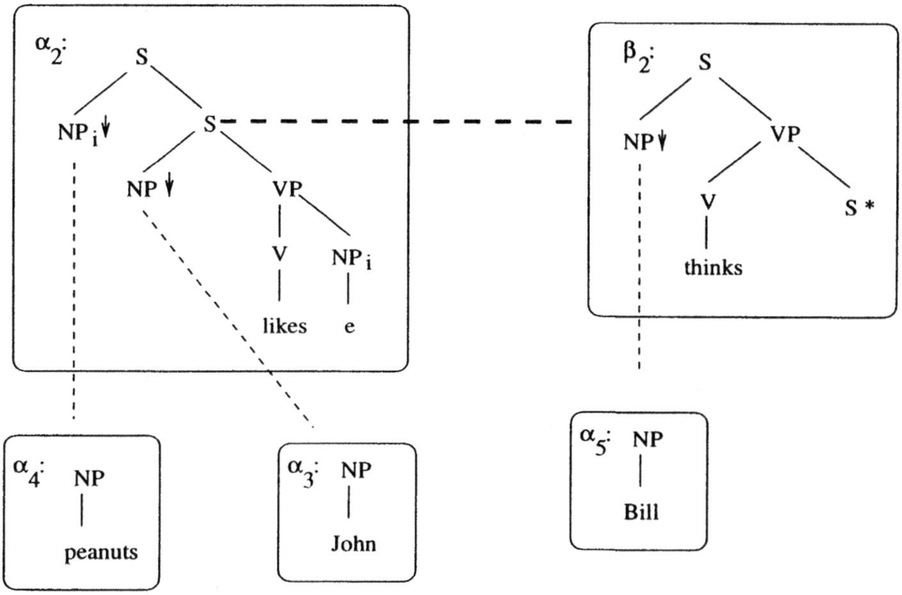

Fig. 5. Example of long-distance topicalization

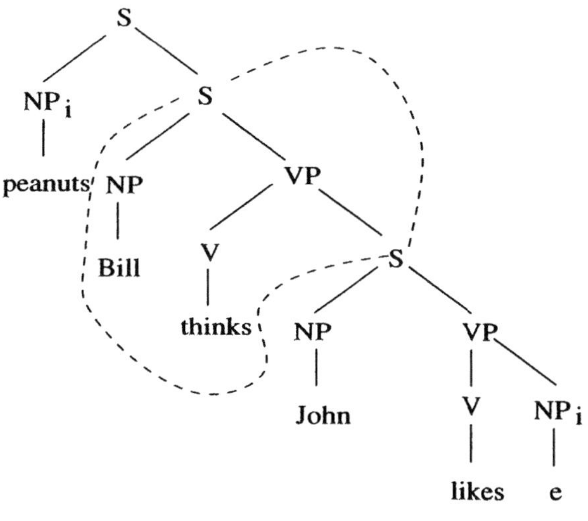

Fig. 6. Result of Figure 5

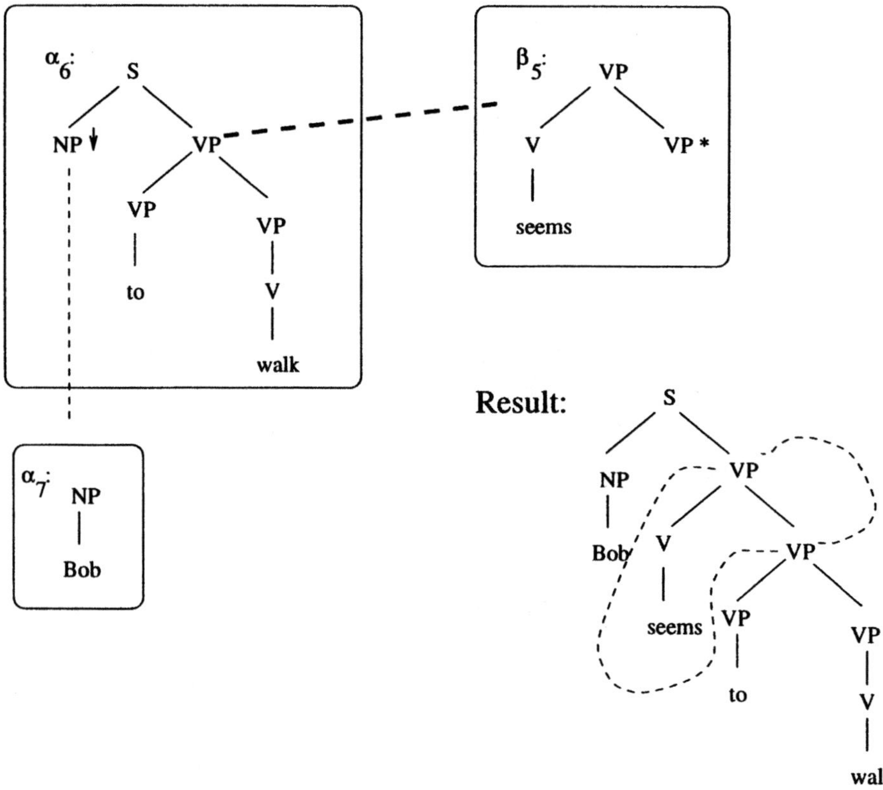

Fig. 7. Raising

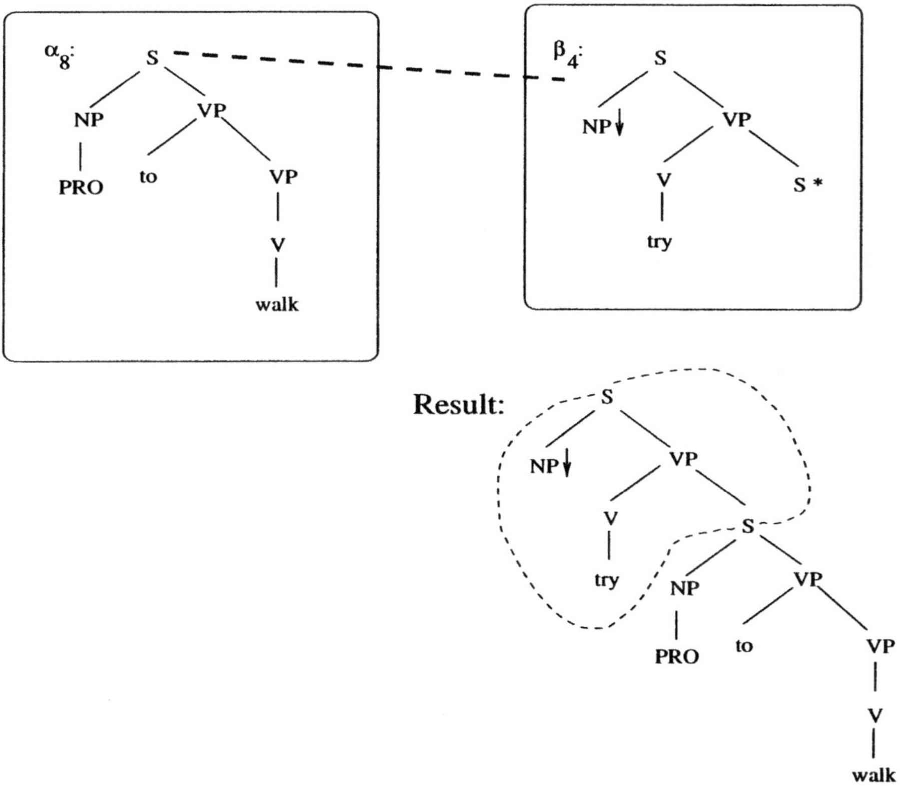

Fig. 8. Sentential Complementation with PRO control

From the point of view of the present paper the main points to note are as follows. All dependencies are represented in the elementary trees. The operations of substitution and adjoining do not affect this localization. We have represented the elementary trees as a *finite* set of trees. Of course, a linguistic theory can be used to specify this finite set. In fact, in some sense, this is all that the linguistic theory has to do and the rest is 'free'. The important point is that the constraints that license the elementary trees are *distinct* from the operations that combine the elementary trees, namely substitution and adjoining. Management of resources (in terms of dependencies) is localized to the elementary trees. The operations that combine the trees do not do any management of these resources. This issue is crucial to the development of the system described in this paper. In the style of resource-sensitive logics the same point can be made by saying that the resource-sensitivity constraints are operating at the level of the elementary structures - elementary trees of LTAG or the basic PPTs of PPTS as will be seen later.

It should be noted that categorial grammar allows for a larger domain of locality than context-free grammar because the arguments appear in the representation of the type associated with the lexical item. However, it does not allow an extended domain of locality as in LTAG, thus not permitting factorization of recursion from the domain of dependencies. This is clearly seen by a comparison of the examples in Figures 5 and 6 with a derivation in categorial grammar.

3 An Overview of PPTS

There are two aspects to the PPTS system: the construction of the basic PPTs, and the inference rules that define how they are manipulated. The finite set of basic PPTs, BPPT, is constructed according to the following schemata, explained in more detail below:

1. Arguments of the type associated with a lexical item are unfolded by introducing assumptions.
2. There is no unfolding past an argument which is not 'selected' by the lexical item.
3. If a *trace* assumption is introduced while unfolding then it must be *locally* discharged, i.e., within the basic PPT which is being constructed.
4. During unfolding a node can be *interpolated* from a conclusion node X to an assumption node Y.

All assumptions introduced in a PPT must be fulfilled by one of the following three operations[1]:

application - the conclusion node of one PPT is linked to an assumption node of another.

[1] This only applies to PPTs that are actually used in a parse. A PPT that is not used is irrelevant to the parse and its assumptions can remain unfulfilled.

stretching - An interior node of a PPT is 'opened up', to create a conclusion node and an assumption node, in order to allow interaction with another PPT.

interpolation - The two ends of an interpolation construction (previously created within a basic PPT) are linked to another PPT.

Rather than describing all four steps above and then the inference rules, we will present them in the following order, since some of the schema naturally fall together with some of the operations. We will describe schema 1 and 'application' together in Section 3.1. Schema 2 is described in Section 3.2 and 'stretching' in Section 3.3 together with a simple example. Schema 3 is described in section 3.4 and schema 4 and 'interpolation' in Section 3.5 together with a simple example.

While traditional categorial grammar rules specify inferences between types, the inference rules for the three operations on PPTs instead specify inferences between proofs. This is a direct consequence of the extended domain of locality in PPTS. (However, the rules for building the set BPPT are similar to those of other categorial grammars).

These three operations are specified by inference rules that take the form of λ-operations, where the body of the λ-term is itself the proof. This is done by adapting a version of typed label-selective λ-calculus - [4]. This extension of λ-calculus uses labelling of abstractions and applications to allow unordered currying. Arguments have both symbol and numeric labels, and the intuitive idea is that the symbolic labels express the possibility of taking input on multiple channels, and the numeric labels expresses the order of input on that channel. The use of this calculus is not critical to our approach. We have used it for convenience only. The linguistic and computational properties do not depend on this choice in any essential manner.

3.1 Unfolding and Application

The PPT for a lexical item is in the form of a λ-term over a proof tree, where the bound variables are the 'unfilled assumptions'. Each bound variable in a PPT has a type associated with it. For clarity of presentation we will not tag each argument with its type, but rather have a type term associated with each λ-term. There is a family of types, `judg` α (judgement of α), each of which specifies a proof of category α. We start with a simple example for the most straightforward of the PPTS operations, proof application. Let the lexical items *Bob*, *likes*, and *Hazel*, have the following PPTs:

$$\left(\frac{\texttt{Bob}}{\texttt{NP}}\right) : (\texttt{judg NP}) \tag{1}$$

$$\lambda_{l1}x.\lambda_{r1}y.\left(\cfrac{x \quad \cfrac{\cfrac{\texttt{likes}}{(\texttt{NP}\backslash\texttt{S})/\texttt{NP}} \quad y}{\texttt{NP}\backslash\texttt{S}}}{\texttt{S}}\right) : \begin{array}{r}\{l1 \Rightarrow (\texttt{judg NP}), r1 \Rightarrow (\texttt{judg NP})\} \\ \rightarrow (\texttt{judg S})\end{array} \tag{2}$$

$$\left(\frac{\texttt{Hazel}}{\texttt{NP}}\right) : \texttt{(judg NP)} \tag{3}$$

Labels l and r signify assumptions that need to be filled from the left or right, respectively. In the label-selective λ-calculus, function application is written in a way analogous to that in standard λ-calculus, with the function on the left and its arguments on the right. As noted in the introduction to Section 3, the labelling of abstractions allows unordered currying. The channel of communications is specified by preceding the argument with ${}_{\hat{p}}$, which signifies application over channel p. This can only take place if the abstraction is also over this channel, as stated by the β-reduction rule for this system:

$$(\lambda_p x.M)_{\hat{p}} N \to [N/x]M$$

The use of the symbolic labels l and r is purely an abstraction, and implies nothing about the actual order of the lexical items. It is instead the parser's responsibility to ensure that correct items are applied along the correct channels. So for the sentence *Bob likes Hazel*, the parser has to control the application of the PPTs for *Bob* and *Hazel* along the l and r channels of the PPT for *likes*. Thus the function-argument structure is abstracted from the word order. Figure 9 shows a derivation for *Bob likes Hazel* using the PPTs (1), (2), and (3).

$$\lambda_{l1} x.\lambda_{r1} y.\left(\frac{x \quad \dfrac{\dfrac{\texttt{likes}}{\texttt{(NP\backslash S)/NP}} \quad y}{\texttt{NP\backslash S}}}{\texttt{S}}\right) {}_{\hat{l1}} \left(\frac{\texttt{Bob}}{\texttt{NP}}\right) {}_{\hat{r1}} \left(\frac{\texttt{Hazel}}{\texttt{NP}}\right)$$

$$\to \quad \lambda_{r1} y.\left(\frac{\dfrac{\texttt{Bob}}{\texttt{NP}} \quad \dfrac{\dfrac{\texttt{likes}}{\texttt{(NP\backslash S)/NP}} \quad y}{\texttt{NP\backslash S}}}{\texttt{S}}\right) {}_{\hat{r1}} \left(\frac{\texttt{Hazel}}{\texttt{NP}}\right)$$

$$\to \quad \left(\frac{\dfrac{\texttt{Bob}}{\texttt{NP}} \quad \dfrac{\dfrac{\texttt{likes}}{\texttt{(NP\backslash S)/NP}} \quad \dfrac{\texttt{Hazel}}{\texttt{NP}}}{\texttt{NP\backslash S}}}{\texttt{S}}\right)$$

Fig. 9. Derivation for *Bob likes Hazel*

3.2 Selectional Restrictions on Unfolding

When unfolding a type we do not unfold a category that is not 'selected' , in the sense described below, by the lexical item. In the example above in Section 3.1 for *likes*, the NPs are both arguments of the lexical item, but this is not always the case. For example, for an adverb with type $\texttt{(NP\backslash S)\backslash(NP\backslash S)}$, such as the lexical item *passionately*, the NPs themselves are not arguments of the lexical item. Therefore, we represent the type of this item as (NP\S)\(NP*\S), where the * marks the NP as not being 'selected' by *passionately*, and *passionately* would have the following PPT:

$$\lambda_{l1} x. \left(\frac{x \quad \dfrac{\texttt{passionately}}{(\texttt{NP}\backslash\texttt{S})\backslash(\texttt{NP}^*\backslash\texttt{S})}}{(\texttt{NP}^*\backslash\texttt{S})} \right) : \{l1 \Rightarrow (\texttt{judg NP}\backslash\texttt{S})\} \rightarrow (\texttt{judg NP}\backslash\texttt{S}) \tag{4}$$

We note here that if the tree for *passionately* was in fact unfolded into the range subtype, resulting in an unfilled assumption for NP as well, the resulting PPT would not be able to be used in a derivation, by the very nature of the operations used to connect different PPTs together. This is of course in stark contrast to more standard categorial grammars. We discuss this point in more detail in Section 3.3.

Another example of selectional restrictions on unfolding arises in the case of raising verbs. A well-known difference between verbs such as *tries* and *seems* is that the arguments for the former are a subject NP and an infinitival sentential complement, while the sole argument for *seems* is an infinitival sentential complement. *Seems* is referred to as a raising verb because the subject of the sentential complement is described as having moved (raised) to the subject position of the sentence. Instead of having movement, PPTS can analyze raising constructions in a way analogous to that of the LTAG analysis [12], as illustrated in Section 2.

First, consider the case of the non-raising verb *tries*.

$$\lambda_{l1} x. \lambda_{r1} y. \left(\frac{x \quad \dfrac{\dfrac{\texttt{tries}}{(\texttt{NP}\backslash\texttt{S})/\texttt{Sinf}} \quad y}{\texttt{NP}\backslash\texttt{S}}}{\texttt{S}} \right) : \begin{array}{r} \{l1 \Rightarrow (\texttt{judg NP}), r1 \Rightarrow (\texttt{judg Sinf})\} \\ \rightarrow (\texttt{judg S}) \end{array} \tag{5}$$

This PPT can simply apply to arguments on the left and right of the appropriate types to derive a sentence such as *Bob tries to walk*[2]. However, the PPT for *seems* would not unfold the NP in NP\S, as the NP in NP*\S is not 'selected' by *seems*:

$$\lambda_{r1} x. \left(\frac{\dfrac{\texttt{seems}}{(\texttt{NP}^*\backslash\texttt{S})/(\texttt{NP}\backslash\texttt{Sinf})} \quad x}{\texttt{NP}^*\backslash\texttt{S}} \right) : \{r1 \Rightarrow (\texttt{judg NP}\backslash\texttt{Sinf})\} \rightarrow (\texttt{judg NP}\backslash\texttt{S}) \tag{6}$$

In this case, the PPT for *walk* would not take a PRO subject but rather a non-PRO NP. In Section 3.5 the interaction of raising verbs with the operation of interpolation is discussed.

[2] We are assuming here that an underlying feature system will ensure that the complement has a PRO subject.

3.3 Stretching

As mentioned above, stretching 'opens up' a node, and is usually done to allow the insertion of an optional modifier. In terms of our specification of PPTs by the label-selective λ-calculus, a proof ready to be stretched becomes an abstraction over an inference rule (or over a proof). For example, for the sentence *Bob likes Hazel passionately*, the intuitive idea is that the $\mathtt{NP\backslash S}$ node in the PPT for *likes* is stretched to form a larger PPT that includes the PPT for *passionately*. For example, when the $\mathtt{NP\backslash S}$ node in the PPT tree in Figure 9 for *Bob likes Hazel* gets stretched, the result is:

$$\lambda_{s1}x.\left(\dfrac{\dfrac{\mathtt{Bob}}{\mathtt{NP}} \qquad \dfrac{\dfrac{\dfrac{\mathtt{likes}}{\mathtt{(NP\backslash S)/NP}} \quad \dfrac{\mathtt{Hazel}}{\mathtt{NP}}}{\mathtt{NP\backslash S}}}{\mathtt{NP\backslash S}}\,(x)}{\mathtt{S}}\right) : \begin{array}{r}\{s1 \Rightarrow \\ (\{l1 \Rightarrow \mathtt{(judg\ NP\backslash S)}\} \\ \to \mathtt{(judg\ NP\backslash S)})\} \\ \to \mathtt{(judg\ S)}\end{array} \tag{7}$$

where $s1$ is meant to be the channel for the stretching operation. Whereas in the previous example the bound variable was an abstraction over a judgement of a base category such as $\mathtt{NP}$, here the bound variable abstracts over an inference rule. The inference rule can itself be considered as a function, and so this stretched PPT can be considered a higher-order function. This PPT is now looking for one argument to give back a $\mathtt{(judg\ S)}$, where that one argument must itself be a PPT that is looking for a $\mathtt{(judg\ NP\backslash S)}$ on its left to give back a $\mathtt{(judg\ NP\backslash S)}$. The tree for *passionately* above is such a tree, and at this point, β-reduction on (7) applied to (4) completes the stretching operation:

$$\lambda_{s1}x.\left(\dfrac{\dfrac{\mathtt{Bob}}{\mathtt{NP}} \qquad \dfrac{\dfrac{\dfrac{\mathtt{likes}}{\mathtt{(NP\backslash S)/NP}} \quad \dfrac{\mathtt{Hazel}}{\mathtt{NP}}}{\mathtt{NP\backslash S}}}{\mathtt{NP\backslash S}}\,(x)}{\mathtt{S}}\right)\ \hat{s1}\ \left[\lambda_{l1}x.\left(\dfrac{x \quad \dfrac{\mathtt{passionately}}{\mathtt{(NP\backslash S)\backslash(NP^{*}\backslash S)}}}{\mathtt{NP^{*}\backslash S}}\right)\right]$$

$$\to \left(\dfrac{\dfrac{\mathtt{Bob}}{\mathtt{NP}} \qquad \dfrac{\dfrac{\dfrac{\mathtt{likes}}{\mathtt{(NP\backslash S)/NP}} \quad \dfrac{\mathtt{Hazel}}{\mathtt{NP}}}{\mathtt{NP\backslash S}} \qquad \dfrac{\mathtt{passionately}}{\mathtt{(NP\backslash S)\backslash(NP^{*}\backslash S)}}}{\mathtt{NP\backslash S}}}{\mathtt{S}}\right)$$

The use of stretching means that so-called spurious ambiguity in a traditional categorial grammar exists in PPTS, although at the level of the composition of trees and not at the level of the resulting derived proof tree. For example, consider the case of two adjective partial proof trees, both unfoldings of $\mathtt{N/N}$ preceding a $\mathtt{N}$. For convenience, call the left adjective tree P1, the right adjective tree P2, and the (righthand-side) $\mathtt{N}$ tree P3. It is possible to apply P2 to P3 and then use the resulting tree as the argument for P1. It is also possible to stretch the $\mathtt{N}$ conclusion node of P2 (i.e., abstract out an inference rule of type $\mathtt{(judg\ N)} \to \mathtt{(judg\ N)}$) and insert the P1 tree (as the desired inference rule), and then apply the resulting tree to P3. This is analogous to the ambiguity that would result in a standard categorial grammar - both (P1 (P2 P3)) and ((P1 P2) P3) are possible, depending on the use of function composition and application. For PPTS, though, the same derived proof tree would result in either case.

3.4 Trace Assumptions

During the unfolding of a type, a trace assumption can be used which must then be discharged within the PPT that is being constructed. After being discharged, the assumption can then be expected to appear on either the left or right, depending on the context. For handling topicalization, it will be on the opposite side from where the trace originally was. This is an example of the notion of an extended domain of locality. For example, in the following PPT for *likes*, the **NP** assumption is discharged, resulting in the category **NP\S**[3].

$$\lambda_{l1}x.\lambda_{l2}y.\left(\dfrac{y \qquad \dfrac{\dfrac{x \qquad \dfrac{\dfrac{\mathtt{likes}}{\mathtt{(NP\backslash S)/NP}} \quad [\mathtt{NP}]^1}{\mathtt{NP\backslash S}}}{\mathtt{S}}}{\mathtt{NP\backslash S}}\,[1]}{\mathtt{S}}\right) : \begin{array}{r}\{l1 \Rightarrow (\mathtt{judg\ NP}),\\ l2 \Rightarrow (\mathtt{judg\ NP})\}\\ \rightarrow (\mathtt{judg\ S})\end{array} \qquad (8)$$

Figure 10 shows how (8) can be used for a simple case of topicalization. The use of trace assumptions and discharge is constrained in certain ways. We will not describe these constraints here.

3.5 Interpolation

Interpolation refers both to a rule that can be used *during* the construction of a basic PPT, and to a rule used to combine two PPTs, at least one of which must have had interpolation used during its construction. For example, the following tree for *walk* has an interpolation from conclusion node **NP\Sinf** to node **NP\S**. This has the effect of requiring that it be used in a raising construction, such as *Bob seems to walk*, as will be shown below.

$$\lambda_{i1}z\lambda_{l1}x.\left(\dfrac{x \qquad \dfrac{\dfrac{\mathtt{walk(inf)}}{\mathtt{NP\backslash Sinf}}}{\mathtt{NP\backslash S}}\,(z)}{\mathtt{S}}\right) : \begin{array}{r}\{l1 \Rightarrow (\mathtt{judg\ NP}),\\ i1 \Rightarrow (\{r1 \Rightarrow (\mathtt{judg\ NP\backslash Sinf})\}\\ \rightarrow (\mathtt{judg\ NP\backslash S}))\}\\ \rightarrow (\mathtt{judg\ S})\end{array} \qquad (9)$$

Interpolation is similar to the stretched tree for *likes* in that it has an abstraction over an inference rule. However, stretching a PPT only happens during

[3] The discharge is marked by a number (e.g., [1] in (8)) to coindex it with the assumption being discharged.

$$\lambda_{l1}x.\lambda_{l2}y.\left(\frac{y \qquad \dfrac{\dfrac{x \qquad \dfrac{\dfrac{\texttt{likes}}{\texttt{(NP\\S)/NP}} \quad [\texttt{NP}]^1}{\texttt{NP\\S}}}{\texttt{S}}}{\texttt{NP\\S}}\,[1]}{\texttt{S}}\right) \hat{l}1 \left(\frac{\texttt{Mary}}{\texttt{NP}}\right) \hat{l}2 \left(\frac{\texttt{Apples}}{\texttt{NP}}\right)$$

$$\rightarrow \qquad \lambda_{l1}y.\left(\frac{y \qquad \dfrac{\dfrac{\dfrac{\texttt{Mary}}{\texttt{NP}} \qquad \dfrac{\dfrac{\texttt{likes}}{\texttt{(NP\\S)/NP}} \quad [\texttt{NP}]^1}{\texttt{NP\\S}}}{\texttt{S}}}{\texttt{NP\\S}}\,[1]}{\texttt{S}}\right) \hat{l}1 \left(\frac{\texttt{Apples}}{\texttt{NP}}\right)$$

$$\rightarrow \qquad \left(\frac{\dfrac{\texttt{Apples}}{\texttt{NP}} \qquad \dfrac{\dfrac{\dfrac{\texttt{Mary}}{\texttt{NP}} \qquad \dfrac{\dfrac{\texttt{likes}}{\texttt{(NP\\S)/NP}} \quad [\texttt{NP}]^1}{\texttt{NP\\S}}}{\texttt{S}}}{\texttt{NP\\S}}\,[1]}{\texttt{S}}\right)$$

Fig. 10. Derivation of *Apples Mary likes*

the course of the derivation. For a tree with interpolation, as in (9), the inference rule abstraction is done during the course of building the basic PPT, that is, before the start of the derivation.

Thus, this PPT for *walk* can be considered to subcategorize for this abstracted inference rule, just as it also subcategorizes for a `(judg NP)`. This will therefore be a different PPT than the PPT that results in the straight unfolding, as discussed in section 3.2.

Continuing with this example, β-reduction is used to assemble (6) and (9):

$$\lambda_{i1}z.\lambda_{l1}x.\left(\frac{x \qquad \dfrac{\dfrac{\texttt{walk(inf)}}{\texttt{NP\\Sinf}}}{\texttt{NP\\S}}\,(z)}{\texttt{S}}\right) \hat{l}1 \left[\lambda_{r1}x.\left(\frac{\dfrac{\texttt{seems}}{\texttt{(NP*\\S)/(NP\\Sinf)}} \quad x}{\texttt{NP*\\S}}\right)\right]$$

$$\rightarrow \qquad \lambda_{l1}x.\left(\frac{x \qquad \dfrac{\dfrac{\texttt{seems}}{\texttt{(NP*\\S)/(NP\\Sinf)}} \quad \dfrac{\texttt{walk(inf)}}{\texttt{NP\\Sinf}}}{\texttt{NP\\S}}}{\texttt{S}}\right)$$

And now a simple application along the l channel can be done with the the PPT for the subject *Bob*, resulting in the proof tree (10) for *Bob seems to walk.*

$$\left(\frac{\dfrac{\texttt{Bob}}{\texttt{NP}} \qquad \dfrac{\dfrac{\texttt{seems}}{(\texttt{NP}^{*}\backslash\texttt{S})/(\texttt{NP}\backslash\texttt{Sinf})} \quad \dfrac{\texttt{walk(inf)}}{\texttt{NP}\backslash\texttt{Sinf}}}{\texttt{NP}\backslash\texttt{S}}}{\texttt{S}}\right) \tag{10}$$

4 Relationships between PPTs, Natural Deduction, and Proof-Nets

4.1 Natural Deduction or Proof-Nets?

The PPTs (basic and derived) look like natural deduction(ND) trees (and proof-nets in some respects). However there are important differences.

In PPTS there are two modes of satisfying (discharging) the hypotheses (or assumptions). An assumption introduced in unfolding during the construction of basic PPTs is satisfied (discharged) by linking it to the conclusion node of another appropriate tree. This discharge is similar to the cut link in the proof-net representation. On the other hand when the assumption is introduced as a 'trace' assumption during the construction of a basic PPT, its discharge is exactly the same kind of discharge in hypothetical reasoning used in ND trees.

The discharge which is similar to the cut link is external to a basic PPT while the discharge similar to the hypothetical reasoning is internal to a basic PPT. This latter discharge is used only during the construction of a basic PPT. It is not used when PPTs are combined. The locality of this internal discharge severely restricts its power, in contrast to its use in ND trees where it can operate in a global manner.

PPTs can also be thought of as compact and linguistically convenient representations of proof-nets. In fact, there is an implicit claim in our paper that PPTs which are close to ND trees with the differences as described above are just the right objects for linguistic description. The unfolding represented in linear logic proof-nets is, in a sense, *excessive* from the linguistic point of view, i.e, it does not provide a compact linguistic representation.

It is worth considering in this context the arguments that have been made against using natural deduction instead of a linear logic proof-net representation. There are well-known limitations of natural deduction for the full linear logic, but when considering intuitionistic linear logic, natural deduction is "a serious candidate" [5], although with reservations. Its seems to us of interest that in the context of PPTS most of those objections (as outlined in [5]) are not relevant.

There are two main objections to using intuitionistic natural deduction[4]. The first concerns the global nature of the resource management - in Girard's words,

[4] Girard lists four objections to using natural deduction. The first is that it can only handle one, and not multiple, conclusions. Since our system is not a multiple-conclusion system, this is irrelevant, and the rest of his objections concern an intu-

> Due to discharge, the introduction rule for linear implication (and the elimination rule for tensor) does not apply to a formula, but to a whole proof. This *global* character of the rule is quite a serious defect. (his emphasis)

We discuss tensor elimination immediately below, but the main point regarding implication introduction is that in PPTS the hypothetical reasoning is *localized* within the domain of a basic PPT, and does not have the global character that Girard criticizes in more standard natural deduction systems. It is also worth pointing out that since the hypothetical reasoning is in effect built into the proof trees as elementary objects to begin with, no issues regarding hypothetical reasoning arise during parsing. This is because the parsing process just consists of putting together these already-built trees, and no more hypothetical reasoning needs to be done[5].

Girard's second objection is that the use of tensor elimination requires the use of an extraneous formula. As far as we can tell, the linear logic accounts of syntax that we have seen do not make essential use of tensor elimination. Mark Johnson (pc) has suggested to us that a possible use of tensor elimination might for possessive NPs, as in *the king of France's dinner*, in which *France's* could have the type $\mathtt{NP} \otimes \mathtt{NP} \backslash (\mathtt{NP}/\mathtt{N})$. Then NP could serve as the argument for the preposition *of* and then *'s* combines with *the king of France* to form a possessive NP that would then combine with, e.g., *dinner*, to get *(the king of france)'s dinner*. This seems to us to perhaps not be a defininitve counter-example since it is at the morphological level, and so could be easily dealt with in PPTS. A more convincing example would be one in which $\otimes$ was introduced during the derivation and needed to be eliminated later in the derivation.

Therefore, we conclude that natural deduction proofs, rather than full-blown proof-nets, are more appropriate for our purposes here[6].

4.2 PPTS as natural deduction

Because of the non-commutativity in the partial proof trees, the natural deduction system used is very close to associative Lambek natural deduction derivation structures ([3], [15]). There are three main differences:

- two different modes of satisfying hypotheses
- use of the stretching operation
- use of a limited exchange rule

---

itionistic version of linear logic. His second criticism is of a more philosophical nature about the elimination rule being upside down, which he says is a "very inessential" criticism. The remaining two objections are discussed in the main text.

5 The PPT representation also makes the parsing polynomially tractable as in the case of parsing LTAGs.

6 It is worth noting that [6] concludes that the mapping between natural deduction proofs to intuitionistic proof-nets is an isomorphism except for tensor elimination.

The first point was discussed in Section 4.1. The second difference arises as a consequence of the method of linking between different PPTs, which has no obvious analog in a Lambek natural deduction system

The third difference arises from the fact that we allow the hypothesis discharge to occur on the opposite side from the hypothesis itself, as illustrated in the example for topicalization in section 3.4. In effect, what this is is a limited permutation rule. The use of a free permutation rule in categorial grammar is known to lead to the 'collapse' of the grammar ([14]). We are allowing this use of permutation only within a basic PPT, and not when the PPTs further combine with each other. In this way, the unfolding of the categories into 'pre-built' trees allows us more control over the introduction of such structural modalities. To illustrate, (11) shows the scheme for topicalization, and (12) shows the same tree in sequent form. The $\backslash I$ rule is not a Lambek rule, since the withdrawn assumption is not on the left periphery, although it can be made into one by explicitly putting in the *exchange* rule, as in (13).

$$\left(\dfrac{\begin{array}{c}A'\\ \vdots\\ NP\end{array} \qquad \dfrac{\dfrac{\begin{array}{c}B\\ \vdots\\ S/NP\end{array} \quad NP}{S}\,/E}{NP\backslash S}\,\backslash I}{S}\,\backslash E\right) \tag{11}$$

$$\left(\dfrac{\Delta \vdash NP \qquad \dfrac{\dfrac{\Gamma \vdash S/NP \quad x : NP \vdash NP}{\Gamma, x : NP \vdash S}\,/E}{\Gamma \vdash NP\backslash S}\,\backslash I}{\Delta, \Gamma \vdash S}\,\backslash E\right) \tag{12}$$

$$\left(\dfrac{\Delta \vdash NP \qquad \dfrac{\dfrac{\dfrac{\Gamma \vdash S/NP \quad x : NP \vdash NP}{\Gamma, x : NP \vdash S}\,/E}{x : NP, \Gamma \vdash S}\,\mathit{exchange}}{\Gamma \vdash NP\backslash S}\,\backslash I}{\Delta, \Gamma \vdash S}\,\backslash E\right) \tag{13}$$

This type of 'limited permutation' is not the same as the use of the ΔP modality in [3], [15], even aside from the issue of the locality of the proof. The ΔP modality is used to handle the problem of non-peripheral extraction, by moving the argument from the periphery to a medial position, and upon discharge resulting in a type $\mathtt{S/\Delta N}$, which is essentially an $\mathtt{S}$ with an $\mathtt{N}$ gap inside somewhere.

4.3 PPTS and Proof-Nets

There has been increasing interest in the last few years regarding the use of a linear logic proof-net system for natural language uses, particularly for categorial grammar systems (e.g., [18], [16], [17]), As just discussed, we take the view that natural deduction (or at least something very much like natural deduction) is more appropriate for a linguistic application than a proof-net representation. However, in some ways PPTS still has very much the 'flavor' of proof-nets - specifically, the linking of unfilled assumptions and conclusions to connect the PPTS can be thought of as something like linking via 'cut' in a proof-net. So it remains an interesting question as to exactly how PPTS compares to a proof-net representation - what would be involved in trying to recast PPTS in such a framework?

A number of questions immediately arise. First, the basic PPTs combine in a non-commutative way. Therefore, some sort of non-commutative proof-net framework is required, such as those developed by [1] or [18]. However, there is also the use of the limited permutation within a basic PPT. So, there needs to be some intermingling of commutativity and non-commutativity in the proof-net. This is akin to the use of some type of structural modality for permutation in linear logic or associative Lambek calculus. [3] propose such a modality for Lambek calculus, and [21] proposes such a modality for permutation in linear logic.

A larger question, however, is how the stretching and interpolation operations would be handled in a proof-net setting. Say a PPT has been reformulated as a proof-net. How can it be 'stretched' apart to permit the insertion of another proof-net? To illustrate, one approach to representing a PPT as a proof-net would be to adopt a Lambek calculus proof-net system ([18]). Figure 11 shows a simple proof net in this style for a transitive verb, using the polarity directions of [16]. This much is straightforward. However, Figure 12 shows a proof-net in this style for an adverb. An immediate difference, of course, in this type of proof-net from that in, say, [16], is that the category is not unfolded all the way, because of the selectional restrictions imposed, as discussed in Section 3.2.

The linking of unfilled assumptions and conclusion can be seen as cut links. What would be needed to simulate the stretching operation? One possibility would be to 'open up' the *likes* tree by extending two 'prongs' that can act as the sites for cut links[7]. The two prongs would originate from the $\mathtt{NP\backslash S}^-$ node in Figure 11, and would need to connect to the two $\mathtt{NP\backslash S}$ nodes in Figure 12.

There is a close connection here to other work on using proof-nets for natural language purposes. [2] presents a logical formulation of Tree Adjoining Grammar

[7] The interpolation operation could be done in a similar way, except with the 'prongs' existing as part of the proof-net to begin with, thus requiring that they be linked to something.

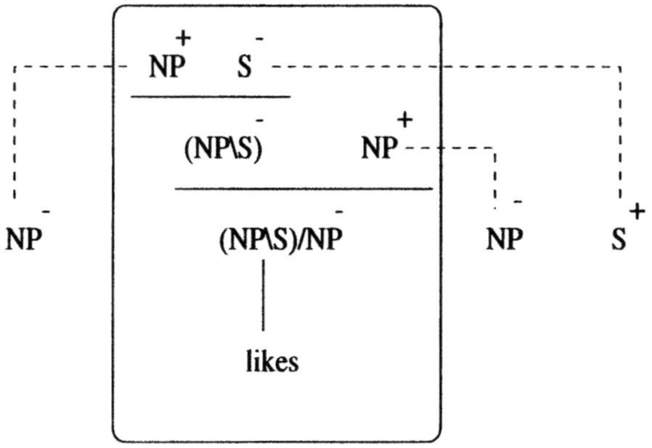

Fig. 11. Proof-net for transitive verb

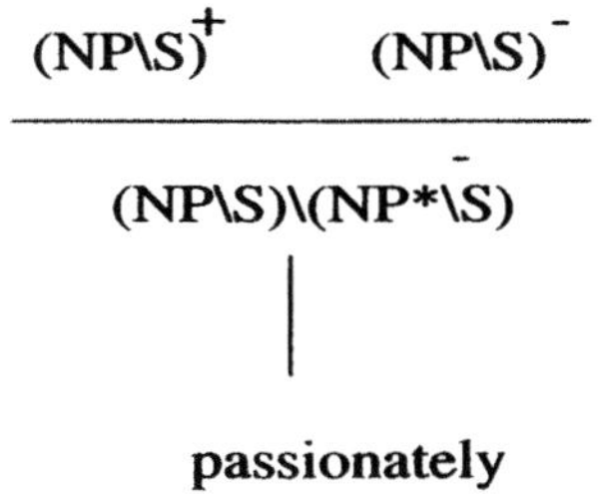

Fig. 12. Proof-net for adverb

using the non-commutative proof-net system of [1][8]. A TAG tree is broken down into a sequent $\Gamma \vdash A$, where Γ is a sequence of formulas representing the links in the TAG tree, and A is the root of the tree. Each such sequent can be rewritten in proof-net form, and a sequence of words is derivable if the associated proof-net consisting of the rewritten sequents can be connected into a valid proof-net. To handle adjunction, they provide a formula of the form $X \multimap X$ when X is a node at which adjunction can take place. The corresponding section of the proof-net is used as a 'handle' for the adjunction rule. A manipulation of the proof-net is done to simulate the adjunction rule of their logical calculus.

This approach to adjunction or stretching is very similar to ours. Essentially, their adjunction formula serves the same purpose as the manipulation in PPTS of a tree to ready it for the stretching operation. A difference is that for them every such possible adjunction node is represented as having already been split apart, while in PPTS that is only done upon demand. Another difference is that since in their system the tree for each word produces several sub-proof-nets, their proof-net representations connect lots of little sub-proofs, some of which have the same origin (i.e., the same TAG tree), and some of which of course do not. Then for clarity they simplify the resulting proof-net by circling "subnets associated to lexical items", and the further simplify by replacing the "internal logical machinery by boxes" to get rid of "superfluous information" since all that is really needed is the information for what corresponds to the substitution and adjunction nodes. For PPTS, this information is what we concentrate on to begin with. This lends futher support, we feel, to our claim that natural deduction trees are more appropriate for natural language uses than full-blown proof-net representation.

There is also a connection to the work of [13], in which 'partial proof-nets' are used as building blocks of their system. These proof-nets are based on POMSET logic, a system based on multiplicative linear logic "enriched with the non-commutative 'before', and which consequently deals with partially ordered multisets instead of ordinary multisets of formulae." For comparison purposes, we discuss here their translation of TAG trees into their system[9] In a manner very similar to that of [2], a TAG tree is broken up into several formulas, which are put together via axiom links to form a partial proof-net. Substitution is done by axiom links[10], and adjunction is done by breaking an axiom link in a par-

[8] The motivation behind the PPTS system is not just to encode LTAG into a categorial framework but rather to construct a categorial framework incorporating key ideas of LTAG.

[9] They also discuss a Lambek calculus embedding, as well as using their partially ordered multisets to handle some phenomena, such as scrambling and clitic climbing, that can only be handled to a limited degree in PPTS (or TAG). Further work on extensions of PPTS analogous to extensions of LTAG is in progress at present.

[10] Note that [2] describe substitution in terms of cut links, and [13] describe it in terms of axiom links. It is not clear to us if this difference in terminology is reflective of any deeper differences, or if it is simply symptomatic of the close connection between cut and axiom links.

tial proof-net, "thus creating two new axiom-links which link previously linked dual nodes in the PPN respectively to two premises of a tensor link", and then performing the adjunction by linking this newly-created tensor link to its dual in another tree. This is analogous to our stretching of a node, together with the actual stretching operation.

Once again, it seems to us that the crucial information about a partial proof-net consists of what axiom links there are to communicate with other partial proof-nets, and which axiom links can be broken to give rise to secondary conclusions. It is also worth noting that their use of tensor and par does not invalidate our earlier suggestions that tensor elimination is not needed for linguistic applications. It is used in [13] to perform the equivalent of the stretching operation, while in PPTS an operation is defined for this purpose. In essense, we trade off the cost of having a separate stretching rule (and even in both [13] and [2], such stretching is done by some otherwise 'abnormal' changes in the system), for the benefit of a greatly simplified representation of the essential linguistic information.

5 Conclusion

We have discussed the relationship between a categorial system (PPTS) based on partial proof trees (PPTs), resource sensitive logics and the nature of syntactic constraints. PPTS incorporates some of the key insights of lexicalized tree adjoining grammar, namely the notion of an extended domain of locality and the consequent factoring of recursion from the domain of dependencies. PPTS therefore inherits the linguistic and computational properties of that system. In particular, we have discussed the relationship between PPTS, natural deduction, and linear logic proof-nets, and argue that natural deduction rather than a proof-net system is more appropriate for the construction of the PPTs. We have also shown how the use of PPTs allows us to 'localize' the management of resources, thereby freeing us from this management as the PPTs are combined. The operations that build the basic PPTs are distinct from those that combine the PPTs. Resource sensitivity considerations enter essentially only during the construction of the basic PPTs.

References

1. M. Abrusci. Phase semantics and sequent calculus for pure noncommutative classical linear propositional logic. In *The Journal of Symbolic Logic*, 56(4):1403-1451, 1991.
2. M. Abrusci, Ch. Fouqueré, J. Vauzeilles. Tree adjoining grammar and noncommutative linear logic. In *this volume*, 1997.
3. G. Barry, M. Hepple, N. Leslie, G. Morrill. Proof figures and structural operators for categorial grammar. In *Proceedings of the Fifth Conference of the European Chapter of the Association for Computational Linguistics.*

4. Jacques Garrigue and Hassan Aït-Kaci. The typed polymorphic label-selective λ-calculus. POPL 1994.
5. Jean-Yves Girard. Linear Logic: Its syntax and semantics. In Girard, Lafont, and Regnier, eds., *Advances in Linear Logic*, Cambridge University Press, Cambridge, England, pp. 1-42.
6. Mark Johnson. Natural deduction and proof nets intuitionistic linear logic. Manuscript, Brown University. 1996.
7. Aravind K. Joshi, K. Vijay-Shanker, and David Weir. The convergence of mildly context-sensitive grammar formalisms. In P. Sells, S. Shieber, and T. Wasow, eds., *Foundational Issues in Natural Language Processing*, Cambridge, MA:MIT Press.
8. Aravind K. Joshi. TAGs in categorial clothing, presented at the *Tree Adjoining Grammar Workshop* (TAG+), Institute for Research in Cognitive Science, University of Pennsylvania, Philadelphia, June 1992. A revised version, 'Unfolded Types', was presented at the Logic and Language Workshop at LSA, Ohio State University, August 1993.
9. Aravind Joshi and Seth Kulick Partial proof trees as building blocks for a categorial grammar. To appear in *Linguistics and Philosophy*, 1997.
10. Aravind K. Joshi and Yves Schabes. Tree adjoining grammars. To appear in Arto Saolmaa and Gzegorz Rosenberg, eds., *Handbook of Formal Languages and Automata*, Vol. 3, Springer-Verlag, Heidelberg, 1997.
11. R. Kasper, B. Kiefer, K. Netter, and K. Vijay-Shanker. Compilation of HPSG to TAG. In *30th Annual Meeting of the Association for Computational Linguistics.*
12. Anthony S. Kroch and Aravind K. Joshi. The linguistic relevance of tree adjoining grammars. Technical Report MS-CIS-85-16, Department of Computer and Information Science, University of Pennsylvania, 1985.
13. Alain Lecomte and Christian Retoré. Words as Modules: a lexicalised grammar in the framework of linear logic proof nets. In Carlos Martin-Vide, editor, *Proceedings of the 2nd International Conference on Mathematical Linguistics*, John Benjamins Publishing Company, Amsterdam, 1997.
14. Michael Moortgat. *Categorial Investigations: Logical and Linguistic Aspects of the Lambek Calculus* Foris, Dordrecht, 1988.
15. Glyn Morrill. *Type-logical grammar.* Kluwer, Dordrecht.
16. Glyn Morrill. *Clausal Proofs and Discontinuity* In *Bulletin of the IGPL*, Vol. 3, No. 2,3, pp. 403-427. 1995.
17. Christian Retoré. Calcul de Lambek et logique linéaire. *Traitement Automatique des Langues* 37(2):39–70.
18. Dirk Roorda. *Resource Logics: proof-theoretical investigations*, Ph.D. dissertation, Universiteit van Amsterdam. 1991.
19. K. Vijay-Shanker. 1992. Using descriptions of trees in a tree adjoining grammar. *Computational Linguistics*, 18(4):481–517.
20. The XTAG-Group. A lexicalized tree adjoining grammar for english. Technical Report IRCS 95-03, University of Pennsylvania. 1995.
21. D.N. Yetter. Quantales and (noncommutative) linear logic. In *Journal of Symbolic Logic* 55, pp. 41-64.

Inessential Features

Marcus Kracht *

II. Mathematisches Institut
Freie Universität Berlin
Arnimallee 3
D-14195 Berlin
kracht@math.fu-berlin.de

Abstract. If one converts surface filters into context free rules, one has to introduce new features. These features are strictly nonlexical, and their distribution is predictable from the distribution of the lexical features. Now, given a (feature based) context free grammar, we ask whether one can identify the nonlexical features. This is not possible; however, the notion of an *inessential feature* offers an approximation. To arrive at a descriptive theory of language one needs to eliminate all the inessential features. One can measure the complexity of a language by the complexity of the formulae needed to define the distribution of inessential features.

1 Introduction

According to the lexicalist doctrine, the features that get used in syntax must be exactly those that are used in the lexicon as well. That is to say, the lexicon already provides the necessary distinctive features on which syntax operates, and there is no need to introduce new ones. We will give two examples. In X–bar–syntax a distinction is drawn between (usually) three levels in the completion of a phrase: the lexical level, the intermediate level and the phrasal level. From a lexicalist perspective, although talk about the various levels is not meaningless, their use in syntax should in principle be eliminable. In other words the status of a constituent in a syntactic structure is not freely assigned by syntax, but follows exactly from the assignment of purely lexical features in the syntactic tree. If something is a phrase in a structure, it necessarily is a phrase in that structure. For example, in

(1.) *John is [very [proud of his son]].*

we have the adjective *proud*, and the adjectival phrase *very proud of his son*. That the latter is a phrase follows from the principles of X–bar–syntax. [2] There is an

* This research has been carried out in collaboration with the Innovationskolleg 'Formale Modelle kognitiver Komplexität' (INK 12/A3) at Potsdam University, funded by the DFG. I wish to thank Jens Michaelis for many useful discussions. Thanks also to Hans Leiß and James Rogers for raising interesting questions.

[2] Notice that strictly speaking, at least the distinction between lexical and phrasal level is justified for a lexicalist. In English, *John* acts like a noun phrase, not like

intuition that syntax should only talk about those features that are given by the lexicon. In other words, syntax and morphology share a pool of features, which we call lexical features. A syntactic theory (and a morphological theory) is not allowed to introduce new features, and computation should proceed using only the given lexical features. This is not a substantial criterion but a criterion that makes it possible to separate lexical from nonlexical features and to provide a complexity measure for the computational system (or syntax) alone. However, in the Minimalist Program it is actually assumed that the computational system performs computations only on the feature complexes of the lexical elements which get inserted from the lexicon. Consequently, Chomsky 1995 has sought to eliminate the levels from X–bar–syntax (see also the discussion thereof in Kracht 1996b).

The other example concerns the slash–feature of GPSG. [3] Here the intuition is somewhat clearer. The slash–feature was introduced to control the dependency between a filler and the corresponding gap. As an example we use simple question formation and topicalization. Consider the contrast between (2.), (3.) and (4.).

(2.) *Alfred is [stealing books].*
(3.) *What is Alfred [stealing]?*
(4.) *Books, Alfred is [stealing].*

Steal is a transitive verb, and it normally expects its object to the right. However, in questions and other constructions, this need not be so. Two solutions offer themselves. One is to supply the object in form of an empty element, and then discuss separately the distribution of such empty elements; another is to revise the context restriction of transitive verbs according to the facts just presented. The first has been implemented in transformational grammar, the latter in GPSG. In GPSG, a transitive verb may occur either in a constituent together with a direct object, or it may form a constituent of the form *transitive verb with an object missing*, which is coded with the help of the slash–feature roughly as tv[slash : np], where tv is the category of transitive verbs. The problem is that the addition of this new feature is inadmissible for a lexicalist. Any transitive verb is equally admissible in the contexts (2′.), (3′.) and (4′.). There is therefore no need to discriminate between words that can be used in one of the contexts and not the other. [4]

(2′.) *Alfred is ____ books.*
(3′.) *What is Alfred ____?*
(4′.) *Books, Alfred is ____.*

---

a noun, and there are a number of phrasal pro–forms with this property, too, e. g. *one*, *such*, *so*.

[3] Notice that what we call features in the sequel are booleans, not features in the sense of GPSG and feature logic.

[4] Actually, this is not quite right. (3′.) can be filled by *doing*, while (2′.) and (4′.) cannot. However, *do* is anyway syntactically distinct from a full verb. Hence, that it discriminates the given contexts need not invalidate our argument.

Thus in both cases we have an instance of features that are not motivated from the lexicon but only from syntax.

2 The Constituent Logic(s)

2.1 The Basic Structures

Some notation shall be fixed for convenience. With M a set, let $\wp(M)$ denote the powerset of M, and let M^* be the set of finite strings of elements from M. An element of M^* is denoted by bold face type, e. g. $\mathbf{x}$. Given binary relations R, S over M, put

$$R \circ S := \{\langle x, z\rangle : (\exists y)(\langle x, y\rangle \in R \text{ and } \langle y, z\rangle \in S)\}$$

Moreover, R^n is defined inductively by $R^0 := \{\langle x, x\rangle : x \in M\}$, $R^{n+1} := R \circ R^n$. Finally, $R^* := \bigcup_{n \geq 0} R^n$ and $R^+ := \bigcup_{n>0} R^n$.

Our original structures are ordered trees — possibly infinitely branching — and decorated with features from a given set F of features. F can in principle be any set (it may even even empty) but it is always required to be *finite*. Here, an *ordered labelled tree over* F is a quadruple $\mathfrak{O} = \langle T, <, L, \xi\rangle$, where $<$ is a tree ordering on T, $\xi : T \to \wp(F)$ is a function, called the *labelling function*, and L an ordering *compatible* with $<$, the *left-of-relation*. $<$ is a *tree ordering* on T if $<$ is a binary relation on T which is transitive, irreflexive, the sets $\{y : y > x\}$ are linear for all x, and there is an r such that $r > x$ for all $x \neq r$. A *leaf* is a node x such that for no y, $y < x$. We write $y \leq x$ if $y < x$ or $y = x$. L is *compatible with* $<$ if it satisfies the following postulates. (l) L is linear on the leaves, (c) xLy iff for all leaves u and v such that $u \leq x$ and $v \leq y$ it holds that uLv. Given a labelled ordered tree, we define two relations $\prec$ (child–of) and $\sqsubset$ (immediate left–sister–of).

$x \prec y$ iff $x < y$ and for no z, $x < z < y$,
$x \sqsubset y$ iff xLy, for no v: $xLvLy$, and for some z: $x \prec z$ and $y \prec z$.

We put $\mathsf{T}(\mathfrak{O}) := \langle T, \prec, \sqsubset, \xi\rangle$. A quadruple $\mathfrak{T} = \langle T, \prec, \sqsubset, \xi\rangle$ where T is a set, $\prec$ and $\sqsubset$ binary relations on T and $\xi : T \to \wp(F)$ a function is called an *F–tree* if it is of the form $\mathsf{T}(\mathfrak{O})$ for some ordered labelled tree $\mathfrak{O}$. The relations $<$ and L can be recovered as follows: $< = \prec^+$, and $L = \prec^* \circ \sqsubset^+ \circ \succ^*$. Therefore, the class of F–trees can be characterized directly. Namely, $\mathfrak{T} = \langle T, \prec, \sqsubset, \xi\rangle$ is a finite F–tree iff (α) – (δ) hold. (α) The transitive closure $\prec^+$ of $\prec$ is a tree ordering, (β) $\sqsubset^+$ and its converse are both irreflexive linear orders, (γ) If $x, y \prec z$ then $x \sqsubset^+ y$, $x = y$ or $y \sqsubset^+ x$, (δ) If $x \prec z$ and $x \sqsubset^+ y$ or $y \sqsubset^+ x$ then also $y \prec z$.

2.2 Modal Languages for Trees

With each $f \in F$ we associate a boolean constant f. (For simplicity, we also write f in place of f.) Our boolean connectives are $\top$, $\wedge$, $\neg$, the others being defined from them in the usual way. We denote by $\mathfrak{Tm}_{Boo}(F)$ the set of boolean terms over F that can be formed in this language. We denote members of $\mathfrak{Tm}_{Boo}(F)$ by a, b etc. We write $\mathsf{a} \leq \mathsf{b}$ if $\mathsf{a} \to \mathsf{b}$ is a boolean tautology. For a set $C \subseteq F$ we put

$$\chi(C) := \bigwedge_{f \in C} \mathsf{f} \wedge \bigwedge_{f \in F-C} \neg \mathsf{f}$$

Each boolean term over F is equivalent to a disjunction of formulae $\chi(C)$ for certain C (for example the disjunctive normal form).

There are a number of languages with which we will talk about these structures. The first three will be introduced in this section. The largest of them is called *Olt* (orientation language over trees). It is identical to propositional dynamic logic (**PDL**) over four basic programs, called *up*, *down*, *left* and *right*. Recall that **PDL** has two sorts of expressions, *programs* and *propositions*. There is a set *Var* of propositional variables, a set F of propositional constants, and a set Π_0 of program constants. Propositions are formed by using boolean connectives. The basic set is $\top$, $\neg$ and $\wedge$, all others are defined in the usual way. Moreover, if α is a program and φ a proposition, then $[\alpha]\varphi$ and $\langle\alpha\rangle\varphi$ are propositions. We assume that $[\alpha]\varphi$ is equivalent with $\neg\langle\alpha\rangle\neg\varphi$. Programs are formed in the following way. Members of Π_0 are programs, called *basic programs*. If α and β are programs, then $\alpha;\beta$, $\alpha \cup \beta$ and α^* are programs as well. We define $\alpha^+ := \alpha;\alpha^*$. Finally, if φ is a proposition, then $\varphi?$ is a program. In our case,

$$\Pi_0 = \{\mathit{left}, \mathit{right}, \mathit{up}, \mathit{down}\}$$

We write $\Diamond_{\uparrow}$ for $\langle \mathit{up} \rangle$, $\Box_{\uparrow}$ for $[\mathit{up}]$, and similar conventions are used for $\Diamond_{\downarrow}$, $\Box_{\downarrow}$, $\Diamond_{\rightarrow}$, $\Box_{\rightarrow}$, $\Diamond_{\leftarrow}$ and $\Box_{\leftarrow}$. Moreover, we write $\Diamond_{\uparrow}^*$ for $\langle \mathit{up}^* \rangle$, $\Box_{\uparrow}^*$ for $[\mathit{up}^*]$, $\Diamond_{\uparrow}^+$ for $\langle \mathit{up}^+ \rangle$ and $\Box_{\uparrow}^+$ for $[\mathit{up}^+]$ (and likewise for *down*, *left* and *right*). There are two more languages which are of interest to us. The first is *BOlt(F)*, the *basic* orientation language, which is a 4–modal language based on the operators $\Box_{\downarrow}$, $\Box_{\uparrow}$, $\Box_{\leftarrow}$ and $\Box_{\rightarrow}$, with additional constants from F. The other language is what we call the *weak* orientation language *WOlt(F)* of Blackburn, de Rijke & Meyer–Viol 1996; it is a modal logic based on the primitive operators $\Box_{\uparrow}$, $\Box_{\uparrow}^*$, $\Box_{\downarrow}$, $\Box_{\downarrow}^*$, $\Box_{\leftarrow}$, $\Box_{\leftarrow}^*$, $\Box_{\rightarrow}$ and $\Box_{\rightarrow}^*$. [5] Both languages can be construed as fragments of **PDL**. Namely, *BOlt(F)* coincides with the $*$–free fragment of **PDL**, also known as **EPDL**. *WOlt(F)* coincides with the $*$–free fragment over Π_1 where

$$\Pi_1 := \Pi_0 \cup \{\mathit{up}^*, \mathit{down}^*, \mathit{left}^*, \mathit{right}^*\}$$

The structures for these logics are the same for all languages, namely generalized Kripke–structures $\mathfrak{T}$ together with a valuation function for the constants from F. Generalized Kripke–structures here are simply called *structures* and are quintuples $\langle T, \prec, \sqsubset, \mathbb{T}, \xi \rangle$ such that T is a non–empty set, $\prec$ and $\sqsubset$ binary relations over T, $\xi : T \to \wp(F)$ and $\mathbb{T} \subseteq \wp(T)$ a system of sets closed under relative complement, intersection and $[\alpha]$, where for $B \subseteq T$

$$[\alpha]B := \{x : (\forall y)(\langle x, y \rangle \in R(\alpha) \to y \in B)\} .$$

[5] This language has a different name in the quoted paper, but we decided to harmonize the terminology here.

Here α is a program of the language and $R(\alpha)$ the associated binary relation in T. $R(\alpha)$ is computed as follows.

$$\begin{array}{lll@{\qquad}lll} R(right) & := & \sqsubset & R(left) & := & \sqsupset \\ R(up) & := & \prec & R(down) & := & \succ \\ R(\alpha;\beta) & := & R(\alpha)\circ R(\beta) & R(\alpha\cup\beta) & := & R(\alpha)\cup R(\beta) \\ R(\alpha^*) & := & R(\alpha)^* & & & \end{array}$$

$\langle T,\prec,\sqsubset,\xi\rangle$ is a Kripke–structure if $\langle T,\prec,\sqsubset,\wp(T),\xi\rangle$ is a generalized Kripke–structure. So, the structures for these languages differ only with respect to the closure properties for the system $\mathbb{T}$. The Kripke–structures do not change. (Readers unfamiliar with generalized Kripke–structures may think of them as Kripke–structures instead. This may go at the expense of precision, but is more intuitive to begin with.)

A *model* is a triple $\mathfrak{M} = \langle\mathfrak{T},\beta,x\rangle$, where $\mathfrak{T}$ is a generalized Kripke–structure, $\beta : Var \to 2^f$ an assignment, and $x \in f$. For a formula φ in $Olt(F)$ $\mathfrak{M} \models \varphi$ is defined by induction on φ.

$$\begin{array}{lcl} \langle\mathfrak{T},\beta,x\rangle \models \top & \Leftrightarrow & \text{true} \\ \langle\mathfrak{T},\beta,x\rangle \models p & \Leftrightarrow & x \in \beta(p) \\ \langle\mathfrak{T},\beta,x\rangle \models \mathsf{f} & \Leftrightarrow & \mathsf{f} \in \xi(x) \\ \langle\mathfrak{T},\beta,x\rangle \models \neg\varphi & \Leftrightarrow & \langle\mathfrak{T},\beta,x\rangle \not\models \varphi \\ \langle\mathfrak{T},\beta,x\rangle \models \varphi\wedge\psi & \Leftrightarrow & \langle\mathfrak{T},\beta,x\rangle \models \varphi;\psi \\ \langle\mathfrak{T},\beta,x\rangle \models \langle\alpha\rangle\varphi & \Leftrightarrow & \text{there is } y \text{ such that } \langle x,y\rangle \in R(\alpha) \text{ and } \langle\mathfrak{T},\beta,y\rangle \models \varphi \end{array}$$

This means in detail that

$$\begin{array}{lcl} \langle\mathfrak{T},\beta,x\rangle \models \Diamond_{\rightarrow}\varphi & \Leftrightarrow & \text{there is } y \sqsupset x \text{ such that } \langle\mathfrak{T},\beta,y\rangle \models \varphi \\ \langle\mathfrak{T},\beta,x\rangle \models \Diamond_{\leftarrow}\varphi & \Leftrightarrow & \text{there is } y \sqsubset x \text{ such that } \langle\mathfrak{T},\beta,y\rangle \models \varphi \\ \langle\mathfrak{T},\beta,x\rangle \models \Diamond_{\downarrow}\varphi & \Leftrightarrow & \text{there is } y \prec x \text{ such that } \langle\mathfrak{T},\beta,y\rangle \models \varphi \\ \langle\mathfrak{T},\beta,x\rangle \models \Diamond_{\uparrow}\varphi & \Leftrightarrow & \text{there is } y \succ x \text{ such that } \langle\mathfrak{T},\beta,y\rangle \models \varphi \\ \langle\mathfrak{T},\beta,x\rangle \models [\alpha;\beta]\varphi & \Leftrightarrow & \langle\mathfrak{T},\beta,x\rangle \models [\alpha][\beta]\varphi \\ \langle\mathfrak{T},\beta,x\rangle \models [\alpha\cup\beta]\varphi & \Leftrightarrow & \langle\mathfrak{T},\beta,x\rangle \models [\alpha]\varphi;[\beta]\varphi \\ \langle\mathfrak{T},\beta,x\rangle \models [\alpha^*]\varphi & \Leftrightarrow & \langle\mathfrak{T},\beta,x\rangle \models \varphi;[\alpha]\varphi;[\alpha^2]\varphi;\ldots \end{array}$$

Furthermore, $\langle\mathfrak{T},\beta\rangle \models \varphi$ if $\langle\mathfrak{T},\beta,x\rangle \models \varphi$ for all $x \in T$, and $\mathfrak{T} \models \varphi$ if $\langle\mathfrak{T},\beta\rangle \models \varphi$ for all valuations β. Given a class $\mathfrak{X}$ of generalized Kripke–structures,

$$\mathsf{Th}\,\mathfrak{X} := \{\varphi \in Olt(F) : (\forall\mathfrak{T}\in\mathfrak{X})(\mathfrak{T}\models\varphi)\}$$

The logic of F–trees is denoted by $\mathbf{CL}(F)$ ($\mathbf{BCL}(F)$, $\mathbf{WCL}(F)$). The reader should be aware of the fact that these logics may admit models which are not based on F–trees. Given a logic Λ, we denote by $\mathsf{Mod}(\Lambda)$ ($\mathsf{Krp}(\Lambda)$, $\mathsf{FKrp}(\Lambda)$) the set of model structures (Kripke–structures, finite Kripke–structures) for Λ. (Notice that generally we do not need to know from what language Λ is drawn.) Even though some of our definitions are parametric in the choice of the language, we will often suppress that dependency unless it is relevant. Also, we speak of an F–**logic** when we mean an extension of the logic of F–trees in one of the languages under consideration. The logics of n–ary branching trees are obtained by adding the (constant) axiom $(\Box^{\rightarrow})^n\bot$.

With a modal logic Λ we associate the following consequence relations. $\Phi \Vdash_\Lambda \phi$ if ϕ can be deduced from Φ and the theorems of Λ by means of modus ponens and the rule $\chi/\Box\chi$, where $\Box$ is any box–like modal operator. (So, in $Olt(F)$ this rule takes the form $\chi/[\alpha]\chi$, where α is a program.) Furthermore, we write $\Phi \vdash_\Lambda \varphi$ if φ can be derived from Φ and the theorems of Λ by modus ponens alone. We call $\vdash_\Lambda$ the *local consequence relation* and $\Vdash_\Lambda$ the *global consequence relation* of Λ. The following holds. $\Phi \vdash_\Lambda \varphi$ iff for all $\mathfrak{T} \in \mathsf{Mod}(\Lambda)$, all valuations β and $x \in T$, if $\langle \mathfrak{T}, \beta, x\rangle \models \Phi$ then $\langle \mathfrak{T}, \beta, x\rangle \models \varphi$. $\Phi \Vdash_\Lambda \varphi$ if for all $\mathfrak{T} \in \mathsf{Mod}(\Lambda)$ and all valuations β, if $\langle \mathfrak{T}, \beta\rangle \models \Phi$ then $\langle \mathfrak{T}, \beta\rangle \models \varphi$. The local deducibility relation has a deduction theorem, that is, for all formulae φ, ψ and sets of formulae Φ

$$\Phi; \varphi \vdash_\Lambda \psi \qquad \Leftrightarrow \qquad \Phi \vdash_\Lambda \varphi \rightarrow \psi$$

A logic Λ is *complete* with respect to a class $\mathfrak{X}$ of frames if $\Lambda = \mathsf{Th}\,\mathfrak{X}$; that is, $\psi \in \Lambda$ exactly when $\mathfrak{T} \models \psi$ for all $\mathfrak{T} \in \mathfrak{X}$. Λ has the *finite model property* of $\Lambda = \mathsf{Th}(\mathsf{FKrp}(\Lambda))$. Λ is *decidable* if there is an algorithm solving for each φ the problem '$\varphi \in \Lambda$' (which is the same as '$\vdash_\Lambda \varphi$'). A logic that has the finite model property and is finitely axiomatizable is decidable.

Say that a logic Λ has the *global finite model property* if whenever $\Phi \nVdash_\Lambda \varphi$ for finite Φ then for some finite $\mathfrak{T} \in \mathsf{Mod}(\Lambda)$ and some valuation β on $\mathfrak{T}$ we have $\langle \mathfrak{T}, \beta\rangle \models \Phi$ but $\langle \mathfrak{T}, \beta\rangle \not\models \varphi$. And say that Λ is *globally decidable* if for finite Φ, the question '$\Phi \Vdash_\Lambda \varphi$' is decidable. If a logic has global finite model property (is globally decidable) then it has the finite model property (is decidable).

2.3 Axiomatizing the Logics of Trees

Let us turn now to the axiomatization of the logic of F–trees. Consider the logic $BCL(F)$, obtained by adding the following axioms to $\mathbf{K}_4$:

(a)	$p \rightarrow \Box^{\rightarrow}\Diamond^{\leftarrow}p$	(b)	$p \rightarrow \Box^{\leftarrow}\Diamond^{\rightarrow}p$
(c)	$p \rightarrow \Box^{\uparrow}\Diamond^{\downarrow}p$	(d)	$p \rightarrow \Box^{\downarrow}\Diamond^{\uparrow}p$
(e)	$\Diamond^{\leftarrow}p \rightarrow \Box^{\rightarrow}p$	(f)	$\Diamond^{\rightarrow}p \rightarrow \Box^{\leftarrow}p$
(g)	$\Diamond^{\uparrow}p \rightarrow \Box^{\uparrow}p$	(h)	$\Diamond^{\downarrow}\Diamond^{\uparrow}p \rightarrow p$
(i)	$\Diamond^{\downarrow}\Diamond^{\leftarrow}p \rightarrow \Diamond^{\downarrow}p$	(k)	$\Diamond^{\downarrow}\Diamond^{\rightarrow}p \rightarrow \Diamond^{\downarrow}p$
(l)	$\Diamond^{\downarrow}\top \rightarrow \Diamond^{\downarrow}\Box^{\rightarrow}\bot \wedge \Diamond^{\downarrow}\Box^{\leftarrow}\bot$	(m)	$\Box^{\uparrow}\bot \rightarrow \Box^{\rightarrow}\bot \wedge \Box^{\leftarrow}\bot$

We note first that the logic of the set of finite F–trees is not axiomatizable in $BOlt(F)$. This is so because the one point structure in which all relations are reflexive is a model for the theory of F–trees. Furthermore, $\mathbf{BCL}(F)$ is Sahlqvist, hence canonical and complete with respect to (possibly infinite) Kripke structures. However, it is already complete with respect to finite F–trees. For let $\varphi \notin \mathbf{BCL}(F)$. Then there is a $\mathfrak{T}$, a Kripke frame for $\mathbf{BCL}(F)$, a valuation β and a point x such that $\langle \mathfrak{T}, \beta, x\rangle \models \neg\varphi$. $\mathfrak{T}$ can be unravelled from x into a (possibly infinite) F–tree $\mathfrak{U}$. Let d be the modal depth of φ, and let y be a point such that x can be reached from y in exactly d steps, going down. It is not hard to show that we can select a finite subtree $\mathfrak{U}$ of $\mathfrak{T}$ of depth at most $2d$ and with root y such that $\mathfrak{U} \models \mathbf{BCL}(F)$ and $\langle \mathfrak{U}, \beta, x \rangle \models \neg\varphi$.

Proposition 1. *The logic* $\boldsymbol{BCL}(F)$ *is complete with respect to finite* F*-trees.*

This theorem is also a direct consequence of Theorem 2.

$\mathbf{WCL}(F)$ (and $\mathbf{CL}(F)$) is obtained from $\mathbf{BCL}(F)$ by adding the following axioms in addition to the axioms for the basic normal logic (here, $\Box^+ := \Box\Box^*$)

$$
\begin{array}{llll}
(n) & \Box_{\uparrow}^+(\Box_{\uparrow}^+ p \to p) \to \Box_{\uparrow}^+ p & (o) & \Box_{\downarrow}^+(\Box_{\downarrow}^+ p \to p) \to \Box_{\downarrow}^+ p \\
(p) & \Box_{\leftarrow}^+(\Box_{\leftarrow}^+ p \to p) \to \Box_{\leftarrow}^+ p & (q) & \Box_{\rightarrow}^+(\Box_{\rightarrow}^+ p \to p) \to \Box_{\rightarrow}^+ p
\end{array}
$$

$$
\begin{array}{llll}
(r) & \Diamond_{\uparrow}\Diamond_{\downarrow} p \leftrightarrow \Diamond_{\leftarrow}^* p \vee \Diamond_{\rightarrow}^* p & & \\
(t) & \Diamond_{\uparrow}^* \Box_{\uparrow} \bot & (t) & \Diamond_{\downarrow}^* \Box_{\downarrow} \bot \\
(u) & \Diamond_{\rightarrow}^* \Box_{\leftarrow} \bot & (v) & \Diamond_{\leftarrow}^* \Box_{\rightarrow} \bot
\end{array}
$$

This axiomatization is not independent.

Theorem 2 (Blackburn & Meyer–Viol & de Rijke). $\boldsymbol{WCL}(F)$ *is complete with respect to finite* F*-trees.*

There are two consequences of this theorem that are worth noting. The global and the local consequence relation are closely interrelated, since it is possible in $\mathbf{WCL}(F)$ and $\mathbf{CL}(F)$ to define the universal modality of Goranky & Passy 1992, denoted here by $\boxtimes$.

Proposition 3 (Goranko & Passy). *Define* $\boxtimes$ *by* $\boxtimes\varphi := \Box_{\uparrow}^* \Box_{\downarrow}^* \varphi$. *Assume that* $\Lambda \supseteq \boldsymbol{(W)CL}(F)$. *Then*

$$\Phi \Vdash_{\Lambda} \phi \quad \Leftrightarrow \quad \boxtimes\Phi \vdash_{\Lambda} \phi$$

Hence if Λ *has the finite model property (is decidable) it has the global finite model property (is globally decidable).*

Proof. Let $\Phi \Vdash_{\Lambda} \varphi$. Assume that $\langle \mathfrak{T}, \beta, x \rangle \models \boxtimes\Phi$ for an F-tree $\mathfrak{T}$. Then for all $y \in T$, $\langle \mathfrak{T}, \beta, y \rangle \models \Phi$, and so $\langle \mathfrak{T}, \beta \rangle \models \Phi$, by definition. Hence $\langle \mathfrak{T}, \beta \rangle \models \varphi$ and so $\langle \mathfrak{T}, \beta, x \rangle \models \varphi$. This shows $\boxtimes\Phi \vdash_{\Lambda} \varphi$. Now assume that $\boxtimes\Phi \vdash_{\Lambda} \varphi$. Then obviously $\boxtimes\Phi \Vdash_{\Lambda} \varphi$. Moreover, $\Phi \Vdash_{\Lambda} \boxtimes\Phi$ and so $\Phi \Vdash_{\Lambda} \varphi$.

This means that the global consequence relation is reducible to the global consequence relation in the present context. The next theorem immediately follows.

Corollary 4. $\boldsymbol{WCL}(F)$ *has the (global) finite model property and is (globally) decidable.*

We can use Theorem 4 to prove a theorem announced in Kracht 1995a.

Theorem 5. $\boldsymbol{CL}(F)$ *is complete with respect to finite trees. Hence* $\boldsymbol{CL}(F)$ *has the (global) finite model property and is (globally) decidable.*

Proof. It suffices to show that $\mathbf{CL}(F)$ has the finite model property. Moreover, we assume $F = \emptyset$. This simplifies the notation somewhat. Let ψ be a formula of $Olt(F)$. We associate a formula $\nabla(\psi)$ with ψ as follows. For each χ in the Fischer–Ladner–Closure of ψ we pick a new variable q_χ. Then $\nabla(\psi)$ is the conjunction of the following formulae

$$\begin{array}{llllll} q_p & \leftrightarrow & p & q_{\neg\chi} & \leftrightarrow & \neg q_\chi \\ q_{\chi\vee\omega} & \leftrightarrow & q_\chi \vee q_\omega & q_{\chi\wedge\omega} & \leftrightarrow & q_\chi \wedge q_\omega \\ q_{\langle\chi?\rangle\omega} & \leftrightarrow & q_{\chi\wedge\omega} & q_{\langle\alpha\cup\beta\rangle\chi} & \leftrightarrow & q_{\langle\alpha\rangle\chi} \vee q_{\langle\beta\rangle\chi} \\ q_{\langle\alpha;\beta\rangle\chi} & \leftrightarrow & q_{\langle\alpha\rangle\langle\beta\rangle\chi} & q_{\langle\alpha^*\rangle\chi} & \leftrightarrow & q_\chi \vee q_{\langle\alpha;\alpha^*\rangle\chi} \\ & & & & & \\ q_{\langle\alpha\rangle\chi} & \leftrightarrow & \langle\alpha\rangle q_\chi & \multicolumn{3}{l}{\alpha \in \{\mathit{up}, \mathit{down}, \mathit{left}, \mathit{right}\}} \end{array}$$

Notice that $\nabla(\psi) \in \mathit{WOlt(F)}$. It is not hard to see that for a model $\langle\mathfrak{T}, \beta\rangle$ based on an F–tree $\mathfrak{T}$, if $\langle\mathfrak{T}, \beta\rangle \models \nabla(\psi)$ then for any formula χ in the Fischer–Ladner–Closure of ψ, $\langle\mathfrak{T}, \beta\rangle \models \chi \leftrightarrow q_\chi$. Hence the following holds

$$\vdash_{\mathbf{CL}} \psi \quad \Leftrightarrow \quad \nabla(\psi) \Vdash_{\mathbf{CL}} q_\psi$$

Furthermore, for $\Phi \subseteq \mathit{WOlt(F)}$ and $\psi \in \mathit{WOlt(F)}$ we have

$$\Phi \Vdash_{\mathbf{CL}} \psi \quad \Leftrightarrow \quad \Phi \Vdash_{\mathbf{WCL}} \psi$$

From right to left is immediate, since $\mathbf{CL}(\mathrm{F})$ extends $\mathbf{WCL}(\mathrm{F})$. Moreover, suppose the right hand side fails. Then there is a model $\mathfrak{M} = \langle\mathfrak{T}, \beta\rangle$ based on a finite tree $\mathfrak{T}$ such that $\mathfrak{M} \models \Phi$ but $\mathfrak{M} \nvDash \psi$. However, $\mathfrak{M}$ also is a model for $\mathbf{CL}(F)$, and so the left hand side fails as well. So, $\vdash_{\mathbf{CL}} \psi$ iff $\nabla(\psi) \Vdash_{\mathbf{WCL}} q_\psi$. Finally, by Proposition 3,

$$\nabla(\psi) \Vdash_{\mathbf{WCL}} q_\psi \quad \Leftrightarrow \quad \vdash_{\mathbf{WCL}} \boxtimes\nabla(\psi) \rightarrow q_\psi$$

Putting these three together we get that $\vdash_{\mathbf{CL}} \psi$ iff $\vdash_{\mathbf{WCL}} \boxtimes\nabla(\psi) \rightarrow q_\psi$. Now suppose that the last fails. Then there exists a finite model $\langle\mathfrak{T}, \beta, x\rangle \models \boxtimes\nabla(\psi); \neg\psi$. Then $\langle\mathfrak{T}, \beta, x\rangle \models \neg\psi$. Moreover, $\mathfrak{T}$ is a model for $\mathbf{CL}(F)$.

Theorem 6. *Let Φ be a finite set of variable–free formulae of Olt(F), and let $\Lambda := \mathbf{Olt}(F) \oplus \Phi$. Then Λ has the (global) finite model property and is (globally) decidable.*

Proof. (The argument is given in Kracht 1995a. Therefore we will just sketch it.) We may work with the case $\Phi = \{\varphi\}$ (for example, let φ be the conjunction of all members of Φ). Now notice that the following holds for all ψ

$$\Vdash_\Lambda \psi \quad \Leftrightarrow \quad \varphi \Vdash_{\mathbf{CL(F)}} \psi \quad \Leftrightarrow^{\ddagger} \quad \vdash_{\mathbf{CL(F)}} \boxtimes\varphi \rightarrow \psi$$

(where ‡ follows from Proposition 3). Now the theorem follows from Theorem 2.

3 Syntactic Codes

3.1 Boolean Grammars

Contrary to the usual definition in the theory of formal languages we will distinguish between the grammar and the lexicon. A language is generated by a pair consisting of a grammar and a lexicon. Recall that a language over a set D is simply a subset of D^*.

Definition 7. Let D and F be sets. An F–**lexicon** for D is a pair $\langle D, \gamma \rangle$, where $\gamma : D \to \wp(F)$. D is called the **dictionary** of $\mathbb{L}$ and γ the **class assignment function.** [6]

The concept of a (context free) grammar for F–trees is defined as follows.

Definition 8. A **context free F–grammar** is a triple $\mathbb{G} = \langle \Sigma, \Omega, R \rangle$ where Σ and Ω are boolean F–terms, called the **start term** and the **stop term**, and $R \subset \mathfrak{Tm}_{Boo}(F) \times \mathfrak{Tm}_{Boo}(F)^+$ a finite set, the set of **rules.** It is required that every term in a rule from R is consistent. Rules are as usual written $\mathsf{x} \to \mathsf{y}_0 \ldots \mathsf{y}_{k-1}$. An F–tree $\mathfrak{T} = \langle T, \prec, \sqsubset, \xi \rangle$ is **generated by** $\mathbb{G}$, in symbols $\mathbb{G} \gg \mathfrak{T}$, if (i.) for the root x: $\chi(\xi(x)) \leq \Sigma$, (ii.) for all leaves y: $\chi(\xi(y)) \leq \Omega$, and (iii.) for all non–leaves z, if $z \succ y_i$, $i < k$, and $y_i \sqsubset y_j$ iff $i < j < k$, then there exists $\mathsf{a} \to \mathsf{b}_0 \ldots \mathsf{b}_{k-1} \in R$ such that $\chi(\xi(z)) \leq \mathsf{a}$ and $\chi(\xi(y_i)) \leq \mathsf{b}_i$ for all $i < k$.

Boolean grammars manipulate only nonterminal symbols in the usual sense of the word. Hence, Ω should not be thought of as a set of nonterminals, but as a description of the lexical nodes. A *grammar* for an actual language is therefore a pair $\langle \mathbb{G}, \mathbb{L} \rangle$, where $\mathbb{G}$ is an F–grammar and $\mathbb{L}$ an F–lexicon.

This split into grammar and lexicon will turn out to be crucial. Given an F–tree $\mathfrak{T}$ and $\mathbf{a} = \langle a_i : i < k \rangle \in D^*$, let $\mathbf{a} \in \mathsf{Y}(\langle \mathfrak{T}, \mathbb{L} \rangle)$ if the leaves of $\mathfrak{T}$ are x_i, $i < k$, and $x_i L x_j$ whenever $i < j$, and for all $i < k$ we have $\gamma(a_i) = \xi(x_i)$. $\mathsf{Y}(\langle \mathfrak{T}, \mathbb{L} \rangle)$ is the set of strings modulo γ represented by $\mathfrak{T}$. For a set S of F–strings we put

$$\mathsf{Lang}(\langle S, \mathbb{L} \rangle) := \bigcup_{\mathfrak{T} \in S} \mathsf{Y}(\langle \mathfrak{T}, \mathbb{L} \rangle)$$

For a grammar $\mathbb{G}$, we let

$$\mathsf{Lang}(\langle \mathbb{G}, \mathbb{L} \rangle) := \bigcup_{\mathbb{G} \gg \mathfrak{T}} \mathsf{Y}(\langle \mathfrak{T}, \mathbb{L} \rangle)$$

We will give two examples of boolean grammars. Both will be needed later. In both cases we do not use the boolean nature of the labels explicitly in the notation, to keep matters simple. Distinct symbols denote distinct atoms of the free boolean algebra generated by the features.

---

[6] For technical convenenience we allow no lexical ambiguity. Also, each $a \in D$ has a unique syntactic category, and all categories are mutually exclusive. See also Section 5.

A Grammar for Movement This grammar generates the language $M := ab^* \cup b^*a$. In transformational terms this language can be generated by writing a right regular grammar that generates b^*a, and then having an optional movement process that 'topicalizes' a. However, there is a regular grammar that generates this language without movement. Put $\Sigma :=$ x, $\Omega :=$ a ∨ b and let the set R of rules be

x	→	a	y
x	→	a	
x	→	b	z
y	→	b	y
y	→	b	
z	→	b	z
z	→	a	

Now $\mathbb{M} := \langle \Sigma, \Omega, R \rangle$. The lexicon is $\langle \{a, b\}, \gamma \rangle$, where $\gamma(a) = \{\mathsf{a}\}$ and $\gamma(b) = \{\mathsf{b}\}$. For let the first rule apply. Then we generate a · y. It is easy to see that y $\to^*$ b^+. If the second rule applies, the string generated is a alone. Now assume that the third rule is applied. Then we get the string b · z. Moreover, z $\to^*$ $\mathsf{b}^* \cdot \mathsf{a}$. Thus, the grammar generates the preterminal strings of the forms $\mathsf{a} \cdot \mathsf{b}^* \cup b^* \cdot \mathsf{a}$. Hence, with the lexicon as given, the language $ab^* \cup b^*a$ is generated, as promised.

A Grammar for Reflexives The next grammar is a simplified grammar for illustrating the behaviour of reflexives. It generates the language

$$R := \{a[d^* \cup c^+d(c \cup d)^* \cup d^+c(c \cup d)^*]\}^*a$$

This language can be more succinctly described as follows. It generates a string **x** exactly if (i) **x** begins and ends with a and (ii) for any occurrence of c, a d must also occur in between the occurrence of c and the next a either to the left or to the right. To phrase condition (ii) into linguistic terminology suppose that this languages is generated by a right regular grammar. Then we may say that each occurrence of a c must a–command an occurrence of d that a–commands the given c. Here, x *a–commands* y if for all nodes z properly dominating x and also dominating an a, z dominates y. To see the connection with reflexives, think of a as being a complementizer, of c as being a reflexives, and of d as an antecedent. With some generosity we see that what is encoded is the requirement that a reflexive only occurs in a sentence that also contains an antecedent. (We trust that reader can see this. A sufficiently realistic grammar would be too complicated for the present paper.) The set S of rules is the following.

u	→	a	
u	→	a	u ∨ q ∨ v ∨ w ∨ x
q	→	a	q ∨ u
v	→	d	v ∨ u

w ∨ y	→	d	y	x ∨ r	→	c	r
y	→	c	z ∨ u	r	→	c	s ∨ u
z	→	c ∨ d	z ∨ u	s	→	c ∨ d	s ∨ u

$\Sigma := \mathsf{x}$, $\Omega := \mathsf{a} \vee \mathsf{c} \vee \mathsf{d}$. $\mathbb{R} := \langle \Sigma, \Omega, S \rangle$. The lexicon is $\langle \{a, c, d\}, \kappa \rangle$ where $\kappa(a) = \{\mathsf{a}\}$, $\kappa(c) = \{\mathsf{c}\}$ and $\kappa(d) = \{\mathsf{d}\}$. (To see that this grammar generates R, let U be the language produced by u. Observe that q produces $a^+ \cdot U$, v produces $d^+ \cdot U$, w produces $d^+c(c \cup d)^* \cdot U$ and x produces $c^+d(c \cup d)^* \cdot U$. Let $P := d^+ \cup d^+c(c \cup d)^* \cup c^+d(c \cup d)^*$ and $Z = a^+ \cup P$. Then we get $U = a \cup (a[Z \cup \{\epsilon\}])U$. So, $U = (a[Z \cup \{\epsilon\}])^* a$. We may actually rewrite this as $(aP)^*a$. So, $U = R$, as required.)

3.2 Quasi Context Free Sets

We say that a set S of finite F–trees is a context–free set if there exists an F–grammar $\mathbb{G}$ such that $S = \{\mathfrak{T} : \mathbb{G} \gg \mathfrak{T}\}$. Now, given a rule $\rho = \mathsf{x} \rightarrow \mathsf{y}_0 \ldots \mathsf{y}_{k-1}$ we define

$$\gamma(\rho) := \mathsf{x} \rightarrow \Diamond(\neg \ominus \top \wedge \mathsf{y}_0 \wedge \ominus(\mathsf{y}_1 \wedge \ominus(\mathsf{y}_2 \wedge \ldots \wedge \ominus(\mathsf{y}_{k-1} \wedge \neg \ominus \top) \ldots)))$$

Given an F–grammar $\mathbb{G} = \langle \Sigma, \Omega, R \rangle$ let

$$\gamma(\mathbb{G}) := (\neg \ominus \top \rightarrow \Sigma) \wedge (\neg \Diamond \top \rightarrow \Omega) \wedge \bigvee_{\rho \in R} \Diamond \top \rightarrow \gamma(\rho)$$

We call $\gamma(\mathbb{G})$ the **characteristic formula** of $\mathbb{G}$. It is not hard to see that for a finite F–tree $\mathfrak{T}$, $\mathbb{G} \gg \mathfrak{T}$ iff $\mathfrak{T} \models \gamma(\mathbb{G})$. The following is now immediate.

Proposition 9. *Let S be a context-free set of finite n-branching F-trees. Then* $\mathsf{Th}\, S$ *is axiomatizable over* $\boldsymbol{CL}_n(F)$ *by formula in* $BOlt(F)$.

The converse need not hold. For a characterization of the language in which only context–free sets can be defined see Rogers 1997.

Let $G \subseteq F$ and $\mathfrak{T} = \langle T, \prec, \sqsubset, \xi, \mathbb{T} \rangle$. Define the **projection** $\mathfrak{T}_G$ of a $\mathfrak{T}$ onto G by $\mathfrak{T}_G := \langle T, \prec, \sqsubset, \zeta, \mathbb{T} \rangle$, where $\zeta(x) := \xi(x) \cap G$. Likewise, the projection S_G of a class S of F–structures is defined by $S_G := \{\mathfrak{T}_G : \mathfrak{T} \in S\}$.

Definition 10. Let S be a set of finite F–trees. S is called **quasi context–free** if there exists a finite set G and a context–free set T of $F \cup G$–trees such that $S = T_F$.

There is a characterization of quasi context–free sets of finite F–trees in Rogers 1994 and Kracht 1995b. This characterization is given in terms of logic.

Grammars define well–formed sets of structures. In our case we assume that these structures are finite F–trees, where F is an arbitrary but fixed set of features. It follows that a grammar may be viewed as a logic. This view has been defended in Kracht 1995a. It is not entirely unproblematic for the reason that logics typically admit infinite structures while grammars do not generate such structures. We will see here that the logics we will be studying in connection with context–free grammars are complete with respect to their finite structures, so that the infinite structures — though not excluded by the logics — can be ignored in practice. This is similar to non–standard models of the real line. The difference between a logic and a grammar is roughly the following. A logical system is just a description of the legitimate objects with no indication of how to obtain one, while a generating device allows to obtain just the right set of structures with no indication of their characteristic properties apart from the immediate ones. For a generating device it is therefore not immediate how to recognize the structures that it produces, though in the case of context sensitive language such recognizing algorithms can easily be obtained (though they may not be efficient, but that is another matter). It would be preferrable if one had a method to mediate between generative systems on the one hand and descriptive systems on the other. Such a method has been proposed in Kracht 1995b. It shows how to construct a grammar from a description. These descriptions may not contain variables, however, and the outcome is always a context-free grammar. Though that is known to be a restriction, since natural languages are not necessarily context-free, we will deal with that case throughout this paper.

Theorem 11 Coding Theorem. *Let Λ be an axiomatic expansion of $\boldsymbol{CL}_n(F)$. Λ is the logic of a quasi context-free set iff $\Lambda = \boldsymbol{CL}_n(F) \oplus \Phi$ for a finite set of variable-free formulae from $Olt(F)$. Moreover, there is an algorithm which, given Φ, computes a set G, formulae $\varphi_g \in Olt(F)$ for $g \in G$, and an $F \cup G$-grammar $\mathbb{G}$ such that (i) the set of finite structures of Λ is exactly the projection to F of the set of $F \cup G$-trees generated by $\mathbb{G}$ and (ii) a $F \cup G$-tree $\mathfrak{T}$ is generated by Λ iff $\mathfrak{T}_F$ is a Λ-structure and $\mathfrak{T} \models \mathsf{g} \leftrightarrow \varphi_g$ for each $g \in G$.*

The theorem expresses not only that given a logic axiomatized by constant formulae there exists a context free grammar over an expanded set of features that generates a set T of which the set of finite Λ-models is a projection. It also says that we can compute formulae that explicitly tell us how the additional features are distributed with respect to the set of original features.

4 Inessential and Eliminable Features

4.1 Inessential Features

In intuitive terms, a feature (by which we mean a boolean constant in this connection) is called *inessential* if its distribution is fixed by the other features. To give an example, [slash : np] is inessential, for it can be reconstructed from a tree in which it is not present. (This claim, however, is not trivial and depends on assumptions on movement in syntax.)

Definition 12. Let S be a set of F-trees and $G \subseteq F$. Put $H := F - G$. G is **inessential in** S if for every $\mathfrak{T} \in S_H$ there exists exactly one $\mathfrak{U} \in S$ such that $\mathfrak{T} = \mathfrak{U}_H$.

(This definition can obviously be generalized to general structures.) Thus, given an arbitrary set of F-trees, and a set G of features, S_H is the projection of S onto the complement of G in F. If $\mathfrak{T} \in S_H$ then, by definition of S_H, there exists at least one $\mathfrak{U}$ of which $\mathfrak{T}$ is the projection. G is inessential in S if there exists no two F–trees of which $\mathfrak{T}$ is the projection, for all $\mathfrak{T} \in S_H$. This means that the features of H alone suffice to identify a tree in S. However, it is by no means clear that given the projection $\mathfrak{T}_H$ of $\mathfrak{T}$ onto H we can produce $\mathfrak{T}$ from $\mathfrak{T}_H$ by some algorithm. In the general case this is impossible. However, in the present discussion we are interested in sets of trees definable by means of axioms. The reader is asked to verify that a set G is inessential in S iff all $\mathsf{g} \in G$ are inessential. Thus, we will often specialize without warning to the case of a single feature rather than a set.

Definition 13. Let Λ be an F–logic Λ and $G \subseteq F$ a set of features. We say that G is **inessential** in Λ if it is inessential in $\mathsf{Mod}(\Lambda)$.

The notion of being inessential can be rephrased in logical terms using the notion of an *implicit definition.*

Definition 14. Let Λ be a logic extending $\mathbf{CL}_n(F)$ and let $\varphi(p, \mathbf{q})$ be a formula. $\varphi(p, \mathbf{q})$ is called a **global implicit definition** of p if

$$\varphi(p, \mathbf{q}); \varphi(r, \mathbf{q}) \Vdash_\Lambda p \leftrightarrow r$$

In this definition, φ may also contain the constants from F. The next theorem considers the case where p replaces the occurrences of a given boolean $\mathsf{f} \in F$. For the purpose of that theorem $\varphi[p/\mathsf{f}]$ is the result of uniformly replacing each occurrence of f by p.

Proposition 15. *Let $\Lambda = \boldsymbol{CL}(F) \oplus \varphi$ be an F–logic. f is inessential in Λ iff $\varphi[p/\mathsf{f}]$ is a global implicit definition of p in Λ. Moreover, if φ is a constant formula, f is inessential in Λ iff it is inessential in $\mathsf{FKrp}(\Lambda)$.*

Proof. Let f be inessential in Λ. Assume that $\langle \mathfrak{T}, \beta \rangle \models \varphi[p/\mathsf{f}]; \varphi[q/\mathsf{f}]$. Then $\langle \mathfrak{T}, \beta, x \rangle \models p$ exactly if $\langle \mathfrak{T}, \beta, x \rangle \models \mathsf{f}$. Hence $\mathfrak{T} \models \varphi$, which implies that $\mathfrak{T} \in \mathsf{Krp}(\Lambda)$. Furthermore, also $\langle \mathfrak{T}, \beta, x \rangle \models q$ iff $\langle \mathfrak{T}, \beta, x \rangle \models \mathsf{f}$, and so $\langle \mathfrak{T}, \beta \rangle \models p \leftrightarrow q$. This shows that $\varphi[p/\mathsf{f}]$ implicitly defines p. The converse is immediate. For the second claim notice that Λ has the finite model property. This implies among other that $\varphi[p/\mathsf{f}]; \varphi[p/\mathsf{f}] \Vdash_\Lambda p \leftrightarrow q$ iff for every finite model $\mathfrak{T}$ and valuation β, if $\langle \mathfrak{T}, \beta \rangle \models \varphi[p/\mathsf{f}]; \varphi[q/\mathsf{f}]$ then $\beta(p) = \beta(q)$.

Theorem 16. *Let $\Lambda = \boldsymbol{CL}(F) \oplus \varphi$ for a constant formula φ and let $\mathsf{f} \in F$. Then it is decidable whether or not f is essential in Λ.*

Proof. f is essential iff $\varphi[p/\mathsf{f}]; \varphi[q/\mathsf{f}] \Vdash_\Lambda p \leftrightarrow q$. By Proposition 3 this is equivalent to

$$\vdash_\Lambda \boxtimes\varphi[p/\mathsf{f}] \wedge \boxtimes\varphi[q/\mathsf{f}]. \rightarrow .(p \leftrightarrow q)$$

Now, Λ is decidable by Theorem 6 and this establishes the claim.

4.2 Eliminable Features

Let Λ be a logic (= grammar) and f an inessential feature. We know then that the distribution of that feature is fixed by the distribution of the other features. Nevertheless, it may not be possible to know in what way it must be distributed.

Definition 17. Let S be a set of F–structures, and $f \in F$. f is **eliminable** in S if there is a formula $\chi(p)$ such that for all $\mathfrak{T} \in S$

$$\langle \mathfrak{T}, \beta \rangle \models \chi(p) \Leftrightarrow \langle \mathfrak{T}, \beta \rangle \models p \leftrightarrow \mathsf{f}$$

Definition 18. Let Λ be a logic and $\varphi(p, \mathbf{q})$ an implicit definition of p. $\psi(\mathbf{q})$ is called a **(corresponding) explicit definition** of p in Λ if $\varphi(p, \mathbf{q}) \Vdash_\Lambda p \leftrightarrow \psi(\mathbf{q})$.

Definition 19. An inessential feature f of $\Lambda \supseteq \mathbf{CL}(F)$ is called **eliminable** if there exists an explicit definition in Λ.

Now assume that f is eliminable in Λ. Then it is inessential, and we have

$$\begin{aligned} \Lambda &= \mathbf{CL}(F) \oplus \varphi \\ &= \mathbf{CL}(F) \oplus \varphi \oplus \mathsf{f} \leftrightarrow \psi \\ &= \mathbf{CL}(F) \oplus \varphi[\psi/\mathsf{f}] \oplus \mathsf{f} \leftrightarrow \psi \end{aligned}$$

Thus, an axiomatization of Λ can be given that uses the structural axiom $\varphi[\psi/\mathsf{f}]$, in which f does no longer occur, plus an explicit axiom $\mathsf{f} \leftrightarrow \psi$ defining the distribution of f. In that case we may simply pass to the language over the set $H := F - \{\mathsf{f}\}$. Define

$$\Lambda^{-f} := \mathbf{CL}(F - \{\mathsf{f}\}) \oplus \varphi[\psi/\mathsf{f}]$$

Then Λ^{-f} axiomatizes the logic of the structures $\mathsf{Mod}(\Lambda)_H$.

Proposition 20. *Let* $\Lambda = \mathbf{CL}(F) \oplus \varphi$ *be an* F*-logic, and* $\mathsf{f} \in F$. *Put* $H := F - \{\mathsf{f}\}$. *Suppose that* f *is eliminable with explicit definition* ψ. *Then*

$$\mathsf{Th}(\mathsf{Mod}(\Lambda)_H) = \mathbf{CL}(F) \oplus \varphi[\psi/\mathsf{f}]$$

A good illustration of these concepts is Chomsky 1995. Here it is argued that the additional features distinguishing levels in X–bar syntax are inessential since they can be deduced from the structure with the categorial labels alone. It is not hard to see that the level attributes are also eliminable. However, eliminability is not always guaranteed.

Theorem 21. *There exists a logic* Λ *axiomatized by constant formulae and an inessential feature which is not eliminable.*

For a proof take the example of Kracht 1995b of a logic $\Lambda \supseteq \mathbf{CL}_3(\{\mathsf{f}, \mathsf{g}\})$ which axiomatizes the logic of ternary branching trees such that g is is true along the branches of a binary branching subtree, while f holds at those leaves exactly where g holds. Then g is inessential. For let $\mathfrak{T} = \langle T, \prec, \sqsubset, \xi \rangle$ be an $\{\mathsf{f}\}$–tree. Then there is at most one way to turn $\mathfrak{T}$ into an $\{\mathsf{f}, \mathsf{g}\}$–tree. Namely, let $\mathfrak{U} := \langle T, \prec, \sqsubset, \zeta \rangle$ such that $\mathsf{f} \in \zeta(x)$ iff $\mathsf{f} \in \xi(x)$ and $\mathsf{g} \in \zeta(x)$ iff there exists a leaf $y \prec^+ x$ such that $\mathsf{f} \in \xi(y)$. Then if $\mathfrak{T}$ is the projection of a $\{\mathsf{f}, \mathsf{g}\}$–tree $\mathfrak{V}$, $\mathfrak{V} = \mathfrak{U}$. So, g is indeed inessential. It it not hard to come up with a formula $\varphi(p, q)$ which implicitly defines p in the way prescribed. But g is not eliminable. A proof can be found in Kracht 1996a.

5 On the Descriptive Complexity of Language

5.1 Naturalizing the Feature System

We are going to exemplify the usefulness of these concepts by illustrating how they allow to determine the complexity of languages. This complexity is not measured in terms of time or space complexity bounds for the recognition problem (or other problems) but rather in terms how of complicated it is to describe the facts of the language. We have considered four languages which we will discuss now: the language of boolean expressions, the basic language, the weak language and the (full) language for F–trees. Suppose that the language is given to us a subset of D^*, D the dictionary. We need to introduce a set F of features to begin with. Already here some assumptions must be made.

Definition 22. Let $S \subseteq D^*$ be a language over D, and let $a \in D$. Put $C_S(a) := \{\langle \mathbf{x}, \mathbf{y} \rangle \in D^* \times D^* : \mathbf{x} \cdot a \cdot \mathbf{y} \in S\}$. Call a and b **syntactically indistinguishable** if $C_S(a) = C_S(b)$.

Let F be a set of features. A *class* (*over* F) is a subset of F. A *class assignment function* on D is a function $\gamma : D \to \wp(F)$. A class assignment is *proper* if $C_S(a) = C_S(b)$ implies $\gamma(a) = \gamma(b)$; it is *minimal* if $\gamma(a) = \gamma(b)$ implies $C_S(a) = C_S(b)$. We are interested in proper and minimal class assignments. Proper assignments are such that they assign the same class to syntactically indistinguishable elements. Minimal assignments put all indistinguishables in one class. Given γ and a class $C \subseteq F$, let $E_\gamma(C) = \{a : \gamma(a) = C\}$ and call it the *lexical extension* of the class C. If the lexical extension of C is not empty, we call C a *lexical class*. Now, if there are for example three classes, there must be at least two features. But then we have four classes, so one of the classes has empty lexical extension and is therefore not lexical. Roughly, the *theory* of the lexicon $\langle D, \gamma \rangle$ is the set of all lexical classes. Formally, we put

$$\mathsf{M}(\gamma) := \bigvee_{E_\gamma(C) \neq \emptyset} \chi(C)$$

Given an F–lexicon $\mathbb{L} = \langle D, \gamma \rangle$ and a set $G \subseteq F$, put $\gamma_G(a) := \wp(a) \cap G$ and $\mathbb{L}_G := \langle D, \gamma_G \rangle$.

Definition 23. Let D be a dictionary, $S \subseteq D^*$ a languange over D and $\mathbb{L} = \langle D, \gamma \rangle$ an F–lexicon. G is a **natural subset** of F if $\mathbb{L}_G$ is a proper and minimal class assignment. If G is natural, $\mathbb{L}_G$ is called the **naturalization** of $\mathbb{L}$ with respect to S. If $\mathbb{L} = \mathbb{L}_G$, $\mathbb{L}$ is called **natural** with respect to S.

A lexicon may possess different naturalizations with respect to one and the same language. To see this, take two features, f_1 and f_2, and assume that only the classes $\{\mathsf{f}_1\}$ and $\{\mathsf{f}_2\}$ are lexical. This is the case with $S = \{ab\}$, and $\gamma(a) = \{\mathsf{f}_1\}$, $\gamma(b) = \{\mathsf{f}_2\}$. Then both $\{\mathsf{f}_1\}$ and $\{\mathsf{f}_2\}$ are natural subsets. (One can also show that natural subsets need even not be equal size. Namely, the boolean algebra of subsets of $\{a, b, c, d\}$ is generated by $\{\{a\}, \{b\}, \{c\}\}$ and also by $\{\{a, b\}, \{b, c\}\}$.) However, take two natural sets G and H. Then each member of H can be expressed as a boolean term over G, and each member of G by a boolean term over H. Since we generally care about definitions only up to interdefinability, we allow ourselves to speak about *the* natural subset and in particular about *the* naturalization of a lexicon.

5.2 Descriptive Complexity

We are now approaching the definition of a complexity hierarchy for languages. The idea is very simply put the following. We require that the language S be the language of a set U of F–trees. We now try to eliminate all features that are not in the natural set. The complexity of the language is measured in terms of the complexity of the defining formulae for the nonnatural features. To make this absolutely restrictive we require that each constituent has a class that is also lexical. This forbids the features to be used in combinations in which they do not occur in the lexicon.

Definition 24. Let S be a set of F–trees, $\mathbb{L} := \langle D, \gamma \rangle$ a lexicon and $L := \mathsf{Lang}(\langle S, \gamma \rangle)$. S is a **natural set of F–trees with respect to** $\mathbb{L}$, if $\mathbb{L}$ is a proper and minimal lexicon with respect to L and for all $\langle T, <, \sqsubset, \xi \rangle \in S$ and all nodes x, $\xi(x)$ is a lexical class.

Definition 25. Let S be a set of F–trees and $\mathbb{L}$ a lexicon. Let G be a subset of F such that S_G is natural with respect to $\mathbb{L}$. Then $T := S_G$ is the **naturalization of** S. Let $\varphi \in \mathit{Olt}(G)$ be such that

$$\mathsf{Th}\, T = \mathbf{CL}(G) \oplus \mathsf{M}(\gamma) \oplus \varphi$$

Then $\mathbf{CL}(G) \oplus \mathsf{M}(\gamma) \oplus \varphi$ is called the **natural theory** of S.

Of course, φ is not uniquely determined. However, it is clear from the definition that the logic $\mathbf{CL}(G) \oplus \mathsf{M}(\gamma) \oplus \varphi$ is uniquely determined by G. Now, if a different natural set is chosen, we get a logic $\mathbf{CL}(H) \oplus \mathsf{M}(\delta) \oplus \psi$, and formulae $\chi_g \in \mathfrak{Tm}_{Boo}(H)$, $g \in G$, $\omega_h \in \mathfrak{Tm}_{Boo}(G)$, $h \in H$, such that

1. $\mathsf{M}(\delta)[\omega_h/\mathsf{h} : h \in H]$ is derivable in $\mathbf{CL}(G) \oplus \mathsf{M}(\gamma)$,
2. $\mathsf{M}(\gamma)[\chi_g/\mathsf{g} : g \in G]$ is derivable in $\mathbf{CL}(H) \oplus \mathsf{M}(\delta)$,

3. $\psi[\omega_h/\mathsf{h} : h \in H]$ is derivable in $\mathbf{CL}(G) \oplus \mathsf{M}(\gamma) \oplus \varphi$,
4. $\varphi[\chi_g/\mathsf{g} : g \in G]$ is derivable in $\mathbf{CL}(H) \oplus \mathsf{M}(\delta) \oplus \psi$.

The two logics are interpretable in each other modulo boolean expressions, and hence the natural theory is unique up to boolean interpretation.

Definition 26. Let S be a set of F–trees, $\mathbb{L}$ a lexicon and G a natural subset. The **descriptive complexity** of S is defined as follows. S has complexity **pc** (**b**, **w**, **pdl**) if for a nonnatural feature f, there exists a formula $\varphi(p)$ from $\mathfrak{Tm}_{Boo}(G)$ ($BOlt(G)$, $WOlt(G)$, $Olt(G)$) such that

$$S_G \models \mathsf{f} \leftrightarrow \varphi[\mathsf{f}/p]$$

The reader may verify that the complexity class does not depend on the choice of G. Moreover, if S is quasi context free and has complexity α where $\alpha \neq pc$, then $\mathsf{Th}\, S$ can be axiomatized by a sentence of complexity α as well. The only exception is pc. Here, the sentence is of complexity b. For take the charactistic axiom of the context free grammar defined in Section 3.1). Now replace in it the unnatural features by their explicit definitions. This returns a formula of identical complexity. In a last step we define the complexity class of a language.

Definition 27. Let D be a dictionary, and $L \subseteq D^*$ a language. L has **complexity** α if there exists a set of features F, a set S of F–trees, and an F–lexicon $\mathbb{L}$ such that $L = \mathsf{Lang}(\langle S, \gamma\rangle)$ and S has complexity α.

5.3 Examples

We are giving examples of languages which are of different complexity class. The languages we choose are simplified languages displaying certain phenomena of natural language. Looking at these examples we will demonstrate that natural language has at least complexity *pdl.*

Languages of Complexity pc. Let us begin with the lowest complexity class. By definition, if L is a context free language of complexity pc, the defining formulae for the nonnatural features are booleans. That means, nonnatural features serve no structural purpose, and we are in effect dealing with a class of grammars that we call *natural.* They are defined as follows.

Definition 28. Let $\langle \mathbb{G}, \mathbb{L}\rangle$ be a grammar for the language $S \subseteq D^*$. We say that $\langle \mathbb{G}, \mathbb{L}\rangle$ is a **natural context free grammar** if the assignment of the lexicon is proper and minimal, and for the theory of the lexicon $\mathsf{M}(\gamma)$ we have $\Sigma \leq \mathsf{M}(\gamma)$, $\Omega \leq \mathsf{M}(\gamma)$ and for every rule $\mathsf{a} \rightarrow \mathsf{b}_0 \ldots \mathsf{b}_{k-1}$, $\mathsf{a} \leq \mathsf{M}(\gamma)$ and $\mathsf{b}_i \leq \mathsf{M}(\gamma)$ for all $i < k$.

The second part of the definition is equivalent to the requirement that $\mathbb{G} \gg \mathfrak{T}$ only if for every node x, $\xi(x) = C_S(a)$ for some $a \in D$.

Consider the case where $D = \{a\}$. Then there are no natural features. In a natural grammar the rules have the form $\top \rightarrow \top \ldots \top$. Hence, a natural context free grammar over the empty set of features is uniquely identifiable by the set of branching numbers for its rules. The reader may verify that the language $\{a\}$ is generated by a natural context free grammar, while $\{a^n\}$ is not, for every $n > 1$. Natural grammars look like a very restricted class of grammars. But they are not. Natural languages are to a large part generable by a natural context free grammar. Simply observe that in many cases a constituent can be replaced in a structure by a single lexical element. The 'nonnaturalness' of natural languages is largely induced by longdistance effects (movement, binding) as well as coordination.

Languages of Complexity b. Languages of complexity *b* allow elements to exercise influence over elements that are a specified number of nodes apart. This is the case for example in case assignment or selection of multiple arguments. It can be shown that all finite languages are of complexity *b*; as we have seen, not all of them are of complexity *pc*. To take a more interesting case, let us discuss the language $M := ab^* \cup b^*a$. We know it can be generated by the grammar $\mathbb{M}$ above. However, only the sets $\{\mathsf{a}\}$ and $\{\mathsf{b}\}$ are natural. Let us take $G := \{\mathsf{a}\}$. We have $\mathsf{M}(\gamma) = (\mathsf{a} \wedge -\mathsf{b}) \vee (\mathsf{b} \wedge -\mathsf{a})$. We have $\mathsf{x} \leftrightarrow \boxdot\bot$, so x is definable in $\mathbf{BCL}(G)$. However, y and z are not definable, as one can at least intuitively see. It does not follow, though, that the language M is not of complexity *b*. To see this, take the following grammar.

$$
\begin{array}{lcll}
\mathsf{x} & \to & \mathsf{a} & \mathsf{b} \\
\mathsf{x} & \to & \mathsf{b} & \mathsf{a} \\
\mathsf{x} & \to & \mathsf{a} & \\
\mathsf{b} & \to & \mathsf{b} & \mathsf{b}
\end{array}
$$

$\Sigma := \mathsf{x}$, $\Omega := \mathsf{a} \vee \mathsf{b}$. This grammar generates M, and we have $\mathsf{x} \leftrightarrow \boxdot\bot$. So M is of complexity *b*, but not of complexity *pc*.

Languages of Complexity w. It is not difficult to see that the language $\{b^n a c^n : n \in \omega\} \cup \{ab^n c^n : n \in \omega\}$ is not of complexity *b*. Take the grammar

$$
\begin{array}{lclll}
\mathsf{x} & \to & \mathsf{a} & & \\
\mathsf{x} & \to & \mathsf{b} & \mathsf{x} & \mathsf{c} \\
\mathsf{y} & \to & \mathsf{a} & \mathsf{z} & \\
\mathsf{z} & \to & \mathsf{b} & \mathsf{z} & \mathsf{c} \\
\mathsf{z} & \to & \mathsf{b} & \mathsf{c} &
\end{array}
$$

$\Sigma := \mathsf{x} \vee \mathsf{y}$, $\Omega := \mathsf{a} \vee \mathsf{b} \vee \mathsf{c}$. Then $\mathsf{z} \leftrightarrow \boxdot^*\neg\mathsf{a}$, $\mathsf{y} \leftrightarrow \boxdot\top \wedge \diamond\mathsf{z}$, and $\mathsf{x} \leftrightarrow \boxdot\bot \wedge \neg\mathsf{y}$. Thus movement in this case can be defined by formulae of complexity *w*. Indeed, we conjecture that movement is in general of complexity *w*, as long as it is into c–commanding position.

Languages of Complexity pdl. Finally, we look at the complexity *pdl*. Take the language R of reflexives. This language is regular. To express the distribution of the additional features we claim that formulae of complexity w are not sufficient. We sketch the argument. An elementary formula α is modally definable if it is equivalent in predicate calculus to a formula that is composed from positive atomic formulae using conjunction, disjunction and restricted quantifiers. Moreover, the formula can be rewritten in such a way that each subformula contains exactly two free variables (see for example Kracht 1996a). To verify that α holds in a structure, one can start a Fraissé–Ehrenfeucht game. Since at every stage of such a game the subformula under consideration contains only two free variables, we can actually check α using a game in which the players play with two pebbles that are placed on the structure and may be moved one at a time in the game along a relation. (Thus the memory is restricted from infinitely many to just two variables.) Now, it is easy to see that for conditions of the form *in between two occurrences of x, if there is a y then there is a z* no winning strategy can be formulated in such a game. For as soon as we have fixed our occurrences of x, we have exhausted our storage capacity. This argument is independent of any structural analysis we assume for the language R. Thus, reflexives require the expressive power of *pdl*.

6 Conclusion

In Rogers 1994 and subsequent work, James Rogers has advocated the use of monadic second order logic as a tool in the analysis of language. This gives rise to yet another language to talk about F–trees, which we denote here by $\mathcal{L}_2(F)$. The $\mathcal{L}_2(F)$–logic of the finite trees is denoted by $\mathbf{MSOlt}(F)$. This gives us the following hierarchy of languages

$$BOlt(F) \subset WOlt(F) \subset Olt(F) \subset \mathcal{L}_2(F)$$

$\mathcal{L}_2(F)$ is expressively sufficient if we assume that for some extension $\mathcal{L}_2(F \cup G)$ by nonlexical features all facts can be expressed. Namely, suppose there exists a G and a φ such that the set S of well–formed F–trees is the projection of a $\mathcal{L}_2(F \cup G)$–definable set T. Then $S = \{\mathfrak{T} : \mathfrak{T} \models (\exists \mathbf{x})\varphi[\mathbf{x}/\mathbf{g}])\}$. Hence, the elimination of a feature (whether it be essential or not) is a trivial matter. This is bought at a price, though. We no longer need to know exactly how the features are distributed with respect to the other features in order to know that they are eliminable. Moreover we contend that the language $Olt(F)$ is sufficient in all respects. To that end we note that all relevant locality domains can be expressed in $Olt(F)$. This of course is far away from being a proof. To turn this into a real argument, one needs to investigate quite closely the role of movement in syntax. This has been done in Rogers 1994 and Kracht 1995b. Both have given explicit reductions to $Olt(F)$ of some theories. Also, in Kracht 1996b it is shown how phrasal levels can be eliminated along the lines requested by Chomsky 1995. We need to warn the reader, however, that the preceding discussion makes sense only with the assumption that natural languages are context free. If not, matters are more complex. In order to be able to deal with natural language in its full complexity, we need to assume different classes of structures, more general than F–trees. The notions developed here can be extended to the general case, and we believe that the results also carry over. This, however, awaits further investigation.

References

Patrick Blackburn, Wilfried Meyer-Viol, and Maarten de Rijke. A Proof System for Finite Trees. In H. Kleine Büning, editor, *Computer Science Logic '95*, number 1092 in Lecture Notes in Computer Science, pages 86 – 105. Springer, 1996.

Noam Chomsky. Bare Phrase Structure. In Gert Webelhuth, editor, *Government and Binding Theory and the Minimalist Program*, pages 385 – 439. Blackwell, 1995.

Valentin Goranko and Solomon Passy. Using the universal modality: Gains and Questions. *Journal of Logic and Computation*, 2:5 – 30, 1992.

Marcus Kracht. Is there a genuine modal perspective on feature structures? *Linguistics and Philosophy*, 18:401 – 458, 1995.

Marcus Kracht. Syntactic Codes and Grammar Refinement. *Journal of Logic, Language and Information*, 1995.

Marcus Kracht. Tools and Techniques in Modal Logic. Habilitationsschrift, Department of Mathematics, FU Berlin, 1996.

Marcus Kracht. On Reducing Principles to Rules. In Maarten de Rijke and Patrick Blackburn, editors, *Specifying Syntactic Structure*, pages 95 – 122, CSLI, 1996.

James Rogers. *Studies in the Logic of Trees with Applications to Grammar Formalisms*. PhD thesis, Department of Computer and Information Sciences, University of Delaware, 1994.

James Rogers. *Strict LT2: regular – Local: recognizable*. this volume, 1997.

Linear Logic as Logic Programming: An Abstract*

Dale Miller

Computer Science Department, University of Pennsylvania
Philadelphia, PA 19104-6389 USA
dale@cis.upenn.edu
http://www.cis.upenn.edu/~dale

The theory of cut-free sequent proofs has been used to motivate and justify the design of a number of logic programming languages. Two such languages, λProlog and its linear logic refinement, Lolli [13], provide for various forms of abstraction (modules, abstract data types, and higher-order programming) but lack primitives for concurrency. The logic programming language, LO (Linear Objects) [2] provides some primitives for concurrency but lacks abstraction mechanisms. Forum is a logic programming presentation of all of linear logic that modularly extends λProlog, Lolli, and LO. This language, therefore, allows specifications to incorporate both abstractions and concurrency.

The motivation for Forum. Below are several examples of logic programming languages. Here we use linear logic connectives as in [9], with the addition of $\Rightarrow$ for intuitionistic implication: $A \Rightarrow B$ denotes $!A \multimap B$.

1. *Horn clauses*, the logical foundation of Prolog, are formulas of the form $\forall \bar{x}(G \Rightarrow A)$ where G may contain occurrences of & and $\top$. (We shall use $\bar{x}$ as a syntactic variable ranging over a list of variables and A as a syntactic variables ranging over atomic formulas.) In such formulas, occurrences of $\Rightarrow$ and $\forall$ are restricted so that they do not occur to the left of the implication $\Rightarrow$. As a result of this restriction, cut-free proofs involving Horn clauses do not contain right-introduction rules for $\Rightarrow$ and $\forall$.
2. *Hereditary Harrop formulas* [17], the logical foundation of λProlog, result from removing the restriction on $\Rightarrow$ and $\forall$ in Horn clauses: that is, such formulas can be built freely from $\top$, &, $\Rightarrow$, and $\forall$. Some presentations of hereditary Harrop formulas and Horn clauses allow certain occurrences of disjunctions ($\oplus$) and existential quantifiers [17]: since such occurrences do not add much to the expressiveness of these languages, they are not considered directly here.
3. The logic at the foundation of *Lolli* is the result of adding $\multimap$ to the connectives present in hereditary Harrop formulas: that is, Lolli programs are freely built from $\top$, &, $\multimap$, $\Rightarrow$, and $\forall$. As with hereditary Harrop formulas, it is possible to also allow certain occurrences of $\oplus$ and $\exists$, as well as the tensor $\otimes$ and the modal !.

* Parts of this abstract are taken from the paper [16].

4. The formulas used in LO are of the form $\forall \bar{x}(G \multimap A_1 \parr \cdots \parr A_n)$ where $n \geq 1$ and G may contain occurrences of &, $\top$, $\parr$, $\bot$. Similar to the Horn clause case, occurrences of $\multimap$ and $\forall$ are restricted so that they do not occur to the left of the implication $\multimap$.

The reason that Lolli does not include LO is the presence of $\parr$ and $\bot$ in the latter. This suggests the following definition for Forum, the intended super-language: allow formulas to be freely generated from $\top$, &, $\bot$, $\parr$, $\multimap$, $\Rightarrow$, and $\forall$. For various reasons, it is also desirable to add the modal ? directly to this list of connectives. Clearly, Forum contains the formulas in all the above logic programming languages.

Since the logics underlying Prolog, λProlog, Lolli, LO, and Forum differ in what logical connectives are allowed, richer languages modularly contain weaker languages. This is a direct result of the cut-elimination theorem for linear logic. Thus a Forum program that does not happen to use $\bot$, $\parr$, $\multimap$, and ? will, in fact, have the same cut-free proofs as are described for λProlog. Similarly, a program containing just a few occurrences of these connectives can be understood as a λProlog program that takes a few exceptional steps, but otherwise behaves as a λProlog program.

Forum is a presentation of all of linear logic since it contains a complete set of connectives. The connectives missing from Forum are directly definable using the following logical equivalences.

$$B^\bot \equiv B \multimap \bot \qquad 0 \equiv \top \multimap \bot \qquad 1 \equiv \bot \multimap \bot$$
$$!B \equiv (B \Rightarrow \bot) \multimap \bot \qquad B \oplus C \equiv (B^\bot \,\&\, C^\bot)^\bot \qquad B \otimes C \equiv (B^\bot \parr C^\bot)^\bot$$
$$\exists x.B \equiv (\forall x.B^\bot)^\bot$$

The collection of connectives in Forum are not minimal. For example, ? and $\parr$, can be defined in terms of the remaining connectives.

$$?B \equiv (B \multimap \bot) \Rightarrow \bot \quad \text{and} \quad B \parr C \equiv (B \multimap \bot) \multimap C$$

The proof that Forum is, in fact, a logic programming language requires showing that if a sequent has a proof in linear logic, it has a proof that is, in a certain formal sense, *goal directed*. The proof of this follows from a result of Andreoli on focusing proofs [1]: for details, see [16].

Applications of Forum. Forum has been used to give specifications in various domains. We list some major extended examples below.

1. Forum can be used as a *logical framework* for the specification of both natural deduction and sequential calculus proof systems. Single conclusion, intuitionistic based systems, such as λProlog and LF [10], have been used to provide satisfactory treatments of natural deduction proof systems [7, 20, 22] but the specifications of sequent calculus in these systems is less than satisfactory [7, 21]. In [16], the multiple conclusion aspects of Forum allowed for natural and flexible presentations of sequent calculus, and Gentzen's LJ calculus [8] is studied in some depth there.

2. In [14], the operational semantics of the π-calculus [18] is specified. Important notions like scope extrusion, mobility, and testing are given simple proof theoretic treatments there.
3. The operational semantics of programming languages provides another area where Forum provides natural specifications.
   (a) Linear logic provides a simple mechanism for modeling state. Algol-like references and state is specified in [15, 16] and in this thesis, [5], Chirimar shows how the richer notion of state in Standard ML can be expressed.
   (b) Concurrency primitives similar to those found in Concurrent ML [23] are presented in [15, 16].
   (c) In [5] Chirimar presents specifications of exceptions and continuations (similar to those found in some implementations of SML). He also shows that these can be added modularly to his specification of call-by-value evaluation and state. With these specifications, he proves various equivalences among program phrases involving references and higher-order features.
   (d) Cervesato and Pfenning [4] similarly specify and analyzed ML-style references in a linear logic language that is similar to the Lolli subset of Forum.
4. Also in his thesis, Chirimar specifies both the sequential and the concurrent (piped-line) operational semantics of the DLX RISC processor [11]. He is able to capture the call-forwarding and early branch resolution optimizations and proves them to be equivalent. He also studies the problem of code equivalence via the Forum specification, and, in particular, analyzes the problem of code rescheduling for DLX.
5. In [3, 6], Bugliesi, Delzanno, Liquori, and Martelli specify and analyze an object-oriented programming language using Forum.

It should also be added that the area of natural language parsing should provide lots of other examples of where linear logic can be used to advantage. For example, Josh Hodas used Lolli to provide a declarative treatment of Filler-Gap Dependency Parsers [12]. See also a similar project in [19].

References

1. Jean-Marc Andreoli. Logic programming with focusing proofs in linear logic. *Journal of Logic and Computation*, 2(3):297–347, 1992.
2. J.M. Andreoli and R. Pareschi. Linear objects: Logical processes with built-in inheritance. *New Generation Computing*, 9(3-4):445–473, 1991.
3. Michele Bugliesi, Giorgio Delzanno, Luigi Liquori, and Maurizio Martelli. A linear logic calculus of objects. In M. Maher, editor, *Proceedings of the Joint International Conference and Symposium on Logic Programming*. MIT Press, September 1996.

4. Iliano Cervesato and Frank Pfenning. A linear logic framework. In *Proceedings, Eleventh Annual IEEE Symposium on Logic in Computer Science*, pages 264–275, New Brunswick, New Jersey, July 1996. IEEE Computer Society Press.
5. Jawahar Chirimar. *Proof Theoretic Approach to Specification Languages*. PhD thesis, University of Pennsylvania, February 1995. Available on the web from `http//www.cis.upenn.edu/~dale/forum/`.
6. Giorgio Delzanno and Maurizio Martelli. Objects in forum. In *Proceedings of the International Logic Programming Symposium*, 1995.
7. Amy Felty. Implementing tactics and tacticals in a higher-order logic programming language. *Journal of Automated Reasoning*, 11(1):43–81, August 1993.
8. Gerhard Gentzen. Investigations into logical deductions. In M. E. Szabo, editor, *The Collected Papers of Gerhard Gentzen*, pages 68–131. North-Holland Publishing Co., Amsterdam, 1969.
9. Jean-Yves Girard. Linear logic. *Theoretical Computer Science*, 50:1–102, 1987.
10. Robert Harper, Furio Honsell, and Gordon Plotkin. A framework for defining logics. *Journal of the ACM*, 40(1):143–184, 1993.
11. J. Hennesy and D. Patterson. *Computer Architecture A Quantitative Approach*. Morgan Kaufman Publishers, Inc., 1990.
12. Joshua Hodas. Specifying filler-gap dependency parsers in a linear-logic programming language. In K. Apt, editor, *Proceedings of the Joint International Conference and Symposium on Logic Programming*, pages 622–636, 1992.
13. Joshua Hodas and Dale Miller. Logic programming in a fragment of intuitionistic linear logic. *Information and Computation*, 110(2):327–365, 1994.
14. Dale Miller. The π-calculus as a theory in linear logic: Preliminary results. In E. Lamma and P. Mello, editors, *Proceedings of the 1992 Workshop on Extensions to Logic Programming*, number 660 in LNCS, pages 242–265. Springer-Verlag, 1993.
15. Dale Miller. A multiple-conclusion meta-logic. In S. Abramsky, editor, *Ninth Annual Symposium on Logic in Computer Science*, pages 272–281, Paris, July 1994.
16. Dale Miller. Forum: A multiple-conclusion specification language. *Theoretical Computer Science*, 165:201–232, 1996.
17. Dale Miller, Gopalan Nadathur, Frank Pfenning, and Andre Scedrov. Uniform proofs as a foundation for logic programming. *Annals of Pure and Applied Logic*, 51:125–157, 1991.
18. Robin Milner, Joachim Parrow, and David Walker. A calculus of mobile processes, Part I. *Information and Computation*, pages 1–40, September 1992.
19. Fernando C. N. Pereira. Prolog and natural-language analysis: into the third decade. In *Proceedings of the 1990 North American Conference on Logic Programming*. MIT Press, 1990.
20. Frank Pfenning. Logic programming in the LF logical framework. In Gérard Huet and Gordon D. Plotkin, editors, *Logical Frameworks*. Cambridge University Press, 1991.

21. Frank Pfenning. Structural cut elimination. In *Proceedings, Tenth Annual IEEE Symposium on Logic in Computer Science*, pages 156–166, San Diego, California, 26–29 1995. IEEE Computer Society Press.
22. Frank Pfenning and Ekkehard Rohwedder. Implementing the meta-theory of deductive systems. In *Proceedings of the 1992 Conference on Automated Deduction*, June 1992.
23. John H. Reppy. CML: A higher-order concurrent language. In *ACM SIGPLAN Conference on Programming Language Design and Implementation*, pages 293–305, June 1991.

Derivational Minimalism

Edward Stabler

University of California, Los Angeles, CA 90024-1543, USA

Abstract. A basic idea of the transformational tradition is that constituents move. More recently, there has been a trend towards the view that all features are lexical features. And in recent "minimalist" grammars, structure building operations are assumed to be feature driven. A simple grammar formalism with these properties is presented here and briefly explored. Grammars in this formalism can define languages that are not in the "mildly context sensitive" class defined by Vijay-Shanker and Weir (1994).

1 Minimalist grammars

Adapting the general framework of [13], a grammar is regarded as a specification of a lexicon and generating functions for building complex expressions:

A *grammar* $G = (V, Cat, Lex, \mathcal{F})$, where	
V is a set,	(non-syntactic features)
Cat is a set,	(syntactic features)
Lex is a set of expressions built from V and Cat,	(the lexicon)
$\mathcal{F}$ is a set of partial functions from tuples of expressions to expressions	(the generating functions)

In the minimalist grammars presented here, expressions will be a certain kind of finite, binary ordered trees with labels only at the leaves. The *language* defined by such a grammar is the closure of the lexicon under the structure building functions, $L(G) = CL(Lex, \mathcal{F})$.

1.1 Trees

A finite tree is given by a set of nodes with a dominance relation of the usual kind, $\tau = (N_\tau, \triangleleft^*_\tau)$. We leave off the subscripts when no confusion will result. We use the following notation:

$x \triangleleft y$	x is the parent of y
$x \triangleleft^+ y$	x properly dominates y
$x \triangleleft^* y$	x dominates y

The root of any tree τ is the minimal element of N, and the *leaves* are the maximal elements. That is, the set of leaves $L_\tau = \{x \mid \sim(\exists y)\ x \triangleleft y\}$.

Constituents are standardly picked out with the dominance relation. The constituent with root node x is the part of the structure that x dominates. The set of nodes dominated by x is $\uparrow x = \{y \in N |\ x \lhd^* y\}$. So then for any leaf x, $\uparrow x = \{x\}$. The subtree τ_x with root x is

$$\tau_x = (\uparrow x, (\lhd^* \restriction \uparrow x)).$$

Our trees are linearly ordered by an additional *precedence* relation, $\tau = (N_\tau, \lhd^*_\tau, \prec^*_\tau)$. We use the following notation:

$x \prec y$	x immediately precedes y
$x \prec^+ y$	x properly precedes y
$x \prec^* y$	x precedes y

We will assume that for any two distinct nodes, either one dominates the other or one precedes the other (but never both), and we assume precedence is inherited through dominance in the usual way:

$$(\forall w, x, y, z)\ \ (x \prec^* y \ \wedge \ x \lhd^* w \ \wedge \ y \lhd^* z) \rightarrow (w \prec^* z)$$

One additional relation is added to tree structures in order to obtain appropriate objects for minimalist grammar. When two constituents combine, one of them always "projects over" the other.[1] To represent that a determiner d *projects over* a noun n to form a DP, we let $<$ represent this relation between the sisters in a tree, writing d<n, and we can adopt the usual notation for the transitive and reflexive, transitive closures of this relation, respectively:

$x < y$	x immediately projects over y
$x <^+ y$	x properly projects over y
$x <^* y$	x projects over y

Regarding the projection relation $<$ as reflexive, we can say that whenever a node has a child, there is a unique child that projects over every child of that parent:

$$(\forall x)\ ((\exists y)(x \lhd y)) \rightarrow ((\exists y)(\forall z)(x \lhd z \rightarrow y < z))$$

---

[1] This approach is inspired by Chomsky's [7, p245] suggestion, "If constituents α, β of K have been formed in the course of computation, one of the two must project – say, α. At the LF interface, maximal K is interpreted as a phrase of the type α (e.g., as a nominal phrase if [the head of K] H(K) is nominal); and it behaves in the same manner in the course of computation." Note that this assumption is empirically loaded, and far from obviously correct. The relevant properties of a complex are not in general determined by just one of the immediate subconstituents. In the minimalist tradition, this fact is accommodated in part by allowing, in certain cases, the projecting head to incorporate features of its sister, and by allowing properties of subconstituents (namely, in our formalization, the -x subconstituents) to influence the elaboration of structure.

Adding $<^*$ to our tree structures, they have the form $\tau = (N_\tau, \triangleleft^*_\tau, \prec^*_\tau, <^*_\tau)$. These are the basic structures of our minimalist grammar.

In terms of such structures, we can define some structural notions that are relevant for the specification of the grammar. Given any tree $\tau = (N, \triangleleft^*, \prec^*, <^*)$ and any $x, y \in N$, x is a *head of* y iff either

y is a leaf and $x = y$, or

$(\exists z)\ (y \triangleleft z\ \wedge\ (\forall w)(y \triangleleft w \rightarrow z <^* w)\ \wedge\ x$ is a head of $z)$.[2]

The following basic results are easily obtained from these definitions.

Proposition 1. *Every head is a leaf, and every leaf is a head of itself.*

Proposition 2. *If x is a head of y then $y \triangleleft^* x$.*

Proposition 3. *Every node y has a unique head x.*

We define the *maximal projection of head* x to be the least node y with head x. That is, the maximal projection y of x is the node $y \in \{z \in N |$ the head of z is $x\}$ such that there is no w in this set with the property that $w \triangleleft^+ y$.

Finally, for convenience, it is useful to call a node x a *specifier of head* y iff

i. x is a maximal projection,
ii. the parent of x has head y, and
iii. $x \prec^+ y$.

And similarly we call a node x a *complement of head* y iff

i. x is a maximal projection,
ii. the parent of x has head y, and
iii. $y \prec^+ x$.

In the linguists' standard depiction of a labeled, ordered tree, the minimal element is at the top, with immediate dominance shown by arcs and linear precedence shown by left-to-right order. Our trees have a third relation, so there is a question about how to depict them. Since we will only be considering binary branching trees, a simple idea presents itself. Since only the leaves are labeled, we can indicate at each internal node, which of the two daughters projects over the other.

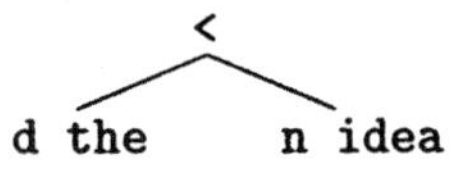

Notice that in this tree, $<$ and $\prec$ coincide. They do not coincide in a tree like the following (which is the way we will represent what linguists call "VP shells"):

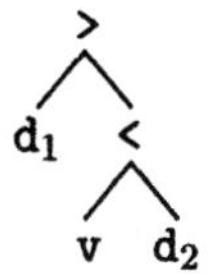

[2] Again, this treatment of heads is inspired by one of Chomsky's [7, pp245-245] suggestions: "It is natural, then, to take the label of [the complex] K [formed from α and β] to be not α itself, but rather H(K), a decision that leads to technical simplification."

It is perhaps enlightening to observe that, rather than letting the left-right dimension of our graphical depiction represent $\prec^*$ we could have let it represent $<$, marking $\prec$ explicitly in the tree to get a different depiction of the same structure:

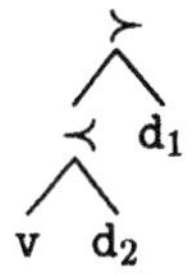

In this kind of presentation, the projecting category is always on the left, while precedence gets explicitly marked. However, we will use the former convention, explicitly indicating the "projects over" relation.

1.2 Features

Vocabulary items are broken into pronounced parts and interpreted parts, $V = (P \cup I)$ The pronounced, *phonetic features* are indicated by placing slashes around the standard orthographic representation of the word. So for example, we will consider the set,

$$P = \{\texttt{/marie/,/quechua/,/speaks/,/believes/,} \ldots\}.$$

The interpreted, *semantic features* are indicated by placing parentheses around standard orthographic representations, as in

$$I = \{\texttt{(marie),(quechua),(speaks),(believes),} \ldots\}.$$

As an abbreviation, we will sometimes use, for example, `marie` to represent the sequence `/marie/(marie)`, and similarly for other vocabulary when corresponding phonetic and interpreted features are simultaneously available.

The *syntactic features* are usefully partitioned into four kinds,

$$Cat = (base \cup select \cup licensors \cup licensees).$$

We introduce each kind of feature in turn.

The basic syntactic categories,

$$base = \{\texttt{c,t,v,d,n,}\ldots\},$$

represent the familiar categories: complementizer, tense, verb, determiner, noun, and so on. For each type of category, there are three ways of "selecting" a constituent of that category. We will use the feature `=n` to indicate the simple selection of a noun phrase; the feature `=N` indicates that a noun phrase is selected and furthermore the phonetic features of the head of the noun phrase are moved to be suffixed to the sequence of phonetic features of the selecting head; and finally the feature `N=` indicates that a noun phrase is selected and furthermore the phonetic features of the head of the noun phrase are moved to be prefixed to the sequence of phonetic features of the selecting head. So the set of possible selection features is:

$$select = \{\texttt{=x},\ \texttt{=X},\ \texttt{X=} \mid \texttt{x} \in base\}.$$

The categories and selection features interact in local, head-head configurations. As we will see, the structure building rule *merge* will cancel a requirement `=x`, `=X`, or `X=` by combining the constituent with this requirement with a constituent of category `x`.

The remaining kinds of features are those involved in phrasal movement, which always involves a head-specifier relationship. In particular, a head will assign a feature $+f$ to a $-f$ constituent that moves covertly to its specifier (movements are explained below), or else a feature $+F$ is assigned to a $-f$ constituent that moves overtly to its specifier. So for example, we can have features that indicate requirements like

$$licensees = \{\texttt{-case},\texttt{-wh},\ \ldots\ \},$$

with corresponding features that indicate assignments, like

$$licensors = \{\texttt{+case},\texttt{+CASE},\texttt{+wh},\texttt{+WH},\ \ldots\ \}.$$

These features $+f$ and $+F$ are the triggers for phrasal movement. The structure building rule *move* will cancel a requirement `-f` by moving the phrase with this feature to the specifier of a head that has either `+f` or `+F`.

No limit has been indicated for the numbers of elements in *base*, *licensees* and *licensors*, but linguists typically assume that these sets will be finite and small. And then, if there are k *licensees* then there will be $2k$ *licensors*.

The features written with capital letters `=X`, `X=`, `+X` are sometimes called *strong features*. (Cf. [22], [7]). Strong features cause phonetic material to move along with the affected syntactic features. The strong/weak distinction provides some control over how much structure moves along with the features that are canceled by the structure building rule. This carrying along of more or less additional structure is sometimes called "pied piping."

We are now in a position to define what counts as a linguistic expression in our minimalist grammars. An *expression* is a finite, binary labeled ordered tree $\tau = (N_\tau, \triangleleft_\tau^*, \prec_\tau^*, <_\tau^*, Label_\tau)$, where the domain of *Label* is just the leaves L of the tree and the range is a regular set,

$$Label : L \rightarrow select^*(licensors)select^*(base)licensees^*P^*I^*.$$

The rationale for this particular ordering of features in the label will become clear below: the syntactic features are canceled in order.

Notice that $Rng(Label) \subset (V \cup Cat)^*$. Furthermore, $\lambda \in Rng(Label)$; that is, "empty nodes" can occur in expressions.

1.3 Minimalist Grammars

A *minimalist* grammar is a 4-tuple $(V, Cat, Lex, \mathcal{F})$, where

$V = (P \cup I)$,
$Cat = (base \cup select \cup licensee \cup licensor)$,
Lex is a finite set of expressions built from V and Cat
(where an "expression" is a tree as defined above), and
$\mathcal{F} = \{merge, move\}$.

To complete this definition, we need only define the generating functions.[3]

The function *merge* is used to allow a head to select and combine with a phrase of an appropriate type on its right. For example the verb `makes` may select a determiner phrase `tortillas` to form the verb phrase `makes tortillas`. In our minimalist grammars, this is a `=x` head merging with a tree of category `x` to yield a tree in which these two features have canceled each other out:

`=d =d v make` + `d tortillas` ⇒

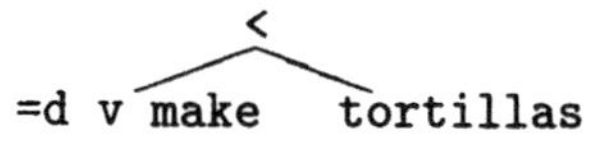

Notice that the canceled features are initial elements of the heads of the trees involved – the structure building rules only cancel initial elements. Notice that the output tree has the verb as its head, as shown by the < at the parent node, and so we would traditionally call the output tree a verb phrase.

Sometimes the phonetic content of the selected head moves to prefix the phonetic material of the selecting head. For example, in Nahuatl, the verb 'make' can select and incorporate the object 'tortilla' as its prefix:

i. Ni-c-chihua in tlaxcal (Nahuatl) [11]
1s-3os-make tortilla

ii. Ni-tlaxcal-chihua
1s-tortilla-make

This is called *head movement with left adjunction,* and in our formalism it is the construction formed when a `X=` head merges with tree of category `x`:[4]

`D= =d v make` + `d tortilla` ⇒

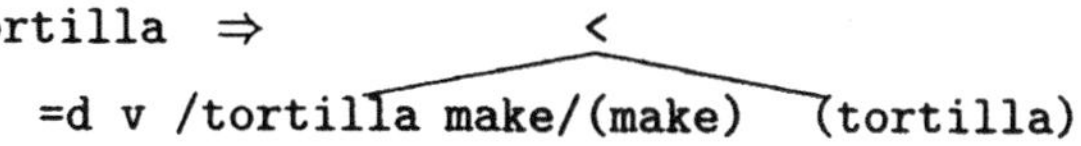

[3] We present the generating functions informally here, and present a more formal statement in the appendix. A detailed presentation can be found in [27].

[4] As the diagram here indicates, the complex that results from incorporation is treated here just as a head with a a sequence of features, but most linguists assume that a more articulated structure is required. See, for example, [22], [29], [15]. Further discussion of head movement and some alternative formalizations are presented in [27].

A third case of *merge* is ***head movement with right adjunction.*** This again is like selection, but the phonetic content of the selected head moves to suffix the phonetic material of the selecting head. We find apparent right adjunction in Sora:

i. Jom-bɔŋ-t-ɛ-n-ji pɔ (Sora) [1]
eat-buffalo-NONPAST-3S-INTR-3PS Q

In minimalist grammars this is the construction formed when a =X head merges with tree of category x.

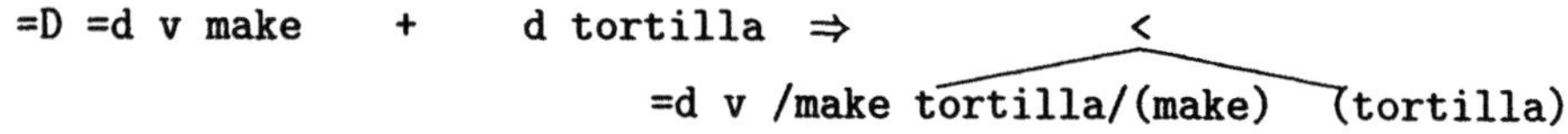
=D =d v make
+
d tortilla
⇒
<
=d v /make tortilla/(make)
(tortilla)

The final case of *merge* is what might be called *shell formation.* This occurs when a head that has already combined with a complement on its right combines with further arguments on its left. In some recent theories, this may occur in verb phrases, on the assumption that all arguments of a verb, including the subject, originate in the verb phrase:

i. I saw [Maria making tortillas]
ii. Chuala mé [na saighdiúirí ag imeacht] (Irish) [8]
heard I the soldiers leaving

This kind of construction is formed when a =x non-head merges with tree of category x:

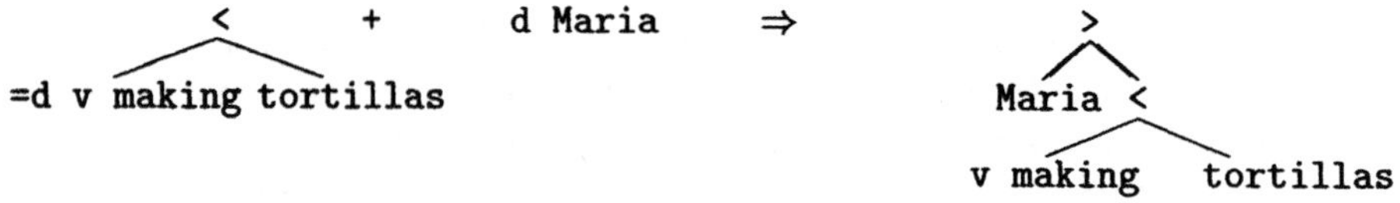
<
=d v making tortillas
+
d Maria
⇒
>
Maria
<
v making
tortillas

The binary function *merge* applies in just the four cases listed here: always canceling one selection feature =x, =X or X= against one corresponding categorial feature x.

The other structure building rule is *move.* This rule is traditionally invoked to form sentences like i-iii from underlying structures that, without these movements, would lead to expressions like i'-iii':

i. which student do I like?
i'. I like which student?
ii. which student did Mary tell you that she thought I would like?
ii'. Mary told you that she thought I would like which student?
iii. that student, I like.
iii'. I like that student.

The movements in i-iii are *overt*: pronounced features are moved, sometimes over many constituent boundaries. In certain other constructions that are arguably structurally similar, it is proposed that there is *covert* movement, as in "quantifier raising" constructions. For example, the pronounced form in i, below, may have a structure of the sort indicated in ii, where the universally quantified phrase has raised to take wide scope over `some student`:

i. `/some student likes every teacher/`

ii. `(every teacher) some student likes /every teacher/`

To build constructions like these, *move* is formalized as a unary operation on expressions.

Overt movement occurs when *move* applies to a tree whose head has an initial feature `+X`, and where the tree contains exactly one `-x` feature. This restriction to one `-x` feature is a kind of "economy" condition: it prevents two embedded `-x` constituents from competing for the first available specifier of a `+x` or `+X` head, so that a `-x` feature is always canceled by the "closest" possible `+x` or `+X` feature. The `-x` head may be arbitrarily deep in the tree. The movement raises the whole maximal projection of the `-x` head up to the specifier of the `+X` head.

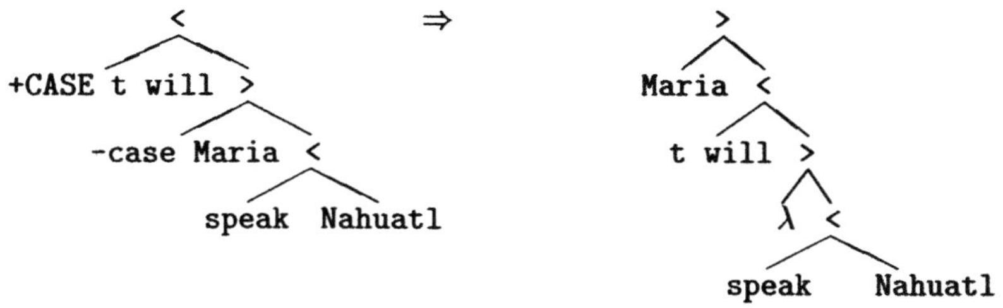

Overt movement leaves behind just a node labeled by the empty sequence of features λ.

Covert movement is similar, except that it is triggered by an initial feature `+x` (rather than a "strong" `+X`), and it does not move the whole `-x` phrase, but only the interpreted and syntactic features. The phonetic features are left behind, as we see in the following "covert object shift:"

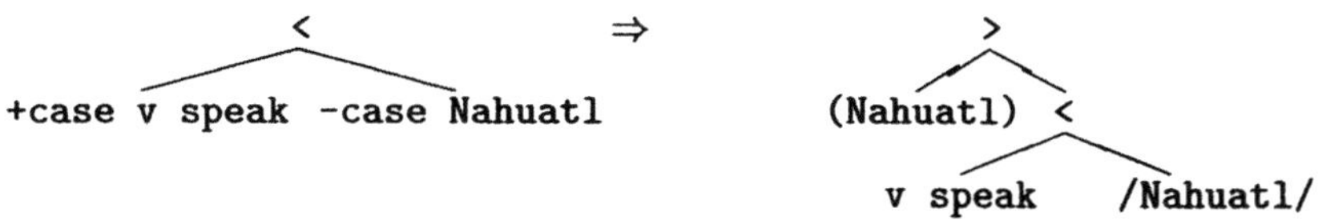

In this simple example, the `-x` constituent is a sister of the `+x` constituent, but as already mentioned, it can be arbitrarily deep in the tree.

2 Examples and basic properties

We explore the effect of varying the lexicon of the minimalist grammars, keeping $\mathcal{F} = \{merge, move\}$ fixed.

2.1 A simple SVO language

This first example is inspired by [7].[5] It embodies particular grammatical assumptions (e.g. the assumption that a language like English may have a "covert object shift"), which other MG grammars will not share.

Let Lex_1 be the set containing the following 12 expressions:

```
d -case maria              d -case quechua
=n d -case some            =n d -case every
n student                  n language
=d +case =d v speaks       =c +case =d v believes
=v +CASE t
=t c                       =t c -case                 =t c -case /that/
```

The following 8 step derivation yields a structure that is pronounced: `/some linguist speaks every language/`. The derivation begins by merging the following two lexical elements:

from the lexicon:

`=n d -case every`   `n language`

Applying *merge* to these two elements, in this order, yields a determiner phrase:

step 1 merge:

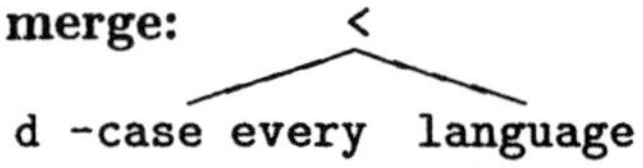

This is a determiner phrase that needs case. It can be merged with the lexical item that is pronounced `/speaks/` to yield the following tree:

step 2 merge:

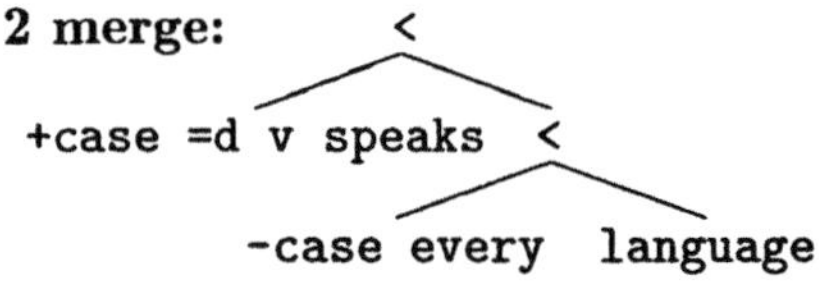

[5] In particular, we are roughly following the proposal [7, p358] made in the following passage: "... both Specs are within the minimal domain of v, so either is available for θ-marking the external argument of a transitive verb. Suppose that we allow this possibility, so that the outer Spec can host the external argument ... Obj can only raise to the inner Spec ... to check the strength feature and undergo overt Case marking. If overt object raising takes place, then Subj will be merged in the outer Spec to receive the external θ-role provided by the configuration ... On these assumptions, it follows that Subj always c-commands Obj within IP." In fact, this kind of proposal has been familiar for some time. It was proposed, for example, in [17] that the position where the object receives case is below the subject, and nevertheless within VP.

The head of the result of step 2 must assign case to its specifier, and there is exactly one `-case` element inside the tree, so *move* applies in step 3 to covertly move the object, leaving the pronounced material behind. (Languages with overt object shift are considered below.)

step 3 move:

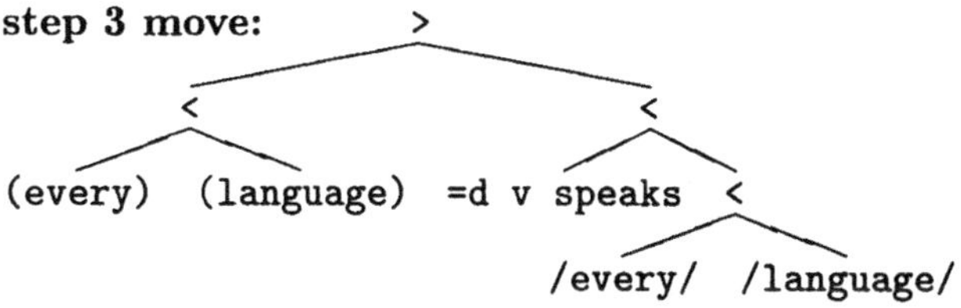

The first feature of the head of the verb phrase formed in step 2 is the selection feature for the subject, so we first build a subject with two new elements from the lexicon:

from the lexicon:

`=n d -case some`   `n linguist`

step 4 merge:

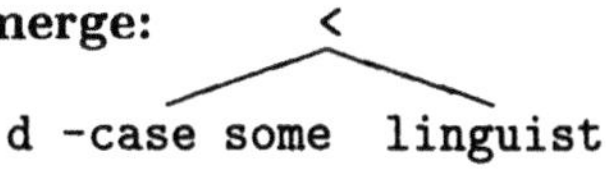

We can now apply merge to the result of step 3 and the result of step 4, in that order, to yield the following "VP shell:"

step 5 merge:

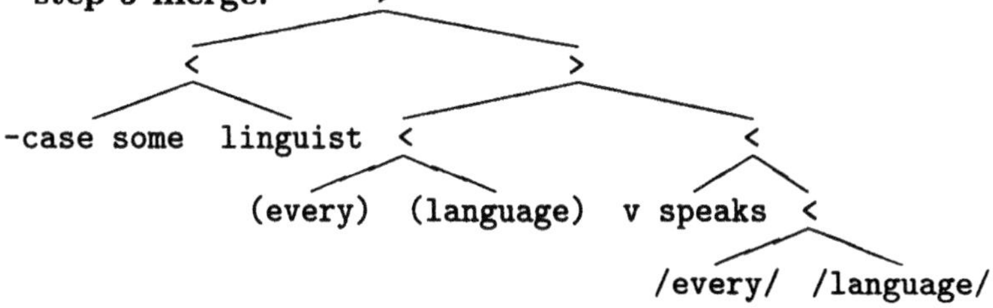

The result of step 5 is a verb phrase, so it is selected by the phonetically empty lexical item that has category `t`. Applying merge to this tense element and the result of step 5, in that order, we obtain:

step 6 merge:

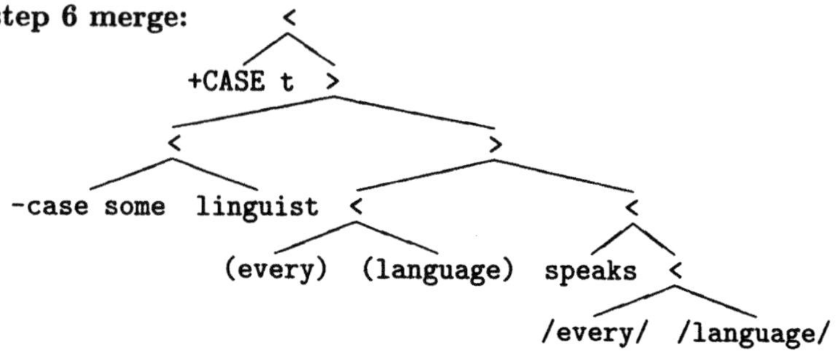

Since the result of step 6 is a tense phrase that must assign case to an overt specifier, move can apply to move the `-case` element to specifier position:

step 7 move:

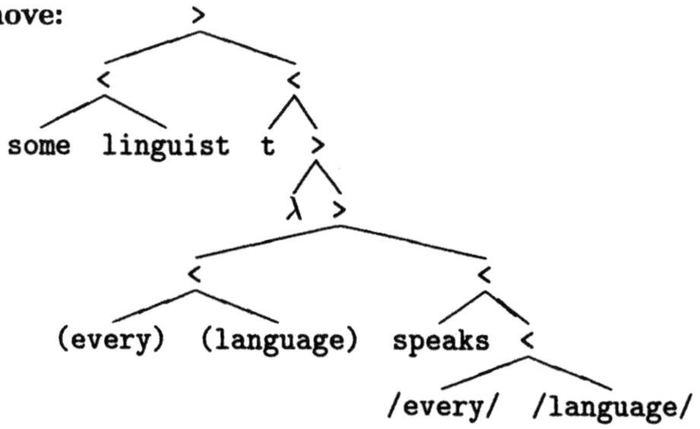

The result of step 7 is a tense phrase, and since tense is selected by the lexical complementizer, *merge* can apply to yield the following tree:

step 8 merge:

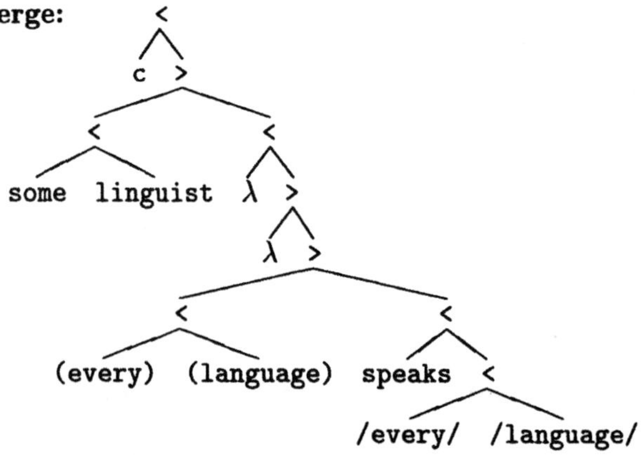

This last tree is *well formed* in the sense that it has no outstanding syntactic features at all except the single category symbol c at its head. (We could imagine that the c is deleted when this structure is integrated into the discourse.) In this case, we will say $\text{MG}_1 \Rightarrow^*$ `some linguist speaks every language`, and we will refer to the language of the grammar, the set of phonetic strings that have well formed syntactic structures as

$$strings(MG_1) = \{s|\ MG_1 \Rightarrow^* s\}.$$

Proposition 4. $MG_1 \Rightarrow^*$ `some linguist speaks every language` *(Furthermore, there is exactly one such derivation.)*

Proposition 5.
$MG_1 \Rightarrow^*$ `maria believes that some student speaks every language`

Proposition 6. $MG_1 \not\Rightarrow^*$ `speaks every`

2.2 SOV languages

If we modify MG_1 so that the verbs are strong case assigners, we get phonetic forms with the SOV word order. Let Lex_2 be the set containing the following 11 expressions:

`d -case maria`	`d -case quechua`
`=n d -case some`	`=n d -case every`
`n student`	`n language`
`=d +CASE =d v speaks`	`=c +CASE =d v believes`
`=v +CASE t`	
`=t c`	`=t c -case`

We present the steps of one sample derivation:

step 1 merge:

step 2 merge:

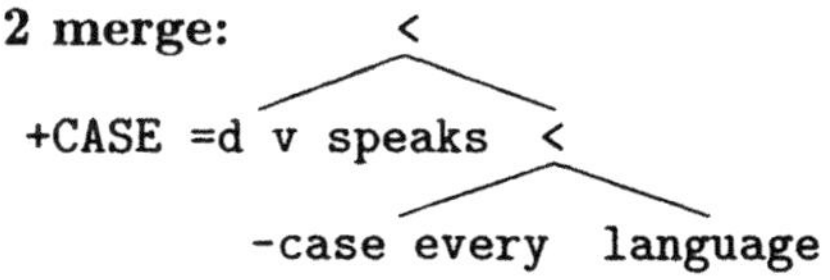

step 3 move:

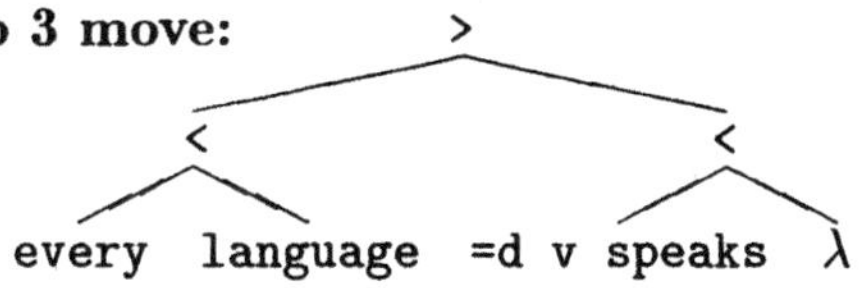

step 4 merge:

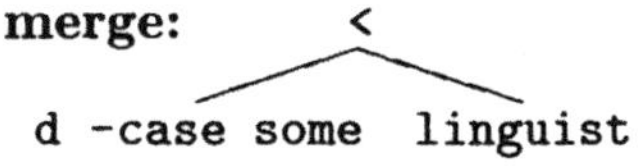

step 5 merge:

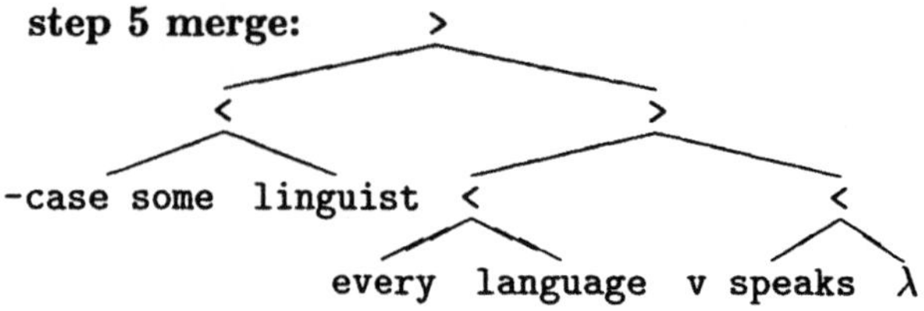

step 6 merge:

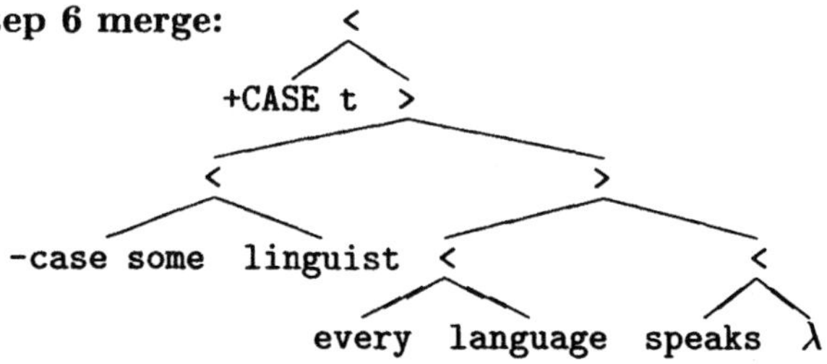

step 7 move:

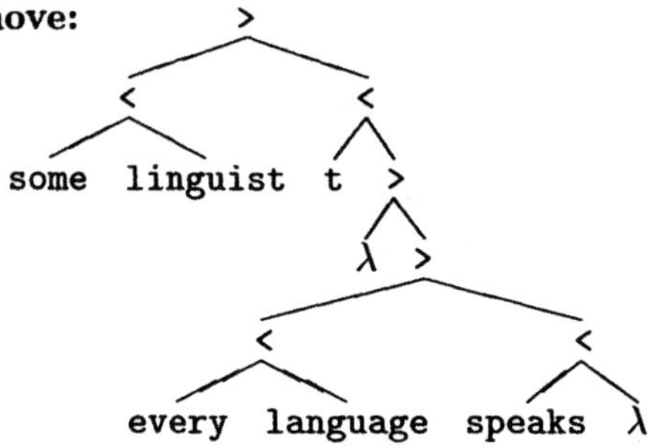

step 8 merge:

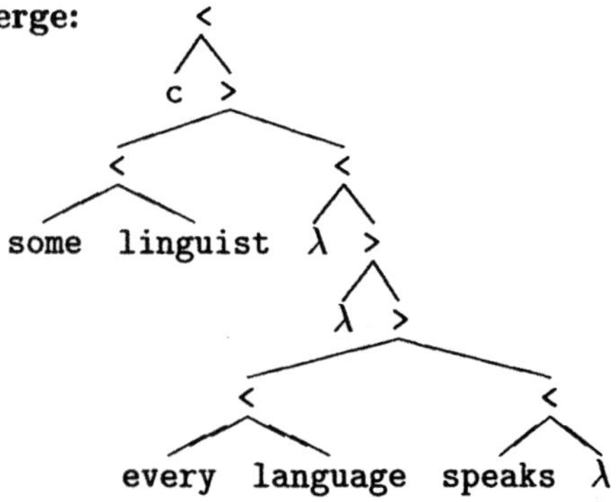

2.3 VSO languages

If we modify MG_1 so that c and t strongly select their complements, triggering head movement with right adjunction, then we get phonetic forms with VSO word order. Let Lex_3 be the set containing the following 11 expressions:

```
d -case maria              d -case quechua
=n d -case some            =n d -case every
n student                  n language
=d +case =d v speaks       =C +case =d v believes
=V +CASE t
=T c                       =T c -case
```

We present one example derivation:

step 1 merge:

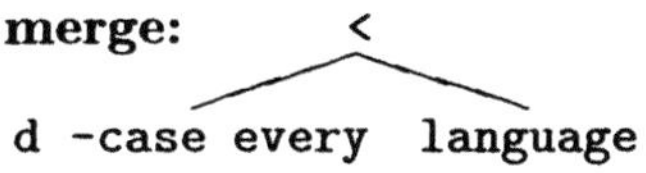

step 2 merge:

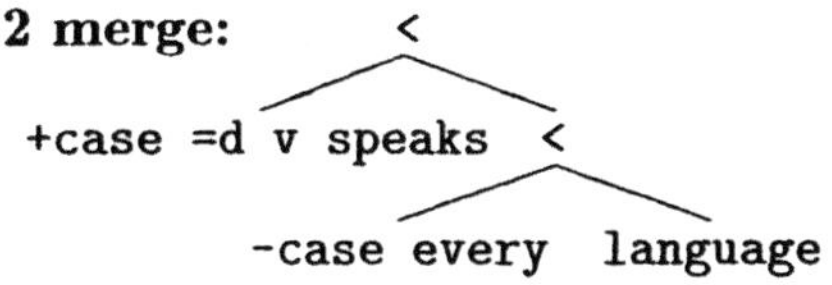

step 3 move:

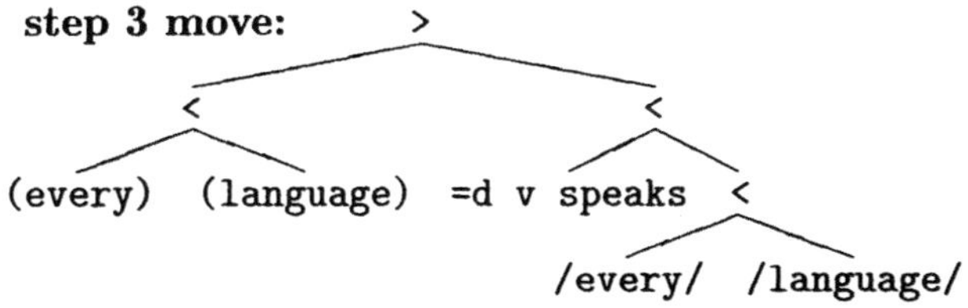

step 4 merge:

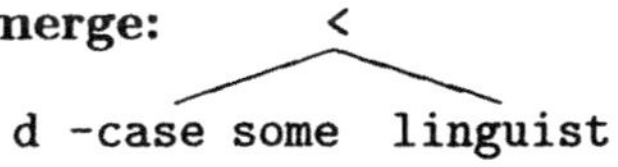

step 5 merge:

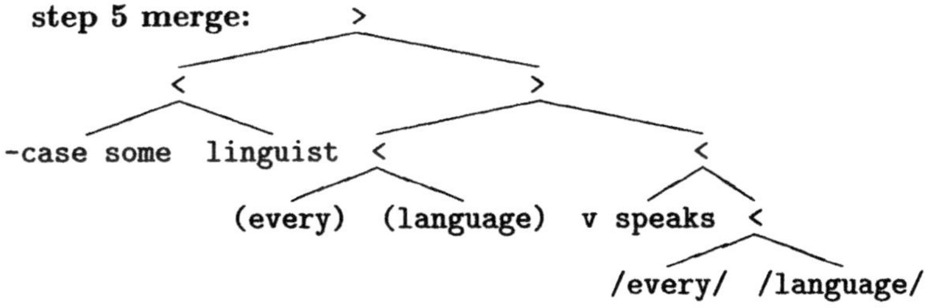

step 6 merge:

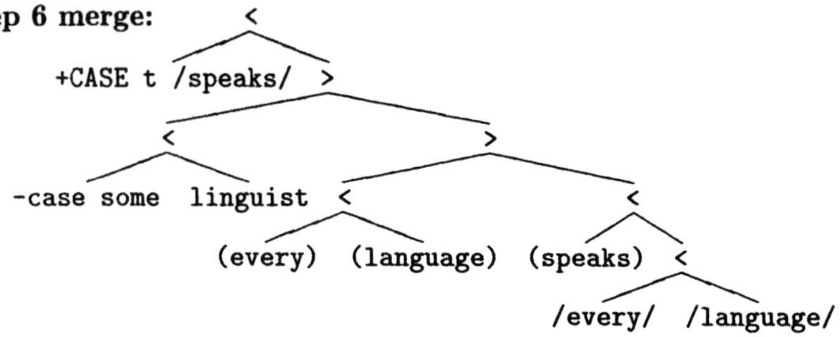

step 7 move:

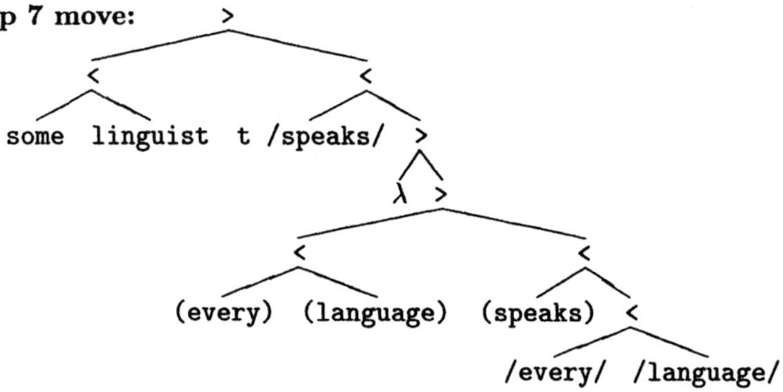

step 8 merge:

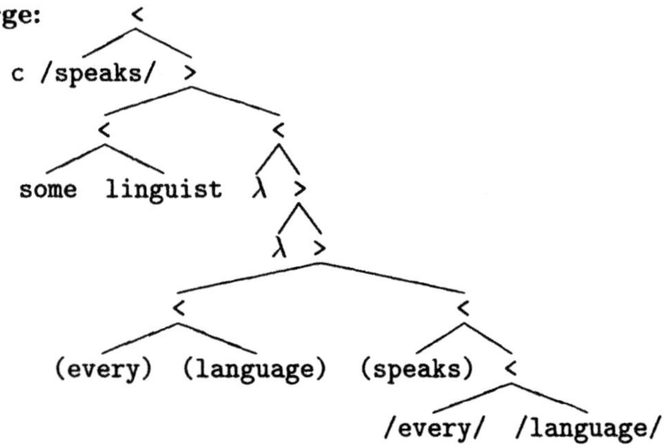

Notice that since `believes` strongly selects its clausal complement, we will get "verb clusters" in the highest c position with this grammar:

step 14 merge:

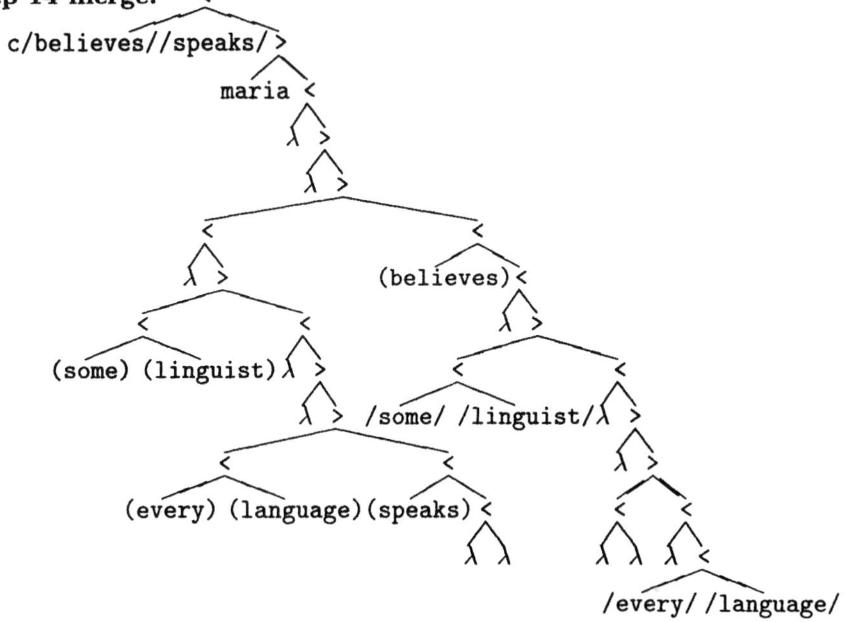

The pronounced positions of the verbs in these clusters exhibit "crossing" dependencies with respect to the pronounced positions of their respective subjects. Using subscripts to indicate which subjects go with which verbs, we derive the following orders of basic constituents in the phonetic form:

$$V_1\ S_1\ O_1$$
$$V_1\ V_2\ S_1\ S_2\ O_2$$
$$V_1\ V_2\ V_3\ S_1\ S_2\ S_3\ O_3$$
$$\ldots$$

2.4 WW languages

Given the previous example, it is no surprise that the MG formalism allows the definition of simple "copying languages." That is, a certain kind of "reduplication" can be defined even though there is no copying operation in the grammar. Consider for example the grammar defined by the following lexicon of 9 elements, Lex_4:

$=V_1$ c	$=V_2$ c	c
$=d_1$ v_1 /1/	$=d_2$ v_2 /2/	
=C $=d_1$ v_1 /1/	=C $=d_2$ v_2 /2/	
d_1 /1/	d_2 /2/	

The exploration of derivations from this lexicon is left to the reader (particularly because the examples in the next two sections are of greater interest).

Proposition 7. *strings*$(MG_4) = \{ww \mid w \in \{1,2\}^*\}$. *(cf. also [9])*

The proof of this claim is based on the fact, easily seen from the lexicon, that for every v_1 introduced in a derivation there must be exactly one corresponding d_1, a for every v_2 introduced in a derivation there must be exactly one corresponding d_2. Furthermore, all the verbs will raise to right adjoin to the highest c, in order, leaving the corresponding d's in their original positions.

2.5 $c^n v^n s^n o^n$

Like other formalisms that can define ww languages, the MG formalism can also define four counting dependencies. Let Lex_5 be the set containing the following 7 expressions:

```
=V c -case /c/    =V c /c/          c
s /s/
o /o/
=o =s v /v/          C= =o +CASE =s v /v/
```

We present one example derivation:

step 1 merge:

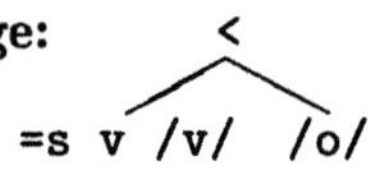

step 2 merge:

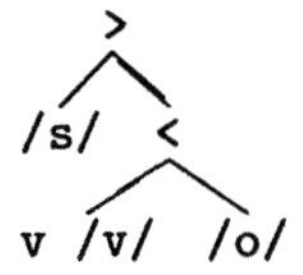

step 3 merge:

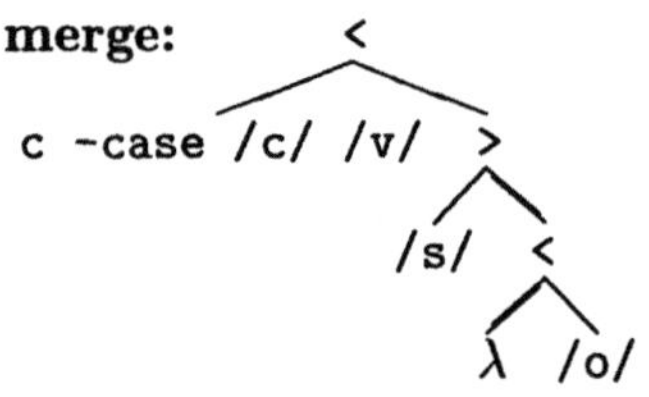

step 4 merge:

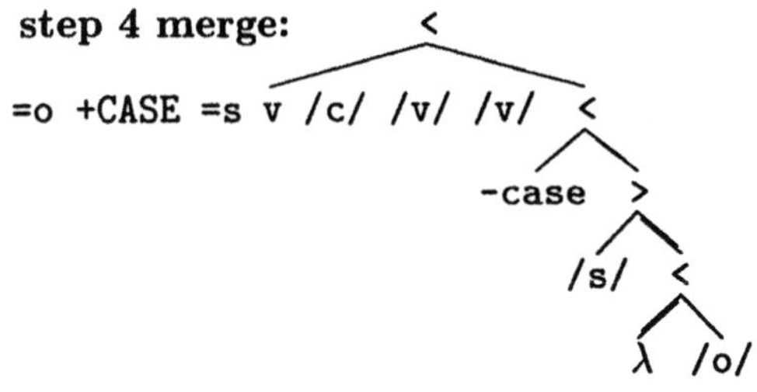

step 5 merge:

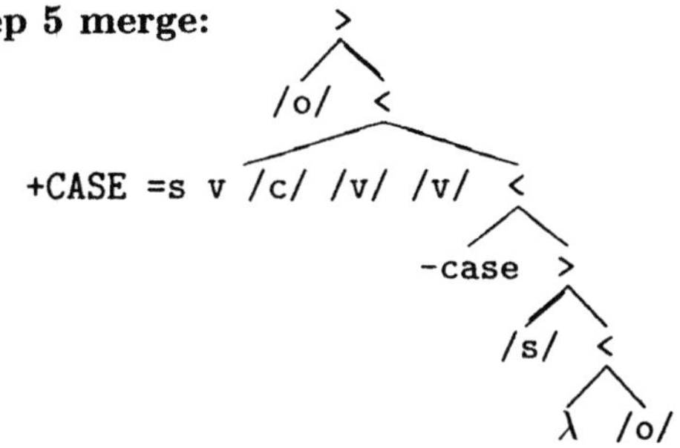

step 6 move:

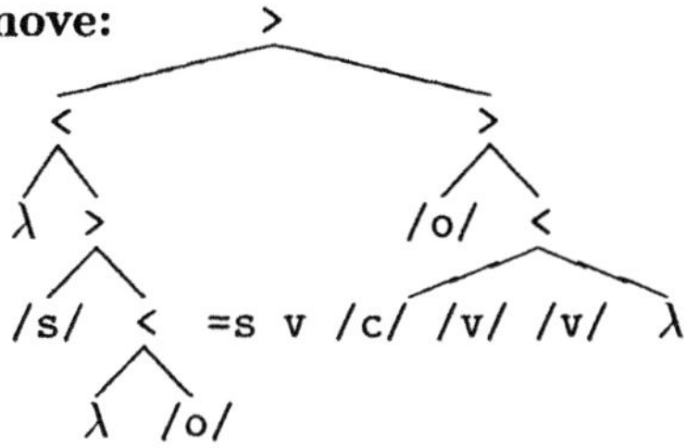

step 7 merge:

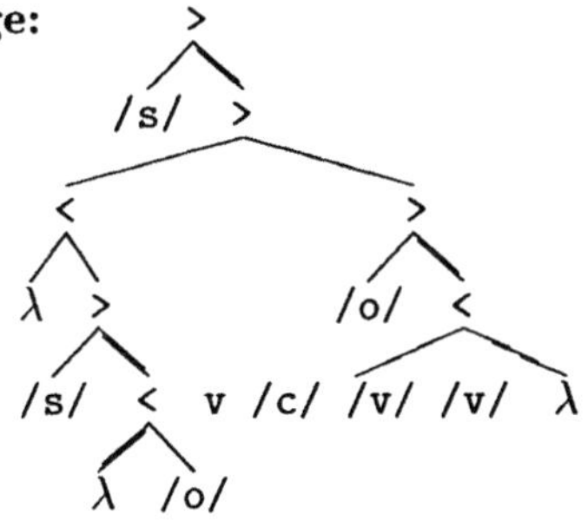

step 8 merge:

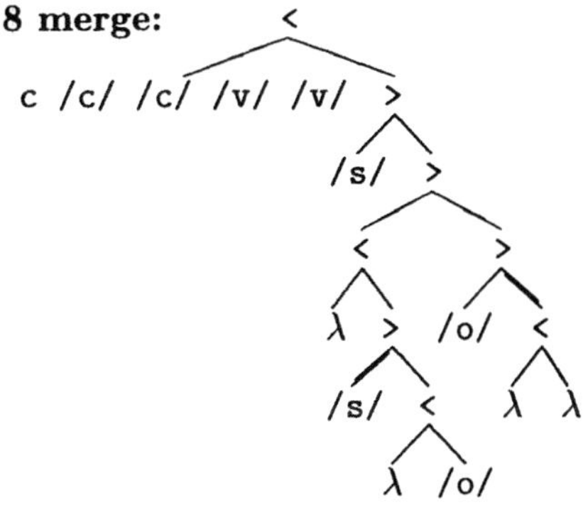

Proposition 8. $strings(MG_5) = \{\mathrm{c}^n\mathrm{v}^n\mathrm{s}^n\mathrm{o}^n \mid n \geq 0\}$.

The proof of this proposition is based on the fact that any derivation of a well-formed structure must use one of the lexical complementizers: (i) `=V c -case /c/` or (ii) `=V c /c/` or (iii) `c`. The derivations in case (iii) are trivial. Any use of (i) in a derivation must have a corresponding use of `C= =o +CASE =s v /v/` to allow for cancellation of the case features – this is the recursive case. And any use of (ii) must have a corresponding use of the non-recursive `=o =s v /v/`. An induction shows that either way, we will have equal numbers of `c,v,s,o`, in the appropriate order.

It is well known that neither $strings(MG_4)$ nor $strings(MG_5)$ are context free languages, but these languages are included in the "mildly context sensitive" class defined by [28], a class definable by tree adjoining grammars, by a certain kind of head wrapping grammars, and by a certain restricted form of combinatory categorial grammar. Let's call these languages TAG languages. It has been argued that we need to be able to define copying (ww) constructions to get Dutch dependencies [4] and to get the Swiss-German string set [25].

Various linguists have argued that human languages cannot be properly handled by formalisms that yield only the TAG languages. [24] argues that we need more power to get the right dependencies in German scrambling. [31] and [23] show that we need more power to get the string sets of number names in English and Chinese. And [20] shows that we need more than TAG power to get the case system of Old Georgian, as that language is described in [2]. Given these proposals, the following, final example is of interest.

2.6 $c^n v^n x^n s^n o^n$

Languages with five counting dependencies are not included in the TAG languages. Notice that the previous example uses strong selection (in particular, head movement with right adjunction) to build up the $c^n v^n$, and it uses XP movement of (the "remnants" of) -case CP to build up the $s^n o^n$, interleaving these two processes properly. While there can be at most one head extraction from any constituent, there can be as many XP movements as there are kinds of licensees. (That is, there can be anywhere from 0 to $|licensees|$ extractions from any constituent.) We use this idea to define a language with more than 4 counting dependencies. This example is based on one formulated by Anoop Sarkar (p.c.).

Let Lex_6 be the following set of 13 expressions:

`=T c /c/`	`c`		
`=V`$_f$ `+D =x t -d`	`=V`$_f$ `=x t -d`	`=V =x t`	`=V +D =x t`
`=o =s v /v/`	`C= =o +F =s v /v/`		
`=o =s v`$_f$ `-f /v/`	`C= =o +F =s v`$_f$ `-f /v/`		
`s /s/`			
`o /o/`			
`x /x/`			

The following derivation of `/c c v v x x s s o o/` in 13 steps illustrates the basic recursion in the grammar. The x's are collected in the highest specifiers of t, the s's and o's are collected in the highest specifiers of v, and the c's and v's all raise to the highest c:

step 1 merge:

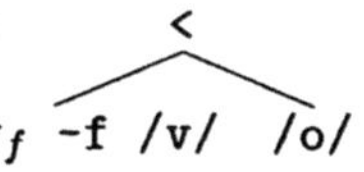

step 2 merge:

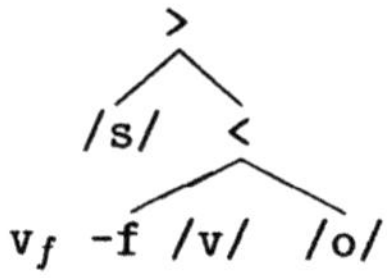

step 3 merge:

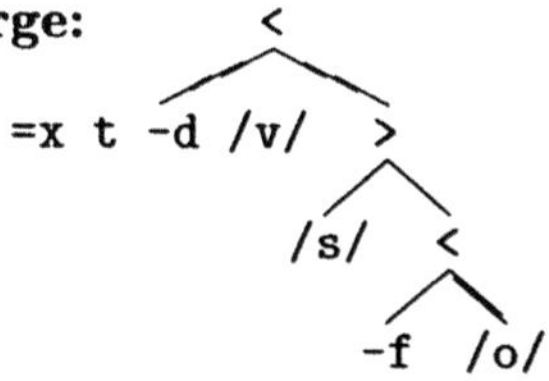

step 4 merge:

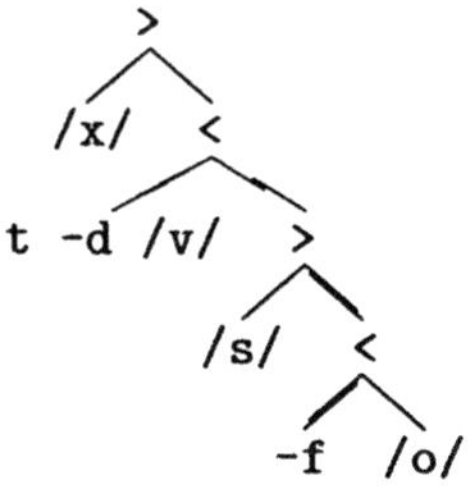

step 5 merge:

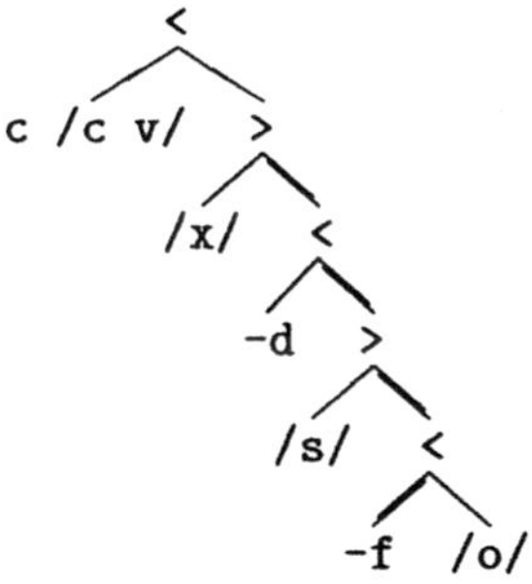

step 6 merge:

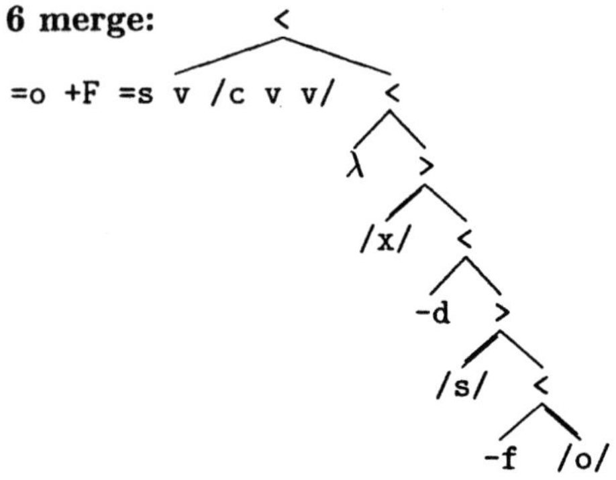

step 7 merge:

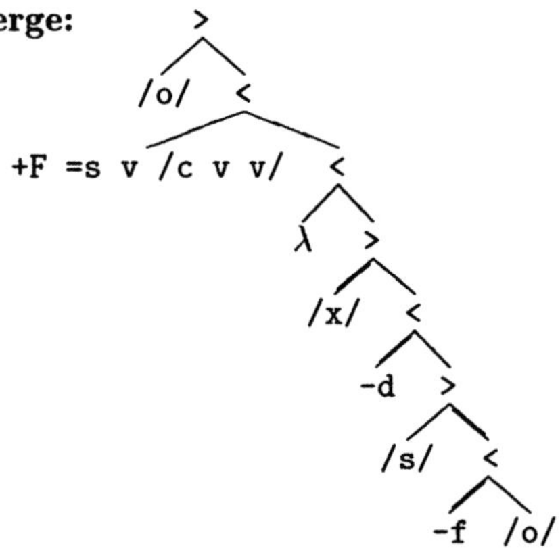

step 8 move:

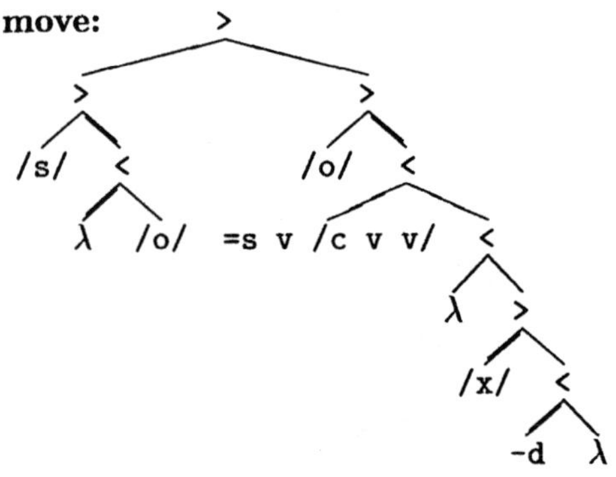

step 9 merge:

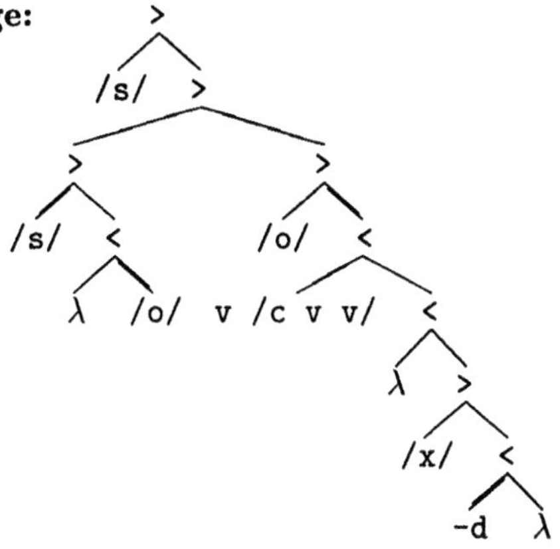

step 10 merge:

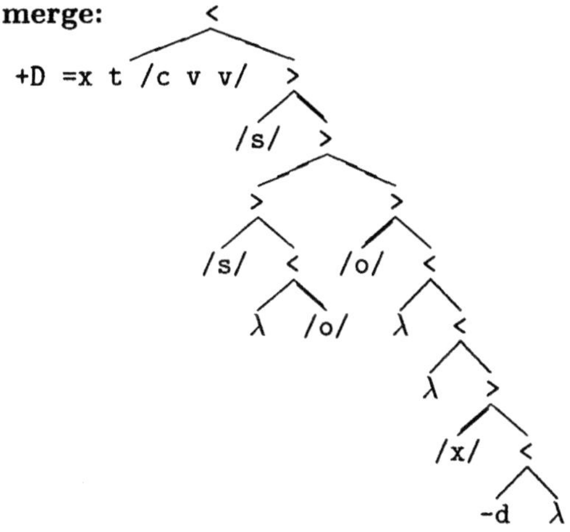

step 11 move:

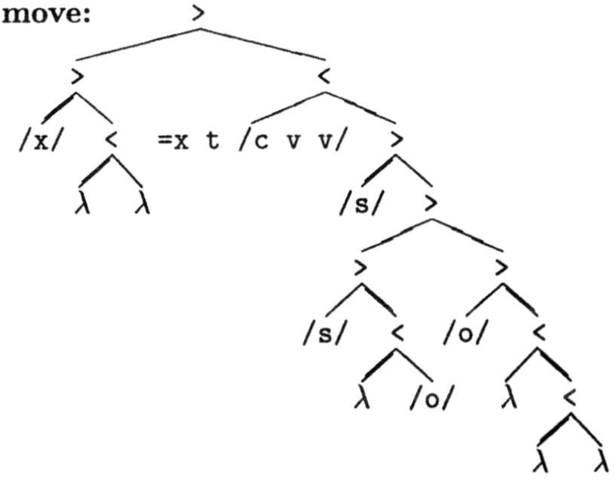

step 12 merge:

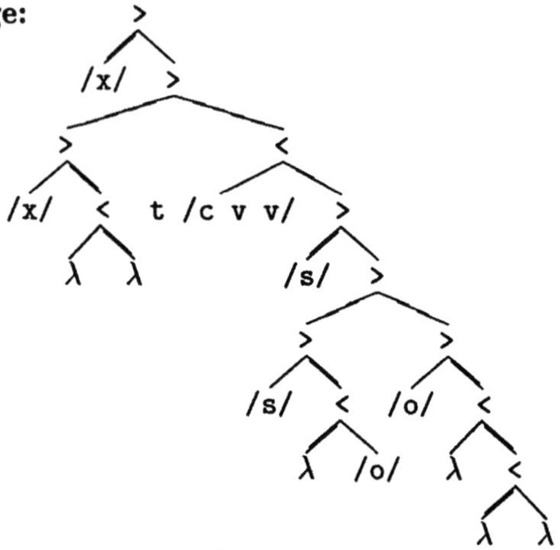

step 13 merge:

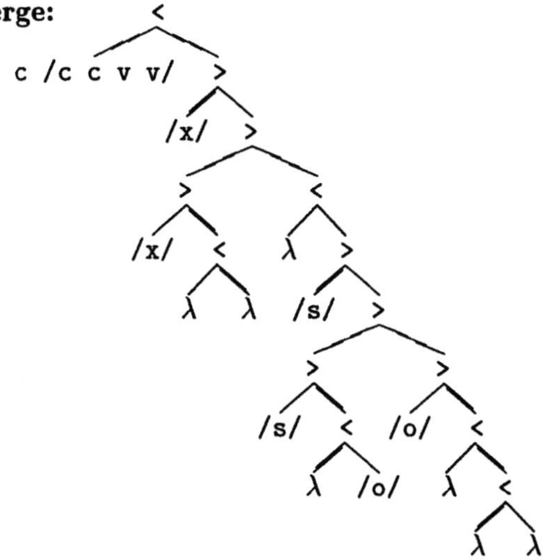

Proposition 9. *strings*$(MG_6) = \{\mathrm{c}^n\mathrm{v}^n\mathrm{x}^n\mathrm{s}^n\mathrm{o}^n | \ n \geq 0\}$.

Languages like this one, with five counting dependencies, are not TAG languages. It remains an open problem to specify how the MG-definable string sets compare to previously studied supersets of the TAG language class.

3 Beyond MGs

Following Chomsky and the earlier transformational tradition, the presentation of minimalist theory here is derivational. Brody [5] presents a representational minimalism that may appear quite different, but Cornell's [10] formalization of "representational minimalism" shows that the two are remarkably close. However, regardless of whether the presentation is derivational or representational, a simple formalism like the one explored in this paper requires some elaboration to handle human languages. For example, consider successive cyclic A-movement, as in

i. John$_i$ is t$_i$ happy
ii. John$_i$ seems t$_i$ to be t$_i$ happy
iii. John$_i$ appears t$_i$ to seem t$_i$ to be t$_i$ happy
iv. ...

One way to allow this assumes that while triggering features like `=d`, `=n`, `+case`, `+CASE` are deleted, the properties of the expressions `d`, `n`, `-case` are optionally not deleted.

Chomsky explores some much more elaborate grammars in [7], considering especially the following ideas:

- Maybe the syntax of human languages defines unordered trees, with $\prec$ imposed on the leaves by non-syntactic conditions.
- Maybe projection need not be explicitly represented in all constructions, because it is fixed by language-universal principles.[6]
- There may be additional "economy principles," acting as a kind of filter on derivations, and potentially defining a different class of languages.
- Maybe the sharp distinction between head movement and phrasal movement can be eliminated in favor of a general account of what "pied pipes" in any movement, and some general minimality condition on movements.

Some of these ideas are explored in a formal setting in [27,30].

The MG grammar formalism is not symmetric with respect to linear order: all movements are leftward, the first selected constituent always attaches to the right of the selector, and all other selected constituents attach to the left. It is interesting to compare the asymmetries in this system with those considered by Kayne in [12]. Given any tree $\tau = (N, \triangleleft^*, \prec^*, <^*)$, define the relations sister S, c-command CC, and asymmetric c-command ACC, all of them binary relations on N, as follows:[7]

---

[6] [7, §4.4.2] suggests that while *merge* is just defined to project one rather than the other of its arguments, in the case of *move* operations, we can deduce from other general assumptions about "checking" and "economy" that in the result, the moved subtree is projected over by its sister.

[7] The formulation of Kayne's view offered here is simplified in two significant respects. First, following [18] and [6], Kayne complicates these definitions for "adjunction structures." These have no exact analog in our system, but our specifiers might be regarded as left-adjoined. Making this adjustment in the claim would not affect the

$$aSb \text{ iff } a \neq b \text{ and for some } c \in N,\ c \lhd a \text{ and } c \lhd b.$$
$$aCCb \text{ iff for some } c,\ aSc \text{ and } c \lhd^* b.$$
$$aACCb \text{ iff } aCCb \text{ and } \neg bACCa.$$

Now define a binary relation R on the leaves of the tree $L = \{x| \sim(\exists y)\ x \lhd y\}$:

$$aRb \text{ iff for some } x, y,\ \ x \lhd^* a,\ \ y \lhd^* b, \text{ and } xACCy.$$

Kayne's hypothesis (the "linear correspondence axiom") is this:

(LCA) In the structures of natural languages, R is a strict linear order on L.

That is, $\forall x, y, z \in L$,
(i) if xRy then $x \neq y$, (irreflexivity)
(ii) if xRy and yRz then xRz, (transitivity)
(iii) if xRy then $\neg yRx$, and (asymmetry)
(iv) if $x \neq y$ then either xRy or yRx. (linearity)
Note that axiom (iii) is redundant, since it is entailed by (i) and (ii), and that it is different from what is usually called antisymmetry ($(xRy \wedge yRx) \rightarrow x = y$). In terms of what languages can be defined, the LCA clearly imposes no restriction at all until it is combined with other constraints, but we can immediately consider whether the LCA is respected in the structures defined by MG grammars.

Clearly, the LCA is not respected in the trees defined by our grammars. For example, in the structure derived in §2.1 (as the result of step 8) the deepest 2 leaves are labeled `/every/` and `/language/`, and these leaves are not linearly ordered by R. There are no nodes x, y such that $xACCy$, x dominates `/every/`, and y dominates `/language/`. Discussing this kind of case, Kayne says [12, pp9-10] that these two nodes "are in too symmetric a relation with one another ... replacing one of the two symmetric nodes by a more complex substructure breaks the symmetry and renders the phrase marker admissible." But notice that in our system this structure is not "symmetric" in any interesting sense: these two nodes enter the derivation as the selecting node and the selected node respectively; one is a complement and one is not; and so on. Given these features, the MG formalism (and any near variant) is going to require syntactic anaylses similar to some of Kayne's, even though it does not use the extra X-bar-like structure required by the LCA to mark the asymmetries. Considering the goal of properly capturing the asymmetries of human linguistic structures, it is not clear that the LCA has any advantage over this or other similar mechanisms that yield an appropriate structural asymmetry in all definable languages.[8]

One other prominent idea in recent transformational grammar is that movement is actually copying and deletion, where deletion is not just a reflex of movement, but a process that is potentially sensitive to other aspects of structure. One empirical motivation for this idea comes from the existence of apparent

very general remarks made here. Second, the LCA below could be taken as applying only to phonetically overt leaves of a tree, rather than to all the leaves, as suggested in [7, p337], for example. Again, for present purposes this adjustment is not relevant.

[8] See [7, §4.8] for further discussion of this point.

"duplication" of phonetically overt substructures, where the duplicated elements are syntactically related but not part of the same word. This happens in a wide range of diverse languages and constructions: for example, in "predicate clefts" [14, §6], in "partial wh-movement" [19], and in "resumptive pronouns" [26]. The attempt to account for these and other phenomena has led to the consideration of grammatical constraints that refer specifically to the presence of phonetic material [26,21,16]. This contrasts with a relatively long-standing tradition according to which phonetic material is not relevant to the principles of grammar. For example, Bouchard [3] argues that the stipulation of properties depending on whether a constituent is empty or not can undermine the empirical force of the grammar. The simple MG formalism presented here follows this older tradition, making phonetic and interpretable material completely irrelevant to the syntactic derivation. The question of how it should be extended to handle duplications of phonetic material is considered in [27].

Appendix: Definition of the structure building operations

An *expression* is a tree τ, as defined in §1.2. An expression is *complex (or a non-head)* iff it has more than one node; otherwise, it is *simple (or a head)*.

In the following definition it will be convenient to say that a tree τ *has feature (or category)* **f** iff the first element of the sequence that labels the head of τ is **f**. And we will say that a tree is *maximal* iff its root is the maximal projection of some head.

We use the standard labelled bracket notation $[_< \tau_0, \tau_1]$ to indicate an expression with immediate subtrees τ_0 and τ_1, in that linear order, where τ_0 projects over τ_1.

$$Dom(merge) = \{[\tau_0,\tau_1] | \begin{array}{ll} \text{either} & \tau_0 \text{ is a head that has feature } \mathtt{=x},\ \mathtt{=X}, \text{ or } \mathtt{X=}, \\ & \text{and } \tau_1 \text{ has category } \mathtt{x}, \\ \text{or} & \tau_0 \text{ is a complex expression that has feature } \mathtt{=x}, \\ & \text{and } \tau_1 \text{ has category } \mathtt{x}\ \} \end{array}$$

$$merge(\tau_0,\tau_1) = \begin{cases} [_< \tau_0', \tau_1'] & \text{if } \tau_0 \text{ is a head that has feature } \mathtt{=x}, \\ & \quad \tau_0' \text{ is like } \tau_0 \text{ except that } \mathtt{=x} \text{ is deleted, and} \\ & \quad \tau_1' \text{ is like } \tau_1 \text{ except that } \mathtt{x} \text{ is deleted} \\ [_< \tau_0', \tau_1'] & \text{if } \tau_0 \text{ is a head that has feature } \mathtt{=X}, \\ & \quad \tau_0' \text{ is like } \tau_0 \text{ except that } \mathtt{=x} \text{ is deleted} \\ & \qquad \text{and its phonetic features are the result of} \\ & \qquad \text{concatenating those of } \tau_0 \text{ and } \tau_1 \text{ in that order,} \\ & \quad \tau_1' \text{ is like } \tau_1 \text{ except } \mathtt{x} \text{ and all phonetic features are deleted} \\ [_< \tau_0', \tau_1'] & \text{if } \tau_0 \text{ is a head that has feature } \mathtt{X=}, \\ & \quad \tau_0' \text{ is like } \tau_0 \text{ except that } \mathtt{=x} \text{ is deleted} \\ & \qquad \text{and its phonetic features are the result of} \\ & \qquad \text{concatenating those of } \tau_1 \text{ and } \tau_0 \text{ in that order,} \\ & \quad \tau_1' \text{ is like } \tau_1 \text{ except } \mathtt{x} \text{ and all phonetic features are deleted} \\ [_> \tau_1', \tau_0'] & \text{if } \tau_0 \text{ is a complex that has feature } \mathtt{=x} \\ & \quad \tau_0' \text{ is like } \tau_0 \text{ except that } \mathtt{=x} \text{ is deleted, and} \\ & \quad \tau_1' \text{ is like } \tau_1 \text{ except that } \mathtt{x} \text{ is deleted} \end{cases}$$

$$Dom(move) = \{\tau| \begin{array}{l}\tau \text{ has a feature } \texttt{+x} \text{ or } \texttt{+X}, \text{ and} \\ \tau \text{ has exactly one proper subtree with the feature } \texttt{-x}\ \}\end{array}$$

$move(\tau) = [_> \tau_0', \tau']$, where
either τ has feature **+X**,
τ_0 is a proper subtree of τ with feature **-x**,
τ_0 is maximal,
τ_0' is like τ_0 except that **-x** is deleted, and
τ' is like τ except that **+X** is deleted and
subtree τ_0 is replaced by a leaf with no features
or τ has feature **+x**,
τ_0 is a proper subtree of τ with feature **-x**,
τ_0 is maximal,
τ_0' is like τ_0 except that **-x** and all phonetic features are deleted,
and τ' is like τ except that **+x** is deleted and
all non-phonetic features in τ_0 are deleted

Acknowledgments: Thanks to Edward Keenan, Thomas Cornell, Sean Fulop, Francois Lamarche, Jeff MacSwan and Anoop Sarkar for stimulating discussions and helpful suggestions on previous versions.

References

1. Mark Baker. *The Polysynthesis Parameter.* Oxford University Press, New York, 1996.
2. Winfried Boeder. Suffixaufname in Kartvelian. In Frans Plank, editor, *Double Case: Agreement by Suffixaufnahme.* Oxford University Press, New York, 1995.
3. Denis Bouchard. *On the Content of Empty Categories.* Foris, Dordrecht, 1984.
4. Joan Bresnan, Ronald M. Kaplan, Stanley Peters, and Annie Zaenen. Cross-serial dependencies in Dutch. *Linguistic Inquiry*, 13(4):613–635, 1982.
5. Michael Brody. *Lexico-Logical Form: A Radically Minimalist Theory.* MIT Press, Cambridge, Massachusetts, 1995.
6. Noam Chomsky. *Barriers.* MIT Press, Cambridge, Massachusetts, 1986.
7. Noam Chomsky. *The Minimalist Program.* MIT Press, Cambridge, Massachusetts, 1995.
8. Sandra Chung and James McCloskey. Government, barriers and small clauses in modern Irish. *Linguistic Inquiry*, 18:173–238, 1987.
9. Thomas L. Cornell. Deriving the *ww* language with μP style. University of Tübingen, 1996.
10. Thomas L. Cornell. Representational minimalism. University of Tübingen, 1996.
11. Jane H. Hill and Kenneth C. Hill. *Speaking Mexicano.* The University of Arizona Press, Tucson, Arizona, 1986.
12. Richard Kayne. *The Antisymmetry of Syntax.* MIT Press, Cambridge, Massachusetts, 1994.
13. Edward L. Keenan and Edward P. Stabler. Abstract syntax. In Anna-Maria Di Sciullo, editor, *Configurations: Essays on Structure and Interpretation*, pages 329–344, Somerville, Massachusetts, 1996. Cascadilla Press. Conference version available at http://128.97.8.34/.

14. Hilda Koopman. *The Syntax of Verbs: From Verb Movement Rules in the Kru Languages to Universal Grammar.* Foris, Dordrecht, 1983.
15. Hilda Koopman. On verbs that fail to undergo V-second. *Linguistic Inquiry*, 26:137–163, 1995.
16. Hilda Koopman. The spec-head configuration. Syntax at Sunset: UCLA Working Papers in Syntax and Semantics, edited by Edward Garrett and Felicia Lee, 1996.
17. Hilda Koopman and Dominique Sportiche. The position of subjects. *Lingua*, 85:211–258, 1991.
18. Robert May. *Logical Form: Its Structure and Derivation.* MIT Press, Cambridge, Massachusetts, 1985.
19. Dana McDaniel. Partial and multiple wh-movement. *Natural Language and Linguistic Theory*, 7:565–604, 1989.
20. Jens Michaelis and Marcus Kracht. Semilinearity as a syntactic invariant. In *Logical Aspects of Computational Linguistics (LACL)*, pages 37–40, 1996.
21. David Pesetsky. Principles of sentence pronunciation. MIT Lecture notes. Available at http://ruccs.rutgers.edu/roa.html, 1994.
22. Jean-Yves Pollock. Verb movement, universal grammar, and the structure of IP. *Linguistic Inquiry*, 20:365–424, 1989.
23. Daniel Radzinski. Chinese number names, tree adjoining languages and mild context sensitivity. *Computational Linguistics*, 17:277–300, 1991.
24. Owen Rambow, K. Vijay-Shanker, and David Weir. D-tree grammars. In *Proceedings of the 33rd Annual Meeting of the Association for Computational Linguistics*, 1995. Available at http://xxx.lanl.gov/cmp-lg/ACL-95-proceedings.html.
25. Stuart M. Shieber. Evidence against the context-freeness of natural language. *Linguistics and Philosophy*, 8(3):333–344, 1985.
26. Ur Shlonsky. Resumptive pronouns as a last resort. *Linguistic Inquiry*, 23:443–468, 1992.
27. Edward P. Stabler. *Acquiring and parsing languages with movement.* Basil Blackwell, Oxford, 1996. Forthcoming. Draft available at http://128.97.8.34/.
28. K. Vijay-Shanker and David Weir. The equivalence of four extensions of context free grammar formalisms. *Mathematical Systems Theory*, 27:511–545, 1994.
29. Sten Vikner. *Verb Movement and Expletive Subjects in the Germanic Languages.* Oxford University Press, New York, 1995.
30. Charles Yang. Minimal computation. Massachusetts Institute of Technology, 1996.
31. Arnold Zwicky. Some languages that are not context free. Technical Report Quarterly Progress Report 70, MIT Research Laboratory of Electronics, Cambridge, Massachusetts, 1963.

Tree Adjoining Grammars in Noncommutative Linear Logic

— Extended Abstract —

V. Michele Abrusci[1], Christophe Fouqueré[2], and Jacqueline Vauzeilles[2]

[1] CILA, Universitá di Bari, 70121 Bari, Italy
[2] LIPN-CNRS URA 1507, Université Paris-Nord, 93430 Villetaneuse

Abstract. This paper[1] presents a logical formalization of Tree-Adjoining Grammar (TAG). TAG deals with lexicalized trees and two operations are available: substitution and adjunction. Adjunction is generally presented as an insertion of a tree inside another, surrounding the subtree at the adjunction node. This seems to be contradictory with standard logical ability. We prove that some logic, namely a fragment of noncommutative intuitionistic linear logic (N-ILL), can serve this purpose. Briefly speaking, linear logic is a logic considering facts as *resources*. N-ILL can then be considered either as an extension of Lambek calculus, or as a restriction of linear logic. We model the TAG formalism in four steps: trees (initial or derived) and the way they are constituted, the operations (substitution and adjunction), and the elementary trees, i.e. the grammar. The sequent calculus is a restriction of the standard sequent calculus for N-ILL. Trees (initial or derived) are then obtained as the closure of the calculus under two rules that mimic the grammatical ones. We then prove the equivalence between the language generated by a TAG grammar and the closure under substitution and adjunction of its logical representation. Besides this nice property, we relate parse trees to logical proofs, and to their geometric representation: *proofnets*. We briefly present them and give examples of parse trees as proofnets. This process can be interpreted as an assembling of blocks (proofnets corresponding to elementary trees of the grammar).

1 Introduction

This paper presents a logical formalization of Tree-Adjoining Grammar (TAG, [8], [9]). TAG deals with lexicalized trees and two operations are available: substitution and adjunction. A set of (elementary) trees is associated to each lexical item. TAG is a tree rewriting system: the parsing process consists in applying operations to trees in order to obtain a (derived) tree whose sequence of leaves is a sentence. Adjunction increases the expressive power of the formalism in such a way that non context-free languages can be represented although the parsing process is done in a polynomial time. Adjunction is generally presented as

[1] An extended version is currently in submission and available as a technical report [5]

an insertion of a tree inside another, surrounding the subtree at the adjunction node. This seems to be contradictory with standard logical ability. We prove hereafter that some logic, namely a fragment of non-commutative intuitionistic linear logic (N-ILL, [2,3]), can serve this purpose. Briefly speaking, linear logic, developed by Girard [6], is a logic considering facts as *resources*. N-ILL can then be considered either as an extension of Lambek calculus, or as a restriction of linear logic. Nevertheless, viewing logical literals as resources allows a straight and natural mapping from a derivational formalism (such as TAG) to such a logic: there is no need for indexing pieces of trees or words of a sentence. Since we are not interested in disjunction in this paper, we only need the intuitionistic part of linear logic. Finally, non-commutativity is necessary insofar as we aspire to take care of word order.

We model the TAG formalism in four steps: trees (initial or derived) and the way they are constituted, the operations (substitution and adjunction), and the elementary trees, i.e. the grammar. Labels occurring in the grammar constitute the set of propositional variables we need. The sequent calculus is a restriction of the standard sequent calculus for N-ILL: there are identity axioms ($A \vdash A$) and rules for introducing connectives ($\otimes$ at left hand side, $\multimapinv$ at right hand side). $\multimapinv$ is the left implication, $\otimes$ is one of the two 'and' connectives available in Linear Logic and its variants. We prove that this restricted calculus is closed under two rules that mimic the grammatical operations. Trees (initial or derived) are then obtained as the closure of the calculus under these two rules. In fact, trees are represented as (provable) sequents in an almost classical way. The right hand side is the variable labeling the mother node of the tree. The left hand side is a sequence of formulas of the following kinds: A for some leaf A of the tree, $A \multimapinv B_1 \otimes \cdots \otimes B_n$ where A is the label of some internal node and B_i are the labels of its daughters, $A \multimapinv A$ whenever A is a node where an adjunction can take place. This latter kind of formula can be grammatically interpreted as if such an A was split into two nodes with the same label, linked by some "soft" relation. The set of elementary trees of a TAG grammar $\mathcal{G}'$ is then represented as a subset M of the sequents in the closure of the calculus under the two previous rules. We then prove the equivalence between the language generated in TAG by such a grammar $\mathcal{G}'$ and the closure under substitution and adjunction of the logical representation M. Note that our interpretation of adjunction is very close to the use of *quasi-trees* described in [13].

Besides this nice property, we relate parse trees to logical proofs, and to their geometric representation: *proofnets*. As for linear logic, there exists in N-ILL a correspondence between proofs and some sort of nets, called proofnets. We briefly present proofnets and give examples of parse trees as proofnets. This enables a new point of view on the parsing process. This process can be interpreted as an assembling of blocks (proofnets corresponding to elementary trees of the grammar), and also as a circulation of information through links relating nodes of the proofnets.

The paper is organized in four parts. Section 2 describes the TAG formalism. We recall the terminology and show how substitution and adjunction operate on trees. Section 3 gives a survey of noncommutative linear logic and relates it to Lambek calculus and linear logic. We propose in section 4 a logical formulation of TAG in a fragment of N-ILL, and prove the correspondence between the two. Section 5 is devoted to the representation of proofs as proofnets.

2 Tree Adjoining Grammars

The Tree Adjoining Grammar formalism (TAG) is a tree generating formalism introduced in [8], linguistically motivated (see for example, [1,10]), and with formal properties studied in [14–16]. A TAG is defined by two finite sets of trees composed by means of the substitution and adjunction operations[2].

Definition 1. A TAG G is a 5-uple (V_N, V_T, S, I, A) where

- V_N is a finite set of non-terminal symbols,
- V_T is a finite set of terminal symbols,
- S is a distinguished non-terminal symbol, the *start* symbol,
- I is a set of *initial* trees,
- A is a set of *auxiliary* trees.

An *elementary* tree is either an initial tree or an auxiliary tree. Both *initial* and *auxiliary* trees are trees with at least one leaf labeled by a terminal node (the grammar is a so-called *lexicalized* one). An *auxiliary* tree must furthermore have a leaf (the *foot* node, marked with a star $\star$) with the same label as the root node. Each non-terminal node is marked as adjoinable or non-adjoinable (in this case, the node is marked *NA*). Each internal node must obviously be labeled by a non-terminal node.[3] A *derived* tree is either an initial tree or a tree obtained from derived trees by means of the two available operations.

In conformity with the literature, we will use α to refer to an initial tree, β to refer to an auxiliary tree, γ to refer to some derived tree. Examples of initial and auxiliary trees are given in fig. 1. Two TAGs are defined: $G_1 = (\{S\}, \{a, b, c, d, \epsilon\}, S, \{\alpha_1\}, \{\beta_1\})$ (ϵ is the empty word) and $G_2 = (\{S, VP, NP, N\}, \{the, man, walks\}, S, \{\alpha_2, \alpha_3, \alpha_4\}, \emptyset)$.

The *substitution* operation is defined as usual. A non-terminal leaf of a tree may be expanded with a tree whose root node has the same label. Leaves that accept substitution are marked with a down arrow $\downarrow$. The *adjunction* operation is a little bit more complicated. It supposes a derived tree with a non-terminal

[2] Originally, there was no need for a substitution operation as initial trees were rooted at S, thus labeling a sentence. We refer here to the Lexicalized-TAG formalism where this constraint disappears on behalf of the substitution operation. However, we maintain the name TAG.

[3] In some versions, non-terminal nodes of elementary trees are labeled by a *set* of (auxiliary) trees that can be adjoined at this node. In the case of an empty set, the node is obviously non-adjoinable. For the sake of clarity, we simplify the definition to only take into account the *boolean* adjoinable property: either the node is adjoinable or it is non-adjoinable (NA).

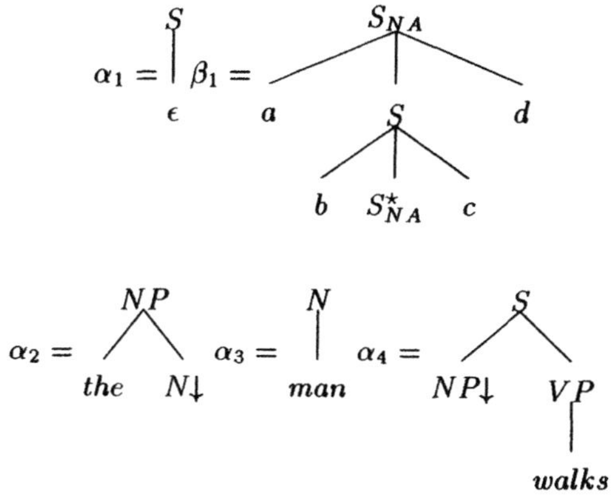

Fig. 1. Elementary trees.

node, say X, possibly internal and not marked NA, and an auxiliary tree with root node X. The operation consists in:

- excising the subtree with root labeled X in the derived tree,
- inserting the auxiliary tree at node labeled X in the derived tree,
- finally, inserting the excised subtree at the foot node (labeled X and marked with a star $\star$) in the auxiliary tree.

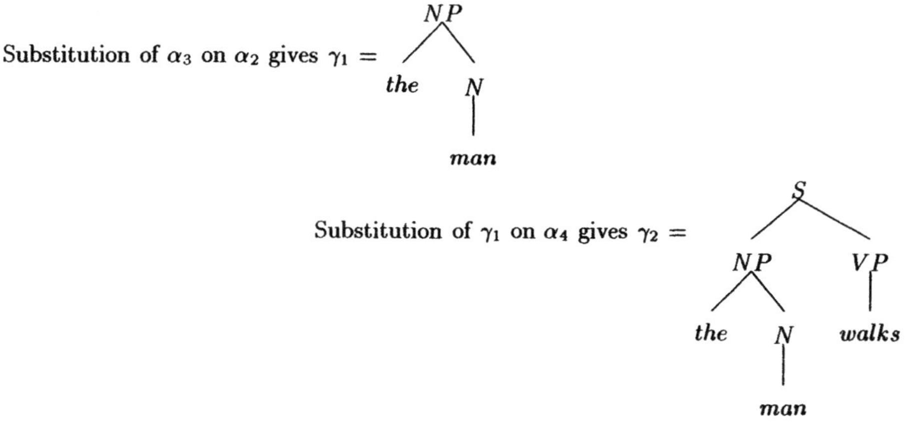

Fig. 2. Substitution results

Examples of these operations are given in fig. 2 and 3. In order to clarify the way adjunction is done, the adjoined tree β_1 has its links dashed in the derived trees γ_3 and γ_4. Obviously, there is only one kind of link. We write $\gamma_1 \Rightarrow_G \gamma_2$ when γ_2 is the result of an adjunction or a substitution of an elementary tree

Adjunction of β_1 on α_1 gives γ_3 =

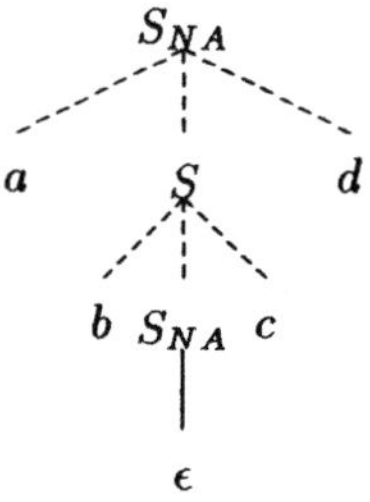

Adjunction of β_1 on γ_3 gives γ_4 =

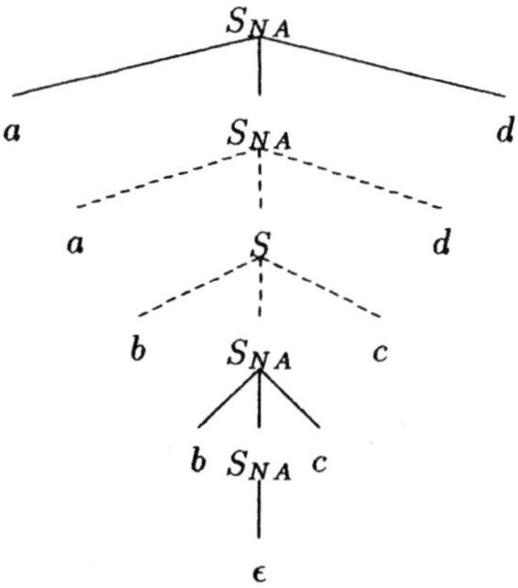

Fig. 3. Adjunction results

of a TAG G on the derived tree γ_1. $\Rightarrow_G^*$ is the reflexive, transitive closure of $\Rightarrow_G$. The set $\{\gamma / \exists \alpha \in G \text{ and } \alpha \Rightarrow_G^* \gamma\}$ is noted $T(G)$. The language $L(G)$ generated by a TAG G is the set of strings, i.e. sequences of leaves of trees in $T(G)$ when the leaves of these trees are only labeled with terminal nodes, and whose root is the start symbol. Hence, $L(G_1) = \{a^n b^n c^n d^n / n \geq 0\}$ and $L(G_2) = \{\textit{the man walks}\}$.

3 Noncommutative Intuitionistic Linear Logic

Linear logic was introduced by Girard [6] as a "resource conscious logic". In other words, while classical logic deals with static descriptions, linear logic considers propositions as finite resources. Hence, 'A' and 'A *and* A' are equivalent in classical logic, this is (generally) not the case in linear logic. The easiest technical way to investigate this difference is to consider the Gentzen sequent calculus for these logics. A *sequent* is of the form $\Gamma \vdash \Delta$ where Γ and Δ stand for sequences of well-formed formulae w.r.t. the language of the logic. It expresses the fact that the (multiplicative) disjunction of formulas in Δ is a consequence of the (multiplicative) conjunction of formulas in Γ. A *sequent calculus* is a set of rules specifying the provable sequents, being given a set of axioms. A *proof* of a sequent is then the successive application of sequent rules beginning with axioms, i.e. a tree with the proved sequent as the root of the tree (at the bottom) and whose leaves are axioms (at the top). Rules of a sequent calculus introduce in some way connectives in the right or left hand side of a sequent. Hence, in the case of a simple calculus, sequent calculus is constructive in the sense that, given a sequent to be proved, there exists a constructive way to find the proof. We refer the reader to [12] for a survey on various systems of deduction and the relations between sequent calculus, Hilbert-style systems and natural deduction. Besides these introduction rules and axioms, we find structural rules that govern the structure of a sequent. In classical logic, the set of structural rules consists in weakening, contraction and exchange (cf fig. 4 where A, B are formulas, $\Gamma, \Gamma', \Delta, \Delta'$ are sequences of formulas). Weakening and contraction allow the arbitrary copy of formulas: having a formula A as a hypothesis or conclusion is equivalent to having it twice (or more). This point of view contradicts the notion of resource, hence these two structural rules are omitted in linear logic. However special connectives, namely the *exponentials* of-course '!' and why-not '?' have these properties. The exchange rule is responsible for commutativity of the comma (in the right side and in the left side): the order of hypotheses or conclusions does not matter. This rule is no longer valid in the noncommutative version of linear logic.

$$\frac{\Gamma \vdash \Delta}{\Gamma, A \vdash \Delta}\ (l - \textit{weakening}) \qquad \frac{\Gamma \vdash \Delta}{\Gamma \vdash \Delta, A}\ (r - \textit{weakening})$$

$$\frac{\Gamma, A, A \vdash \Delta}{\Gamma, A \vdash \Delta}\ (l - \textit{contraction}) \qquad \frac{\Gamma \vdash \Delta, A, A}{\Gamma \vdash \Delta, A}\ (r - \textit{contraction})$$

$$\frac{\Gamma, B, A, \Gamma' \vdash \Delta}{\Gamma, A, B, \Gamma' \vdash \Delta}\ (l - \textit{exchange}) \qquad \frac{\Gamma \vdash \Delta, B, A, \Delta'}{\Gamma \vdash \Delta, A, B, \Delta'}\ (r - \textit{exchange})$$

Fig. 4. Structural rules

However, and this is already true in linear logic, the logical interpretation of 'and' and 'or' is not as simple as it is in classical logic. We need to distinguish two 'and' ($\otimes$ 'times', & 'with') and two 'or' ($⅋$ 'par', $\oplus$ 'plus'), hence inducing four constants: $1, \top, \bot, 0$ (respective neutral elements for the previous connectives). In fact, connectives are related in such a way that they form two groups: the multiplicative group ($\otimes, ⅋, 1, \bot$) and the additive group ($\&, \oplus, \top, 0$). We only use hereafter the multiplicative group. There are obviously fundamental reasons for this proliferation but these explanations are outside the scope of this paper. The negation and the implication are however of special interest. In (commutative) linear logic, there are only one negation $\cdot^{\bot}$ and one (linear) implication $\multimap$. In the noncommutative case, they have also to be split: there are a pre- ${}^{\bot}\cdot$ and a post- negation $\cdot^{\bot}$ and a pre- $\circ\!-$ and a post- implication $\multimap$. These two implications have to be related with the two operations in Lambek calculus: $\multimap$ with $\backslash$ and $\circ\!-$ with $/$. The implications may be defined in the following way:

$B \circ\!- A \equiv B \parr^{\perp} A$ and $A -\!\circ B \equiv A^{\perp} \parr B$. We give in fig. 5 the one-sided sequent calculus for the multiplicative fragment of noncommutative linear logic N-LL, and in fig. 6 the two-sided sequent calculus for the multiplicative fragment of intuitionistic noncommutative linear logic N-ILL: sequent calculus for N-LL and sequent calculus for N-ILL satisfy the cut-elimination theorem[4]; however we make use of cut-rules in section 4. Note that if $\Gamma \vdash A$ is provable in the multiplicative intuitionistic noncommutative linear logic, then $\vdash (\Gamma^*)^{\perp}, A^*$ is provable in the multiplicative noncommutative linear logic, where:

- for each formula A of intuitionistic noncommutative linear logic, A^* is a formula of noncommutative linear logic defined as follows
  - $p^* = p$, for every propositional letter p
  - $(B \otimes C)^* = B^* \otimes C^*$, $(B -\!\circ C)^* = (B^*)^{\perp} \parr C^*$, $(B \circ\!- C)^* = B^* \parr^{\perp}(C^*)$
- for each finite sequence $A_1, \ldots, A_n$ of formulas of intuitionistic noncommutative linear logic, $(A_1, \ldots, A_n)^* = (A_1)^*, \ldots, (A_n)^*$
- for each finite sequence $A_1, \ldots, A_n$ of formulas of noncommutative linear logic, $(A_1, \ldots, A_n)^{\perp} = (A_n)^{\perp}, \ldots, (A_1)^{\perp}$

We give hereafter two examples of proofs in order to show the way the sequent calculus can be used. We choose logical translations of a Lambek grammar to pinpoint the obvious relation with Lambek formalism. The first one (fig. 7) is a straightforward translation in a Lambek style, being given the two implications. The second proof (fig. 8) interprets the Lambek grammar in a derivation-style, we only need one implication and the connective times. The proofs use cuts: they can be withdrawn as the logic enjoys the cut-elimination theorem, but we think it can help understanding the process. Moreover, we associate to each lexical item a (provable) sequent we use as a proper axiom (label 'lex'). The following sections include other examples and emphasize the usefulness of noncommutative linear logic in the linguistic domain. The lexicon in a Lambek-style is the following one:

John	: NP
gives	: ((NP\ S)/NP)/NP
Mary	: NP
a	: NP/N
book	: N

4 The calculus $\mathcal{A}$ (a fragment of N-ILL)

The formalization of TAG in N-ILL relies mainly on a logical presentation of the two operations substitution and adjunction together with a correspondence between proofs and trees. As already shown in the previous section, the substitution operation is nothing else but the application of some sort of cut-rule we call the *atomic cut-rule*. Interpreting the adjunction operation is really the main difficulty. The adjunction results from two atomic cut-rules between the sequent corresponding to the adjunction tree and two suitable sequents corresponding

[4] For each proof, there exists a cut-free proof with the same conclusion.

Alphabet:

- propositional letters: $a, b, c, \ldots$
- for each propositional letter p and each integer $n > 0$

$$p^{\overbrace{\perp \cdots \perp}^{n \text{ times}}} \text{ and } {}^{\overbrace{\perp \cdots \perp}^{n \text{ times}}}p$$

- connectives: $\otimes, \wp$

Formulas: usual definition
Sequents: $\vdash \Gamma$ where Γ is a finite sequence of formulas
Metalinguistic definition of $A^{\perp}$ and ${}^{\perp}A$ s.t. ${}^{\perp}(A^{\perp}) = ({}^{\perp}A)^{\perp} = A$, for every formula A:

$$(p^{\overbrace{\perp \cdots \perp}^{n \text{ times}}})^{\perp} = p^{\overbrace{\perp \cdots \perp}^{n+1 \text{ times}}} \qquad ({}^{\overbrace{\perp \cdots \perp}^{n \text{ times}}}p)^{\perp} = {}^{\overbrace{\perp \cdots \perp}^{n-1 \text{ times}}}p$$

$${}^{\perp}(p^{\overbrace{\perp \cdots \perp}^{n \text{ times}}}) = p^{\overbrace{\perp \cdots \perp}^{n-1 \text{ times}}} \qquad {}^{\perp}({}^{\overbrace{\perp \cdots \perp}^{n \text{ times}}}p) = {}^{\overbrace{\perp \cdots \perp}^{n+1 \text{ times}}}p$$

$$(B \otimes C)^{\perp} = C^{\perp} \wp B^{\perp} \qquad (B \wp C)^{\perp} = C^{\perp} \otimes B^{\perp}$$

$${}^{\perp}(B \otimes C) = {}^{\perp}C \wp {}^{\perp}B \qquad {}^{\perp}(B \wp C) = {}^{\perp}C \otimes {}^{\perp}B$$

Rules of sequent calculus:

$$\frac{}{\vdash A^{\perp}, A}\ (axiom) \qquad \frac{\vdash \Gamma_1, A, \Gamma_2 \quad \vdash A^{\perp}, \Delta}{\vdash \Gamma_1, \Delta, \Gamma_2}\ (cut_1) \qquad \frac{\vdash \Gamma, A \quad \vdash \Delta_1, A^{\perp}, \Delta_2}{\vdash \Delta_1, \Gamma, \Delta_2}\ (cut_2)$$

$$\frac{\vdash \Delta_1, A, B, \Delta_2}{\vdash \Delta_1, A \wp B, \Delta_2}\ (r\, \wp) \qquad \frac{\vdash \Gamma_1, A, \Gamma_2 \quad \vdash B, \Delta}{\vdash \Gamma_1, A \otimes B, \Delta, \Gamma_2}\ (r_1 \otimes) \qquad \frac{\vdash \Gamma, A \quad \vdash \Delta_1, B, \Delta_2}{\vdash \Delta_1, \Gamma, A \otimes B, \Delta_2}\ (r_2 \otimes)$$

Fig. 5. Language and sequent calculus for Multiplicative Noncommutative Linear Logic

Alphabet:

- propositional letters: $a, b, c, \ldots$
- connectives: $\otimes, \circ\!-, -\!\circ$

Formulas: usual definition
Sequents: $\Gamma \vdash A$ where Γ is a finite sequence of formulas and A is a formula
Rules of sequent calculus:

$$\frac{}{A \vdash A}\ (axiom) \qquad \frac{\Gamma \vdash A \quad \Gamma_1, A, \Gamma_2 \vdash B}{\Gamma_1, \Gamma, \Gamma_2 \vdash B}\ (cut)$$

$$\frac{\Gamma \vdash A \quad \Delta \vdash B}{\Gamma, \Delta \vdash A \otimes B}\ (r - \otimes) \qquad \frac{\Gamma_1, A, B, \Gamma_2 \vdash C}{\Gamma_1, A \otimes B, \Gamma_2 \vdash C}\ (l - \otimes)$$

$$\frac{\Gamma_1, A, \Gamma_2 \vdash C \quad \Delta \vdash B}{\Gamma_1, A \circ\!- B, \Delta, \Gamma_2 \vdash C}\ (l - \circ\!-) \qquad \frac{\Gamma, B \vdash A}{\Gamma \vdash A \circ\!- B}\ (r - \circ\!-)$$

$$\frac{\Gamma_1, A, \Gamma_2 \vdash C \quad \Delta \vdash B}{\Gamma_1, \Delta, B -\!\circ A, \Gamma_2 \vdash C}\ (l - -\!\circ) \qquad \frac{B, \Gamma \vdash A}{\Gamma \vdash B -\!\circ A}\ (r - -\!\circ)$$

Fig. 6. Language and sequent calculus for Multiplicative Noncommutative Intuitionistic Linear Logic

to two subparts of the tree where adjunction is done. However, it remains to prove that there is only one way to combine the pieces, the substitution node being given, and that the order of the elements are as requested. For that purpose, we show that for a suitable fragment of N-ILL there is a unique way to decompose a sequent $\Gamma, a \circ\!- A, \Delta \vdash B$ into $\Gamma, a, \Delta_2 \vdash B$ and $\Delta_1 \vdash A$. In this section, we clarify the calculus $\mathcal{A}$ used to interpret TAG: it includes a cut rule and an adjunction rule that mimic the grammatical operations. According with the previous remarks, these two rules are correct w.r.t. the logic. We give the basic properties satisfied by this calculus $\mathcal{A}$. In order to model TAG in N-ILL, we first construct the set $\mathcal{G}$ of subtrees of depth 1 of trees appearing in a TAG grammar $\mathcal{G}'$. The TAG grammar $\mathcal{G}'$ is then a subset of the closure $\mathcal{T}(\mathcal{G})$ under substitution (possibly with the declaration of adjunction nodes annotated in this case subst*) and adjunction of the set $\mathcal{G}$. The interpretation of elements of $\mathcal{G}$ as provable sequents of $\mathcal{A}$ is straightforward. This leads to a calculus $\mathcal{A}(\mathcal{G})$ where the operations are restricted w.r.t. $\mathcal{G}$. The TAG grammar $\mathcal{G}'$ is then in correspondence with a subset $\mathrm{M}(\mathcal{G}')$ of $\mathcal{A}(\mathcal{G})$ and we prove the equivalence between the language generated by $\mathcal{G}'$ and the set of sequents obtained by closure on $\mathrm{M}(\mathcal{G}')$ by the cut and adjunction rules[5]. Proofs of propositions are postponed until the annex. The various components of our approach are summarized below.

[5] We note M instead of $\mathrm{M}(\mathcal{G}')$ whenever there is no ambiguity.

$$\dfrac{}{NP, (((NP \multimap S) \circ\!- NP) \circ\!- NP) \circ\!- gives, gives, NP, NP \vdash S}\,(\mathrm{lex}) \quad \dfrac{}{NP \circ\!- Mary, Mary \vdash NP}\,(\mathrm{lex})$$

$$\dfrac{}{NP, (((NP \multimap S) \circ\!- NP) \circ\!- NP) \circ\!- gives, gives, NP \circ\!- Mary, Mary, NP \vdash S}\,(\mathrm{cut})$$

$$\dfrac{}{(NP \circ\!- N) \circ\!- a, a, N \vdash NP}\,(\mathrm{lex}) \quad \dfrac{}{N \circ\!- book, book \vdash N}\,(\mathrm{lex})$$

$$\dfrac{}{(NP \circ\!- N) \circ\!- a, a, N \circ\!- book, book \vdash NP}$$

$$\dfrac{}{NP \circ\!- John, John \vdash NP}\,(\mathrm{lex}) \quad \dfrac{}{NP, (((NP \multimap S) \circ\!- NP) \circ\!- NP) \circ\!- gives, gives, NP \circ\!- Mary, Mary, (NP \circ\!- N) \circ\!- a, a, N \circ\!- book, book \vdash S}\,(\mathrm{cut})$$

$$\dfrac{}{NP \circ\!- John, John, (((NP \multimap S) \circ\!- NP) \circ\!- NP) \circ\!- gives, gives, NP \circ\!- Mary, Mary, (NP \circ\!- N) \circ\!- a, a, N \circ\!- book, book \vdash S}\,(\mathrm{cut})$$

Fig. 7. Proof of *John gives Mary a book*: (Lambek-style) two implications

$$\dfrac{}{S \circ\!- NP \otimes VP, NP, VP \circ\!- V \otimes NP \otimes NP, V \circ\!- gives, gives, NP, NP \vdash S}\,(\mathrm{lex}) \quad \dfrac{}{NP \circ\!- Mary, Mary \vdash NP}\,(\mathrm{lex})$$

$$\dfrac{}{S \circ\!- NP \otimes VP, NP, VP \circ\!- V \otimes NP \otimes NP, V \circ\!- gives, gives, NP \circ\!- Mary, Mary, NP \vdash S}\,(\mathrm{cut})$$

$$\dfrac{}{NP \circ\!- Det \otimes N, Det \circ\!- a, a, N \vdash NP}\,(\mathrm{lex}) \quad \dfrac{}{N \circ\!- book, book \vdash N}\,(\mathrm{lex})$$

$$\dfrac{}{NP \circ\!- Det \otimes N, Det \circ\!- a, a, N \circ\!- book, book \vdash NP}\,(\mathrm{cut})$$

$$\dfrac{}{NP \circ\!- John, John \vdash NP}\,(\mathrm{lex}) \quad \dfrac{}{S \circ\!- NP \otimes VP, NP, VP \circ\!- V \otimes NP \otimes NP, V \circ\!- gives, gives, NP \circ\!- Mary, Mary, NP \circ\!- Det \otimes N, Det \circ\!- a, a, N \circ\!- book, book \vdash S}\,(\mathrm{cut})$$

$$\dfrac{}{S \circ\!- NP \otimes VP, NP \circ\!- John, John, VP \circ\!- V \otimes NP \otimes NP, V \circ\!- gives, gives, NP \circ\!- Mary, Mary, NP \circ\!- Det \otimes N, Det \circ\!- a, a, N \circ\!- book, book \vdash S}\,(\mathrm{cut})$$

Fig. 8. Proof of *John gives Mary a book*: one implication and times

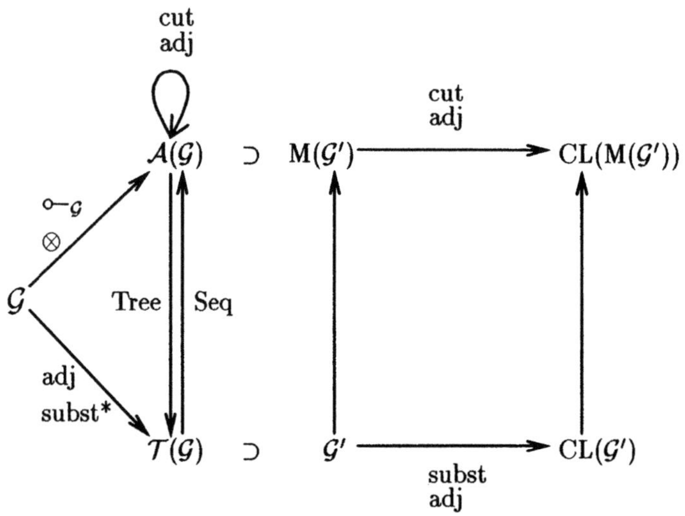

Consider the following fragment $\mathcal{A}$ of the non-commutative intuistionistic linear logic (N-ILL).

Definition 2 (The calculus $\mathcal{A}$).

- Alphabet of $\mathcal{A}$: propositional letters $a, b, \ldots$, connectives $\otimes, \multimap$,
- Formulas: usual definition. A is a *simple* $\otimes$*–formula* iff A is a propositional letter or A is a formula $b_1 \otimes \cdots \otimes b_n$ where $b_1, \ldots, b_n$ are propositional letters.
- Sequents: $\Gamma \vdash A$, where Γ is a finite sequence of formulas and A is a formula,
- Sequent calculus:
  - Axiom: $a \vdash a$
  - Rules: $$\frac{\Gamma \vdash A \quad \Delta \vdash B}{\Gamma, \Delta \vdash A \otimes B}\,(\otimes) \qquad \frac{\Gamma \vdash A \quad \Gamma_1, a, \Gamma_2 \vdash B}{\Gamma_1, a \multimap A, \Gamma, \Gamma_2 \vdash B}\,(\multimap)$$

Axiom and rules are restricted as follows: a stands for a propositional letter, A, B stand for simple $\otimes$–formulas.

Proposition 3 (Main properties of calculus $\mathcal{A}$). *(proofs in [5])*

1. *If $\Gamma \vdash A \otimes B$ is provable in $\mathcal{A}$, then*
   - *A and B are simple $\otimes$–formulas;*
   - *there is a unique pair (Γ_1, Γ_2) s.t. $\Gamma = \Gamma_1, \Gamma_2$ and both the sequents $\Gamma_1 \vdash A$ and $\Gamma_2 \vdash B$ are provable in $\mathcal{A}$.*
2. *If $\Gamma, a \multimap A, \Delta \vdash B$ is provable in $\mathcal{A}$, then*
   - *A and B are simple $\otimes$–formulas;*
   - *there is a unique pair (Δ_1, Δ_2) s.t. $\Delta = \Delta_1, \Delta_2$ and both the sequents $\Delta_1 \vdash A$ and $\Gamma, a, \Delta_2 \vdash B$ are provable in $\mathcal{A}$.*

   Such a pair (Δ_1, Δ_2) will be called "the splitting pair for Δ in $\Gamma, a \multimap A, \Delta \vdash B$". Note that this pair can be computed easily: the first element Δ_1 of the splitting pair must satisfy a counting condition on each variable occurring in it (see [5]).

3. The calculus $\mathcal{A}$ is closed under the atomic cut-rule *(i.e. substitution rule)*

$$\frac{\Gamma \vdash a \quad \Delta_1, a, \Delta_2 \vdash A}{\Delta_1, \Gamma, \Delta_2 \vdash A}\ (cut)$$

i.e.: if the sequents $\Gamma \vdash a$ and $\Delta_1, a, \Delta_2 \vdash A$ are provable in $\mathcal{A}$, then the sequent $\Delta_1, \Gamma, \Delta_2 \vdash A$ is also provable in $\mathcal{A}$.

4. The calculus $\mathcal{A}$ is closed under the adjoining rule

$$\frac{\Gamma_1, a, \Gamma_2 \vdash a \quad \Delta, a \multimap a, \Lambda \vdash b}{\Delta, \Gamma_1, \Lambda_1, \Gamma_2, \Lambda_2 \vdash b}\ (adj)$$

where (Λ_1, Λ_2) is the splitting pair of Λ in $\Delta, a \multimap a, \Lambda \vdash b$.

Note that Λ_1 and Λ_2 are *uniquely defined* from the premises, so the previous deduction is really a logical rule.

Definition 4 (The calculus $\mathcal{A}(\mathcal{G})$). Let $\mathcal{G}$ be a family of labeled trees, of depth 1, not of the form $X \multimap X$. Let $\mathcal{T}(\mathcal{G})$ be the closure of $\mathcal{G}$ under the rules:

- substitution with or without the declaration of a new internal point on which the adjoining operation may be applied,
- adjoining operation.

$\mathcal{A}(\mathcal{G})$ is the calculus obtained from $\mathcal{A}$ as follows:

- propositional letters are exactly all the labels of the trees in $\mathcal{G}$,
- the rule $(\multimap)$ is restricted as follows:

$$\frac{\Gamma \vdash A \quad \Gamma_1, a, \Gamma_2 \vdash B}{\Gamma_1, a \multimap A, \Gamma, \Gamma_2 \vdash B}\ (\multimap, \mathcal{G})$$

  where A, B are simple $\otimes$–formulas of the language of $\mathcal{A}(\mathcal{G})$, a is a propositional letter of the language of $\mathcal{A}(\mathcal{G})$ and one of the following cases occurs:
  - A is a
  - A is a propositional letter b different from a, and the tree 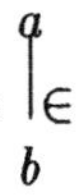

$\in \mathcal{G}$
  - A is $b_1 \otimes \cdots \otimes b_n$, and the tree 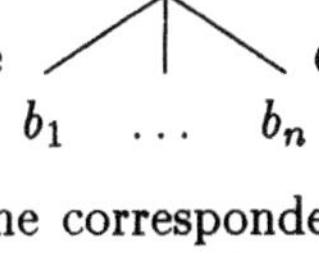

$\in \mathcal{G}$

The following propositions state the correspondence between sequents and trees. The first two provide a precise translation between the two notions. Basically, a sequent $\Gamma \vdash a$ (in the previous language) is the logical equivalent of a tree with root a, and there is exactly one formula in Γ for each leaf, for each subtree (of depth 1), for each adjunction node, and nothing else. *Seq()* (resp. *Tree()*) associates a sequent to each tree (resp. each sequent), and we prove the two are converse. The last three propositions are properties concerning the logical counterpart of a TAG grammar. The last one is in fact the most important: the closure under (logical) adjunction and substitution of the set of sequents corresponding to a set of elementary trees is exactly the set of sequents corresponding to the closure under (grammatical) adjunction and substitution of this set of elementary trees. In other words, the logical and grammatical calculi coincide, i.e. the restricted logical calculus we defined above and the TAG calculus.

Proposition 5 (Main properties of calculus $\mathcal{A}(\mathcal{G})$). *The properties 1-4 of $\mathcal{A}$ are also properties of $\mathcal{A}(\mathcal{G})$. Moreover the following properties hold for $\mathcal{A}(\mathcal{G})$:*

- *To $T \in \mathcal{T}(\mathcal{G})$, we associate a sequent Seq(T) of $\mathcal{A}(\mathcal{G})$ s.t.:*
  - *if a is the root of T, and the terminal points of T (ordered from left to right) are $a_1, \ldots, a_m$, then Seq(T) is*
    $$\Gamma \vdash a$$
    where in Γ the sequence of all the occurring propositional variables is $a_1, \ldots, a_m$ and in Γ there is a formula $c \multimapinv c$ iff c is an internal point of T on which the adjoining operation may be operated;
  - *Seq(T) is provable in $\mathcal{A}(\mathcal{G})$.*
- *To every provable sequent $\Gamma \vdash A$ in $\mathcal{A}(\mathcal{G})$, we associate Tree($\Gamma \vdash A$) s.t.*
  - *if A is a propositional letter, then Tree($\Gamma \vdash A$) $\in \mathcal{T}(\mathcal{G})$ where the root is A, the terminal points (from left to right) are exactly all the propositional letters occurring in Γ and in the same order in which they occur in Γ, and the internal points on which the adjoining operation may be operated are exactly all the propositional letters c s.t. $c \multimapinv c$ occurs in Γ;*
  - *if A is $b_1 \otimes \cdots \otimes b_n$, and so $\Gamma = \Gamma_1 \ldots \Gamma_n$ with the sequents $\Gamma_i \vdash b_i$ provable in $\mathcal{A}(\mathcal{G})$ for every $1 \leq i \leq n$, then Tree($\Gamma \vdash A$) is a sequence $T_1, \ldots, T_n$ of trees $\in \mathcal{T}(\mathcal{G})$, s.t. $T_i =$ Tree($\Gamma_i \vdash b_i$).*
- *If $\Gamma \vdash a$ is provable in $\mathcal{A}(\mathcal{G})$, then Seq(Tree($\Gamma \vdash a$)) $= \Gamma \vdash a$. If T is a tree of $\mathcal{G}$, then Tree(Seq(T)) $= T$.*
- *Let M be a set of provable sequents in $\mathcal{A}(\mathcal{G})$. Define CL(M) as follows:*
  - *$M \subseteq$ CL(M)*
  - *(closure under atomic cut-rule)*
    if $\Gamma \vdash a \in$ CL(M) and $\Delta_1, a, \Delta_2 \vdash B \in$ CL(M), then $\Delta_1, \Gamma, \Delta_2 \vdash B \in$ CL(M)
  - *(closure under adjoining operation) if $\Gamma_1, a, \Gamma_2 \vdash a \in$ CL(M) and $\Delta, a \multimapinv a, \Lambda \vdash b \in$ CL(M), then $\Delta, \Gamma_1, \Lambda_1, \Gamma_2, \Lambda_2 \vdash b \in$ CL(M), where (Λ_1, Λ_2) is the splitting pair of Λ in $\Delta, a, \Lambda \vdash b$;*
  - *nothing else belongs to CL(M).*
- *If $\Gamma \vdash A \in$ CL(M), then $\Gamma \vdash A$ is provable in $\mathcal{A}(\mathcal{G})$.*
- *If $\mathcal{G}' \subseteq \mathcal{T}(\mathcal{G})$, let CL($\mathcal{G}'$) be the closure of $\mathcal{G}'$ under:*
  - *substitution;*
  - *adjoining operation.*

  Clearly, CL($\mathcal{G}'$) $\subseteq \mathcal{T}(\mathcal{G})$.
  Let $M = \{Seq(T)/T \in \mathcal{G}'\}$, then $CL(M) = \{Seq(T)/T \in CL(\mathcal{G}')\}$.

Starting from this last proposition, it is not too difficult to prove that the language accepted by a TAG grammar $\mathcal{G}'$ is exactly the language accepted by M($\mathcal{G}'$). We can define the language accepted by such a calculus in the following way. Let us take only those sequents in CL(M($\mathcal{G}'$)) whose right part is the propositional variable S (the start symbol of the grammar), and such that propositional variables of the left part of the sequent correspond to terminal symbols of the grammar, i.e. words of the language. The language accepted by M($\mathcal{G}'$) is then the set of sequences of words in the same order as they appear in the previous sequents.

Example 6. Grammar $\mathcal{G}'_1 = \{$ 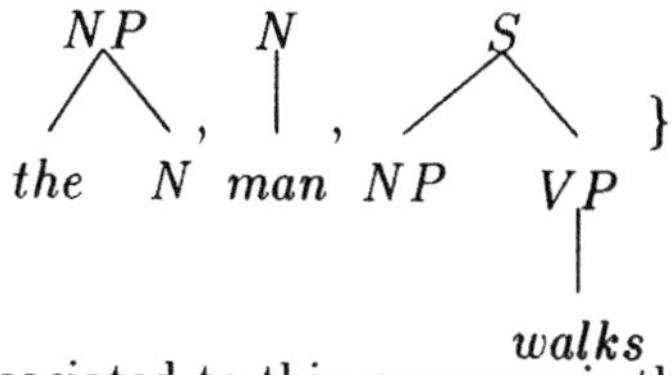 $\}$

The set of sequents M_1 associated to this grammar is the following one:

$M_1 = \{$

$NP \multimap the \otimes N, the, N \vdash NP,$

$N \multimap man, man \vdash N,$

$S \multimap NP \otimes VP, NP, VP \multimap walks, walks \vdash S$

$\}$

The analysis of "the man walks" corresponds to the following proof in $\mathcal{A}(\mathcal{G}'_1)$:

$$\dfrac{\dfrac{NP \multimap the \otimes N, the, N \vdash NP \quad N \multimap man, man \vdash N}{NP \multimap the \otimes N, the, N \multimap man, man \vdash NP} \quad S \multimap NP \otimes VP, NP, VP \multimap walks, walks \vdash S}{S \multimap NP \otimes VP, NP \multimap the \otimes N, the, N \multimap man, man, VP \multimap walks, walks \vdash S}$$

Example 7. Grammar $\mathcal{G}'_2 = \{$ 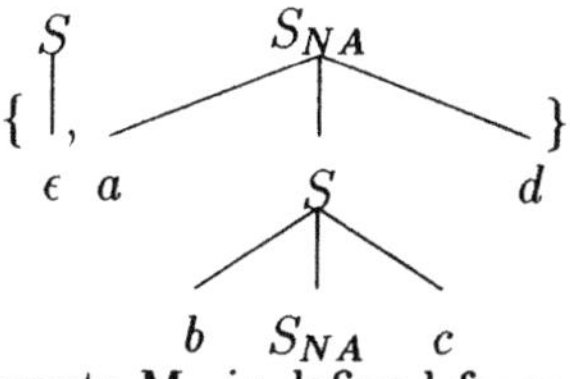 $\}$

The associated set of sequents M_2 is defined from $\mathcal{G}'_2$

$M_2 = \{$

$S \multimap a \otimes S \otimes d, a, S \multimap S, S \multimap b \otimes S \otimes c, b, S, c, d \vdash S,$

$S \multimap S, S \multimap \epsilon, \epsilon \vdash S$

$\}$

The analysis of "aabbccdd" corresponds to the proof of the following sequent. We have decomposed the different elements of the left part according to the adjunction rule.

$$\underbrace{S \multimap a \otimes S \otimes d, a,}_{\Delta} \underbrace{S \multimap a \otimes S \otimes d, a, S \multimap S, S \multimap b \otimes S \otimes c, b,}_{\Gamma_1} \underbrace{S \multimap b \otimes S \otimes c, b, S, c,}_{\Lambda_1} \underbrace{c, d,}_{\Gamma_2} \underbrace{d}_{\Lambda_2} \vdash S$$

5 TAG analysis using noncommutative proof nets

A proof in sequent calculus contains many useless properties in its contexts. Girard has defined in a purely geometric way [6] a class of graphs of formulas, called *proof-nets*: to each proof of a sequent $\vdash \Gamma$ in the one-sided sequent calculus for multiplicative linear logic corresponds a proof-net whose conclusions are exactly the formulas in Γ, and to each proof-net corresponds at least one proof of the sequent $\vdash \Gamma$ in the one-sided sequent calculus for multiplicative linear logic (where Γ is a sequence of all the conclusions of the proof-net). Similarly, Abrusci [3] defined in a purely geometric way a class of graphs, called *noncommutative proof nets*: to each proof of a sequent $\vdash \Gamma$ in the one-sided sequent calculus for multiplicative noncommutative linear logic corresponds a noncommutative proof-net with conclusions Γ, and to each noncommutative proof-net with conclusions Γ corresponds at least one proof of the sequent $\vdash \Gamma$ in the one-sided sequent calculus for multiplicative noncommutative linear logic. Therefore, to each proof of $\Gamma \vdash A$ in the sequent calculus for intuistionistic multiplicative noncommutative linear logic corresponds a noncommutative proof-net with conclusions $(\Gamma^*)^\perp, A^*$.

5.1 Noncommutative proofnets

To every proof π of a sequent $\vdash \Gamma$ in the one-sided sequent calculus for multiplicative noncommutative linear logic, we can associate (by induction on the construction of the proof π) a *noncommutative proofnet with conclusions* Γ, i.e. an oriented planar graph π' of occurrencies of formulas s.t.:

- the conclusions of π' are exactly the formulas in Γ;
- π' is a noncommutative proof structure, i.e. it is constructed by means of the following links[6]:
    - Axiom-link (two conclusions, no premise) 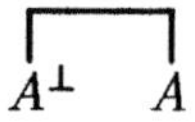

    - Cut-link (two premises, no conclusion) 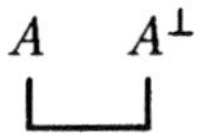

    - $\otimes$-link (two premises, one conclusion) 

    - $⅋$-link (two premises, one conclusion) 

  and every occurrence of formula is a premise of at most one link and is conclusion of exactly one link;
- the translation of π is a proofnet, i.e. it admits no shorttrip. A shorttrip is a trip that does not contain each node twice. A trip is a sequence of nodes, going from one node to another according to the graph and to a switch for each times-link and each par-link, in a bideterministic way: the traversal of nodes is done according to fig. 9 but without taking into account the labels of nodes (see below);
- every assignment for π' is total;
- π' induces the linear order Γ of the conclusions.

An *assignment* for a proof structure π' is made in the following way. Let us associate two integer variables left-N and right-N to each node N computed as in fig. 9. The left variable of a node labeled by a propositional variable A is named

[6] The par link is graphically distinguished from the times link. However this is only sugar as the graph has really only one kind of edge.

x^A. A *special trip* is a trip from the left variable to the right variable of some node. It follows the links given by the graph but the switch for times must be at right, the switch for par must be at left. Moreover the switch for par is used only if right-C occurs before right-B in the special trip from left-A. At the same time it imposes constraints between integer variables as defined in the following figure, where $\rightarrow$ means the transition from a variable to another variable. The assignment is *total* when the set of constraints can be satisfied. The precedence relation on the conclusions of π' is defined s.t. A precedes B iff right-A = left-B + 1. Then π' *induces the linear order of the conclusions* iff the precedence relation is a chain and each conclusion occurs exactly once in the chain.

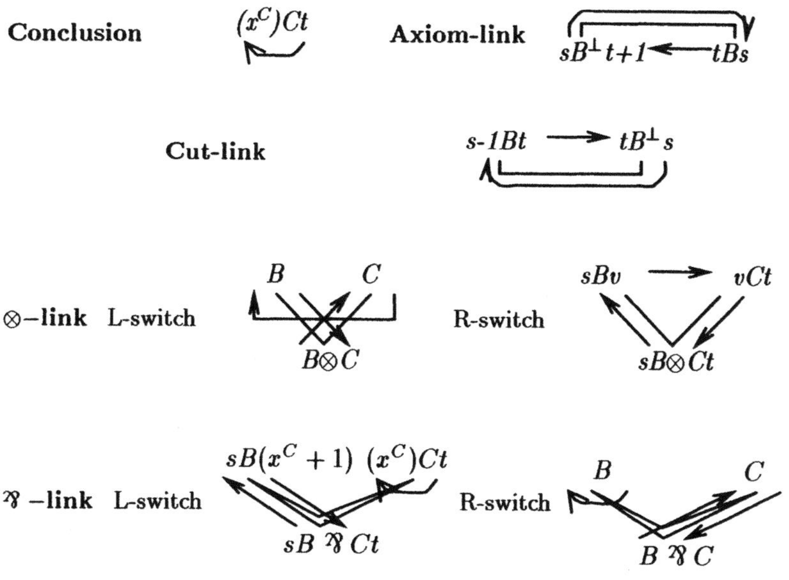

Fig. 9. Travels through proof structures

Precise definitions, examples, explanations and the proof of the following theorem can be found in [4].

Theorem 8. *π' is a noncommutative proof net with conclusions Γ iff there exists a proof π of the sequent $\vdash \Gamma$ in the sequent calculus for multiplicative noncommutative linear logic s.t. π' is associated to π.*

Note that every noncommutative proofnet is a planar graph.

5.2 Parsing examples

We give in this section two simple examples of parses. The aim of this section is to show the strong connection between the structure of proofs of sequents and a standard TAG derived structure. Moreover, it emphasizes the interest of a proofnet approach as the syntax (and parsing process) is concretely designed as a logical manipulation of logical structures. In the conclusion, we briefly mention that this can also give a logical formalization of D-trees [13].

The first example requires only composition, i.e. the cut-rule from the logical point of view. We first give the sequents (provable in $\mathcal{A}$) associated with the lexical items. Their meanings are straightforward, e.g. '*John* and *Mary* are noun phrases (NP)', '*saw* requires a complement NP to obtain a verb phrase (VP) and a subject NP to obtain a sentence (S)'. Note that VP is an adjunction node so the sequent associated to the item *saw* includes the formula $VP \multimapinv VP$. The next example uses this specification.

John $NP \multimapinv John, John \vdash NP$

Mary $NP \multimapinv Mary, Mary \vdash NP$

saw $S \multimapinv NP \otimes VP, NP, VP \multimapinv VP, VP \multimapinv V \otimes NP, V \multimapinv saw, saw, NP \vdash S$

The proof associated to the analysis of *John saw Mary* requires two cuts. The two sequent proofs given in fig. 10 are the only two possibilities for this sentence in the fragment $\mathcal{A}(\mathcal{G})$. This pinpoints the fact that the order in which the cuts are made is not significant w.r.t. the derived structure. Proofnets allow expression of this equivalence. Hence the two proofs have the same associated proofnet given in fig. 11. For the sake of clarity, the cut rules are bold lines, and we circle subnets associated to lexical items. Obviously, if we delete the two cut lines, we are left with three proofnets representing (provable) sequents. Such a proofnet contains still superfluous information. As the only available operations in $\mathcal{A}(\mathcal{G})$ are (i) the cut-rule and (ii) the adjunction rule on a propositional variable, we only need to keep nodes referring to (i) conclusions of the proofnet that are propositional variables or negation of propositional variables (a cut can be made on such a literal), and (ii) the fact that there exists a subgraph of the following form (corresponding to the existence of a formula $A \multimapinv A$ in the left part of a sequent, i.e. its negation $A \otimes A^{\perp}$ in the one-sided associated sequent):

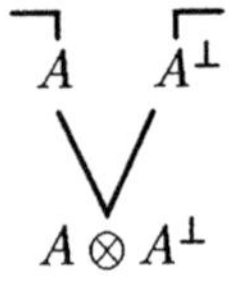

We can then simplify the graph and replace the internal logical machinery by black boxes (big black circles in the figure). The conclusions of the basic proofnets are labeled: outputs (i.e. conclusions that are propositional variables) are drawn as closed half circles, inputs (i.e. conclusions that are negation of propositional variables) are drawn as open half circles. Plain lines link black boxes to black boxes or conclusions, and subgraphs corresponding to adjunction points are drawn as dashed lines. The previous proofnet is then redrawn as in fig. 14 right.

$$\dfrac{NP \mathrel{\circ\!\!-} John, John \vdash NP \qquad \dfrac{S \mathrel{\circ\!\!-} NP \otimes VP, NP, VP \mathrel{\circ\!\!-} VP, VP \mathrel{\circ\!\!-} V \otimes NP, V \mathrel{\circ\!\!-} saw, saw, NP \vdash S \quad NP \mathrel{\circ\!\!-} Mary, Mary \vdash NP}{S \mathrel{\circ\!\!-} NP \otimes VP, NP, VP \mathrel{\circ\!\!-} VP, VP \mathrel{\circ\!\!-} V \otimes NP, V \mathrel{\circ\!\!-} saw, saw, NP \mathrel{\circ\!\!-} Mary, Mary \vdash S}}{S \mathrel{\circ\!\!-} NP \otimes VP, NP \mathrel{\circ\!\!-} John, John, VP \mathrel{\circ\!\!-} VP, VP \mathrel{\circ\!\!-} V \otimes NP, V \mathrel{\circ\!\!-} saw, saw, NP \mathrel{\circ\!\!-} Mary, Mary \vdash S}$$

$$\dfrac{NP \mathrel{\circ\!\!-} Mary, Mary \vdash NP \qquad \dfrac{S \mathrel{\circ\!\!-} NP \otimes VP, NP, VP \mathrel{\circ\!\!-} VP, VP \mathrel{\circ\!\!-} V \otimes NP, V \mathrel{\circ\!\!-} saw, saw, NP \vdash S \quad NP \mathrel{\circ\!\!-} John, John \vdash NP}{S \mathrel{\circ\!\!-} NP \otimes VP, NP \mathrel{\circ\!\!-} John, John, VP \mathrel{\circ\!\!-} VP, VP \mathrel{\circ\!\!-} V \otimes NP, V \mathrel{\circ\!\!-} saw, saw, NP \vdash S}}{S \mathrel{\circ\!\!-} NP \otimes VP, NP \mathrel{\circ\!\!-} John, John, VP \mathrel{\circ\!\!-} VP, VP \mathrel{\circ\!\!-} V \otimes NP, V \mathrel{\circ\!\!-} saw, saw, NP \mathrel{\circ\!\!-} Mary, Mary \vdash S}$$

Fig. 10. $\mathcal{A}(\mathcal{G})$-proofs of *John saw Mary*

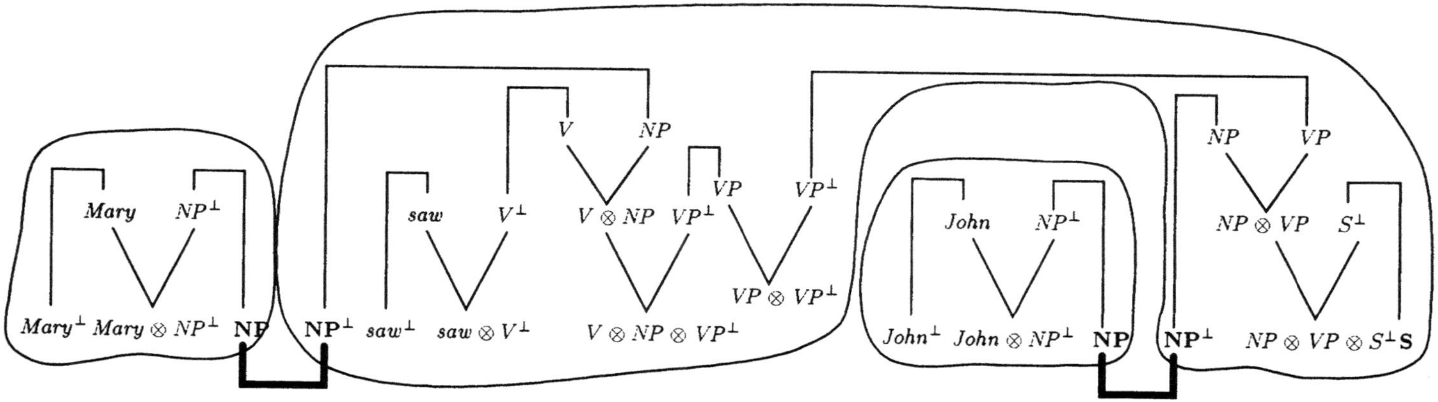

Fig. 11. *John saw Mary*

We obviously find the derived tree (neglecting some minor differences). The logical proofnet can then be seen as an "explanation" of the structure of the tree, that is to say the operations available on the tree are the result of some focus of what can be done on the proofnet. On the one hand the use of black boxes is necessary to clarify the structure of the analysis, on the other hand this hides proof details that can be useful for some linguistic operations (as is the case for adjunction w.r.t. the classical structure of a derived tree). We show in [5] another application of such a (logical) refinement.

The next example includes the two operations composition and adjunction, i.e. two cut-rules and an adjunction rule. In fig. 12 the adjunction rule is represented as a double thick dashed line: this (logically) mimics the adjunction as it can be described in the derived tree given in fig. 14 left. Note that the adverb has to be placed after the complement (rightmost in the proofnet) in order to keep the graph planar. The proofnet in fig. 13 is the proofnet corresponding to a cut-free proof. The sequent associated to the adverb *today* is the following one:

$today\ VP \multimapinv VP \otimes today, VP, today \vdash VP$

6 Conclusion

The use of logics to describe Natural Language is not a new idea. Work on e.g. Lambek calculus and logic programming are famous examples (see e.g. [11], ... on how to use sequent calculus for natural language processing). However, linguistic formalisms have fundamentally evolved these two decades. Though theoretical research has been done on unification and attribute-value structures, operations on syntactic trees have been investigated mainly by comparing different solutions [16,15]. We consider here another way to look at these operations (see also [7]). We focus on the adjunction operation available in Tree Adjoining Grammars as it seems to be the most simple way to augment the expressive power of a formalism. We prove that Noncommutative Intuitionistic Linear Logic is a natural logical means and we define a fragment equivalent to TAG. We show furthermore to which extent geometric representations of proofs (proofnets) may be useful to understand how black boxes (i.e. relations between nodes in a syntactic tree) help simplifying a parse but also hide interesting mechanisms. There is still a lot to do in this direction. Among other things, Generalized Categorial Grammars have also to be logically investigated, the objective being to relate the current available operations and to complete this set. The previous discussions show also the relationship between our point of view and the idea of quasi-trees developed by Vijay-Shanker [13]. He proposes to consider *partial descriptions of trees*, i.e. adjunction nodes are represented by means of loose relations whose meaning is a domination relation. In this case, the adjunction operation is identified with a pair of substitution operations. The strong relation with what precedes is clear. However, in order to take into account exactly this presentation the axiom of identity $A \vdash A$, where A is a propositional variable, has to be added to the

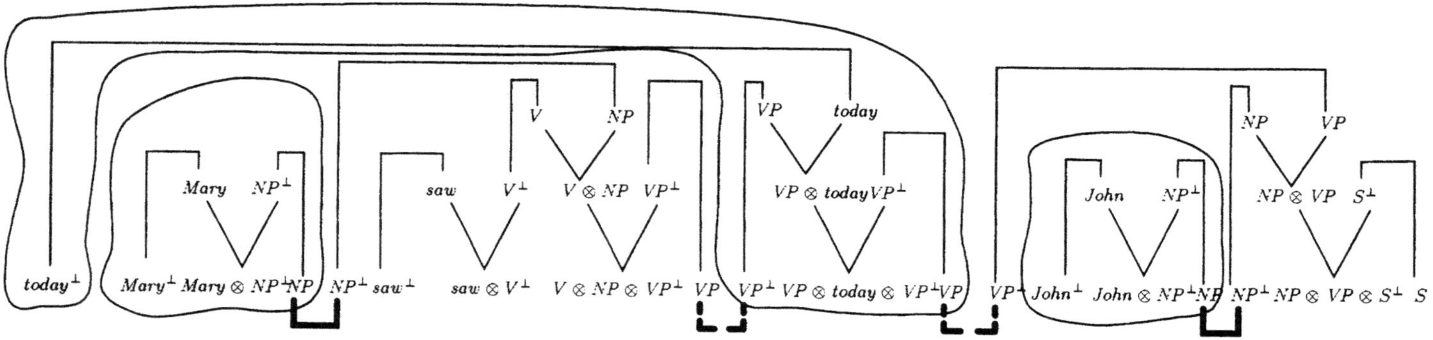

Fig. 12. *John saw Mary today*

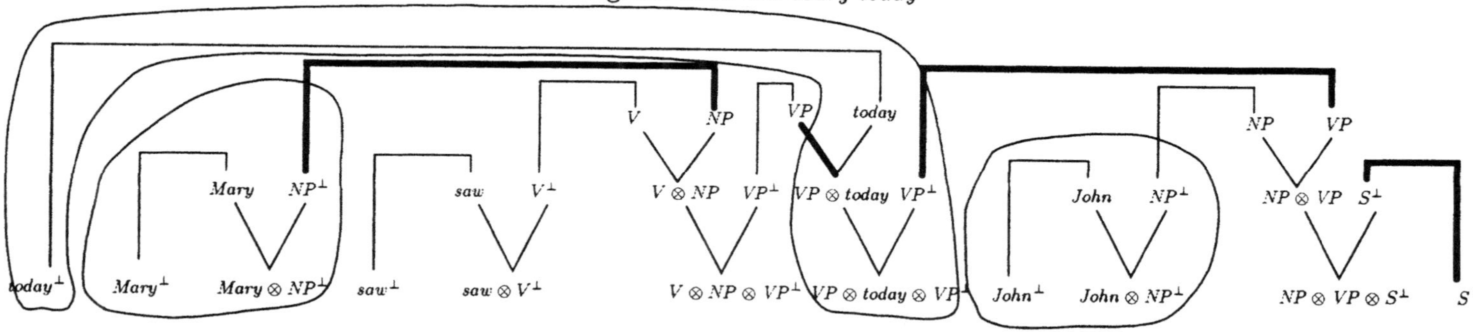

Fig. 13. Cut-free proofnet for *John saw Mary today*

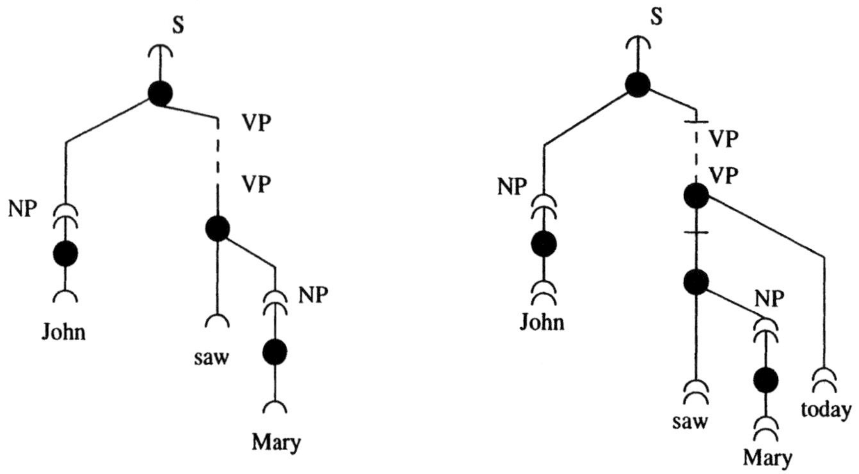

Fig. 14. (left) Simplified proof for *John saw Mary.* (right) Simplified proof for *John saw Mary today*

calculus $\mathcal{A}(\mathcal{G})$ given in section 4. In this way, adjunction nodes can be deleted from sequents. In this new calculus, the following rule is satisfied:

$$\frac{A \vdash A \quad \Gamma, A \multimapinv A, \Delta \vdash B}{\Gamma, \Delta \vdash B} \; (adjunction)$$

Hence, we obtain the following equivalence:

Proposition 9. *A parse tree is* correct

iff each pair of nodes in a domination relation have the same label
iff there is a proof whose conclusions that are propositional variables are the words of the sentence in the same order, and without any formula of the form $A \multimapinv A$.

References

1. A. Abeillé, K. Bishop, S. Cote, and Y. Schabes. A lexicalized tree-adjoining grammar for english. Technical Report MS-CIS-90-24, LINC LAB 170, Computer Science Department, University of Pennsylvania, Philadelphia, PA, 1990.
2. M. Abrusci. Noncommutative intuitionnistic linear propositional logic. *Zeitschrift für Mathematische Logik und Grundlagen der Mathematik*, 36:297–318, 1990.
3. M. Abrusci. Phase semantics and sequent calculus for pure noncommutative classical linear propositional logic. *The Journal of Symbolic Logic*, 56(4):1403–1451, 1991.
4. M. Abrusci. Noncommutative proof nets. In J.-Y. Girard, Y. Lafont, and L. Regnier, editors, *Advances in Linear Logic*, volume 222, pages 271–296. Cambridge University Press, 1995. Proceedings of the Workshop on Linear Logic, Ithaca, NewYork, June 1993.

5. M. Abrusci, C. Fouqueré, and J. Vauzeilles. Tree adjoining grammars in non-commutative linear logic. Technical Report 97-03, LIPN, Université Paris-Nord, France, 1997. In submission.
6. J.-Y. Girard. Linear logic. *Theoretical Computer Science*, 50:1–102, 1987.
7. A.K. Joshi and S. Kulick. Partial proof trees, resource conscious logic and syntactic constraints. In *(this volume)*, 1997.
8. A.K. Joshi, L.S. Levy, and M. Takahashi. Tree adjunct grammars. *Journal of Computer and System Sciences*, 10(1):136–163, 1975.
9. Aravind Joshi and Yves Schabes. Tree-adjoining grammars. In Grzegorz Rozenberg and Arto Salomaa, editors, *Handbook of Formal Languages*, volume 3 – Beyond Words, chapter 2, pages 69 – 124. Springer-Verlag, 1996.
10. A.S. Kroch and A.K. Joshi. Linguistic relevance of tree adjoining grammars. Technical Report MS-CIS-85-18, LINC LAB 170, Computer Science Department, University of Pennsylvania, Philadelphia, PA, 1985.
11. J. Lambek. The mathematics of sentence structure. *Am. Math. Monthly*, 65:154–169, 1958.
12. G. Sundholm. Systems of deduction. In D. Gabbay and F. Guenthner, editors, *Handbook of Philosophical Logic*, volume 1, pages 133–188. D. Reidel Publishing Company, 1983.
13. K. Vijay-Shanker. Using descriptions of trees in a tree adjoining grammar. *Computational Linguistics*, 18(4):481–517, 1992.
14. K. Vijay-Shanker and A.K. Joshi. Some computational properties of tree adjoining grammars. In *23rd Meeting of the Association for Computational Linguistics*, pages 82–93, 1985.
15. K. Vijay-Shanker and D.J. Weir. The equivalence of four extensions of context-free grammars. *Mathematical Systems Theory*, 27:511–545, 1994.
16. K. Vijay-Shanker and D.J. Weir. Parsing some constrained grammar formalisms. *Computational Linguistics*, 19(4):591–636, 1994.

Constructing Different Phonological Bracketings from a Proof Net

Denis Bechet and Philippe de Groote

Projet Calligramme
INRIA-Lorraine – CRIN – CNRS
615, rue du Jardin Botanique - B.P. 101
54602 Villers-lès-Nancy Cedex – FRANCE
e-mail: bechet@loria.fr, degroote@loria.fr

Abstract. We state and prove Roorda's interpolation theorem in the framework of proof-net theory. This allows us to transform any proof-net into some other proof-net that matches some given (phonological or prosodic) bracketing.

1 Introduction

Almost a decade ago, Girard invented linear logic together with the notion of proof-net [7]. Girard's proof-nets have been subsequently adapted to the Lambek calculus by Roorda [16] and, since then, many authors have advocated the notion of proof-net as the right parsing structure in the framework of categorial grammars [11, 13, 14, 16]. Nevertheless, if one wants to take this proposal seriously, one must be able to perform, on the proof-nets, all the computations that one usually performs on Gentzen's sequential derivations.

From a theoretical standpoint, the above possible objection is actually not a problem. Indeed, by Girard's sequentialisation theorem, one may always associate to any proof-net some corresponding sequential derivation. Therefore, any piece of information that can be computed from a sequential derivation may be computed from a proof-net. From a methodological and algorithmic point of view, however, one does not want to make the *détour* of sequentialising the proof-nets: one wants to compute information directly from the proof-nets.

In a recent paper [5], Retoré and one of the authors of the present paper have shown how to get semantic readings directly from proof-nets. In the same spirit, we show, in this paper, how to assign a phonological term to any proof-net (using Moortgat's phonological algebra), and how to transform a given proof-net in order to get different phonological bracketings. Technically, the main difficulty consists of stating and proving, in the framework of the proof-nets, Roorda's interpolation theorem [16]. This problem is solved in Section 7.

The paper is organised as follows. The next section is a short review of the Lambek calculus. Section 3 introduces Moortgat's phonological algebra together with a sequent calculus that assigns some bracketing to any derivation of a given sequent. Section 4 shows how to transform a derivation in order to stick to some given bracketing. Section 5 is a brief introduction to proof-net theory. Section 6 explains how to read the phonological bracketing associated with a proof directly from the corresponding proof-net. Finally, in Section 7, we state and prove our main technical result, i.e., Roorda's interpolation theorem in the framework of proof-net theory.

2 The Lambek calculus

The Lambek calculus, introduced as a logical basis for categorial grammars almost four decades ago [9], may be defined as the non-commutative intuitionistic multiplicative fragment of linear logic.[1]

The formulas (or types) of the Lambek calculus are built from an alphabet of atomic formulas ($\mathcal{A}$) according to the following grammar:

$$\mathcal{F} \ ::= \ \mathcal{A} \mid \mathcal{F} \bullet \mathcal{F} \mid \mathcal{F} \backslash \mathcal{F} \mid \mathcal{F} / \mathcal{F}$$

where formulas of the form $A \bullet B$ correspond to conjunctions (or products), formulas of the form $A \backslash B$ correspond to direct implications (i.e., A *implies* B), and formulas of the form A/B to retro-implications (i.e., A *is implied by* B).

The deduction relation of the calculus is defined by means of the following system:

Identity rules

$$A \vdash A \quad \text{(ident)} \qquad\qquad \frac{\Gamma \vdash A \quad \Delta_1, A, \Delta_2 \vdash B}{\Delta_1, \Gamma, \Delta_2 \vdash B} \quad \text{(cut)}$$

Logical rules

$$\frac{\Gamma, A, B, \Delta \vdash C}{\Gamma, A \bullet B, \Delta \vdash C} \quad (\bullet \text{ left}) \qquad\qquad \frac{\Gamma \vdash A \quad \Delta \vdash B}{\Gamma, \Delta \vdash A \bullet B} \quad (\bullet \text{ right})$$

$$\frac{\Gamma \vdash A \quad \Delta_1, B, \Delta_2 \vdash C}{\Delta_1, \Gamma, A \backslash B, \Delta_2 \vdash C} \quad (\backslash \text{ left}) \qquad\qquad \frac{A, \Gamma \vdash B}{\Gamma \vdash A \backslash B} \quad (\backslash \text{ right})$$

$$\frac{\Gamma \vdash A \quad \Delta_1, B, \Delta_2 \vdash C}{\Delta_1, B/A, \Gamma, \Delta_2 \vdash C} \quad (/ \text{ left}) \qquad\qquad \frac{\Gamma, A \vdash B}{\Gamma \vdash B/A} \quad (/ \text{ right})$$

where Greek uppercases range over sequences of formulas.

It is to be noted that the above system does not include any structural rule. In particular, the absence of the exchange rule is responsible for the non-commutativity of the connectives. This, in turn, explains the presence of two different implications.

[1] This is not entirely true because empty sequences of hypotheses are not allowed in the sequents of the original Lambek calculus. We do not insist on this restriction since the results presented in this paper hold in both system (i.e., the Lambek calculus with or without the empty sequence).

3 Moortgat's phonological algebra

Following Moortgat [12], one defines the phonological algebra associated with a set of tokens $\mathcal{V}$ as the structure freely generated from $\mathcal{V}$ by a binary operation "+", and one adds to this structure an identity element ε such that for any $a \in \mathcal{V}$, $(a+\varepsilon) = a$ and $(\varepsilon + a) = a$. Notice that, apart from these identity laws, the phonological algebra does not obey any law. In particular, "+" is not associative.

The purpose of the phonological algebra is to associate with any Gentzen derivation a phonological term that would reflect some prosodic phrasing [10, 12]. This may be achieved by decorating sequents with phonological terms:

$$a : A \vdash a : A \quad \text{(Id)} \qquad \frac{\Gamma \vdash t : A \qquad \Delta, a : A, \Theta \vdash u : B}{\Delta, \Gamma, \Theta \vdash u[a{:=}t] : B} \ \text{(Cut)}$$

$$\frac{\Gamma \vdash t : A \qquad \Delta, b : B, \Theta \vdash u : C}{\Delta, \Gamma, a : A \backslash B, \Theta \vdash u[b{:=}(t+a)] : C} \ (\backslash\text{L}) \qquad \frac{a : A, \Gamma \vdash t : B}{\Gamma \vdash t[a{:=}\varepsilon] : A \backslash B} \ (\backslash\text{R})$$

$$\frac{\Gamma \vdash t : A \qquad \Delta, b : B, \Theta \vdash u : C}{\Delta, a : B/A, \Gamma, \Theta \vdash u[b{:=}(a+t)] : C} \ (/\text{L}) \qquad \frac{\Gamma, a : A \vdash t : B}{\Gamma \vdash t[a{:=}\varepsilon] : B/A} \ (/\text{R})$$

where a and b range over tokens; t and u range over the terms of the phonological algebra; $t[a{:=}u]$ denotes the term obtained by substituting u for a, in t; in Rules (\R) and (/R), the token a is fresh.

4 Rebracketing by interpolation

Because of Rule (Cut), the phonological bracketing associated to a given derivation is not invariant under cut-elimination. This is due to the following fact: the Lambek calculus is associative whereas the phonological algebra is not. This apparent mismatch is actually not a drawback but entails the property of *structural completeness* [2], which may be used, for instance, to settle conflicts between intonational and syntactic phrasing.

Example 4.1 Syntactic phrasing: (pierre + (écoute + (marie + chanter))) (1)

$$\cfrac{\text{m}{:}SN \vdash \text{m}{:}SN \qquad \cfrac{x{:}SV \vdash x{:}SV \qquad \cfrac{\text{p}{:}SN \vdash \text{p}{:}SN \qquad z{:}P \vdash z{:}P}{\text{p}{:}SN, y{:}SN\backslash P \vdash (\text{p}+y){:}P}}{\text{p}{:}SN, \text{e}{:}(SN\backslash P)/SV, x{:}SV \vdash (\text{p}+(\text{e}+x)){:}P}}{\text{p}{:}SN, \text{e}{:}(SN\backslash P)/SV, \text{m}{:}SN, \text{c}{:}SN\backslash SV \vdash (\text{p}+(\text{e}+(\text{m}+\text{c}))){:}P}$$

Intonational phrasing: ((pierre + écoute) + (marie + chanter)) (2)

$$\dfrac{\dfrac{\dfrac{y{:}SV \vdash y{:}SV \quad \dfrac{\mathrm{p}{:}SN \vdash \mathrm{p}{:}SN \quad w{:}P \vdash w{:}P}{\mathrm{p}{:}SN,\ z{:}SN\backslash P \vdash (\mathrm{p}+z){:}P}}{\mathrm{p}{:}SN,\ \mathrm{e}{:}(SN\backslash P)/SV,\ y{:}SV \vdash (\mathrm{p}+(\mathrm{e}+y)){:}P}}{\mathrm{p}{:}SN,\ \mathrm{e}{:}(SN\backslash P)/SV \vdash (\mathrm{p}+\mathrm{e}){:}P/SV} \quad \dfrac{\mathrm{m}{:}SN \vdash \mathrm{m}{:}SN \quad \dfrac{y{:}SV \vdash y{:}SV \quad z{:}P \vdash z{:}P}{x{:}P/SV,\ y{:}SV \vdash (x+y){:}P}}{x{:}P/SV,\ \mathrm{m}{:}SN,\ \mathrm{c}{:}SN\backslash SV \vdash (x+(\mathrm{m}+\mathrm{c})){:}P}}{\mathrm{p}{:}SN,\ \mathrm{e}{:}(SN\backslash P)/SV,\ \mathrm{m}{:}SN,\ \mathrm{c}{:}SN\backslash SV \vdash ((\mathrm{p}+\mathrm{e})+(\mathrm{m}+\mathrm{c})){:}P}\ (\mathrm{cut})$$

The difficulty in finding a derivation that corresponds to a given prosodic phrasing such as (2) consists in guessing the needed *cut formulas*—P/SV, in our simple example—[10]. When working in the Lambek calculus with product, the problem of guessing the cut formulas may be circumvented by using Roorda's interpolation theorem [16]. This lemma, however, is stated in the framework of the sequent calculus. Therefore, if one wants to stick to the formalism of proof-nets, one has to answer the two following questions:

- how to assign phonological terms to proof-nets;
- how to compute interpolants from proof-nets.

Sections 6 and 7 are devoted to these two questions while the next section is a crash review of proof-net theory.

5 Proof-nets for the Lambek calculus

Proof-nets, which have been introduced by Girard [7] as an appropriate way of representing proofs in linear logic, are defined as a special class of graph whose nodes are decorated with formulas.

In this section, we review the usual notion of multiplicative proof-net (i.e., the notion of proof-net that fits classical multiplicative linear logic). Then we explain briefly how this notion may be adapted to the Lambek calculus (i.e., how to take *intuitionism* and *non-commutativity* into account). The reader who would like to know more details on the subject is referred to [15, 16].

We first introduce the formulas of multiplicative linear logic. They obey the following grammar:

$$\mathcal{F} \ ::= \ \mathcal{A}^+ \ | \ \mathcal{A}^- \ | \ \mathcal{F} \otimes \mathcal{F} \ | \ \mathcal{F} \parr \mathcal{F}$$

Where the connectives "$\otimes$" and "$\parr$" are respectively called *tensor* and *par*.

Then, we consider the following *links* that are respectively called *axiom*, $\otimes$*-link*, $\parr$*-link*, and *cut*:

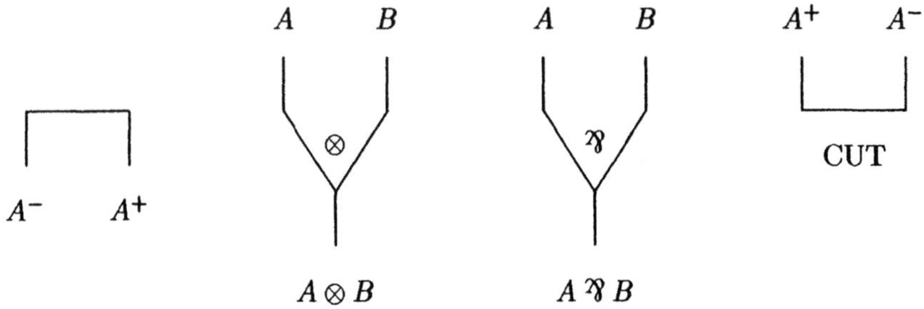

where

- the formulas A^- and A^+ are defined to be the conclusions of the *axiom*;
- the formula $A \otimes B$ is defined to be the conclusion of the $\otimes$-*link* while the formulas A and B are defined to be its left and right premises;
- the formula $A \parr B$ is defined to be the conclusion of the $\parr$-*link* while the formulas A and B are defined to be its left and right premises;
- the formulas A^+ and A^- are defined to be the premises of the *cut*;
- when A is not an atomic formula, the formula A^+ is simply defined to be A itself while the formula A^- is defines according to the following inductive clauses:

$$(A \otimes B)^- = A^- \parr B^-$$
$$(A \parr B)^- = A^- \otimes B^-$$

Note that we distinguish between the left and the right premise only for the $\otimes$-link and the $\parr$-link. There is no notion of left and right premise for a cut. Similarly, There is no notion of left and right conclusion for an axiom.

The notion of link allows the notion of *proof-structure* to be defined.

A proof-structure is a set of (occurrences of) formulas connected by links, such that every (occurrence of a) formula is a conclusion of exactly one link and is a premise of at most one link. The (occurrences of) formulas that are not the premise of any link are called the conclusions of the proof-structure.

Given a proof-structure, the graph obtained by removing all the axioms is called a *proof-frame*. In fact such a proof-frame is nothing but a forest of syntactic trees of formulas.

Proofs in linear logic will be represented by proof-structures. It is not the case, however, that every proof-structure corresponds to some actual proof in the sequent calculus. In fact, the proof-structures that correspond to actual proofs are defined to be the proof-nets. Now, the keystone of proof-net theory is that these proof-nets may be globally characterised by giving some correctness criterion that allows them to be discriminated from the other proof-structures (therefore the notion of proof-net may be defined without making any explicit reference to the sequent calculus). In order to introduce such a correctness criterion, which is due to Danos and Regnier [4], we must define the notion of *switching*.

A switching of a proof-structure is a selection for every $\parr$-link between the *left* or the *right* position. The graph underlying such a switching is obtained by replacing each $\parr$-link by a single edge as follows:

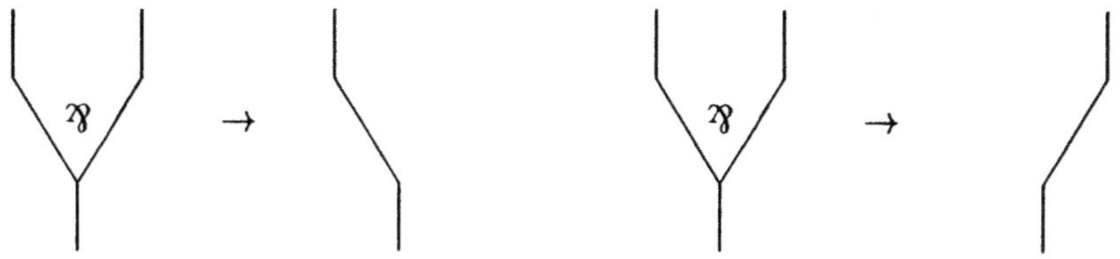

left position right position

We are now in a position to define formally the notion of multiplicative proof-net: *a proof-structure is a proof-net if and only if for every possible switching the underlying graph is connected and acyclic.*

As we said, we must take intuitionism and non-commutativity into account in order to accommodate the above notion of proof-net to the Lambek calculus. To this end, the following positive and negative translations are introduced:

1. $(A)^+ = A^+$, if A^+ is atomic,
2. $(A \setminus B)^+ = B^+ \parr A^-$,
3. $(A/B)^+ = B^- \parr A^+$,
4. $(A \bullet B)^+ = B^+ \otimes A^+$,
5. $(A)^- = A^-$, if A^+ is atomic,
6. $(A \setminus B)^- = A^+ \otimes B^-$,
7. $(A/B)^- = A^- \otimes B^+$,
8. $(A \bullet B)^- = A^- \parr B^-$.

These translations allow us to transform any intuitionistic sequent $A_0, \cdots, A_n \vdash B$ of the Lambek calculus into a sequence $A_0^-, \cdots, A_n^-, B^+$ of formulas of multiplicative linear logic. Then, to allow for non-commutativity amounts to specifying some planarity constraints. This leads to the following definition.

A *non-commutative intuitionistic multiplicative proof-net* associated to a sequent $A_0, \cdots, A_n \vdash B$ is a multiplicative proof-net whose conclusions are $A_0^-, \cdots, A_n^-, B^+$ and that may be represented by a topological planar graph [1, p. 16] such that:

1. the topological planar representation respects the notion of left and right premise;
2. all the conclusions appear on the external boundary of the representation;
3. when following the external boundary counterclockwise one meets the conclusions in the order $A_0^-, \cdots, A_n^-, B^+$ (up to a circular permutation);
4. the contour of each (bounded) face contains exactly one $\parr$-link (this last condition, which is redundant for the cut-free proof-nets, is mandatory in the presence of cuts).

Note that such proof-nets are intuitionistic because they have only one positive conclusion (B^+). This conclusion will be called the output conclusion while the other ones ($A_0^-, \cdots, A_n^-$) will be called the input conclusions.

In fact we may incorporate the above positive and negative translations within the proof-nets in order to make explicit the notion of link for the Lambek calculus. This leads to the ⅋-links and ⊗-links given by Fig. 1. The signs (+ and −) that appear at the level of the premises and conclusions of these links are called *positive* and *negative polarities* (or, respectively, *output* and *input polarities*). Note that the polarities assigned to the premises of a link determine unequivocally the polarity assigned to its conclusion. A priori, there are four different ways of assigning polarities to the two premises of a link. However, some of these possible configurations are forbidden, namely the +/+ assignment for the ⅋-link and the −/− assignment for the ⊗-link. This is due to the intuitionistic nature of the Lambek calculus.

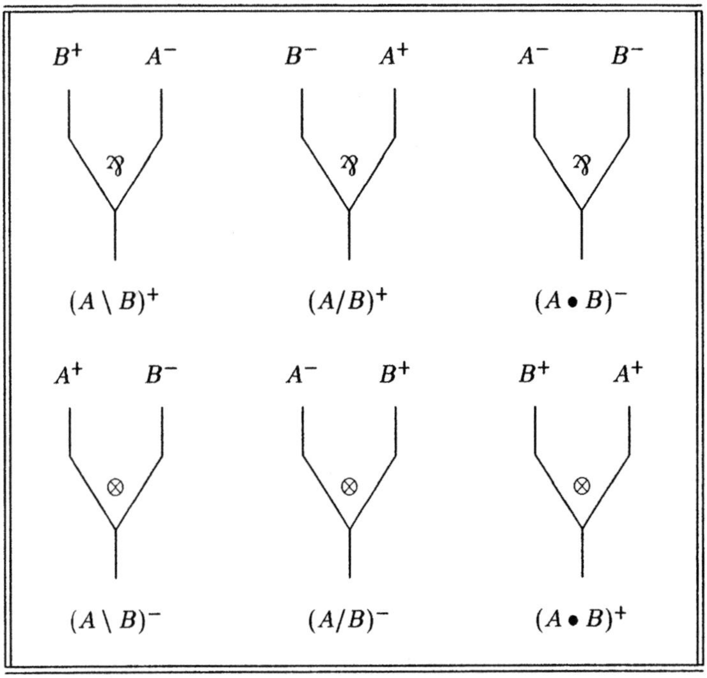

Fig. 1. ⅋-links and ⊗-links for the Lambek calculus

From now on, we will say proof-net for non-commutative intuitionistic multiplicative proof-net.

The above notion of proof-net satisfies the following property that justifies that non-commutative intuitionistic multiplicative proof-nets correspond to the proof-nets of the Lambek calculus.

Proposition 5.1 *A sequent* $\Gamma \vdash B$ *is provable in the Lambek calculus if and only if there exists an associated proof-net.* □

The only-if-part of this proposition may be easily established by induction on the derivations of the sequent calculus. The if-part, which corresponds to Girard's sequentialisation theorem, can be proven using the *splitting ⅋-link method* due to Danos [3].

A ⅋-link occurring in a proof-net is called *splitting* if its removal splits the proof-net in two parts, one connected to the two premises and one to the conclusion of the link (see Fig. 2).

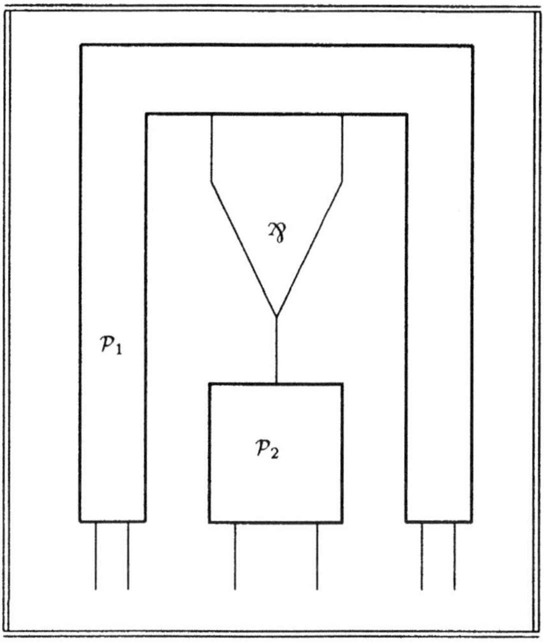

Fig. 2. A splitting ⅋

The splitting-⅋ method is based on the following lemma.

Lemma 5.2 *Any proof-net that contains at least one ⅋-link contains a splitting ⅋-link on the external boundary of its topological planar representation.*

This lemma is proven in [3] for classical multiplicative linear logic. The proof is similar in the intuitionistic, non-commutative case. The only novelty, which is due to our non-commutative setting, is that the splitting ⅋ must be on the external boundary of the proof-net [6].

Given a splitting ⅋ (see Fig. 2), the two parts $\mathcal{P}_1$ and $\mathcal{P}_2$ induce two smaller proof-nets. The part connected to the two premises (i.e., $\mathcal{P}_1$) is directly a proof-net. The part connected to the conclusion (i.e., $\mathcal{P}_2$) with an additional axiom is a proof-net. This fact allows the sequentialisation theorem to be proven by induction on the size of the proof-nets.

6 Reading the phonological bracketing from a proof-net

In [16, pp. 39-40], Roorda defines a procedure that assigns a string to each node of a proof-net. This procedure may be adapted (actually simplified) in order to compute the phonological term associated to a given proof-net.

Technically, we work with the phonological algebra generated by a set $\mathcal{V} = \mathcal{P} \cup \mathcal{X}$, where $\mathcal{P}$ and $\mathcal{X}$ are two disjoint sets, respectively called the set of parameters and the set of variables. The terms that do not contain variables will be called proper terms.

The computation of the proper phonological term associated to a proof-net goes as follows:

1. Assign to each input conclusion (negative conclusion) of the proof-net a different parameter (In practice, the atomic constituents of the phrase); assign to the output conclusion (positive conclusion) of the proof-net a variable (say x).
2. Assign to each node of the proof-net a term (or a variable) according to the unfolding described in Fig. 3.
3. Consider the unification problem made of the constraints associated to some of the links, and of the equations "*variable* = *term*" resulting from the axiomatic links. By solving this unification problem, one finds a proper term for the variable x. This term is the phonological term associated to the proof-net.

Roorda's results [16] ensure that the unification problem involved in the computation of a phonological term always admits a solution. Moreover, it is easy to show that the phonological term associated to a proof-net (according to our procedure) is the same as the one that would be obtained by considering some corresponding sequential proof. Notice that the unfolding procedure that we give is actually a simplification of Roorda's: in particular, associative unification is not needed.

7 Interpolation on proof-nets

Roughly speaking, Roorda's interpolation theorem says that whenever a sequent $\Gamma, \Psi, \Delta \vdash A$ is provable, there exists a formula I (called an interpolant) such that the two sequents $\Psi \vdash I$ and $\Gamma, I, \Delta \vdash A$ are provable. In addition, the atomic subformulas of I must obey some occurrence conditions (see [16] for details).

Now consider a proof-net, say Π, with n input conclusions C_i^- $(1 \leq i \leq n)$ and one output conclusion C^+. In order to state an interpolation problem for this proof-net, one must distinguish some consecutive input conclusions, say $C_j^-, C_{j+1}^-, \ldots, C_{j+k}^-$. Then a solution to this interpolation problem consists of one formula I and two proof-nets Π_1 and Π_2 such that:

1. the input conclusions of Π_1 are $C_j^-, C_{j+1}^-, \ldots, C_{j+k}^-$, and its output conclusion is I^+;

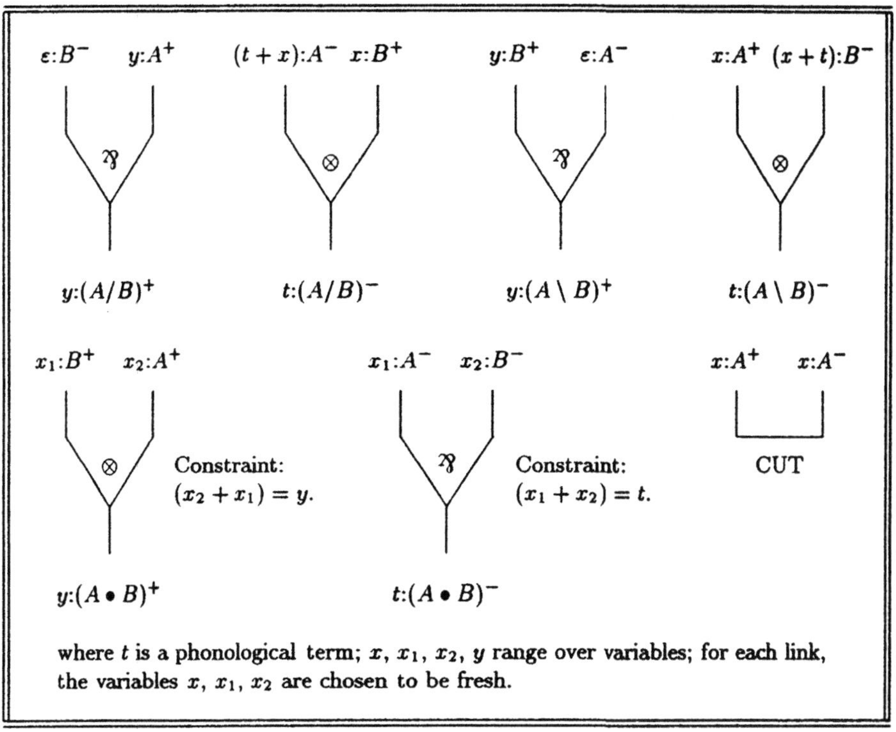

Fig. 3. unfolding

2. the input conclusions of Π_2 are $C_1^-, C_{j-1}^-, I^-, C_{j+k+1}^-, \ldots, C_n^-$, and its output conclusion is C;
3. in Π_1 (resp. Π_2), there is no axiomatic link both conclusions of which would belong to the proof-frame associated to I^+ (resp. I^-);
4. in Π_1 (resp. Π_2), all the axiomatic links no conclusion of which belong to the proof-frame associated to I^+ (resp. I^-) were already existing in Π.

More abstractly, but equivalently, an interpolation problem consists of a proof-net Π together with a set of n axiomatic links whose removal splits the proof-net Π into two disconnected parts M_1 and M_2 (see Fig.4). These parts, which are not proof-nets, will be called modules. Without lost of generality, consider that the output conclusion of Π is a conclusion of M_2. Then, a solution to this interpolation problem consists of a formula I of length n such that the proof-structure obtained by

1. linking the module M_1 to the proof-frame I^+ using n axioms,
2. linking the conclusions of the proof-frames I^+ and I^- by a cut,
3. linking the proof-frame I^- to the module M_2 using n axioms,

is a proof-net (see Fig. 5).

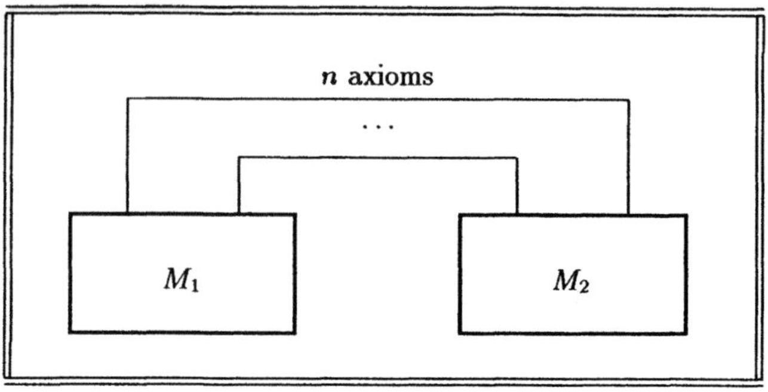

Fig. 4. Interpolation problem

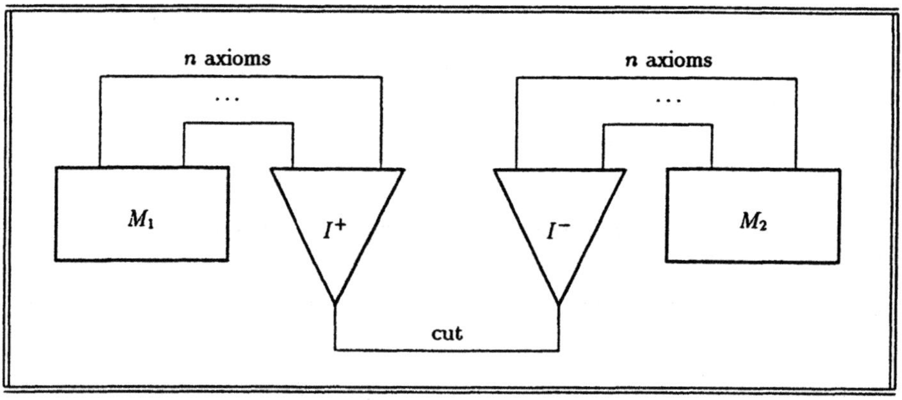

Fig. 5. Solution to the interpolation problem

In order to show that any interpolation problem admit a solution, we establish two key lemmas.

Lemma 7.1 *Consider a proof-net containing a set of n cuts* $(n > 1)$ *whose removal splits the proof-net into two disconnected modules (see Fig.6). Then, there exist, among these n cuts, two cuts and one of the two modules* M_1 *or* M_2 *(say* M_i*) such that for any switching, the two corresponding conclusions are always connected by a path belonging to* M_i*. Moreover, one may always find two such cuts that are adjacent.*

Proof. The second part of the proposition, which concerns the fact that the cuts may be found adjacent, is rather involved and quite long because of numerous cases and subcases. The difficulty arises from the fact that one must use *planarity arguments* that cannot be easily formalised. For this reason, we reserve the complete proof for a long paper and establish only the first part of the proposition.[2]

[2] Consequently, in the present paper, our proof of the interpolation theorem is only complete for the (intuitionistic) commutative case.

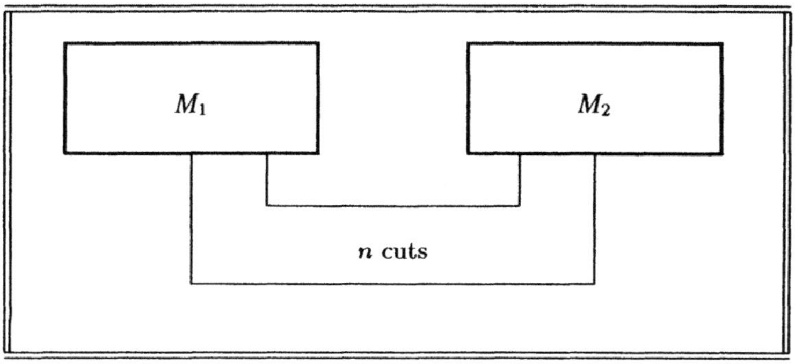

Fig. 6.

The proof is by induction on the number of ⅋-links in the proof-net.

If the proof-net does not contain any ⅋-link, it has only axioms, cuts and ⊗-links. Therefore, there is only one possible switching (the empty one). Then, because any proof-net is connected, there exist two cuts that are connected inside the same module (M_1 or M_2).

If the proof-net $\mathcal{P}$ has at least one ⅋-link, there exists, by Lemma 5.2, a splitting ⅋-link that induces two proof-nets $\mathcal{P}_1$ and $\mathcal{P}_2$. The n initial cuts are then divided in two sets A and B belonging respectively to the proof-nets $\mathcal{P}_1$ and $\mathcal{P}_2$ (see Fig. 7). There are three cases:

- The number of cuts in A is greater or equal to 2. Then we are done by applying the induction hypothesis to the proof-net $\mathcal{P}_1$.
- The number of cuts in B is greater or equal to 2. Then we apply the induction hypothesis on the proof-net $\mathcal{P}_2$.
- The numbers of cuts in A and B are exactly one in both cases. Then the two cuts may not be connected within the module that does not contain the splitting ⅋ (see Fig. 7). This implies that they must be connected, for any switching, by a path belonging to the other module. □

The above lemma, which provides the most important part of the interpolation theorem, yields the next lemma as an almost direct consequence.

Lemma 7.2 *Consider a proof-net containing a set of n cuts whose removal splits the proof-net into two disconnected modules (see Fig. 6). Then, there exist, among these n cuts, two adjacent cuts that may be replaced by a single cut between a "⊗" and a "⅋" in such a way that the resulting proof-structure is a proof-net (see Fig. 8).*

Proof. This proposition is a consequence of the previous lemma. For the configuration of Fig. 6, we can apply the previous lemma and find two adjacent cuts connected, for any switching, by a path belonging to one of the modules (say M_i). Now, we can add a ⅋-link on the side of M_i and a ⊗-link on the other side as is shown on Fig. 8.

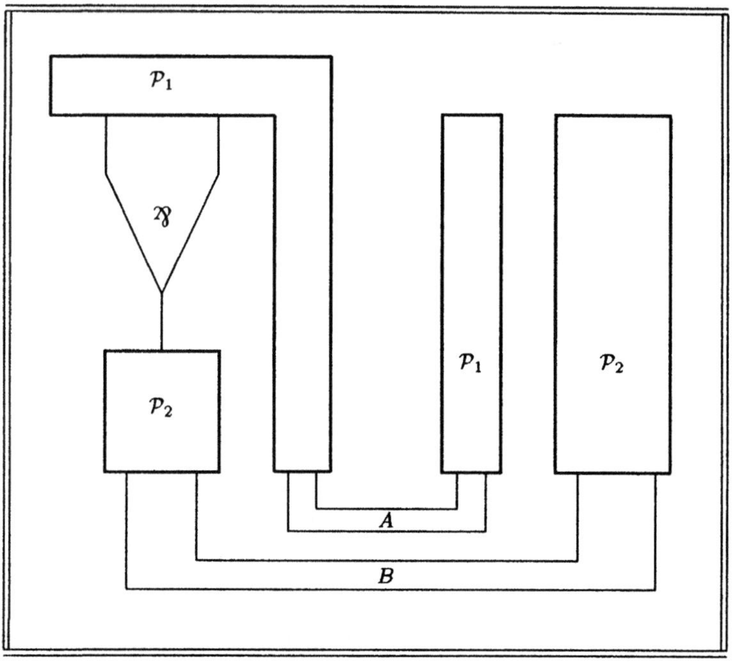

Fig. 7.

Now, it remains to prove: firstly, that this construction is always possible (it could be impossible for polarity reasons); secondly, that it yields a proof-net (i.e., a *correct* proof-structure).

Regarding the polarity problem, we must decide which sort of ⅋-link we add: $+/-$, $-/+$, or $-/-$ (this determines the sort of $\otimes$-link to add, by duality). In fact, there is no degree of freedom here because we must respect the polarities of the initial proof-net. However, we must prove that the polarities of the premises of the new ⅋-link are not both output (because that corresponds to the configuration $+/+$ which is forbidden in the intuitionistic proof-nets).

Consider a switching such that all the $+/-$ ⅋-links are switched on the left and all the $-/+$ ⅋-links are switched on the right. The graph underlying this switching is a tree whose root is the output conclusion of the original proof-net and whose edges (starting from the root) "go up" through positive formulas, cross the axioms in the output/input direction, "go down" through negative formulas, and cross the cuts in the input/output direction. Therefore, there exist two paths from the root of the tree to the two negative premises of the two cuts of interest. On the other hand, there also exists, for this switching, a path between the two premises of the ⅋-link we are going to add. Therefore, if these two premises were positive, there would exist a path between the two positive premises of the two cuts. This would make a cycle, which is a contradiction.

It remains to prove that the construction is correct. Any switching of the new proof-structure is determined by a switching of the initial proof-net together

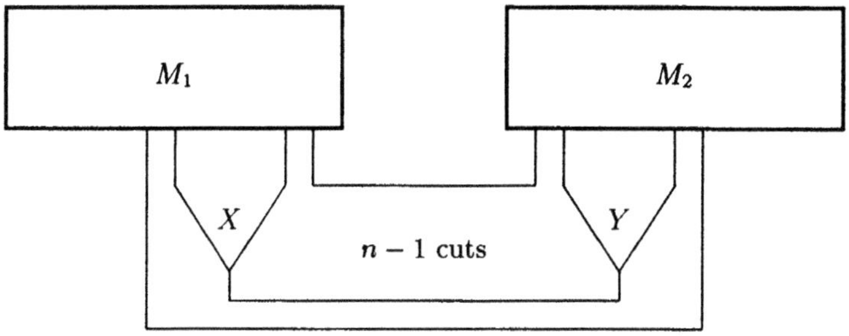

where X is a $\otimes$ and Y is a ⅋, or conversely.

Fig. 8.

with a switch for the additional ⅋-link. For the initial proof-net, we know that the graph has no cycle and is connected. We know that there exists a path between the two selected cuts in $\mathcal{M}_i$. This path remains in the new proof-structure. So the additional $\otimes$-link does not create a new cycle in the graph. For the same reason, because the initial proof-net is connected for any switching, the new one is also connected. Thus the new proof-structure is correct and is, by definition, a proof-net. □

We are now in a position to prove the interpolation theorem.

Theorem 7.3 *Any interpolation problem admits a solution.*

Proof. Given a proof-net such as the one in Fig. 4, one easily obtains a proof-net such as the one in Fig. 5 by replacing each of the n axioms by a path made of one axiom, one cut, and one axiom. Then, one may obtain an interpolant by iterating the key lemma. □

The proof of this theorem gives an algorithm to compute interpolants. The method is as follows:

1. Let n be the number of axioms that splits the given proof-net in two disconnected modules. Replace each of these axioms by a path *axiom-cut-axiom*.
2. If $n = 1$ then stop. (the interpolation problem is already solved)
3. Otherwise, find two adjacent cuts that obey the property described in Lemma 7.2. This corresponds to finding, in a module, two conclusions that are connected for any *switching* [4]. This last property is reminiscent of the notion of *empire* and may be checked using Girard's closure conditions on empires [8].
4. Replace the two adjacent cuts by a single cut as specified in Lemma 7.2.
5. Decrease n by 1 and go to step 2.

This algorithm, which works on proof-nets, does not use any sequentialisation of the proof-nets. Its complexity is at most $m * n^2$, where m is the size of the proof-net and n is the number of axioms that splits the proof-net in two parts. This cubic complexity corresponds actually to a rough estimate. Using tabularisation techniques, we could obtain a sub-quadratic algorithm.

8 Concluding remarks

We said, in Section 3, that the difficulty in finding a derivation corresponding to a given prosodic phrasing consists in guessing the cut formulas. In fact, this difficulty is not a technical one. Indeed, when working in the Lambek calculus with product, one may always group together two constituents of type A and B by assigning them the type $(A \bullet B)$. Such a trivial solution, of course, is not satisfactory.

The real problem in guessing the cut formulas is to provide the prosodic constituents with categorial types *that make sense.* With respect to this, the use of interpolation seems promising. Indeed, an interpolant may be interpreted as a type whose every atomic subtype specifies an actual interaction with the *external world.* This means, in our case, interactions between the constituent (to which the interpolant is assigned as a type) and the rest of the phrase.

Nevertheless, working with interpolants does not settle the problem completely because, in general, an interpolation problem admits several solutions. Therefore, what is now needed is a mathematical classification of these different solutions that would allow some canonical choice to be made.

References

[1] C. Berge. *Graphs.* North-Holland, second revised edition edition, 1985.

[2] W. Buszkowski. Generative power of categorial grammars. In R. T. Oehrle, E. Bach, and D. Wheeler, editors, *Categorial Grammars and Natural Languages Structures*, pages 69–94. Reidel, 1988.

[3] V. Danos. *Une application de la logique linéaire à l'étude des processus de normalisation et principalement du lambda calcul.* Thèse de doctorat, Université de Paris VII, 1990.

[4] V. Danos and L. Regnier. The structure of multiplicatives. *Archive for Mathematical Logic*, 28:181–203, 1989.

[5] Ph. de Groote and C. Retoré. On the semantic readings of proof-nets. In G.-J. Kruijff, G. Morrill, and D. Oehrle, editors, *Formal Grammar*, pages 57–70. Eighth European Summer School in Logic Language and Information, August 1996.

[6] A. Fleury. Private communication.

[7] J.-Y. Girard. Linear logic. *Theoretical Computer Science*, 50:1–102, 1987.

[8] J.-Y. Girard. Quantifiers in linear logic II. Technical Report 19, Equipe de Logique Mathêmatique, Université de Paris VII, 1991.

[9] J. Lambek. The mathematics of sentence structure. *Amer. Math. Monthly*, 65:154–170, 1958.

[10] A. Lecomte. Prosodie et stratégie de calcul. Communication à la journée ATALA "Interaction prosodie-syntaxe", Février 1996.

[11] A. Lecomte and C. Retoré. Pomset logic as an alternative categorial grammar. In *Proceedings of the Conference of the European Summer School in Logic, Language and Information*, Barcelona, 1995.

[12] M. Moortgat. *Categorial Investigations: logical and linguistic aspects of the lambek calculus*. Foris Publications, 1988.

[13] M. Moortgat. Categorial type logic. In J. van Benthem and A. ter Meulen, editors, *Handbook of Logic and Language*, chapter two. Elsevier, to appear.

[14] G. Morrill. Memoisation of categorial proof nets: parallelism in categorial processing. In V. M. Abrusci and C. Casadio, editors, *Proofs and Linguistic Categories, Proceedings 1996 Roma Workshop*. CLUEB, 1996.

[15] C. Retoré. Calcul de lambek et logique linéaire. *Traitement Automatique de Langues*, 37(2):39–70, 1997.

[16] D. Roorda. *Resource Logics: proof-theoretical investigations*. PhD thesis, University of Amsterdam, 1991.

Vagueness and Type Theory

Pascal Boldini

Université Paris X-Nanterre
200 Avenue de la République
92001 Nanterre cedex
France
boldini@modalx.u-paris10.fr

Abstract. The aim of this essay is to show that one can give a proof-theoretical semantics to vague predicates (most of the observational predicates). The starting point is the critic of the truth-conditional analysis of vagueness in terms of degrees of truth, and the solution proposed is based of the anti-realist principle *meaning is use*. Therefore the problem of vague is replaced by the problem of graduality.
Through the example of the predicate *to be small* are presented the principles of the anti-realist approach. The semantical representation of the predicate is a formula of the Intuitionistic Type Theory of Martin-Löf (TT). This formula is introduced in a context (in the sense of TT) which formalizes the conditions of use. Among the contextual parameters is required a contextual "objective" property B which must have *bounds*. Hence in a given context a paraphrase of the assertion *a is small* is *a is small enough in order to satisfy B*.
From this point of view, the logical puzzles called sorits illustrate the relevance of the proof-theoretical approach. They appear as pedagogical devices which stress the difference between the semantical content of a proposition and its logical behaviour. The semantical content defined in proof-theoretical terms supports graduality, whereas the logical behaviour forbids it.

1 Motivations

There are two complementary motivations for this work,

- a semantical one: is proof-theoretical semantics relevant at the lexical level?
- a philosophical one: is it possible to give an anti-realist account for the graduality of most of the observational predicates?

1.1 The lexical issue

The introduction, by P. Martin-Löf in the 70's, of the Intuitionistic Type Theory ([6]) has created the theoretical conditions for the development of a proof-theoretical semantics for natural language. Up to now, this work has been principally carried out by A. Ranta and G. Sundholm, and has proved successful[1] in the analysis of quantification and reference ([10], [12], [13]).

Like any logical semantics, the domain of relevance of proof-theoretical semantics is the propositional level. This is not a restriction. As a matter of fact logical semantics is in the same position as any semantics since this level is the only observable in linguistics. The general problem in semantics is to infer semantical information from this level to inferior ones like the lexical level. From this point of view, the perspectives offered by classical logic are very poor (even in the case of quantifiers and connectives). The consequence is that it is difficult to connect the logical approach to the non-logical trend in semantical research.

Through the example of the predicate *to be small*, I illustrate the superiority of a logical semantics based on TT for this purpose. The main technical reason for such a superiority is that TT demands and allows a precise formalization of the context. Consequently, many contextual elements gain a logical status (*e.g.* proof-objects), whereas they were rejected in the rag-bag domain of pragmatics by the classical approach.

1.2 The philosophical issue

The topic of vagueness appears in the debate between realism and anti-realism in semantics. For example, in the chapter X of his book, *The norm of truth*, Pascal Engel ([4]) criticizes the anti-realism *à la* Dummet ([2], [3]), because it cannot give a satisfactory account of the coherence of vague predicates. In this debate, the so-called *sorit paradoxes* play an important role. Famous examples of such paradoxes are:

- The Megaric Sorit of the Heap

$$\frac{\begin{array}{c}\texttt{If you remove one grain, a heap of wheat is still a heap}\\ \texttt{If you remove two grains, a heap of wheat is still a heap}\\ \vdots\end{array}}{\texttt{Two grains of wheat form a heap}}$$

- Wang's Paradox

$$\frac{\begin{array}{l}\texttt{0 is small}\\ \texttt{If } n \texttt{ is small, then } n+1 \texttt{ is small}\end{array}}{\texttt{Every integer is small}}$$

At first sight, these paradoxes are arguments for the anti-realist in semantics: they suggest that vague predicates have no definite truth conditions.

However it is still possible to argue for a truth-conditional approach. Actually these predicates seem to follow a particular logic: a *logic of vagueness*. Such

[1] A good example is anaphora. The proof-theoretical formalizations of "donkey-sentences" (Every man who owns a donkey beats it) are compositional in the sense that the constituents of the sentence are constituents of the formula, whereas classical formalizations are clearly *ad hoc*.

formalisms (*e.g.* [5], or the popular fuzzy logic) are truth-conditional, and the notion of degree of truth formalizes, in a simple and direct way, the tolerance (or graduality) of such predicates. In addition to that they explain the paradoxes, showing how the degree of truth decreases along the chain of inferences.

This achievement changes the status of the sorits. Since they are not arguments against the truth-conditional point of view, they must be considered as a semantical phenomenon worth of interest. Hence the anti-realist cannot hold anymore his dogmatic and negative position, he has to provide a precise account of the behaviour of vague predicates.

1.3 Structure of the article

The paper is structured as follows. Section 2 recalls the basic principles of proof-theoretical semantics and discusses the ontological status of the proofs. Section 3 is devoted to the study of a particular predicate: *to be small.* This study begins with the mathematical use of the predicate (section 3.1). From this particular case are deduced the contextual parameters required for the use of the predicate. Among them, the most important is a contextual property B with ***bounds.*** Section 3.2 extends the analysis to the general use and proposes a semantical representation of to *to be small* as a formula of TT introduced in a context (in the sense of TT) formalizing the conditions of use. Section 4 examines the semantical and logical relations between the predicate *to be small* and the contextual predicate B. It shows that these predicates are not generally equivalent, and even if it is the case, they have not the same semantical content in proof-theoretical terms. Section 5 defends the monadic status of the predicate against relativist solutions in terms of hidden arguments (*to be small* is *to be small relatively to somebody or something*). Section 6 shows how comparative judgements are formalized in the same context as simple judgements. Section 7 goes back to the problem of sorits (Wang's Paradox in this case). The conclusion of the sorit is blocked since the required proof by induction can not be generally performed for the formula representing the predicate. Moreover the role of the sorit is explained. It is a logical game which compels us to shift from logical representations which support graduality to equivalent one which do not support it any more and which have not the same semantical content. Section 8 concludes with the main points revealed by this anti-realist approach to vagueness, and with some pointers to further research.

2 Proof-theoretical semantics

The principles of a proof-theoretical semantics are presented and discussed in [12]. In this section I just want to make everything clear about a possible source of confusion: realism about proofs.

The fundamental principle of proof-theoretical semantics is strictly intuitionist and goes back to Heyting: the meaning of a proposition is not a truth value, but "what is to count as a proof of the proposition" ([14], p. 298). A part of the history of theoretical computer science is the history of the application of this conception through the ***propositions as types*** or ***propositions as sets*** principles. The project has been made easier by the evident constructive content of computing, which allows a clear identification between proof-objects and programs. Unfortunatly the situation is not so favourable in the case of natural language.

The nature of the proof-objects set a legitimate ontological problem which must not lead to new forms of realism (*e.g.* Proofs are formal proofs.) or to aporetic questions (*e.g.* What is the proof of a proof?, etc...). A detailed discussion of this topic is beyond the scope of this paper (good starting points are [7] and [14]), hence I will assume that the ***propositions as sets*** principle still holds in the case of natural language provided that the concept of proof is extended to *any process* of knowledge acquisition (intellectual or perceptive).

3 A case study: *to be small*

In this section I consider an example of vague predicate: *to be small*, and its associated sorit: Wang's paradox.

I propose a semantical representation of the predicate by a formula of TT, introduced in a context (in the sense of TT) which formalizes the conditions of use. The semantical representation is motivated by a close inspection of the conditions of use in mathematical practice.

The rules required for the formalizations and deductions are Σ, and Π formation/introduction/elimination rules:

- Π-formation

$$\frac{A\,\mathsf{Set} \qquad \begin{array}{c}[x:A]\\ \vdots \\ B(x)\,\mathsf{Set}\end{array}}{(\Pi x \in A)B(x)\,\mathsf{Set}}$$

- Π-introduction (Π-i)

$$\frac{\begin{array}{c}[x:A]\\ \vdots \\ b(x):B(x)\end{array}}{(\lambda x)b(x):(\Pi x \in A)B(x)}$$

- Π-elimination (Π-e)

$$\frac{c:(\Pi x \in A)B(x) \qquad a:A}{Ap(c,a):B(a)}$$

- Σ-formation

$$\frac{\begin{matrix} & [x \in A] \\ & \vdots \\ A\,\mathsf{Set} & B(x)\,\mathsf{Set}\end{matrix}}{(\Sigma x : A)B(x)\,\mathsf{Set}}$$

– Σ-introduction (Σ-i)

$$\frac{a : A \qquad b : B(a)}{(a, b) : (\Sigma x : A)B(x)}$$

– Σ-elimination (Σ-e)

$$\frac{\begin{matrix} & [x : A,\ y : B(x)] \\ & \vdots \\ c : (\Sigma x \in A)B(x) & d(x, y) : C((x, y))\end{matrix}}{E(c,\ (x, y)d(x, y)) : C(c)}$$

with the fundamental type equality $Prop = Set$.

In practice we will use the two derived rules ($p(c) \equiv E(c,\ (x, y)x)$, and $q(c) \equiv E(c,\ (x, y)y)$) for Σ-elimination:

$$\frac{c : (\Sigma x : A)B(x)}{p(c) : A} \qquad \frac{c : (\Sigma x : A)B(x)}{q(c) : B(p(c))}$$

3.1 Mathematical use

Like any specialized human activity, mathematical practice is not carried inside a specific language apart from the ordinary one, it is carried inside an idiolect which contains specific predicates (*e.g. prime, differentiable*) and ordinary ones (*e.g. small, tall, fast*).

The working mathematician does not use an ordinary predicate like *to be small* as an abbreviation for a precise, sophisticated, and "purely" mathematical one, he uses it in a productive and dynamic way (*cf.* [11]). When he asserts *a is small*, $a : \mathsf{N}$, he means that *he knows* (= he can prove) that $a : \mathsf{N}$ satisfies a given contextual property $B : (\mathsf{N})\mathsf{Prop}$, the form of which is in most cases : $g(a) \leq \varepsilon$, $g : (\mathsf{N})\mathsf{R}, \varepsilon : \mathsf{R}$ (*e.g.* $n \log n \leq 10^{-3}$).

Although they are contextual, the "objective" properties $B : (\mathsf{N})\mathsf{Prop}$ are not arbitrary. They belong to a particular class: properties with "bounds". To put it precisely, there exists some $u : \mathsf{N}$ such that, if $B(u)$ *true*, then for all $x \leq u$, $B(x)$ *true*.

In most cases, an upper bound (a *frontier*, *cf.* 7.2) can be determined effectively, but this arithmetical result has nothing to do with the contextual use of the property $B : (\mathsf{N})\mathsf{Prop}$. My opinion is that if the use of the predicate *to be small* requires the existence of such a property, it does not require the knowledge of the theoretical upper bound. On the contrary, I would say that a flexible and widespread use of *to be small* requires the practical ignorance of such a theoretical bound.

Therefore, the context wich formalizes the conditions of use, simply express the fact that B has bounds:

$$[B : (\mathsf{N})\mathsf{Prop},\ c : (\Sigma u : \mathsf{N})(\Pi x : \mathsf{N})(x \leq u \to B(x))].$$

Inside this context the assertion *a is small* means that a is inferior to some bound of the property B.

The process of formalization can be decomposed in three stages.

1. We consider the set of bounds of B.
   Based on the *propositions = sets* principle, the definition of subsets in TT gives:
   $$(\Sigma u : \mathsf{N})(\Pi x : \mathsf{N})(x \leq u \to B(x)),$$
   the proposition introduced in the context.
2. We consider an element of this set: $v : (\Sigma u : \mathsf{N})(\Pi x : \mathsf{N})(x \leq u \to B(x))$. By the Σ-elimination rule we know that its first projection $p(v) : \mathsf{N}$ is an integer, and its second projection is a proof:
   $$q(v) : (\Pi x : \mathsf{N})(x \leq p(v) \to B(x)).$$
3. We express that the integer a is inferior to the value of the bound, *i.e* to $p(v)$ the first projection of v.

The output of this analysis is the semantical representation of *to be small* as the formation rule:

$$\frac{B : (\mathsf{N})\mathsf{Prop} \qquad\qquad c : (\Sigma u : \mathsf{N})(\Pi x : \mathsf{N})(x \leq u \to B(x))}{\begin{array}{l} a\, is\ small : \mathsf{Prop} \\ a\, is\ small = (\Sigma v : (\Sigma u : \mathsf{N})(\Pi x : \mathsf{N})(x \leq u \to B(x)))(a \leq p(v)) : \mathsf{Prop} \end{array}}$$

The formula introduced by the rule is a progressive conjunction, where $p(v) : \mathsf{N}$ is the integer (the bound in a classical setting) produced by the Σ-elimination rule.

Remark A (multi-sortal) classical formulation of the same ideas would be:

$$(a\, is\ small) = (\exists v : \mathsf{N})((\forall x : \mathsf{N})(x \leq v \to B(x)) \wedge (a \leq v)).$$

The superiority of the type theoretic solution lies in the fact that the existence of a set of bounds for B is independent of the assertion, and appears as a real constituent of the formula. Of course, this is not the case in the classical solution.

3.2 General use

A predicate like *to be small* has a very extended use. Actually it is always possible to assign a meaning to a sentence NP is small, where NP is a given noun phrase. Since the type of a noun phrase is a set, *to be small* is a polymorphic predicate of type : $(X : \mathsf{Set})(X)\mathsf{Prop}$.

Therefore, among the conditions of use (presuppositions) we must introduce a set $A : \mathsf{Set}$ (*e.g. Child, Dog, Apartment*) depending on the context. Following the same line as for mathematical use, I pretend that an "objective" contextual property $B : (A)\mathsf{Prop}$ is required in order to assert *a is small* where $a : A$. Examples of such properties are *to be nursed, not to be able to walk*, for a child, or *I feel uncomfortable in, a surface area inferior to* $100m^2$ for an apartment. The diversity of these contextual properties explain why a realist approach to meaning is hopeless.

Sometimes the contextual property is an exact metric constraint like in the last example. In most cases the metric or ordinal aspect is only implicit, it appears in dialogs when people argue about the validity of a judgement of smallness. Nevertheless this ordinal dimension is part of the conditions of use, since a justification should be required of anybody who makes such a judgement. Moreover this aspect is linked to an important characteristic (noticed in the mathematical use (3.1)) of the contextual properties $B : (A)\mathsf{Prop}$: they must have bounds.

In order to express these ideas, a representation function (utility, measurement) $f : A \rightarrow \mathsf{N}$, must appear in the context. Examples of such functions are *age, height, surface area*, or *number of rooms*, depending on the type A of the objects. The presupposition that there exists a set of bounds for the property $B : (A)\mathsf{Prop}$ is settled in the context $[A : \mathsf{Set}, B : (A)\mathsf{Prop}, f : A \rightarrow \mathsf{N}]$, and formalized by:

$$c : (\Sigma u : \mathsf{N})(\Pi x : A)(f(x) \leq u \rightarrow B(x)).$$

Two remarks:

1. The bounds are integers depending on the representation function, hence they are no "natural" bounds. Since we do not require any extra property for the representation function, the values of the bounds do not necessarily represent objects $a : A$.
2. There is no intrinsic relation (any realistic link) between the representation function and the property B. The thesis is that the former is simply required by the use, and not by internal characteristics of B.

An alternative consists in providing A with an order $\leq_A$: $A \times A \rightarrow \mathsf{Prop}$. The corresponding formalization would be:

$$c : (\Sigma u : A)(\Pi x : A)(x \leq_A u \rightarrow B(x)).$$

This solution appears as a direct generalization of the one proposed for mathematical use. Nevertheless two reasons make me prefer the previous one:

1. With its representation function, the first solution also generalizes the mathematical case: put $f = \lambda x.x : \mathsf{N} \rightarrow \mathsf{N}$.

2. The presupposition that A comes equipped with an order is too demanding from a pragmatic perspective. Analysis of real discourse shows that if there is an order on A, it is only manifested or constructed in the use, through a representation function based on a cultural norm.

The conclusion of this discussion is that the context formalizing the conditions of use is:

$$[A : \mathsf{Set},\ B : (A)\mathsf{Prop},\ f : A \rightarrow \mathsf{N},\ c : (\Sigma u : \mathsf{N})(\Pi x : A)(f(x) \leq u \rightarrow B(x))].$$

In this context, the judgment *a is small*, $a : A$, means that there exists a bound v for the property $B : (A)\mathsf{Prop}$ such that $f(a)$ the representation of a is inferior to $p(v)$ the "integer component" of v. We obtain the formation rule:

$$\frac{A : \mathsf{Set}\ \ B : (A)\mathsf{Prop}\ \ f : A \rightarrow \mathsf{N}\ \ c : (\Sigma u : A)(\Pi x : A)(f(x) \leq u \rightarrow B(x))}{\begin{array}{l} a\, is\, small : \mathsf{Prop} \\ a\, is\, small = (\Sigma v : (\Sigma u : \mathsf{N})(\Pi x : A)(f(x) \leq u \rightarrow B(x)))(f(a) \leq p(v)) : \mathsf{Prop}\end{array}}$$

4 Equality, equivalence, or implication?

In this section, I defend this logical representation against an objection that may have appeared in the reader's mind: " your sophisticated representation reduces simply to a contextual definition of the predicate ***to be small*** by the contextual predicate B!"

I will argue in two steps. First, I show that generally there is no logical equivalence between the propositions *a is small* and $B(a)$. Second, even in such cases of equivalence, we cannot consider logical equivalence as a redefinition.

4.1 Implication

An easy deduction[2] proves: $(a\, is\, small) \rightarrow B(a)\ true$.

$$\dfrac{\dfrac{\dfrac{\dfrac{y : a\, is\, small}{p(y) : (\Sigma u : \mathsf{N})(\Pi x : A)(f(x) \leq u \rightarrow B(x))}\,\Sigma e}{q(p(y)) : (\Pi x : A)(f(x) \leq p(p(y)) \rightarrow B(x))}\,\Sigma e \quad a : A}{Ap(q(p(y)), a) : f(a) \leq p(p(y)) \rightarrow B(a)}\,\Pi e \qquad q(y) : f(a) \leq p(p(y))}{Ap(Ap(q(p(y)), a), q(y)) : B(a)}\,\Pi e$$

Generally we cannot prove the converse. This amounts to the fact that to an element $a : A$ such that $B(a)$ *true* does not necesseraly correspond a bound $f(a)$ for B. In other terms, a particular two years old child can still be nursed, without entailing that every younger child is nursed.

[2] All the deductions in the paper correspond to very elementary reasonings. I adopt the formal presentation hoping that it will give to the reader unfamiliar with TT a flavour of the system.

4.2 Equivalence

There are cases of equivalence. They occur when there is a direct connection between the property $B : (A)\mathsf{Prop}$ and the representation function $f : A \to \mathsf{N}$. The simplest examples are provided by properties expressing numerical constraints like:

$$B(a) = f(a) \leq u_0 : \mathsf{Prop},\ [a : A, u_0 : \mathsf{N}].$$

The implication $(f(a) \leq u_0) \to$ (*a is small*) is easy to prove since u_0 is an obvious bound for the property.

$$\dfrac{\dfrac{y : f(a) \leq u_O \qquad \dfrac{\dfrac{\dfrac{[x : A]^1}{\lambda z.z : f(x) \leq u_O \to f(x) \leq u_O}}{\lambda x.\lambda z.z : (\Pi x : A)(f(x) \leq u_O \to f(x) \leq u_O)}\,\Pi i_1}{(u_0, \lambda x.\lambda z.z) : (\Sigma u : \mathrm{N})(\Pi x : A)(f(x) \leq u \to f(x) \leq u_O)}\,\Sigma i}{y : f(a) \leq p((u_0, \lambda x.\lambda z.z))}\,\mathrm{ext}}{((u_0, \lambda x.\lambda z.z), y) : (\Sigma w : (\Sigma u : \mathrm{N})(\Pi x : A)(f(x) \leq u \to f(x) \leq u_O))(f(a) \leq p(w))}\,\Sigma i$$

Truth-conditional semantics identify[3] two equivalent propositions since they have the same contents, and this identification is the source of well known difficulties in the application of any tarskian theory of truth to natural language[4] (*The snow is white* has the same content as *The grass is green*).

As to the proof-theoretical point of view, it distinguishes between equivalence and equality. In TT, equality between propositions (or sets) is one of the four basic forms of judgements. As a consequence, two equal propositions p and q have the same proofs, whereas equivalence means that there exists procedures that *transform* proofs of p into proofs of q and conversely. Actually, this directly follows from the principles developped in (2):

1. The content of a proposition is given by its proofs.
2. A realist theory of proofs is a non-sense.

In consequence the equivalence (*a is small*) $\leftrightarrow f(a) \leq u_0$ is taken for what it is: a logical result, not a semantical one. This means that like Achilles in the famous article of Lewis Carroll ([1]), you can use this result to try to convince your interlocutor that he says *a is small* because $f(a) \leq u_0$. But still like Achilles you will not be able to *force* her or him to agree.

---

[3] I am forced to employ this imprecise term, since for the classical conception equality between propositions is meta-theoretical, contrary to the proof-theoretical one where there are internal judgements of equality between propositions.

[4] Some of these difficulties can be overcome within a holist approach to natural language, *cf.* the whole work of Davidson.

4.3 A rejected alternative

Similar arguments justify my preference for the formalization

$$(\Sigma v : (\Sigma u : \mathsf{N})(\Pi x : A)(f(x) \leq u \rightarrow B(x)))(f(a) \leq p(v))$$

instead of:

$$(\Pi x : A)(f(x) \leq f(a) \rightarrow B(x))$$

They are indeed equivalent, due to the transivity and reflexivity of the order relation (the terms *trans* and *reflex* in the formal proofs), but they have not the same semantical (proof-theoretical) content. Here are the proofs:

$$\dfrac{\dfrac{\dfrac{\dfrac{\dfrac{\dfrac{y : (a\ is\ small)}{p(y) : (\Sigma u : \mathrm{N})(\Pi x : A)(f(x) \leq u \rightarrow B(x))}\,\Sigma e}{q(p(y)) : (\Pi x : A)(f(x) \leq p(p(y)) \rightarrow B(x))}\,\Sigma e \qquad [x : A]^2}{Ap(q(p(y)), x) : f(x) \leq p(p(y)) \rightarrow B(x)}\,\Pi e \qquad \dfrac{[z : f(x) \leq f(a)]^1 \quad q(y) : f(a) \leq p(p(y))}{trans(z, q(y)) : f(x) \leq p(p(y))}}{Ap(Ap(q(p(y)), x), trans(z, q(y))) : B(x)}\,\Pi e}{\lambda z.Ap(Ap(q(p(y)), x), trans(z, q(y))) : f(x) \leq f(a) \rightarrow B(x)}\,\Pi i_1}{\lambda x.\lambda z.Ap(Ap(q(p(y)), x), trans(z, q(y))) : (\Pi x : A)(f(x) \leq f(a) \rightarrow B(x))}\,\Pi i_2$$

and conversely,

$$\dfrac{\dfrac{y : (\Pi x : A)(f(x) \leq f(a) \rightarrow B(x))}{(f(a), y) : (\Sigma u : \mathrm{N})(\Pi x : A)(f(x) \leq u \rightarrow B(x))}\,\Sigma i \qquad reflex(a) : f(a) \leq f(a)}{((f(a), y), reflex(a)) : (\Sigma w : (\Sigma u : \mathrm{N})(\Pi x : A)(f(x) \leq u \rightarrow B(x)))(f(a) \leq p(w))}\,\Sigma i$$

5 Hidden parameters

The conditions of use are formalized by a context which consists in a declaration of four parameters. Such an introduction of parameters seems to bring our solution close to very old analyses. A recurrent idea since the antiquity is that *to be small* is not a monadic predicate but a dyadic one with a hidden argument: to be small is to be small relatively to somebody or something.

This is a particular case of the widespread opinion[5] which says that the application of observational predicates is determined by typical examples: *to be red* is to be red relatively to a set of exemplary red things. Of course, this approach cannot satisfy an anti-realist since it gives a mysterious and transcendantal role to these elected examplars. Moreover, in a more analytic point of view, it is clear that the predicate *to be exemplarily red* presents the same problems as the common observational predicate.

It could be suggested that my solution consists in replacing the paraphrase,

---

[5] In this discussion, I follow the lines of P. Engel, [4].

to be small ≡ to be small *relatively to* an exemplary object

by the paraphrase,

to be small ≡ to be small *relatively to* the contextual property B.

But this is misleading since the term *relatively to* has not the same meaning in the two sentences. In the first paraphrase the meaning is ordinal, *a is small* means that a (its representation $f(a)$ in the general case) is inferior to a pre-existing norm of smallness. In the second paraphrase, the meaning of *relatively to* is less precise, it is simply said that the definition of *to be small* depends on a contextual property. In fact, the correct paraphrase is:

to be small ≡ to be small *enough in order to* satisfy the contextual property B.

Hence the predicate is truly monadic. There is no hidden argument, there are hidden parameters: the four conditions of use declared in the context.

6 Smaller than

The four conditions of use are required and manifested when simple judgements are combined with judgements of comparison in elementary reasonnigs like: John is small, Paul is smaller than John, hence Paul is small.

Clearly, a judgment of comparison introduces an implicit scale. The point is that we do not need extra assumptions to formalize it. We put the formation rule:

$$\frac{A : \mathsf{Set}\ \ B : (A)\mathsf{Prop}\ \ f : A \to \mathsf{N}\ \ c : (\Sigma u : A)(\Pi x : A)(f(x) \leq u \to B(x))}{\begin{array}{l} a\ \textit{is smaller than}\ b : \mathsf{Prop} \\ a\ \textit{is smaller than}\ b = f(a) \leq f(b) : \mathsf{Prop}\end{array}}$$

Notice that the formula uses only the representation function f, but the whole context is required since the function is contextually dependent.

In such a context, the deduction

$$\frac{\begin{array}{l} b\ \textit{is small} \\ a\ \textit{is smaller than}\ b\end{array}}{a\ \textit{is small}}$$

can be performed. The assumption y : b *is small* gives $q(y) : f(b) \leq p(p(y))$ and $p(y) : (\Sigma u : \mathsf{N})(f(x) \leq u \to B(x))$ by (Σ-e). Then we apply a transivity assumption,

$$trans : f(a) \leq f(b) \to (f(b) \leq p(p(y)) \to f(a) \leq p(p(y)))$$

to the assumption z : a *is smaller than* b and to $q(y)$ in order to obtain:

$$Ap(Ap(trans, z), q(y)) : f(a) \leq p(p(y)).$$

Hence we can introduce by (Σ-i) the term:

$$(p(y), Ap(Ap(trans, z), q(y))) : (\Sigma w : (\Sigma u : \mathsf{N})(f(x) \leq u \to B(x)))(f(a) \leq p(w))$$

which proves that a *is small.*

7 Back to the sorit

I only consider Wang's paradox:

$$\frac{\begin{array}{l}0 \text{ is small}\\ \text{If } n \text{ is small, } n+1 \text{ is small}\end{array}}{\text{Every integer is small}}$$

Three reasons legitimate this restriction:

1. a general solution for the *to be small* case follows the same lines since the construction of the corresponding sorits involves explicitely a representation function;
2. moreover these sorits, which should motivate such an extension, appear as unnatural and theoretical constructs;
3. the case of the heap-like sorits deserve a specific analysis since the questions involved seem to be more related to another problem: the problem of mass nouns.

7.1 The induction

The canonical proof associated to the sorit is a proof by induction. With the formalization proposed, the induction step is:

$$\text{(I)}\quad \begin{array}{c} y : (\Sigma v : (\Sigma u : \mathsf{N})(\Pi x : \mathsf{N})(x \leq u \rightarrow B(x)))(a \leq p(v)) \\ \vdots \\ e(a,y) : (\Sigma v : (\Sigma u : \mathsf{N})(\Pi x : \mathsf{N})(x \leq u \rightarrow B(x)))(\mathsf{succ}(a) \leq p(v)) \end{array}$$

From the assumption we know (*cf.* 4.1, 4.3) that $p(p(y)) : \mathsf{N}$ is a bound of B (the proof term is $q(p(y)) : (\Pi x : \mathsf{N})(x \leq p(p(y)) \rightarrow B(x))$), and that $a \leq p(p(y))$. Therefore the only *logical* way to build the proof term $e(a, y)$, is to prove that $\mathsf{succ}(p(p(y))$ is a bound of B. Hence the induction step reduces to:

$$\text{(II)}\quad \begin{array}{c} q(p(y)) : (\Pi x : \mathsf{N})(x \leq p(p(y)) \rightarrow B(x)) \\ \vdots \\ e'(a,y) : (\Pi x : \mathsf{N})(x \leq \mathsf{succ}(p(p(y))) \rightarrow B(x)) \end{array}$$

Since $p(p(y)) : \mathsf{N}$ is a bound of B, $\mathsf{succ}(p(p(y)) : \mathsf{N}$ is a bound if and only if $\mathsf{succ}(p(p(y))$ satisfies B. Therefore we are led to prove:

$$\text{(III)}\quad \begin{array}{c} q(p(y)) : (\Pi x : \mathsf{N})(x \leq p(p(y)) \rightarrow B(x)) \\ \vdots \\ e''(a,y) : B(\mathsf{succ}(p(p(y)))) \end{array}$$

To summarize, in order to perform the induction step corresponding to the vague predicate, we have to perform an induction step corresponding to the contextual predicate B.

As a matter of fact, the different steps correspond to three equivalent propositions :

$$(\Pi a : \mathsf{N})(a \textit{ is small}) \leftrightarrow (\Pi a : \mathsf{N})(\Pi x : \mathsf{N})(x \leq a \rightarrow B(x)) \leftrightarrow (\Pi a : \mathsf{N})B(a).$$

These propositions make more explicit the conditions of truth, and particularly, the last one reveals why the induction step can't be generally performed. Consequently it gives the constructivist way to block the derivation of the paradox.

7.2 From a bound to a frontier

Nevertheless there is more to learn in these different inductions. The last form of the induction step:

$$\text{(III)} \quad \begin{array}{c} q(p(y)) : (\Pi x : \mathsf{N})(x \leq p(p(y)) \rightarrow B(x)) \\ \vdots \\ e''(a, y) : B(\mathsf{succ}(p(p(y)))) \end{array}$$

is generally impossible to perform, because it is contrary to the very idea of bound. In the idea of bound there is the idea of *frontier*, and this is the aspect which is crucial for this third induction, whereas it is minor in the conditions of use.

Let me precise the distinction between bound and frontier. The presupposition

$$v : (\Sigma u : \mathsf{N})(\Pi x : \mathsf{N})(x \leq u \rightarrow B(x)),$$

which appears in the conditions of use insists on the "downward closed" aspect in the idea of bound, it does not mention that some bounds are frontiers, *i.e* that a property holds before and not after.

When I use the predicate *to be small*, only the existence of bounds matters in the first sense. I don't need to know the best one (the upper bound, which exists since we deal with integers) which is a frontier. On the contrary, when performing the induction step, I consider any bound, hence I have to deal with the frontier. This is the fact that the third induction step reminds us.

Therefore we can say that the transition from the form (I) of the induction to the form (III) is parallel to a transition from an idea of bound as introduced in the conditions of use to an idea of bound as frontier. The significant point for our concern is that this process goes with the disappearance of graduality.

7.3 How graduality disappears

My claim is that the form (I) of the induction supports the common sense agreement to the graduality of vague predicates, whereas the form (III) does not.

To put it informally, the form (I) asks for bounds such that their successor is a bound (this is enough to guarantee the transition, if *a is small* then succ*(a) is small*). We can say in a provocative way that it is almost the case! The case of failure is the case stressed by the third form of the induction: the case of frontiers.

It is time now to gather all the elements dicussed so far, in order to draw a complete picture of this type theoretic approach to the sorit.

1. The common sense intuition that vague predicates support graduality is legitimate. The semantical representation based on the conditions of use, supports graduality in most cases.
2. The sorit is a pedagogical device that reveals the limits of graduality, in a logical context. That logical game suggests a proof by induction which forces us to give up the original semantical representation for an equivalent one which does not support graduality any more.
3. Contrary to the truth conditional analysis, I introduce a distinction between the *semantical representation* and the *logical behaviour*. The paradoxical aspect of the sorits is based on the confusion between these two dimensions. In the sorit, *to be small* and the contextual property B have the same logical behaviour since the conclusions $(\Pi a : \mathsf{N})(a\ is\ small)$ and $(\Pi a : \mathsf{N})B(a)$ are equivalent. Nevertheless the propositions *a is small* and $B(a)$ are not equivalent (*c.f.* 4.1).

8 Conclusion

This study has drawn some principles which should be fruitfully applied to many observational predicates.

1. The problem of vagueness is constituted by a truth-conditional *a priori*. Based on the conditions of use, the anti-realist approach to meaning reformulate the question in terms of graduality. The notion of graduality is not absolute, but relative to contextual forms of representation and to contextual "objective" properties.
2. The semantical representation of the predicates is deduced from the analysis of the conditions of use. This analysis must specify the knowledge required in order to use the predicate. Moreover this semantical representation must be distinguished from logically equivalent ones which do not have the same content (in terms of knowledge). The role of the sorits is to exemplify this distinction.

Type theory is a promising framework in order to extend the research to many problems concerning graduality. For example, heap-like sorits can be analyzed as enonciations which create (implicitely) inductive types for the objects under predication. A reasonable approach consists in formalizing these types by some of the inductives types provided by TT, hence the corresponding canonical proofs will give the correct framework for a logical and semantical study of the sorit.

References

1. L. Carroll. What the tortoise said to achilles. *Mind*, 4, 1895.
2. M. Dummet. What is a theory of meaning ? In Evans and McDowell, editors, *Truth and Meaning*, pages 67–197. Oxford University Press, 1976.
3. M. Dummet. *Truth and Other Enigmas*. Duckworth, London, 1978.
4. P. Engel. *The norm of truth, an introduction to the philosophy of logic*. Harvester Wheatsheaf. Hemel Hempstead, 1991.
5. J. Goguen. The logic of inexacts concepts. *Synthese*, 1967.
6. P. Martin-Löf. *Intuitionistic type theory*. Bibliopolis, 1984.
7. P. Martin-Löf. On the meanings of the logical constants and the justifications of the logical laws. In *Atti degli incontri di logica mathematica*, volume 2, pages 203–281. Università di Siena, 1985.
8. A. Ranta. Propositions as games as types. *Synthese*, 76:377–395, 1988.
9. A. Ranta. Intuitionistic categorial grammar. *Linguistics and Philosophy*, 14:203–239, 1991.
10. A. Ranta. *Type-theoretical grammar*. Clarendon, Oxford, 1994.
11. S. Shapiro. Logic, ontology, mathematical practice. *Synthese*, 79:13–50, 1989.
12. G. Sundholm. Proof theory and meaning. In D. Gabbay and F. Guenthner, editors, *Handbook of Philosophical Logic*, volume 3. D. Reidel, 1986.
13. G. Sundholm. Constructive generalized quantifiers. *Synthese*, 79:1–12, 1989.
14. G. Sundholm. Proof-theoretical semantics and fregean identity criteria for propositions. *The Monist*, 77(3):294–314, 1994.

A Natural Language Explanation for Formal Proofs

Yann Coscoy*

INRIA-Sophia-Antipolis

Introduction

We study formal proofs conceived to be checked automatically. These proofs are rarely used. We think that it is partly due to the fact that it is very difficult for a human to understand the connection between what he considers a mathematical proof and its formal representation. We are interested in automatically producing text explaining these formal representations. We have chosen to produce text in natural language using the traditional vocabulary of mathematics.

More precisely, we work on a formalism called *Calculus of Inductive Constructions*, which uses a functional representation of proofs. The objective of this formalism is to allow an automatic proof checking by a simple machine. Each aspect, simplicity and automation, imposes its own specificity to the proof representation. On the one hand, the proofs contain a lot of trivialities that would be considered useless by human readers. On the other hand, some information that would be very useful to these same human readers are omitted.

In previous work [3], we have developed a machine that translates proofs of the *Calculus of Inductive Constructions* into natural language. The text produced by this machine has the same structure as the formal proof. These texts are not satisfactory. They are in general too verbose, and sometimes they omit important information. In this article, we will present an improvement of this translation based on a more precise choice of the information we include in the text.

1 A brief survey of *Calculus of Constructions*

The *Calculus of Inductive Constructions* is a formalism used to represent proofs. It is an extension of *Calculus of Constructions*, which belongs itself to a family of functional formalisms called λ-calculi. We will briefly present the pure λ-calculus, then we will introduce the λ-calculus with dependent types, and then the *Calculus of Constructions*. (We will present the *Calculus of Inductive Constructions* later in section 4.)

* Supported by *Direction de la Recherche et de la Technologie, (DGA France)*

1.1 Pure λ-calculus

The terms of λ-calculus are called "λ-terms" or "λ-expressions". They are defined by the grammar:

$$t \ := \ v \mid c \mid (t\ t) \mid \lambda v.\, t$$

The "v" and "c" represent variables and constants. They are simply denoted by names. The "$(t\ t)$" represents applications. The term $(F\ A)$ denotes the application of the function F to an argument A. This corresponds to the more traditional notation $F(A)$. The "$\lambda v.\, t$" represents functions definitions. The term $\lambda x.\, T$ represents the function that maps the variable x to the term T. In mathematical texts, the more traditional notation is $x \mapsto T[x]$. The square brackets are used to make clear that T can depend on x. In λ-calculus this dependency is implicit.

There exist three rewriting rules which can be used to transform a λ-term into an equivalent λ-term.

$$(\alpha\text{-conversion})\ \Gamma \vdash \lambda x.\, M \longmapsto \lambda y.\, M\{x/y\} \ \texttt{if not}\ y \in Free(M)$$

$$(\beta\text{-reduction})\ \Gamma \vdash (\lambda x.\, M\ N) \longmapsto M\{x/N\}$$

$$(\delta\text{-reduction})\ \Gamma \vdash c \longmapsto D \ \texttt{if}\ c{:}= D \in \Gamma$$

The α-conversion corresponds to the renaming of local variables. The β-reduction specify how to compute the results of functions. The notation $M\{x/N\}$ means that the variable x must be substituted by the argument N within the body M of the function. The δ-reduction means that a constant can be substituted by its definition.

If the function F is defined by $F{:}= \lambda x.\, (x + a)$, then, $(F\ 3)$ can be δ-reduced in $(\lambda x.\, (x + a)\ 3)$. And, this expression can be α-converted in $(\lambda y.\, (y + a)\ 3)$ or β-reduced in $3 + a$.

This system, called pure λ-calculus, gives very few guarantees about the correctness of the defined functions. To avoid this disadvantage, several extensions of this formalism attribute *types* to λ-expressions. The *Calculus of Constructions* is one of these extensions. It is a λ-calculus with "dependent" types.

1.2 λ-calculus with dependent types

To give a mathematical meaning to λ-expressions, a *type* is attributed to each of them. The notation $M{:}T$ is used to express "M has type T". Types can be constructed with other types or other expressions. We can for example define a type Nat to designate natural numbers. So, we can for any natural n define the type $(list\ Nat\ n)$ to designate the lists of length n of natural numbers.

Consider now the function which maps a natural n to the list of length $2 * n$ that contains a repetition of 0. The domain of the function is Nat and its range is $(list\ Nat\ (2 * n))$ where n is the argument of the function. The type of this function is a *dependent* type because the range depends of the effective argument of the function. We denote the type of this function $\forall n{:}\, Nat.\, (list\ Nat\ (2 * n))$.

Consider now another function on naturals and lists that maps the natural n to the list of length 3 that contains three times n. This list has formally type $\forall n\colon Nat.(list\ Nat\ 3)$. In this case, the range $(list\ Nat\ 3)$ does not depend on the argument n. We can use a simpler notation $Nat \rightarrow (list\ Nat\ 3)$.

1.3 Proof representation

Some types, e.g., Nat or $(list\ Nat\ n)$, represent sets, but others represent propositions. To distinguish them, the *Calculus of Constructions* defines two special symbols, Set and $Prop$, called *sorts*. The types which represent sets are themselves of type Set whereas the types which represent propositions are themselves of type $Prop$.

The Curry-Howard isomorphism defines a direct correspondence between types and propositions. The symbols "∀" and "→" of types actually correspond to the symbols "∀" and "⇒" of logic. This correspondence is such that if the type T represents a proposition, then any λ- term of type T represents a proof of this proposition. Checking that the λ-term follows the typing rules guarantees that the proof is valid.

2 Background

The system of translation from λ-terms into natural language presented in this section has been described in a earlier publication. A more complete description can be found in [3].

2.1 The main idea of translation

We use the word "proof" to designate a λ-term whose type is a proposition. Each proof is constructed by an operator of λ-calculus with some subterms. The subterms whose type is a proposition are also proofs. This construction of a proof with subterms can be considered as an elementary reasoning step. We determine the intuitive meaning of each of these steps studying the types of the subexpressions. Then, we produce a sentence expressing this step. This sentence contains the type of the constructed λ-term because this type represents the proposition that is proved by this part of the proof. All these sentences are grouped together in a text whose structure is precisely the structure of the λ-term.

2.2 A little development on relations

Here, we introduce the formal development on relations that we use to illustrate this article. A relation is a binary predicate on a set. This is formally defined as a function that takes as arguments a set and two elements of this set and then gives a proposition. So, we define the constant *Rel* by:

$$Rel\colon= \forall U\colon Set.\, U \rightarrow U \rightarrow Prop$$

The inverse of a relation can be formally defined with a function Inv that takes as argument a set and a relation on this set and then gives another relation. This function should have the type $\forall U\colon Set.\,(Rel\ U) \to (Rel\ U)$. It is defined by:

$$Inv := \lambda U\colon Set.\,\lambda R\colon (Rel\ U).\,\lambda x, y\colon U.\,(R\ y\ x)$$

Transitivity is a predicate on relations. It can be defined by a function $Trans$ that takes as arguments a set, a relation on this set, and then gives a proposition. This function has type $\forall U\colon Set.\,(Rel\ U) \to Prop$. Its definition is:

$$Trans := \lambda U\colon Set.\,\lambda R\colon (Rel\ U).\,\forall x, y, z\colon U.\,(R\ x\ y) \Rightarrow (R\ y\ z) \Rightarrow (R\ x\ z)$$

We can notice that the proposition $(R\ x\ y) \Rightarrow (R\ y\ z) \Rightarrow (R\ x\ z)$ that could be understood as $(R\ x\ y) \Rightarrow ((R\ y\ z) \Rightarrow (R\ x\ z))$ is logically equivalent to the proposition $((R\ x\ y) \wedge (R\ y\ z)) \Rightarrow (R\ x\ z)$. It is a curryfied form that is more natural in λ-calculus.

Next, we want to prove that if a relation is transitive, then its inverse relation is also transitive. This assertion is formally expressed by:

$$\forall U\colon Set.\,\forall R\colon (Rel\ U).\,(Trans\ U\ R) \Rightarrow (Trans\ U\ (Inv\ U\ R))$$

The proof that we have chosen starts by introducing an arbitrary set U and a transitive relation R. It continues by introducing three elements x, y, and z such that $(Inv\ U\ R\ x\ y)$ and $(Inv\ U\ R\ y\ z)$. Then it uses the hypothesis of transitivity and the definition of Inv to prove $(Inv\ U\ R\ x\ z)$. The λ-term that formally represents this proof is:

$$\begin{array}{l} \lambda U\colon Set.\,\lambda R\colon (Rel\ U).\,\lambda trans\colon (Trans\ U\ R). \\ \quad \lambda x, y, z\colon U.\,\lambda h_1\colon (Inv\ U\ R\ x\ y).\,\lambda h_2\colon (Inv\ U\ R\ y\ z). \\ \qquad (trans\ z\ y\ x\ h_2\ h_1) \end{array}$$

2.3 A first translation

The λ-abstractions correspond to proofs of propositions with universal quantifiers. The term $\lambda x\colon T.\,M$ (with $M\colon P$ and $P\colon Prop$) is a proof, in three steps, of $\forall x\colon T.\,P$. The proof starts by introducing an arbitrary variable x of type T. It continues with the proof M of P with this variable. Then it concludes by generalizing the proposition P to any variable x. It is always possible to translate one of these proofs by:

Consider an arbitrary x of type T. «M» We have proven $\forall x\colon T.\,P$.

Such a translation is always correct, but it is too general. It expresses correctly the structure of the proof, but it does not express its intuitive nature. The conciseness of the formalism allows an overloading of λ-abstractions, this means that they are used to introduce terms of several natures. We determine the nature of the variable x by studying its type T, then we can generate an appropriate sentence.

If T is one of the sorts *Prop* or *Set*, then x represents respectively a proposition or a set. When T is not a sort, we study its type. If T has type *Prop*, it is itself a proposition, and the λ-abstraction corresponds to the introduction of a hypothesis. But if T has type *Set*, the λ-abstraction corresponds to the introduction of an arbitrary element x of set T. We can translate the beginning of our little example with these specific sentences:

Consider an arbitrary set U.
  Consider an arbitrary R of type $(Rel\ U)$.
    Assume $(Trans\ U\ R)$ $(trans)$.
      Consider an arbitrary element x of U.
        Consider an arbitrary element y of U.
          Consider an arbitrary element z of U.
            Assume $(Inv\ U\ R\ x\ y)$ (h_1).
              Assume $(Inv\ U\ R\ y\ z)$ (h_2).
                «$(trans\ z\ y\ x\ h_2\ h_1)\colon(R\ z\ x)$»
              We have proven $(Inv\ U\ R\ y\ z) \Rightarrow (R\ z\ x)$.
            We have proven $(Inv\ U\ R\ x\ y) \Rightarrow (Inv\ U\ R\ y\ z) \Rightarrow (R\ z\ x)$.
          We have proven $\forall z\colon U.\,(Inv\ U\ R\ x\ y) \Rightarrow (Inv\ U\ R\ y\ z) \Rightarrow (R\ z\ x)$.
        We have proven $\forall y,z\colon U.\,(Inv\ U\ R\ x\ y) \Rightarrow (Inv\ U\ R\ y\ z) \Rightarrow (R\ z\ x)$.
      We have proven $\forall x,y,z\colon U.\,(Inv\ U\ R\ x\ y) \Rightarrow (Inv\ U\ R\ y\ z) \Rightarrow (R\ z\ x)$.
    We have proven $(Trans\ U\ R) \Rightarrow \forall x,y,z\colon U.\ \cdots$.
  We have proven $\forall R\colon(Rel\ U).\,(Trans\ U\ R) \Rightarrow \forall x,y,z\colon U.\ \cdots$.
We have proven $\forall U\colon Set.\,\forall R\colon(Rel\ U).\,(Trans\ U\ R) \Rightarrow \forall x,y,z\colon U.\ \cdots$.

We now translate the central part of the proof *i.e.* $(trans\ z\ y\ x\ h_2\ h_1)$. We also proceed by type analysis, we can determine that this application corresponds to the mathematical application of hypothesis *trans* to two subproofs. These two subproofs are the variables h_2 and h_1 that represent hypotheses. We can complete the text by:

* With hypothesis *trans* we have $(Trans\ U\ R)$.
* With hypothesis h_2 we have $(Inv\ U\ R\ y\ z)$.
* With hypothesis h_1 we have $(Inv\ U\ R\ x\ y)$.
Applying the first result to the two others we get $(R\ z\ x)$.

2.4 A shorter translation

The text that we obtain by grouping these two parts is obviously too long and too repetitive. To avoid this, we use more complex sentences that express several proof steps at a time. For λ-abstractions, we use a sentence that introduces simultaneously several variables. For applications, we take advantage of the fact that all subproofs are hypotheses to produce one single sentence. The text that we finally get is:

Theorem: *Trans_R_imp_Trans_Inv_R.*
Statement: $\forall U{:}\,Set.\forall R{:}\,(Rel\ U).(Trans\ U\ R) \Rightarrow (Trans\ U\ (Inv\ U\ R))$.
Proof:
Consider a set U and a R of type $(Rel\ U)$ such that
$(Trans\ U\ R)$ $(trans)$; then consider three elements x, y and z of U such that $(Inv\ U\ R\ x\ y)$ (h_1) and $(Inv\ U\ R\ y\ z)$ (h_2).
Applying hypothesis *trans* to hypotheses h_2 and h_1 we get $(R\ z\ x)$.
Q.E.D.

However, we are not satisfied with this text, some information is lacking. For example, to understand this proof, it is necessary to known that the final result $(R\ z\ x)$ is equivalent to $(Inv\ U\ R\ x\ z)$. This equivalence is not expressed in the text because it is not in the λ-term. However, it can be found by studying the type expressions of the subproofs.

3 The types expressions

The type expressions we include in the text are to allow human readers to understand the development of the proof. We have not yet specified how these expressions are obtained. There exist several classical algorithms that can compute then. But, while in the *Calculus of Constructions* a λ-term has only one type, this type can be represented by different expressions. The expression computed depends on the algorithm used. All these expressions are formally equivalent, but we want to obtain the one which is easiest to understand for human readers.

3.1 Motivation for computing types

We actually do not compute one but two type expressions for each subproof. The first expression, called the *expected* type, corresponds to the proposition this subproof has to prove. This expression does not depend on the subproof itself but only on its location within the global proof. The second expression computed for a subproof is called the *constraint* type. This expression depends of the structure of the subproof. It indicates the direction the proof will follow. When the proof is correct, these two expressions are formally equivalent. This equivalence can be checked automatically, but this in no way implies that it is easy to understand for human readers.

3.2 The algorithm

The main algorithm:

The algorithm consists on a recursive top-down traversal of the λ-term that annotates each subproof with its two type expressions T_e and T_c. The algorithm has to be initialized with the expected type of the proof we want to annotate. When the proof concerns a theorem, this type is simply the statement of the theorem. The algorithm then computes the constraint type of the proof and the expected type of its subproofs. At this point it can recursively annotate the subproofs. The judgment $\Gamma, T_e \vdash M \leadsto M_{T_c}^{T_e}$ must be understood as "In an environment Γ, for an expected type T_e, the proof M must be the annotated with T_e and T_c". The following inference rules determine the way in which these annotations are computed.

$$\text{(VAR)}\ \Gamma, T_e \vdash v \leadsto v_{T_c}^{T_e}\ \texttt{if}\ (v{:}\,T_c) \in \Gamma$$

$$\text{(CONST)}\ \Gamma, T_e \vdash c \leadsto c_{T_c}^{T_e}\ \texttt{if}\ (c{:}\,T_c) \in \Gamma$$

$$\text{(LAMBDA)}\ \frac{\Gamma \vdash T_e \rhd \forall x{:}\,T_2.\,T_3 \qquad (x{:}\,T_1) + \Gamma, T_3 \vdash M \leadsto M'}{\Gamma, T_e \vdash (\lambda x{:}\,T_1.\,M) \leadsto (\lambda x{:}\,T_1.\,M')_{\forall x:T_2.\,T_3}^{T_e}}$$

$$\text{(APP1)}\ \frac{\begin{array}{c}\Gamma \vdash M{:}\,T_1 \qquad \Gamma \vdash T_1 \rhd \forall x{:}\,T_2.\,T_3 \\ \Gamma, \forall x{:}\,T_2.\,T_3 \vdash M \leadsto M' \qquad \Gamma, T_2 \vdash N \leadsto N'\end{array}}{\Gamma, T_e \vdash (M\ N) \leadsto (M'\ N')_{T_3\{x/N\}}^{T_e}}\ \texttt{if}\ \Gamma \vdash T_2{:}\,Prop$$

$$\text{(APP2)}\ \frac{\Gamma \vdash M{:}\,T_1 \qquad \Gamma \vdash T_1 \rhd \forall x{:}\,T_2.\,T_3 \qquad \Gamma, \forall x{:}\,T_2.\,T_3 \vdash M \leadsto M'}{\Gamma, T_e \vdash (M\ N) \leadsto (M'\ N)_{T_3\{x/N\}}^{T_e}}\ \texttt{if not}\ \Gamma \vdash T_2{:}\,Prop$$

The rule APP2 corresponds to the case where the type of N is not a proposition. In this case, N is not a proof and we do not compute annotations for it. The algorithm uses two auxiliary algorithms. The types inference algorithm computes the types of the applications' heads. The weak head normal-form algorithm is used when a type must be put in the form $\forall x{:}\,T_1.\,T_2$.

A simple type inference algorithm:

We have chosen the simplest type inference algorithm because it does not reduce the constants. This way, the type we obtain is quite abstract. The judgment $\Gamma \vdash M{:}\,T$ must be understood as "In the context Γ, the term M has type T".

$$\text{(VAR)}\ \Gamma \vdash v{:}\,T\ \texttt{if}\ (v{:}\,T) \in \Gamma$$

$$\text{(CONST)}\ \Gamma \vdash c{:}\,T\ \texttt{if}\ (c{:}\,T) \in \Gamma$$

$$\text{(APP)}\ \frac{\Gamma \vdash M{:}\,T_1 \qquad \Gamma \vdash T_1 \rhd \forall x{:}\,T_2.\,T_3}{\Gamma \vdash (M\ N){:}\,T_3\{x/M\}}$$

$$\text{(LAMBDA)}\ \frac{(x{:}\,T_1) + \Gamma \vdash M{:}\,T_2}{\Gamma \vdash (\lambda x{:}\,T_1.\,M){:}\,\forall x{:}\,T_1.\,T_2}$$

$$\text{(PROD)}\ \frac{(x{:}\,T_1) + \Gamma \vdash T_2{:}\,s}{\Gamma \vdash (\forall x{:}\,T_1.\,T_2){:}\,s}$$

The calculus of weak head normal-form:

The weak head normal form of an expression has the property that if a type is the type of a λ-abstraction or the type of the head of an application, its weak head normal-form has the form $\forall x{:}T_1.T_2$. We have chosen this algorithm because it reduces a minimum number of constants and we want to keep the type expressions as abstract as possible. The algorithm we present is simpler than the classical one. It is because we only use it to reduce types into the form $\forall x{:}T_1.T_2$.

The judgment $\Gamma \vdash T_1 \rhd T_2$ should be understood as "In a context Γ, type T_1 has the weak head normal-form T_2.

$$\text{(PROD)}\ \Gamma \vdash \forall x{:}T_1.T_2 \rhd \forall x{:}T_1.T_2$$

$$\text{(LAMBDA)}\ \Gamma \vdash \lambda x{:}T_1.T_2 \rhd \lambda x{:}T_1.T_2$$

$$\text{(CONST)}\ \frac{\Gamma \vdash D \rhd M}{\Gamma \vdash c \rhd M}\quad \texttt{if } (c{:=}\,D) \in \Gamma$$

$$\text{(BETA)}\ \frac{\Gamma \vdash M\{x/N\} \rhd M'}{\Gamma \vdash (\lambda x{:}T.M\ N) \rhd M'}$$

$$\text{(APP)}\ \frac{\Gamma \vdash M \rhd M' \quad \Gamma \vdash (M'\ N) \rhd M_1}{\Gamma \vdash (M\ N) \rhd M_1}\quad \texttt{if not } M = \lambda x{:}T.M_2$$

Dealing with α-conversion:
With these algorithms, it is possible to apparently get an incoherence between the names of the variables used in types and the names used in λ-terms. For example, the type of the proof $\lambda x{:}T.M$ can be $\forall a{:}T.P$. This is not a formal incoherence but it can lead to some dislinking text. We prefer to use in the types the same names that are in the proof. So, if the computed type for proof $\lambda x_1{:}T_1.\cdots\lambda x_n{:}T_n.M$ is $\forall a_1{:}T'_1.\cdots\forall a_n{:}T'_n.T$, we rename it in $\forall x_1{:}T'_1.\cdots\forall x_n{:}T'_n.T$.

3.3 The complete translation

We now have a proof where each subproof is annotated by two type expressions. We can use the sentences of the previous translation briefly described in section 2. We only have to adapt them when the expected and constraint types differ. In this case, we use a sentence of the form "We have proven T_c which is equivalent to T_e." The new translation in its complete form is:

Consider a set U.
  Consider a R of type $(Rel\ U)$.
    Assume $(Trans\ U\ R)$ $(trans)$.
      Consider an element x of U.
        Consider an element y of U.
          Consider an element z of U.
            Assume $(Inv\ U\ R\ x\ y)$ (h_1).
              Assume $(Inv\ U\ R\ y\ z)$ (h_2).
                * With hypothesis $trans$ **we have** $(Trans\ U\ R)$ **which is equivalent to** $\forall x, y, z{:}\, U. (R\ x\ y) \Rightarrow \cdots$.
                * With hypothesis h_2 **we have** $(Inv\ U\ R\ y\ z)$ **which is equivalent to** $(R\ z\ y)$.
                * With hypothesis h_1 **we have** $(Inv\ U\ R\ x\ y)$ **which is equivalent to** $(R\ y\ x)$.
                Applying the first result to the two others **we get** $(R\ z\ x)$ **which is equivalent to** $(Inv\ U\ R\ x\ z)$.
              We have proven $(Inv\ U\ R\ y\ z) \Rightarrow (Inv\ U\ R\ x\ z)$.
            We have proven $(Inv\ U\ R\ x\ y) \Rightarrow (Inv\ U\ R\ y\ z) \Rightarrow (Inv\ U\ R\ x\ z)$.
          We have proven $\forall z{:}\, U. (Inv\ U\ R\ x\ y) \Rightarrow \cdots$.
        We have proven $\forall y, z{:}\, U. (Inv\ U\ R\ x\ y) \Rightarrow \cdots$.
      We have proven $\forall x, y, z{:}\, U. (Inv\ U\ R\ x\ y) \Rightarrow \cdots$ **which is equivalent to** $(Trans\ U\ (Inv\ U\ R))$.
    We have proven $(Trans\ U\ R) \Rightarrow (Trans\ U\ (Inv\ U\ R))$.
  We have proven $\forall R{:}\, (Rel\ U). (Trans\ U\ R) \Rightarrow (Trans\ U\ (Inv\ U\ R))$.
We have proven $\forall U{:}\, Set. \forall R{:}\, (Rel\ U). (Trans\ U\ R) \Rightarrow (Trans\ U\ (Inv\ U\ R))$.

This text is now complete. It should be compared with the text presented in section 2.3. All the information that could be useful to the reader are exposed. For example the equivalence between $(R\ z\ x)$ and $(Inv\ U\ R\ x\ z)$ was lacking in the first text. It is now expressed in the sentence "$\cdots$ **we get** $(R\ z\ x)$ **which is equivalent to** $(Inv\ U\ R\ x\ z)$".

3.4 More complex sentences

Again, the text we obtain is excessively verbose. As for the previous translation, we want to use more complex sentences. We also want to avoid giving too many type expressions. Nevertheless, we must be sure to keep all the useful information in the text.

λ-abstractions

It is not useful to translate the λ-abstractions one by one. It is often possible to introduce several variables in a single sentence. However, we cannot do this in every case because this contraction makes the types of intermediate λ-abstractions disappear. We do not describe this contraction directly on the text but on the λ-term with a conditional rewriting rule. We denote a multiple λ-abstraction with the notation $\lambda x_1{:}T_1; x_2{:}T_2. M$.

$$\left(\lambda x_1 \colon T_1; \cdots x_i \colon T_i . \, (\lambda x_{i+1} \colon T_{i+1}; \cdots x_{i+j} \colon T_{i+j} . \, M)^{T'_e}_{T'_c}\right)^{T_e}_{T_c}$$
$$\downarrow \; if \; T'_e = T'_c$$
$$(\lambda x_1 \colon T_1; \cdots x_{i+j} \colon T_{i+j} . \, M)^{T_e}_{T_c}$$

This rule makes the type annotations T'_e and T'_c disappear. Nevertheless, by construction, we know how to easily derive T'_e from T_c. When T_c remains present, the disappearance of T'_e (and of T'_c if it is equal to T'_e) does not deprive the reader of information.

Applications

The application of a function to several arguments is formally decomposed into several applications each with a single argument. But it is often useful to consider this set of applications as a single application. This is put in concrete form with the usual rule that allows to denote the applications $((f \; a_1) \; a_2)$ with the notation $(f \; a_1 \; a_2)$. As with λ-abstractions, this rule makes the type of the intermediate application disappear. So, we use a conditional rewriting rule.

$$\left((M \; a_1 \cdots a_i)^{T'_e}_{T'_c} \; a_{i+1} \cdots a_{i+j}\right)^{T_e}_{T_c}$$
$$\downarrow \; if \; T'_e = T'_c$$
$$(M \; a_1 \cdots a_{i+j})^{T_e}_{T_c}$$

By construction, T_c is the specialization of T'_e to the arguments $a_{i+1} \cdots a_{i+j}$. With this condition, it is not useful for a human reader, to keep T'_e (or T'_c if it is equal to T'_e) when T_c remains present in the text.

Variables and constants

When all the subproofs of an application are variables or constants, it is more natural to produce a unique sentence which translates at the same time the application and all of its subproofs. We use this rule with the condition that, for each subproof, the expected type must be equal to the constraint type. Another rule, used to reduce the verbosity of the text, is to omit the constraint type of variables or constants because these types are immediately accessible.

Our example

The text after the contractions is:

> **Theorem:** $Trans\_R\_imp\_Trans\_Inv\_R$.
> **Statement:** $\forall U{:}\,Set.\forall R{:}\,(Rel\ U).(Trans\ U\ R) \Rightarrow (Trans\ U\ (Inv\ U\ R))$.
> **Proof:**
> Consider a set U and a R of type $(Rel\ U)$ such that $(Trans\ U\ R)$ $(trans)$.
> Consider three elements x, y and z of U such that $(Inv\ U\ R\ x\ y)$ (h_1) and $(Inv\ U\ R\ y\ z)$ (h_2).
> * With hypothesis $trans$ we get $\forall x, y, z{:}\,U.(R\ x\ y) \Rightarrow (R\ y\ z) \Rightarrow (R\ x\ z)$
> * With hypothesis h_2 we get $(R\ z\ y)$.
> * With hypothesis h_1 we get $(R\ y\ x)$.
> Applying the first result to the two others we get $(R\ z\ x)$ which is equivalent to $(Inv\ U\ R\ x\ z)$.
> We have proven $\forall x, y, z{:}\,U.(Inv\ U\ R\ x\ y) \Rightarrow (Inv\ U\ R\ y\ z) \Rightarrow (Inv\ U\ R\ x\ z)$ which is equivalent to $(Trans\ U\ (Inv\ U\ R))$.
> **Q.E.D.**

This text should be compared with the text obtained in section 2.4. This text represents the totality of the proof. It is very precisee. A human reader doesn't need so many details. Next, we look into suppressing information that the human reader deems useless.

3.5 The *well-known* simple definitions

To obtain shorter text, we want to suppress some information. This information will be type information. More precisely it will be information on equivalence between expected and constraint types.
We want allow the rules of contraction of λ-terms defined in section 3.4 to permit more type annotations to disappear. To do this, we change the conditions $T'_e = T'_c$ of these rules by conditions $T'_e \approx T'_c$. This new notation means that T'_e and T'_c does not need to be equal but simply *close*.

It is simply a restriction of the definition of equivalence. To determine if two propositions are equivalent, we compute their normal form. This normal form is obtained by a complete β-reduction (by computing the results of all applications of functions) and by a complete δ-reduction (by substituting all constants by they definitions). Then we check if both normal forms are α-convertible (equal after an adequate renaming of binded variables).

The definition of closeness is parameterized by a list of constants. This list contains the constants that the reader considers as *well-known*. To determine if two expressions are *close*, we compute some weak normal form. This weak normal form is obtained by a complete β-reduction and a partial δ-reduction. We reduce only the *well-known* constants. Then we also check if the two weak normal forms are α-convertible. We have defined an initial list of well-known constants, but the reader can modify this list to adapt the translation to his knowledge.

In our example, if the reader adds the constant *Trans* to this list, he will obtain a shorter text. This text will not explain the proof steps concerning definition of *Trans*. However, he will continue to explain the ones concerning definition of *Inv*:

Theorem: *Trans_R_imp_Trans_Inv_R.*
Statement: $\forall U{:}\, Set.\, \forall R{:}\, (Rel\ U).\, (Trans\ U\ R) \Rightarrow (Trans\ U\ (Inv\ U\ R))$.
Proof:
Consider a set U and a R of type $(Rel\ U)$ such that $(Trans\ U\ R)$ $(trans)$; and three elements x, y and z of U such that $(Inv\ U\ R\ x\ y)$ (h_1) and $(Inv\ U\ R\ y\ z)$ (h_2).
* With hypothesis h_2 we get $(R\ z\ y)$.
* With hypothesis h_1 we get $(R\ y\ x)$.
Applying hypothesis *trans* to these two results we get $(R\ z\ x)$ which is equivalent to $(Inv\ U\ R\ x\ z)$.
Q.E.D.

4 The *inductive* extension of *Calculus of Constructions*

In this section, we describe briefly the extension of the *Calculus of Constructions* known as the *Calculus of Inductive Constructions*. Then, we present the adaptation of our translation system to this new formalism.

4.1 Inductive definitions

Inductive definitions have been added to the *Calculus of Constructions* to increase its expressivity. They allow one to define types by constructors and allow to introduce induction. For example, in the *Calculus of Inductive Constructions* the disjunction is not a primitive of the language. It is inductively defined for any arbitrary propositions A and B. The notation used to define it in the *Coq* system is:

$$\begin{aligned}&\text{Inductive } or\ [A, B{:}\, Prop] : Prop :=\\ &\quad or_{intro}l{:}\, A \Rightarrow (or\ A\ B)\\ &\quad |\ or_{intro}r{:}\, B \Rightarrow (or\ A\ B).\end{aligned}$$

This definition defines an inductive constant $or{:}\, Prop \to Prop \to Prop$ used to build propositions. It also defines two constructors:
$or_{intro}l{:}\, \forall A, B{:}\, Prop.\, A \Rightarrow (A \vee B)$ and $or_{intro}r{:}\, \forall A, B{:}\, Prop.\, B \Rightarrow (A \vee B)$, which allow one to *introduce* this constant. It also defines an *elimination* rule of this constant. All the uses of an inductive definition are made by an *introduction* with one of its constructors, or by an *elimination* with the `Elim` operator. They are always explicit in the λ-term.

4.2 Adaptation of the translation

The sentences used for introducing an inductive constant are very closed to the ones used for applying a hypothesis. They have the form:

$$(or_{intro}l\ A\ B\ M) \leadsto \boxed{\begin{array}{l} *\ \text{«}M\text{»}\ \text{we have } A. \\ \text{So, with constructor } or_{intro}l \text{ we have } A \vee B. \end{array}}$$

For the elimination of inductive constants we defined other sentences that are used to bring out the structure of a proof by cases. The elimination of a disjunction will give the text:

$$\begin{array}{l} < P > \texttt{Elim}\ M\ \texttt{with} \\ \quad \lambda h\colon A.\, M_A \\ \quad \lambda h\colon B.\, M_B \\ \quad \textbf{end} \end{array} \leadsto \boxed{\begin{array}{l} \text{«}M\colon A \vee B\text{»} \\ \text{So by definition of } or \text{ we have two cases :} \\ \text{Case 1.:} \\ \qquad \text{We have } A\ (h_1). \\ \qquad\quad \text{«}M_A\text{»} \\ \text{Case 2.:} \\ \qquad \text{We have } B\ (h_1). \\ \qquad\quad \text{«}M_B\text{»} \\ \text{So we have proven } P. \end{array}}$$

We have also defined some sentences for the inductive constants with either no constructors or one constructor.

4.3 Adaptation of type calculus

Concerning the algorithm that computes type annotations, the eliminations behave in a way similar to applications. To compute the expected types of the arguments of an application, it is necessary to compute a type expression of the application's head and reduce it to a weak head normal-form. To compute the expected types of an elimination's subproofs, it is necessary to compute a type expression of the eliminated term and reduce it to a weak normal form.

The constructors have reactions very similar to the constants. We can extend the algorithms defined in section 3.2, by adding some inference rules.

The main algorithm:

$$\text{(ELIM1)}\ \frac{\begin{array}{c} \Gamma \vdash M\colon T_1 \qquad \Gamma \vdash T_1 \triangleright T_2 \qquad \Gamma, T_2 \vdash M \leadsto M' \\ \Gamma, F(\Gamma, T_2, T_c, i) \vdash N_i \leadsto N_i' \ \ \texttt{for}\ i \in \{1 \cdots n\} \end{array}}{\Gamma, T_e \vdash \left(\begin{array}{l} < T_c > \texttt{Elim}\ M\ \texttt{with} \\ \quad N_1 \cdots N_n \\ \ \textbf{end} \end{array}\right) \leadsto \left(\begin{array}{l} < T_c > \texttt{Elim}\ M'\ \texttt{with} \\ \quad N_1' \cdots N_n' \\ \ \textbf{end} \end{array}\right)_{T_c}^{T_e}}$$

$$\texttt{if}\ \Gamma \vdash T_2\colon Prop$$

$$\frac{\begin{array}{c}\Gamma \vdash M : T_1 \qquad \Gamma \vdash T_1 \rhd T_2 \\ \Gamma, F(\Gamma, T_2, T_c, i) \vdash N_i \rightsquigarrow N'_i \ \ \texttt{for}\ i \in \{1 \cdots n\}\end{array}}{(\text{ELIM2})\ \Gamma, T_e \vdash \left(\begin{array}{c} < T_c > \texttt{Elim}\ M\ \texttt{with} \\ N_1 \cdots N_n \\ \texttt{end} \end{array}\right) \rightsquigarrow \left(\begin{array}{c} < T_c > \texttt{Elim}\ M'\ \texttt{with} \\ N'_1 \cdots N'_n \\ \texttt{end} \end{array}\right)^{T_e}_{T_c}}$$

$$\texttt{if not}\ \Gamma \vdash T_2 : Prop$$

The rule *ELIM*2 corresponds to the case where M is not a proof. The notation $F(\Gamma, T_2, T_c, i)$ represents the function of the *Calculus of Inductive Constructions* that computes the type of ith case of an elimination depending on the type of the eliminated term and the constraint type of the elimination.

The inference type algorithm:

$$(\text{IND CONSTANT})\ \Gamma \vdash C : T\ \texttt{if}\ (C : T) \in \Gamma$$

$$(\text{IND CONSTRUCT})\ \Gamma \vdash C_{intro} i : T\ \texttt{if}\ (C_{intro} i : T) \in \Gamma$$

$$(\text{ELIM})\ \Gamma \vdash \begin{array}{c} < T > \texttt{Elim}\ M\ \texttt{with} \\ N_1 \cdots N_n \\ \texttt{end} \end{array} : T$$

The weak head normal form algorithm:

The weak head normal-form we compute for the expected type of eliminated terms are $(C\ a_1 \cdots a_p)$ where C is the inductive constant and where $a_1 \cdots a_p$ are its parameters.

$$\frac{\Gamma \vdash (N_i\ a_{p+1} \cdots\ a_m) \rhd M_1}{(\text{IOTA})\ \Gamma \vdash \left(\begin{array}{c} < T > \texttt{Elim}\ (C_{intro} i\ a_1 \cdots\ a_m)\ \texttt{with} \\ N_1 \cdots N_n \\ \texttt{end} \end{array}\right) \rhd M_1}$$

$$\texttt{if}\ \Gamma \vdash (C_{intro} i\ a_1 \cdots\ a_m) : (C\ a'_1 \cdots a'_p)$$

$$\frac{\Gamma \vdash M \rhd M_1 \qquad \Gamma \vdash \left(\begin{array}{c} < T > \texttt{Elim}\ M_1\ \texttt{with} \\ N_1 \cdots N_n \\ \texttt{end} \end{array}\right) \rhd M_2}{(\text{ELIM}) \qquad \Gamma \vdash \left(\begin{array}{c} < T > \texttt{Elim}\ M\ \texttt{with} \\ N_1 \cdots N_n \\ \texttt{end} \end{array}\right) \rhd M_2}$$

$$\texttt{if not}\ M = (C_{intro} i\ a_1 \cdots\ a_m)$$

4.4 The adaptation of our example

In our example, to define the constants *Trans* and *Inv*, instead of simple definitions, we could have use inductive definitions with one constructor.

Inductive $Trans\ [U : Set;\ R : (Rel\ U)] : Prop :=$
$\quad Trans_{intro} : (\forall x, y, z : U. (R\ x\ y) \Rightarrow (R\ y\ z) \Rightarrow (R\ x\ z)) \Rightarrow (Trans\ U\ R).$

Inductive $Inv\ [U : Set;\ R : (Rel\ U);\ x, y : U] : Prop :=$
$\quad Inv_{intro} : (R\ y\ x) \Rightarrow (Inv\ U\ R\ x\ y).$

A formal proof of our assertion with these new definitions is:

$$
\begin{array}{l}
\lambda U\!: Set.\, \lambda R\!: (Rel\ U).\, \lambda trans\!: (Trans\ U\ R). \\
\quad < (Trans\ U\ (Inv\ U\ R)) > \texttt{Elim}\ trans\ \texttt{with} \\
\quad\quad \lambda trans'\!: \forall x, y, z\!: U.\, (R\ x\ y) \Rightarrow (R\ y\ z) \Rightarrow (R\ x\ z). \\
\quad\quad\quad (Trans_{intro}\ U\ (Inv\ U\ R) \\
\quad\quad\quad\quad \lambda x, y, z\!: U.\, \lambda h_1\!: (Inv\ U\ R\ x\ y).\, \lambda h_2\!: (Inv\ U\ R\ y\ z). \\
\quad\quad\quad\quad\quad (Inv_{intro}\ U\ R\ x\ z \\
\quad\quad\quad\quad\quad\quad (trans'\ z\ y\ x \\
\quad\quad\quad\quad\quad\quad\quad < (R\ z\ y) > \texttt{Elim}\ h_2\ \texttt{with}\ \ \lambda h_2'\!: (R\ z\ y).\, h_2'\ \ \textbf{end} \\
\quad\quad\quad\quad\quad\quad\quad\quad < (R\ y\ x) > \texttt{Elim}\ h_1\ \texttt{with}\ \ \lambda h_1'\!: (R\ y\ x).\, h_1'\ \ \textbf{end}))) \\
\quad \textbf{end}
\end{array}
$$

This proof is bigger than the previous one. It is because all uses of the definitions of $Trans$ and Inv are done explicitly with introductions (application of a constructor C_{intro}) and by eliminations (use of operator `Elim`). The text we obtain is:

Theorem: $Trans\_R\_imp\_Trans\_Inv\_R$.
Statement: $\forall U\!: Set.\, \forall R\!: (Rel\ U).\, (Trans\ U\ R) \Rightarrow (Trans\ U\ (Inv\ U\ R))$.
Proof:
Consider a set U and a R of type $(Rel\ U)$ such that
$(Trans\ U\ R)$ $(trans)$.
We use definition of $Trans$ with hypothesis $trans$.
We have $\forall x, y, z\!: U.\, (R\ x\ y) \Rightarrow (R\ y\ z) \Rightarrow (R\ x\ z)$ $(trans')$.
Consider three elements x, y and z of U such that $(Inv\ U\ R\ x\ y)$ (h_1) and $(Inv\ U\ R\ y\ z)$ (h_2).
 * Using definition of Inv with hypothesis h_2 we get $(R\ z\ y)$
 * Using definition of Inv with hypothesis h_1 we get $(R\ y\ x)$
 Applying hypothesis $trans'$ to these two results we get $(R\ z\ x)$
 So, applying definition of Inv, we get $(Inv\ U\ R\ x\ z)$.
We have proven $\forall x, y, z\!: U.\, (Inv\ U\ R\ x\ y) \Rightarrow (Inv\ U\ R\ y\ z) \Rightarrow (Inv\ U\ R\ x\ z)$.
So, using definition of $Trans$ we have $(Trans\ U\ (Inv\ U\ R))$.
Q.E.D.

This text is similar to the text of section 3.4 although $Trans$ and Inv are defined in a different way.

5 The *well-known* inductive definitions

As for simple definitions, we are now going to define a list of *well-known* inductive definitions. All the transformations we define in this section are parameterized by this list.

We had descrided in section 3.5, how to hide the use of simple definitions by suppressing type annotations. But, we cannot adapt this method to inductive definitions. Each use of an inductive definition (elimination or introduction) appears explicitly in the proof structure. To hide these proof steps, we modify directly the λ-term before producing the text.

These transformations produce λ-terms which may not be well-typed. These λ-terms can no longer be checked by the type checkers of the *Calculus of Inductive Constructions.* This is due to the fact that they represent incomplete proofs. If we want to validate the λ-terms, which we obtain after the transformations, it will be necessary to reconstruct a complete proof.

5.1 Omitting an introduction

The introductions of an inductive constant are done by applying a constructor. When the definition of the introduced constant is *well-known*, and when this application has a unique subproof, it is possible to mingle the application and its subproof. In the λ-term we syntactically substitute the application by its subproof. We use the rewriting rule:

$$(C_{intro}i\ a_1 \cdots a_p\ N^{T_{e2}}_{T_{c2}})^{T_{e1}}_{T_{c1}} \longmapsto N^{T_e=T_{e1}}_{T_c=T_{c2}}$$

For example, we can consider a proof with an *or* introduction. In this proof h as type A.

$$(C_{intro}l\ A\ B\ h^A_A)^{A\vee B}_{A\vee B} \qquad \longmapsto \qquad h^{A\vee B}_A$$

With hypothesis h we have A. So, by definition of *or* we get $A \vee B$.	$\longmapsto$	With hypothesis h we have $A \vee B$.

5.2 Omitting an elimination

The rule we are going to define concerns uniquely the elimination of a variable that is introduced by a λ-abstraction and then immediately eliminated by an `Elim` operator. We use this rule if the type of the variable is a well-known constant with exactly one constructor. This is like a proof by cases with one unique case.

$$\left(\lambda x{:}T.\ <P>\ \texttt{Elim}\ x^{T_{e3}}_{T_{c3}}\ \texttt{with}\ N^{T_{e2}}_{T_{c2}}\texttt{end}\right)^{T_{e1}}_{T_{c1}} \longmapsto N^{T_e=T_{e1}}_{T_c=T_{c2}}\ \texttt{if}\ \begin{array}{l} T_{e3} \approx T_{c3}\ \text{and} \\ \texttt{not}\ x \in Free(N) \end{array}$$

The condition $T_{e3} \approx T_{c3}$ limits this transformation to situations where the reader can easily realize that the type of x is the well-known inductive constant. The condition not $x \in Free(N)$ guarantees that the variable x is not used in another part of the proof.

As an example, we can see the effect of this transformation on a proof using an *and* elimination:

$$\left(\begin{array}{l} \lambda h_1{:}A \wedge B. \\ \quad <P>\ \texttt{Elim}\ h_1\ \texttt{with} \\ \quad\quad \left(\begin{array}{l}\lambda h_2{:}A.\ \lambda h_3{:}B. \\ \quad M\end{array}\right)^{A\Rightarrow B\Rightarrow P}_{A\Rightarrow B\Rightarrow P} \\ \quad \texttt{end} \end{array}\right)^{A\wedge B\Rightarrow P}_{A\wedge B\Rightarrow P} \longmapsto \left(\begin{array}{l}\lambda h_2{:}A.\ \lambda h_3{:}B. \\ \quad P\end{array}\right)^{A\wedge B\Rightarrow P}_{A\Rightarrow B\Rightarrow P}$$

Assume $A \wedge B$ (h_1). We use h_1 with definition of *and*. We have A (h_2) and B (h_3). «$M{:}P$» So, we have proven $A \Rightarrow B \Rightarrow P$. So, we have proven $A \wedge B \Rightarrow P$.	$\longmapsto$	Assume A (h_2) and B (h_3). «$M{:}P$» So, we have proven $A \wedge B \Rightarrow P$.

5.3 Choosing type expressions

For these two transformations, we substitute a term M with types T_{e1} and T_{c1}, by a subterm N with types T_{e2} and T_{c2}. We have to specify the type annotations T_e and T_c of the resulting term.

The expected type of a proof is defined by its location within the global proof. It corresponds to a proof obligation. we choose $T_e{:}= T_{e1}$ as expected type of resulting term. The constraint of a proof describes what the proof actually shows. It depends on the structure of the proof. We choose $T_c{:}= T_{c2}$ as constraint type for the resulting proof.

Initially the constraint and expected types of a proof are equivalent. But, after one of these transformations the two type annotations of the resulting proof are not formally equivalent. The previous definition of closeness is no more adapted. So, before the transformations we annotate each subproof with the closness of its type annotation. Then, after a transformation, we decide that $T_e{:}= T_{e1}$ and $T_c{:}= T_{c2}$ should be considered as closed if both T_{e1} and T_{c1}, and T_{e2} and T_{c2} are closed.

5.4 Our example

If the inductive definition of *Trans* is considered as well-known, our example becomes:

Theorem: *Trans_R_imp_Trans_Inv_R.*
Statement: $\forall U{:}\,Set.\forall R{:}\,(Rel\ U).\,(Trans\ U\ R) \Rightarrow (Trans\ U\ (Inv\ U\ R))$.
Proof:
Consider a set U and a R of type $(Rel\ U)$ such that $\forall x,y,z{:}\,U.\,(R\ x\ y) \Rightarrow (R\ y\ z) \Rightarrow (R\ x\ z)$ ($trans'$) and consider three elements x, y and z of U such that $(Inv\ U\ R\ x\ y)$ (h_1) and $(Inv\ U\ R\ y\ z)$ (h_2).
 * Using definition of Inv with hypothesis h_2 we get $(R\ z\ y)$
 * Using definition of Inv with hypothesis h_1 we get $(R\ y\ x)$
 Applying hypothesis $trans'$ to these two results we get $(R\ z\ x)$
 So, applying definition of Inv, we get $(Inv\ U\ R\ x\ z)$.
Q.E.D.

This text is very close to the text obtained with simple definitions in section 3.5. Its formulation is a little different, but its structure and its detail level are the same. We keep this text as the final translation.

6 Other transformations of the λ-term

There is no reason to limit the transformations of the λ-term to these simple cases. While an abusive use of transformations can prevent the reconstruction of the complete proof and simply make the text incomprehensible, there are other applications for such transformations. In proof systems, the associative operators are often inductively defined with a binary representation that does not take advantage of associativity. This representation forces one to use successive introductions or eliminations. Transformations of the λ-term can group all of these proof steps into one.

Consider the logical operators of conjunction and disjunction. An elimination of the proposition $A \vee (B \vee C)$ must be done in two steps with two successive `Elim` operators. We transform the proof to use only one elimination:

$$\begin{array}{l} <P>\ \texttt{Elim}\ M_1^{T_e=A\vee(B\vee C)}\ \texttt{with} \\ \quad \lambda h_1{:}A.\ M_2^{T_e=P} \\ \quad \lambda h_2{:}B\vee C. \\ \quad\quad <P>\ \texttt{Elim}\ h_2\ \texttt{with} \\ \quad\quad\quad \lambda h_3{:}B.\ M_3^{T_e=P} \\ \quad\quad\quad \lambda h_4{:}C.\ M_4^{T_e=P} \\ \quad\quad \textbf{end} \\ \textbf{end} \end{array} \quad\longmapsto\quad \begin{array}{l} <P>\ \texttt{Elim}\ M_1^{T_e=A\vee(B\vee C)}\ \texttt{with} \\ \quad \lambda h_1{:}A.\ M_2^{T_e=P} \\ \quad \lambda h_3{:}B.\ M_3^{T_e=P} \\ \quad \lambda h_4{:}C.\ M_4^{T_e=P} \\ \textbf{end} \end{array}$$

«$M_1^{T_e=A\vee(B\vee C)}$»
By definition of *or* have two cases.
Case 1.:
  We have A (h_1).
    «$M_2^{T_e=P}$»
Case 2.:
  We have $B \vee C$ (h_2).
    Using h_2, we have $B \vee C$.
    By definition of *or* have two cases.
    Case 2.1.:
    We have B (h_3).
      «$M_3^{T_e=P}$»
    Case 2.2.:
    We have C (h_4).
      «$M_4^{T_e=P}$»
So, we have proven P.

$\longmapsto$

«$M_1^{T_e=A\vee(B\vee C)}$»
By definition of *or* have three cases.
Case 1.:
  We have A (h_1).
    «$M_2^{T_e=P}$»
Case 2.:
  We have B (h_3).
    «$M_3^{T_e=P}$»
Case 3.:
  We have C (h_4).
    «$M_4^{T_e=P}$»
So, we have proven P.

The dual case is the introduction of the conjunction operator. The introduction of $A \wedge (B \wedge C)$ has to be done with two applications of constructor and_{intro}. We transform the λ-term to get only one application:

$$(and_{intro}\ A\ (B\wedge C)\ M_1\ (and_{intro}\ B\ C\ M_2\ M_3)) \longmapsto (and_{intro}\ A\ B\ C\ M_1\ M_2\ M_3)$$

* «$M_1^{T_e=A}$»
  * «$M_2^{T_e=B}$»
  * «$M_3^{T_e=C}$»
* By definition of *and* we have $B \wedge C$.
By definition of *and* we have $A \wedge (B \wedge C)$.
	$\longmapsto$	* «$M_1^{T_e=A}$»
		* «$M_2^{T_e=B}$»
		* «$M_3^{T_e=C}$»
		By definition of *and* we have $A \wedge (B \wedge C)$.

7 Conclusion and future work

This work has been implemented and it is now distributed with the *Coq* system[2]. For future work, we still want to improve the quality of the translation. We also want to give to the user more ways to personalize the text production and to adapt it to the mathematical theory he is interested in. We want to develop the proof transformations done before the verbalization. We want to define a set of correct proof transformation and find a strategy to use them. A interesting application of these transformations can be to produce of text that does not really explain the proofs but just give the main ideas.

A possible extension can be to translate also the logic formulæ into english[1][6]. We are also studying the possibility of using natural language not only for output but also for input[5] or for formal representation of proofs[6]. This means that we must be able to generate a text from a λ-term and then to reconstruct the λ-term from this text.

References

1. D. Chester, *The translation of Formal Proofs into English*, Artificial Intelligence 7 (1976), 261-278, 1976.
2. C. Cornes, J. Courant, J-C. Filliâtre, E. Gimenez, G. Huet, P. Manoury, C. Muñoz, C. Murthy, C. Parent, C. Paulin-Mohring, A. Saïbi, B. Werner, *The Coq Proof Assistant Reference Manual*, INRIA.
3. Y. Coscoy, G. Kahn, L. Théry, *Extracting Text from Proofs*, in *Typed Lambda Calculus and Applications*, volume 902 of *Lecture Notes in Computer Science*. Springer-Verlag.
4. X. Huang, *Human Oriented Proof Presentation: A Reconstructive Approach*, SEKI Report SR-SR-94-07, UNIVERSITÄT DES SAARLANDES,.
5. K. Prazmowski, P.Rudnicki *Mizar-MSE Primer* Warsaw University, University of Alberta.
6. A. Ranta, *Type Theory and the Informal Language of Mathematics*, in Proceedings of the 1993 Types Worshop, Nijmegen, LNCS 806, 1994.

Models for Polymorphic Lambek Calculus

Martin Emms

Centrum für Informations- und Sprachverarbeitung, München

Abstract. An adaptation of *string-semantic* models to the Polymorphic Lambek Calculus is studied. We note that if quantifiers range over arbitrary sets of strings, the polymorphic calculus is incomplete. The semantics is refined so that quantifiers range over sets of strings that are the interpretation of categories, and we prove a completeness result. In addition some other models are considered and there are speculations on the relevance of model theory to linguistics.

1 Monomorphic Grammars and Models

In this paper we investigate models of the polymorphic Lambek calculus, an extension of the Lambek calculus with quantification of category variables. Several notions of model for the quantifier-free calculus are considered and extended to the polymorphic case. The Lambek calculus, and its polymorphic extension have their foremost application in linguistic analysis. By way of motivation for the later results, this section discuss the significance of model theory for linguistics. The section is somewhat speculative; the two research streams, linguistic and model-theoretic, are substantial, but concerning their confluence little has been said. Besides the material introducing the calculi and models, the later sections can be read independently of this one.

1.1 Calculi and grammars

First some preliminaries. Categorial grammar formalisms can generally be seen as logics. Since the connection was made most strikingly by Lambek, and especially in the last decade, explorations have been made of a number of parameters of variation in these logics. One parameter is *language* of the logic. We will use $\mathcal{L}$, followed by a series of connectives drawn from the set $\{\bullet, \mathbf{1}, /, \backslash, \forall, \exists\}$ to specify a particular language, and refer to elements of such a language as categories or sometimes formulae.

Both the Adjukiewicz/Bar-Hillel [2] [3] and Lambek [16] categorial grammar formalisms are based on the same language $\mathcal{L}(/, \backslash)$. They differ with respect to the sequents over $\mathcal{L}(/, \backslash)$ that they accept. The sets of sequents with which we will be concerned will be defined by calculi based on the rules in Figures 1.

These rules derive intuitionistic sequents from intuitionistic sequents, where an intuitionistic sequent is an antecedent sequence of formulae, followed by '$\Rightarrow$', and then a single formula. Concerning the notation we point out that w, x, y range over formulae, U, V, T range over sequences of formulae. $x[y/Z]$ stands for

$$x \Rightarrow x$$

$$\frac{U, y, V \Rightarrow w \qquad T \Rightarrow x}{U, y/x, T, V \Rightarrow w}/\mathrm{L} \qquad \frac{T, x \Rightarrow y}{T \Rightarrow y/x}/\mathrm{R}$$

$$\frac{T \Rightarrow x \qquad U, y, V \Rightarrow w}{U, T, x\backslash y, V \Rightarrow w}\backslash\mathrm{L} \qquad \frac{x, T \Rightarrow y}{T \Rightarrow x\backslash y}\backslash\mathrm{R}$$

$$\frac{U, x, y, V \Rightarrow w}{U, x\bullet y, V \Rightarrow w}\bullet\mathrm{L} \qquad \frac{T_1 \Rightarrow x \qquad T_2 \Rightarrow y}{T_1, T_2 \Rightarrow x\bullet y}\bullet\mathrm{R}$$

$$\frac{U, x[y/Z], V \Rightarrow w}{U, \forall Z.x, V \Rightarrow w}\forall\mathrm{L} \qquad \frac{T \Rightarrow x}{T \Rightarrow \forall X.x[X/Z]}\forall\mathrm{R},\ Z!$$

$$\frac{U, x, V \Rightarrow w}{U, \exists X.x[X/Z], V \Rightarrow w}\exists\mathrm{L},\ Z! \qquad \frac{T \Rightarrow x[y/X]}{T \Rightarrow \exists X.x}\exists\mathrm{R}$$

$$\frac{U, V \Rightarrow w}{U, \mathbf{1}, V \Rightarrow w}\mathbf{1}\ \mathrm{L} \qquad \Rightarrow \mathbf{1}$$

$$\frac{T_1, T_2 \Rightarrow w}{T_1, x, T_2 \Rightarrow w}\mathrm{Weak} \qquad \frac{T_1, x, x, T_2 \Rightarrow w}{T_1, x, T_2 \Rightarrow w}\mathrm{Contr} \qquad \frac{\pi(T) \Rightarrow w}{T \Rightarrow w}\mathrm{Perm}$$

Fig. 1. Identity axiom, and rules for $/,\backslash,\bullet,\forall,\exists,\mathbf{1}$,Structural Rules

the substitution of y for Z in x, defined to include a change of bound variable to avoid accidental capture. The side condition 'Z!' is that Z is not free below the line, and X is not free in $QZ.x$, this latter part allowing $QX.x[X/Z]$ to be an alphabetic variant of $QZ.x$.

The Adjukiewicz/Bar-Hillel formalism is based on the calculus obtained by taking the identity axiom scheme, together with (/L) and (\L), whilst the Lambek formalism takes additionally the (/R) and (\R) rules. In order to have systematic names for other choices, we use $\mathrm{L}^{\langle c_i\rangle_{1\leq i\leq n}}$ for (the set of sequents derivable using) the calculus obtained by taking the identity axiom scheme, together with the rules associated with each of the connectives c_i, with in the case of $\forall$L and $\exists$R, the obvious proviso that formula y substituted for the bound variable be drawn from the appropriate language: $\mathcal{L}(\langle c_i\rangle_{1\leq i\leq n})$. The calculi including the second-order quantifiers we will refer to as ***polymorphic***. In none of the calculi $\mathrm{L}^{\langle c_i\rangle_{1\leq i\leq n}}$ are the structural rules of Figure 1 admissible, and hence all may be referred to as non-commutative, linear logics. For any of the calculi that may be defined in this way, the derivability of the following Cut rule can be shown (by an inductive argument on the sizes of the premise proofs of a Cut[1])

$$\frac{T \Rightarrow x \qquad U, x, V \Rightarrow w}{U, T, V \Rightarrow w}\text{Cut}$$

Where L is a sequent calculus for a categorial language $\mathcal{L}$, there is a standard conception of how this may be put to work to define a grammar[2]. First let us call a relation $R \subseteq V^+ \times \mathcal{L}$, L- *closed* if whenever $(s_1, x_1) \in R, \ldots, (s_n, x_n) \in R$, and $\text{L} \vdash x_1, \ldots, x_n \Rightarrow y$ then $(s_1 \ldots s_n, y) \in R$ (where V^+ is the closure of V under concatenation).

Definition 1 (L-grammar) *Where V is a vocabulary, $\mathcal{L}$ some categorial language,* L *a sequent calculus for this language, and G_0 some finite relation on $V \times \mathcal{L}$ (known as the lexicon), the* L-grammar *G is the least relation on $V^+ \times \mathcal{L}$, satisfying i. $G_0 \subseteq G$ and ii. G is* L*-closed.*

For any relation $R \subseteq A \times B$, we use $(x)_R$, for $\{a \in A \mid (a, x) \in R\}$. Then choosing some distinguished category, x_0, the set $(x_0)_G$ can be seen as the *language generated by G.*

Example 1: Adjukiewicz grammar : let $V = \{a, b, c\}$, $\mathcal{L} = \{/, \backslash\}$, $G_0 = \{(a, \text{np}), (b, \text{s/s}), (b, \text{np}\backslash\text{np}), (c, \text{np}\backslash\text{s})\}$, L = identity axiom + (/L) + (\L). Then the values of $(\cdot)_G$ on some of the categories are:
$(\text{np})_G = \{ab^p \mid p \geq 0\}$
$(\text{s})_G = \{b^p ab^q c \mid p \geq 0,\ q \geq 0\}$
$(\text{np}\backslash\text{np})_G = \{b\}$
$(\text{s/s})_G = \{b\}$
$(\text{np}\backslash\text{s})_G = \{c\}$

Example 2: Lambek grammar : as above, but with $\text{L} = \text{L}^{/,\backslash}$. Then the values of $(\cdot)$ on some of the categories are:
$(\text{np})_G = \{ab^p \mid p \geq 0\}$
$(\text{s})_G = \{b^p ab^q c \mid p \geq 0,\ q \geq 0\}$
$(\text{np}\backslash\text{np})_G = \{b^p \mid p \geq 1\}$
$(\text{s/s})_G = \{b^p \mid p \geq 1\}$
$(\text{np}\backslash\text{s})_G = \{b^p c \mid p \geq 0\}$

1.2 String semantic models

An L-grammar is a relation between V^+ and $\mathcal{L}$, where $\mathcal{L}$ is some categorial language. In the case of $\mathcal{L}(/, \backslash)$, such relations occur also in the so-called *string-semantic* models of $\mathcal{L}(/, \backslash)$, albeit in the form of functions $[\![\cdot]\!] : \mathcal{L} \rightarrow 2^{V^+}$: a

[1] Lambek's proof of Cut elimination for $\text{L}^{/,\bullet,\backslash}$ by induction on the complexity of the Cut formula, does not work for the polymorphic calculi. The absence of the contraction rule, however, allows a similarly simple proof to be given by induction on proof size. See [[12]].

[2] Due to Cut Elimination, restricting the s_i in the definition to members of V does not change G

category x receives an interpretation $[\![x]\!] \subseteq V^+$, subject to constraints generated by the connective structure of x

Definition 2 (String semantic model of $\mathcal{L}(/, \backslash)$) *$\langle S, \bullet, [\![]\!]\rangle$ is a string-semantic model if $\langle S, \bullet\rangle$ is a free semigroup and $[\![]\!]$ maps categories to subsets of S according to*
1. $[\![x/y]\!] = \{a \in S : \forall b \in [\![y]\!], a\bullet b \in [\![x]\!]\}$
2. $[\![y\backslash x]\!] = \{a \in S : \forall b \in [\![y]\!], b\bullet a \in [\![x]\!]\}$

Any such model is uniquely determined by the values of the basic categories, so that one can alternatively define the models by an interpretation for the basic categories, to be extended according to the above two conditions. We have made one departure from [4] in the above definition, omitting a requirement that S be the closure under $\bullet$ of some *finite* vocabulary V. The class of all string-semantic models we will refer to as S^{inf}. The corresponding class with finitely generated S, we will refer to as S [3].

Example 3: String Semantic Model : the values of $[\![\cdot]\!]$ on the basic categories are given first, followed by implied values on some of the categories:

$[\![\text{np}]\!] = \{ab^p \mid p \geq 0\}$
$[\![\text{s}]\!] = \{b^p ab^q c \mid p \geq 0,\ q \geq 0\}$
$[\![\text{np}\backslash\text{np}]\!] = \{b^p \mid p \geq 1\}$
$[\![\text{s/s}]\!] = \{b^p \mid p \geq 1\}$
$[\![\text{np}\backslash\text{s}]\!] = \{b^p c \mid p \geq 0\}$

The Lambek calculus generates exactly the inclusions true in all such models [4]. More exactly, if we say a sequent is *satisfied by a model*, $M \models x_1, \ldots, x_n \Rightarrow y$ iff $[\![x_1]\!]\bullet \ldots \bullet[\![x_n]\!] \subseteq [\![y]\!]$, then

Theorem 1 (Buszkoswki 1982). $\text{L}^{/,\backslash} \vdash x_1, \ldots, x_n \Rightarrow y$ *iff for all models* $M \in S$, $M \models x_1, \ldots, x_n \Rightarrow y$.

There is a harder to prove version of this [18] for the language $\mathcal{L}(/, \backslash, \bullet)$ and the calculus $\text{L}^{/,\backslash,\bullet}$, where the conditions on $[\![\cdot]\!]$ are extended with:

$$[\![x\bullet y]\!] = \{a \in S : \exists b_1 \in [\![x]\!], \exists b_2 \in [\![y]\!], a = b_1\bullet b_2\}$$

Theorem 2 (Pentus 1993). $\text{L}^{/,\backslash,\bullet} \vdash x_1, \ldots, x_n \Rightarrow y$ *iff for all models* $M \in S$, $M \models x_1, \ldots, x_n \Rightarrow y$.

1.3 Other models

The string-semantic models are very concrete, and *construct* the value of a category as a set of strings. A somewhat more abstract semantics has also been investigated, which simply assumes the existence of objects which may serve as the values of categories. These are the *residuated semi-group* models.

[3] Thus S denotes the same class of models as it does in [4].

Definition 3 (Residuated Semigroup) $\langle M, \bullet, /, \backslash \rangle$ *is a residuated semi group if M is closed under* $\bullet$, $/$, $\backslash$, *the operation* $\bullet$ *is associative, M is partially ordered, and the operations relate to the ordering in the following way:*

$$a \leq c/b \text{ iff } a \bullet b \leq c \text{ iff } b \leq c \backslash a$$

Following [5], we will refer to the class of all residuated semi-groups as RES. Where C varies over connectives, and $\mathbf{C}$ over the corresponding operation, we define a RES-model as follows:

Definition 4 (RES model) $\langle M, \bullet, /, \backslash, [\![]\!] \rangle$ *is a RES-model if:* $\langle M, \bullet, /, \backslash \rangle \in RES$, *and where C is '/','\\','•'* $[\![C(x,y)]\!] = \mathbf{C}([\![x]\!], [\![y]\!])$.

If we say a sequent is satisfied by a model, $\langle R, [\![]\!] \rangle \models x_1, \ldots, x_n \Rightarrow y$ iff $[\![x_1]\!] \bullet \ldots \bullet [\![x_n]\!] \leq [\![y]\!]$ then

Theorem 3 (Buszkowski 1986). $\mathrm{L}^{(/,\backslash,\bullet)} \vdash x_1, \ldots, x_n \Rightarrow y$ *iff for all models* $\langle M, [\![]\!] \rangle$, $\langle M, [\![]\!] \rangle \models x_1, \ldots, x_n \Rightarrow y$

The S^{inf}-completeness of $\mathrm{L}^{(/,\backslash,\bullet)}$ actually entails RES-completeness, but the direct proof of RES completeness is however much easier. S^{inf}-completeness of $\mathrm{L}^{(/,\backslash)}$ entails RES-completeness. The adaptation of the direct proof from the $\mathrm{L}^{(/,\backslash,\bullet)}$ case fails.

The move from string semantics to residuated semi-groups involved one kind of abstraction, abandoning the idea that the value of a category is a set of strings. The *ternary frame semantics* represents another direction of abstraction, in which categories are still interpreted as sets of strings, but the interrelation of these items is abstractly defined by a 3-place 'accessibility' relation.

Definition 5 (Associative Ternary Frame) $\langle W, R \rangle$ *is an associate ternary frame if W is a non-empty set, R a ternary relation on W satisfying,*

$$\forall x, y, z, u \in W(\exists s(Rxys \wedge Rszu) \text{ iff } \exists t(Rxtu \wedge Ryzt))$$

Definition 6 (Associative Ternary Frame Model) $\langle W, R, [\![]\!] \rangle$ *is an associative ternary frame model if* $\langle W, R \rangle$ *is an associative ternary frame, and* $[\![]\!]$ *assigns the categories subsets of W, subject to:*

$$[\![a \bullet b]\!] = \{x : \exists y, z(Ryzx \wedge y \in [\![a]\!] \wedge z \in [\![b]\!])\}$$
$$[\![a \backslash b]\!] = \{x : \forall y, z(Ryxz \wedge y \in [\![a]\!] \longrightarrow z \in [\![b]\!])\}$$
$$[\![b/a]\!] = \{x : \forall y, z(Rxyz \wedge y \in [\![a]\!] \longrightarrow z \in [\![b]\!])\}$$

If we say a sequent is *satisfied by a model,* $\langle W, R, [\![]\!] \rangle \models x_1, \ldots, x_n \Rightarrow y$, iff $[\![x_1 \bullet \ldots \bullet x_n]\!] \subseteq [\![y]\!]$ then

Theorem 4 (Dosen 1990). $\mathrm{L}^{(/,\backslash,\bullet)} \vdash a \Rightarrow b$ *iff every interpretation relative to every associative ternary frame satisfies* $a \Rightarrow b$

From a S^{inf} model a ternary frame model can quickly be constructed, taking the strings as the worlds and the accessibility relationship as $R(a, b, a \bullet b)$. Thus completeness of $\mathrm{L}^{(/,\backslash,\bullet)}$ and $\mathrm{L}^{(/,\backslash)}$ wrt the S^{inf} class implies completeness wrt ternary frames.

Analogs of the 3 above-mentioned model classes for polymorphic calculi will be considered in later sections, the primary emphasis being on the string semantic models.

1.4 Connection between grammars and string-semantic models

The question arises as to whether the model-theoretic results have any linguistic significance. Certainly amongst categorial grammarians the *string-semantics* results are treated as legitimising the sequent rules of $\mathrm{L}^{(/,\backslash)}$ and $\mathrm{L}^{(/,\backslash,\bullet)}$. Thus a linguistic problem which seems to not be Lambek solvable is typically not taken as a prompt to consider further, string-semantically *invalid* sequents, but as a prompt to *extend* the categorial language[4].

In this section I argue that a rationale can be given to this way of proceeding. Consider the sceptical position first. The sceptic says that the mere fact that a given set of sequents are exactly the M-valid sequents for *a* particular notion of model M provides no rationale for the use of these and only these sequents for defining grammars. For the semantics to provide such a rationale it must *reflect* the intended linguistic application. A parallel case is provided by Peano arithmetic. There is *a* notion of model according to which what is first order provable from the Peano axioms is exactly what is true in all models of the axioms. As an axiomatisation of arithmetic, however, one is still entitled to expect more than this to follow from the axioms, as the notion of model countenances *non-standard* models of the axioms.

We try to answer the sceptic now, considering the string-semantics. We will concentrate on $\mathrm{L}^{/,\backslash}$. Given an $\mathrm{L}^{/,\backslash}$-grammar $G \subseteq V^+ \times \mathcal{L}(/,\backslash)$ and an *interpretation* $[\![\cdot]\!] : \mathcal{L}(/,\backslash) \rightarrow 2^{V^+}$ one can ask the questions whether the *interpretation extends the grammar*:

$$(x)_G \subseteq [\![x]\!], \text{ for all } x \in \mathcal{L}(/,\backslash)$$

and the converse for whether the *grammar extends the interpretation.*

We consider first conditions under which it will obtain that an interpretation extends the grammar. An easy proof using the soundness of $\mathrm{L}^{/,\backslash}$ wrt string-semantic interpretations gives that if the model extends the values $(x)_{G_0}$, then it extend the values $(x)_G$.

Lemma 5. *If $G \subseteq V^+ \times \mathcal{L}(/,\backslash)$ is an $\mathrm{L}^{/,\backslash}$-grammar, and $[\![\cdot]\!] \in \mathcal{L} \rightarrow 2^{V^+}$ is the interpretation of a $\mathcal{L}(/,\backslash)$-model, then*

if $(x)_{G_0} \subseteq [\![x]\!]$ for all $x \in \mathcal{L}(/,\backslash)$ then $(x)_G \subseteq [\![x]\!]$ for all $x \in \mathcal{L}(/,\backslash)$

[4] The Combinatory Categorial Grammar school is an exception to this, preferring to keep the language fixed, and increase the admitted sequents

This makes the string-semantics relevant to the definition of G if we see G as attempting to give the fullest possible picture of what must hold in all interpretations which extend a given lexicon G_0.

We assume we are seeking to analyse a given language, say English, or any language for which there is no pre-existing *definition*. We assume that the categorisations facts about this language can be represented as the values of an interpretation $[\![\cdot]\!]$ on the *atomic categories* of $\mathcal{L}(/,\backslash)$. This is actually to assume nothing, as the valuation of *atomic* categories in a string-semantic model can be freely chosen .

Our to-be-analysed language has no pre-existing definition, and hence the interpretation of $\mathcal{L}(/,\backslash)$ is unknown. However certain facts will obtain which the analysis should respect. These may be individual categorisations (eg. 'a is an s') or generalisations (eg. 'whenever b is followed by an s an s results'). These then are constraints on the $\mathcal{L}(/,\backslash)$-interpretation that we are seeking to specify (eg. $a \in [\![\mathrm{s}]\!]$, $b \in [\![\mathrm{s/s}]\!]$). We would now like to know what further categorisations holds in all models which extend these lexical constraints. We can argue that the G we obtain from a lexicon (eg. $G_0 = \{(a, s), (b, s/s)\}$), by applying the definition of an $\mathrm{L}^{(/,\backslash)}$-grammar, gives us as good a picture as possible of this.

We have just seen that the *soundness* of $\mathrm{L}^{(/,\backslash)}$ gives that what G delivers is guaranteed to hold in all models which extend the lexicon. Thus G makes claims which can be relied upon concerning what holds in all models of the lexicon. With the soundness of $\mathrm{L}^{(/,\backslash)}$, if some $(a, x) \in G$ is a miscategorisation, we can assume that one of the lexical assumptions is mistaken. Suppose that $\mathrm{L}^{(/,\backslash)}$ were not *complete*, so that for some sequent representing an inclusion true in all models, $\mathrm{L}^{(/,\backslash)}$ did not derive it. Closing G_0 with this inclusion gives categorisations which hold in all models which extend G_0. Thus a G based on a complete calculus will give a fuller picture of what holds in all models of the lexicon than a G based on an incomplete calculus. With G based on an incomplete calculus, it will arise that some genuine consequence of a lexical hypothesis remains concealed.

Thus soundness of $\mathrm{L}^{(/,\backslash)}$ is desirable if G is to give reliable information about what holds in all models of the lexicon. Completeness of $\mathrm{L}^{(/,\backslash)}$ is desirable if G is not to miss information which obviously holds in all models of the lexicon.

We have that G is a member of the set $\{R \mid R$ is a subrelation of all interpretations extending $G_0\}$. The greatest element and therefore least upper bound of this set is clearly the intersection of interpretations extending G_0. A remaining open question[5] is whether G is also the least upper bound of this set:

Question 6. G is equal to the intersection of interpretations extending G_0.

An important aspect of the above discussion was that G was regarded as an *approximation* of the categorisation facts concerning the language to be analysed. Other considerations enter in if we would like to take G as 'the final answer'. In this case one takes the values of $(x)_G$ for atomic x to define $[\![x]\!]$. Given that G, including $(x)_G$ for atomic x, represents at best the *intersection* of all

[5] First posed by Hans Leiss, p.c.

interpretations extending G_0, there is no reason to assume that the interpretation based on $(x)_G$ for atomic x is also an interpretations extending G_0.

Buszkowski[4] gives the name *correctness* to the property of being a G such that when the interpretation is defined by $[\![x]\!] = (x)_G$ for atomic x, the interpretation extends the lexicon, and hence by Lemma 5, extends G. In the light for the foregoing discussion, this choice of term is an unfortunate one. A grammar G which is not in Buszkowski's sense *correct*, need not be seen as in any sense *wrong*, paradoxical as this may sound: the grammar completely and faithfully says what must hold in all models of the lexicon. When a grammar is not correct in Buszkowski's sense this simply means it is not model defining.

Our earlier example of a Lambek grammar *is* correct. The interpretation defined by $[\![x]\!] = (x)_G$ for atomic x, is the interpretation which was our example string-semantic model, and the model extends the lexicon. Not every Lambek grammar is correct. Consider an attempt to prove from $[\![x]\!] = (x)_G$, for x atomic, that the interpretation extends G, that is $(x)_G \subseteq [\![x]\!]$. We try to make an induction on the complexity of categories. Suppose for some α we have $\alpha \in (x/y)_G$. We require $\alpha \in [\![x/y]\!]$. Thus for all $\beta \in [\![y]\!]$, we require $\alpha\beta \in [\![x]\!]$. However, by induction we can hope only to have $(y)_G \subseteq [\![y]\!]$. For those $\beta \in (y)_G \cap [\![y]\!]$, we have $\alpha\beta \in (x)_G$, and hence by induction $\alpha\beta \in [\![x]\!]$, which is what we require. However, for those $\beta \in [\![y]\!] - (y)_G$, we have no argument for $\alpha\beta \in (x)_G$, and hence none for $\alpha\beta \in [\![x]\!]$.

For such negatively occurring y we need $[\![y]\!] \subseteq (y)_G$, in addition to $(y)_G \subseteq [\![y]\!]$. Let us define $arg(x/y) = arg(y\backslash x) = \{y\} \cup arg(x)$, with $arg(x) = \emptyset$, for atomic x, and $Lex(G_0) = \{x : \text{there is } \alpha \in V, \text{ with } (\alpha, x) \in G_0\}$

Theorem 7. *If* $[\![x]\!] = (x)_G$, *for atomic* x, *and* $(y)_G = [\![y]\!]$ *for all* $y \in \bigcup arg(x)_{x \in Lex(G_0)}$, *then* $[\![\cdot]\!]$ *extends* G *(i.e. is correct).*

Proof. (Sketch) Define $val(x/y) = \{x/y\} \cup val(x)$, with $val(x) = \{x\}$, for atomic x. One shows $(x)_G \subseteq [\![x]\!]$, for all $x \in \bigcup val(y)_{y \in Lex(G_0)}$, which suffices by Lemma 5 given $Lex(G_0) \subseteq \bigcup val(y)_{y \in Lex(G_0)}$. □

Buszkowski discusses two ways in which the condition in this theorem could get fulfilled. One is that all $x \in \bigcup arg(y)_{y \in Lex(G_0)}$ are atomic. The other is that for all subtypes of $x \in Lex(G_0)$, there is a lexical item occurring in $(x)_{G_0}$, and this lexical item occurs in no $(y)_{G_0}$ for $x \neq y$. The condition in the lemma is then fulfilled because it then holds that $(x)_G = [\![x]\!]$ for *all* subtypes of $x \in Lex(G_0)$. The following theorem is essentially Theorem 3 of [4], whose proof we omit.

Theorem 8 (Buszkowski,1982). *If* $[\![x]\!] = (x)_G$ *for atomic* x, *and for all subtypes of* $x \in Lex(G_0)$, *there is* $\alpha \in (x)_{G_0}$ *with* $\alpha \notin (y)_{G_0}$ *for* $x \neq y$, *then for all subtypes* y *of* $x \in Lex(G_0)$, $[\![y]\!] = (y)_G$.

It is to be noted that Theorem 8 shows $(x)_G = [\![x]\!]$ only for $x \in \bigcup sub(y)_{y \in Lex(G_0)}$. Buszkowski goes on to show that there it is never the case that $(x)_G = [\![x]\!]$, for *all* x. We noted earlier that our example of a Lambek model is obtained from the our example of a Lambek grammar by setting $[\![x]\!] = (x)_G$ for atomic x. We noted also that the model extends G. A counterexample to $(x)_G = [\![x]\!]$ is provided by np/(s/s), where $[\![\text{np}/(\text{s}/\text{s})]\!] = \{ab^p \mid p \geq 0\}$, and $(\text{np}/(\text{s}/\text{s}))_G = \emptyset$.

2 Polymorphic Grammars and Models

Polymorphism is an aspect of linguistic formalisms deserving study in its own right, appearing as it does either explicitly or implicitly in many of them. There is explicit appeal in 'cross-categorial' approaches to coordination, and implicit appeal in the lexical entries of unification based frameworks: quantifying over all consistent extensions of a given feature structure, or over all specialisations of a first order term. In previous work, I have investigated various aspects of a polymorphic extension of the original Lambek grammar formalism. So, in addition to basic categories, one has *category variables*, and where x is a category, so also is $QX.x$, $Q \in \{\forall, \exists\}$. The rules for quantifiers are given in Figure 1

See [16] and [12] for proofs that derivability is preserved under substitution throughout for a free variable, and under change of a bound variable. A basic linguistic motivation for the extended calculus is that Chomsky's (now proven) conjecture that the Lambek calculus characterises only CF languages, is not true of the polymorphic extension [7]. Also concretely various linguistic phenomena including quantification, coordination, and extraction are tackled via polymorphism in [6], [9], [10]. Via a decidability result for a particular class of sequents, [8] also shows how these polymorphic accounts may be handled computationally, though [11] proves undecidability in the general case. Our main aim here is to study whether model theoretic results for the Lambek calculus generalise to its basic polymorphic extension. Using again Definition 1 of L-grammar, we give the following example of a polymorphic grammar

Example 4: Polymorphic grammar : let $V = \{a, b, c\}$, $\mathcal{L} = \{/, \backslash, \forall\}$, $\text{L} = \text{L}^{(/,\backslash,\forall)}$, and let G_0 be given by the following table:

$$G_3 \begin{cases} a & t/(t/e) & t/(e\backslash t) & \forall X.t/(X\backslash t)/(X/e) \\ b & t/(t/(e\backslash s)) & t/((e\backslash s)\backslash t) & \forall X.t/(X\backslash t)/(X/(e\backslash s)) \\ c & t/(t/(s\backslash t)) & t/((s\backslash t)\backslash t) & \forall X.t/(X\backslash t)/(X/(s\backslash t)) \\ & t/(t/(s\backslash(t\backslash t))) & t/((s\backslash(t\backslash t))\backslash t) & \forall X.t/(X\backslash t)/(X/(s\backslash(t\backslash t))) \end{cases}$$

then $(t)_G = \{perm(abc)^p \mid p \geq 1\}$ (a non-CF language, see [7])

2.1 Polymorphic String Semantic Models

In the monomorphic case, models were defined to include an interpretation function $[\![]\!]$ defined on all categories, whose operation on complex categories was, however, completely determined by its operation on atomic categories. In the polymorphic case it is more convenient to isolate as I a partial function defined only on basic categories.

Definition 7 (Polymorphic string-semantic model) $\langle S, \bullet, \mathcal{V}, I\rangle$ *is a* polymorphic string-semantic *model if* $\langle S, \bullet\rangle$ *is a free semigroup,* $\mathcal{V} \subseteq \mathcal{P}(S)$*,* $\mathcal{V}$ *non-empty, and I maps basic categories into* $\mathcal{V}$*.*

$\mathcal{V}$ will be referred to as the *range of quantification*. To handle variables in the polymorphic case, the denotation of a category is defined with respect to a model (see above) and an *assignment*, where this a function in $\mathcal{V}^{VAR}$. If g is an assignment, and A a set in $\mathcal{V}$, then g_X^A is the unique assignment h such that (i) $h(Y) = g(Y)$, for $Y \neq X$, and (ii) $h(X) = A$ otherwise.

Definition 8 (Denotation) *If* $M = \langle S, \bullet, \mathcal{V}, I\rangle$ *is polymorphic string-semantic model, and* g *an assignment in* $\mathcal{V}^{VAR}$*, then* $[\![x]\!]^g$ *is defined as follows*
1. for basic x, $[\![x]\!]^g = I(x)$
2. for variables X, $[\![X]\!]^g = g(X)$
3. $[\![x/y]\!]^g = \{a \in S : \forall b \in [\![y]\!]^g, a\bullet b \in [\![x]\!]^g\}$
4. $[\![y\backslash x]\!]^g = \{a \in S : \forall b \in [\![y]\!]^g, b\bullet a \in [\![x]\!]^g\}$
5. $[\![\forall X.y]\!]^g = \bigcap\{[\![y]\!]^{g_X^A} : A \in \mathcal{V}\}$
6. $[\![\exists X.y]\!]^g = \bigcup\{[\![y]\!]^{g_X^A} : A \in \mathcal{V}\}$

Clearly for categories lacking free variables, the denotation does not depend on the assignment. Satisfaction is now defined with respect to a model and an assignment: $M, g \models x_1, \ldots, x_n \Rightarrow y$ iff $[\![x_1]\!]^g\bullet\ldots\bullet[\![x_n]\!]^g \subseteq [\![y]\!]^g$.

The question with which we will be concerned is *which* subsets of S occur in $\mathcal{V}$. Three conditions that one might impose on the range of quantification $\mathcal{V}$ of a polymorphic string-semantic model $\langle S, \bullet, \mathcal{V}, I\rangle$ are:

Condition 1 $\mathcal{V} = \mathcal{P}(S)$
Condition 2 $\mathcal{V}$ *covers the categories*:
$\{[\![x]\!]^g : x \text{ a category, } g \text{ an assignment}\} \subseteq \mathcal{V}$
Condition 3 $\mathcal{V}$ is *covered by the closed categories*:
$\mathcal{V} \subseteq \{[\![x]\!]^g : x \text{ is a closed category, } g \text{ is an assignment}\}$

PS_1^{inf}, PS_2^{inf} and $PS_{2,3}^{inf}$ indicate that particular conditions on $\mathcal{V}$ are in force. Note Condition 1 entails Condition 2. The simplest option, that *all* subsets of S should be available turns out to be incorrect; it is for this reason a range of quantification is given as an explicit parameter in the definition of the model [6]. We also note for PS_2^{inf} models, that I does not affect whether we have a PS_2^{inf} model: it suffices if we have $[\![x]\!]^g \in \mathcal{V}$, for all assignments and *constant-free* categories, as the denotation of a constant-containing category will coincide with that of some constant-free category.

2.1.1 PS_1^{inf}-Incompleteness of $\mathrm{L}^{(/,\backslash,\forall,\exists)}$

The PS_1^{inf} class chooses the quantifier range to be simply the power set of the underlying set of strings, the most obvious candidate for the semantics of

[6] Thus our models are very akin to the so-called *general models* of 2nd Order logic, introduced by [15].

the quantified calculi. We show now PS_1^{inf}-incompleteness of $L^{(/,\backslash,\forall,\exists)}$. Not all instances of the schemata in the lefthand column of the table below are derivable (if for example x and y are assumed to be atomic then one can easily see that all attempts at a proof will fail). Yet all instances of these schemata are satisfied in all PS_1^{inf} models, for the reasons indicated, in the righthand column (where M is an arbitrary PS_1^{inf} model $\langle S, \bullet, I\rangle$, and g an arbitrary assignment):

Satisfied in all M, g	*Holds for any M, any g*
1. $\forall X.X/X \Rightarrow y$	$[\![\forall X.X/X]\!]^g = \emptyset$
2. $\forall X.X\backslash X/X \Rightarrow y$	$[\![\forall X.X\backslash X/X]\!]^g = \emptyset$
3. $\forall X.(X/y)\backslash X \Rightarrow y$	$[\![\forall X.(X/y)\backslash X]\!]^g \subseteq [\![y]\!]^g$
4. $x \Rightarrow \exists X.y/(X/X)$	$[\![\exists X.y/(X/X)]\!]^g = S$
5. $x \Rightarrow \exists X.y/(X\backslash X/X)$	$[\![\exists X.y/(X\backslash X/X)]\!]^g = S$

Proof. Let M be an arbitrary PS_1^{inf} model $\langle S, \bullet, I\rangle$, and g an arbitrary assignment

Equations 1, 4 : We note that $\{b\}/\{b\} = \emptyset$, where $b \in S$. For suppose $a \in \{b\}/\{b\}$. Then $a{\bullet}b \in \{b\}$, which implies $a{\bullet}b = b$, contradicting that the algebras are free.[7] So, when $B = \{b\}$, $[\![X/X]\!]^{g^B_X} = \emptyset = [\![\forall X.X/X]\!]^g$. Since for any $A \subseteq S$, we have $A/\emptyset = S$, we have $[\![y/(X/X)]\!]^{g^B_X} = S = [\![\exists X.y/(X/X)]\!]^g = S$.

Equations 2, 5 : $\{b\}\backslash\{b\}/\{b\} = \emptyset$, since supposing $a \in \{b\}\backslash\{b\}/\{b\}$, gives $b{\bullet}a{\bullet}b = b$, contradicting that the algebras are free. So where $B = \{b\}$, $[\![X\backslash X/X]\!]^{g^B_X} = \emptyset = [\![\forall X.X\backslash X/X]\!]^g$. Also $[\![y/(X\backslash X/X))]\!]^{g^B_X} = S = [\![\exists X.y/(X\backslash X/X)]\!]^g$.

Inclusion 3 : First suppose $[\![y]\!]^g$ is empty. For all B we require $[\![\forall X.((X/y)\backslash X)]\!]^g \subseteq [\![(X/y)\backslash X]\!]^{g^B_X}$, but when $B = \emptyset$, the right-hand side is $S\backslash\emptyset$, which is empty. Hence $[\![\forall X.((X/y)\backslash X)]\!]^g$ is empty. Now assume $[\![y]\!]^g$ is non-empty, and suppose $q \in [\![\forall X.(X/y)\backslash X]\!]^g$, and $q \notin [\![y]\!]^g$. For all $B \subseteq S$, we have $q \in [\![(X/y)\backslash X]\!]^{g^B_X}$. Choose $B = b{\bullet}[\![y]\!]$, for some b. Then $b \in [\![X/y]\!]^{g^B_X}$, and so we require $b{\bullet}q \in b{\bullet}[\![y]\!]^g$, which implies that $q \in [\![y]\!]^g$.

□

These counterexamples can change when empty antecedents are permitted and an identity element is included, but counterexamples remain. $\forall X.((X\backslash X)/X)$ is empty when $S \neq \{\epsilon\}$ and otherwise denotes $\{\epsilon\}$. The same is true of $\forall X.((X\backslash X\backslash X)/X)$, and hence $\forall X.((X\backslash X)/X) \Rightarrow \forall X.((X\backslash X\backslash X)/X)$ is valid. It is not derivable.

We do not wish to extend the calculus to suit the PS_1^{inf} semantics. We would like to give the category $\forall X.(X\backslash X)/X$ to and, but a complete calculus must allow any y to be derived from this category, so that and would satisfy the subcategorisation requirements of any word. Under the assumption that $\mathcal{V} = \mathcal{P}(S)$, and:$\forall X.(X\backslash X)/X$ means says every set of strings is closed under

[7] More generally when there is a longest string in B, $B/B = \emptyset$

the operation of inserting and between members, which is not simply not true. Restricting to sets of strings that are the denotation of a *category*, however, closure under insertion of and is more reasonable. So for sets *which are the value of a category* we suggest that $\mathcal{V}$ just contain the values of categories, which Conditions 2 and 3 give different ways of formalising.

2.1.2 PS_2^{inf} Soundness and Completeness of $\mathrm{L}^{(/,\backslash,\forall)}$

In this section we prove:

Theorem 9. $\mathrm{L}^{(/,\backslash,\forall)} \vdash x_1, \ldots, x_n \Rightarrow y$ *iff for all models* $M \in PS_2^{inf}$, *and assignments* g, $M, g \models x_1, \ldots, x_n \Rightarrow y$

We note that for the soundness direction, $\bullet$ and $\exists$ can easily be included. For the completeness direction, the inclusion of $\bullet$ brings problems well known from the monomorphic case. The inclusion of $\exists$ also brings problems, discussed later in the paper.

Proof. PS_2^{inf}-soundness of $\mathrm{L}^{(/,\backslash,\forall)}$ is proved by induction on the size of a proof. In the following (M, g) is always a pair with $M = \langle S, \bullet, \mathcal{V}, I\rangle \in PS_2^{inf}$, and $g \in \mathcal{V}^{VAR}$.

Consider a proof of $T \Rightarrow x$. The leaves are instances of $x \Rightarrow x$, and are therefore satisfied by every (M, g). It suffices to show that the rules of the calculus preserve this property of being satisfied by every (M, g). The cases for Cut, /L,/R,\L,\R are minor alterations of the corresponding cases in the proof of the string-semantic soundness of $\mathrm{L}^{(/,\backslash)}$, and we give just the quantifier cases, including $\exists$. The argument for $\forall$L and $\exists$R uses that $\mathcal{V}$ meets Condition 2.

Case: $\forall$L. Suppose we obtain the sequent U, $\forall X.x$, $V \Rightarrow w$ from U, $x[y/X]$, $V \Rightarrow w$, that the premise is satisfied by every (M, g) and that the conclusion is not. Hence for some (M, g), there are $\mathbf{u} \in [\![U]\!]^g$, $a \in [\![\forall X.x]\!]^g$, $\mathbf{v} \in [\![V]\!]^g$ such that $\mathbf{u}a\mathbf{v} \notin [\![w]\!]^g$. Since $a \in [\![\forall X.x]\!]^g$, then for any $B \in \mathcal{V}$, $a \in [\![x]\!]^{g^X_B}$. Because $M \in PS_2^{inf}$, we have $[\![y]\!]^g \in \mathcal{V}$, and choosing $B = [\![y]\!]^g$, we have $[\![x]\!]^{g^X_B} = [\![x[y/X]]\!]^g$. Therefore $a \in [\![x[y/X]]\!]^g$, and therefore U, $x[y/X]$, $V \Rightarrow w$ is not satisfied by (M, g), which is a contradiction.

Case: $\exists$R (similar to $\forall$L). Suppose we obtain the sequent $T \Rightarrow \exists X.x$ from $T \Rightarrow x[y/X]$, that the premise is satisfied by every (M, g) and that the conclusion is not. Hence for some (M, g), there are $\mathbf{t} \in [\![T]\!]^g$, such that $\mathbf{t} \notin [\![\exists X.x]\!]^g$. So for no $B \in \mathcal{V}$, $\mathbf{t} \in [\![x]\!]^{g^X_B}$. Because $M \in PS_2^{inf}$, we have $[\![y]\!]^g \in \mathcal{V}$, and choosing $B = [\![y]\!]^g$, we have $[\![x]\!]^{g^X_B} = [\![x[y/X]]\!]^g$. Therefore $\mathbf{t} \notin [\![x[y/X]]\!]^g$, and therefore $T \Rightarrow x[y/X]$ is not satisfied by (M, g), which is a contradiction.

Case:$\forall$R. Suppose we obtain the sequent $T \Rightarrow \forall X.x[X/Z]$, where $Z \notin FV(T)$, and $X \notin FV(\forall Z.x)$, from $T \Rightarrow x$, and that the premise is satisfied by every (M, g) and that the conclusion is not. Hence for some (M, g), there is $\mathbf{t} \in [\![T]\!]^g$, $\mathbf{t} \notin [\![\forall X.x[X/Z]]\!]^g$. Therefore for some $B \in \mathcal{V}$, $\mathbf{t} \notin [\![x[X/Z]]\!]^{g^X_B}$. By the choice

of X, $[\![x[X/Z]]\!]^{g_B^X} = [\![x]\!]^{g_B^Z}$. Also since $Z \notin FV(T)$, $[\![T]\!]^g = [\![T]\!]^{g_B^Z}$. Therefore we have $\mathbf{t} \in [\![T]\!]^{g_B^Z}$, and $\mathbf{t} \notin [\![x]\!]^{g_B^Z}$. So we have that $T \Rightarrow x$ is not a satisfied by (M, g_B^Z), which is a contradiction.
Case:$\exists$L (similar to $\forall$R). Suppose we obtain the sequent $U, \exists X.x[X/Z], V \Rightarrow w$, where $Z \notin FV(U, V, w)$, and $X \notin FV(\exists Z.x)$, from U, x, $V \Rightarrow w$, and that the premise is satisfied by every (M, g) and that the conclusion is not. Hence for some (M, g) there are $\mathbf{u} \in [\![U]\!]^g$, $\mathbf{v} \in [\![V]\!]^g$, $a \in [\![\exists X.x[X/Z]]\!]^g$, such that $\mathbf{u}a\mathbf{v} \notin [\![w]\!]^g$. For some $B \in \mathcal{V}$, $a \in [\![x[X/Z]]\!]^{g_B^X}$. By the choice of X, $[\![x[X/Z]]\!]^{g_B^X} = [\![x]\!]^{g_B^Z}$. Also since $Z \notin FV(U, V, w)$, $[\![U]\!]^g = [\![U]\!]^{g_B^Z}$, $[\![V]\!]^g = [\![V]\!]^{g_B^Z}$, $[\![w]\!]^g = [\![w]\!]^{g_B^Z}$. Therefore we have $\mathbf{u} \in [\![U]\!]^{g_B^Z}$, $a \in [\![x[y/X]]\!]^{g_B^Z}$, $\mathbf{v} \in [\![V]\!]^{g_B^Z}$, and $\mathbf{u}a\mathbf{v} \notin [\![w]\!]^{g_B^Z}$, so $U, x, V \Rightarrow w$ is not satisfied by (M, g_B^Z), which is a contradiction.

We now prove PS_2^{inf}-completeness of $\text{L}^{(/,\backslash,\forall)}$. S^{inf} completeness of $\text{L}^{(/,\backslash)}$can be proved, by taking the semigroup of sequences of categories under the operation of sequence concatenation. The set of sequences which derive a category x, which we notate as $\mathcal{A}[x]$ ('antecedents of x'), is then used to give a canonical interpretation. The following proof pursues the same strategy, with an added twist owing to the presence of *assignments.* We define a canonical model, $M^c = \langle S^c, \bullet^c, \mathcal{V}^c, I^c \rangle$ thus:

S^c = all non-empty sequences of categories, $\bullet^c$ = sequence concatenation
$\mathcal{V}^c = \{\mathcal{A}[x] : x \text{ is a category}\}$
$I^c(x) = \mathcal{A}[x]$, where x is a basic category

Note that $\mathcal{P}(S^c) \neq \mathcal{V}^c$: no finite set can be $\mathcal{A}[x]$ for example. Thus $M^c \notin PS_1^{inf}$, which is good, otherwise the properties of M^c would contradict our claim of PS_1^{inf}-incompleteness.

We relate every assignment g from variables to values in $\mathcal{V}^c$ to (an equivalence class) of *substitutions.* We say a substitution σ 'IS ALLOWED BY g' if for each variable, X, $g(X) = \mathcal{A}[\sigma(X)]$. σ refers here to an *infinite simultaneous substitution*, mapping each variable to some category. Such a σ is extended in the obvious way to a function applying to every category[8]. Note that by the definition of 'IS ALLOWED BY', more than one substitution may be allowed by g. We first observe the following concerning $\mathcal{A}[x]$:

Lemma 10. *If* $\mathcal{A}[x] = \mathcal{A}[x']$, *then* $\mathcal{A}[x/y] = \mathcal{A}[x'/y]$, $\mathcal{A}[y/x] = \mathcal{A}[y/x']$, $\mathcal{A}[x\bullet y] = \mathcal{A}[x'\bullet y]$, $\mathcal{A}[y\bullet x] = \mathcal{A}[y\bullet x']$, $\mathcal{A}[QX.x] = \mathcal{A}[QX.x']$.

Proof If $\mathcal{A}[x] = \mathcal{A}[x']$, then $x \Rightarrow x'$ and vice-versa. Using these one can show $x/y \Rightarrow x'/y$, $y/x \Rightarrow y/x'$, $x\bullet y \Rightarrow x'\bullet y$, $y\bullet x \Rightarrow y\bullet x'$, $QX.x \Rightarrow QX.x'$, and vice-versa. From these, the desired identities of antecedents follow. □

---

[8] In application to a quantified term, $\forall Y.y$, such that Y occurs free in $\sigma(X_i)$ for one of $X_i \in FV(\forall Y.y)$, there is a change of bound variable to the first variable not in $FV(\forall Y.y)$ nor $\sigma(X_i)$ for any $X_i \in FV(\forall Y.y)$.

We define a relation F whose first argument is a pair $\langle x, g\rangle$ consisting of a category x and an assignment g from variables to values in $\mathcal{V}^c$, and whose second argument is a member of $\mathcal{V}$:

$$F(\langle x, g\rangle, A) \text{ iff } A = \mathcal{A}[\sigma(x)] \text{ , for some } \sigma \text{ allowed by } g$$

F is a function We show that if σ_1, σ_2 are two substitutions allowed by the same assignment (that is for all variables, $\mathcal{A}[\sigma_1(X_i)] = \mathcal{A}[\sigma_2(X_i)]$), then $\mathcal{A}[\sigma_1(x)] = \mathcal{A}[\sigma_2(x)]$. The substitutions σ_1 and σ_2 may precipitate changes of bound variable in x, but because the antecedents of categories which differ from each other only by a change of bound variable are identical, we can assume that σ_1 and σ_2 are such as to cause no change of bound variable. Then we use Lemma 10 for each of the free-variables of x, and for each of its occurrences, in order to infer that $\mathcal{A}[\sigma_1(x)] = \mathcal{A}[\sigma_2(x)]$. Henceforth we write $F(x, g)$ for the unique A such that $F(\langle x, g\rangle, A)$.

$F(x, g) = [\![x]\!]^g$ We show now the denotation function $[\![]\!]$ and F are the same function.

Case: variable, X.
$F(X, g)$
$= \mathcal{A}[\sigma(X)]$ for any σ allowed by g
$= \mathcal{A}[\sigma(X)]$ where $g(X) = \mathcal{A}[\sigma(X)]$
$= g(X)$

Case: basic category, x. $F(x, g)$
$= \mathcal{A}[\sigma(x)]$, for any σ allowed by g
$= \mathcal{A}[x]$, because $x = \sigma(x)$
$= I(x) = [\![x]\!]^g$

Case: $[\![x/y]\!]^g$. Let σ be an arbitrary substitution allowed by g, and write $\tilde{x}$ for $\sigma(x)$, and $\tilde{y}$ for $\sigma(y)$. We need to show that
$\{T \in S : \forall T_1 \in S (\text{if } L \vdash T_1 \Rightarrow \tilde{y}, \text{then } L \vdash T, T_1 \Rightarrow \tilde{x})\} = \{T \in S : L \vdash T \Rightarrow \tilde{x}/\tilde{y}\}$.
Left to Right. Note, $L \vdash \tilde{y} \Rightarrow \tilde{y}$, hence $L \vdash T,\ \tilde{y}\ \Rightarrow \tilde{x}$, hence $L \vdash T \Rightarrow \tilde{x}/\tilde{y}$ (by /R)
Right to Left. Let T_1 be arbitrarily chosen such that $L \vdash T_1 \Rightarrow \tilde{y}$. Hence $L \vdash \tilde{x}/\tilde{y}, T_1 \Rightarrow \tilde{x}$ (by /L), hence $L \vdash T, T_1 \Rightarrow \tilde{x}$ (by Cut, assuming $L \vdash T \Rightarrow \tilde{x}/\tilde{y}$)

Case $[\![\forall X.x]\!]^g$. Let σ be an arbitrary substitution allowed by g. Let $\sim$ denote the relation between categories when they differ by changes of bound variable. Because $\mathcal{A}[z] = \mathcal{A}[z']$, when $z \sim z'$, we can assume that $\forall X.x$ is such that the substitution σ causes no changes of bound variable. Let σ_X^z be the substitution differing from σ only by assigning z to X. We need:
$\cap\{\mathcal{A}[\sigma_X^y(x)] : \mathcal{A}[y] \in \mathcal{V}\} = \mathcal{A}[\sigma(\forall X.x)]$.
Left to Right. Suppose for all $\mathcal{A}[y] \in \mathcal{V}$, $T \in \mathcal{A}[\sigma_X^y(x)]$. Pick $Z \notin FV(T, \sigma(Y))$, where $Y \in FV(\forall X.x)$. We have $L \vdash T \Rightarrow \sigma_X^Z(x)$, hence $L \vdash T \Rightarrow \forall Z.\sigma_X^Z(x)$. By the choice of Z, $\forall Z.\sigma_X^Z(x) \sim \sigma(\forall X.x)$. Hence $L \vdash T \Rightarrow \sigma(\forall X.x)$.
Right to Left. Suppose $T \in \mathcal{A}[\sigma(\forall X.x]$, i.e. $L \vdash T \Rightarrow \forall X.\sigma_X^X(x)$. Hence for all y, $L \vdash T \Rightarrow (\sigma_X^X(x))[y/X]$ (By Cut, and $\forall$L). Suppose $T \notin \cap\{\mathcal{A}[\sigma_X^y(x)] : \mathcal{A}[y] \in \mathcal{V}\}$. Then for some $\mathcal{A}[y] \in \mathcal{V}$, $T \notin \mathcal{A}[\sigma_X^y(x)]$. But $\sigma_X^y(x) \sim (\sigma_X^X(x))[y/X]$, therefore $L \not\vdash T \Rightarrow (\sigma_X^X(x))[y/X]$ which is a contradiction.

M^c is in PS_2^{inf} Since $[\![x]\!]^g = F(x, g) = \mathcal{A}[\sigma(x)]$, for some σ allowed by g, we

have that $[\![x]\!]^g \in \mathcal{V}^c$, and therefore $M^c \in PS_2^{inf}$.

M^c is a countermodel to underivable sequents Suppose for all g, $[\![x_1]\!]^g \bullet \ldots \bullet [\![x_n]\!]^g \subseteq [\![y]\!]^g$. Let σ^* be an identity substitution. Let g^* be such that $g^*(X) = \mathcal{A}[X]$, then σ^* is allowed by g^*. We have $L \vdash x_i \Rightarrow x_i$. Because $\mathcal{A}[x_i] = \mathcal{A}[\sigma^*(x_i)] = F(x_i, g^*)$ $= [\![\sigma^*(x_i)]\!]^{g^*} = [\![x_i]\!]^{g^*}$, we have $x_i \in [\![x_i]\!]^{g^*}$. Therefore under the supposition, we have $x_1, \ldots, x_n \in [\![y]\!]^{g^*} = \mathcal{A}[\sigma^*(y)] = \mathcal{A}[y]$, and therefore $L \vdash x_1, \ldots, x_n \Rightarrow y$. □

2.1.3 Examples of $PS_{2,3}^{inf}$ Models

Completeness for the $PS_{2,3}^{inf}$ class is an open question. We make the modest contribution of showing that models in this class exist [9].

Example Six: *S is any set of strings closed under concatenation. $\mathcal{V} = \{S\}$, the interpretation is such that for basic categories, $I(x) = S$.* For Condition 2, we simply check that $\mathcal{V}$ is closed under $/,\backslash$, and $\cap$ and $\cup$. Because $\mathcal{V}$ contains only one set, Condition 2 entails Condition 3.

Example Seven:*S is any set of strings closed under concatenation, $\mathcal{V} = \{S, \emptyset\}$, the interpretation is such that for basic categories $I(x) \in \mathcal{V}$.* We note $[\![\exists X.X]\!]^g = S \cup \emptyset = S$, and that $[\![\forall X.X]\!]^g = S \cap \emptyset = \emptyset$. Thus $\mathcal{V}$ meets Condition 3. For Condition 2, we check that $\mathcal{V}$ is closed under $/,\backslash$, and pairwise $\cap$, and $\cup$. This gives that unions and intersections over arbitrary subsets of $\mathcal{V}$ are contained in $\mathcal{V}$.

Example Eight: S: $\{\alpha, \beta\}^+$, $\mathcal{V} = \{\{\alpha\beta\}, \{\alpha\}, \{\beta\}, \emptyset, S\}$, *and we assume that for some basic category,* s, $I(\mathrm{s}) = \{\alpha\beta\}$, *for some basic category,* np, $I(\mathrm{np}) = \{\alpha\}$, *and that all further basic categories have a value identical to one of these.*

For Condition 3 we note that $\mathcal{V} = \{[\![\mathrm{s}]\!]^g, [\![\mathrm{np}]\!]^g, [\![\mathrm{np}\backslash\mathrm{s}]\!]^g, [\![\forall X.X]\!]^g, [\![\exists X.X]\!]^g\}$. Note $\mathcal{V}$ is not closed under the union of *arbitrary* subsets. For Condition 2, however, we require less than this. Define a *spectrum* of x, relative to an assignment g and a variable X as $\{[\![x]\!]^{g_A^X} : A \in \mathcal{V}\}$. Condition 2 may be reformulated as the requirement that all spectra are subsets of $\mathcal{V}$, and this we will show, considering only categories with no vacuous quantification (vacuous quantifiers can be discarded without changing the denotation). The property is entailed by:

all spectra sp_1, sp_2 of x are (i) in $\mathcal{P}(\mathcal{V})$ and (ii) if x is complex then for all $B_1, B_2 \in \{\{\alpha\}, \{\beta\}, \{\alpha\beta\}\}$, $B_1 \in sp_1$, $B_2 \in sp_2$ implies $B_1 = B_2$. (1)

Proof. We show this by induction on the complexity of a category x. Consider variables and basic categories. Clearly the spectra of these are subsets of $\mathcal{V}$, and

[9] The examples furnish also further PS_2^{inf} models, in addition to the example M^c of the completeness proof.

so we have (i). Because x is not complex, (ii) is trivially true. Now for induction assume we have the property for all categories of complexity less than n and consider a category, x of complexity n. We give only the $\exists X.y$ case.

Case $x = \exists X.y$. Let sp be a spectrum of $\exists X.y$, for some assignment g and variable Z. Consider $[\![\exists X.y]\!]^{g_Z^A}$, for some $A \in \mathcal{V}$. This is $\bigcup sp_A$, where sp_A is the spectrum of y for g_Z^A and the variable X. By induction, $sp_A \subseteq \mathcal{V}$. When y is not complex, then sp_A is either a singleton subset of $\mathcal{V}$ or $\mathcal{V}$ itself, and so $\bigcup sp_A \in \mathcal{V}$. When y is complex, then by induction we have that sp_A contains at most one member of $\{\{\alpha\}, \{\beta\}, \{\alpha\beta\}\}$. This gives that $\bigcup sp_A \in \mathcal{V}$. Therefore $sp \subseteq \mathcal{V}$, i.e. (i). We must now show (ii) because $\exists X.y$ is complex. First note that if y is not complex, $y = X$, and the unique spectrum of $\exists X.y$ is $\{S\}$, and so (ii) is trivially satisfied. So suppose y is complex and suppose $B_1, B_2 \in \{\{\alpha\}, \{\beta\}, \{\alpha\beta\}\}$, such that $B_1 \in sp_1(\exists X.y)$ and $B_2 \in sp_2(\exists X.y)$ and suppose that $B_1 \neq B_2$. This implies spectra sp'_1 and sp'_2 of y and $B'_1, B'_2 \in \{\{\alpha\}, \{\beta\}, \{\alpha\beta\}\}$, such that $B'_1 \neq B'_2$, which contradicts our inductive assumption.

□

2.1.4 Open questions

Existential Quantifier The above completeness proof does not extend to the case with $\exists$. As with $\bullet$, the canonical model does not conform to the condition imposed by the connective. Consider $\exists X.a/(X/X)$, and assume that it contains no free variables. In the canonical model we need that $[\![\exists X.a/(X/X)]\!]^g = \mathcal{A}[\sigma(\exists X.a/(X/X))]$, for all σ allowed by g. Since $\exists X.a/(X/X) \in \mathcal{A}[\exists X.a/(X/X)]$, we require $\exists X.a/(X/X) \in [\![\exists X.a/(X/X)]\!]^g$, which holds iff $\exists X.a/(X/X) \in [\![a/(X/X)]\!]^{g_X^A}$ for some $A = \mathcal{A}[y] \in \mathcal{V}$, which holds iff $\exists X.a/(X/X) \Rightarrow a/(y/y)$ for some y. But there is no such y. For supposing there was such a y, then consideration of possible proofs gives that for some variable Z not occurring in y, we have $L \vdash Z \Rightarrow y$ and $L \vdash y \Rightarrow Z$. By the soundness of L, then these two sequents are satisfied in every model and assignment, and this could only be the case if every model had a singleton range of quantification, which is not the case.

Finite set of atomic strings M^c is not in PS_2. For the monomorphic calculus, there is a construction assigning to each underivable sequent a countermodel, taking V to be the subcategories of the given sequent. For V categories, the set of antecedents *over* V is the value, and the interpretation is extended to non-V categories. For $\text{L}^{(/,\backslash,\forall)}$ isolating the interpretation of V categories from non-V is impossible: the quantified V categories depend on $\mathcal{V}$, which itself must contain the values of all categories. PS_2 completeness is therefore an open question.

2.2 Connection between polymorphic grammars and string-semantics

In a similar way to the monomorphic case, we can establish a connection between the model-theory and the grammars. Since we have defined grammars with respect to a finite vocabulary, the most relevant model class is PS_2. It is reasonable to assume that in G_0, lexical items are assigned closed categories, and that the interesting part of the $L^{/,\backslash,\forall}$-closure G concerns also closed categories.

Given an $L^{/,\backslash,\forall}$-grammar G and a polymorphic model $\langle S, \bullet, \mathcal{V}, I\rangle$, we say the model *extends the grammar* when:

$$(x)_G \subseteq [\![x]\!]^g, \text{ for all (closed) } x \in \mathcal{L}(/, \backslash, \forall)$$

and the converse when the grammar extends the model. As in the monomorphic case, we have that if the model extends the values of $(x)_{G_0}$, then it extends the values $(x)_G$.

PS_2 soundness follows from PS_2^{inf}, and this gives that what G delivers is guaranteed to hold in all PS_2 models which extend the lexicon.

Suppose that $L^{(/,\backslash,\forall)}$ were not PS_2^{inf}-complete, so that for some sequent representing an inclusion true in all models, $L^{(/,\backslash,\forall)}$ did not derive it. Closing G_0 with this inclusion gives categorisations which are present in all PS_2^{inf}-models. Thus a G based on a complete calculus will give a fuller picture of what holds in all models of the lexicon than a G based on an incomplete calculus.

Whilst PS_2-completeness remains an open question, we still do not know whether G gives an incomplete picture of what holds in all PS_2 models.

The polymorphic pendant of Buszkowski's notion of a correct grammar has not yet been explored by the present author. In the polymorphic case, there are two parameters to be extracted from the grammar, the interpretation and the range of quantification. For $\mathcal{V}$ there are two possibilities: either $\mathcal{V} = \{(x)_G \mid x \text{ is closed category}\}$, or $\mathcal{V} \subset \{(x)_G \mid x \text{ is a closed category}\}$. The latter possibility is motivated by the fact that in a typical polymorphic grammar, the grammar will define a $(x)_G$, for many complex x which play no role in the derivations of the categorisations that one is primarily interested in. A model may most easily be obtained in such cases fulfilling $(x)_G \subseteq [\![x]\!]^g = S$.

2.3 Other Models for Quantified Calculi

We considered a polymorphic analog of the residuated semigroup models. For the quantified calculi we assign a value to a category relative to an assignment as usual, and interpret universal and existential quantifiers via greatest lower and least upper bounds.

Definition 9 (*PRES* **model)** $\langle M, \bullet, /, \backslash, [\![]\!]\rangle$ *is a RES-model if:* $\langle M, \bullet, /, \backslash\rangle \in$ *RES, and* $[\![]\!]$ *assigns members of M to categories in accordance to:*

1. $[\![C(x,y)]\!]^g = \mathbf{C}([\![x]\!]^g, [\![y]\!]^g)$.
2. $[\![x]\!]^g = g(x)$, *if x is variable*
3. $[\![x]\!]^{g_1} = [\![x]\!]^{g_2}$, *if x is basic*
4. $[\![\forall X.x]\!]^g = g.l.b\ (\{[\![x]\!]^{g^A_X} : A \in M\})$
5. $[\![\exists X.x]\!]^g = l.u.b\ (\{[\![x]\!]^{g^A_X} : A \in M\})$

Theorem 11. $L^{(/,\backslash,\bullet,\forall,\exists)} \vdash x_1, \ldots, x_n \Rightarrow y$ *iff for all models* $\langle M, \bullet, /, \backslash, [\![]\!]\rangle \in$ *PRES, and assignments g,* $[\![x_1]\!]^g, \ldots, [\![x_n]\!]^g \leq [\![y]\!]^g$

Proof. A canonical model $\langle M, /, \backslash, \bullet, [\![]\!]\rangle$ is defined with: $M = \{\mathcal{A}[x] : x$ is a category$\}$, $\mathbf{C}(\mathcal{A}[x], \mathcal{A}[y]) = \mathcal{A}[C(x,y)]$, for $\mathbf{C} = /, \backslash, \bullet$, $\mathcal{A}[x] \leq \mathcal{A}[y]$ iff $x \Rightarrow y$, and $[\![x]\!]^g = \mathcal{A}[\sigma(x)]$, for any substitution σ allowed by g. We show that this is a PRES-model.

Case x is basic: the interpretation is clearly independent of assignment.
Case x is a variable, X. Suppose $g(X) = \mathcal{A}[y]$. $[\![X]\!]^g = \mathcal{A}[\sigma(X)] = \mathcal{A}[y]$
Case Where C is a binary connective $[\![C(x,y)]\!]^g$. Let σ be allowed by g. We require $[\![C(x,y)]\!]^g = \mathbf{C}([\![x]\!]^g, [\![y]\!]^g)$. $\mathbf{C}([\![x]\!]^g, [\![y]\!]^g) = \mathbf{C}(\mathcal{A}[\sigma(x)], \mathcal{A}[\sigma(y)])=$ $\mathcal{A}[C(\sigma(x), \sigma(y))] = \mathcal{A}[\sigma(C(x,y))]$.
Case $[\![\forall X.x]\!]^g$. We require that $\mathcal{A}[\sigma(\forall X.x)]$ is the g.l.b. of $\{\mathcal{A}[\sigma^y_X(x)] : \mathcal{A}[y] \in M\}$.
$\mathcal{A}[\sigma(\forall X.x)]$ is a l.b.: we require that for any y, $\mathcal{A}[\sigma(\forall X.x)] \leq \mathcal{A}[\sigma^y_X(x)]$, i.e $L \vdash \sigma(\forall X.x) \Rightarrow \sigma^y_X(x)$. We can assume without loss of generality that σ precipitates no changes of bound variables in $\forall X.x$, i.e. $\sigma(\forall X.x) = \forall X.\sigma^X_X(x)$. Therefore by a ($\forall$L) inference, $L \vdash \sigma(\forall X.x) \Rightarrow \sigma^y_X(x)$.
$\mathcal{A}[\sigma(\forall X.x)]$ is a g.l.b.: Let $\mathcal{A}[z]$ be a l.b. of $\{\mathcal{A}[\sigma^y_X(x)] : \mathcal{A}[y] \in M\}$. That is suppose for any y, $L \vdash z \Rightarrow \sigma^y_X(x)$. If Z is some variable not free in x, nor $\sigma(Y)$, where $Y \in FV(x)$, then $\sigma(\forall X.x) \sim \forall Z.\sigma^Z_Z(x[Z/X]) \sim \forall Z.\sigma^Z_X(x)$. Let Z be also not free in z. We have $L \vdash z \Rightarrow \sigma^Z_X(x)$, and by the choice of Z, we have $L \vdash z \Rightarrow \forall Z.\sigma^Z_X(x)$. Therefore $L \vdash z \Rightarrow \sigma(\forall X.x)$, and $\sigma(\forall X.x)$ is the g.l.b.
Case $[\![\exists X.x]\!]^g$: similar to $\forall X.x$

It is easy to show that for any underivable sequent there is an assignment that leaves it unsatisfied: the assignment allows a null substitution. This completes the proof of Theorem 11. □

It is to be noted that Theorem 11 concerns the calculus with product, whereas Theorem 9 concerns a product-free calculus. The *PRES*-completeness of the *product-free* calculi remains an open question.

We consider also a polymorphic version of the associative ternary frame semantics.

Definition 10 (Polymorphic associative ternary frame interpretation) *$\langle W, R, \mathcal{V}, [\![]\!]\rangle$ is quantified associative ternary frame model if conditions on W and R from Definition 6 obtain, $\mathcal{V} \subseteq \mathcal{P}(W)$, $[\![]\!]$ is subject to the further conditions;*

$[\![x]\!]^g = g(x)$ *of x is a variable*
$[\![x]\!]^g$ *is independent of g if x is basic*
$[\![\forall X.x]\!]^g = \cap\{[\![x]\!]^{g^A_X} : A \in \mathcal{V}\}$
$[\![\exists X.x]\!]^g = \cup\{[\![x]\!]^{g^A_X} : A \in \mathcal{V}\}$

Theorem 12. $\text{L}^{(/,\backslash,\bullet,\forall,\exists)} \vdash x_1, \ldots, x_n \Rightarrow y$ *iff for all polymorphic associative ternary frame interpretations, where $\mathcal{V}$ covers the categories, $[\![x_1\bullet \ldots \bullet x_n]\!]^g \subseteq [\![y]\!]^g$*

The proof is omitted here. Soundness is easily shown by induction on the size of derivations. Completeness is easily shown by combining the well known canonical model construction for associative ternary frames with the technique used in the proof of Theorem 9.

3 Directions for future work

Okada [17] proves completeness results for an adaptation of Girard's Phase Space semantics [13], [14]. In the terminology of [17], the monomorphic (quantifier-free) case involves an *Intuitionistic Phase Space*, $D \subseteq 2^S$, S being a commutative monoid, and with D closed under linear implication ($= /$), and arbitrary intersections. S^{inf} models for $\mathrm{L}^{(/,\backslash)}$ can probably be seen as a version of this lacking commutativity, a unit, closure under intersection, and with closure under $/,\backslash$. A *classical* phase spaces require $A = \bot/(\bot/A)$, for all A in D, for some distinguished member $\bot$ of D. For the monomorphic case, soundness and completeness results for phase spaces have been obtained for linear logic in both classical [13] and intuitionistic [1] [17] variants.

In contrast to the string-semantics, $x \otimes y$ is treated as the smallest element of D containing $x \times y$ (the same as $\bot/(\bot/(x \times y))$ in classical phase spaces). Pentus' tricky proof [18] of S-completeness of $\mathrm{L}^{(/,\backslash,\bullet)}$ can probably be seen as completeness for a non-commutative variant of intuitionistic phase-spaces, with D additionally closed under $\times$.

Okada proves soundness and completeness of second order linear logic for *2nd Order Phase Spaces*, where one additionally has (for the numbering and notation refer to [17]):

P4 : every formula A is associated with a subset $\langle A \rangle$ of D, known as the candidate

P5 : for every formula B, for every $\alpha \in \langle B \rangle$, $A^*[\alpha/X] \in \langle A[B/X] \rangle$

and universal quantification is then handled via:

L10 : for any $\zeta : D \to D$, $\forall X.\zeta(X) = \bigcap\{\zeta(\alpha) \mid \alpha \in \langle B \rangle,\ B \text{ a formula}\}$

The exact connection between Okada's results and the results here is a topic for future work, and we end with some speculations concerning this. Perhaps our $\mathcal{V}$ can be seen as the union of the candidates of a second order phase space. PS_2^{inf} models and second order phase spaces share the feature that quantification is not handled by quantification over arbitary subsets of the underlying algebra. Can our PS_1^{inf}-incompleteness result be seen as an incompleteness result for second order phase spaces, where $D = 2^S$? Besides dropping commutativity, the PS_2^{inf} models also lack any requirement that $\mathcal{V}$ be closed under arbitary intersections. Requiring that quantifier ranges are closed under $/,\backslash$, and $\bigcap$, gives our Condition 2, so PS_2^{inf}-soundness gives soundness for the PS^{inf} models with such a closure. Whether completeness also holds for such models, and whether this is essentially Okada's (intuitionistic) result remain open questions.

Complete or not under such closures, there remains a question whether such an intersection is linguistically plausible. Requiring such a closure can be expected to make it harder to find a PS model extending a given polymorphic grammar: the universal quantifiers range over more sets, and correspondingly the denotations of the quantified categories get smaller.

References

1. V. Michele Abrusci. Sequent calculus for intuitionistic linear propositional logic. In P.P.Petkov, editor, *Proceedings of the Summer School and Conference on Mathematical Logic*. Plenum Press, 1990.
2. Kazimierz Ajdukiewicz. Die syntaktische konnexität. *Studia Philosophica*, 1, 1935.
3. Yehoshua Bar-Hillel. A quasi arithmetic notation for syntactic description. *Language*, 29, 1953.
4. Wojczech Buszkowski. Compatibility of a categorial grammar with an associated category system. *Zeitschrift für mathematische Logik und Grundlagen der Mathematik*, 28, 1982.
5. Wojczech Buszkowski. Completeness results for lambek syntactic calculus. *Zeitschrift für mathematische Logik und Grundlagen der Mathematik*, 32, 1986.
6. Martin Emms. Logical ambiguity. PhD Thesis, Centre of Cognitive Science, Edinburgh, 1992.
7. Martin Emms. Extraction covering extensions of the lambek calculus are not context free. In P. Dekker and M. Stokhof, editors, *Proceedings of Ninth Amsterdam Colloquium*, pages 268–286, 1993.
8. Martin Emms. Parsing with polymorphism. In *Sixth Annual Conference of the European Association for Computational Linguistics*, 1993.
9. Martin Emms. Some applications of categorial polymorphism. In DYANA *Deliverable R1.3.A*. ILLC, University of Amsterdam, 1993.
10. Martin Emms. Movement in labelled and polymorphic calculi. In *Proceedings of 1st Rome Workshop on Linear Logic and Categorial Grammar*, 1994.
11. Martin Emms. Undecidability result for polymorphic lambek calculus. In *Tenth Amsterdam Colloquium Proceedings*, 1995.
12. Martin Emms and Hans Leiß. Cut elimination in the second order lambek calculus. In DYANA *Deliverable R1.1.A*. ILLC, University of Amsterdam, 1993.
13. J.-Y. Girard. Linear logic. *Theoretical Computer Science*, 50(1–102), 1987.
14. J-Y. Girard. Linear logic: Syntax and semantics. In J.-Y.Girard, Y.Lafont, and L.Regnier, editors, *Advances in Linear Logic*, London Mathematical Society Lecture Note Series. Cambridge University Press, 1995. to appear.
15. Leon Henkin. Completeness in the theory of types. *Journal of Symbolic Logic*, 15:81–91, 1950.
16. Joachim Lambek. The mathematics of sentence structure. *American Mathematical Monthly*, 65:154–170, 1958.
17. Mitsuhiro Okada. Phase semantics for higher order completeness, cut-elimination and normalization proofs. In J.-Y. Girard, M. Okada, and A. Scedrov, editors, *Linear'96*, volume 3 of *Electronic Notes in Computer Science*. Elsevier, 1996. (available from http://pigeon.elsevier.nl/mcs/tcs/pc/menu.html).
18. Mati Pentus. Lambek grammar is l-complete. available by ftp, 1993.

Sloopy Identity

Claire Gardent

Computerlinguistik
Universität des Saarlandes
D-66041 Saarbrücken
E-mail: claire@coli.uni-sb.de

Abstract. Although sloppy interpretation is usually accounted for by theories of ellipsis, it often arises in non-elliptical contexts. In this paper, a theory of sloppy interpretation is provided which captures this fact. The underlying idea is that sloppy interpretation results from a semantic constraint on parallel structures and the theory is shown to predict sloppy readings for deaccented and paycheck sentences as well as relational-, event-, and one-anaphora. It is further shown to capture the interaction of sloppy/strict ambiguity with quantification and binding. Finally, it is compared with other approaches to sloppy identity, in particular [4,12] and [5].

1 Introduction

Sloppy interpretation involves two clauses: a **source** or antecedent clause and a **target** clause that is, a clause containing a proform (the **target proform**). When the antecedent of the target proform also contains a proform (the **source proform**), a sloppy interpretation may arise. In this case, the interpretation of the target proform differs from the interpretation of its source antecedent in the interpretation of the source proform. For instance, in:

Example 1. Jon^1 [washes his_1 car]^2. Peter does_2 too.

the VP-ellipsis *does* has, among others, the sloppy interpretation *washes Peter's car* (indeed, this is the preferred reading). The interpretation is sloppy because whereas in the source clause *Jon washes his car* the source proform *his* is interpreted as *Jon*, in the target clause *Peter does too*, it is re-interpreted as *Peter*.

Although it is most often associated with VP-ellipsis, the phenomenon of sloppy identity is in fact very pervasive, and can occur in a wide range of configurations for instance: deaccenting (example 2 where the deaccented material is in bold face), paycheck sentences (example 3), VPE as a source proform (examples 4 and 5), non-pronominal referential elements involving implicit arguments (examples 6 and 7), event anaphora (examples 8 and 9) and *one*-anaphora (example 10)[1].

[1] The material occuring between brackets represents the interpretation being considered, in this case, the sloppy interpretation. Most examples are from [15].

Example 2. Jon^1 took his$_1$ wife to the station. No, BILL **took his wife to the station**. *(Bill took Bill's wife to the station)*

Example 3. Jon^1 spent [his$_1$ paycheck]^2 but Peter saved it$_2$. *(Peter saved Peter's paycheck)*

Example 4. I'll [help you]^1 if you [want me to$_1$]^2. I'll kiss you even if you don't$_2$. *(I'll kiss you even if you don't want me to kiss you)*

Example 5. When Harry [drinks]^1, I always conceal [my belief that he shouldn't$_1$]^2. When he gambles, I can't conceal it$_2$. *(When he gambles, I can't conceal my belief that he shouldn't gamble)*

Example 6. Jon went to a local bar to watch the Super-bowl, and Bob did too. *(Bob went to a bar local to Bob)*

Example 7. George drove to the nearest hospital, and Fred did too. *(Fred drove to the hospital nearest to Fred)*

Example 8. Jon^1 got shot by his$_1$ father. That happened to Bob too. *(Bob got shot by Bob's father)*

Example 9. Jon^1 kissed his$_1$ wife, and Bill followed his example (Dahl, 1972) *(Bill kissed Bill's wife)*

Example 10. Although Jon^1 bought a picture of his$_1$ son, Bill snapped one himself. *(Bill snapped a picture of Bill's son)*

In short, sloppy interpretation can result from many combinations of source and target proform. Nevertheless most theories of sloppiness are restricted either to VPE or to Paycheck Pronouns thus failing to capture this obvious generalisation.

What are the constraints on sloppy interpretation? We claim that parallelism plays a fundamental role in triggering sloppiness. Specifically, it seems that sloppy interpretation is only possible when the antecedent of the source proform has a parallel counterpart in the target clause (cf. [4]). The following examples illustrate this. In example (11), *Jon* has a parallel counterpart in the target clause and consequently, a sloppy interpretation is possible. This sloppy interpretation is however not available in (12) where *Bill* has no parallel counterpart.

Example 11. The policeman who arrested Bill^1 [forgot to read him$_1$ his$_1$ rights]^2 and so did$_2$ the policeman who arrested Jon.

Example 12. The policeman who arrested Bill^1 [forgot to read him$_1$ his$_1$ rights]^2 and so did$_2$ Peter.

Of course, sloppy/strict ambiguity is not systematic in that interaction with other linguistic phenomena may block one or the other of the two possible readings. For instance in (13), interaction with quantification results in ruling out a strict reading. Similarly, in example (14), interaction with binding excludes a strict reading. Finally, example (15) shows that the sloppy/strict ambiguity is sensitive to the Pronoun/PN distinction: the source proform must be a pronoun (and not a proper name) for sloppiness to be possible.

Example 13. Every^1 man believes he$_1$ is a fool. No, PETER believes he is a fool. (sloppy only)

Example 14. Mary persuaded Jon^1 to shave himself$_1$. No, Mary persuaded PETER to shave himself. (sloppy only)

Example 15. Jon's mother loves Jon and Bill's mother does too (strict only)

In summary, a theory of sloppiness should be general enough to encompass the various configurations in which sloppy/strict ambiguity may arise while correctly accounting for the parallelism constraint illustrated by examples (11) and (12). Furthermore, it should predict the interaction of sloppy/strict ambiguity with such independent phenomena as quantification, binding theory and syntactic categorisation.

In this paper, I present a theory of sloppiness which adheres to these requirements. The proposed analysis is based on a simple parallelism constraint which is claimed to govern the interpretation of parallel propositions. In essence, this constraint requires that parallel structures share a non-trivial part of their semantics. Crucially, this constraint is stated in terms of equations and solved using Higher-Order Unification. It is the use of this particular mechanism which allows us to make the appropriate linguistic predictions: the multiple solutions generated by HOU mirror the sloppy/strict of natural language.

However, HOU is also known to systematically over-generate in that it yields solutions which although they are mathematically valid, are linguistically incorrect. To overcome this problem, we use a form of HOU developed for guiding inductive theorem proving, namely Higher-Order Coloured Unification (HOCU). The basic idea is that HOCU provides a general framework in which to model the interface between semantic construction and other levels of linguistic information. As we shall see, this yields a linguistically plausible way of avoiding over-generation.

The paper is structured as follows. Section 2 sketches the fundamentals of HOCU, and presents the analysis we propose. Section 3 shows that this analysis predicts the fact that both ellipsis and deaccenting may give rise to sloppy/strict ambiguity, section 4 that it naturally extends to paycheck pronouns, and section 5 that it encompasses those cases of sloppy/strict ambiguity in which the source proform is a VP-ellipsis. In section 6, I review the remaining sloppy/strict configurations and briefly indicate how they can be dealt with. Section 7 focuses on the interaction of sloppiness with quantification, binding and syntax. Section 8 compares the approach with previous proposals and in particular [12], [4] and [5]. Section 9 concludes with pointers to further research.

2 The analysis

Our analysis of sloppy identity falls out of an independent constraint on parallel structures. In [8], I argue that this constraint yields a simple treatment of deaccenting and of its relationship to ellipsis. In this paper, I show that it also provides a general theory of sloppy identity.

The parallelism constraint is a semantic constraint which governs the interpretation of parallel structures. Following [4] (henceforth, DSP), we take the structuring of parallelism as given, that is, we assume that parallel elements are known. The language used for semantic representation is the typed lambda calculus and discourse anaphors such as ellipses and discourse pronouns are represented by free variables of the appropriate type. For instance, a VP-ellipsis is assigned the semantic representation $P_{(e,t)}$ that is, a property variable. The parallelism constraint is as follows.

> Given *SSem* and *TSem*, the semantic representations of the source and target utterances and $SP_1, \ldots, SP_n, TP_1, \ldots, TP_n$, the semantic representations of the source and target parallel elements, the interpretation of parallel utterances must obey the following equations:

$$SSem = A(SP_1), \ldots, (SP_n)$$
$$TSem = A(TP_1), \ldots, (TP_n)$$

Crucially, these equations are resolved using Higher–Order Coloured Unification. Given the equation $(M = N)$, the unification problem consists in finding a well-formed coloured substitution of terms for free variables that will make M and N equal in the theory of $\alpha\beta\eta$–identity. For instance, given the equation $l(j,m) = R(j)$, a possible solution is the substitution which assigns $\lambda x.l(x,m)$ to R, written $\{R \leftarrow \lambda x.l(x,m)\}$. As a result, any free variable occuring in the equations (and in particular any free variable representing a discourse anaphor) is assigned a value. As we shall see, this method yields a uniform account of sloppy/strict ambiguity.

What precisely is Higher-Order Coloured Unification (HOCU) and how does it differ from standard HOU? For a precise description of HOCU, the reader is referred to [14]. Briefly, the important difference is that HOCU operates on a variant of the simply typed λ-calculus where symbol occurrences other than bound variables can be annotated with *colours*. Further, colours can be either constants or variables and restrict the unification process as follows. Colour variables unify both with colour variables and with colour constants. In contrast, a colour constant can only unify with the same colour constant. Further, variables labelled with colour constants are subject to the following restriction.

> For any colour constant c and any c–coloured variable V_c, a well–formed coloured substitution must assign to V_c a c–monochrome term i.e., a term whose symbols are c–coloured.

Why use HOCU? As we have already shown (cf. [9]), the intuition is that colours allows us to create an interface between semantic construction and other sources of linguistic knowledge. In this paper, we shall see that it is particularly useful in avoiding over-generation. We now illustrate this point by a simple example. Consider (16).

Example 16. Jon[1] likes his$_1$ wife. Peter does too.

In an HOU setting, the parallelism constraint yields the following equations for this discourse (recall that ellipses are represented using free variables; thus here R represents the ellipsis *does too*):

$$l(j,\ wife\_of(j)) = A(j)$$
$$R(p) = A(p)$$

Resolution of the first equation yields a total of 4 solutions, namely:

$$\{A \leftarrow \lambda x.l(x,\ wife\_of(x))\}$$
$$\{A \leftarrow \lambda x.l(x,\ wife\_of(j))\}$$
$$\{A \leftarrow \lambda x.l(j,\ wife\_of(x))\}$$
$$\{A \leftarrow \lambda x.l(j,\ wife\_of(j))\}$$

Linguistically, only the first two solutions are valid. The last two are invalid because they would yield an incorrect semantics for the discourse in (16), namely:

Jon likes Jon's wife and Jon likes Peter's wife.
Jon likes Jon's wife and Jon likes Jon's wife.

Intuitively, the problem is that the term occurrence representing the source subject appears in the target representation, and that it may not do so. To capture this intuition, DSP introduce the *Primary Occurrence Restriction* (POR) which in essence aims at ensuring that the term(s) representing the source parallel element(s) do not occur in the solution.

Primary Occurrence Restriction
Given a labeling of occurrences as either primary or secondary, the POR excludes from the set of linguistically valid solutions, any solution which contains a primary occurrence.

Within the HOCU framework, the POR finds a natural encoding: primary occurrences are p-coloured whilst the free variable representing an ellipsis is s-coloured. Since a well-formed coloured substitution only assigns to a c-coloured free variable (where c is a colour constant), a c-monochrome term, it follows that the term assigned to an ellipsis variable (R_{s}) may not contain any primary occurrence (because primary occurrences are p-coloured and p$\neq$ s). Coming back to example (16), the HOCU equations are (here and in what follows, we ignore irrelevant colours; A, B are colour variables):

$$l(j_{\mathsf{p}},\ wife\_of(j_{\mathsf{A}})) = A_{\mathsf{B}}(j_{\mathsf{p}})$$
$$R_{\mathsf{s}}(p_{\mathsf{p}}) = A_{\mathsf{B}}(p_{\mathsf{p}})$$

For which, the following substitutions are well-formed coloured substitutions

$$\{R_{\mathsf{s}} \leftarrow \lambda x.l(x,\ wife\_of(x)), A_{\mathsf{B}} \leftarrow \lambda x.l(x,\ wife\_of(x))\}$$
$$\{R_{\mathsf{s}} \leftarrow \lambda x.l(x,\ wife\_of(j_{\mathsf{s}})), A_{\mathsf{B}} \leftarrow \lambda x.l(x,\ wife\_of(j_{\mathsf{A}}))\}$$

but not these:

$$\{R_{\mathsf{s}} \leftarrow \lambda x.l(j_{\mathsf{P}},\ wife\_of(x)), A_{\mathsf{B}} \leftarrow \lambda x.l(j_{\mathsf{P}},\ wife\_of(x))\}$$
$$\{R_{\mathsf{s}} \leftarrow \lambda x.l(j_{\mathsf{P}},\ wife\_of(j_{\mathsf{s}})), A_{\mathsf{B}} \leftarrow \lambda x.l(j_{\mathsf{P}},\ wife\_of(j_{\mathsf{A}}))\}$$

To summarise: because HOU can yield several solutions (rather than a single one), it allows us to capture the sloppy/strict ambiguity displayed in natural language discourse. And because we use HOCU (rather than straight HOU), we can eliminate from the set of solutions, those solutions that are linguistically invalid. For more details on the applications of HOCU to natural language semantics, we refer the reader to ([9]). In what follows, we will omit colours unless they are used for something else than the POR. Concretely, this means that colours will only re-appear in section 7, where we concentrate on the interaction between semantic construction and other sources of linguistic information.

3 Sloppy identity in ellipsis and deaccenting contexts

It has often been observed (cf. [19,1,18]) that VP-ellipsis and deaccenting (i.e. prosodic reduction) share a number of interpretive similarities and in particular that they both give rise to sloppy/strict ambiguity. Thus in (18), the target VP *took his wife to the station* is deaccented, and like the elided VP in (17), it can be interpreted either strictly or sloppily (upper letters indicate prosodic prominence and bold face deaccented material).

Example 17. Jon[1] took his$_1$ wife to the station. No, BILL did.

Example 18. Jon[1] took his$_1$ wife to the station. No, BILL **took his wife to the station.**

Interestingly, this is exactly what the parallelism constraint predicts. Thus in the VPE case, the parallelism constraint requires that the following equations hold:

$$tk(j,\ wife\_of(j), s) = A(j)$$
$$R(b) = A(b)$$

Resolving the first equation yields two possible values for A:

$$\{A \leftarrow \lambda x.tk(x,\ wife\_of(x), s)\}$$
$$\{A \leftarrow \lambda x.tk(x,\ wife\_of(j), s)\}$$

And consequently, the target clause receives two interpretations, either $tk(b,\ wife\_of(b), s)$ or $tk(b,\ wife\_of(j), s)$ – as required. Now consider the deaccenting case. As for the ellipsis case, we assume that anaphors in the source are resolved whereas discourse anaphors in the target are represented using free variables (alternatively, we could resolve them first and let HOU filter unsuitable resolutions out). Specifically, the target pronoun *his* is represented by the free variable x and the equations to be solved are:

$$tk(j,\ wife\_of(j), s) = A(j)$$
$$tk(b,\ wife\_of(x), s) = A(b)$$

The first equation is resolved as before, thereby yielding two possibilities for the second equation:

$$tk(b,\ wife\_of(x), s) = tk(b,\ wife\_of(b), s)$$
$$tk(b,\ wife\_of(x), s) = tk(b,\ wife\_of(j), s)$$

It follows that x can unify either to j or to b and accordingly, the target pronoun *his* is interpreted as either strict (*Jon*) or sloppy (*Bill*).

Another interesting fact about sloppy interpretation in deaccenting and VP ellipsis contexts is that it may involve an extended domain of licensing that is, a domain that extends beyond the clausal level. For instance, [18] notes that in (19) and (20), both the deaccented *I was bad-mouthing her* and the elliptical *I was* can be assigned the sloppy interpretation: *I was bad-mouthing Sue* even though *Sue* is not part of the anaphoric clause.

Example 19. First, Jon told Mary^1 I was bad-mouthing her$_1$, and then he told SUE I was.

Example 20. First, Jon told Mary^1 I was bad-mouthing her$_1$, and then he told SUE I was bad-mouthing her.

More generally, the interpretation of both ellipsis and deaccenting can depend on elements which occur outwith their governing categories. This suggests that the semantic licensing of these two phenomena occurs at the sentential rather than at the clausal level. Again this falls out of the parallelism constraint: since this constraint operates on utterance representations, it is not restricted to clauses but may indifferently apply either to clauses or to sentences. Specifically, the analysis for the above examples goes as follows.

For the ellipsis case, the equations are:

$$t(j, m, bm(i, m)) = A(m)$$
$$t(x, s, R(i)) = A(s)$$

Solving the first equation yields $\lambda z.t(j, z, bm(i, z))$ and $\lambda z.t(j, z, bm(i, m))$ as possible values for A. By substitution and β-reduction $A(s)$ is then either $t(j, s, bm(i, s))$ or $t(j, s, bm(i, m))$ and the resulting equations are resolved by the following substitutions:

$$\{x \leftarrow j, R \leftarrow \lambda z.bm(z, m)\}$$
$$\{x \leftarrow j, R \leftarrow \lambda z.bm(z, s)\}$$

where the first solution yields the strict reading, the second the sloppy. Resolution of the deaccenting case can similarly be summarised as follows. This time, the equations resulting from the parallelism constraint are:

$$t(j, m, bm(i, m)) = A(m)$$
$$t(x, s, bm(i, y)) = A(s)$$

As before, resolving the first equation yields two possible values for A namely, $\lambda z.t(j,z,bm(i,z))$ and $\lambda z.t(j,z,bm(i,m))$. Similarly, $A(s)$ is then either $t(j,s,bm(i,s))$ or $t(j,s,bm(i,m))$. Consequently, (20) also receives both a strict and a sloppy interpretation.

Finally, deaccenting may involve more complex cases of sloppy interpretation as illustrated by the following examples.

Example 21. Jon^1 said he$_1$ was clever. No, PETER said he was intelligent.

Example 22. The policeman who arrested Jon^1 forgot to read him$_1$ his$_1$ rights and so did the one PETER got collared by.

Example (21) is a straightforward deaccenting example where the deaccented material differs in its lexical realisation from its source counterpart; example (22) is more complex and involves both deaccenting and VP-ellipsis. Both cases trigger a sloppy/strict ambiguity in the interpretation of the target clause.

The important point is that in such cases, ellipsis and deaccenting differ in the semantic relation they require to hold between source and target utterances. In the ellipsis case, the relation is one of syntactic identity: the semantic representation of the ellipsis in the target clause must be identical with the semantic representation of part of the source clause. In the case of deaccenting, the relation is more subtle. Consider (23) for instance.

Example 23. First, JON called Mary a Republican and then PETER insulted her.

[18] argues that in such cases, entailment is involved in licensing prosodic reduction: (23) is licensed by the implication that 'if x calls y a republican, then x insults y' and consequently, the deaccented clause is interpreted as *Peter insulted Mary.* Note that through the entailment, *her* is resolved to *Mary.*

However, Rooth himself notes that the licensing relation between a deaccented sentence and its source, need not always be entailment. Thus in examples (24), (25) and (26), there is clearly no entailment relation holding between source and target clause.

Example 24. He bit her and then SHE punched HIM.

Example 25. Tell me who assaulted whom? HE bit HER.

Example 26. First, a policeman arrested Peter and then PAUL got collared by one.

Rather, the requirement seems to be that the two clauses entail a (reasonably specific) common proposition of a more general form. For instance, the deaccenting in (26) seems to be licensed by the fact that both x *arrest* y and x *collared* y entail that x *did something nasty to* y (note that if I say *First, a policeman arrested Peter and then PAUL was invited to TEA by one*, I have to stress *was invited to TEA*). More specifically, one could follow [19] and argue that deaccenting is licensed provided $(X_S \supset Y) \wedge (X_T \supset Y)$ where X_S, X_T are the semantic representations of the source and target clauses respectively, and Y is such that it subsumes X_S and X_T and it is entailed by X_S and X_T.

Now, whatever the relation is, which holds between a deaccented clause and its source, the above data is clearly problematic for the HOU approach. In such cases, the semantic representation of the deaccented material will differ from that of its parallel counterpart in the source and therefore HOU (which is essentially a matching operation on syntactic structures) will fail thus failing to account for some perfectly acceptable discourses.

There is an intuitively natural solution to this problem. As we already argued in [10,8], a variant of HOU is required to deal with the semantics of deaccenting namely, HOU augmented with logical relations (HOU+R, cf. [16]). Crucially, this form of unification takes into account not only syntactic $\alpha\beta\eta$-identity, but also any logical relation we care to specify. For instance, if the specified relation is entailment, the equation $(M = N)$ will be solved by HOU+R if either M and N syntactically unify or if it can be proved that M entails N. The point is that whatever the relation is which we find, holds between a deaccented clause and its source, we can integrate it into the HOU framework (provided it's a logical relation). Briefly, the HOU+R approach consists in combining HOU with theorem proving. Specifically, each time an intermediate equation $(M = N)$ of type t is found, the theorem prover is called to try and prove that $R(M, N)$ (where R is the specific relation HOU is incremented with). Thus, if we assume that source and target clause must share a common property, any attempt to solve $(M = N)$ will trigger the attempt to prove that $(M \supset Y) \wedge (N \supset Y)$ where Y subsumes both M and N. For a more detailed presentation of HOU+R, we refer the reader to [16]; for a discussion of how this form of unification can be used for deaccenting, see [10,8]. We now briefly sketch how such cases can be handled within the HOU+R framework. Consider example (22) with sloppy interpretation *The policeman who Peter got collared by forgot to read Peter Peter's rights.* The equations to be resolved are:

$$\exists x[po(x) \wedge ar(x,j) \wedge f(x, rd(x,j,j'sr))] = A(j)$$
$$\exists x[Q(x) \wedge col(x,p) \wedge R(x)] = A(p)$$

Solving the first equation yields (we concentrate on the sloppy reading):

$$\{A \leftarrow \lambda z.\exists x[po(x) \wedge ar(x,z) \wedge f(x, rd(x,z,z'sr))]\}$$

Consequently, the second equation becomes

$$\exists x[Q(x) \wedge col(x,p) \wedge R(x)] = \exists x[po(x) \wedge ar(x,p) \wedge f(x, rd(x,p,p'sr))]$$

For which, a possible solution is: $\{Q \leftarrow \lambda z.po(z), R \leftarrow \lambda z.f(z, rd(z,p,p'sr))\}$ After substitution, the lhs of the equation is then:

$$\exists x[po(x) \wedge col(x,p) \wedge f(x, rd(x,p,p'sr))]$$

That is, the underspecified semantics of the target *so did the one Peter got collared by* has correctly been resolved to *the policeman who arrested Peter forgot to read Peter Peter's rights.* Note however that the equation is not solved. Rather, we've reached a situation in which no free variable occurs but still left and right-hand sides are not identical. Within the HOU+R setting, an attempt will then be made to prove that R holds between both sides of the equation. In this case, the theorem prover must prove that both sides of the equations entail a common more general proposition. Specifically, it must be proved that:

$$\exists x[po(x) \wedge ar(x,p) \wedge f(x, rd(x,p,p'sr)) \supset Y] \wedge$$
$$\exists x[po(x) \wedge col(x,p) \wedge f(x, rd(x,p,p'sr)) \supset Y]$$

Since tableaux are refutation systems, we in fact try to prove the negation of this formula and aim for a contradiction. During the proof process, each conjunctive formula can be broken down into its conjuncts which are then added to the current tableau branch. Conversely, a disjunctive formula triggers a branching of the tree whereby each new branch is labelled with one of the disjuncts. Universal and existential formulas license the addition of an instantiation of this formula to the current branch (whereby the instantiation drops the quantifier and replaces the bound variable by an unused free variable in the case of a universal and by a new skolem term in the case of an existential). Finally, if both X_1 and $\neg X_2$ occur on the same tableau branch, and if a substitution can be found which makes X_1 and X_2 equal, the branch is closed. When all tableau branches are closed, the theorem is proved (for a more precise definition of the tableau method, see e.g. [6]). The tableau for the above example can be sketched as follows. In a first phase, we get (we abbreviate $f(x, rd(x,p,p'sr))$ to $fr(x,p)$):

$$(1) \quad \forall x \forall y[ar(x,y) \supset nasty(x,y)]$$
$$(2) \quad \forall x \forall y[col(x,y) \supset nasty(x,y)]$$
$$(3) \quad ar(v_1,v_2) \supset nasty(v_1,v_2)$$
$$(4) \quad col(v_3,v_4) \supset nasty(v_3,v_4)$$
$$(5) \quad \neg(\exists x[po(x) \wedge ar(x,p) \wedge fr(x,p) \supset Y] \wedge \exists x[po(x) \wedge col(x,p) \wedge fr(x,p) \supset Y])$$
$$(6) \quad \neg\exists x[po(x) \wedge ar(x,p) \wedge fr(x,p) \supset Y] | \neg\exists x[po(x) \wedge col(x,p) \wedge fr(x,p) \supset Y]$$

1 and 2 formalise the fact that we assume a context where *if x arrests y, then x is nasty to y* and further *if x collars y, then x is nasty to y*. 3 and 4 are from 1 and 2 by instantiation (where v_i are new free variables). 5 is the negation of what has to be proved. Since $\neg(X \wedge Y)$ is a disjunctive formula, the tableau branches and its disjuncts $\neg X$ and $\neg Y$ are added to the new branches. We now show the continuing derivation for the left branch (the right branch develops in a similar way). For readability, we add lines 3 and 6 of the beginning tableau to the continuing tableau.

$$
\begin{array}{c}
(3)\ \ ar(v_1, v_2) \supset nasty(v_1, v_2) \\
(6)\ \ \neg\exists x[po(x) \wedge ar(x,p) \wedge fr(x,p) \supset Y] \\
(7)\ \ \neg[po(v_1) \wedge ar(v_1,p) \wedge fr(v_1,p) \supset Y] \\
(8)\ \ po(v_1) \wedge ar(v_1,p) \wedge fr(v_1,p) \\
(9)\ \ \neg Y \\
(10)\ \ po(v_1) \\
(11)\ \ ar(v_1,p) \\
(12)\ \ fr(v_1,p) \\
\begin{array}{c|c}
(13)\ \ \neg ar(v_1, v_2) & nasty(v_1, v_2) \\
\{v_2 \leftarrow p\} & \{Y \leftarrow nasty(v_1, v_2)\} \\
\star & \star
\end{array}
\end{array}
$$

7 is from 6 by instantiation. Since $\neg(X \supset Y)$ is a conjunctive formula with conjuncts X and $\neg Y$, lines 8 and 9 are added to the tableau (from 7). Similarly, lines 10, 11 and 12 are from line 8 (because line 8 is labelled with a conjunctive formula). At this stage, the disjunctive formula in (3) is used and the tree branches yielding (13). By using the indicated bindings, we derive the contradictions $\neg ar(v_1, p) \wedge ar(v_1, p)$ for the leftmost branch, and $\neg\ nasty(v_1, p) \wedge nasty(v_1, p)$ for the rightmost one. Since both branches are closed, the tableau is closed and proposition (1) is proved. Thus HOU+R succeeds thereby yielding the appropriate sloppy interpretation for the target clause *So did the one Peter got collared by.*

4 Paycheck Pronouns

Why does the parallelism constraint predict paycheck pronouns? Intuitively, the reason is that as in the ellipsis case, the λ-term shared by source and target utterances may contain the representation of a pronoun. When the antecedent of this pronoun is a parallel element, HOU predicts that this pronoun can behave sloppily. Let us see in more detail how this works. Consider example (27).

Example 27. Jon^1 spent [his$_1$ paycheck]^2 but Peter saved it$_2$.

The pronoun *it* occurring in the second clause has a sloppy interpretation in that it can be interpreted as meaning *Peter's paycheck*, rather than *Jon's paycheck*. In the literature such pronouns are known as *paycheck pronouns* and are treated as introducing a definite whose restriction is pragmatically given (cf. e.g. [2]). Within our proposal, we can straightforwardly capture this intuition by assigning paycheck pronouns the following representation:

$$\text{Pro} \leadsto \lambda Q.\exists x[P(x) \wedge \forall y[P(y) \rightarrow y = x] \wedge Q(x)] \text{ with } P \in \ \mathit{wff}_{(e \rightarrow t)}$$

That is, paycheck pronouns are treated as definites whose restriction (P) is a variable of type $(e \rightarrow t)$. Furthermore, we assume that paycheck pronouns like VP-ellipses, occur in parallel structures and hence are subject to the parallelism constraint. Under these assumption the following equations must hold (we abbreviate $\lambda Q.\exists x[P(x) \wedge \forall y[P(y) \rightarrow y = x] \wedge Q(x)]$ to$\lambda Q.\exists_1 x[P(x) \wedge Q(x)]$):

$$\exists_1 x[pc\_of(x, j) \wedge sp(j, x)] = A(j, sp)$$
$$\exists_1 x[P(x) \wedge sa(p, x)] = A(p, sa)$$

Resolving the first equation yields $\lambda y.\lambda O.\exists_1 x[pc\_of(x, y) \wedge O(y, x)]$ as a value for A so that $A(p, sa) = \exists_1 x[pc\_of(x, p) \wedge sa(p, x)]$ and $\{P \leftarrow \lambda y.pc\_of(y, p)\}$. That is, the target clause is correctly assigned the sloppy interpretation: *Peter saved Peter's paycheck.*

5 Source proform: VPE

So far, we have considered cases of sloppy interpretation in which the source proform is a pronoun. Interestingly however, the source proform can also be a VP ellipsis. This is illustrated by the following examples (from [12]).

Example 28. I'll [help you]^1 if you [want me to$_1$]^2. I'll kiss you even if you don't$_2$.

Example 29. When Harry [drinks]^1, I always conceal [my belief that he shouldn't$_1$]^2. When he gambles, I can't conceal it$_2$.

	Source Utterance	Target Utterance
Configuration	$\text{NP}^j, \ldots, [_{VP}, \ldots, \boxed{\text{PRO}}_j, \ldots,]^i$	$, \ldots, \boxed{\text{VPE}}_i, \ldots,$
Example	*Jon$_j$ [$_{VP}$ washes $\boxed{\textit{his}}_j$ car]^i*	*Peter $\boxed{\textit{does}}_i$ too.*
Configuration	$\text{VP}^j, \ldots, [_{VP}, \ldots, \boxed{\text{VPE}}_j, \ldots,]^i$	$, \ldots, \boxed{\text{VPE}}_i, \ldots,$
Example	*I'll [help you]^j, if you [$_{VP}$ want me $\boxed{\textit{to}}_j$]^i*	*I'll kiss you even if you $\boxed{\textit{don't}}_i$.*
Configuration	$\text{NP}^j, \ldots, [_{NP}, \ldots, \boxed{\text{PRO}}_j, \ldots,]^i$	$, \ldots, \boxed{\text{PRO}}_i, \ldots,$
Example	*Jon$_j$ spent [$_{NP}$ $\boxed{\textit{his}}_j$ paycheck]^i*	*but Peter saved $\boxed{\textit{it}}_i$.*
Configuration	$\text{VP}^j, \ldots, [_{NP}, \ldots, \boxed{\text{VPE}}_j, \ldots,]^i$	$, \ldots, \boxed{\text{PRO}}_i, \ldots,$
Example	*When Harry [drinks]$_j$, I conceal [$_{NP}$ my belief that he $\boxed{\textit{shouldn't}}_j$]^i*	*When he gambles, I can't conceal $\boxed{\textit{it}}_i$.*

Table 1. Ellipsis, Pronouns and sloppiness

In (28), the target proform is a VPE whose antecedent contains a VPE. In other words, the source proform is a VPE. Similarly, in (29), the target proform is a pronoun with a VPE as a source proform. Both examples have a sloppy interpretation: *I'll kiss you even if you don't want me to kiss you* (instead of *help you* in the source clause) and *I can't conceal the belief that he shouldn't gamble* (instead of *he shouldn't drink* in the source clause).

What these (and the previous) examples show, is that sloppy interpretation is independent of whether the source and the target proforms are VPEs or pronominal anaphors. A correct theory of sloppy interpretation must therefore be general enough to encompass all possible cases in a uniform way. This is predicted by our account where sloppy interpretation follows, not from the treatment of VPE and paycheck pronouns, but from their interaction with the parallelism constraint. In what follows we show that our approach accounts for examples (28) and (29) thus covering the four possible configurations for sloppy interpretation illustrated in table (1) where boxes surround the source and target proforms. Consider (28) first. Assuming that the parallel elements are *help* and *kiss* respectively, the parallelism constraint requires that

$$\begin{array}{l} h(i, you) \leftarrow wt(you, h(i, you)) = A(h) \\ k(i, you) \leftarrow P(you)) = A(k) \end{array}$$

Resolution of the first equation yields $\lambda R.(R(i, you) \leftarrow wt(you, R(i, you)))$ as a possible value for A so that the value for $A(k)$ is:

$$\lambda R.(R(i, you) \leftarrow wt(you, R(i, you))(k) = A(k)$$

or equivalently $k(i, you) \leftarrow wt(you, k(i, you))$. Indirectly then, the value of P is now $\lambda x.wt(i, k(i, x))$ so that the VPE occurring in the second clause is correctly interpreted as meaning *want me to kiss you.*

Similarly, the derivation for (29) proceeds as follows. This time we assume that *drinks* and *gambles* are the parallel elements so that the parallelism constraint gives rise to the following equations:

$$\begin{array}{l} dk(h) \rightarrow \exists x[bel(x, sn(dk(h))) \wedge hide(i, x)] = A(dk) \\ gb(h) \rightarrow \exists x[P(x) \wedge hide(i, x)] = A(gb) \end{array}$$

Resolving the first equation yields $\lambda R.(R(h) \rightarrow \exists x[bel(x, sn(R(h))) \wedge hide(i, x)])$ as a possible value for A. By β-reduction, the value of $A(gb)$ is then $gb(h) \rightarrow \exists x[bel(x, sn(gb(h))) \wedge hide(i, x)]$ and P is resolved to $\lambda y.bel(y, sn(gb(h)))$. That is the second clause of the target utterance is interpreted as meaning *I can't conceal my belief that Harry shouldn't gamble* and thereby the pronoun *it* is sloppily resolved to *my belief that Harry shouldn't gamble.*

6 Other sloppy constructions

[15] lists a number of constructions where sloppy/strict ambiguity is possible. We now consider these cases. The first construction involves implicit referential arguments and is exemplified in (30).

Example 30. Jon went to a local bar to watch the Super-bowl, and Bob did too. *(Bob went to a bar local to Bob/Jon)*

If these implicit arguments are taken to be present in the semantic representation, those cases are unproblematic. For instance, the equations for (30) are:

$$\begin{array}{l}\exists x[\; bar(x) \wedge\; loc(x,j) \wedge\; went(j,x,\;\; watch(j,sb))] = A(j) \\ R(b) = A(b)\end{array}$$

Solving the first equation yields two solutions for A, namely

$$\begin{array}{l}\{A \leftarrow \lambda z.\exists x[\; bar(x) \wedge\; loc(x,z) \wedge\; went(z,x,\;\; watch(z,sb))]\} \\ \{A \leftarrow \lambda z.\exists x[\; bar(x) \wedge\; loc(x,j) \wedge\; went(z,x,\;\; watch(z,sb))]\}\end{array}$$

The first solution yields the sloppy reading and the second, the strict.

Another construction listed in [15] is one involving either pronominal (31) or definite (32) event anaphora.

Example 31. Jon got shot by his father. That happened to Bob too. (*Bob got shot by Bob/Jon's father*)

Example 32. Jon kissed his wife, and Bill followed his example (Dahl, 1972) (*Bill kissed Jon/Bill's wife*)

Here the question arises as to how expressions such as *that happened* and *followed x's example* should be represented. Without going into any details about these constructions, it seems reasonable to assume that these expressions are essentially anaphors in that their meaning is determined by the context. Under this assumption, the second clause of (31) and (32) is then represented as $R(b)$ and the equations for e.g. (31) are:

$$\begin{array}{r}shot(f(j),j) = A(j) \\ R(b) = A(b)\end{array}$$

As usual, resolution of the first equation gives us two solutions, one sloppy ($\{R \leftarrow \lambda z.\; shot(f(z),z)\}$) and one strict ($\{R \leftarrow \lambda z.\; shot(f(j),z)\}$).

One-anaphora also permits sloppy/strict ambiguity.

Example 33. Although Jon bought a picture of his son, Bill snapped one himself.

We can capture this by treating one-anaphora similarly to paycheck pronouns that is, as definites whose restriction is pragmatically given. Under this assumption, the equations for (33) are:

$$\begin{array}{l}\exists x[pic\_of(x,j's\;\; son) \wedge bo(j,x)] = A(j,bo) \\ \exists x[P(x) \wedge sna(b,x)] = A(b,sna)\end{array}$$

The sloppy interpretation is given by the solution

$$\{A \leftarrow \lambda z \lambda y.\exists x[pic\_of(x,z's\;\; son) \wedge y(z,x)]\}$$

and the strict reading by the second solution

$$\{A \leftarrow \lambda z \lambda y.\exists x[pic\_of(x,j's\;\; son) \wedge y(z,x)]\}$$

7 Interaction with syntax and quantification

As should be clear from the above discussion, our analysis predicts a systematic ambiguity between strict and sloppy interpretation. However, there are certain constraints on this ambiguity which result from the interaction of parallelism with other linguistic phenomena. We now consider these constraints.

Syntax Categorial information can affect sloppy/strict ambiguity. Thus although (34) has two readings, one strict and one sloppy, (35) can only have the strict reading.

Example 34. Jon^1's mother loves him$_1$ and Bill's mother does too (sloppy/strict)

Example 35. Jon's mother loves Jon and Bill's mother does too (strict only)

Within the standard (that is, non-coloured) HOU framework, such examples are problematic because (34) and (35) have the same semantic representation and therefore, there is no way in which they can be distinguished. In other words, both examples will be predicted to be sloppy/strict ambiguous. However within the HOCU framework, colours can be used to create an interface between semantic construction and other levels of linguistic information. In section 2, we saw that pronouns are variable coloured and hence can give rise either to a strict or to a sloppy interpretation of the target. For full NPs, we stipulate that they be s-coloured. Given this, the equations for (35) are:

$$l(m(j_{\mathsf{p}}), j_{\mathsf{s}}) = A_{\mathsf{B}}(j_{\mathsf{p}})$$
$$R_{\mathsf{s}}(m(b_{\mathsf{p}})) = A_{\mathsf{B}}(b_{\mathsf{p}})$$

Crucially, resolution of the first equation yields only one solution, not two, namely $A_{\mathsf{B}} = \lambda z.l(m(z), j_{\mathsf{s}})$ – this yields the strict reading. By contrast, the sloppy reading is ruled out because the corresponding substitution $\{A_{\mathsf{B}} \leftarrow \lambda z.l(m(z), z)\}$ is not a unifier for the given equations. To see this, it suffices to apply this substitution to the right-hand side of the equation, $A_{\mathsf{B}}(j_{\mathsf{p}})$. This yields $\lambda z.l(m(z), z)(j_{\mathsf{p}})$ which by β-reduction is equivalent to $l(m(j_{\mathsf{p}}), j_{\mathsf{p}})$. But this does not unify with the left-hand side of the equation because of the colour-clash on the second occurrence of j. Hence the sloppy reading is ruled out.

Scope constraints Quantification also constrains sloppiness. This is illustrated by the following examples.

Example 36. Every^1 man believes he$_1$ is a fool. No, PETER believes he is a fool. (sloppy only)

Example 37. Jon lost a^1 book and never got it$_1$ back. No, Peter lost a PEN and never got it back (sloppy only)

In both (36) and (37), the source pronoun has a quantified antecedent and furthermore, this quantified NP does not scope over the target utterance. As a result, only the sloppy interpretation is possible. The strict interpretation is ruled out because it would involve a free variable, the variable introduced by the source quantified antecedent and occuring in the target representation. Under our analysis, this constraint simply follows from general constraints on substitutions which essentially say that a free variable may never become bound and vice-versa. Thus for (36), the parallelism constraint requires that the following equations hold (as in DSP, when a proper name has a quantified parallel element, we use the type-raised representation of proper names to guarantee parallelism of types):

$$\forall x[b(x) \rightarrow bel(x, f(x))] = A(\lambda P.\forall x[b(x) \rightarrow P(x)])$$
$$bel(p, f(y)) = A(\lambda P.P(p))$$

To obtain the strict reading, the second equation needs to be resolved as follows:

$$\{A \leftarrow \lambda Q.Q(\lambda z.bel(z, f(x)), y \leftarrow x\}$$

Applying this substitution to the first equation, we then get

$$\begin{aligned} A(\lambda P.\forall x[b(x) \rightarrow P(x)]) &= \lambda Q.Q(\lambda z.bel(z, f(x))(\lambda P.\forall x[b(x) \rightarrow P(x)]) \\ &= \lambda P.\forall x[b(x) \rightarrow P(x)](\lambda z.bel(z, f(x))) \end{aligned}$$

And at this point, the restrictions on well-formed substitutions requires that x be renamed. Hence x can never be bound by the source quantifier *every man*.

Binding constraints As is illustrated by the following example, the binding constraints also play a role in constraining strict interpretation.

Example 38. Mary persuaded Jon[1] to shave himself$_1$. No, Mary persuaded PETER to shave himself. (sloppy only)

Here only the sloppy interpretation is possible. The most obvious explanation for the missing strict reading (*Peter shaved Jon*) is that the resulting structure would violate condition A of the binding theory according to which a reflexive must be bound in its governing category. Now recall that we only require *discourse* pronouns to be represented by free variables. In contrast, we take reflexive and bound pronouns to be resolved at the sentential level and hence represented either as constants or as bound variables. Given this, the lack of strict reading in (38) above, straightforwardly follows from the parallelism constraint. The equations are:

$$pe(m, sh(j, j)) = A(j)$$
$$pe(m, sh(p, p)) = A(p)$$

So that the only possible solution is $\{A \leftarrow \lambda x.pe(m, sh(x, x))\}$. In particular, the solution which would yield a strict reading namely, $\{A \leftarrow \lambda x.pe(m, sh(x, j))\}$ is not a unifier since it cannot solve both equations simultaneously.

8 Comparison with other approaches

In this section, we briefly compare it with three alternative proposals: DSP's treatment of ellipsis (because it is closely related to our proposal); Hardt's dynamic theory of ellipsis (because it uses a dynamic rather than a static semantics and is in this sense, fundamentally different from our proposal) and Fiengo and May's LF approach (because contrary to our analysis which works on flat semantic representations, this approach involves structured objects namely, logical forms).

Let us first examine how our proposal relates to DSP's treatment of ellipsis. In DSP's analysis, the semantic representation of the source clause is constrained to be equal to $R(S_1,, \ldots, S_n)$ where R is the semantic representation of the target ellipsis and $S_1,, \ldots, S_n$ are the semantic representations of the source parallel elements (that is, the elements of the source clause which have an overt parallel counterpart in the target clause). Reformulating DSP's analysis in a way that makes it more comparable to our proposal, we then have that the interpretation of an elliptical clause must obey the following constraint:

$$S = R(S_1), \ldots, (S_n)$$
$$T = R(T_1), \ldots, (T_n)$$

where R is the semantic representation of the target ellipsis; S and T represent the source and the target clause and $S_1, \ldots, S_n, T_1, \ldots, T_n$ represent the source and the target parallel elements respectively.

This looks a lot like our parallelism constraint. There is one important difference though: DSP's analysis requires that the semantically underspecified element whose value is to be determined by HOU, be the semantic representation of a VP-ellipsis. By contrast, we only require that this semantically underspecified element be the semantics shared by two parallel propositions.

This difference has several important consequences. First, it allows the treatment of deaccenting (because the free variable R may represent overt rather than elided material). Second, it captures the extended domain of licensing involved in both ellipsis and deaccenting context (because the free variable need not represent an ellipsis but may extend over overt material *containing* an ellipsis). Third, it enables a general theory of sloppy identity (since sloppiness is linked to parallelism, not just ellipsis). Fourth, it allows us to preserve the assumption that VPEs denote properties (in DSP's analysis, the variable representing the VPE is a relation of varying arity). This allows compatibility with Montague-type grammars that is, grammars where the semantic type of a constituent is defined by a mapping from syntactic categories into types.

We now turn to Hardt's approach. In a dynamic setting, anaphors can be viewed as denoting functions from contexts to semantic objects. Specifically, an ellipsis can be viewed as a function from contexts to properties. As [7,12] show, this simple observation suffices to predict sloppy/strict ambiguity: if the antecedent of an ellipsis contains a pronoun, the value of this pronoun in the source context may differ from its value in the target context. [12] further shows that in a dynamic setting where pronouns and ellipsis are uniformly treated as function from contexts to semantic objects, the free interplay between pronouns, ellipsis and sloppy identity discussed in section 5 simply falls out.

There are at least two main differences between Hardt's and our proposal. First, Hardt's proposal does not impose a parallelism constraint on sloppy identity. This has pros and cons. On the positive side, this means that the approach encounters no difficulty in accounting for examples such as (22), where the non-contrastive material in the target differs from its parallel counterpart in the source. However, it also means that sloppy identity is unrestricted. In particular, a sloppy interpretation for (12) cannot be ruled out.

The second difference involves directionality. Dynamic semantics is inherently directional in that within the semantic representation, the term representing an anaphor must be preceded by the term representing its antecedent. As a result, the dynamic approach correctly predicts that (39) lacks a sloppy interpretation that is, the reading *this year, I voted for Harry* (example from [12]). Note that by contrast, the HOU approach will predict both a strict and a sloppy reading for the elliptic clause.

Example 39. Tom^1 is always causing me problems. Last year, I didn't vote for him_1 and Tom got mad at me. This year, I did, and HARRY got mad at me.

The blessing is mixed however, for consider the following example.

Example 40. Tom is always causing me problems. Last year, he got mad at me because I didn't vote for him and THIS year, HARRY got mad at me because I did.

In this case, *Harry* does precede the ellipsis and consequently, the dynamic approach predicts a sloppy reading. However, just as in (39), this reading is simply not there. In short, I don't think example (39) is a very decisive argument in favour of the dynamic approach. As example (40) shows, the lack of sloppy reading is due not to linear order, but to some other factor, possibly the semantics of the contrast relation which holds between target and source or possibly, the fact that *Tom* is the current discourse topic.

Finally, we consider [5]'s account (henceforth, FM). Under this account, ellipsis is taken to involve syntactic reconstruction and furthermore, different types of NPs are represented differently. For instance, a proper name is always represented by an α-occurrence but a pronoun can be represented either as a β- or as an α-occurrence. Importantly, reconstruction is sensitive to the $\alpha - \beta$ distinction so that specific constraints on reconstruction can be stated which in essence, aim at capturing the effect of binding on ellipsis reconstruction. In particular, FM's approach predicts the difference between full NPs and pronouns discussed in section 7. It also accounts for the fact that example (41) lacks a strict-sloppy reading that is, the reading *Peter said Max saw Peter's mother.*

Example 41. Max^1 said he_1 saw his_1 mother and Peter^2 did too

The HOCU approach presented here cannot explain this missing reading for the simple reason that Co-indexed pronouns have identical representations and are thus handled identically. Although I do no think the problem unsolvable, I will leave it for now as an open issue.

9 Conclusion

We have presented a uniform treatment of sloppy interpretation which is general enough to cover the cases of sloppy/strict ambiguity observed in the literature. Moreover the treatment integrates a parallelism constraint which restricts sloppy interpretation to those cases where the antecedent of the source proform has a parallel counterpart in the target clause.

There are two obvious directions for further research. The first direction concerns the determination of parallelism. A real weakness of the present paper is that parallel elements are taken as given. This undermines the predictive power of the approach in that there is a definite leeway in deciding what the parallel elements can or may be. Roughly, there are two types of approach to this problem. Either, the parallel elements are determined through some general constraint on parallelism and contrast (cf. e.g. [13]), or they are defined through some matching mechanism on semantic representations such as priority union (cf. e.g. [17,11]). Both have their merits but it seems fair to say that while the general discourse level approach is too vague to be useful for our purpose, the more precise approach advocated by the matching proposals is too restrictive to be empirically very appropriate. To attain a theory of parallelism structuring, an integration of both methods is called for, which combines the general insights of discourse theories of parallelism with the precision of a given matching operation.

The second line of research which needs pursuing concerns the interaction of sloppy/strict ambiguity with other linguistic phenomena. In section 7, we have seen that colours allow for the integration of non-semantic information into the semantic construction process. However, we have also seen cases in which colours are not enough (cf. section 8). In particular, our analysis fails to predict the 'eliminative puzzles of ellipsis'. That is, it fails to capture the fact that in discourses with n referring elements in the source, less that 2^n readings are actually available (cf. [3,5]) and some readings are ruled out. For these cases and more generally, for a full treatment of how semantic construction interacts with other levels of linguistic information, a more sophisticated apparatus is needed. This is the subject of another paper.

Acknowledgments

I would like to thank Daniel Hardt for comments and criticisms on previous versions of this paper. The work reported here was funded by the Deutsche Forschungsgemeinschaft in Sonderforschungsbereich SFB–378, Project C2 (LISA).

References

1. Noam Chomsky and Howard Lasnik. *Syntax: An International Handbook of Contemporary Research*, chapter Principles and Parameter Theory. Walter de Gruyter, 1991. To appear.
2. Robin Cooper. The interpretation of pronouns. In F. Heny and H.S. Schnelle, editors, *Syntax and Semantics*, number 10, pages 61–93. 1979.
3. Östen Dahl. On so-called sloppy identity. Gothenburg Papers in Theoretical Linguistics 11, University of Göteborg, 1972.
4. Mary Dalrymple, Stuart Shieber, and Fernando Pereira. Ellipsis and higher-order unification. *Linguistics and Philosophy*, 14:399–452, 1991.
5. Robert Fiengo and Robert May. *Indices and Identity*. MIT Press, Cambridge, 1994.
6. Melvin Fitting. *First-Order Logic and Automated Theorem Proving*. Springer Verlag, 1990.
7. Claire Gardent. Dynamic semantics and vp ellipsis. In Jan van Eijck, editor, *Logics in AI*, pages 251–267, Amsterdam, The Netherlands, 1990. Springer-Verlag.
8. Claire Gardent. Parallelism, hou and deaccenting. CLAUS Report 85, University of Saarbrücken, January 1997.
9. Claire Gardent and Michael Kohlhase. Higher–order coloured unification and natural language semantics. In *Proceedings of the 34th Annual Meeting of the Association for Computational Linguistics*. ACL, Santa Cruz, 1996.
10. Claire Gardent, Michael Kohlhase, and Noor van Leusen. Corrections and Higher-Order Unification. In *Proceedings of KONVENS96*, pages 268–279. De Gruyter, Bielefeld, Germany, 1996.
11. Claire Grover, Chris Brew, Suresh Manandhar, and Marc Moens. Priority union and generalisation in discourse grammar. In *Proceedings of the 31th Annual Meeting of the Association for Computational Linguistics*, 1994.
12. Daniel Hardt. Dynamic interpretation of verb phrase ellipsis. Ms., University of Villanova, 1996.
13. Jerry Hobbs. *Literature and Cognition*. Number 21 in CSLI Lecture Notes. CSLI, 1990.
14. Dieter Hutter and Michael Kohlhase. A coloured version of the λ-calculus. In William McCune, editor, *Proceedings of the 14th Conference on Automated Deduction*, LNAI, Townsville, Australia, 1997. Springer Verlag. forthcoming.
15. Andrew Kehler. *Interpreting Cohesive Forms in the Context of Discourse Inference*. PhD thesis, Harvard University, 1995.
16. Michael Kohlhase. Higher-order tableaux. In *Proceedings of the Tableau Workshop*, Koblenz, Germany, 1995.
17. H. Prüst, R. Scha, and M. van den Berg. Discourse grammar and verb phrase anaphora. *Linguistics and Philosophy*, 17:261–327, 1994.
18. Mats Rooth. Ellipsis redundancy and reduction redundancy. In Steve Berman and Arild Hestvik, editors, *Proceedings of the Stuttgart Ellipsis Workshop*, University of Stuttgart, 1992.
19. Christopher Tancredi. *Deletion, Deaccenting and Presupposition*. PhD thesis, Massachusetts Institute of Technology, 1992.

A Family of Decidable Feature Logics which Support HPSG-Style Set and List Constructions[†]

Stephen J. Hegner

Department of Computer Science and Electrical Engineering
Votey Building
University of Vermont
Burlington, VT 05405 USA
hegner@emba.uvm.edu

Abstract. A desirable goal of constraint-based parsing is that the whole process should be one of pure algorithmic constraint satisfaction; the implementor should not need to specify any control information, or be aware of how the underlying system implements control. Unfortunately, most existing tools are Turing complete, and hence require additional control information by virtue of their computational power. In this work, a first step towards automatic cosntraint-based parsing of HPSG is provided, in the form of a family of decidable (for satisfiability) logics in which set and list constructions may be expressed in a uniform fashion, and constraints such as the Nonlocal Feature Principle may be recaptured succinctly.

1 Introduction

1.1 Motivation and Overview

In [22, p. 10], it is argued that parsing of (at least a sizeable fragment of) Head-Driven Phrase-Structure Grammar (hereafter HPSG) should be decidable. Under the assumption of decidability, parsing may be performed via purely algorithmic *constraint satisfaction*. The user provides only declarative constraints, and need not supply any control information. In practice, the situation is not so ideal. Existing tools for working with feature logics in general, and HPSG in particular, such as ALE [1], CUF [5], and TFS [24], are *Turing complete*, meaning that they are general enough to allow representation of any computational process, including undecidable ones. While some simple problems may be solved within these frameworks without the specification of control information, this is not the case for many of the essential constraints of HPSG. Thus, it is up to the user, at least in part, to supply parts of the parsing algorithm (or at least to respect how the underlying system implements control).

[†] Portions of this work were prepared while the author was a visiting research fellow at the Department of Informatics, University of Bergen, supported by a grant from the Norwegian Research Council,.

In the work reported here, as a step towards fully automatic parsing of HPSG, a family of decidable feature logics which support some of the key constructs of HPSG is presented. These logics are focused particularly upon the constructs which require sets and/or lists, and have two notable features which distinguish them from other efforts known to the author.

Sets and lists are treated uniformly, using the same construction, and duplicate values are supported. In HPSG, both sets and lists occur in fundamental ways. For example, in filler-gap constructions, the SLASH binding feature consists of an *unordered* multiset of structures, i.e., a set in which duplicates are allowed. While there is no order structure on the elements of the multiset, the possibility that several of the elements will be identical can occur, and must be supported in any formalism. On the other hand, the value of COMP-DTRS is always a (totally ordered) *multilist* of signs, i.e., a list in which the same element may occur more than once. Since multisets and multilists are are variations of the same idea (a collection of objects with order structure), it seems natural that they should be represented using similar constructs. Among other benefits, this would imply that multisets and multilists will be represented by feature structures of similar size and depth, and corresponding operations on multisets and multilists will be of the same complexity. Furthermore, partially ordered sets, should they be needed, may easily be introduced.

The model structure of the associated logic is one of a traditional feature structure, augmented to support multicollections. The sentences necessary to represent (set-oriented) binding dependencies such as the *nonlocal feature principle*, as well as list-oriented dependencies such as the *subcategorization principle*, are expressible. In particular, operations such as union and disjoint union, as well as list concatenation, are expressible. To the best of the author's knowledge, this is the only work to treat multisets and lists uniformly within a decidable feature-structure framework. Manandhar [17], Carpenter [3], and Moshier and Pollard [19] have all developed elegant decidable feature logics which supports set constructions. However, neither supports lists as a fundamental type. In [14], Kepser gives a proof that the feature logic of King [15] is decidable, but this logic does not provide any special constructs for sets or lists; rather, lists must constructed as trees of features, with sets taken to be equivalence classes of lists.

Decidability is proven by mapping the logic into a sorted first-order logic, and then using variants of well-known decidability results in that context. By using this approach, the great wealth of knowledge regarding decidability of first-order theories [6] may be brought to bear on the problem. The approach used in this work employs a typed generalization of the Schönfinkel-Bernays quantificational class (no $\exists$ quantifier occurs within the scope of a $\forall$ quantifier) to many-sorted logics. The types of the logic are constructed by forming a cartesian product of the underlying types of HPSG (called *sorts* in [22]) and a group of three special types used to distinguish ordinary values from multicollections. Roughly speaking, in this generalization, whenever a quantifier ordering of the form $(\forall x)(\exists y)$ occurs, the types of x and y must be such that infinite recursive construction of terms is impossible, and so the

Herbrand universe remains finite. It is shown that the desired class of HPSG constraints may be expressed within this class.

1.2 Prerequisites and Scope

It is assumed that the reader has a reasonable knowledge of order structures [4] first-order logic in general and the expansion theorem in particular [16, Ch, 9], and many-sorted logics [8], as well as some acquaintance with notation for regular languages [16, Ch. 2], and the logical representation of feature structures [7]. For an understanding of the examples, as well as for the motivation for this work, some acquaintance with HPSG [21], [22] would prove very helpful.

Because of space constraints, it has been necessary to limit background material, condense the number and scope of examples, and to limit proofs to sketches of the techniques.

2 Basic Concepts

2.1 Multicollections and Multicollection-Extended Feature Structures

2.1.1 Partially ordered sets. Partially ordered sets (posets) will usually be represented by boldface roman letters, with the underlying set denoted by the corresponding non-bold roman letter. Unless otherwise stipulated, the associated order is denoted by $\leq$. For a set L, $\mathsf{Poset}(L)$ denotes the set of all posets whose underlying set is a subset of L. Consult [4] for more comprehensive information.

2.1.2 Multicollections. The notion of a *multiset*, i.e., a set in which an element may occur several times, is well known [23]. A *multilist* is defined similarly. The construct which we employ to recapture multisets and multilists is termed a *multicollection*, which is a set S which is indexed by a poset of *tags*. Formally, *multicollection* is a triple $\mathbf{C} = (S, \mathbf{P}, f)$ in which S is a set, called the *base set*, $\mathbf{P}$ is a poset, called the *tag set*, and $f : P \to S$ is a surjective function, called the *tagging function*. $\mathbf{C}$ is a *multiset* (resp. *multilist*) if $\mathbf{P}$ is a trivial partial order (resp. total order).

As a simple example, let $S = \{a, b, c\}$, let $P = \{x_1, x_2, x_3, x_4\}$, and let $f : P \to S$ be defined by $x_1 \mapsto a$, $x_2 \mapsto b$, $x_3 \mapsto c$, and $x_4 \mapsto b$. Then, with $\leq$ the trivial partial order in which $x_i \leq x_j \Rightarrow i = j$, $\mathbf{C}$ is the multiset $\{a, b, c, b\}$ in which b occurs twice, and with $\leq$ the partial order generated by $x_1 \leq x_2 \leq x_3 \leq x_4$, then $\mathbf{C}$ is the multilist $[a\ b\ c\ b]$, in which b occurs in both the second and in the fourth position. With $\leq$ the ordering generated by $x_1 \leq x_2$ and $x_1 \leq x_3$, a multicollection which is neither a multiset nor a multilist is obtained.

2.1.3 Multicollection contexts and systems. In this work, multicollections will live at certain nodes of a feature structure, and the multicollections at distinct nodes must be related to each other in a particular way. Specifically, the set of tags must be global, although the ordering relationship among the tags may be local. To recapture this idea, the following notion is employed. A *multicollection context* is a triple $\mathbf{K} = (L, S, I)$ of sets in which L is the *global tag set*, S is the *object set*, and I is the *context set.* A multicollection system over $\mathbf{K}$ is a set of multicollections whose tagging functions agree whenever they overlap. In other words, in a multicollection system, the tag alone determines the associated member of the base set; it does not matter which of the multicollections in the system is considered. Formally, a *multicollection system* over $\mathbf{K}$ is a pair $\mathbf{D} = (\gamma, \eta)$ with $\gamma : L \to S$ a total function, called the *global tagging function*, and $\eta : I \to \mathsf{Poset}(L)$ a total function, called the *context function.* The global tagging function gives the *global* association (i.e., over all multicollections in the system) of tags to elements, while the context function gives the *local* ordering within each multicollection. Thus, while tagging is global to the entire system, ordering is local to the particular multicollection.

As an abuse of notation, we sometimes use the notation $\eta(I)$ to denote the underlying set of the poset. Context will always make it clear which is meant, the entire poset or just the underlying set. The multicollection system $\mathbf{D}$ defines the family $\mathbf{Sys}(D) = \{\mathbf{C}_i = (S_i, \mathbf{P}_i, f_i) \mid i \in I\}$ of multicollections in which $\mathbf{P}_i = \eta(i)$, $S_i = \gamma(P_i)$, and $f_i = \gamma_{|P_i}$. (The notation $\gamma_{|P_i}$ identifies a function with the same action as γ, but with its domain restricted to P_i.)

These rather involved constructs are best understood within the context of of a multicollection-extended feature structure (2.1.5 below), and so an example which illustrates these ideas is deferred until that point.

2.1.4 Feature contexts. A feature context is just a set of parameters which underlie the feature structures of a given context. Formally, an *untyped feature context* is a pair $C = (F, A)$ in which F is a finite set, called the set of *features*, and A is a finite set, called the set of *atoms*. As a notational convention, throughout the rest of this section, an untyped feature context $C = (F, A)$ is fixed.

2.1.5 Multicollection-extended feature structures. Within the current literature, there are several different formalisms for recapturing feature structures. A popular one is the so-called *Kasper-Rounds* [13] representation, in which the feature structure is modelled as a finite-state automaton. An extension of the Kasper-Rounds formalism which integrates multicollections into the structures is employed in this work. Formally, a *multicollection-extended feature structure* (*MEFS* for short) is an eight-tuple $M = (Q, \delta, \alpha, q_o, L, C, \gamma, \eta)$ in which:

(mefs-i) Q is a finite set, called the set of *object states.*

(mefs-ii) C is a finite set, called the set of *multicollection states.*

(mefs-iii) L is a finite set, called the set of *object indices.*

(mefs-iv) $\delta : Q \times F \to Q \cup C$ is a partial function, called the *state-transition function.*

(mefs-v) $\alpha : Q \to A$ is an injective partial function, called the *constant-assignment function.*

(mefs-vi) (γ, η) is a multicollection system over (L, Q, C).

(mefs-vii) $q_o \in Q$ is called the *initial state.*

(mefs-viii) The sets Q, C, L, and F are pairwise disjoint.
(mefs-ix) Given $q \in Q$, if $\alpha(q)\downarrow$, then $\delta(q,e)\uparrow$ for all $e \in F$. (Notation: $f(x)\downarrow$ (resp. $f(x)\uparrow$) means that $f(x)$ is defined (resp. undefined)).

Figure 1 depicts an example, which should help to clarify these ideas, as well as those of 2.1.3. There are two flavors of states, *object states* (the q_i's

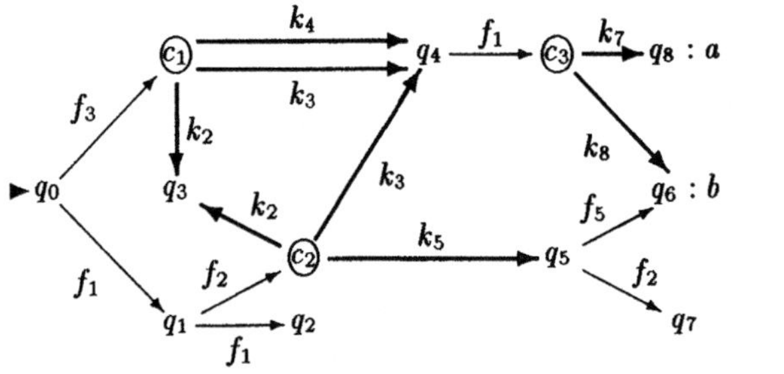

Order information at collection nodes:
At c_1: $k_4 \leq k_2 \leq k_3$.
At c_2: No nontrival ordering.
At c_3: $k_7 \leq k_8$.

Fig. 1. An Example MEFS

in the example) and *multicollection states* (the c_i's in the example, circled for emphasis), and two types of edges, *feature edges* (labelled with members of the underlying set F of features, f_i's in the example) and *tag edges* (shown in bold lines, and labelled with object indices, k_i's in the example). Each object state is similar to a state in an ordinary feature structure, while each multicollection state is the root of a multicollection. The feature edges are defined by the transition function δ, the definition of tag edges involves the multicollection system, and will be addressed shortly. The root node is q_0 in the example and is labelled by the short ingoing arrowhead.

At a given multicollection node c, the base set of the multicollection is just the set of all $q \in Q$ such that there is an edge from c to q. The tag set is the set of all $k \in L$ such that there is an edge from c with label k. The tagging function identifies the association of tag edge labels to the states at the end of the edge. In the example, at c_1, the base set is $\{q_3, q_4\}$, the tag set is $\{k_2, k_3, k_4\}$, and the tagging function assigns $k_2 \mapsto q_3$, $k_3 \mapsto q_2$, and $k_3 \mapsto q_4$. The ordering on the elements of the tag set is specified separately, to the right of the graph; in this case $k_4 \leq k_2 \leq k_3$.

A critical property of MEFS's is that *sinks of tag edges are global values*; that is, all tag edges labelled with the same tag name terminate at the same node. Thus, the k_3 edge emanating from c_1 and that emanating from c_2 **must** point to the same node. This is recaptured succinctly within the definition of a multicollection system (2.1.3); the global tagging function is γ, with each local tagging function a restriction of it. On the other hand, note that *tag ordering is local*; for example, $k_2 \leq k_3$ at c_1, while k_2 and k_3 are incomparable at c_2. Indeed, the multicollections at c_1 and c_3 are multilists, while that at c_2 is a multiset.

The sink of a tag edge must be an object node, so that multicollections cannot be nested directly. However, an element of a multicollection may have a feature which identifies another multicollection (e.g., f_1 from q_4 to c_3). This simplifies the mathematical aspects, and does not seem to impose any major roadblocks in knowledge representation.

MEFS($\mathcal{C}$) denotes the set of all MEFS's over $\mathcal{C}$.

2.1.6 The extended transition function. In the classical Kasper-Rounds formalism, the extended transition function is just the function of that name which is derived from the associated automaton. In the case of an MEFS, the definition is somewhat more complex, because the function γ of the multicollection system embedded within the MEFS is used to define transitions out of tag nodes. Formally, let $M = (Q, \delta, \alpha, q_o, L, C, \gamma, \eta)$ be a MEFS. Define the *extended transition function* for M to be the partial function $(\delta+\gamma)^* : (Q \cup C) \times (F \cup L)^* \to Q \cup C$ given by the following conditions.

(i) For each $q \in Q \cup C$, $(\delta + \gamma)^*(q, \epsilon) = q$. ($\epsilon$ denotes the empty string.)

(ii) For each $q \in Q$, $f \in F$, $(\delta + \gamma)^*(q, f)\downarrow$ iff $\delta(q, f)\downarrow$; $(\delta + \gamma)^*(q, f) = \delta(q, f)$ in this case.

(iii) For each $c \in C$, $k \in L$, $(\delta + \gamma)^*(c, k)\downarrow$ iff $k \in \eta(c)$; $(\delta + \gamma)^*(c, k) = \gamma(k)$ in this case.

(iv) For each $q \in Q$ and $k \in L$, $(\delta + \gamma)^*(q, k)\uparrow$.

(v) For each $c \in C$, $f \in F$, $(\delta + \gamma)^*(c, f)\uparrow$.

(vi) For any $q \in Q \cup C, \omega \in (F \cup L)^*, b \in F \cup L$, $(\delta+\gamma)^*(q, \omega \cdot b)\downarrow$ iff $(\delta+\gamma)^*(q, \omega)\downarrow$ and $\delta((\delta + \gamma)^*(q, \omega), b)\downarrow$, and then $(\delta + \gamma)^*(q, \omega \cdot b) = \delta((\delta + \gamma)^*(q, \omega), b)$.

Notice that the definition of $(\delta + \gamma)^*$ does not depend upon the ordering of elements in the multicollection. In terms of the example of Fig. 1, $(\delta + \gamma)^*$ may be determined from the graph alone, without any reference to the ordering table to its right. The string $\rho \in (F \cup L)^*$ is an *actual path* for M if $(\delta + \gamma)^*(q_o, \rho)\downarrow$. The set of all actual paths for M is denoted ActPath(M).

2.2 Typed Multicollection-Extended Feature Structures

HPSG is founded upon typed feature structures. Thus, to recapture constraints within that framework, it is imperative that the notion of an MEFS be extended to a typed domain. While it is often the case that one starts with *partial* type systems, an adequate theory generally requires that it be extensible to a total one. For details on conditions under which such extensions are possible, consult [9]. In this report, we shall confine attention to the situation in which the order structure is total.

2.2.1 Bounded semilattices and type hierarchies. A common framework for modelling type hierarchies, and the one appropriate for HPSG, is that of a *bounded meet semilattice*, which is a quadruple $\mathbf{T} = (T, \bot, \top, \sqcap)$ in which T is a set, called the *underlying set*; $\sqcap : T \times T \to T$ is a total function, called the *meet operator*, which is associative, commutative, and idempotent; $\bot \in T$ (resp. $\top \in T$) is called the *least element*, (resp. *greatest element*); $\bot \sqcap x = \bot$ and $\top \sqcap x = x$ for all $x \in T$. The symbol $\sqsubseteq$ is used to denote the order relation induced by the semilattice. For more information on semilattices, consult [4].

For the purposes of this paper, a *type hierarchy* is a bounded, finite meet semilattice. Throughout the rest of this paper, we let $\mathbf{T}$ be a type hierarchy.

2.2.2 Typed feature contexts and typed MEFS's. A typed feature context plays the same role in the definition of typed MEFS's that an ordinary feature context plays in the definition of ordinary MEFS's. Formally, a *typed feature context* is a quadruple $\mathcal{C} = (F, A, \mathbf{T}, \mu)$, in which F is a finite set, called the set of *features*; A is a finite set, called the set of *atoms*; $\mathbf{T}$ is a type hierarchy; and $\mu : A \to T \setminus \{\bot\}$ is a total function, called the *constant typing function*.

The definition of a typed MEFS provided here is patterned after that of Carpenter [2], which details the extension of the Kasper-Rounds representation to the typed context. Formally, let $\mathcal{C}$ be a typed feature context over $\mathbf{T}$. A *typed MEFS* over $\mathcal{C}$ is a nine-tuple $M = (Q, \delta, \alpha, q_o, L, C, \gamma, \eta, \theta)$ in which

(tmefs-i) $(Q, \delta, \alpha, q_o, L, C, \gamma, \eta)$ is an MEFS.

(tmefs-ii) $\theta : Q \cup C \cup L \to T$ is a total function, called the *typing function.*

Thus, object states (Q), multicollection states (C), and object indices (L) all have type. This typing function is subject to the following constraints.

(tmefs-iii) For all $c \in C$ and $k \in L$, $k \in \eta(C)$ implies that $\theta(k) \sqsubseteq \theta(c)$.

(tmefs-iv) For all $k \in L$ and $q \in Q$, $\gamma(k) = q$ implies that $\theta(q) \sqsubseteq \theta(k)$.

(tmefs-v) For all $q \in Q$, $\alpha(q)\downarrow$ implies that $\theta(q) \sqsubseteq \mu(\alpha(q))$.

The collection of all typed MEFS's over $\mathcal{C}$ is denoted $\mathsf{TMEFS}(\mathcal{C})$. The *extended transition function* $(\delta{+}\gamma)^*$ for a typed MEFS is defined exactly as for an untyped MEFS.

2.3 The Logic of Typed MEFS's

2.3.1 The logical sort system of a type hierarchy. The *base sort system* for MEFS's is the triple $\mathsf{BaseSort} = \{\mathsf{Obj}, \mathsf{Coll}, \mathsf{Tag}\}$. The *syntactic sort system generated by* $\mathbf{T}$, denoted $\mathbf{CESort(T)} = (\mathsf{CESort}(\mathbf{T}), \bot, \top, \sqcap)$, is the meet semilattice defined by the Cartesian product $((T \setminus \{\bot\}) \times \mathsf{BaseSort}) \cup \{\top, \bot\}$. The meet operator $\sqcap$ is defined by $(t_1, s_1) \sqcap (t_2, s_2) = (t_1 \sqcap t_2, s_1)$ if both $t_1 \sqcap t_2 \neq \bot$ and $s_1 = s_2$; otherwise $(t_1, s_1) \sqcap (t_2, s_2) = \bot$. The symbols $\bot$, $\top$, and $\sqcap$ have double duty, associated with both the underlying type hierarchy $\mathbf{T}$ and the syntactic sort system $\mathbf{CESort(T)}$. Similarly, since $(t, s) \sqcap \top = (t, s)$ for any $(t, s) \in \mathbf{T} \setminus \{\bot\} \times \mathsf{BaseSort}$, $(\top, s)$ will often be abbreviated to s; e.g., $\mathsf{Tag} = (\top, \mathsf{Tag})$. This should cause no confusion, since context will always make clear which interpretation is correct. Also, $\sqsubseteq$ is used to denote the order relation on $\mathbf{CESort(T)}$, as well as the order relation on $\mathbf{T}$.

2.3.2 Variable contexts and typed MEFS feature contexts. An *MEFS variable context* over $\mathbf{T}$ is a $\mathsf{CESort}(\mathbf{T}) \setminus \{\top, \bot\}$-indexed set $\mathcal{V} = \{\mathbf{V}_r \mid r \in \mathsf{CESort}(\mathbf{T}) \setminus \{\top, \bot\}\}$ of variables such that, for $r_1 \neq r_2$, $\mathbf{V}_{r_1} \cap \mathbf{V}_{r_2} = \emptyset$.

To aid in recognizing the type of a variable, the following convention is used. For $t \in T$, variables in $\mathbf{V}_{(t,\mathsf{Obj})}$ are usually written as lowercase letters from the end of the alphabet, with $t \in T$ written as a superscript. Subscripts may be used to distinguish variables, if necessary. Examples include x^t, y^t, z_1^t, and z_2^t. A similar convention is used for variables in $\mathbf{V}_{(t,\mathsf{Coll})}$, except that uppercase letters are used. Examples include X^t, Y^t, Z_1^t, and Z_2^t. Variables in $\mathbf{V}_{(t,\mathsf{Tag})}$ are represented by the special letter ℓ, with subscript and superscript conventions as in the other two cases. Examples include ℓ^t, ℓ_1^t, and ℓ_2^t. In each of these cases, if $t = \top$, then we may omit the superscript entirely, and write, e.g., x, X_1, or ℓ.

For $s \in \mathsf{BaseSort}$, $\mathbf{V}_s$ denotes the set $\bigcup\{\mathbf{V}_{(t,s)} \mid t \in T \setminus \{\bot\}\}$. The symbol $\mathbf{V}$ denotes $\mathbf{V}_{\mathsf{Obj}} \cup \mathbf{V}_{\mathsf{Coll}} \cup \mathbf{V}_{\mathsf{Tag}}$. When we have a variable of an unspecified type, that is, an element of $\bigcup \mathcal{V}$, the Greek letter ν, possibly with a subscript, will be used to represent it.

A *typed MEFS context with variables* is a pair $\mathcal{K} = (\mathcal{C}, \mathcal{V})$ in which $\mathcal{C} = (F, A, \mathbf{T}, \mu)$ is a typed feature context and $\mathcal{V}$ is a MEFS variable context over $\mathbf{T}$. Throughout the rest of this paper, unless noted to the contrary, we let $\mathcal{K} = (\mathcal{C}, \mathcal{V})$ be a typed MEFS context with variables.

2.3.3 Description paths and feature terms. Description paths generalize the feature terms of the Kasper-Rounds framework. The generalization must account for both the edge labelling and the order structure of the embedded multicollections. It is important to note that while feature names are part of the underlying language (as embodied in the underlying typed MEFS context $\mathcal{K}$), tag names are not. The language of description paths uses tag variables (members of $\mathbf{V}_{\mathsf{Tag}}$) within paths to represent tag edges; these variables must then be bound by the logical expression in which the description path is used.

A *simple description path* (or just *SD path*) over $\mathcal{K}$ is any element of the regular set $(F \cdot (\mathbf{V}_{\mathsf{Tag}} + \epsilon))^*$. A simple description path may be thought of as a path through a feature structure, but with tags replaced by tag variables. The restrictions that two tags may not occur in a row, and that the root of a feature structure must be an object state, are built into the regular expression. For example, $f_3\ell_1 f_1\ell_2$ is a simple description path which "fits" the example of Fig. 1, in the sense that upon substituting k_4 for ℓ_1 and k_7 for ℓ_2, an actual path of the MEFS is obtained.

A *description path* over $\mathcal{K}$ is a simple description, followed by an optional *terminator*. As in the Kasper-Rounds formalism, a terminator may be of the form $:x$ or $:a$, in which $x \in \mathbf{V}_{\mathsf{Obj}}$ and $a \in A$. Thus, $f_3\ell_1 f_1\ell_2 : x$ and $f_3\ell_1 f_1\ell_2 : a$ are description paths. For a simple description path which ends with an element of F, a terminator of the form $: X$ is also permitted, with $X \in \mathbf{V}_{\mathsf{Coll}}$. Thus, $f_3\ell_1 f_1 : X$ is a description path, but $f_3\ell_1 f_1\ell_2 : X$ is not. Finally, for a simple description path ending in an element of F, a terminator may be of the form $[\ell_1 \le \ell_2]$ is also permitted, so that $f_3\ell_1 f_1[\ell_2 \le \ell_3]$ is a description path. The set of all description paths over $\mathcal{K}$ is denoted $\mathsf{DPath}(\mathcal{K})$.

Informally, the set of feature terms is the closure of the set of description paths under the usual logical connectives. Formally, the set of *typed collection extended feature terms*, denoted $\mathsf{FT}(\mathcal{K})$, is the smallest set such that $\{\top, \bot\} \cup \mathsf{DPath}(\mathcal{K}) \subseteq \mathsf{FT}(\mathcal{K})$, and whenever $\varphi_1, \varphi_2 \in \mathsf{FT}(\mathcal{K})$, then $(\varphi_1 \wedge \varphi_2)$, $(\varphi_1 \vee \varphi_2)$, $(\neg\varphi_1) \in \mathsf{FT}(\mathcal{K})$ as well. As per usual mathematical conventions, parentheses may be dropped in feature terms when no confusion can result, so one may write terms such as $(\varphi_1 \wedge \neg\varphi_2 \wedge \varphi_3)$, for example.

2.3.4 Assignments. Let $M = (Q, \delta, \alpha, q_o, L, C, \gamma, \eta, \theta) \in \mathsf{TMEFS}(\mathcal{C})$. A $(\mathcal{K}, M)$-assignment associates with each variable an object of the appropriate sort. More formally, a $(\mathcal{K}, M)$-*assignment* is a function $\beta : \mathbf{V} \to Q \cup C \cup L$ with the property that $\beta(\mathbf{V}_{\mathsf{Obj}}) \subseteq Q$; $\beta(\mathbf{V}_{\mathsf{Coll}}) \subseteq C$; $\beta(\mathbf{V}_{\mathsf{Tag}}) \subseteq L$; and for each $t \in T \setminus \{\bot\}$ and $s \in \mathsf{BaseSort}$, $\theta(\beta(\mathbf{V}_{(t,s)})) \sqsubseteq t$. $\mathsf{Asgn}(\mathcal{K}, M)$ denotes the set of all $(\mathcal{K}, M)$-assignments.

As noted above, description paths may not contain tags; they may only contain variables with tag types. The application of an assignment generates a "true" path through a typed MEFS by replacing tag variables with true tags. Given $\rho \in \mathsf{SDPath}(\mathcal{K})$, $\beta\langle\rho\rangle$ denotes the string which is obtained by replacing each variable $\nu \in \mathbf{V}_{\mathsf{Tag}}$ occurring in ρ with $\beta(\nu)$. For example, if $\rho = f_3\ell_1 f_1[\ell_2 \leq \ell_3]$ and β is any assignment which maps $\ell_1 \mapsto k_4$, $\ell_2 \mapsto k_7$, and $\ell_3 \mapsto k_8$, then $\beta\langle\rho\rangle = f_3 k_4 f_1[k_7 \leq k_8]$, a "ground term" (not a legal feature term) which may be interpreted as true or false in a given structure (true in the case of Fig. 1).

2.3.5 Satisfiability. Let $M = (Q, \delta, \alpha, q_o, L, C, \gamma, \eta, \theta) \in \mathsf{TMEFS}(\mathcal{C})$. Informally, for a given feature term ρ, $\mathsf{Sat}(M, \rho)$ is the set of all truth assignments β for which $\beta\langle\rho\rangle$ is a "ground term" which is interpreted as true in M. For example, with M as given in Fig. 1 and ρ and β as defined at the end of 2.3.4 above, $\beta \in \mathsf{Sat}(M, \rho)$, while any β' which does not satisfy either $\ell_1 \mapsto k_4$ or $\ell_1 \mapsto k_3$ is not in $\mathsf{Sat}(M, \rho)$. Formally, for any feature term φ, $\mathsf{Sat}(M, \varphi)$ is a subset of $\mathsf{Asgn}(\mathcal{K}, M)$, defined in cases as follows.

(i) $\mathsf{Sat}(M, \rho) \Leftrightarrow \beta\langle\rho\rangle \in \mathsf{ActPath}(M)$.

(ii) $\mathsf{Sat}(M, \rho{:}\nu) \Leftrightarrow (\beta\langle\rho\rangle \in \mathsf{ActPath}(M)$ and $(\delta + \gamma)^*(q_o, \beta\langle\rho\rangle) = \beta(\nu))$.

(iii) $\mathsf{Sat}(M, \rho{:}a) \Leftrightarrow (\beta\langle\rho\rangle \in \mathsf{ActPath}(M)$ and $\alpha((\delta + \gamma)^*(q_o, \beta\langle\rho\rangle)) = a)$.

(iv) $\mathsf{Sat}(M, \rho[\ell_1 \leq \ell_2]) \Leftrightarrow (\beta\langle\rho\rangle \in \mathsf{ActPath}(M)$ and $(\delta + \gamma)^*(q_o, \rho) \in C$ and

$$\beta(\ell_1) \leq_{\eta((\delta+\gamma)^*(q_o,\rho))} \beta(\ell_2)).$$

(v) For $\varphi_1, \varphi_2 \in \mathsf{FT}(\mathcal{K})$, $\mathsf{Sat}(M, (\varphi_1 \wedge \varphi_2)) = \mathsf{Sat}(M, \varphi_1) \cap \mathsf{Sat}(M, \varphi_2)$.

(vi) For $\varphi_1, \varphi_2 \in \mathsf{FT}(\mathcal{K})$, $\mathsf{Sat}(M, (\varphi_1 \vee \varphi_2)) = \mathsf{Sat}(M, \varphi_1) \cup \mathsf{Sat}(M, \varphi_2)$.

(vii) For $\varphi \in \mathsf{FT}(\mathcal{K})$, $\mathsf{Sat}(M, (\neg\varphi)) = \mathsf{Asgn}(\mathcal{K}, M) \setminus \mathsf{Sat}(M, \varphi)$.

For a set $\Phi \subseteq \mathsf{FT}(\mathcal{K})$, define $\mathsf{Sat}(M, \Phi) = \bigcap\{\mathsf{Sat}(M, \varphi) \mid \varphi \in \Phi\}$.

2.3.6 Variable substitution. To formalize the action of quantifiers, it is necessary to formalize the idea of altering a $(\mathcal{K}, M)$-assignment on exactly one variable. Formally, let $M = (Q, \delta, \alpha, q_o, L, C, \gamma, \eta, \theta) \in \mathsf{TMEFS}(\mathcal{C})$, let $\beta \in \mathsf{Asgn}(\mathcal{K}, M)$, let $s \in \mathsf{BaseSort}$, and let $r \in Q \cup C \cup L$, subject to the constraint that if $s = \mathsf{Obj}$, then $r \in Q$; if $s = \mathsf{Coll}$, then $r \in C$; if $s = \mathsf{Tag}$, then $r \in L$. Then, for $t \in T \setminus \{\bot\}$ and $\nu_1 \in \mathbf{V}_{(t,s)}$, define $\beta[\nu_1 \leftarrow r] \in \mathsf{Asgn}(\mathcal{K}, M)$ by

$$\beta[\nu_1 \leftarrow r](\nu_2) = \begin{cases} r & \text{if } \nu_1 = \nu_2; \\ \beta(\nu_2) & \text{otherwise.} \end{cases}$$

provided that $\theta(r) \sqsubseteq t$. If $\theta(r) \not\sqsubseteq t$, then $\beta[\nu_1 \leftarrow r]$ is undefined.

2.3.7 Quantified feature terms. The quantification of feature terms proceeds in a manner virtually identical to that for many-sorted first-order logic. A *typed MEFS quantifier* is a symbol of the form $\forall_\tau$ or $\exists_\tau$, with $\tau \in \mathsf{CESort}(\mathbf{T}) \setminus \{\top, \bot\}$. The *sort* of the quantifier is τ. As a notational abbreviation, for $s \in \mathsf{BaseSort}$, we will sometimes write $\forall_s$ (resp. $\exists_s$) for $\forall_{(\top,s)}$ (resp. $\exists_{(\top,s)}$).

A *typed MEFS quantifier term* is a string of the form $(Q\nu)$ in which Q is a typed MEFS quantifier and $\nu \in \mathbf{V}$, with Q and ν of the same sort. (In that which follows, the quantifier subscript may be dropped when the sort may be determined from the variable; thus, $(\forall_{(t,\mathsf{Obj})}x^t)$ may be abbreviated to $(\forall x^t)$, and $(\exists_{(\top,\mathsf{Tag})}\nu)$ may be abbreviated to $(\exists\nu)$. These conventions will be used in the sorted first-order logic of Sec. 3.1 as well.)

A *typed MEFS quantifier string* is a (possibly empty) sequence of typed MEFS quantifier terms. A typed MEFS quantifier string is *clean* if no variable in $\mathbf{V}$ occurs in more than one of its quantifier terms.

A *quantified typed feature term* is a string φ of the form $\xi\psi$, in which ξ is a clean quantifier string and ψ is a typed MEFS feature term. In this case, we call ξ the *prefix* of φ and denote it by $\mathsf{Prefix}(\varphi)$. Likewise, we call ψ the *matrix* of φ and denote it by $\mathsf{Matrix}(\psi)$. The set of all quantified feature terms (over the context $\mathcal{K}$) is denoted $\mathsf{QFT}(\mathcal{K})$. We identify $\mathsf{FT}(\mathcal{K})$ with the subset of $\mathsf{QFT}(\mathcal{K})$ consisting of all quantified feature terms whose prefix is empty.

A variable $\nu \in \mathbf{V}$ is *free in* $\varphi \in \mathsf{QFT}(\mathcal{K})$ if it occurs in $\mathsf{Matrix}(\varphi)$, but not in $\mathsf{Prefix}(\varphi)$. A quantified typed feature term is a *sentence* if it contains no free variables. $\mathsf{QFS}(\mathcal{K})$ denotes the set of elements of $\mathsf{QFT}(\mathcal{K})$ which are sentences.

2.3.8 Satisfiability for typed quantified feature terms. In the following, let $M = (Q, \delta, \alpha, q_o, L, C, \gamma, \eta, \theta) \in \mathsf{TMEFS}(\mathcal{C})$, let $t \in T$ and let $\varphi \in \mathsf{QFT}(\mathcal{K})$.

$\mathsf{Sat}(M, (\exists_{(t,\mathsf{Obj})}x^t)\varphi) = \{\beta \in \mathsf{Asgn}(\mathcal{K}, M) \mid (\exists q \in Q)(\beta[x^t \leftarrow q] \in \mathsf{Sat}(M, \varphi))\}$.
$\mathsf{Sat}(M, (\exists_{(t,\mathsf{Tag})}X^t)\varphi) = \{\beta \in \mathsf{Asgn}(\mathcal{K}, M) \mid (\exists c \in C)(\beta[X^t \leftarrow c] \in \mathsf{Sat}(M, \varphi))\}$.
$\mathsf{Sat}(M, (\exists_{(t,\mathsf{Coll})}\ell^t)\varphi) = \{\beta \in \mathsf{Asgn}(\mathcal{K}, M) \mid (\exists k \in L)(\beta[\ell^t \leftarrow k] \in \mathsf{Sat}(M, \varphi))\}$.
$\mathsf{Sat}(M, (\forall_{(t,\mathsf{Obj})}x^t)\varphi) = \{\beta \in \mathsf{Asgn}(\mathcal{K}, M) \mid (\forall q \in Q)(\beta[x^t \leftarrow q] \in \mathsf{Sat}(M, \varphi))\}$.
$\mathsf{Sat}(M, (\forall_{(t,\mathsf{Tag})}X^t)\varphi) = \{\beta \in \mathsf{Asgn}(\mathcal{K}, M) \mid (\forall c \in C)(\beta[X^t \leftarrow c] \in \mathsf{Sat}(M, \varphi))\}$.
$\mathsf{Sat}(M, (\forall_{(t,\mathsf{Coll})}\ell^t)\varphi) = \{\beta \in \mathsf{Asgn}(\mathcal{K}, M) \mid (\forall k \in L)(\beta[\ell^t \leftarrow k] \in \mathsf{Sat}(M, \varphi))\}$.

2.3.9 Proposition — characterization of sentences. *Let* $M \in \mathsf{TMEFS}(\mathcal{C})$ *and* $\varphi \in \mathsf{QFS}(\mathcal{K})$. *Then either* $\mathsf{Sat}(M, \varphi) = \mathsf{Asgn}(\mathcal{K}, M)$ *or else* $\mathsf{Sat}(M, \varphi) = \emptyset$.

Proof. The proof is similar to that for first-order logic, as may be found in [18, 11.6]. □

2.3.10 Example: The Nonlocal Feature Principle of HPSG. The *Nonlocal Feature Principle* of HPSG [22, p. 164] is representative of the class of constraints that this theory targets for representation. Figure 2 depicts the abstract setting in which this constraint may be described. In general, the edges labelled by subscripted λ's may represent sequences of feature edges, rather than single edges. The bolder edges, labelled with subscripted k's, are tag edges. For any S, let $\mathbf{C}_S$ denote the multicollection rooted at node c_S. It is assumed

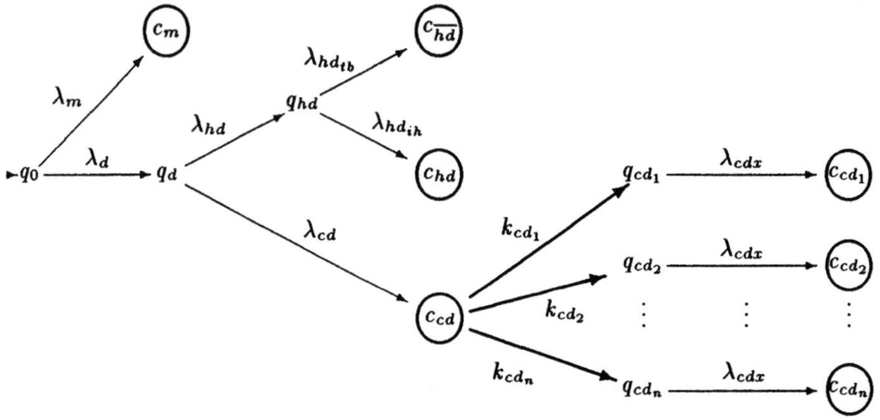

Fig. 2. Abstract Setting for the Nonlocal Feature Principle of HPSG

that $\mathbf{C}_{cd}$ is a multilist, while all other multicollections are multisets. The overall constraint may be expressed succinctly, if somewhat informally, as

$$\mathbf{C}_m = (\mathbf{C}_{hd} \cup (\bigcup_{i=1}^{n} \mathbf{C}_{cd_i})) \setminus \mathbf{C}_{\overline{hd}}$$

In other words, the multiset node c_m is the (multiset) union of the multisets at node c_{hd} and at nodes c_{cd_i}, $1 \leq i \leq n$, less the elements in the multiset at node $c_{\overline{hd}}$. The fact that $\mathbf{C}_{\mathrm{cd}}$ is a multilist (as opposed to a multiset) is of no consequence to this abstraction, although it is certainly important in the linguistic model of HPSG.

For those familiar with HPSG, here is a concretization of the paths of Fig. 2, at least for common situations. These definitions assume that q_0 is of type *headed structure.*[1]

$$\begin{aligned} \lambda_d &= \text{DTRS} \\ \lambda_{hd} &= \text{HEAD-DTR} \\ \lambda_{cd} &= \text{COMP-DTRS} \\ \lambda_m = \lambda_{hd_{ih}} = \lambda_{cdx} &= \text{SYNSEM} \mid \text{NONLOCAL} \mid \text{INHERITED} \mid \text{SLASH} \\ \lambda_{hd_{tb}} &= \text{SYNSEM} \mid \text{NONLOCAL} \mid \text{TO-BIND} \mid \text{SLASH} \end{aligned}$$

A quantified feature term which represents this constraint is the following.

$$(\forall \ell_{\tau_1})(\exists \ell_{\tau_2})$$
$$(\lambda_m \ell_{\tau_1} \Leftrightarrow ((\lambda_d \lambda_{hd} \lambda_{hd_{ih}} \ell_{\tau_1} \vee \lambda_d \lambda_{cd} \ell_{\tau_2} \lambda_{cdx} \ell_{\tau_1}) \wedge \neg \lambda_d \lambda_{hd} \lambda_{hd_{tb}} \ell_{\tau_1})) \quad (1)$$

[1] This example covers the case in which the only daughters of a headed structure, other than the head daughter, are the complement daughters. However, a headed structure may have other forms of daughters, including a marker daughter, an adjunct daughter, and a filler daughter. For simplicity, such daughters are not modelled here, although the extension of the example described here to include these cases is completely straightforward.

In the context of HPSG, τ_1 is the type *local*, and τ_2 is the type *sign*.

Strictly speaking, the symbol $\Leftrightarrow$ is not allowed in quantified feature terms, but may easily be eliminated in the usual way. It remains to express the order constraints. The following two sentences recapture that $\mathbf{C}_m$ is a multiset and that $\mathbf{C}_{cd}$ is a multilist, respectively. The other multisets are characterized similarly.

$$(\forall \ell_1)(\forall \ell_2)(\lambda_m[\ell_1 \leq \ell_2] \Rightarrow \lambda_m[\ell_2 \leq \ell_1]) \tag{2}$$

$$(\forall \ell_1)(\forall \ell_2)((\lambda_d\lambda_{cd}\ell_1 \vee \lambda_d\lambda_{cd}\ell_2) \Rightarrow (\lambda_d\lambda_{cd}[\ell_1 \leq \ell_2] \vee \lambda_d\lambda_c[\ell_2 \leq \ell_1])) \tag{3}$$

3 Decidability

3.1 Embedding into a First-Order Logic

The approach to establishing satisfiability which is taken in this paper is that of embedding the typed MEFS feature logic into a typed first-order logic. This approach has the distinct advantage that much is known about techniques for establishing decidability for satisfiability of first-order logics, and that wealth of knowledge may be drawn upon in establishing the desired result.

3.1.1 Some essential notation. The *rank* of a relation symbol is a sequence defining the sorts of its arguments. The set of all domain elements of sort τ which occur in the model M is denoted $\mathsf{Dom}(M,\tau)$. The value that symbol X assumes under interpretation M is denoted X^M. For a set Φ of sentences, $\mathsf{Mod}(\Phi)$ denotes the set of all models of Φ, while $\mathsf{Mod}_f(\Phi)$ denotes the set of all finite models of Φ. Because we work with two distinct logics, there are two distinct notions of satisfiability. As already defined in 2.3.6 and 2.3.9, $\mathsf{Sat}(M,\varphi)$ denotes the set of $(\mathcal{K},M)$-assignments which satisfy the typed feature term φ with respect to the typed MEFS M. On the other hand, $\mathsf{FOSat}(M,\varphi)$ denotes the set of first-order truth assignments which satisfy the (many-sorted) first-order formula φ with respect to the first-order model M, in the logic $\mathsf{Logic}(\mathcal{K})$ defined in 3.1.2 below.

3.1.2 The first-order logic of a typed MEFS context. The *many-sorted first-order logic corresponding to* $\mathcal{K}$, denoted $\mathsf{Logic}(\mathcal{K})$, is the first-order logic, with equality, which is defined as follows.

(i) The set of sorts of $\mathsf{Logic}(\mathcal{K})$ is precisely $\mathsf{CESort}(\mathbf{T})$.

(ii) The language contains precisely the following relation symbols.

- For each $f \in F$, there is a relation symbol Attr_f, with rank $(\mathsf{Obj},\mathsf{Obj})$.
- For each $f \in F$, there is a relation symbol AttrC_f, with rank $(\mathsf{Obj},\mathsf{Coll})$.
- For each $a \in A$, there is a relation symbol Const_a, with rank (Obj).
- There is a relation symbol $\mathsf{TagOrder}$, with rank $(\mathsf{Coll},\mathsf{Tag},\mathsf{Tag})$.
- There is a relation symbol TagVal, with rank $(\mathsf{Tag},\mathsf{Obj})$.
- There is a relation symbol $\mathsf{TagUsed}$, with rank (Tag).

(iii) There is one constant symbol, $\mathsf{InitState}$, of type Obj.

(iv) There are no non-nullary function symbols.

3.1.3 First-order representation of an MEFS. Let $M = (Q, \delta, \alpha, q_o, L, C, \gamma, \eta, \theta)$ be a typed MEFS. The *first-order representation of* M, denoted $\mathsf{FO}(M)$, is the interpretation in $\mathsf{Logic}(\mathcal{K})$ which describes M. Informally, $\mathsf{Attr}_f^{\mathsf{FO}(M)}(q_1, q_2)$ (resp. $\mathsf{AttrC}_f^{\mathsf{FO}(M)}(q, c)$) means that there is a feature edge in M from q_1 to q_2 (resp. from q_1 to c) labelled f. $\mathsf{TagOrder}^{\mathsf{FO}(M)}(c, k_1, k_2)$ records that $k_1 \leq k_2$ at node c. $\mathsf{TagVal}^{\mathsf{FO}(M)}(k, q)$ records that tag k is assigned the value at q, and that the types of a and q are compatible. $\mathsf{TagUsed}^{\mathsf{FO}(M)}(k)$ just records that the tag k is used in M. The formal specification is as follows.
(i) $\mathsf{Dom}(\mathsf{FO}(M), (t, \mathsf{Obj})) = \{q \in Q \mid \theta(q) \sqsubseteq t\}$.
(ii) $\mathsf{Dom}(\mathsf{FO}(M), (t, \mathsf{Coll})) = \{c \in C \mid \theta(c) \sqsubseteq t\}$.
(iii) $\mathsf{Dom}(\mathsf{FO}(M), (t, \mathsf{Tag})) = \{k \in L \mid \theta(k) \sqsubseteq t\}$.
(iv) $\mathsf{Attr}_f^{\mathsf{FO}(M)}(q_1, q_2)$ iff $q_1, q_2 \in Q$ and $\delta(q_1, f) = q_2$.
(v) $\mathsf{AttrC}_f^{\mathsf{FO}(M)}(q, c)$ iff $q \in Q$, $c \in C$, and $\delta(q, f) = c$.
(vi) $\mathsf{Const}_a^{\mathsf{FO}(M)}(q)$ iff $q \in \mathsf{Dom}(\mathsf{FO}(M), (\mu(a), \mathsf{Obj}))$ and $\alpha(q) = a$.
(vii) $\mathsf{TagOrder}^{\mathsf{FO}(M)}(c, k_1, k_2)$ iff $c \in C$, $k_1, k_2 \in \eta(c)$, and $k_1 \leq_{\eta(c)} k_2$.
(viii) $\mathsf{TagVal}^{\mathsf{FO}(M)}(k, q)$ iff $k \in L$, $q \in Q$, and $\gamma(k) = q$.
(ix) $\mathsf{TagUsed}^{\mathsf{FO}(M)}(k)$ iff $k \in L$ and there is a $c \in C$ such that $\delta(c, k)\downarrow$.
(x) $\mathsf{InitState}^{\mathsf{FO}(M)} = q_o$.

3.1.4 The axiom system. To ensure that a structure over the logic $\mathsf{Logic}(\mathcal{K})$ represents a typed MEFS, it is necessary to enforce certain axioms. The *first-order axiom system* $\mathsf{FAxioms}(\mathcal{K})$ for the typed MEFS context $\mathcal{K}$ is defined to be the following set.
(i) For each $a \in A$:
(i-a) $(\forall x)(\forall y)((\mathsf{Const}_a(x) \wedge \mathsf{Const}_a(y)) \Rightarrow (x = y))$.
(ii) For each $f \in F$:
(ii-a) $(\forall x)(\forall y)(\forall z)((\mathsf{Attr}_f(x, y) \wedge \mathsf{AttrC}_f(x, z)) \Rightarrow \bot)$.
(ii-b) $(\forall x)(\forall y)(\forall z)((\mathsf{Attr}_f(x, y) \wedge \mathsf{Attr}_f(x, z)) \Rightarrow y = z)$.
(ii-c) $(\forall x)(\forall y)(\forall z)((\mathsf{AttrC}_f(x, y) \wedge \mathsf{AttrC}_f(x, z)) \Rightarrow y = z)$.
(iii) $(\forall X)(\forall \ell_1)(\forall \ell_2)$
$$(\mathsf{TagOrder}(X, \ell_1, \ell_2) \Rightarrow (\mathsf{TagOrder}(X, \ell_1, \ell_1) \wedge \mathsf{TagOrder}(X, \ell_2, \ell_2))).$$
(iv) $(\forall X)(\forall \ell_1)(\forall \ell_2)(\forall \ell_3)$
$$((\mathsf{TagOrder}(X, \ell_1, \ell_2) \wedge \mathsf{TagOrder}(X, \ell_2, \ell_3)) \Rightarrow \mathsf{TagOrder}(X, \ell_1, \ell_3)).$$
(v) $(\forall X)(\forall \ell_1)(\forall \ell_2)((\mathsf{TagOrder}(X, \ell_1, \ell_2) \wedge \mathsf{TagOrder}(X, \ell_2, \ell_1) \Rightarrow \ell_1 = \ell_2))$.
(vi) $(\forall X)(\forall \ell)(\mathsf{TagOrder}(X, \ell, \ell) \Rightarrow \mathsf{TagUsed}(\ell))$.
(vii) $(\forall \ell)(\exists y)(\mathsf{TagUsed}(\ell) \Rightarrow \mathsf{TagVal}(\ell, y))$.
(viii) $(\forall \ell)(\forall x)(\forall y)((\mathsf{TagVal}(\ell, x) \wedge \mathsf{TagVal}(\ell, y)) \Rightarrow x = y)$.
Condition (i) states that constant a can be associated with at most one object state; (ii) states that there is at most one edge leaving a given object node with a given feature label; conditions (iii)-(v) state that $\mathsf{TagOrder}$ is a partial order; condition (vi) states that any tag at node X is used; condition (vii) states that the value associated with a given tag is global.

3.1.5 Proposition. *If* $M \in \mathsf{TMEFS}(\mathcal{C})$, *then* $\mathsf{FO}(M) \in \mathsf{FAxioms}(\mathcal{K})$. □

The proof of 3.1.5 is a straightforward verification. Thus, the first order representation of any typed MEFS satisfies the axioms of 3.1.4.

3.1.6 Representation of a feature term as a first-order formula. To establish an equivalence between the logic of typed MEFS's and these axioms, it must also be shown that any (finite) model of these axioms represents an MEFS. This task is somewhat intricate, and requires a substantial dose of complex notation. To simplify the presentation in this abbreviated paper, the idea of this representation will be illustrated, with the formal details left to the reader. The idea is a natural extension of that introduced for ordinary feature structures in [10], [11]. Consider the feature term $\varphi = f_1 f_2 \ell_1 f_1[\ell_2 \leq \ell_3]$, which might be used in the representation of the example of Fig. 1. One first-order representation is

$$(\exists x_0)(\exists x_1)(\exists x_2)(\exists x_3)(\exists x_4)(\exists X_1)(\exists X_2)\ (\mathsf{InitState} = x_0 \wedge \mathsf{Attr}_{f_1}(x_0, x_1) \wedge \mathsf{AttrC}_{f_2}(x_1, X_1) \wedge \mathsf{Attr}_{f_1}(x_2, X_2) \wedge \mathsf{TagVal}(\ell_1, x_2) \wedge \mathsf{TagVal}(\ell_2, x_3) \wedge \mathsf{TagVal}(\ell_3, x_4) \wedge \mathsf{TagOrder}(X_1, \ell_1, \ell_1) \wedge \mathsf{TagOrder}(X_2, \ell_2, \ell_3)) \tag{4}$$

Similarly, a first-order formula representing $\varphi' = f_1 f_2 \ell_1 f_1 : a$ is

$$(\exists x_0)(\exists x_1)(\exists x_2)(\exists x_3)(\exists X_1)(\exists X_2)\ (\mathsf{InitState} = x_0 \wedge \mathsf{Attr}_{f_1}(x_0, x_1) \wedge \mathsf{AttrC}_{f_2}(x_1, X_1) \wedge \mathsf{Attr}_{f_1}(x_2, X_2) \wedge x_3 = a \wedge \mathsf{TagVal}(\ell_1, x_2) \wedge \mathsf{TagVal}(\ell_2, x_3) \wedge \mathsf{TagOrder}(X_1, \ell_1, \ell_1) \wedge \mathsf{TagOrder}(X_2, \ell_2, \ell_2)) \tag{5}$$

These two examples illustrate most of the key ideas of the representation. A variable, of the appropriate sort, is introduced for each node which the path requires. The predicates have the meanings identified in 3.1.3. Note that some predicates are implied by the axioms of 3.1,4, and need not be included explicitly. For example, $\mathsf{TagOrder}(X_2, \ell_2, \ell_2)$, $\mathsf{TagOrder}(X_2, \ell_3, \ell_3)$, $\mathsf{TagUsed}(\ell_1)$, $\mathsf{TagUsed}(\ell_2)$, and $\mathsf{TagUsed}(\ell_3)$ may be added as conjuncts to the representation of φ without altering the semantics. Nonetheless, since all such representations are equivalent in the presence of the schema of 3.1.4, the terminology "the" first order representation of φ, notationally $\mathsf{FO}(\varphi)$, will be used in that which follows.

All quantifiers introduced in this representation are existential. In translating a feature term, any quantifiers on that term are placed outside of the the scope of these translation quantifiers. Thus, for quantified feature term, $\psi = (\forall \ell_1)(\exists \ell_2)(\exists \ell_3)(f_1 f_2 \ell_1 f_1[\ell_2 \leq \ell_3])$, the full quantifier prefix, to be applied to the conjunct of atoms identified in (4) above, would be $(\forall \ell_1)(\exists \ell_2)(\exists \ell_3)(\exists x_0)(\exists x_1)(\exists x_2)(\exists x_3)(\exists x_4)(\exists X_1)(\exists X_2)$. The string $(\forall \ell_1)(\exists \ell_2)(\exists \ell_3)$ is $\mathsf{Prefix}(\psi)$, and the string $(f_1 f_2 \ell_1 f_1[\ell_2 \leq \ell_3])$ is $\mathsf{Matrix}(\psi)$, in the notation of 2.3.7. $\mathsf{FO}(\varphi)$ is then defined to be $\mathsf{Prefix}(\varphi) \cdot \mathsf{FO}(\mathsf{Matrix}(\psi))$. Note that $\mathsf{FO}(\mathsf{Matrix}(\psi)) = \varphi$ is the formula of (4). The full formal result relating satisfiability of quantified feature terms to the satisfiability of first-order formulas is the following.

3.1.7 Proposition. *Let* $\varphi \in \mathsf{QFT}(\mathcal{K})$, *and let* $M \in \mathsf{TMEFS}(\mathcal{C})$. *Then* $\mathsf{Sat}(M,\varphi) = \mathsf{FOSat}(\mathsf{FO}(M),\mathsf{FO}(\varphi))$. □

The proof of 3.1.7 is a tedious but straightforward inductive argument. We are now in a position to provide the complement of 3.1.3; namely the definition of a canonical typed MEFS associated with a first-order model.

3.1.8 The canonical MEFS of a first-order model. Let $\mathcal{I} \in \mathsf{Mod}_f(\mathsf{FAxioms}(\mathcal{K}))$. Define the *canonical typed MEFS corresponding to* $\mathcal{I}$, denoted $\mathsf{TMEFS}(\mathcal{I}) = (Q^{\mathcal{I}}, \delta^{\mathcal{I}}, \alpha^{\mathcal{I}}, q_o^{\mathcal{I}}, L^{\mathcal{I}}, C^{\mathcal{I}}, \gamma^{\mathcal{I}}, \eta^{\mathcal{I}}, \theta^{\mathcal{I}})$, as follows. Start by defining the relation $\mathsf{AttrL}^{\mathcal{I}}$ of rank $(\mathsf{Coll},\mathsf{Obj})$ by $\mathsf{AttrL}^{\mathcal{I}}(X,x)$ iff $(\exists \ell)(\mathsf{TagOrder}(X,\ell,\ell) \wedge \mathsf{TagVal}(\ell,x))$. Then let $\mathsf{Attr}^{\mathcal{I}}$ to be the binary relation defined by $(\bigcup_{e\in F} \mathsf{Attr}_e^{\mathcal{I}}) \cup (\bigcup_{e\in F} \mathsf{AttrC}_e^{\mathcal{I}}) \cup \mathsf{AttrL}^{\mathcal{I}}$. Next, let $\overline{\mathsf{Attr}}^{\mathcal{I}}$ be the transitive closure of Attr. We are now set to make the definitions.

(a) $Q^{\mathcal{I}} = \{q \in \mathsf{Dom}(\mathcal{I},\mathsf{Obj}) \mid \overline{\mathsf{Attr}}^{\mathcal{I}}(\mathsf{InitState},q)\}$.

(b) $C^{\mathcal{I}} = \{x \in \mathsf{Dom}(\mathcal{I},\mathsf{Coll}) \mid \overline{\mathsf{Attr}}^{\mathcal{I}}(\mathsf{InitState},X)\}$.

(c) $L^{\mathcal{I}} = \{\ell \in \mathsf{Dom}(\mathcal{I},\mathsf{Tag}) \mid (\exists X \in C^{\mathcal{I}})(\mathsf{TagOrder}(X,\ell,\ell))\}$.

(d) $\delta^{\mathcal{I}}$ is defined by $\delta^{\mathcal{I}}(q,e)\downarrow$ iff $q \in Q^{\mathcal{I}}$ and either $(\exists r \in Q^{\mathcal{I}})(\mathsf{Attr}_e^{\mathcal{I}}(q,r))$ or else $(\exists c \in C^{\mathcal{I}})(\mathsf{AttrC}_e^{\mathcal{I}}(q,c))$. In this case, $\delta^{\mathcal{I}}(q,e)$ is defined to be the unique r or c found by this construction. The uniqueness follows from rule (ii) of 3.1.4.

(e) For $q \in Q^{\mathcal{I}}$, $\alpha^{\mathcal{I}}(q)\downarrow$ iff $(\exists a \in A)(\mathsf{Const}_a(q))$, and then $\alpha^{\mathcal{I}}(q) = a$.

(f) For $k \in L^{\mathcal{I}}$, $\gamma^{\mathcal{I}}(k)$ is defined iff $(\exists q \in Q^{\mathcal{I}})(\mathsf{TagVal}(k,q))$ holds. In this case, the value of $\gamma^{\mathcal{I}}(k)$ is this q.

(g) For $c \in C^{\mathcal{I}}$, $\eta^{\mathcal{I}}(c)$ is defined to be the poset whose underlying set is $\{k \mid \mathsf{TagOrder}^{\mathcal{I}}(c,k,k)\}$, with $k_1 \leq_c k_2$ iff $\mathsf{TagOrder}^{\mathcal{I}}(c,k_1,k_2)$.

(h) The typing function $\theta^{\mathcal{I}}$ is defined as follows.

- For $q \in Q^{\mathcal{I}}$, $\theta^{\mathcal{I}}(q) = \sqcap\{t \in T \mid q \in \mathsf{Dom}(\mathcal{I},(t,\mathsf{Obj}))\}$.
- For $c \in C^{\mathcal{I}}$, $\theta^{\mathcal{I}}(c) = \sqcap\{t \in T \mid c \in \mathsf{Dom}(\mathcal{I},(t,\mathsf{Coll}))\}$.
- For $k \in L^{\mathcal{I}}$, $\theta^{\mathcal{I}}(k) = \sqcap\{t \in T \mid k \in \mathsf{Dom}(\mathcal{I},(t,\mathsf{Tag}))\}$.

3.1.9 Proposition. *Let* $\mathcal{I} \in \mathsf{Mod}_f(\mathsf{FAxioms}(\mathcal{K}))$. *Then* $\mathsf{TMEFS}(\mathcal{I}) \in \mathsf{TMEFS}(\mathcal{C})$, *and for any* $\varphi \in \mathsf{QFT}(\mathcal{K})$, $\mathsf{Sat}(\mathsf{TMEFS}(\mathcal{I}),\varphi) = \mathsf{FOSat}(\mathcal{I},\mathsf{FO}(\varphi))$. □

The proof is once again a tedious but straightforward induction. The finiteness of $\mathcal{I}$ is essential, since a set of sentences in $\mathsf{Logic}(\mathcal{K})$ may certainly have infinite models, which will by definition not be typed MEFS's. In 3.2.5, an applicable condition on a set of sentences which ensures that the existence of a model implies the existence of finite model will be established.

3.2 Decidability of the First-Order Theory

3.2.1 The Schönfinkel-Bernays class. In single-sorted first-order logic, the *Schönfinkel-Bernays* class (or *SB class*, for short) of sentences, without function symbols, has the property that no existential quantifier occurs within the scope of a universal quantifier. Thus, in prenex normal form, such a sentence has the general form $(\exists x_1)\cdots(\exists x_m)(\forall y_1)\cdots(\forall y_n)\varphi$. It is well known that any sentence in this class (and hence any finite set of such sentences) is decidable for satisfiability [6, p. 212]. The proof rests upon the fact that the Herbrand universe [16, 9.4] of the functional form of the sentence (i.e., the sentence obtained by Skolemizing all existential variables) involves no non-nullary function symbols, and hence is finite with a predetermined size bound.

The SB class has been used to establish the decidability of a logic for feature structures [10], [11]. However, in the context of this paper, both the axiom system (3.1.4) and typical constraints to be modelled (2.3.11) involve formulas outside outside of the SB class. Fortunately, it is possible to extend the idea of the SB class to many-sorted logics in such a way that existential quantifiers may lie with in the scope of universal ones, yet decidability is preserved.

3.2.2 Quantifier classes in many-sorted logics. In a single-sorted logic, a quantifier language is just a set of strings over the alphabet $\{\forall, \exists\}$. The quantifier language associated with the SB class is thus the regular set $\exists^*\forall^*$. The extension of the notion of quantifier language to the many-sorted case is identical, save that the quantifiers are tagged.

A *quantifier language* over a set S of sorts (e.g., $S = \mathsf{CESort}(\mathbf{T})$) is a set of strings $\mathcal{Q}$ over the alphabet $\{\forall_\tau \mid \tau \in S\} \cup \{\exists_\tau \mid \tau \in S\}$. The *closure* of $\mathcal{Q}$ is $\overline{\mathcal{Q}} = \{Q^1_{\tau_1} Q^2_{\tau_2} .. Q^k_{\tau_k} \mid (\forall i : 1 \leq i \leq k)(Q^i \in \{\forall, \exists\}$ and $\exists \tau'_i \in S$ with $\tau_i \sqsubseteq \tau'_i$ and $Q^1_{\tau'_1} Q^2_{\tau'_2} .. Q^k_{\tau'_k} \in \mathcal{Q})\}$. The closure of $\mathcal{Q}$ thus contains all strings obtained by replacing type subscripts on quantifiers by more specific types. $\mathcal{Q}$ is *closed* if $\mathcal{Q} = \overline{\mathcal{Q}}$. Given a formula φ in prefix-matrix form, the *quantifier string* of φ is the string $\mathsf{QuantStr}(\varphi)$ obtained from $\mathsf{Prefix}(\varphi)$ by deleting all parentheses and variables (but preserving or restoring type markers on quantifiers). For example, in $\mathsf{Logic}(\mathcal{K})$, both $(\forall_{(s_1,\mathsf{Obj})} x^{s_1})(\exists_{(s_2,\mathsf{Coll})} Y^{s_2})(\exists_{(\top,\mathsf{Tag})} \ell^\top)$ and its abbreviation $(\forall x^{s_1})(\exists Y^{s_2})(\exists \ell)$ (see 2.3.8(b)) become $\forall_{(s_1,\mathsf{Obj})}\exists_{(s_2,\mathsf{Coll})}\exists_{(\top,\mathsf{Tag})}$. Given an S-sorted first-order logic $\mathcal{L}$, the *quantifier class* for the quantifier language $\mathcal{Q}$, denoted $\mathsf{QuantClass}(\mathcal{Q}, \mathcal{L})$, is the set of all sentences φ in the language of $\mathcal{L}$ in prefix-matrix form such that $\mathsf{QuantStr}(\varphi) \in \mathcal{Q}$.

3.2.3 Functional forms, the Herbrand universe and expansion. The ideas of this paragraph, for the single-sorted case, are discussed in [16, Sec. 9.4]. Only the items necessary to extend these concepts to the many-sorted context are presented here. Given a sentence, the *functional form* is obtained by Skolemizing all existential variables. A key difference is that, in the many-sorted case, functions have rank. For example, the Skolemization of axiom 3.1.4(vii) yields $(\forall \ell)(\mathsf{TagUsed}(\ell) \Rightarrow \mathsf{TagVal}(\ell, f_y(\ell)))$. The Skolem function f_y has rank $\mathsf{Obj} \rightarrow \mathsf{Tag}$; that is, the single argument must be of sort Obj, and the result will be of sort Tag.

The *Herbrand universe* consists of all formal terms obtained by composition of all functions, Skolem and otherwise. If there is no term of a given maximal sort s, a special constant term a_s is introduced and added to the Herbrand universe. For $\mathsf{Logic}(\mathcal{K})$ and the axioms of 3.1.4, there is one constant symbol from the language InitState (of sort Obj), and just one Skolem function, the f_y defined above. The composite term $f_y(\mathsf{InitState})$ is of type Tag. It is necessary to add one additional constant symbol a_{Coll}, corresponding to the maximal sort Coll, to ensure that the Herbrand universe contains at least one element of each sort. Notice, though, that because of the rank constraints, the function f_y cannot compose recursively, and so the Herbrand universe for 3.1.4 is finite, consisting of just the three terms $\{\mathsf{InitState}, f_y(\mathsf{InitState}), a_{\mathsf{Coll}}\}$.

The *Herbrand expansion* consists of all ground terms of the underlying formulas formed by using the Herbrand universe as the underlying domain space. If the Herbrand universe is finite and of determinable size, so too will be the Herbrand expansion of a finite set of formulas (such as those of 3.1.4). Since a set of sentences has a model iff its Herbrand expansion does, and a model of the Herbrand expansion is a model of the original set of sentences, finiteness of the Herbrand expansion provides not only a framework for establishing the existence of a model, but for its finiteness as well. We now turn to the issue of determining conditions under which the Herbrand universe remains finite and of determinable size.

3.2.4 Generalized SB quantifier languages. Let S be a set of sorts and $\mathcal{Q}$ be a quantifier language over S. Define $R_{\mathcal{Q}} \subseteq S \times S$ by $(\tau_1, \tau_2) \in R_{\mathcal{Q}}$ iff there is a string $\sigma \in \mathcal{Q}$ with $\forall_{\tau_1}$ preceding $\exists_{\tau_2}$. Define $R_{\mathcal{Q}}^{\sqsubseteq} = \{(\tau_1, \tau_2) \mid (\exists \tau_3)(\exists \tau_4)((\tau_3, \tau_4) \in R_{\mathcal{Q}}$ and $\tau_1 \sqsubseteq \tau_3$ and $\tau_2 \sqsubseteq \tau_4)\}$, with $R_{\mathcal{Q}}^{\sqsubseteq +}$ its transitive closure. Call $\mathcal{Q}$ a *generalized SB-quantifier class* if $(\tau_1, \tau_2) \in R_{\mathcal{Q}}^{\sqsubseteq +}$ implies $\tau_1 \sqcap \tau_2 = \bot$.

3.2.5 Theorem. *Let S be a set of sorts, $\mathcal{L}$ an S-sorted first-order logic with no non-nullary function symbols and only finitely many constant symbols, and $\mathcal{Q}$ a generalized SB-quantifier class. Then* QuantClass($\mathcal{Q}, \mathcal{L}$) *is decidable for satisfiability, and any finite $\Phi \subseteq$* QuantClass($\mathcal{Q}, \mathcal{L}$) *which has a model has a finite model.*

Proof sketch. The proof hinges upon establishing that the Herbrand universe is finite, and of determinable size. Once that is established, we may make use of the fact that a formula is satisfiable iff its Herbrand expansion is [16, Thm. 9.4.1].

To establish that the Herbrand universe is finite. it suffices to show that for no function symbol f is it possible to have a term of the form $f(\ldots, t, \ldots)$ for which f occurs in t. Let $\mathcal{Q}$ denote the quantifier class for the given set of sentences, and assume that t is a term involving a chain of function symbols $(f_0, f_1, \ldots f_k)$, in which $f_0 = f$ and for each i, $0 \le i \le k-1$, a term of the form $f_i(-)$ occurs as the $\alpha(i)^{th}$ argument to f_{i-1}. Let τ_i denote the range sort of f_i, and let $\tau_{\alpha(i)}$ denote the domain type in f_i of the argument position in which the f_{i+1} term occurs. Then $(\tau_{\alpha(i)}, \tau_i) \in R_{\mathcal{Q}}^{\sqsubseteq +}$ for $0 \le i \le k-1$, and since $\tau_{i+1} \sqsubseteq \tau_{\alpha(i)}$, it follows that $(\tau_{i+1}, \tau_i) \in R_{\mathcal{Q}}^{\sqsubseteq}$ for $0 \le i \le k-1$. Thus $(\tau_k, \tau_0) \in R_{\mathcal{Q}}^{\sqsubseteq +}$. Thus $f_k \neq f_0$, and so no terms can involve recursive applications of any function symbol. The number of distinct terms is finite and strictly bounded, whence the Herbrand expansion has the same property. Decidability, as well as finiteness of the model, follows as outlined above.

A final point to consider is the decidability of a finite set of sentences, as opposed to a single sentence. However, it is straightforward to establish that $\mathsf{QuantClass}(\mathcal{Q}, \mathcal{L})$ must be closed under conjunctions, since the relation $R_{\mathcal{Q}}^{\sqsubseteq +}$ is constructed from all strings in $\mathcal{Q}$, and not just a single string. In other words, the elements of $R_{\mathcal{Q}}^{\sqsubseteq +}$ generated by a "best" prefix of $\varphi_1 \wedge \varphi_2$ are also generated by $\mathsf{Prefix}(\varphi_1)$ and $\mathsf{Prefix}(\varphi_2)$. □

3.2.6 A family of decidable classes of typed MEFS feature logics. *Let $\mathcal{Q}_1$ be a generalized SB quantifier class which is a subset of $(\{\forall_{(s,\mathsf{Tag})} \mid s \in T \setminus \{\bot\}\} \cup \{\exists_{(s,\mathsf{Tag})} \mid s \in T \setminus \{\bot\}\})^*$, and let $\mathcal{Q}_2 = (\{\exists_{(s,\mathsf{Obj})} \mid s \in T \setminus \{\bot\}\} \cup \{\exists_{(s,\mathsf{Coll})} \mid s \in T \setminus \{\bot\}\})^*$. Then any finite family of quantified typed feature sentences over the quantifier class $\mathcal{Q}_1 \cdot \mathcal{Q}_2 = \{\sigma_1 \cdot \sigma_2 \mid \sigma_1 \in \mathcal{Q}_1$ and $\sigma_2 \in \mathcal{Q}_2\}$ is decidable for satisfiability.*

Proof sketch. At first glance, this may appear to be a simple application of 3.2.5. However, 3.2.5 is a theorem about first-order logic, while this result concerns typed feature logic. Let $\varphi \in \mathsf{QFS}(\mathcal{K})$ be such that $\mathsf{QuantStr}(\varphi) \in \mathcal{Q}_1 \cdot \mathcal{Q}_2$. The process of translation of φ to $\mathsf{FO}(\varphi)$, as described in 3.1.6, introduces additional quantifiers. In the translation, feature terms are replaced with the equivalent formulas identified in 3.1.6. There are two key points to note. First of all, the quantifiers which are added will lie within the scope (and thus to the right of) the quantifiers of φ. Second. all quantifiers in the replacement terms are existential and of a subsort of either Obj or else of Coll. Some of the original feature terms may be negated, which complements the affected quantifiers to universal. However, these feature terms do not lie in one another's scope, so, for each term in the translation, the quantifiers will be either all existential or else all universal. The universal quantifiers of this added sequence may thus be moved inside of the existential ones, resulting in a quantifier sequence of the form $\exists_{\tau_1}\exists_{\tau_2}..\exists_{\tau_{k_1}}\forall_{\upsilon_1}\forall_{\upsilon_2}..\forall_{\upsilon_{k_2}}$, with each τ_i and each υ_i of one of the forms (s, Obj) or (s, Coll), for some $s \in T \setminus \{\bot\}$. In other words, if we define $\mathcal{Q}_3 = (\{\forall_{(s,\mathsf{Obj})} \mid s \in T \setminus \{\bot\}\} \cup \{\forall_{(s,\mathsf{Coll})} \mid s \in T \setminus \{\bot\}\})^*$, then this added quantifier sequence will be in $\mathcal{Q}_2 \cdot \mathcal{Q}_3$. The translated first order formula will thus have a total quantifier sequence in $\mathcal{Q}_1 \cdot \mathcal{Q}_2 \cdot \mathcal{Q}_2 \cdot \mathcal{Q}_3$, which reduces to just $\mathcal{Q}_1 \cdot \mathcal{Q}_2 \cdot \mathcal{Q}_3$. It is clear that $(\mathcal{Q}_1 \cdot \mathcal{Q}_2 \cdot \mathcal{Q}_3)^{\sqsubseteq +} = (\mathcal{Q}_1 \cdot \mathcal{Q}_2)^{\sqsubseteq +}$, since there are no existential quantifiers to the right of any of the universal quantifiers in $\mathcal{Q}_3$. We are thus left with the problem of analyzing the original quantifier class $\mathcal{Q}_1 \cdot \mathcal{Q}_2$. It is a straightforward verification that this is an SB quantifier class, thus completing the proof. □

3.2.7 Example: decidability of the Nonlocal Feature Principle. The constraints of the Nonlocal Feature Principle of HPSG are expressed by equations (1)–(3), in 2.3.11. To establish decidability, these constraints must be combined with the axiom system $\mathsf{FAxioms}(\mathcal{K})$ of 3.1.4, and the resulting set of typed feature sentences tested for satisfiability. It is easy to see that the conditions of 3.2.6 applies to this set, rendering it satisfiable.

4 Limitations and Further Directions

The work abstracted here is only a beginning of an effort towards fully automated parsing of HPSG, for several reasons. First of all, certain critical, but not all, set and list operations are expressible in a decidable quantifier class of our language. Further work is necessary to establish a universal framework for expressing a wider variety of set and list constructions.

Second, the only specialized constructions which are considered are those based upon sets and lists. Other equally important forms, such as *linear precedence constraints*, are not addressed.

Third, while the logic presented is decidable for the representation of constraints at a single level, it is not decidable for what Kepser [14] calls *grammaticality*; that is, it is not decidable for recursively embedded constraints. For example, the Nonlocal Feature Principle must hold at every node which is type both *phrase* and *headed-structure*, and not just at one particular node. (It should be pointed out the neither the logic of King [15] nor the logic of Manandhar [17] are shown to be decidable for grammaticality, and in all likelihood they do not have this property.) It is the belief of this author that the decidability of grammaticality cannot be established without some reference to input size; decidability of grammaticality must be tied to size-bounding information computed from the input string, in a spirit similar to off-line parsing of LFG [20] (but without reference to a context-free skeleton, of course). Johnson [12] does provide a system, based upon first-order logic, in which grammaticality is established via off-line parsability, but the formalism is closer to LFG than to HPSG, in that is is built around a context-free skeleton. Furthermore, it does not support types or lists as an explicit construct.

Fourth, the expression of even simple constraints is quite tedious. Thus, at a very minimum, some enclosing package of syntactic sugar which makes is relatively simple to represent key constraints in a simple fashion must be developed.

Finally, it must be acknowledged that decidability does not necessarily imply tractability. Once a decidable logic is identified, the issue of finding means of incorporating it into computationally tractable algorithms remains. Nonetheless, it is possible to envision embedding a decidable logic, such as the one described here, into a larger, more general system such as CUF, TFS, or ALE. This would enable a larger class of constraints to be solved without explicit specification of control information.

References

1. B. Carpenter. ALE: The Attribute Logic Engine user's guide. Technical report, Carnegie Mellon University, Laboratory for Computational Linguistics, 1992.
2. B. Carpenter. *The Logic of Typed Feature Structures*. Cambridge University Press, 1992.
3. B. Carpenter. Set descriptions for logic programming. Paper presented at the 3rd ASL/LSA Conference on Logic and Language. Also referenced under the title: An attribute-value logic for sets, 1993.

4. B. A. Davey and H. A. Priestly. *Introduction to Lattices and Order.* Cambridge University Press, 1990.
5. M. Dorna. The CUF user's manual. Technical report, Institut für maschinelle Sprachverarbeitung, Universität Stuttgart, 1994.
6. B. Dreben and W. D. Goldfarb. *The Decision Problem: Solvable Classes of Quantificational Formulas.* Addison-Wesley, 1979.
7. J. E. Fenstad, T. Langholm, and E. Vestre. Representations and interpretations. In M. Rosner and R. Johnson, editors, *Computational Linguistics and Formal Semantics*, pages 31–95. Cambridge University Press, 1992.
8. J. H. Gallier. *Logic for Computer Science.* John Wiley and Sons, 1986.
9. S. J. Hegner. Distributivity in incompletly specified type hierarchies: Theory and computational complexity. In J. Dörre, editor, *Computational Aspects of Constraint-Based Linguistic Description II, DYANA-2, ESPRIT Basic Research Project 6852, Deliverable R1.2B*, pages 29–120. DYANA, 1994. Also available as LLI Technical Report No. 4, University of Oslo, Department of Linguistics.
10. M. Johnson. Features and formulas. *Computational Linguistics*, 17:131–151, 1991.
11. M. Johnson. Computing with features as formulas. *Computational Linguistics*, 20(1):1–25, 1994.
12. M. Johnson. Two ways of formalizing grammar. *Linguistics and Phil.*, 17, 1994.
13. R. T. Kasper and W. C. Rounds. The logic of unification in grammar. *Linguistics and Phil.*, 13:35–58, 1990.
14. S. Kepser. A satisfiability algorithm for a typed feature logic. Sonderforschungsberiech 340, Teilprojekt B4, Universities of Stuttgart and Tübingen, 1993.
15. P. King. *A Logical Formalism for Head-Driven Phrase Structure Grammar.* PhD thesis, University of Manchester, 1989.
16. H. R. Lewis and C. H. Papadimitriou. *Elements of the Theory of Computation.* Prentice-Hall, 1981.
17. S. Manandhar. An attributive logic of set descriptions and set operations. In *Proceedings of the 32nd Annual Meeting of the ACL*, pages 255–262, 1994.
18. J. D. Monk. *Mathematical Logic.* Springer-Verlag, 1976.
19. M. A. Moshier and C. J. Pollard. The domain of set-valued feature structures. *Linguistics and Phil.*, 17:607–631, 1994.
20. F. C. N. Pereira and D. H. D. Warren. Parsing as deduction. In *Proceedings of the 21st Annual Meeting of the ACL*, pages 137–144, 1983.
21. C. Pollard and I. A. Sag. *Information-Based Syntax and Semantics*, volume 1: Fundamentals of *CSLI Lecture Notes No. 13.* CSLI, 1987.
22. C. Pollard and I. A. Sag. *Head-Driven Phrase Structure Grammar.* University of Chicago Press, 1994.
23. S. Sahni. *Concepts in Discrete Mathematics.* Camelot Publishing, 1985.
24. R. Zajac. Notes on the Typed Feature System, Version 4, January 1991. Technical report, Universität Stuttgart, Institut für Informatik, Project Polygloss, 1991.

Language Understanding: A Procedural Perspective*

Ruth Kempson[1], Wilfried Meyer Viol[2] and Dov Gabbay[3]

[1] Department of Linguistics, SOAS, University of London,
e-mail: rk@soas.ac.uk
[2] Department of Computing, Imperial College, University of London,
e-mail: wm3@doc.ic.ac.uk
[3] Department of Computing, Imperial College, University of London,
e-mail: dg@doc.ic.ac.uk

Abstract. In this paper we introduce the data structures and process structure of an incremental parser which reflects the underspecified nature of the information encoded in the NL string. We show how this parser can deal with so called crossover phenomena in a way other systems cannot. The parser is formulated within the LDS framework and constructs parse trees with the help of a modal logic for finite trees. *wh*-expressions are interpreted as constituents with underspecified tree location. The dynamics of the parser is formulated in terms of transition system in which the transitions between the parser states are effected by deduction rules.

1 Introduction

In this paper we will introduce the data structures and the process structure of a natural language parser which incrementally creates a (set of) labelled logical form(s), possible interpretation(s), while traveling through a NL string in a left-to-right, word-by-word fashion. The underlying aim is to model the process of understanding reflecting at each step the partial nature of the information encoded in the string and the ways in which this information is enriched by mechanisms which fix some particular interpretation. We describe an application for the model dealing with the interaction of *wh* expressions and anaphora. The compilation of logical formulas interpreting NL strings is formalized within an LDS framework ([3]) in which *labels* guide the parser in the goal-directed process of constructing an *ordered tree of declarative units*. Declarative units consist of pairs of *sequences of labels* followed by a *content formula*. The *formula* of a declarative unit represents the *content* of the words supplied in the course of a parse. The *labels* annotate this content with linguistic *features* and *control* information guiding the direction of the parse process. Declarative units are represented as finite sets of formulas. In the course of a parse the content

* This research was supported by the UK Engineering and Physical Sciences Research Council under grant reference GR/K67397,

and number of these *feature sets* grows incrementally. Moreover, these sets implicitly label an *ordered tree structure*, the syntactic tree of the representation under development: that is, one set of feature specifications can be *daughter* or *sister* to another set. This tree structure is formalized within a *Modal Logic of Finite Trees* (eg. [1], [11]) in which modalities refer to relations within trees. For instance, $\langle d\rangle\phi$ holds at a tree node if ϕ holds at a daughter node.
Dynamically, the formal model is the parser as a ***transition system***. The ***states*** of the transition system correspond to ***state descriptions*** of the parser. The ***transitions*** of the system correspond to ***inference steps between state descriptions***. In this sense we represent parsing as ***deduction***. The execution of the transitions is delegated to so-called goal-directed ***tasks***. A task contains a record of what has been achieved on the way to the goal of the task, and what remains to be done. Passing along the string these tasks start by being ***declared*** (nothing has been achieved yet) and incrementally move to being ***satisfied*** (nothing remains to be done). In this sense our parser resembles the one of D. Milward [15]. At every point in the parsing process the information gathered up to that point is captured in a sequence of ***task states***. A task may spawn new (sub)tasks. The *goal* of the entire procedure is the satisfaction of the top level task with goal type t, at the last word of a string. The steps involved in the satisfaction of such tasks include steps of type deduction (modus ponens), but, unlike categorial grammars (eg [17]), such familiar deductive steps form but one type of transition from task state to task state. At the conclusion of a successful parse the satisfied tasks can be seen to label a (parse) tree.
The dynamic aspect of our parser is similar in spirit to the work undertaken within the framework of *evolving algebras* (see [5] and especially [7] and [8]). Not suprisingly, the transition system we develop can be formulated within this framework. On the other hand, our interest is mainly in the ***detail*** of the left-to-right ***parsing*** as it pertains to long distance dependencies (and their interaction with anaphoric processes). For a description at this level of detail the generality of the evolving algebra framework is not required.

2 Data Structures

The object of our parser is the compilation of logical formulas. This determines the data structures required. There are four of them: *Content Formulas*, *Declarative Units*, *Task States*, and *Parse States*. **Content Formulas** essentially represent the contribution to *content* of the words in a string. The language of these formulas is a term logical one with variable binding term operators like ϵ and τ to accommodate quantification. They constitute the *formula part* of declarative units. An example

$$(a) \qquad Man(\epsilon x Man(x)) \wedge Walk(\epsilon x Man(x))$$

representing "a man walks". For more information about variable binding term operators and motivation for their use in linguistics, see [13], [14]. The logical formula to be compiled for a given string consists of a labelled content formula of semantic type t. The labelled formulas, **declarative units** (DU's), are constructed in the course of the parse. So at any moment in the process we must be able to describe the *partial declarative units* present. This description consists of a set of DU-formulas. An example where a is the content formula above

$$(b) \qquad \{Tn(m), Ty(t), Tense(p), Fo(a)\}$$

The goal of the parsing process is to construct a declarative unit of type t using all the words of the string. The construction of a declarative unit is delegated to a *(sub)task*. A (sub)task can be in one of three **task states**: *Declared*, the task is declared but no material has been collected to complete the task. *In progress*, DU-formulas have been collected but not enough to construct a labelled formula of the required type. And finally *Satisfied*, when enough material has been collected to construct a formula of the required type. An example of a satisfied task state for b the declarative unit above

m	**show** t
	b

$_1$

A **Parse State**, finally, is then completely described by a sequence of task states D, the position of the reading head in the string, and a pointer to the task presently under consideration.

Sc	Po	Le
$l(s)$	1	k

$\cdot D$

The following paragraphs describe these data structures in more detail

2.1 Content Formulas

Definition 1 Language
Terms and Formulas of the language L_C for a non-empty set C of quantifier operators are built from individual variables in V, meta variables M, predicate variables in $\mathcal{P}$, individual constants in A, and predicate constants in P as follows

1. the set T_C of L_C-*terms* is defined by
   (a) all elements of A or M are in T_C
   (b) if $x \in V$, $a \in A$, $c \in C$ and $\phi[a/x]$ in $FORM_C$, then $(cx, \phi) \in T_C$.
2. the set Λ_C of *lambda terms* of L_C is defined by
   if $X \in V$, $a \in A$, $\phi[a/X] \in FORM_C \cup T_C$ then $\lambda X.\phi \in \Lambda_C$.
   If $X \in \mathcal{P}$, $a \in A$, $\phi[a/X] \in FORM_C \cup T_C$ then $\lambda X.\phi \in \Lambda_C$,
3. the set $FORM_C$ of L_C-*formulas* is defined by
   (a) if $t_1, \ldots, t_n \in T_C$, and P an n-place predicate of L. then $Pt_1 \ldots t_n \in FORM_C$
   (b) if $\phi, \phi' \in FORM_C$ then $\phi\#\phi' \in FORM_C$, where $\# \in \{\wedge, \vee, \leftrightarrow, \rightarrow\}$.

Notice that λ may bind variables within the scope of elements of C but not vice versa. Moreover in elements of T_C and $FORM_C$ there occur no free variables.

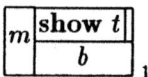

Example 1 We will represent the content of a word like *some* by

$$\lambda P(\epsilon x, P(x))$$

It is a function requiring an instance of (the type of) P (for instance, $\lambda y \cdot Man(y)$) to become a complete object (of type e), i.e., *epsilon* terms.

$$(\epsilon x, Man(x))$$

2.2 Declarative Units

Declarative units consists of pairs of *sequences of labels* followed by a *content formula.*

$$\underbrace{\langle l_1, \ldots l_n \rangle}_{\text{Sequence of labels}} \; : \; \underbrace{\phi}_{\text{Content Formula}}$$

Declarative units constitute the components of the representation to be constructed. The *formula* of a declarative unit is the side representing the *content* of the words supplied in the course of a parse. The *labels* annotate this content with linguistic *features* and *control* information guiding the direction of the parse process.
In the course of a parse declarative units are built. In order to be able to describe growth and construction of these units, they will be represented as finite sets of *atomic DU-formulas*

$$\{C_1(l_1), \ldots, C_n(l_n), Fo(\phi)\}.$$

The *label categories* $C_1, \ldots C_n$ can be seen as *feature dimensions.* $C(l)$ states the association of feature dimension C with feature value l. In fact, the formula $C_i(l)$ is an atomic formula interpreted on a model over $\mathcal{L}$. We recognize two special feature dimensions:

- The *type* dimension Ty with values from $\langle Lab_{Ty}(e, cn, t), \rightarrow, \cdot \rangle$ consisting of types over e, cn and t. This feature determines the combinatorial properties of the declarative unit.
- The *Tree Node* dimension Tn with values chosen from the node set Lab_{Tn} of an *ordered linked tree* $\mathcal{T} = \langle Lab_{Tn}, \leq, <, L \rangle$ (where $\leq$ is the *dominance* relation, $<$ the *precedence* relation, and L the *link* relation). On these trees the relations R_u, R_d, R_l, R_r, and R_L are defined: *mother-of, daughter-of, left-sister-of, right-sister-of and linked-to relations.* We will also consider the reflexive and transitive closures R_i^*, $i \in \{u, d, l, r, L\}$ of these relations. These relations are interpreted by *modalities* in our language in the standard way.

Definition 2 (Language of Declarative Units) The language of *declarative units* is a first order language with *Non-logical Vocabulary*:

1. a denumerable number of sorted constants from *Lab* for $i \leq n$, where $\mathcal{L}_i = \langle Lab_i, R^1, \ldots, R_i^m \rangle$ structures the set of *feature values* in *Lab*,

2. *monadic predicates Fo* ('*Formula*'), Ty ('*Type*'), Tn ('*Tree node*'), C_i, $i \leq n$ and identity '$=$',
3. *modalities* $\langle u\rangle$ (up),$\langle d\rangle$ (down) ,$\langle l\rangle$ (left), $\langle r\rangle$ (right), $\langle L\rangle$ (link) and their starred versions $\langle d\rangle^*$, $\langle u\rangle^*$, $\langle l\rangle^*$, $\langle r\rangle^*$. We will use the abbreviation $\langle\#\rangle^n$, $n \in \mathbb{N}$, for

$$\underbrace{\langle\#\rangle\ldots\langle\#\rangle}_{n \text{ times}}$$

Formulas:

1. If $j \in L_C$ then $Fo(j)$ is an (atomic) DU-formula.
   If $k \in Lab_1$ then $Ty(k)$ is an (atomic) DU-formula.
   If $k \in Lab_2$ then $Tn(k)$ is an (atomic) DU-formula.
   If $k \in Lab_i$, $2 < i \leq n$, then $C_i(k)$ is an (atomic) DU-formula.
   If t, t' are variables or individual constants, then $t = t'$ is an (atomic) DU-formula.
2. If ϕ and ψ are DU-formulas and x, then $\phi\#\psi$ is a DU-formula for $\# \in \{\wedge, \vee, \rightarrow, \leftrightarrow\}$.
   If x is a variable and ϕ a DU-formula, then $\forall x\phi$ and $\exists x\phi$ are DU-formulas.
   If M is a modality and ϕ a DU-formula, then $M\phi$ is a DU-formula.

This language we use to formulate properties of declarative units and their rules.

- Declarative units are related to each other through their *tree node feature*: If $Tn(n)$ is an element of a partial declarative unit DU_i, we may represent as follows:

  $$\begin{array}{ccc} \text{Tree Node } n & & \text{labelled formula} \\ Tn(n) & \longleftarrow \; i \; \longrightarrow & \{C_1(l)\ldots C_k(l')\} \end{array}$$

  That is, unit i is located at node n. We have the modal entity of a *decorated tree node*. If $m, n \in Lab_{Tn}$ such that $m \leq n$ and $Tn(m) \in DU_1, Tn(n) \in DU_2$ then $DU_1 \leq DU_2$. This we can call ***absolute addressing***. But there are also *relative* ways of expressing tree relations. For instance, allowing declarative units to contain non-atomic *addresses*, if $Tn(m) \in DU_1$, $\langle l\rangle Tn(m) \in DU_2$, and $\langle u\rangle^* Tn(m) \in DU_3$, then $DU_1 \leq DU_3$ and $DU_1 < DU_2$.

  $$DU_1 = \{Tn(m)\ldots C_k(l')\} \quad < \quad DU_2 = \{\langle l\rangle Tn(m)\ldots C'_k(l')\}$$

- A set of declarative units structured as a tree represents an *application* tree: declarative units at daughters combine to give a declarative unit at the mother. For instance, applications of the rule of Modus Ponens.

  $$\frac{\langle e,\ldots\rangle : \phi \qquad\qquad \langle e \rightarrow t,\ldots\rangle : \psi}{\langle t,\ldots\rangle : \psi(\phi)}$$

for declarative units get the *meta description*

$$\frac{\langle d\rangle(Ty(e) \wedge Fo(\phi)) \wedge \langle d\rangle(Ty(e \rightarrow t) \wedge Fo(\psi))}{Ty(t) \wedge Fo(\psi(\phi))}$$

An item has Type Feature t and Form Feature $\psi(\phi)$ if it has daughters with Type Features $e \rightarrow t$ and t and Form Features ψ and ϕ respectively.
- We will use the following modal principles more or less implicitly (here $\# \in \{u, d, l, r, L\}$)
  1. $\langle\#\rangle^{-1}[\#]\phi \rightarrow \phi$ where $\langle u\rangle = \langle d\rangle^{-1}$, $\langle l\rangle = \langle r\rangle^{-1}$: mother-of is the converse of daughter-of and left-of the converse of right-of.
  2. $\langle\#\rangle^{*}\phi \leftrightarrow (\phi \vee \langle\#\rangle\langle\#\rangle^{*}\phi)$. For instance, stating that $\langle d\rangle^{*}\phi$ holds at a tree node n is equivalent to stating that ϕ holds at n or $\langle d\rangle^{*}\phi$ holds at a daughter of n.

2.3 Task States

In the course of a parse both the set of (partial) declarative units and the set of features connected to a particular (partial) declarative unit grows. The *Complete Declarative Units* (*Du's*) are *maximally consistent* subsets of $\mathcal{A}$. A *Du* is finite (modulo identity) and has the form

$$\{C_1(l_1), \ldots, C_n(l_n), Fo(\phi)\}$$

The growth of the structure of (partial) declarative units corresponding to an NL string is described in terms of transitions between *Task States*. With each declarative unit there corresponds one task. A Task State is a description of the state of a task. A task is completely described by the following four feature dimensions: **Goal (G)**. Values on this dimension are the *semantic types* in the label set Ty. This feature indicates which semantic object is under construction. **Tree Node (TN)**. Values are elements of the label set Tn. The 'top-node' in Tn will be denoted by 1. This feature fixes the location of the task in question within a tree structure. **Discrepancy (TODO)**. Values are (finite sequences of) DU-formulas. This dimension tells us what has to be found/constructed before the goal object can be constructed. **Result (DONE)**. Values are lists, sequences, of DU-formulas. These values will be the partial declarative units of the Incremental Model. We will represent the task state $TS(i)$ by

<table>
<tr><td rowspan="2">TN</td><td>show G</td><td>TODO</td></tr>
<tr><td colspan="2">DONE</td></tr>
</table>

i

We can distinguish three kinds of task states: **Task Declarations**: Nothing has yet been achieved with respect to a goal G, G is in TODO, DONE is empty. **Tasks in Progress**: both DONE and TODO are non empty. If G is the goal and if things are set up right, then $DONE, TODO \Rightarrow G$. **Satisified Tasks** There is nothing left to be done. TODO is empty *Soundness* of the deductive system amounts to the fact that the goal G can be computed, derived, from α in case TODO is empty.[4]

[4] Here in particular the similarities with the evolving algebra paradigm are evident.

2.4 Parse States

A parse state

$$\langle \begin{array}{|c|c|c|}\hline Sc & Po & Le \\ \hline s & p & l \\ \hline \end{array}(S)\rangle,$$

finally, consists of a ***bookkeeping device*** $\begin{array}{|c|c|c|}\hline Sc & Po & Le \\ \hline s & p & l \\ \hline \end{array}$ and a sequence S of task states. In the bookkeeping device, the value of ***pointer*** Po, p, is a natural number $p \leq l$. This value gives the task state in S currently under consideration. s Gives the value of the ***string counter*** Sc which represents the location of the reading head in the string. Finally, the length of the string of tasks state S is l, the value of Le.

3 Dynamics

The ***dynamics*** of the parse process consists of reaching a final parse state starting from the initial state where the ***transitions*** in the process are licensed, driven, by the words in a string. Concretely, the dynamics of the parsing process, is the dynamics of ***demand satisfaction***: given the tree modalities, the presence of a modal formula of the form $\langle d \rangle \phi$ as TODO gives an ***unsatisfied demand***, a so-called ***defect***[5]: it requires action. The ***task states*** of LDS_{NL} can be seen as sets of DU-formulas together with demands to be dealt with. The parsing process then essentially consists of attempts to use the words of a string to satisfy the overall demand to construct an entity of the truth-value type t. The course from initial parse state to a final one is guided by *Transition Rules*.

3.1 Basic Transition Rules

In the following the symbols $X, Y, Z, \ldots$ will range over individual DU-formulas, the symbols $\alpha, \beta, \ldots$ will range over (possibly empty) sequences of such formulas, D, $D', \ldots$ will range over (possibly empty) sequences of tasks, and $w_i, w_{i+1}, \ldots$ will range over words.

The start of a parsing sequence is a single task state, the *Axiom state*. The last element of such a sequence is the *Goal* state. The number of task states in a parse state grows by applications of the Subgoal- and Adjunction rules. Tasks become satisfied by applications of the Scanning and Thinning.

1. **Axiom**

$$\begin{array}{|c|c|c|}\hline Sc & Po & Le \\ \hline 0 & 1 & 1 \\ \hline \end{array}\left(1 \begin{array}{|l|l|}\hline \textbf{show t} & Ty(t) \\ \hline & \\ \hline \end{array} \right)_1$$

[5] We know this from completeness proofs in modal logic of the so-called ***step-by-step*** variety. In contrast to the situation in modal logic, however, satisfying nodes (maximally consistent sets) need to be eventually *licensed* by the words in a given string, consistency alone is not enough.

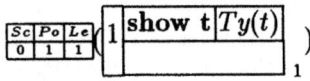

Goal

$$\left(\begin{array}{|c|c|c|}\hline Sc & Po & Le \\\hline l(s) & 1 & k \\\hline\end{array}\right| \left|\begin{array}{c}\boxed{1} \end{array}\right| \begin{array}{|c|}\hline \textbf{show } t \\\hline Ty(t), \alpha \\\hline\end{array}_1 \cdot D\right)$$

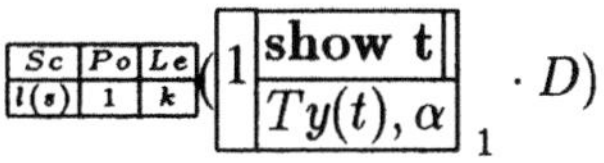

where s is a string with length $l(s)$ and all elements of D are *satisfied* task states.

In the Axiom state nothing has been done yet and it is required to construct an object of type t; in the Goal state this requirement has been fulfilled.

2. **String processing.** Essentially, only the words occurring in the string allow us to add information in the DONE compartment of a task state. This is formalized in the Scanning rule. When a formula occurs both in the DONE and in the TODO compartment, then it may be removed from the latter. This is the way TODO is emptied. The Thinning rule expresses this.

(a) **Scanning**

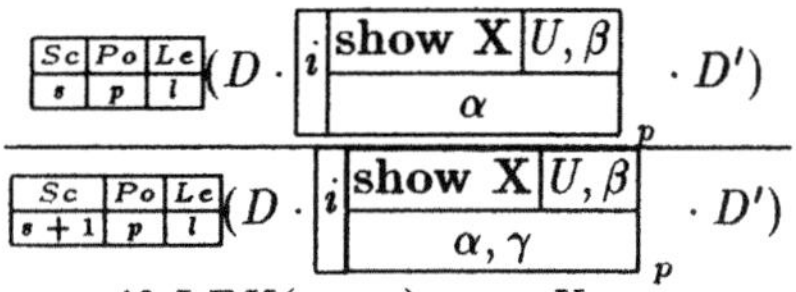

if $LEX(w_{s+1}) = \gamma$, $U \in \gamma$

The expression $LEX(w_{s+1}) = Y$ refers to the lexical entry for the word w_{j+1}. This is a set of DU-formulas possibly containing U; if this set contains the *trigger* in the TODO box, then it may be added to the DONE box. In that case, the *Thinning* rule allows us to remove the demand from the TODO box.

(b) **Thinning**

$$\begin{array}{|c|c|c|}\hline Sc & Po & Le \\\hline s & p & l \\\hline\end{array}\left(D \cdot \left|\begin{array}{c} i \end{array}\right| \begin{array}{|c|c|}\hline \textbf{show } X & U, \beta \\\hline \multicolumn{2}{|c|}{\alpha, \gamma} \\\hline\end{array}_p \cdot D'\right)$$

$$\rule{3cm}{0.4pt}$$

$$\begin{array}{|c|c|c|}\hline Sc & Po & Le \\\hline s+1 & p & l \\\hline\end{array}\left(D \cdot \left|\begin{array}{c} i \end{array}\right| \begin{array}{|c|c|}\hline \textbf{show } X & \beta \\\hline \multicolumn{2}{|c|}{\alpha, \gamma} \\\hline\end{array}_p \cdot D'\right)$$

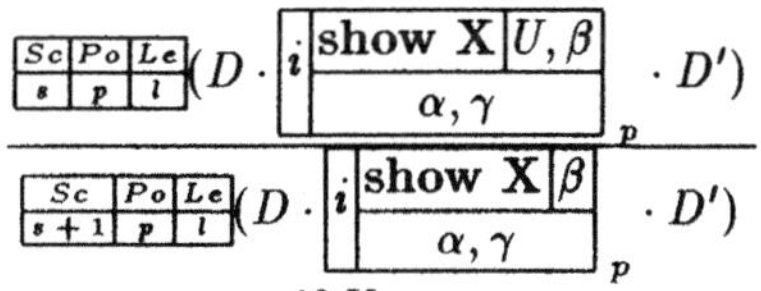

if $U \in \gamma$

This is the only rule allowing us to remove elements from TODO; we can only end up with satisfied tasks (empty TODO's) by fulfilling the requirements.

1. **Mode of Combination.** The following two rules deal with the processing of information available at a specific task node. The first rule, Introduction, analyses a requirement into subrequirements as specified by syntactic or logical rules present. The second rule, Elimination, combines — or rewrites — information that has been acquired, again according to the rules present.

(a) **Introduction**

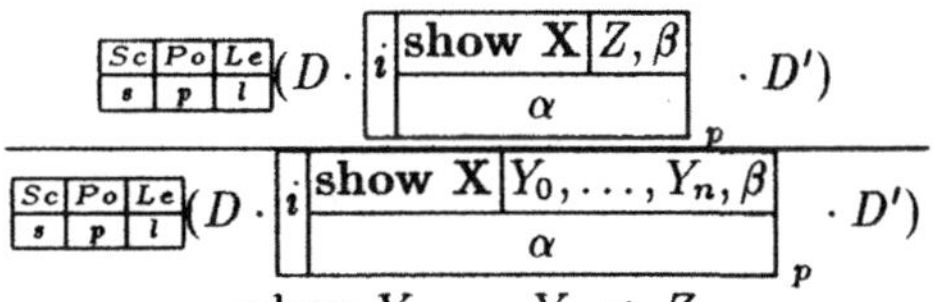

where $Y_0, \ldots, Y_n \Rightarrow Z$

Here $Y_0, \ldots, Y_n \Rightarrow Z$ is some mode of combination: a requirement (Z) is analysed into subrequirements $(Y_1, \ldots, Y_n)$. For instance for function application we have

$$\langle d \rangle Ty(X), \langle d \rangle Ty(X \rightarrow Y) \Rightarrow Ty(Y)$$

So, Introduction gives

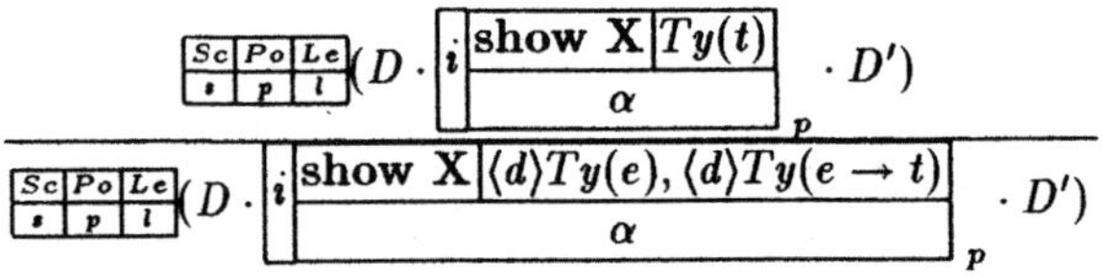

(b) **Elimination**

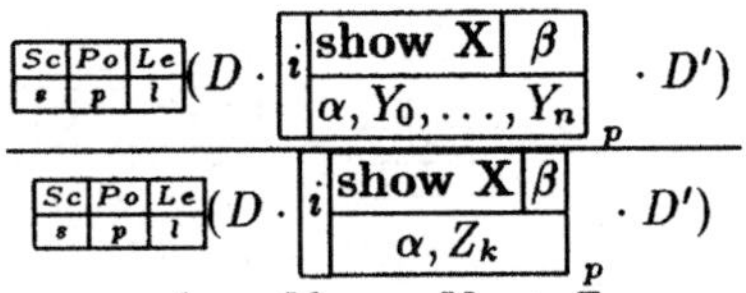

where $Y_0, \ldots, Y_n \Rightarrow Z$

The inverse of Introduction. This inverse relation guarantees that an empty TODO compartment corresponds to a DONE compartment which can derive the goal.

2. **Tree Extending Processes**. The following rules deal with the creation of the linked tree structure. Two rules deal with the building up of structure: the Subgoal rule creates the trees proper, and the Adjunction rule creates *linkages*. When a requirement at node $Tn(i)$ involves an existential modality, e.g. $\langle d \rangle Ty(e)$, "there is a daughter of type e", then the Subgoal rule creates such a daughter — at node $\langle u \rangle Tn(i)$ — with the requirement $Ty(e)$. The Adjunction rule only connects the top node of a new tree (still to be developed) — at node $\langle L \rangle^{-1} Tn(i)$ — to a *satisfied* task state — at node $Tn(i)$: adjuncts are 'superfluous' with respect to demand satisfaction. Having created new structure, the Completion rule tells us how to propagate the information through the tree once the requirements have been fulfilled.

(a) **Subgoal**

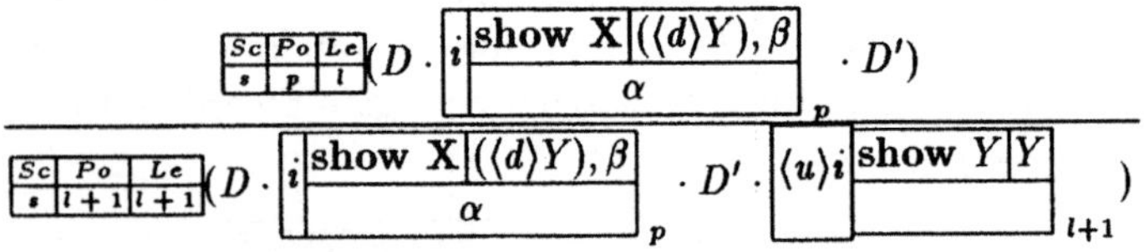

Here a subtask is constructed in order to satisfy some demands in TODO of task i. When there are no demands then structures can be coordinated through *adjunction*.

(b) Y-**Adjunction**

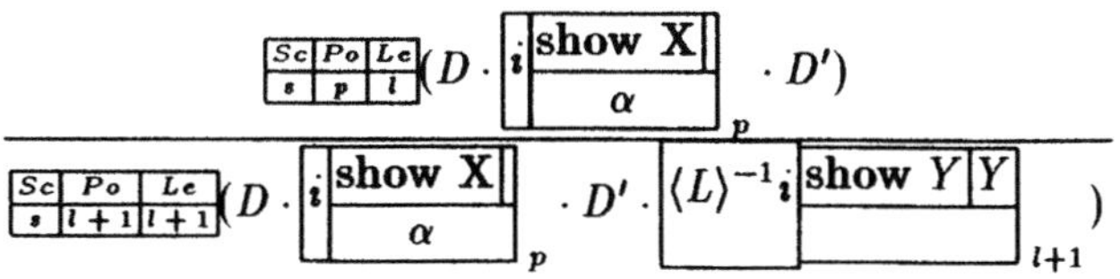

(c) **Completion**

$$
\frac{\boxed{\begin{array}{|c|c|c|}\hline Sc & Po & Le \\\hline s & p & l \\\hline\end{array}}(D \cdot {}_i\boxed{\begin{array}{c}\text{show } X|\beta \\\hline \alpha\end{array}}{}_j \cdot D' \cdot \langle\#\rangle^{-1}{}_i\boxed{\begin{array}{c}\text{show } Y \\\hline U_0\ldots,U_n\end{array}}{}_p \cdot D'')}{\boxed{\begin{array}{|c|c|c|}\hline Sc & Po & Le \\\hline s & j & l \\\hline\end{array}}(D \cdot {}_i\boxed{\begin{array}{cc}\text{show } X & \beta \\\hline \alpha(\langle\#\rangle(U_0\ldots,U_n))\end{array}}{}_j \cdot D' \cdot \langle\#\rangle^{-1}{}_i\boxed{\begin{array}{c}\text{show } Y \\\hline U_1\ldots,U_n\end{array}}{}_p \cdot D'')}
$$

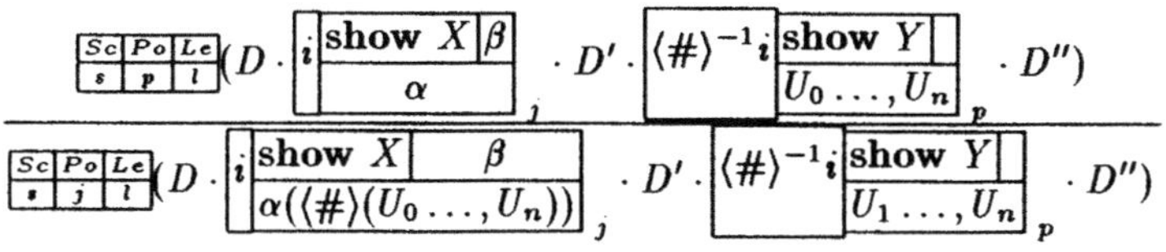

The completion rule combines both structures created by *Subgoal* and those created by *Y-Adjunction*.

This concludes the statement of the *basic transition rules*. Each of these rules rewrites (concludes from) a single premise to a conclusion modulo some side conditions. Notice that rewriting can only take place at task states highlighted by the task pointer. This means that there may be rules required to shift this pointer. These rules won't be described here.

Remark 1 (Lexical Rules) We give a taste of the way lexical rules are formulated in this set-up. In the Lexicon we associate with a word w a set Y of DU-formulas

$$Lex(w) = Y$$

If the TODO feature of the task state at the pointer has value X, which we will abbreviate as $Tod(X)$, and $X \in Y$, then the information Y of w may be used (see the Scanning rule). Every word is entered relative to a context consisting of a *parse state*, that is a sequence of task states and a pointer, Po, a natural number $Po := n$ pointing to the n'th element of the sequence of length $Le := l$ and a string counter $Sc = j$. For instance,

1. If $Tod(Ty(x))$,
     $Lex(w_{j+1}) = Y, Ty(x) \in Y$,
   then **Scan**.

For instance, $x = e$, $Y = \{Ty(e), Fo(\textbf{John})\}$. The task under consideration requires an item of type e, and the word to be processed, *John*, is of that type.

2. If $Tod(Ty(x))$,
     $Lex(w_{j+1}) = Y, Ty(y \to x) \in Y$,
   then a) apply **Introd.**: $Tod(\langle d\rangle Ty(y \to x)), (\langle d\rangle Ty(y))$,
       b) apply **Subgoal**,
       c) apply **Scan**.

For instance, $x = e \to t$, $y = e$, $Y = \{Ty(e \to (e \to t)), Fo(\textbf{Love})\}$. The task under consideration requires a VP $(e \to t)$, but gets a transitive verb $(e \to (e \to t))$; $e \to t$ is split in $e \to (e \to t)$ and e, and scanning then leaves $Tod(\langle d\rangle(Ty(e)))$.

3.2 Wh-Rules

Besides the basic transition rules our system includes special purpose rules, for instance, for dealing with *wh* expressions. For sentence initial *wh* the premise parse state consists of the Axiom; for relative clause *wh*, *t-Adjunction* first creates an Axiom state linked to the head, next *Gap Adjunction* is applied to the fresh axiom.

Gap Adjunction

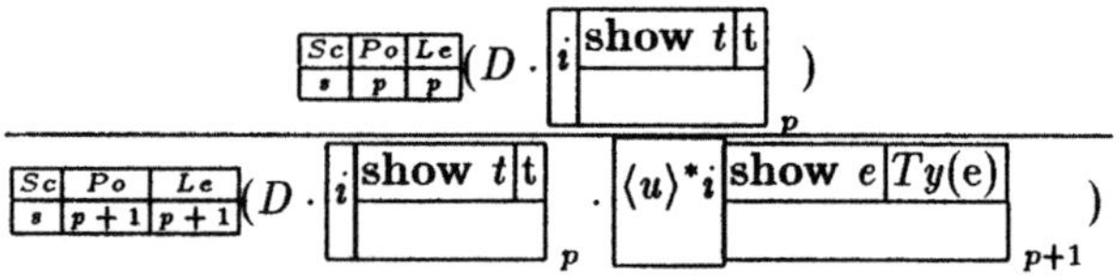

Now there is a node of type e 'dangling' at an unspecified location below the adjoint clause. This is our dynamic representation of long distance dependencies. The kind of *wh* word determines the subsequent actions through the lexicon. For instance, if *wh*= *who*, then the *wh* phrase consists of this single word and $Fo(Wh) \wedge Ty(e)$ is put in DONE. On the other hand, if *wh*= *which*, then we are dealing with a proper *wh*-phrase and Introduction splits $Ty(e)$ in $\langle d\rangle Ty(cn \rightarrow e)$ and $\langle d\rangle Ty(cn)$ and places $Fo(Wh) \wedge Ty(cn \rightarrow e)$ in DONE of the $\langle d\rangle Ty(cn \rightarrow e)$ daughter.
The *wh* constituent with underspecified location becomes fixed at the location of the *gap*. This is the import of the following rule.

Gap Resolution

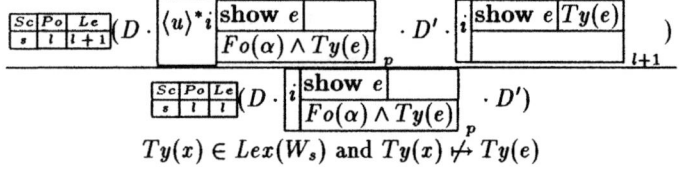

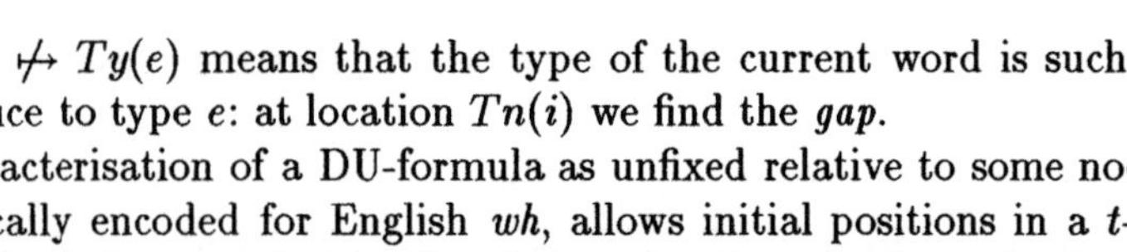

$$Ty(x) \in Lex(W_s) \text{ and } Ty(x) \not\rightarrow Ty(e)$$

Here $Ty(x) \not\rightarrow Ty(e)$ means that the type of the current word is such that it cannot reduce to type e: at location $Tn(i)$ we find the *gap*.
So the characterisation of a DU-formula as unfixed relative to some node i, an option lexically encoded for English *wh*, allows initial positions in a t-task to under-specify their tree relation. *Resolution* of such underdetermined specification takes place locally at some node i whose TODO specification is satisfied not by the specification of the next lexical input but by the presented floating constituent.
The adjunction and Wh-rules may apply to satisfied e- and satisfied cn-tasks. These correspond respectively to *non restrictive* and *restrictive* relative clause strategies. Both applications are driven by lexical specifications.

In case of *unrestricted relative clauses* we have the following sequence of rule applications:

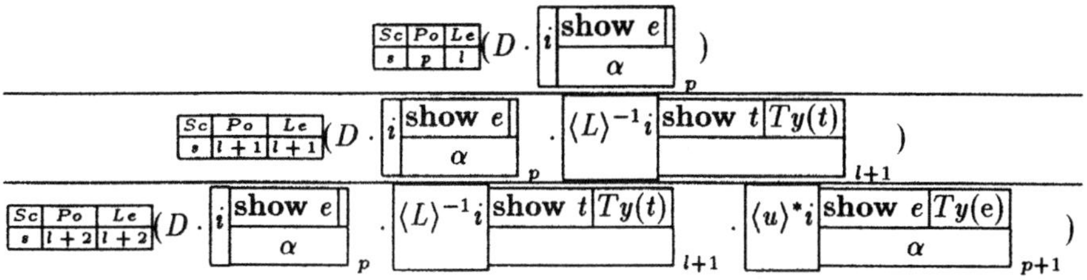

First t-adjunction is applied and then Gap adjunction. Notice that the dangling constituent is 'loaded' with the information of the satisfied e-task that constitutes the head of the relative clause.
For *restricted relative clauses* we proceed as follows:

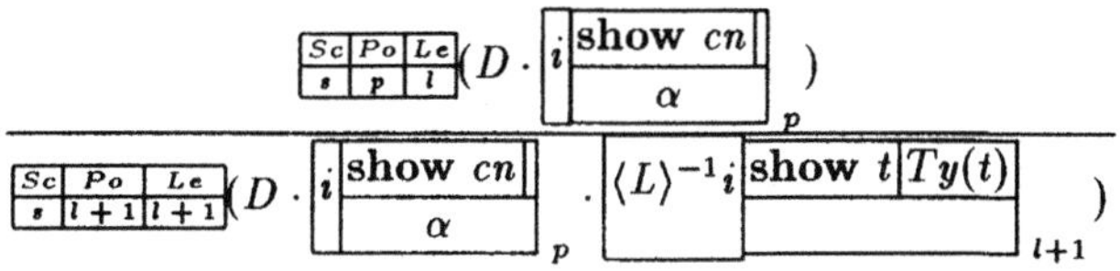

Here, (due to the type clash), no information of the head is loaded into the dangling component. When the gap is resolved and the restricted relative clause finished, then the Completion rule 'merges' the head with the relative clause. This requires a principle like

$$Fo(\lambda y\phi) \wedge Ty(cn), \langle L\rangle(Fo(\beta[Wh/y]) \wedge Ty(t)) \Rightarrow Fo(\lambda y(\phi \wedge \beta))$$

This principle allows the Elimination rule, after Completion, to merge, for instance,

$$Fo(\lambda y Man(y)) \wedge Ty(cn) \text{ and } Fo(Walks(Wh)) \wedge Ty(t)$$

to

$$Fo(\lambda y(Man(y) \wedge walks(y))) \wedge Ty(cn).$$

4 Application of the Model - Crossover: A Dynamic Perspective

Before we can discuss the application of this framework to the treatment of crossover phenomena we need a characterisation of underspecificity and its resolution in context. We define contextual resolution to be the selection of some suitable syntactic choice, given what is independently made available. Anaphora resolution, for example, involves a choice relative to the constraints the particular lexical item imposes. Pronouns are defined as meta variables of the form $u_{\mathbf{pro}}$

$$Lex(he) = \{Ty(e), Fo(u_{pro}), Gender(male), \langle u \rangle Ty(t), ...\}$$

Determiners also may project such meta variables, eg the definite and demonstrative determiners. The instantiation of the meta variable 'u_{pro}' must be a formula in some ***satisfied task*** or a formula which has been derived elsewhere in the discourse sequence. This holds for all anaphoric expressions. The process is presumed to be on-line, and subject to a locality restriction specific to pronominals (following [18]). [6] The novelty of our account of *wh* lies in the characterisation of initial *wh* expressions as projecting an unfixed constituent, and in the sensitivity of anaphora resolution to the progressive accumulation of information. A benefit of looking at *wh* phenomena from this perspective is that phenomena classified as mysteries are predicted - eg the interaction of *wh* construal and anaphora resolution called "crossover". The restriction, provisionally described, is that a pronominal cannot be construed as bound by the *wh* expression if the gap which the *wh* is to bind is to the right of the pronominal:

(1) *Who$_i$ does Joan think that he$_i$ worries e$_i$ is sick?

(2) *Who$_i$ does Joan think that his$_i$ mother worries e$_i$ is sick?

(3) *Whose$_i$ exam results$_j$ was he$_i$ certain e$_j$ would be better than anyone else's?

(4) Who$_i$ does John think e$_i$ worries his$_i$ mother is sick?

(5) Who$_i$ does Joan think e$_i$ worries that he$_i$ is sick?

(6) Whose$_i$ exam results$_j$ e$_j$ were so striking that he$_i$ was suspected of cheating?

This restriction is context-sensitive, being apparently rescinded in some circumstances. Within the GB paradigm, the phenomenon has been argued ([12]) to subdivide into at least three different phenomena. "Strong crossover" is the restriction which prohibits a pronoun from being interpreted as dependent on a c-commanding operator if it both precedes and c-commands the trace bound by that operator, said to be due to the name- like properties of the empty-category (a principle C effect) - (1). "Weak crossover" is a restriction that precludes a pronoun from being bound by some c-commanding operator in the presence of a following trace, when the pronoun does not c-command that trace - (2). This distinction is not made in the categorial grammar account ([2]). There, crossover arises from the interaction between two different types of quantifying in process, in both cases discharging some initial assumption constructed for the purpose of preserving local semantic compositionality. *wh* binding involves a regular quantifying operation, with a constructed assumption locally combining with other

[6] Exceptions to the on-line restriction are invariably language- and construction-particular, and must be specifically encoded.

premises and then being discharged at some arbitrary point in the compilation of content. The output of this rule, being of the form $\lambda x.\psi$, combines with the higher type *wh* expression to yield a propositional formula with the variable associated with the *wh* suitably binding the abstracted position. Anaphora resolution is seen as a specialised variant of quantifying in, a process which discharges an assumption corresponding to the pronominal in the presence of some antecedent, without any alteration in the resulting type assignment ([6]). The precluded order is predicted to be underivable because though the gap assumption could be discharged in the presence of the pronominal, this would leave nothing for the *wh* to apply to, and vacuous application is debarred.

The problem in both accounts is that the phenomenon is predicted in virtue of the configurational relation between the parts, yet weak crossover effects display context-sensitivity. Nonrestrictive relative clause constructions, parasitic gap constructions, and *easy to please* constructions, all fail to display weak crossover effects:

(7) John, who_i his_i mother had regularly ignored e_i fell ill during the exam period.

(8) *John, who_i Sue thinks he_i doesn't believe e_i is sick, fell ill during the exam.

(9) Which_i of the team did the judge put away e_i without his_i mother being able to see?

(10) Sam_i is all too easy for his_i mother to ignore e_i.

The categorial account does not extend to these data; and the Principles and Parameter account requires a number of additional principles ([12]).[7]

Data such as (7), (9),(10) are said to constitute a discrete phenomenon of "weakest crossover" in which the empty category is a pronominal epithet and not a 'true variable'. This division into a third category is however problematic, as demonstrated in detail by [20]; and in any case, as Postal reminds us, there are data which fall within the strong crossover classification such as (3), (6) which nevertheless display exactly the same context-sensitivity as weak crossover phenomena:

[7] The asymmetry of context-sensitivity as between strong crossover and weak crossover environments is particularly puzzling for the Categorial analysis of [2]. On this analysis, principle B is but a pragmatic effect which discourages co-referential readings in a given locally restricted environment (cf. [6] who explicitly excludes any account of principle B effects from the account of anaphoric binding). If the circumstances in which a weak crossover effect fails to hold is to be explained as a pragmatic phenomenon of incidental co-reference, then there is no reason to preclude a similar effect of pragmatic coreference in example 8. In particular, there is no basis for invoking any locality restriction, since the surface sequence of expressions provides no basis for predicting that such a restriction might be applicable.

(11) John, whose$_i$ mother$_j$ I told him$_i$ e$_j$ had refused the operation, was very upset.

(12) John, whose$_i$ exam results$_j$ he$_i$ had been certain e$_j$ would be better than anyone else's, failed dismally.

There is also puzzling variation across languages, which remain intransigent, given this mode of explanation.
Looked at from the dynamics of processing, the data are unproblematic. Formulas characterised as holding at some node $\langle u\rangle^* m$ do not have a fixed position in the configuration, and do not have an identified position from which to project the information contained in that formula. Without any such identification, as in *wh* questions, the information contained therein will not be visible for the purpose of pronominal resolution, unless it is identified independently of its position. The effect of *wh* resolution when it applies is indeed to determine this position within the configuration. Hence the primary crossover restriction **wh* ...pronoun ...gap (for both weak, strong, and extended strong crossover data)[8].

This restriction does not apply invariably in relative clauses, because of the different information made available at the outset of processing the different types of structure. In processing a question, no information is available at all about the *wh* expression:

(13) Who did you see?

In processing a relative clause construed *non restrictively* information is made available from the outset about the nature of the *wh*-expression[9].

(14) John, who you saw, was a linguist.

Because such a *wh* expression is identified as 'John', it can count as an antecedent for the pronominal.
In restrictive relative construals however, where *t*-adjunction links a clause to a *cn*-task, no information is transferred from the initially completed *cn*-task to the linked structure (because of the type clash between the type *cn* and the type of the *wh* variable), and so, as in questions, the DU-formula $Fo(Wh) \wedge Ty(e)$ remains invisible until after the identification of the tree node from which it is to project its content. So dependence of the pronominal on the *wh* is impossible:[10]

[8] The lack of crossover effect in parasitic gaps or *easy to please* constructions is predicted to be unproblematic, since in these cases, the previous expression (the true gap or the subject of *easy*) will provide the antecedent for the pronoun.

[9] Definite and indefinite determiners are the two primary types of determiner which license both restrictive and nonrestrictive construals. In both cases, adjunction is to a completed term of the formula language, either in the case of definites as an instantiated formula analogous to pronominals, or in the case of indefinites as a completed epsilon term (with no dependency needing to be compiled). Cf. [14].

[10] The data here are notoriously unclear (hence the term "weak crossover"), and linguists have differed in their decision as to how to classify these data. Some examples

(15) Every child who$_i$ his$_i$ brother ignored e$_i$ throughout his party was clearly ill at ease.

(16) At least one woman who$_i$ her$_i$ cousin refused to cooperate with e$_i$ reported the matter to the authorities.

The asymmetry between (17) and (18) is not covered by this process of identifying the *wh* relativiser; but it can be explained straightforwardly by the way information projected by the *wh* expression is transferred node by node through the emerging structure to its point of resolution.

(17) *John, who$_i$ Sue knows he$_i$ thinks e$_i$ will fail, did surprisingly well.

(18) John, who$_i$ Sue knows e$_i$ thinks he$_i$ will fail, did surprisingly well.

This successive transfer of information gives rise to the following prediction. With *wh* identified independently by a given antecedent α in nonrestrictive construals of the *wh* element, the formula '$\langle d\rangle^*(Fo(\alpha) \wedge Ty(e))$' carried down will be local everywhere along the chain of nodes intervening between its projection and its resolution. In consequence there will be locality clashes with any pronominal itself projecting Ty(e) onto a task-state along that chain. The restriction on identification of pronominals is that any DU-formula '$Fo(u_{\text{pro}}) \wedge Ty(e)$' within a given task **Show** t or **Show** e, could not be identified with any other DU-formula '$Fo(\alpha) \wedge Ty(e)$' of type e as also being a minor premise to the same task. If, then, the carried down $\langle d\rangle^*$ specification '$\langle d\rangle^*(Fo(\alpha) \wedge Ty(e))$' and the projection from the pronoun agree on the type specification, then the identification of u_{pro} as α is precluded. If, on the other hand, either the pronominal being projected or this specification is within a determiner, then the pronominal and the *wh* element are not local w.r.t. each other. Hence the asymmetry between (8) and (7).

Since the DU-formula '$Fo(\alpha) \wedge Ty(e)$' projected from the *wh* expression is part of the information available at the intervening task states despite not yet having its combinatorial role fixed, this analysis further predicts that anaphora resolution in nonrestrictive relatives with the order *wh* pronoun will parallel non-relative sentences in which a name as antecedent is followed by a pronoun. (19) is predicted to parallel (20) (both *wh* and the definite NP precede the pronominal *his*). (12) parallels (21) (both *John's exam results* and *whose exam results* precede the pronominal). Similarly (22) and (23):

(19) The bastard who$_i$ his$_i$ mother worshipped.

---

seem to display a weak crossover effect, in particular relatives clauses modifying a quantified determiner head as in (15-16), others do not. Judgments are much less clear with definites and generic construals, where there appears to be interference from the implication implicit in such construals that the resulting expression is independently identifiable: (i) The man who$_i$ his$_i$ mother systematically ignored e$_i$ made a good parent. (ii) The children who$_i$ their$_i$ mother systematically helps e$_i$ with their homework do well. In the face of this somewhat unclear data we adopt the view that restrictive relatives display crossover effects as in questions. Cf. Also footnote 11.

(20) The bastard$_i$ worships his$_i$ mother.

(21) John$_i$'s exam results gave him$_i$ a nasty shock.

(22) *Joan behind whom$_i$ she$_i$ looked e$_i$ nervously, coughed.

(23) *Behind Joan$_i$ she$_i$ looked nervously.

This principle-B style of analysis will not apply at all to construals of relative sequences as adjuncts on the *cn*-task, because the consequence of building an adjunct structure on the *cn* task is that no information will be transferred into the building of the adjoined structure, so no potential antecedent is made available, and their construal is predicted to be controlled solely by the lack of availability of an antecedent - hence the lack of context-sensitivity in such cases, parallelling questions (modulo the caveat of footnote 10 as already discussed). [11]

Striking confirmation of this procedural approach comes from Chinese, which provides a test case. Chinese has two relative strategies, one in which the entire relative precedes the Determiner plus nominal, the other in which the Determiner precedes the relative sequence with its nominal head following. The analysis proposed here predicts no possibility of anaphoric dependence between a pronominal within the relative in the first strategy, and allows anaphoric dependence as in English for the second. This prediction is correct. In the first strategy, with no identification that the sequence is a relative clause as in (24)-(25), there are only created TODO tasks associated with the initial expression, so even where it is the verb that is initial, there is no completed task to provide an antecedent for the pronominal:

(24) *Ta$_i$ muqin hushi e$_i$ de mei ge ren$_i$ dou mei kao jige.
he mother ignore rel every CL man all not test pass
Everyone who$_i$ his$_i$ mother ignored e$_i$ failed the test.

(25) *e$_i$ Hushi ta$_i$ muqin de mei ge ren$_i$ dou mei kao jige.
ignore he mother rel every CL man all not test pass
Everyone who$_i$ ignored his$_i$ mother failed the test.

[11] The account in the text presumes that the identification of pronominal occurring within a relative sequence will either make use of the information made available by the *wh* element, if any, or, if not, by some information which is identified independently from outside that structure. There is a third possibility. Given that the building of the adjoined structure for a relative sequence construed restrictively is an adjunction to a *cn*-task itself part of an unsatisfied *e*-task containing the projection of a determiner plus nominal, then the question arises whether the formula projected by that unsatisfied *e*-task can be used as the basis for assigning a value to a pronominal occurring within the relative sequence. The answer is that, in some languages, the answer seems to be yes. While English speakers are hesitant about many crossover judgments with restrictive relatives, particularly if the head is a definite determiner, French speakers display no hesitation over all weak crossover sequences, finding all to be fully acceptable. Some languages (and other dialects of English) accordingly seem to be less sensitive to the requirement that the term used for anaphora resolution be fully identified.

In the second strategy, if the pronominal intervenes between the determiner and gap it will not allow dependence of the pronominal on the relativiser or the head, as in English.

(26) *Mei ge ta_i muqin hushi de ren_i dou mei kao jige.
every CL he mother ignore DE man all not test pass
Everyone who_i his_i failed the test.

But if the gap in the relative sequence precedes the pronominal then the coincidence of the disjunctive specification induced by the triggering of the need to build a relative clause and the TODO tasks created by the verb, ensure that the disjunction is resolved and the position can duly act as antecedent for a pronominal:

(27) Mei ge e_i hushi ta_i muqin de ren_i dou mei kao jige.
every CL ignore he mother DE man all not test pass
Everyone who_i ignored his_i mother failed the test.

These data follow as an immediate consequence of the analysis proposed here. On the contrary, however, the crucial data (25), (27) are not characterisable as a crossover phenomenon on either GB or categorial analyses, and no unifying analysis seems possible.

5 Conclusion

A distinguishing feature of this account of crossover has been the underspecification of constituent structure. The concept of structural underspecification is close to the concept of functional uncertainty of Kaplan and Zaenen articulated within the LFG framework ([9]), but in that analysis the uncertainty is defined in terms of thematic roles which are structural primitives. The consequent transfer of content for the initial expression through the tree configuration is like the slash mechanism of HPSG ([18]), though in HPSG such transfer is defined as a mechanism of upward feature percolation. Like categorial grammar analyses, the basic mode of combination is type-deduction, and *wh* expressions are defined to ensure the combination of the content projected by the *wh* expression with expressions with which it is not contiguous (cf eg [16], [17]). However unlike categorial grammar accounts, this is not defined through some suitable type assignment, and no semantic mode of combination is defined between the *wh* expression and its sister expressions in the string. Seen in the most general terms, the account we have proposed presents the claim that the concept of context-dependence and its resolution is structurally defined, and that resolution of any underspecification of either denotation or structure is determined on a left-right basis that broadly follows the order in which the interpretation is presented. A surprising prediction follows immediately from this claim, distinguishing it from other frameworks: a sharp asymmetry is predicted between left-dislocation of *wh* expressions which occurs freely in language, and right-dislocated *wh* expressions which are predicted not to occur. Under this account, postposing of *wh* elements out of their structurally licensed position to the right periphery of a sentence is precluded. The lexical projection of a DU-formula with an underspecified tree node, with no further input to provide a means of resolution, would lead to inconsistency and predicted illformedness. Predicted is the non-occurrence of any question such as (28), with the *wh*-expression right-dislocated, in contrast to the wellformedness of its left-dislocated counterpart (29):

(28) *You think e_i saw Bill at the market who_i?
(29) Who_i do you think e_i saw Bill at the party ?

So far as we know, this prediction is not only correct across all languages, but cannot be made to follow directly from any other framework.

References

1. Blackburn, P. & Meyer-Viol, W.: 1994, ' Linguistics, logic and finite Trees', *Bulletin of the IPGL* 2:2-39.
2. Dowty, D.: 1992, "Variable-free' syntax, variable-binding syntax, the natural deduction Lambek calculus and the crossover constraint', *Proceedings of the 1992 West Coast Conference on Formal Linguistics*.
3. Gabbay, D.: 1996, *Labelled Deductive Systems*, Oxford University Press.
4. Gabbay, D. & Kempson, R.: 1992, 'Natural-language content: a proof-theoretic perspective', *Proceedings of 8th Amsterdam Semantics Colloquium*. Amsterdam.
5. Gurevich, Y.: 1991, 'Evolving algebras: A tutorial introduction', *Bulletin of the European Association for Theoretical Computer Science*, 43,264-286.
6. Hepple, M.: 1990, *The Grammar of Processing of Order and Dependency: A Categorial Grammar*, PhD Dissertation, University of Edinburgh.
7. Johnson, D., Moss, L.: 1995, 'Dynamic Intrepretations of Constraint-Based Grammar Formalisms', *Journal of Logic, Language, and Information*, 4:61-79.
8. Johnson, D., Moss, L.: 1995, 'Grammar formalisms viewed as evolving algebras', *Linguistics and Philosophy*.
9. Kaplan, R. and Zaenen, A.: 1989, 'Long-distance dependencies, constituent structure, and functional uncertainty', in Baltin, M. and Kroch, A. (eds.) *Alternative Conceptions of Phrase Structure*, pp. 17- 42. University of Chicago Press, Chicago.
10. Kempson, R., Meyer-Viol, W., Gabbay, D., (forthcoming), 'Syntactic computation as labelled deduction: *wh* a case study', Borsley, B. & Roberts, E. (eds.)*Syntactic Categories*. Academic Press.
11. Kracht, M.: 1995, 'Syntactic codes and Grammar Refinement', *Journal of Logic, Language, and Information* 4:41-60.
12. Lasnik, H. & Stowell, T.: 1991, 'Weakest crossover' *Linguistic Inquiry* 22, 687-720.
13. Meyer-Viol, W.: 1995, *Instantial Logic*, PhD Dissertation, University of Utrecht.
14. Meyer-Viol, W., Kibble, R., Kempson, R., Gabbay, D.: 1996, 'Indefinites as Epsilon Terms: A Labelled deduction Account', *Proceeding of the Second International Workshop on Computational Semantics*, Tilburg.
15. Milward, D.: 1994, 'Dynamic Dependency Grammar', *Linguistic and Philosophy*, 17:561-605.
16. Moortgat, M.: 1988, *Categorial Investigations*, Fores, Dordrecht.
17. Morrill, G.: 1994, *Type-Logical Grammar*, Kluwer, Dordrecht.

18. Pollard, C. & Sag, I.: 1994, *Head-Driven Phrase Structure Grammar*, University of Chicago Press, Chicago.
19. Postal. P.: 1972, *Cross-over Phenomena*, Holt, Rinehart & Winston.
20. Postal, P.: 1993, 'Remarks on weak crossover effects', *Linguistic Inquiry* 24, 539-56.

The Automatic Deduction of Classificatory Systems from Linguistic Theories (Abridged)*

Paul John King[1] and Kiril Ivanov Simov[2]

[1] Breuningstr. 19, 72072 Tübingen, Germany, king@sfs.nphil.uni-tuebingen.de
[2] Laboratory for Linguistic Modelling, Bulgarian Academy of Sciences, Acad. G. Bonchev Str. 25A, Sofia 1113, Bulgaria, kivs@bgcict.acad.bg

Abstract. Classifying linguistic objects is a widespread and important linguistic task, and computational linguistics often requires the deduction of a classificatory system from a general linguistic theory. Since hand deducing a classificatory system may consume much effort and introduce errors, a device that effectively deduces accurate classificatory systems from general linguistic theories would benefit computational linguistics. We present a prototypical abstract device that automatically deduces classificatory systems from finite linguistic theories.

1 Introduction

Classifying linguistic objects is a widespread and important linguistic task. For example, the benefits of a classification of words according to their inflectional paradigms are apparent for an inflectionally simple language, such as English, and even more so for an inflectionally complex language, such as Bulgarian, in which inflection is a ubiquitous and indispensable part of syntactic processing. For example, the MORPHO-ASSISTANT system of [11] and [12] constructs a dictionary acquisition module by means of a classificatory system for Bulgarian inflectional morphology built by Paskaleva, Avgustinova, Damova and Simov.

A *classificatory system* comprises (i) a *classification*, a set of *labels* that indicate sets of objects, and (ii) an *index*, an algorithm that computes from limited information about an object the label of the class to which the object belongs. Some linguistic theories give classificatory systems implicitly, others explicitly. Linguists usually prefer implicit classificatory systems, since they enable the expression of linguistic intuitions as general theories, but computer scientists usually prefer explicit classificatory systems, since they enable such tasks as fast look-up of tabulated data, automated knowledge acquisition, controlled linguistic inference, etc. Thus, computational linguistics often requires the deduction of a classificatory system from a general linguistic theory. Hand deducing a classificatory system may consume much effort and risks unwittingly violating the theory from which it is deduced, with disastrous consequences if, say, the classification

* This paper is an abridged version of [7]. The authors wish to thank the Seminar für Sprachwissenschaft, Tübingen, for hosting the writing of this paper, and the Internationales Zentrum, Tübingen, for funding Simov's visit to the Seminar. This paper is due in equal parts to both authors.

subsumes two classes under one label, or the index assigns some object a wrong label. Thus, a device that effectively deduces an accurate classificatory system from a general linguistic theory would greatly benefit computational linguistics. We present here an abstract prototype of such a device.

Our experiences show that such a device should ideally compute a classificatory system possessing at least the following five qualities:

(Q1) Each pair of distinct labels in the classification should indicate inherently disjoint sets of objects, to ensure that each object receives a unique label.

(Q2) No label in the classification should indicate an inherently empty set of objects, to prune out intrinsically useless labels.

(Q3) The labels of the classification should indicate sets of objects that are neither too narrow nor too broad, to ensure that the classification truly captures the intuitions of the theory from which it is deduced.

(Q4) The index should correctly assign each object the label of the class to which the object belongs, for obvious reasons.

(Q5) The index should efficiently assign each object the label of the class to which it belongs, to facilitate rapid classification of objects.

Qualities (Q3) and (Q5) require control mechanisms to compute an optimal classificatory system from a given input linguistic theory. Here, we address only qualities (Q1), (Q2) and (Q4) in order to establish that automatically generating a classificatory system from a general linguistic theory is at all possible.

We present a classification as a special disjunctive normal form, called an *exclusive matrix*, in the SRL (Speciate Re-entrant Logic) of [5]. The elements of the exclusive matrix, called *clauses*, are the labels of the classification. Our device has two parts. The first effectively deduces a semantically equivalent exclusive matrix from an arbitrary finite SRL theory. The second deduces from the exclusive matrix an *index tree*, a finite structure of queries and responses that, together with a fixed traversal algorithm, constitutes an index.

The paper is structured as follows: Section 2 illustrates a classificatory system by giving a common example, and motivates the need for a device to automatically generate classificatory systems from general theories by describing a linguistically important classificatory system that cannot be easily hand deduced. Section 3 reviews the relevant aspects of SRL. Sections 4 and 5 give respectively the first and second parts of our device. Section 6 concludes the paper.

2 Illustration and Motivation

Classifying words according to their inflectional paradigms is a simple classificatory system. For example, each German noun has eight declensions, a singular and a plural declension for each of the cases nominative, accusative, genitive and dative. The declension of each German noun can be classified according to how its nominative singular declension is modified by affixation and umlauting, and almost all German nouns exhibit one of the following patterns:

	Singular				Plural			
	Nom.	Acc.	Gen.	Dat.	Nom.	Acc.	Gen.	Dat.
(D1)	—	—	—s	—	—	—	—	—n
(D2)	—	—	—(s)	—	¨—	¨—	¨—	¨—n
(D3)	—	—	—(s)	—	—e	—e	—e	—en
(D4)	—	—	—(s)	—	¨—e	¨—e	¨—e	¨—en
(D5)	—	—	—s	—	—er	—er	—er	—ern
(D6)	—	—	—s	—	¨—er	¨—er	¨—er	¨—ern
(D7)	—	—	—(s)	—	—s	—s	—s	—s
(D8)	—	—	—(s)	—	—n	—n	—n	—n
(D9)	—	—n	—n(s)	—n	—n	—n	—n	—n

Thus, (D1)–(D9) is a classification in which each pattern is a label that indicates the class of German nouns whose declensions exhibit the pattern.[3] There is also an index, since the nominative singular and genitive singular declensions of a noun determine all of its singular declensions, and the nominative plural declension further determines all of its plural declensions.[4] However, not all German nouns exhibit a regular declension pattern. For example, the German noun 'Herz' (heart) exhibits the following pattern:

Singular				Plural			
Nom.	Acc.	Gen.	Dat.	Nom.	Acc.	Gen.	Dat.
Herz	Herz	Herzens	Herzen	Herzen	Herzen	Herzen	Herzen

No pattern in (D1)–(D9) indicates a class containing 'Herz'. Worse, the index wrongly assigns 'Herz' pattern (D9), giving the accusative singular declension of 'Herz' as 'Herzen'. Clearly, we can modify our classification to provide a label that indicates a class containing 'Herz' by adding the following pattern:

(D10)	—	—	—ns	—n	—n	—n	—n	—n

We can then modify our index in order to assign 'Herz' the appropriate pattern: To classify a noun, if the genitive singular declension appends nothing or 's' to the nominative singular form then the declension pattern is among (D1)–(D8), and the nominative plural declension determines all declensions of the noun. If the genitive singular declension appends 'n' to the nominative singular declension, then the declension pattern of the noun must be (D9). If the genitive singular declension appends 'ns' to the nominative singular declension then the declension pattern is (D9) or (D10), and the accusative singular declension determines all declensions of the noun.

[3] Note however that some German nouns have additional letters (typically 'e' and 's') inserted into some of their declensions, with the inserted letters regularly determined by additional factors such as dialect, style and rhythm.

[4] Indeed, all German dictionaries exploit this index, in that each entry for a noun gives only its nominative singular, genitive singular and nominative plural declensions.

In order to better motivate the need for a device to automatically deduce classificatory systems from general linguistic theories, we now give an example of a linguistically important classificatory system that does not presently exist, and whose hand deduction would involve an inordinate amount of work. In a highly lexicalized grammar, the lexical entries in a theory of a natural language constrain word behavior. Such constraints apply both internally to limit the structure of individual words, and externally to limit the possible sister constituents that can occupy specific positions within larger linguistic structures. Subcategorization is an example of the external application of such constraints. For example, in the HPSG (Head-driven Phrase Structure Grammar) of [8] and [9], the principle type of linguistic structure is the *sign*, where signs include both words and phrases. Each sign bears, among other things, a complex of syntactic and semantic objects called a *synsem object*. In turn, each synsem object bears, among other things, a finite list of synsem objects called a *subcat list*. The subcat list serves to restrict which signs a given sign can take as sister constituents within a larger sign.

> "The SUBCAT value of a sign is in essence the sign's valence, that is, a specification of what other signs the sign in question must combine with in order to become *saturated*. More precisely, the SUBCAT value is a list of *synsem* objects, corresponding to the SYNSEM values of the other signs selected as complements by the sign in question." [9, p. 23]

Suppose that a new lexical entry, constraining a new word, is added to a HPSG theory. Two converse problems may arise. The new constraints on the subcat list of the new word and the existing constraints on the synsem objects of the existing words may allow some existing words to wrongly occupy certain positions on the subcat list of the new word. Conversely, the new constraints on the synsem object of the new word and the existing constraints on the subcat lists of the existing words may allow the new word to wrongly occupy certain positions on the subcat lists of some existing words. To prevent both problems, the writer of a lexicon for a HPSG theory must bear in mind the synsem objects and subcat lists that the theory currently licenses, and how they may interact with the synsem objects and subcat lists that each new lexical entry licenses. This is a daunting, perhaps overwhelming, task as the lexicon grows to license tens or hundreds of thousands of words. In practice, the lexicon writer informally deduces from the current theory tacit classifications of synsem objects and subcat lists, and ensures that each new lexical entry licenses words whose synsem objects and subcat lists fall into classes indicated by appropriate labels in the classifications. However, the informality of the classifications can lead the lexicon writer to overlook subtle or unexpected interactions between synsem objects and subcat lists, and the tacitness of the classifications can allow a lexicon writer working as part of a team to add a lexical entry that accords with their idiosyncratic classifications but conflicts with those of their colleagues. Thus, it is good practice for lexicon writers to work with explicit and formally proven classifications, particularly if the lexicon is intended to be large or produced by a team of writers. The utility of a device to automatically deduce classificatory systems from general linguistic theories is obvious in such circumstances.

3 Speciate Re-entrant Logic

The SRL of [5] is a sound, complete (see [5]) and decidable (see [4]) logic designed specifically to support formalisms for both the information-based HPSG of [8] and the object-based HPSG of [9]. Here we review only those aspects of SRL that are germane to the present paper, and discuss neither the logic of SRL nor the use of SRL to express a HPSG theory (see instead [5], [4] and [6]).

Underlying a typical interpretable logic is the intuition that an assertion is a finite and syntactically well-formed string of symbols that is either true or false when interpreted. Underlying SRL is the intuition that a description is a finite and syntactically well-formed string of symbols that is either true or false *of an object* when interpreted. For example, the English description 'it is black' is true of a soot particle but false of a snow flake when interpreted. To capture these intuitions, SRL provides a class of formal languages, each comprising a signature and a class of interpretations. Each signature provides the nonlogical symbols from which descriptions are syntactically constructed. Each interpretation provides a universe of objects, and assigns each nonlogical symbol a meaning from which is generated a denotation function that assigns each description the collection of objects in the universe of which the description is true. In the present paper, we work in a subclass of SRL comprising those formal languages with what we call a *computable* signature, since this ensures the termination of the algorithms we subsequently present.

Definition 1. Triple $\langle \text{Spec}, \text{Feat}, \text{Appr} \rangle$ is a *computable signature* iff

Spec is a finite set,

Feat is a countable set, and

Appr is a total recursive function from Spec $\times$ Feat to *Pow*(Spec).

Suppose that Sign $= \langle \text{Spec}, \text{Feat}, \text{Appr} \rangle$ is a computable signature. We call each member of Spec a *species* in Sign, each member of Feat a *feature* in Sign, and Appr the *appropriateness function* in Sign. For notational facility, we henceforth work with respect to an implicit computable signature Sign $= \langle \text{Spec}, \text{Feat}, \text{Appr} \rangle$, and assume that none of the symbols $:$, $\sim$, $\approx$, $\not\approx$, $\neg$, $\wedge$, $\vee$, $\rightarrow$, [and] is a species or a feature.

Definition 2. Triple $\mathcal{I} = \langle \mathcal{U}, \mathcal{S}, \mathcal{F} \rangle$ is an *interpretation* iff

$\mathcal{U}$ is a set,

$\mathcal{S}$ is a total function from $\mathcal{U}$ to $\mathcal{S}$,

$\mathcal{F}$ is a total function from Feat to the set of partial functions from $\mathcal{U}$ to $\mathcal{U}$, and

for each $\varphi \in$ Feat, for each $v \in \mathcal{U}$,

$\mathcal{F}(\varphi)(v)$ is defined iff $\text{Appr}\langle \mathcal{S}(v), \varphi \rangle \neq \emptyset$, and

if $\mathcal{F}(\varphi)(v)$ is defined then $\mathcal{S}(\mathcal{F}(\varphi)(v)) \in \text{Appr}\langle \mathcal{S}(v), \varphi \rangle$.

Suppose that $\mathcal{I} = \langle \mathcal{U}, \mathcal{S}, \mathcal{F} \rangle$ is an interpretation. We call $\mathcal{U}$ the *universe* in $\mathcal{I}$, each member of $\mathcal{U}$ an *object* in $\mathcal{I}$, $\mathcal{S}$ the *species denotation function* in $\mathcal{I}$, and

$\mathcal{F}$ the *feature denotation function* in $\mathcal{I}$. Each species denotes one member of a set of disjoint sets that cover $\mathcal{U}$, and $\mathcal{S}$ assigns each object in $\mathcal{I}$ the species that denotes the unique set to which the object belongs: for each $\sigma \in \text{Spec}$, σ denotes $\{v \in \mathcal{U} \mid \mathcal{S}(v) = \sigma\}$. Each feature denotes a partial function from $\mathcal{U}$ to $\mathcal{U}$, and $\mathcal{F}$ assigns each feature the partial function it denotes: for each $\varphi \in \text{Feat}$, φ denotes $\mathcal{F}(\varphi)$. The appropriateness function encodes – and the last line in the definition of an interpretation enforces – a relationship between the denotations of species and features: for each $\sigma \in \text{Spec}$, for each $\varphi \in \text{Feat}$, if $\text{Appr}\langle\sigma, \varphi\rangle = \emptyset$ then the denotation of φ acts upon no object in the denotation of σ, and if $\text{Appr}\langle\sigma, \varphi\rangle \neq \emptyset$ then the denotation of φ acts upon each object in the denotation of σ to yield an object in the denotation of some species in $\text{Appr}\langle\sigma, \varphi\rangle$.

Definition 3. Term and Desc are the smallest sets such that

$: \in \text{Term}$,
for each $\tau \in \text{Term}$, for each $\varphi \in \text{Feat}$, $\tau\varphi \in \text{Term}$,
for each $\tau \in \text{Term}$, for each $\sigma \in \text{Spec}$, $\tau \sim \sigma \in \text{Desc}$,
for each $\tau_1 \in \text{Term}$, for each $\tau_2 \in \text{Term}$, $\tau_1 \approx \tau_2 \in \text{Desc}$,
for each $\tau_1 \in \text{Term}$, for each $\tau_2 \in \text{Term}$, $\tau_1 \not\approx \tau_2 \in \text{Desc}$,
for each $\delta \in \text{Desc}$, $\neg\delta \in \text{Desc}$,
for each $\delta_1 \in \text{Desc}$, for each $\delta_2 \in \text{Desc}$, $[\delta_1 \wedge \delta_2] \in \text{Desc}$,
for each $\delta_1 \in \text{Desc}$, for each $\delta_2 \in \text{Desc}$, $[\delta_1 \vee \delta_2] \in \text{Desc}$, and
for each $\delta_1 \in \text{Desc}$, for each $\delta_2 \in \text{Desc}$, $[\delta_1 \rightarrow \delta_2] \in \text{Desc}$.

We call each member of Term a *term*, each member of Desc a *description*, and each subset of Desc a *theory*.

Definition 4. For each interpretation $\mathcal{I} = \langle \mathcal{U}, \mathcal{S}, \mathcal{F} \rangle$,

$\mathcal{T}_\mathcal{I}$ is the total function from Term to the set of partial functions from $\mathcal{U}$ to $\mathcal{U}$ such that

for each $v \in \mathcal{U}$,
$\mathcal{T}_\mathcal{I}(:)(v)$ is defined and $\mathcal{T}_\mathcal{I}(:)(v) = v$,
for each $\tau \in \text{Term}$, for each $\varphi \in \text{Feat}$, for each $v \in \mathcal{U}$,
$\mathcal{T}_\mathcal{I}(\tau\varphi)(v)$ is defined iff $\mathcal{T}_\mathcal{I}(\tau)(v)$ and $\mathcal{F}(\varphi)(\mathcal{T}_\mathcal{I}(\tau)(v))$ are defined, and
if $\mathcal{T}_\mathcal{I}(\tau\varphi)(v)$ is defined then $\mathcal{T}_\mathcal{I}(\tau\varphi)(v) = \mathcal{F}(\varphi)(\mathcal{T}_\mathcal{I}(\tau)(v))$,

$\mathcal{D}_\mathcal{I}$ is the total function from Desc to $Pow(\mathcal{U})$ such that

for each $\tau \in \text{Term}$, for each $\sigma \in \text{Spec}$,
$$\mathcal{D}_\mathcal{I}(\tau \sim \sigma) = \{ v \in \mathcal{U} \mid \mathcal{T}_\mathcal{I}(\tau)(v) \text{ is defined and } \mathcal{S}(\mathcal{T}_\mathcal{I}(\tau)(v)) = \sigma \},$$
for each $\tau_1 \in \text{Term}$, for each $\tau_2 \in \text{Term}$,
$$\mathcal{D}_\mathcal{I}(\tau_1 \approx \tau_2) = \left\{ v \in \mathcal{U} \,\middle|\, \begin{array}{l} \mathcal{T}_\mathcal{I}(\tau_1)(v) \text{ and } \mathcal{T}_\mathcal{I}(\tau_2)(v) \text{ are defined,} \\ \text{and } \mathcal{T}_\mathcal{I}(\tau_1)(v) = \mathcal{T}_\mathcal{I}(\tau_2)(v) \end{array} \right\},$$
for each $\tau_1 \in \text{Term}$, for each $\tau_2 \in \text{Term}$,
$$\mathcal{D}_\mathcal{I}(\tau_1 \not\approx \tau_2) = \left\{ v \in \mathcal{U} \,\middle|\, \begin{array}{l} \mathcal{T}_\mathcal{I}(\tau_1)(v) \text{ and } \mathcal{T}_\mathcal{I}(\tau_2)(v) \text{ are defined,} \\ \text{and } \mathcal{T}_\mathcal{I}(\tau_1)(v) \neq \mathcal{T}_\mathcal{I}(\tau_2)(v) \end{array} \right\},$$

for each $\delta \in \text{Desc}$, $\mathcal{D}_\mathcal{I}(\neg\delta) = (\mathcal{U} \setminus \mathcal{D}_\mathcal{I}(\delta))$,
for each $\delta_1 \in \text{Desc}$, for each $\delta_2 \in \text{Desc}$,
$\mathcal{D}_\mathcal{I}([\delta_1 \wedge \delta_2]) = \mathcal{D}_\mathcal{I}(\delta_1) \cap \mathcal{D}_\mathcal{I}(\delta_2)$,
for each $\delta_1 \in \text{Desc}$, for each $\delta_2 \in \text{Desc}$,
$\mathcal{D}_\mathcal{I}([\delta_1 \vee \delta_2]) = \mathcal{D}_\mathcal{I}(\delta_1) \cup \mathcal{D}_\mathcal{I}(\delta_2)$, and
for each $\delta_1 \in \text{Desc}$, for each $\delta_2 \in \text{Desc}$,
$\mathcal{D}_\mathcal{I}([\delta_1 \rightarrow \delta_2]) = (\mathcal{U} \setminus \mathcal{D}_\mathcal{I}(\delta_1)) \cup \mathcal{D}_\mathcal{I}(\delta_2)$, and

$\Theta_\mathcal{I}$ is the total function from $Pow(\text{Desc})$ to $Pow(\mathcal{U})$ such that
for each $\theta \subseteq \text{Desc}$, $\Theta_\mathcal{I}(\theta) = \{v \in \mathcal{U} \mid \text{for each } \delta \in \theta,\ v \in \mathcal{D}_\mathcal{I}(\delta)\}$.

Suppose that $\mathcal{I}$ is an interpretation. We call $\mathcal{T}_\mathcal{I}$ the *term denotation function* in $\mathcal{I}$, $\mathcal{D}_\mathcal{I}$ the *description denotation function* in $\mathcal{I}$, and $\Theta_\mathcal{I}$ the *theory denotation function* in $\mathcal{I}$. A term is the symbol : followed by a finite string of features, and denotes the functional composition of the denotations of its constituent features. Description $\tau \sim \sigma$ is true of object v iff term τ denotes a function defined on v to yield an object in the denotation of species σ. Description $\tau_1 \approx \tau_2$ is true of object v iff terms τ_1 and τ_2 denote functions defined on v to yield one and the same object. Description $\tau_1 \not\approx \tau_2$ is true of object v iff terms τ_1 and τ_2 denote functions defined on v to yield two different objects. Description $\neg\delta$ is true of object v iff δ is false of v. Description $[\delta_1 \wedge \delta_2]$ is true of object v iff δ_1 is true of v and δ_2 is true of v. Description $[\delta_1 \vee \delta_2]$ is true of object v iff δ_1 is true of v or δ_2 is true of v (or both). Description $[\delta_1 \rightarrow \delta_2]$ is true of object v iff δ_2 is true of v whenever δ_1 is true of v. Each description denotes the set of objects of which it is true. Theory θ is true of object v iff each description in θ is true of v. Each theory denotes the set of objects of which it is true. Notice that for each $\tau_1 \in \text{Term}$, for each $\tau_2 \in \text{Term}$, description $\tau_1 \not\approx \tau_2$ is not strictly part of the SRL syntax of [5], but is semantically equivalent to $[[\tau_1 \approx \tau_1 \wedge \tau_2 \approx \tau_2] \wedge \neg\tau_1 \approx \tau_2]$, and is thus a harmless meta-syntactic addition that enables us to eliminate negation ($\neg$) and implication ($\rightarrow$) in the exclusive matrices of the next section, while ensuring that every finite theory has a semantically equivalent exclusive matrix.

Definition 5. For each $\theta \subseteq \text{Desc}$,
θ is *satisfiable* iff for some interpretation $\mathcal{I}$, $\Theta_\mathcal{I}(\theta) \neq \emptyset$.

Thus, a theory is satisfiable iff it is true of some object in some interpretation.

In order to prepare the ground for the exclusive matrices of the next section, we now move beyond the SRL syntax and semantics of [5] and introduce some further definitions of our own.

Definition 6.

$\text{Atom}^\text{K} = \{\tau \sim \sigma \mid \tau \in \text{Term and } \sigma \in \text{Spec}\}$
$\qquad \cup \{\tau_1 \approx \tau_2 \mid \tau_1 \in \text{Term and } \tau_2 \in \text{Term}\}$, and
$\text{Atom}^\text{C} = \text{Atom}^\text{K} \cup \{\tau_1 \not\approx \tau_2 \mid \tau_1 \in \text{Term and } \tau_2 \in \text{Term}\}$.

We call each member of $\mathrm{Atom}^{\mathrm{K}}$ a *King atomic description*, and each member of $\mathrm{Atom}^{\mathrm{C}}$ a *Carpenter atomic description*, after the atomic descriptions in the logics of [5] and [1] respectively. Clearly, $\mathrm{Atom}^{\mathrm{K}} \subseteq \mathrm{Atom}^{\mathrm{C}}$.

Definition 7.
$\mathrm{Lite}^{\mathrm{K}} = \mathrm{Atom}^{\mathrm{K}} \cup \{\neg\delta \mid \delta \in \mathrm{Atom}^{\mathrm{K}}\}$, and
$\mathrm{Lite}^{\mathrm{C}} = \mathrm{Atom}^{\mathrm{C}} \cup \{\neg\delta \mid \delta \in \mathrm{Atom}^{\mathrm{C}}\}$.

We call each member of $\mathrm{Lite}^{\mathrm{K}}$ a *King literal*, and each member of $\mathrm{Lite}^{\mathrm{C}}$ a *Carpenter literal*, where a literal is either an atomic description or the negation of an atomic description. Clearly, $\mathrm{Lite}^{\mathrm{K}} \subseteq \mathrm{Lite}^{\mathrm{C}}$.

Definition 8. $\mathrm{Clau} = \mathit{FinPow}(\mathrm{Lite}^{\mathrm{C}})$ and $\mathrm{Matr} = \mathit{FinPow}(\mathrm{Clau})$.[5]

We call each member of Clau a *clause*, and each member of Matr a *matrix*.

Definition 9. For each interpretation $\mathcal{I} = \langle \mathcal{U}, \mathcal{S}, \mathcal{F} \rangle$, $\mathcal{M}_{\mathcal{I}}$ is the total function from Matr to $\mathit{Pow}(\mathcal{U})$ such that
for each $\mu \in \mathrm{Matr}$, $\mathcal{M}_{\mathcal{I}}(\mu) = \{v \in \mathcal{U} \mid \text{for some } \theta \in \mu,\ v \in \Theta_{\mathcal{I}}(\theta)\}$.

Suppose that $\mathcal{I}$ is an interpretation. We call $\mathcal{M}_{\mathcal{I}}$ the *matrix denotation function* in $\mathcal{I}$. Matrix μ is true of object v iff each literal in some clause in μ is true of v. Each matrix denotes the set of objects of which it is true. Clearly, each matrix represents a disjunctive normal form description: for each $\{\{\delta_{i,j} \mid 1 \leq j \leq n_m\} \mid 1 \leq i \leq m\} \in \mathrm{Matr}$, for each interpretation $\mathcal{I}$,
$\mathcal{M}_{\mathcal{I}}(\{\{\delta_{i,j} \mid 1 \leq j \leq n_m\} \mid 1 \leq i \leq m\}) = \mathcal{D}_{\mathcal{I}}(\bigvee_{i=1}^{m}(\bigwedge_{j=1}^{n_m} \delta_{i,j}))$.

Definition 10. *Subterm* is the total function from Matr to $\mathit{Pow}(\mathrm{Term})$ such that for each $\mu \in \mathrm{Matr}$, $\mathit{Subterm}(\mu) =$

$$\left\{ \tau \in \mathrm{Term} \;\middle|\; \begin{array}{l} \text{for some } \theta \in \mu, \text{ for some } \omega \in \mathrm{Feat}^*,^{6} \\ \quad \text{for some } \sigma \in \mathrm{Spec},\ \tau\omega \sim \sigma \in \theta \text{ or } \neg\tau\omega \sim \sigma \in \theta, \text{ or} \\ \quad \text{for some } \tau' \in \mathrm{Term},\ \tau\omega \approx \tau' \in \theta \text{ or } \neg\tau\omega \approx \tau' \in \theta, \text{ or} \\ \quad \text{for some } \tau' \in \mathrm{Term},\ \tau' \approx \tau\omega \in \theta \text{ or } \neg\tau' \approx \tau\omega \in \theta, \text{ or} \\ \quad \text{for some } \tau' \in \mathrm{Term},\ \tau\omega \not\approx \tau' \in \theta \text{ or } \neg\tau\omega \not\approx \tau' \in \theta, \text{ or} \\ \quad \text{for some } \tau' \in \mathrm{Term},\ \tau' \not\approx \tau\omega \in \theta \text{ or } \neg\tau' \not\approx \tau\omega \in \theta \end{array} \right\}.$$

Thus, for each $\mu \in \mathrm{Matr}$, $\mathit{Subterm}(\mu)$ is the set of subterms of terms occurring in literals in clauses in μ.

4 Classification

An exclusive matrix is a matrix meeting several syntactic conditions such that each individual clause in an exclusive matrix is satisfiable, but the union of each pair of distinct clauses in an exclusive matrix is unsatisfiable. The first part of

[5] For each set X, $\mathit{FinPow}(X)$ is the set of finite subsets of X.
[6] For each set X, X^* is the set of finite strings of members of X.

our device is an algorithm called `Class` that effectively deduces from each finite theory an exclusive matrix that is semantically equivalent to the theory. Thus, `Class` effectively deduces from a finite theory an exclusive matrix that constitutes a classification with qualities (Q1) and (Q2).

Each clause in an exclusive matrix is nonempty and positive, in the sense that each literal in the clause is an atomic description, not the negation of an atomic description. Moreover, each clause in an exclusive matrix meets several conditions that we discuss informally immediately after giving the formal definition of an exhaustive matrix.

Definition 11. μ is an *exclusive matrix* iff

$\mu \in$ Matr, and

for each $\theta \in \mu$,

$\theta \subseteq \text{Atom}^{\text{C}}$,

$: \approx : \in \theta$,

for each $\tau \in$ Term, for each $\varphi \in$ Feat,

if $\tau\varphi \approx \tau\varphi \in \theta$ then $\tau \approx \tau \in \theta$,

for each $\tau_1 \in$ Term, for each $\tau_2 \in$ Term,

if $\tau_1 \approx \tau_2 \in \theta$ then $\tau_2 \approx \tau_1 \in \theta$,

for each $\tau_1 \in$ Term, for each $\tau_2 \in$ Term, for each $\tau_3 \in$ Term,

if $\tau_1 \approx \tau_2 \in \theta$ and $\tau_2 \approx \tau_3 \in \theta$ then $\tau_1 \approx \tau_3 \in \theta$,

for each $\tau_1 \in$ Term, for each $\tau_2 \in$ Term, for each $\varphi \in$ Feat,

if $\tau_1 \approx \tau_2 \in \theta$, $\tau_1\varphi \approx \tau_1\varphi \in \theta$ and $\tau_2\varphi \approx \tau_2\varphi \in \theta$

then $\tau_1\varphi \approx \tau_2\varphi \in \theta$,

for each $\tau \in$ Term,

$\tau \approx \tau \in \theta$ iff for some $\sigma \in$ Spec, $\tau \sim \sigma \in \theta$,

for each $\tau_1 \in$ Term, for each $\tau_2 \in$ Term, for each $\sigma_1 \in$ Spec, for each $\sigma_2 \in$ Spec,

if $\tau_1 \approx \tau_2 \in \theta$, $\tau_1 \sim \sigma_1 \in \theta$ and $\tau_2 \sim \sigma_2 \in \theta$ then $\sigma_1 = \sigma_2$,

for each $\tau \in$ Term, for each $\sigma_1 \in$ Spec, for each $\varphi \in$ Feat, for each $\sigma_2 \in$ Spec,

if $\tau \sim \sigma_1 \in \theta$ and $\tau\varphi \sim \sigma_2 \in \theta$ then $\sigma_2 \in \text{Appr}\langle\sigma_1, \varphi\rangle$,

for each $\tau \in$ Term, for each $\sigma \in$ Spec, for each $\varphi \in$ Feat,

if $\tau \sim \sigma \in \theta$, $\text{Appr}\langle\sigma, \varphi\rangle \neq \emptyset$ and $\tau\varphi \in \mathit{Subterm}(\mu)$

then $\tau\varphi \approx \tau\varphi \in \theta$,

for each $\tau_1 \in$ Term, for each $\tau_2 \in$ Term,

if $\tau_1 \not\approx \tau_2 \in \theta$ then $\tau_1 \approx \tau_1 \in \theta$ and $\tau_2 \approx \tau_2 \in \theta$,

for each $\tau_1 \in$ Term, for each $\tau_2 \in$ Term,

if $\tau_1 \approx \tau_1 \in \theta$ and $\tau_2 \approx \tau_2 \in \theta$ then $\tau_1 \approx \tau_2 \in \theta$ or $\tau_1 \not\approx \tau_2 \in \theta$, and

for each $\tau_1 \in$ Term, for each $\tau_2 \in$ Term,

$\tau_1 \approx \tau_2 \notin \theta$ or $\tau_1 \not\approx \tau_2 \notin \theta$.

The easiest way to grasp an intuitive understanding of an exhaustive matrix μ is to consider, for some clause θ in μ, the binary relations $\equiv$ and $\not\equiv$ on terms induced by $\approx$ and $\not\approx$ in θ: for each $\tau_1 \in$ Term, for each $\tau_2 \in$ Term,

$\tau_1 \equiv \tau_2$ iff $\tau \approx \tau_2 \in \theta$, and

$\tau_1 \not\equiv \tau_2$ iff $\tau \not\approx \tau_2 \in \theta$.

$\equiv$ is an equivalence relation on a finite, nonempty and subsort-closed domain of terms. $\equiv$ also has the following 'growth' property: for each $\tau_1 \in$ Term, for each $\tau_2 \in$ Term, for each $\varphi \in$ Feat,

if $\tau_1 \equiv \tau_2$,

$\tau_1\varphi$ is in the domain of $\equiv$, and

$\tau_2\varphi$ is in the domain of $\equiv$

then $\tau_1\varphi \equiv \tau_2\varphi$.

Moreover, each equivalence class in $\equiv$ is labeled with a unique species, and $\equiv$ must never violate the appropriateness function Appr: for each $\tau \in$ Term, for each $\sigma_1 \in$ Spec, for each $\varphi \in$ Feat, for each $\sigma_2 \in$ Spec,

if σ_1 labels the $\equiv$ equivalence class of τ, and

σ_2 labels the $\equiv$ equivalence class of $\tau\varphi$

then $\sigma_2 \in \text{Appr}\langle\sigma_1, \varphi\rangle$.

However, fulfilling Appr is only compulsory if all the terms involved are subterms of terms already occurring in literals in clauses in μ: for each $\tau \in$ Term, for each $\sigma \in$ Spec, for each $\varphi \in$ Feat,

if σ labels the $\equiv$ equivalence class of τ, and

$\text{Appr}\langle\sigma, \varphi\rangle \neq \emptyset$

then $\tau\varphi$ is in the domain of $\equiv$

provided $\tau\varphi$, and hence τ, are in $\mathit{Subterm}(\mu)$.

We write Excl for the set of exclusive matrices. Notice that for each $\mu \in$ Excl, for each μ',

if $\mu' \subseteq \mu$ then $\mu' \in$ Excl.

The utility of exclusive matrices as classifications resides in the following two propositions, both proved in [7].

Proposition 12. *For each* $\mu \in$ Excl, *for each* $\theta_1 \in \mu$, *for each* $\theta_2 \in \mu$,
if $\theta_1 \cup \theta_2$ *is satisfiable then* $\theta_1 = \theta_2$.

Proposition 13. *For each* $\mu \in$ Excl, *for each* $\theta \in \mu$,
θ *is satisfiable.*

Thus, if each clause θ in an exclusive matrix μ is considered to be a label that indicates the denotation of θ then proposition 12 shows that each two distinct labels in μ indicate disjoint sets, and proposition 13 shows that no individual label in μ necessarily indicates the empty set. Thus, μ constitutes a classification with qualities (Q1) and (Q2).

We now turn to the algorithm **Class** that effectively deduces a semantically equivalent exclusive matrix from a finite theory. **Class** employs three component algorithms, **Matrix**, **Goetz** and **Atomic**, and we give each in turn before giving **Class**. We first give **Matrix**. Since the SRL descriptions are the propositional logic formulae with propositional variables simultaneously replaced by atomic descriptions, each of the numerous algorithms that compute semantically equivalent disjunctive normal forms of propositional logic formulae yields an algorithm that computes semantically equivalent disjunctive normal forms of SRL descriptions. Further, for each interpretation $\mathcal{I}$,

$\Theta_{\mathcal{I}}(\emptyset) = \mathcal{D}_{\mathcal{I}}(: \approx :)$,

for each $n \in \mathbb{N}$, for each $\{\delta_0, \ldots, \delta_n\} \subseteq \text{Desc}$,

$\Theta_{\mathcal{I}}(\{\delta_0, \ldots, \delta_n\}) = \mathcal{D}_{\mathcal{I}}([\delta_0 \wedge \ldots \wedge \delta_n])$, and

for each disjunctive normal form $\bigvee_{i=1}^{m}(\bigwedge_{j=1}^{n_m} \delta_{i,j}) \in \text{Desc}$,

$\mathcal{D}_{\mathcal{I}}(\bigvee_{i=1}^{m}(\bigwedge_{j=1}^{n_m} \delta_{i,j})) = \mathcal{M}_{\mathcal{I}}(\{\{\delta_{i,j} \mid 1 \leq j \leq n_m\} \mid 1 \leq i \leq m\})$.

Thus, there clearly exists an algorithm **Matrix** that computes a total function from *FinPow*(Desc) to Matr such that for each $\theta \in$ *FinPow*(Desc), for each interpretation $\mathcal{I}$,

$\Theta_{\mathcal{I}}(\theta) = \mathcal{M}_{\mathcal{I}}(\texttt{Matrix}(\theta))$.

We next give **Goetz**.

Definition 14. $\rightharpoondown$ is the smallest binary relation on Matr $\times$ Matr such that for each $\mu \in$ Matr, for each $\theta \in$ Clau,

for each $\delta \in \text{Atom}^{\text{C}}$,

if $\theta \notin \mu$, $\delta \in \theta$ and $\neg\delta \in \theta$ then $\mu \cup \{\theta\} \rightharpoondown \mu$,

if $\theta \notin \mu$ and $: \approx : \notin \theta$ then $\mu \cup \{\theta\} \rightharpoondown \mu \cup \{\theta \cup \{: \approx :\}\}$,

for each $\tau \in$ Term, for each $\varphi \in$ Feat,

if $\theta \notin \mu$, $\tau\varphi \approx \tau\varphi \in \theta$ and $\tau \approx \tau \notin \theta$ then $\mu \cup \{\theta\} \rightharpoondown \mu \cup \{\theta \cup \{\tau \approx \tau\}\}$,

for each $\tau_1 \in$ Term, for each $\tau_2 \in$ Term,

if $\theta \notin \mu$, $\tau_1 \approx \tau_2 \in \theta$ and $\tau_2 \approx \tau_1 \notin \theta$ then $\mu \cup \{\theta\} \rightharpoondown \mu \cup \{\theta \cup \{\tau_2 \approx \tau_1\}\}$,

for each $\tau_1 \in$ Term, for each $\tau_2 \in$ Term, for each $\tau_3 \in$ Term,

if $\theta \notin \mu$, $\tau_1 \approx \tau_2 \in \theta$, $\tau_2 \approx \tau_3 \in \theta$ and $\tau_1 \approx \tau_3 \notin \theta$
then $\mu \cup \{\theta\} \rightharpoondown \mu \cup \{\theta \cup \{\tau_1 \approx \tau_3\}\}$,

for each $\tau_1 \in$ Term, for each $\tau_2 \in$ Term, for each $\varphi \in$ Feat,

if $\theta \notin \mu$, $\tau_1 \approx \tau_2 \in \theta$, $\tau_1\varphi \approx \tau_1\varphi \in \theta$, $\tau_2\varphi \approx \tau_2\varphi \in \theta$ and $\tau_1\varphi \approx \tau_2\varphi \notin \theta$
then $\mu \cup \{\theta\} \rightharpoondown \mu \cup \{\theta \cup \{\tau_1\varphi \approx \tau_2\varphi\}\}$,

for each $\tau \in$ Term,

if $\theta \notin \mu$, $\tau \approx \tau \in \theta$ and for each $\sigma \in$ Spec, $\tau \sim \sigma \notin \theta$
then $\mu \cup \{\theta\} \rightharpoondown \mu \cup \{\theta \cup \{\tau \sim \sigma\} \mid \sigma \in \text{Spec}\}$,

for each $\tau \in$ Term, for each $\sigma \in$ Spec,

if $\theta \notin \mu$, $\tau \sim \sigma \in \theta$ and $\tau \approx \tau \notin \theta$ then $\mu \cup \{\theta\} \rightharpoondown \mu \cup \{\theta \cup \{\tau \approx \tau\}\}$, for each $\tau_1 \in$ Term, for each $\tau_2 \in$ Term, for each $\sigma_1 \in$ Spec, for each $\sigma_2 \in$ Spec,

if $\theta \notin \mu$, $\tau_1 \approx \tau_2 \in \theta$, $\tau_1 \sim \sigma_1 \in \theta$, $\tau_2 \sim \sigma_2 \in \theta$ and $\sigma_1 \neq \sigma_2$

then $\mu \cup \{\theta\} \rightharpoondown \mu$,

for each $\tau \in$ Term, for each $\sigma_1 \in$ Spec, for each $\varphi \in$ Feat, for each $\sigma_2 \in$ Spec,

if $\theta \notin \mu$, $\tau \sim \sigma_1 \in \theta$, $\tau\varphi \sim \sigma_2 \in \theta$ and $\sigma_2 \notin \text{Appr}\langle\sigma_1, \varphi\rangle$

then $\mu \cup \{\theta\} \rightharpoondown \mu$,

for each $\tau \in$ Term, for each $\sigma \in$ Spec, for each $\varphi \in$ Feat,

if $\theta \notin \mu$, $\tau \sim \sigma \in \theta$, $\text{Appr}\langle\sigma, \varphi\rangle \neq \emptyset$, $\tau\varphi \in \mathit{Subterm}(\mu \cup \{\theta\})$ and $\tau\varphi \approx \tau\varphi \notin \theta$

then $\mu \cup \{\theta\} \rightharpoondown \mu \cup \{\theta \cup \{\tau\varphi \approx \tau\varphi\}\}$,

for each $\tau_1 \in$ Term, for each $\tau_2 \in$ Term,

if $\theta \notin \mu$, $\tau_1 \not\approx \tau_2 \in \theta$ and $\tau_1 \approx \tau_1 \notin \theta$ then $\mu \cup \{\theta\} \rightharpoondown \mu \cup \{\theta \cup \{\tau_1 \approx \tau_1\}\}$,

for each $\tau_1 \in$ Term, for each $\tau_2 \in$ Term,

if $\theta \notin \mu$, $\tau_1 \not\approx \tau_2 \in \theta$ and $\tau_2 \approx \tau_2 \notin \theta$ then $\mu \cup \{\theta\} \rightharpoondown \mu \cup \{\theta \cup \{\tau_2 \approx \tau_2\}\}$,

for each $\tau_1 \in$ Term, for each $\tau_2 \in$ Term,

if $\theta \notin \mu$, $\tau_1 \approx \tau_1 \in \theta$, $\tau_2 \approx \tau_2 \in \theta$, $\tau_1 \approx \tau_2 \notin \theta$ and $\tau_1 \not\approx \tau_2 \notin \theta$

then $\mu \cup \{\theta\} \rightharpoondown \mu \cup \{\theta \cup \{\tau_1 \approx \tau_2\}, \theta \cup \{\tau_1 \not\approx \tau_2\}\}$, and

for each $\tau_1 \in$ Term, for each $\tau_2 \in$ Term,

if $\theta \notin \mu$, $\tau_1 \approx \tau_2 \in \theta$ and $\tau_1 \not\approx \tau_2 \in \theta$ then $\mu \cup \{\theta\} \rightharpoondown \mu$.

$\rightharpoondown$ is adapted from the rewrite rules of [2] used in [4], and is best understood intuitively as a set of left-to-right rewrite rules. Ignoring all nonatomic literals, each rule in $\rightharpoondown$ acts upon a clause θ in a matrix μ iff θ violates some or other condition for μ being exclusive, and the rule either modifies θ to better conform μ to the exhaustive matrix conditions or deletes θ entirely. A matrix is terminal iff no rewrite rule in $\rightharpoondown$ applies to it.

Definition 15. For each $\mu \in$ Matr,

μ is *terminal* iff for no $\mu' \in$ Matr, $\mu \rightharpoondown \mu'$.

There clearly exists an algorithm `Goetz` that computes a total function from Matr to {Provisional, Terminal} $\times$ Matr such that for each $\mu \in$ Matr,

if μ is terminal

then $\texttt{Goetz}(\mu) = \langle\text{Terminal}, \mu\rangle$

else for some $\mu' \in$ Matr,

$\mu \rightharpoondown \mu'$ and $\texttt{Goetz}(\mu) = \langle\text{Provisional}, \mu'\rangle$.

Next, `Atomic` is an algorithm that deletes the nonatomic literals from the clauses in a matrix. Thus, `Atomic` computes the total function from Matr to Matr such that for each $\mu \in$ Matr,

$\texttt{Atomic}(\mu) = \{\theta \cap \text{Atom}^{\text{C}} \mid \theta \in \mu\}$.

Finally, `Class` is the following algorithm: for each $\theta \in \mathit{FinPow}(\text{Desc})$,

read θ;
set $\langle \mathtt{f}, \mathtt{m} \rangle := \mathtt{Goetz}(\mathtt{Matrix}(\theta))$;
while $\mathtt{f} =$ Provisional;
  set $\langle \mathtt{f}, \mathtt{m} \rangle := \mathtt{Goetz}(\mathtt{m})$;
write $\mathtt{Atomic}(\mathtt{m})$.

Thus, `Class` converts a finite theory to a semantically equivalent matrix, applies the rewrite rules in $\rightarrow_\tau$ repeatedly until a terminal matrix is produced, and deletes all nonatomic literals from the clauses in the terminal matrix. [7] proves that `Class` computes a semantically equivalent exclusive matrix from each finite theory.

Proposition 16. `Class` *computes a total function from FinPow*(Desc) *to* Excl *such that for each* $\theta \in$ *FinPow*(Desc), *for each interpretation* $\mathcal{I}$,
$\Theta_{\mathcal{I}}(\theta) = \mathcal{M}_{\mathcal{I}}(\mathtt{Class}(\theta))$.

Thus, proposition 16 shows that `Class` computes an exclusive matrix μ from a finite theory θ such that the denotations of μ and θ are identical under all interpretations. Thus, `Class` effectively deduces from θ an exclusive matrix that constitutes a classification of the denotation of θ with qualities (Q1) and (Q2).

To illustrate `Class` and the classifications it deduces, consider the following simple example. Suppose that

Spec $= \{a, b, c\}$,
Feat $= \{x, y\}$,
Appr is the total function from Spec $\times$ Feat to *Pow*(Spec) such that
  Appr$\langle a, x \rangle = \{b, c\}$,
  Appr$\langle a, y \rangle = \{b, c\}$,
  Appr$\langle b, x \rangle = \emptyset$,
  Appr$\langle b, y \rangle = \emptyset$,
  Appr$\langle c, x \rangle = \emptyset$, and
  Appr$\langle c, y \rangle = \emptyset$, and
$\theta = \{[{:}x \sim b \rightarrow {:}y \sim c], [{:}x \sim c \rightarrow {:}x \approx {:}y]\}$

Clearly,
 $\langle$Spec, Feat, Appr$\rangle$ is a computable signature,
 $\theta \subseteq$ Desc, and
 for each interpretation $\mathcal{I} = \langle \mathcal{U}, \mathcal{S}, \mathcal{F} \rangle$, for each $v \in \mathcal{U}$,
  $v \in \Theta_{\mathcal{I}}(\theta)$ iff v is of the form

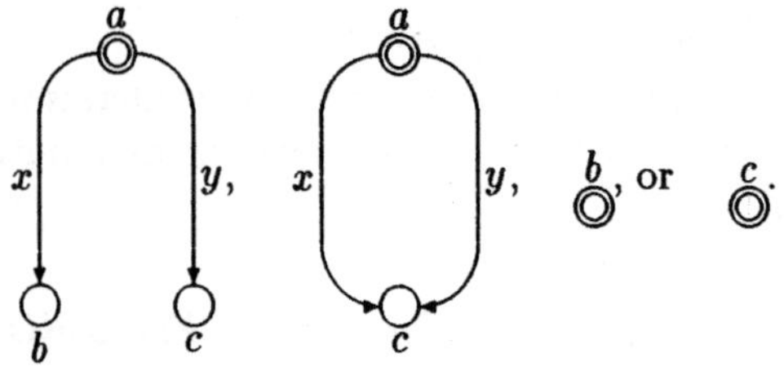

Since, for each interpretation $\mathcal{I}$,

$$\mathcal{M}_{\mathcal{I}}(\theta) = \mathcal{D}_{\mathcal{I}}\left(\begin{bmatrix} [\neg{:}x \sim b \wedge \neg{:}x \sim c] \\ \vee[\neg{:}x \sim b \wedge {:}x \approx {:}y] \\ \vee[{:}y \sim c \wedge \neg{:}x \sim c] \\ \vee[{:}y \sim c \wedge {:}x \approx {:}y] \end{bmatrix}\right),$$

we can suppose that

$$\mathtt{Matrix}(\theta) = \left\{\begin{Bmatrix} \neg{:}x \sim b, \\ \neg{:}x \sim c \end{Bmatrix}, \begin{Bmatrix} \neg{:}x \sim b, \\ {:}x \approx {:}y \end{Bmatrix}, \begin{Bmatrix} {:}y \sim c, \\ \neg{:}x \sim c \end{Bmatrix}, \begin{Bmatrix} {:}y \sim c, \\ {:}x \approx {:}y \end{Bmatrix}\right\}.$$

Then $\mathtt{Class}(\theta) = \{P, Q, R, S\}$, where

$$P = \{ : \approx :, : \sim b \},$$

$$Q = \{ : \approx :, : \sim c \},$$

$$R = \left\{\begin{array}{l} : \approx :, {:}x \approx {:}x, {:}y \approx {:}y, {:}x \approx {:}y, {:}y \approx {:}x, \\ : \not\approx {:}x, {:}x \not\approx :, : \not\approx {:}y, {:}y \not\approx :, \\ : \sim a, {:}x \sim c, {:}y \sim c \end{array}\right\}, \text{ and}$$

$$S = \left\{\begin{array}{l} : \approx :, {:}x \approx {:}x, {:}y \approx {:}y, \\ : \not\approx {:}x, {:}x \not\approx :, : \not\approx {:}y, {:}y \not\approx :, {:}x \not\approx {:}y, {:}y \not\approx {:}x, \\ : \sim a, {:}x \sim b, {:}y \sim c \end{array}\right\}.$$

Clearly, for each interpretation $\mathcal{I} = \langle \mathcal{U}, \mathcal{S}, \mathcal{F} \rangle$, for each $v \in \mathcal{U}$,

$v \in \Theta_{\mathcal{I}}(P)$ iff v is of the form 

,

$v \in \Theta_{\mathcal{I}}(Q)$ iff v is of the form 

,

$v \in \Theta_{\mathcal{I}}(R)$ iff v is of the form 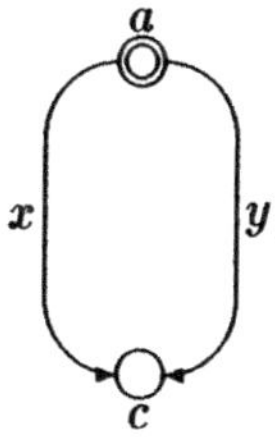

, and

$v \in \Theta_{\mathcal{I}}(S)$ iff v is of the form 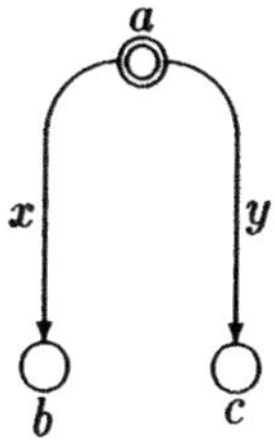

.

Thus, for each interpretation $\mathcal{I}$, $\mathtt{Class}(\theta)$ is a classification of $\Theta_{\mathcal{I}}(\theta)$.

5 Index

An index tree is a finite tree such that each inner node bears a query, each edge bears a response, and each outer node bears a clause. An index tree analyzes an exclusive matrix iff the tree represents an analysis of the matrix in terms of queries and responses. The second part of our device is an algorithm called

`Index` that effectively deduces from each nonempty exclusive matrix an index tree that analyzes the matrix, whereupon, for each object the matrix is true of, a fixed algorithm called `Clause` effectively deduces – from the index tree and the responses offered by a human or computer oracle to queries posed by `Clause` concerning the object – the unique clause in the matrix that is true of the object. Thus, `Index` effectively deduces from a nonempty exclusive matrix an index tree that together with `Clause` constitutes an index with quality (Q4).[7]

We first define a query, a response, an oracle, and disclosure.

Definition 17.

$\text{Quer} = \{\boxed{\tau} \mid \tau \in \text{Term}\} \cup \{\boxed{\tau_1, \tau_2} \mid \tau_1 \in \text{Term and } \tau_2 \in \text{Term}\}$, and

$\text{Resp} = \{\boxed{\sigma} \mid \sigma \in \text{Spec}\} \cup \{\boxed{-}, \boxed{\approx}, \boxed{\not\approx}, \boxed{\pm}, \boxed{\mp}, \boxed{=}\}$.

We call each member of Quer a *query* and each member of Resp a *response*. For each interpretation $\mathcal{I} = \langle \mathcal{U}, \mathcal{S}, \mathcal{F} \rangle$, for each $v \in \mathcal{U}$,

for each $\tau \in \text{Term}$,

$\boxed{\tau}$ represents the query "What is $\mathcal{S}(\mathcal{T}_\mathcal{I}(\tau)(v))$?", to which

$\boxed{\sigma}$ represents, for each $\sigma \in \text{Spec}$, the response "$\mathcal{T}_\mathcal{I}(\tau)(v)$ is defined and $\mathcal{S}(\mathcal{T}_\mathcal{I}(\tau)(v)) = \sigma$", and

$\boxed{-}$ represents the response "$\mathcal{T}_\mathcal{I}(\tau)(v)$ is undefined", and

for each $\tau_1 \in \text{Term}$, for each $\tau_2 \in \text{Term}$,

$\boxed{\tau_1, \tau_2}$ represents the query "Does $\mathcal{T}_\mathcal{I}(\tau_1)(v) = \mathcal{T}_\mathcal{I}(\tau_2)(v)$?", to which

$\boxed{\approx}$ represents the response "$\mathcal{T}_\mathcal{I}(\tau_1)(v)$ and $\mathcal{T}_\mathcal{I}(\tau_2)(v)$ are defined and $\mathcal{T}_\mathcal{I}(\tau_1)(v) = \mathcal{T}_\mathcal{I}(\tau_2)(v)$",

$\boxed{\not\approx}$ represents the response "$\mathcal{T}_\mathcal{I}(\tau_1)(v)$ and $\mathcal{T}_\mathcal{I}(\tau_2)(v)$ are defined and $\mathcal{T}_\mathcal{I}(\tau_1)(v) \neq \mathcal{T}_\mathcal{I}(\tau_2)(v)$",

$\boxed{\pm}$ represents the response "$\mathcal{T}_\mathcal{I}(\tau_1)(v)$ is defined and $\mathcal{T}_\mathcal{I}(\tau_2)(v)$ is undefined",

$\boxed{\mp}$ represents the response "$\mathcal{T}_\mathcal{I}(\tau_1)(v)$ is undefined and $\mathcal{T}_\mathcal{I}(\tau_2)(v)$ is defined", and

$\boxed{=}$ represents the response "$\mathcal{T}_\mathcal{I}(\tau_1)(v)$ and $\mathcal{T}_\mathcal{I}(\tau_2)(v)$ are undefined".

Definition 18. For each interpretation $\mathcal{I} = \langle \mathcal{U}, \mathcal{S}, \mathcal{F} \rangle$, for each $v \in \mathcal{U}$, $Accurate^v_\mathcal{I}$ is the total function from Quer to Resp such that

for each $\tau \in \text{Term}$,

$$Accurate^v_\mathcal{I}(\boxed{\tau}) = \begin{cases} \boxed{\mathcal{S}(\mathcal{T}_\mathcal{I}(\tau)(v))} & \text{if } \mathcal{T}_\mathcal{I}(\tau)(v) \text{ is defined} \\ \boxed{-} & \text{if } \mathcal{T}_\mathcal{I}(\tau)(v) \text{ is undefined, and} \end{cases}$$

[7] The empty matrix is of no interest, since for each interpretation $\mathcal{I}$, $\mathcal{M}_I(\emptyset) = \emptyset$: there are no objects for an index to classify.

for each $\tau_1 \in$ Term, for each $\tau_2 \in$ Term,

$$Accurate^{v}_{\mathcal{I}}(\boxed{\tau_1, \tau_2}) = \begin{cases} \boxed{\approx} \text{ if } \mathcal{T}_{\mathcal{I}}(\tau_1)(v) \text{ and } \mathcal{T}_{\mathcal{I}}(\tau_2)(v) \text{ are defined and} \\ \qquad \mathcal{T}_{\mathcal{I}}(\tau_1)(v) = \mathcal{T}_{\mathcal{I}}(\tau_2)(v) \\ \boxed{\not\approx} \text{ if } \mathcal{T}_{\mathcal{I}}(\tau_1)(v) \text{ and } \mathcal{T}_{\mathcal{I}}(\tau_2)(v) \text{ are defined and} \\ \qquad \mathcal{T}_{\mathcal{I}}(\tau_1)(v) \neq \mathcal{T}_{\mathcal{I}}(\tau_2)(v) \\ \boxed{\pm} \text{ if } \mathcal{T}_{\mathcal{I}}(\tau_1)(v) \text{ is defined and} \\ \qquad \mathcal{T}_{\mathcal{I}}(\tau_2)(v) \text{ is undefined} \\ \boxed{\mp} \text{ if } \mathcal{T}_{\mathcal{I}}(\tau_1)(v) \text{ is undefined and} \\ \qquad \mathcal{T}_{\mathcal{I}}(\tau_2)(v) \text{ is defined} \\ \boxed{=} \text{ if } \mathcal{T}_{\mathcal{I}}(\tau_1)(v) \text{ and } \mathcal{T}_{\mathcal{I}}(\tau_2)(v) \text{ are undefined.} \end{cases}$$

Clearly, $Accurate^{v}_{\mathcal{I}}(\kappa)$ is the accurate response to query κ about object v in interpretation $\mathcal{I}$. An *oracle* is an algorithm that computes a total function from Quer to Resp. We write Orac for the set of oracles. For each $o \in$ Orac, for each interpretation $\mathcal{I} = \langle \mathcal{U}, \mathcal{S}, \mathcal{F} \rangle$, for each $v \in \mathcal{U}$, o *discloses* v under $\mathcal{I}$ iff o computes $Accurate^{v}_{\mathcal{I}}$. Thus, an oracle discloses an object under an interpretation iff the oracle accurately responds to all queries concerning the object. For example, an oracle disclosing objects under a natural language could be a machine database for the objects of the natural language, or a human being with mature competence in the natural language.

We next define the important notion of a residue. Suppose that an exclusive matrix μ is known to be true of an object v. Suppose, also, that a reasonable query κ about v elicits the accurate response ρ, where, by reasonable, we mean that κ concerns only subterms of terms occurring in literals in clauses in μ. On the basis of μ, κ and ρ, it is possible to determine an exclusive matrix $\mu' \subseteq \mu$ such that μ' is known to be true of v. We call μ' the residue of μ, κ and ρ.

Definition 19. *Residue* is the total function from Matr $\times$ Quer $\times$ Resp to Matr such that for each $\mu \in$ Matr,

for each $\tau \in$ Term,

for each $\sigma \in$ Spec, $Residue\langle \mu, \boxed{\tau}, \boxed{\sigma} \rangle = \{\theta \in \mu \mid \tau \sim \sigma \in \theta\}$,

$Residue\langle \mu, \boxed{\tau}, \boxed{-} \rangle = \{\theta \in \mu \mid \tau \approx \tau \notin \theta\}$,

$Residue\langle \mu, \boxed{\tau}, \boxed{\approx} \rangle = \emptyset$,

$Residue\langle \mu, \boxed{\tau}, \boxed{\not\approx} \rangle = \emptyset$,

$Residue\langle \mu, \boxed{\tau}, \boxed{\pm} \rangle = \emptyset$,

$Residue\langle \mu, \boxed{\tau}, \boxed{\mp} \rangle = \emptyset$, and

$Residue\langle \mu, \boxed{\tau}, \boxed{=} \rangle = \emptyset$, and

for each $\tau_1 \in$ Term, for each $\tau_2 \in$ Term,

for each $\sigma \in$ Spec, $Residue\langle \mu, \boxed{\tau_1, \tau_2}, \boxed{\sigma} \rangle = \emptyset$,

$Residue\langle \mu, \boxed{\tau_1, \tau_2}, \boxed{-} \rangle = \emptyset$,

$Residue\langle \mu, \boxed{\tau_1, \tau_2}, \boxed{\approx} \rangle = \{\theta \in \mu \mid \tau_1 \approx \tau_2 \in \theta\}$,

$$Residue\langle \mu, \boxed{\tau_1, \tau_2}, \boxed{\not\approx} \rangle = \{\theta \in \mu \mid \tau_1 \not\approx \tau_2 \in \theta\},$$
$$Residue\langle \mu, \boxed{\tau_1, \tau_2}, \boxed{\pm} \rangle = \{\theta \in \mu \mid \tau_1 \approx \tau_1 \in \theta \text{ and } \tau_2 \approx \tau_2 \notin \theta\},$$
$$Residue\langle \mu, \boxed{\tau_1, \tau_2}, \boxed{\mp} \rangle = \{\theta \in \mu \mid \tau_1 \approx \tau_1 \notin \theta \text{ and } \tau_2 \approx \tau_2 \in \theta\}, \text{ and}$$
$$Residue\langle \mu, \boxed{\tau_1, \tau_2}, \boxed{=} \rangle = \{\theta \in \mu \mid \tau_1 \approx \tau_1 \notin \theta \text{ and } \tau_2 \approx \tau_2 \notin \theta\}.$$

Notice that for each $\mu \in$ Matr, for each $\kappa \in$ Quer, for each $\rho \in$ Resp,
$Residue\langle \mu, \kappa, \rho \rangle \subseteq \mu$.
Thus, for each $\mu \in$ Excl, for each $\kappa \in$ Quer, for each $\rho \in$ Resp,
$Residue\langle \mu, \kappa, \rho \rangle \in$ Excl.

Definition 20. For each $\mu \in$ Matr,

$$\text{Quer}_\mu = \{\boxed{\tau} \mid \tau \in Subterm(\mu)\} \cup \{\boxed{\tau_1, \tau_2} \mid \tau_1 \in Subterm(\mu) \text{ and } \tau_2 \in Subterm(\mu)\}.$$

[7] proves the following proposition.

Proposition 21. *For each* $\mu \in$ Excl, *for each interpretation* $\mathcal{I} = \langle \mathcal{U}, \mathcal{S}, \mathcal{F} \rangle$, *for each* $v \in \mathcal{U}$, *for each* $\kappa \in \text{Quer}_\mu$,
if $v \in \mathcal{M}_\mathcal{I}(\mu)$
then $Residue\langle \mu, \kappa, Accurate^v_\mathcal{I}(\kappa) \rangle \neq \emptyset$, *and*
$v \in \mathcal{M}_\mathcal{I}(Residue\langle \mu, \kappa, Accurate^v_\mathcal{I}(\kappa) \rangle)$.

We can now define an index tree, and the analysis of an exclusive matrix.

Definition 22. Quadruple $\langle \mathfrak{N}, \mathfrak{I}, \mathfrak{O}, \mathfrak{L} \rangle$ is an *index tree* iff
$\mathfrak{N} \in FinPow(\text{Resp}^*)$,
$\varepsilon \in \mathfrak{N}$,[8]
for each $\nu \in \text{Resp}^*$, for each $\rho \in$ Resp, if $\nu\rho \in \mathfrak{N}$ then $\nu \in \mathfrak{N}$,
$\mathfrak{I} = \{\nu \in \mathfrak{N} \mid \text{for some } \rho \in \text{Resp}, \nu\rho \in \mathfrak{N}\}$,
$\mathfrak{O} = \{\nu \in \mathfrak{N} \mid \text{for each } \rho \in \text{Resp}, \nu\rho \notin \mathfrak{N}\}$,
$\mathfrak{L}$ is a total function from $\mathfrak{N}$ to Quer $\cup$ Clau,
for each $\nu \in \mathfrak{I}$, $\mathfrak{L}(\nu) \in$ Quer, and
for each $\nu \in \mathfrak{O}$, $\mathfrak{L}(\nu) \in$ Clau.

Suppose that $\mathfrak{T} = \langle \mathfrak{N}, \mathfrak{I}, \mathfrak{O}, \mathfrak{L} \rangle$ is an index tree. We call each member of $\mathfrak{N}$ a *node* in $\mathfrak{T}$, each member of $\mathfrak{I}$ an *inner node* in $\mathfrak{T}$, each member of $\mathfrak{O}$ an *outer node* in $\mathfrak{T}$, and $\mathfrak{L}$ the *labeling* in $\mathfrak{T}$. For each $\nu \in \mathfrak{N}$, we say $\mathfrak{L}(\nu)$ *labels* ν in $\mathfrak{T}$. $\mathfrak{T}$ can be pictured as a finite tree with labeled nodes and labeled directed edges. The nodes are the members of $\mathfrak{N}$, the root node is ε, each inner node has some directed edge leaving it, and each outer node has no directed edge leaving it. Query $\mathfrak{L}(\nu)$ labels each inner node ν, and clause $\mathfrak{L}(\nu)$ labels each outer node ν.

[8] ε is the empty string.

There is a directed edge from node ν_1 to node ν_2 labeled with response ρ iff $\nu_2 = \nu_1\rho$. For example, if

$\mathfrak{N} = \{\varepsilon, \rho_0, \rho_1, \rho_1\rho_2, \rho_1\rho_3\}$,
$\mathfrak{I} = \{\varepsilon, \rho_1\}$,
$\mathfrak{D} = \{\rho_0, \rho_1\rho_2, \rho_1\rho_3\}$, and
$\mathfrak{L}$ is the total function from $\mathfrak{N}$ to Quer $\cup$ Clau, such that
$\mathfrak{L}(\varepsilon) = \kappa_0 \in$ Quer,
$\mathfrak{L}(\rho_0) = \theta_0 \in$ Clau,
$\mathfrak{L}(\rho_1) = \kappa_1 \in$ Quer,
$\mathfrak{L}(\rho_1\rho_2) = \theta_1 \in$ Clau, and
$\mathfrak{L}(\rho_1\rho_3) = \theta_2 \in$ Clau.

then $\langle\mathfrak{N}, \mathfrak{I}, \mathfrak{D}, \mathfrak{L}\rangle$ is an index tree that can be pictured as

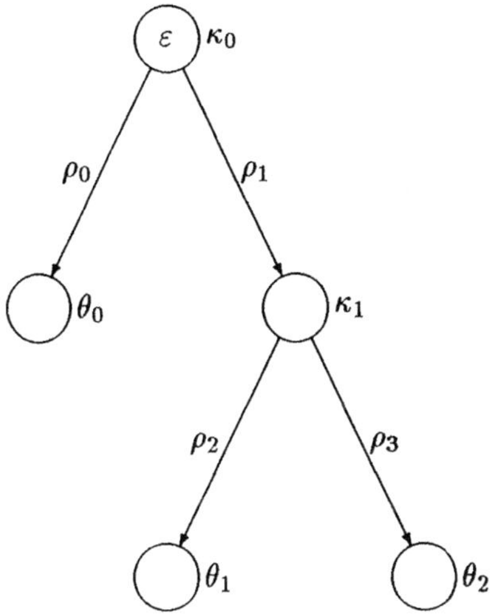

We write Tree for the set of index trees. Notice that for each $\langle\mathfrak{N}, \mathfrak{I}, \mathfrak{D}, \mathfrak{L}\rangle \in$ Tree, for each $\nu \in \mathfrak{N}$,

either $\nu \in \mathfrak{I}$ or $\nu \in \mathfrak{D}$.

Definition 23. For each $\mathfrak{T} = \langle\mathfrak{N}, \mathfrak{I}, \mathfrak{D}, \mathfrak{L}\rangle \in$ Tree,

$\mathfrak{M}$ is a *marking* of $\mathfrak{T}$
iff $\mathfrak{M}$ is a total function from $\mathfrak{N}$ to Excl,
for each $\nu \in \mathfrak{I}$, $\mathfrak{L}(\nu) \in \text{Quer}_{\mathfrak{M}(\nu)}$,
for each $\nu \in \mathfrak{I}$, for each $\rho \in$ Resp,
if $\mathit{Residue}\langle\mathfrak{M}(\nu), \mathfrak{L}(\nu), \rho\rangle \neq \emptyset$
then $\nu\rho \in \mathfrak{N}$ and $\mathfrak{M}(\nu\rho) = \mathit{Residue}\langle\mathfrak{M}(\nu), \mathfrak{L}(\nu), \rho\rangle$, and
for each $\nu \in \mathfrak{D}$, $\mathfrak{M}(\nu) = \{\mathfrak{L}(\nu)\}$.

Suppose that $\mathfrak{T} = \langle\mathfrak{N}, \mathfrak{I}, \mathfrak{D}, \mathfrak{L}\rangle$ is an index tree, and $\mathfrak{M}$ is a marking of $\mathfrak{T}$. For each $\nu \in \mathfrak{N}$, we say $\mathfrak{M}(\nu)$ *marks* ν in $\mathfrak{T}$ under $\mathfrak{M}$. Notice that for each $\mathfrak{T} =$

$\langle \mathfrak{N}, \mathfrak{I}, \mathfrak{O}, \mathfrak{L} \rangle \in$ Tree, for each marking $\mathfrak{M}$ of $\mathfrak{T}$, for each $\nu \in \mathfrak{N}$,
$\mathfrak{M}(\nu) \neq \emptyset$.

An index tree $\mathfrak{T}$ analyzes an exclusive matrix μ iff μ marks the root node under some marking of $\mathfrak{T}$.

Definition 24. For each $\mathfrak{T} \in$ Tree, for each $\mu \in$ Excl,
$\mathfrak{T}$ *analyzes* μ iff for some marking $\mathfrak{M}$ of $\mathfrak{T}$, $\mathfrak{M}(\varepsilon) = \mu$.

Notice that for each $\mathfrak{T} = \langle \mathfrak{N}, \mathfrak{I}, \mathfrak{O}, \mathfrak{L} \rangle \in$ Tree, for each $\mu \in$ Excl,
if $\mathfrak{T}$ analyzes μ then for each $\nu \in \mathfrak{O}$, $\mathfrak{L}(\nu) \in \mu$.

We now turn to the algorithm `Clause` that effectively deduces – from an index tree that analyzes an exclusive matrix, and an oracle that discloses an object in the denotation of the matrix – the unique clause in the matrix that is true of the object. `Clause` is the following algorithm: for each $\langle \mathfrak{N}, \mathfrak{I}, \mathfrak{O}, \mathfrak{L} \rangle \in$ Tree, for each $o \in$ Orac,

read $\langle \mathfrak{N}, \mathfrak{I}, \mathfrak{O}, \mathfrak{L} \rangle$, o;
set $\mathtt{p} := \varepsilon$;
while $\mathtt{p} \in \mathfrak{I}$;
    set $\mathtt{r} := o(\mathfrak{L}(\mathtt{p}))$, $\mathtt{p} := \mathtt{pr}$;
write $\mathfrak{L}(\mathtt{p})$.

Thus, `Clause` uses an oracle o to navigate from the root node of an index tree $\mathfrak{T}$ towards an outer node. If `Clause` is currently at an inner node then `Clause` poses the query that labels the node to o, and uses the response of o to determine which daughter node to go to next. If `Clause` is currently at an outer node then `Clause` outputs the clause that labels the node. [7] proves that the nature of a marking ensures that if $\mathfrak{T}$ analyzes an exclusive matrix μ and o discloses some object v in the denotation of μ then `Clause` outputs the unique clause in μ that is true of v.

Proposition 25. `Clause` *computes a partial function from* Tree × Orac *to* Clau *such that for each* $\mathfrak{T} \in$ Tree, *for each* $o \in$ Orac, *for each* $\mu \in$ Excl, *for each interpretation* $\mathcal{I}$, *for each* $v \in \mathcal{M}_{\mathcal{I}}(\mu)$,
if $\mathfrak{T}$ *analyzes* μ *and* o *discloses* v *under* $\mathcal{I}$
then `Clause`$\langle \mathfrak{T}, o \rangle$ *is defined,* `Clause`$\langle \mathfrak{T}, o \rangle \in \mu$ *and* $v \in \Theta_{\mathcal{I}}(\mathtt{Clause}\langle \mathfrak{T}, o \rangle)$.

Thus, proposition 25 shows that `Clause` computes – from an index tree $\mathfrak{T}$ that analyzes an exclusive matrix μ and an oracle that discloses an object v in the denotation of μ – the unique clause in μ that is true of v. Thus, `Clause` and $\mathfrak{T}$ together constitute an index for μ with quality (Q4).

We lastly turn to the algorithm `Index` that effectively deduces from a nonempty exclusive matrix μ an index tree that analyzes μ. `Index` employs three component algorithms, `Weight`, `Query` and `Grow`, and we give each in turn before giving `Index`. Firstly, `Weight` is an algorithm that determines, for each matrix and each query, the cardinality of the largest residue: `Weight` computes the total function from Matr × Quer to $\mathbb{N}$ such that for each $\mu \in$ Matr, for each $\kappa \in$ Quer,

$\texttt{Weight}\langle\mu,\kappa\rangle = \mathit{Max}\{\mathit{Card}(\mathit{Residue}\langle\mu,\kappa,\rho\rangle) \mid \rho \in \mathrm{Resp}\}$.[9]

Thus, $\texttt{Weight}\langle\mu,\kappa\rangle$ computes how uninformative is the least informative response to query κ with respect to matrix μ. Secondly, **Query** is an algorithm that computes, for each nonempty exclusive matrix, a reasonable query with the smallest weight: **Query** computes a total function from Excl $\setminus \{\emptyset\}$ to Quer such that for each $\mu \in \mathrm{Excl} \setminus \{\emptyset\}$,

$\texttt{Query}(\mu) \in \mathrm{Quer}_\mu$, and
$\texttt{Weight}\langle\mu,\texttt{Query}(\mu)\rangle = \mathit{Min}\{\texttt{Weight}\langle\mu,\kappa\rangle \mid \kappa \in \mathrm{Quer}_\mu\}$.[10]

Thus, $\texttt{Query}(\mu)$ indicates a most telling query κ with respect to nonempty exclusive matrix μ, in the sense that the least informative response to κ is no less informative than the least informative response to any other query. Thirdly, **Grow** is an algorithm that computes, for each nonempty exclusive matrix and each query, a list of all response with nonempty residues, together with their residues: **Grow** computes the total function from $(\mathrm{Excl} \setminus \{\emptyset\}) \times \mathrm{Quer}$ to $\mathit{FinPow}(\mathrm{Resp} \times (\mathrm{Excl} \setminus \{\emptyset\}))$ such that for each $\mu \in \mathrm{Excl} \setminus \{\emptyset\}$, for each $\kappa \in \mathrm{Quer}$,

$\texttt{Grow}\langle\mu,\kappa\rangle = \{\langle\rho, \mathit{Residue}\langle\mu,\kappa,\rho\rangle\rangle \in \mathrm{Resp} \times \mathrm{Matr} \mid \mathit{Residue}\langle\mu,\kappa,\rho\rangle \neq \emptyset\}$.

Finally, **Index** is the following algorithm: for each $\mu \in \mathrm{Excl} \setminus \{\emptyset\}$,

```
read μ;
set I := ∅, O := ∅, L := ∅, W := ⟨⟨ε, μ⟩⟩;
while W = ⟨⟨ν0, μ0⟩, ..., ⟨νm, μm⟩⟩;
      if μ0 = {θ};
      then set O := O ∪ {ν0}, L := L ∪ {⟨ν0, θ⟩}, W := ⟨⟨ν1, μ1⟩, ..., ⟨νm, μm⟩⟩;
      else if Grow⟨μ0, Query(μ0)⟩ = ⟨⟨ρ1, μ'1⟩, ..., ⟨ρl, μ'l⟩⟩;
           then set I := I ∪ {ν0},
                    L := L ∪ {⟨ν0, Query(μ0)⟩},
                    W := ⟨⟨ν1, μ1⟩, ..., ⟨νm, μm⟩, ⟨ν0ρ1, μ'1⟩, ..., ⟨ν0ρl, μ'l⟩⟩;
write ⟨I ∪ O, I, O, L⟩.
```

Suppose that $\mu \in \mathrm{Excl} \setminus \emptyset$. **Index** incrementally builds from scratch an index tree $\mathfrak{T}$ that analyzes μ. **Index** has three registers, **I**, **O** and **L**, in which it builds up the inner nodes, outer nodes and labeling of $\mathfrak{T}$. These registers are initially empty. It also has a working register **W** in which a sequence of node/nonempty-exclusive-matrix pairs keeps track of the relevant parts of a tacit marking of $\mathfrak{T}$. **W** is initially set to $\langle\langle\varepsilon,\mu\rangle\rangle$, indicating that matrix μ marks the root node in $\mathfrak{T}$. **Index** considers each node/matrix pair in **W** in turn until **W** is empty. If **Index** is considering a node/matrix pair $\langle\nu_0,\mu_0\rangle$ in which μ_0 is a singleton $\{\theta\}$ then

Index deems ν_0 to be an outer node with mark μ_0 and label θ,
updates **I**, **O** and **L** accordingly, and
deletes $\langle\nu_0,\mu_0\rangle$ from the head of **W**.

---

[9] For each set X, $\mathit{Card}(X)$ is the cardinality of X. For each nonempty finite $X \subseteq \mathbb{N}$, $\mathit{Max}(X)$ is the largest member of X.

[10] For each nonempty $X \subseteq \mathbb{N}$, $\mathit{Min}(X)$ is the smallest member of X.

If **Index** is considering a node/matrix pair $\langle \nu_0, \mu_0 \rangle$ in which μ_0 is a nonsingleton then

> **Index** deems ν_0 to be an inner node with mark μ_0 and label $\mathtt{Query}(\mu_0)$,
>
> updates I, O and L accordingly,
>
> deletes $\langle \nu_0, \mu_0 \rangle$ from the head of **W**,
>
> uses $\mathtt{Grow}\langle \mu_0, \mathtt{Query}(\mu_0) \rangle$ to generate a list of all responses to $\mathtt{Query}(\mu_0)$ with nonempty residues in μ, together with the residues, and
>
> for each response/nonempty-exclusive-matrix pair $\langle \rho, \mu' \rangle$ in the list, appends the node/matrix pair $\langle \nu_0 \rho, \mu' \rangle$ to the tail of **W**.

Thus, one can think of **W** as a list of node/matrix pairs awaiting consideration by **Index**. If **Index** deems the node of a node/matrix pair in **W** an inner node then **Index** uses **Grow** to calculate the daughters of the node and the matrices that mark them, and appends these node/matrix pairs to **W** for subsequent consideration. If **Index** deems the node of a node/matrix pair in **W** an outer node then **Index** calculates no daughters of the node. If **W** is empty then **Index** outputs $\mathtt{I} \cup \mathtt{O}$, I, O and L – that is, the nodes, inner nodes, outer nodes and labeling of $\mathfrak{T}$. [7] proves that **Index** computes from each nonempty exclusive matrix an index tree that analyzes the matrix.

Proposition 26. **Index** *computes a total function from* Excl $\setminus \{\emptyset\}$ *to* Tree *such that for each* $\mu \in$ Excl $\setminus \{\emptyset\}$,

> $\mathtt{Index}(\mu)$ *analyzes* μ.

Thus, proposition 26 shows that **Index** computes from a nonempty exclusive matrix μ an index tree that analyzes μ. Thus, **Index** effectively deduces from μ an index tree that together with **Clause** constitutes an index for μ with quality (Q4). Notice that **Index** improves upon our earlier index-deducing algorithm of [10], in that our earlier algorithm computes an index that runs **Query** repeatedly in order to classify an object, whereas **Index** bears all of the high computational cost of repeatedly running **Query** while computing an index that never runs **Query**.

To illustrate **Index** and the indices it deduces, consider the following continuation of the simple example at the end of the previous section. Upon input $\mathtt{Class}(\theta) = \{P, Q, R, S\}$, the registers of **Index** are initialized such that

$$\langle \mathtt{I} \cup \mathtt{O}, \mathtt{I}, \mathtt{O}, \mathtt{L} \rangle \text{ is empty and } \mathtt{W} = \Big[\langle \varepsilon, \{P, Q, R, S\} \rangle \Big].$$

Since **W** is not empty, **Index** begins the first performance of its while loop, considering node/matrix pair $\langle \varepsilon, \{P, Q, R, S\} \rangle$. Since $\{P, Q, R, S\}$ is not a singleton, **Index** must compute $\mathtt{Query}(\{P, Q, R, S\})$, and to this end, **Index** must compute $\mathtt{Weight}\langle \{P, Q, R, S\}, \kappa \rangle$ for each $\kappa \in \mathrm{Quer}_{\{P,Q,R,S\}}$, where

$$\mathrm{Quer}_{\{P,Q,R,S\}} = \left\{ \begin{array}{l} \boxed{:}, \boxed{:x}, \boxed{:y}, \\ \boxed{:, :}, \boxed{:, :x}, \boxed{:, :y}, \\ \boxed{:x, :}, \boxed{:x, :x}, \boxed{:x, :y}, \\ \boxed{:y, :}, \boxed{:y, :x}, \boxed{:y, :y} \end{array} \right\}.$$

For example,

$$Residue\langle\{P,Q,R,S\},\boxed{:},\boxed{a}\rangle = \{R,S\},$$
$$Residue\langle\{P,Q,R,S\},\boxed{:},\boxed{b}\rangle = \{P\},$$
$$Residue\langle\{P,Q,R,S\},\boxed{:},\boxed{c}\rangle = \{Q\},$$
$$Residue\langle\{P,Q,R,S\},\boxed{:},\boxed{-}\rangle = \emptyset,$$
$$Residue\langle\{P,Q,R,S\},\boxed{:},\boxed{\approx}\rangle = \emptyset,$$
$$Residue\langle\{P,Q,R,S\},\boxed{:},\boxed{\not\approx}\rangle = \emptyset,$$
$$Residue\langle\{P,Q,R,S\},\boxed{:},\boxed{\pm}\rangle = \emptyset,$$
$$Residue\langle\{P,Q,R,S\},\boxed{:},\boxed{\mp}\rangle = \emptyset, \text{ and}$$
$$Residue\langle\{P,Q,R,S\},\boxed{:},\boxed{=}\rangle = \emptyset.$$

Thus
$$\texttt{Weight}\langle\{P,Q,R,S\},\boxed{:}\rangle = 2.$$

In fact,
$$\texttt{Weight}\langle\{P,Q,R,S\},\boxed{:x}\rangle = 2,$$
$$\texttt{Weight}\langle\{P,Q,R,S\},\boxed{:y}\rangle = 2,$$
$$\texttt{Weight}\langle\{P,Q,R,S\},\boxed{:,:}\rangle = 4,$$
$$\texttt{Weight}\langle\{P,Q,R,S\},\boxed{:,:x}\rangle = 2,$$
$$\texttt{Weight}\langle\{P,Q,R,S\},\boxed{:,:y}\rangle = 2,$$
$$\texttt{Weight}\langle\{P,Q,R,S\},\boxed{:x,:}\rangle = 2,$$
$$\texttt{Weight}\langle\{P,Q,R,S\},\boxed{:x,:x}\rangle = 2,$$
$$\texttt{Weight}\langle\{P,Q,R,S\},\boxed{:x,:y}\rangle = 2,$$
$$\texttt{Weight}\langle\{P,Q,R,S\},\boxed{:y,:}\rangle = 2,$$
$$\texttt{Weight}\langle\{P,Q,R,S\},\boxed{:y,:x}\rangle = 2, \text{ and}$$
$$\texttt{Weight}\langle\{P,Q,R,S\},\boxed{:y,:y}\rangle = 2.$$

Thus, $\texttt{Query}(\{P,Q,R,S\})$ can be any of $\boxed{:}$, $\boxed{:x}$, $\boxed{:y}$, $\boxed{:,:x}$, $\boxed{:,:y}$, $\boxed{:x,:}$, $\boxed{:x,:x}$, $\boxed{:x,:y}$, $\boxed{:y,:}$, $\boxed{:y,:x}$ and $\boxed{:y,:y}$. Suppose that
$$\texttt{Query}(\{P,Q,R,S\}) = \boxed{:}.$$

Then
$$\texttt{Grow}\langle\{P,Q,R,S\},\texttt{Query}(\{P,Q,R,S\})\rangle$$
$$= \{\langle\boxed{a},\{R,S\}\rangle,\langle\boxed{b},\{P\}\rangle,\langle\boxed{c},\{Q\}\rangle\},$$

and upon completing the first performance of its while loop, the registers of **Index** are such that

$$\langle \texttt{I} \cup \texttt{O}, \texttt{I}, \texttt{O}, \texttt{L}\rangle = \textcircled{\varepsilon}\,\boxed{:} \text{ and } \texttt{W} = \begin{bmatrix} \langle\boxed{a},\{R,S\}\rangle, \\ \langle\boxed{b},\{P\}\rangle, \\ \langle\boxed{c},\{Q\}\rangle \end{bmatrix}.$$

Since **W** is not empty, **Index** begins the second performance of its while loop, considering node/matrix pair $\langle\boxed{a},\{R,S\}\rangle$. Since $\{R,S\}$ is not a singleton, **Index** must compute $\mathtt{Query}(\{R, S\})$. Since

$\mathtt{Weight}\langle\{R, S\}, \boxed{:}\rangle = 2,$

$\mathtt{Weight}\langle\{R, S\}, \boxed{:x}\rangle = 1,$

$\mathtt{Weight}\langle\{R, S\}, \boxed{:y}\rangle = 2,$

$\mathtt{Weight}\langle\{R, S\}, \boxed{:, :}\rangle = 2,$

$\mathtt{Weight}\langle\{R, S\}, \boxed{:, :x}\rangle = 2,$

$\mathtt{Weight}\langle\{R, S\}, \boxed{:, :y}\rangle = 2,$

$\mathtt{Weight}\langle\{R, S\}, \boxed{:x, :}\rangle = 2,$

$\mathtt{Weight}\langle\{R, S\}, \boxed{:x, :x}\rangle = 2,$

$\mathtt{Weight}\langle\{R, S\}, \boxed{:x, :y}\rangle = 1,$

$\mathtt{Weight}\langle\{R, S\}, \boxed{:y, :}\rangle = 2,$

$\mathtt{Weight}\langle\{R, S\}, \boxed{:y, :x}\rangle = 1,$ and

$\mathtt{Weight}\langle\{R, S\}, \boxed{:y, :y}\rangle = 2,$

$\mathtt{Query}(\{R, S\})$ can be any of $\boxed{:x}$, $\boxed{:x, :y}$ and $\boxed{:y, :x}$. Suppose that

$\mathtt{Query}(\{R, S\}) = \boxed{:x}.$

Then

$\mathtt{Grow}\langle\{R, S\}, \mathtt{Query}(\{R, S\})\rangle = \{\langle\boxed{b}, \{S\}\rangle, \langle\boxed{c}, \{R\}\rangle\},$

and upon completing the second performance of its while loop, the registers of **Index** are such that

$\langle \mathtt{I} \cup \mathtt{O}, \mathtt{I}, \mathtt{O}, \mathtt{L}\rangle =$ 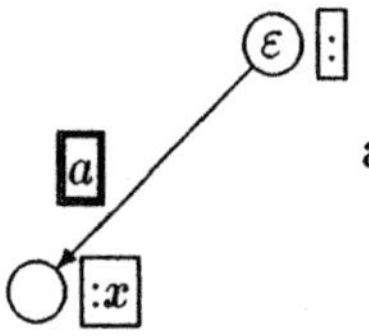

and $\mathtt{W} = \begin{bmatrix} \langle\boxed{b}, \{P\}\rangle, \\ \langle\boxed{c}, \{Q\}\rangle, \\ \langle\boxed{a\,b}, \{S\}\rangle, \\ \langle\boxed{a\,c}, \{R\}\rangle \end{bmatrix}.$

Since **W** is still not empty, **Index** begins the third performance of its while loop, considering node/matrix pair $\langle\boxed{b}, \{P\}\rangle$. However, since $\{P\}$ is a singleton, **Index** need not compute $\mathtt{Query}(\{P\})$. Instead, upon completing the third performance of its while loop, the registers of **Index** are such that

$\langle \mathtt{I} \cup \mathtt{O}, \mathtt{I}, \mathtt{O}, \mathtt{L}\rangle =$ 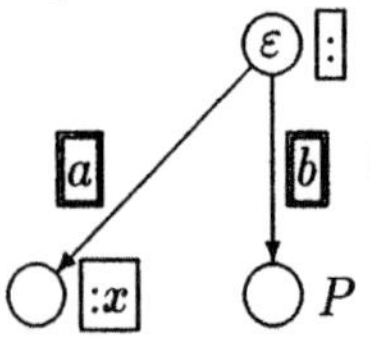

and $\mathtt{W} = \begin{bmatrix} \langle\boxed{c}, \{Q\}\rangle, \\ \langle\boxed{a\,b}, \{S\}\rangle, \\ \langle\boxed{a\,c}, \{R\}\rangle \end{bmatrix}.$

Index performs its while loop three more times. Upon completing the fourth performance, the registers of **Index** are such that

$\langle \mathtt{I} \cup \mathtt{O}, \mathtt{I}, \mathtt{O}, \mathtt{L}\rangle =$ 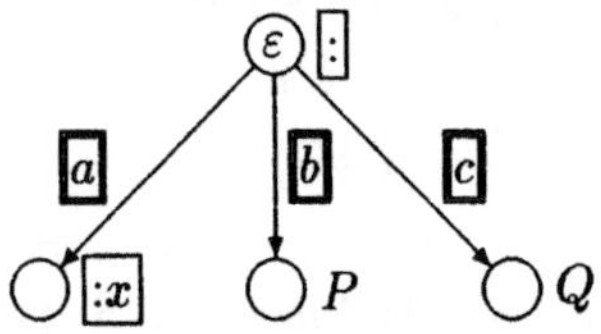

and $\mathtt{W} = \begin{bmatrix} \langle\boxed{a\,b}, \{S\}\rangle, \\ \langle\boxed{a\,c}, \{R\}\rangle \end{bmatrix},$

upon completing the fifth, they are such that

$\langle \mathtt{I} \cup \mathtt{O}, \mathtt{I}, \mathtt{O}, \mathtt{L} \rangle =$

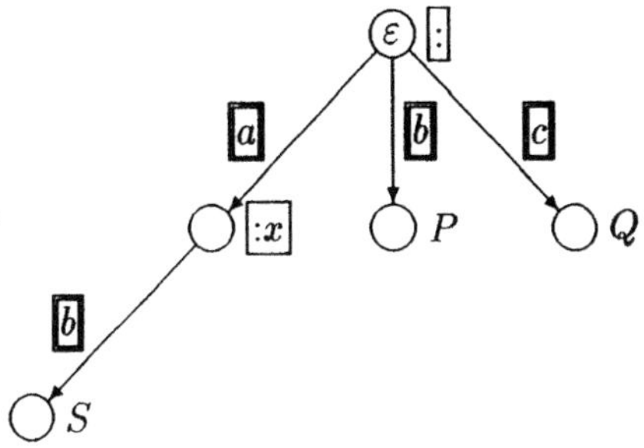

and $\mathtt{W} = \left[\langle \boxed{a}\boxed{c}, \{R\} \rangle \right]$,

and upon completing the sixth, they are such that

$\langle \mathtt{I} \cup \mathtt{O}, \mathtt{I}, \mathtt{O}, \mathtt{L} \rangle =$

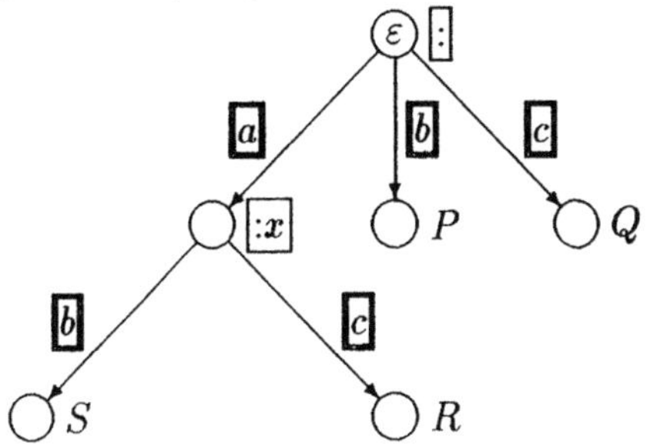

and $\mathtt{W} = []$.

Since **W** is now empty, **Index** outputs

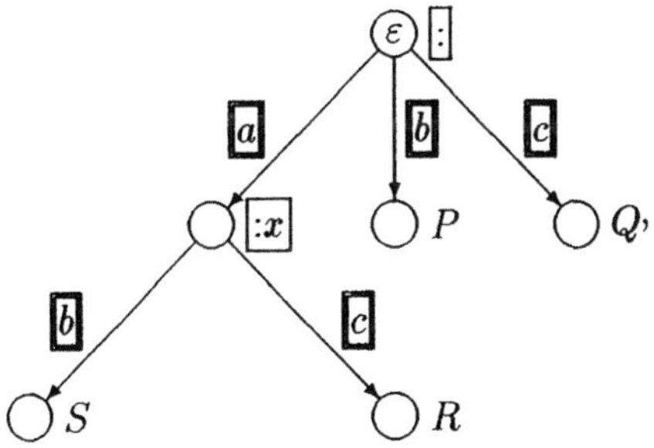

an index tree $\mathfrak{T}$ that, under marking

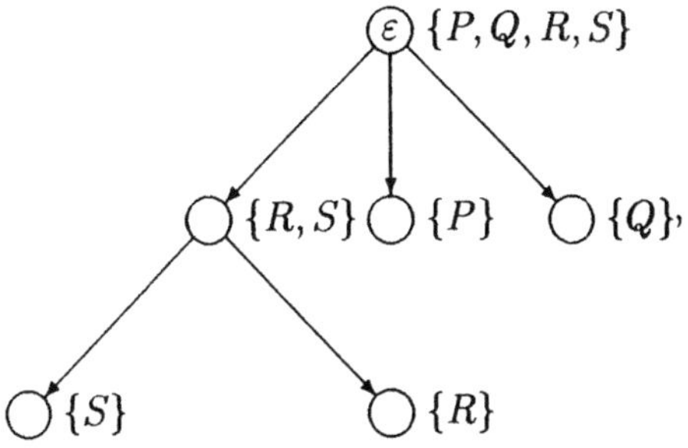

analyzes $\mathtt{Class}(\theta)$. Thus, $\mathfrak{T}$ enables any object in the denotation of θ to be classified, according to the classification $\mathtt{Class}(\theta)$, with responses to at most two queries.

6 Conclusions

In this paper we have presented a device that computes from a finite SRL theory (i) an exhaustive matrix whose constituent clauses denote disjoint, exhaustive and not necessarily-empty subsets of the denotation of the theory, and (ii) an index tree that enables a fixed traversal algorithm to interrogate an oracle in order to determine for each object in the denotation of the theory the unique clause in the exhaustive matrix that is true of the object. Thus, our device effectively deduces from a finite linguistic theory a classificatory system with qualities (Q1), (Q2) and (Q4). We conclude by making four points about our device.

Firstly, our device is computationally expensive – `Class` and `Index` are time exponential or worse – and makes no attempt to compute classificatory systems meeting qualities (Q3) and (Q5). Nonetheless, our device shows that the automatic deduction of classificatory systems meeting qualities (Q1), (Q2) and (Q4) is possible in principle. Only future research can show if the automatic deduction of classificatory systems meeting qualities (Q1)–(Q5) is possible in practice.

Secondly, an index queries an external oracle in order to elicit sufficient information to classify an object. However, certain inferential processes, such as parsing and generation, themselves pose queries, but to a classification, in order to further instantiate their current information about some objects. Though this is not strictly indexing, we envisage extending our index along the lines of [3] in order to yield a device that can efficiently support such inferencing.

Thirdly, given the complexity of natural language, a linguistic theory can easily overlook certain linguistic objects. If a classificatory system accurately deduced from a theory fails to classify an object then the object is identified as theoretically overlooked, thus indicating that a revision of the theory is necessary. Unfortunately, our device deduces from a theory a classificatory system that can occasionally classify an object the theory is not true of, much like the first classification of Sect. 2 classifies 'Herz' as exhibiting pattern (D9). To overcome this shortcoming, and render our device more scientifically useful, we must modify our device so that if `Clause` classifies an object then `Clause` seeks confirmation that the indicated clause is actually true of the object.

Lastly, our device deliberately delivers a classification with quality (Q1), but one can argue that the labels in a classification should name a hierarchy of subsets, not a partition. However, let quadruple $\langle \mathcal{L}, \ll, \mu, \# \rangle$ be an *exclusive hierarchy* iff

$\langle \mathcal{L}, \ll \rangle$ is a pre-order,

$\mu \in \text{Excl}$,

$\#$ is a total function from $\mathcal{L}$ to $Pow(\mu)$, and

for each $\lambda_1 \in \mathcal{L}$, for each $\lambda_2 \in \mathcal{L}$,

$\lambda_1 \ll \lambda_2$ iff $\#(\lambda_1) \supseteq \#(\lambda_2)$.

Intuitively, $\langle \mathcal{L}, \ll \rangle$ is a hierarchical classification such that for each $\lambda \in \mathcal{L}$,

λ is a label, and

for each interpretation $\mathcal{I}$, λ indicates $\bigcup_{\mu \in \#(\lambda)} \mathcal{M}_{\mathcal{I}}(\mu)$.

Meets, joins, etc. can be added to $\langle \mathcal{L}, \ll \rangle$ as required, and our index easily modified to suit. Though not all hierarchies can be construed as exclusive hierarchies, we believe that the majority of important linguistic hierarchies can be so construed.

References

[1] Bob Carpenter. *The Logic of Typed Feature Structures.* Cambridge Tracts in Theoretical Computer Science, number 32. Cambridge University Press, Cambridge, England. 1992.

[2] Thilo Götz. "A normal form algorithm for King's descriptive formalism." Term paper. Seminar für Sprachwissenschaft, Eberhard-Karls-Universität, Tübingen, Germany. 1993.

[3] Peter Graf. *Term Indexing.* Lecture Notes in Artificial Intelligence 1053. Springer-Verlag, Berlin, Germany. 1995.

[4] Stephan Kepser. "A satisfiability algorithm for a typed feature logic." SFB 340 technical report 60. IBM Deutschland GmbH, Heidelberg, Germany. 1994.

[5] Paul J. King. *A Logical Formalism for Head-Driven Phrase Structure Grammar.* Doctoral thesis. The University of Manchester, Manchester, England. 1989.

[6] Paul J. King. "An expanded logical formalism for head-driven phrase structure grammar." SFB 340 technical report 59. IBM Deutschland GmbH, Heidelberg, Germany. 1994.

[7] Paul J. King and Kiril Iv. Simov. "The automatic deduction of classificatory systems from linguistic theories." Unpublished manuscript. 1997.

[8] Carl J. Pollard and Ivan A. Sag. *Information-Based Syntax and Semantics*, vol. 1. CSLI Lecture Notes 13. CSLI, Stanford, California, USA. 1987.

[9] Carl J. Pollard and Ivan A. Sag. *Head-Driven Phrase Structure Grammar.* University of Chicago Press, Chicago, Illinois, USA. 1994.

[10] Kiril Simov and Paul J. King. "Indexing of linguistic knowledge." In *Proc. Logical Aspects of Computational Linguistics* (lecture abstracts), pages 81–84. Nancy, France. 1996.

[11] Kiril Simov, Galia Angelova and Elena Paskaleva. "MORPHO-ASSISTANT: The proper treatment of morphological knowledge." In *Proc.* COLING'90, vol. 3, pages 453–457. Helsinki, Finland. 1990.

[12] Kiril Simov, Elena Paskaleva, Mariana Damova and Milena Slavcheva. "MORPHO-ASSISTANT: A knowledge-based system for Bulgarian morphology." In *Proc. Third Conference on Applied Natural Language Processing* (systems demonstrations), pages 17–18. Trento, Italy. 1992.

A Belief-Centered Treatment of Pragmatic Presupposition

Lucia H.B.Manara *[1] and Anne De Roeck[2]

[1] Departamento de Computação
Universidade Estadual Paulista
São José do Rio Preto-SP-Brazil
manalh@essex.ac.uk
[2] Department of Computer Science
University of Essex
Colchester - Essex CO4 3SQ, UK
deroe@essex.ac.uk

Abstract. Traditional, semantic, accounts of presupposition centre on truth conditional treatments relying on entailments. In contrast, our work concentrates on the investigation of presupposition as a pragmatic phenomenon which interacts with agents' beliefs. Several accounts (e.g., [1],[2],[5],[6],[7],[8],[23]) have taken contextual factors into account. However, they run into problems caused by the consequences of the basic possible world based notions of propositionhood they deploy, which prevent the formulation of partial, revisable information states.
Starting from a notion of proposition developed in property theory ([20],[21],[22]), we develop a formal model of contexts as partial beliefs entertained by agents, who do not necessarily hold accurate or compatible views. We show how this model can be exploited in the treatment of the projection problem for conditionals, conjunctions and disjunctions. We show that a treatment along these lines provides an adequate model of complex presuppositional behaviour, including the projection problem. We contrast our results with those obtained in other approaches.

1 Introduction

Traditional semantic accounts of presupposition, concerned primarily with truth conditions and entailment, lead to various well-known problems. We can point, mainly, to the following:

(i) Negation preserves presupposition ([4],[19]). Semantic theories of presupposition are built on a definition that takes into account the fact that presuppositions are sustained by both positive sentences and their negative counterpart. This could be captured by the definition below. (see [5] and [23]).

$$A \textit{ presupposes } B \textit{ if and only if } A \models B \textit{ and } \neg A \models B.$$

* Supported by a grant from the CNPq - Brazil, grant number 200492/92-6

However, under the standard definition of negation and entailment only tautologies are presupposed by a sentence, because only tautologies may be entailed by a sentence and its negation. (see Gazdar [5]). This suggests it is impossible to retain classical two-valued logic.
Several variations on these definitions, using three-valued logics or a kind of bivalence with truth value gaps, have been developed. Their proponents are committed to the claim that negation in natural language is ambiguous in order to capture the presuppositions of positive and negative sentences and to account for the fact that the sentence (1) below is not contradictory. See [5] for a critique of these theories.

(1) The King of France is not bald, for France has no king.

(ii) The example (1) shows that under certain conditions presuppositions are defeasible. This seems particularly the case for negative sentences. Defeasibility is non-monotonic, which makes it impratical to define under a classical notion of entailment.

(iii) The distinctive behaviour of presupposition in complex sentences (the projection problem) shows that presuppositions survive in linguistic contexts where entailments cannot. It was originally anticipated by Langendoen and Savin([11]) that the presuppositions of a sentence should be compositional, in the sense that the presuppositions of all constituents of a complex sentence will be projected as presuppositions of the complex sentence. This is not the case, and the particular behaviour of presuppositions in complex sentences turns out to be a really distinctive characteristic of presuppositions. For example, consider the sentences below.

(2) The King of France is (not) bald.
(3) There is a King of France.
(4) If there is a King of France, then the King of France is (not) bald.
(5) If John is right, then the King of France is (not) bald.
(6) Either there is no King of France, or the King of France is (not) bald.

(3) is presupposed by (2) and (5) but not by (4) and (6). In these cases the presupposition of the second sentence component follows from the first one.

(iv) Semantic accounts of presupposition do not cater for the dependency of presuppositions on contextual information. The example below provides evidence against any context-independent semantic theory of presupposition, and has been taken, in discussions, to show the context dependence of presuppositions.

(7) If Nixon invites Angela Davis to the White House, he will regret having invited a black militant.

Nixon will have invited a black militant is an elementary presupposition of the consequent of (7). If the context of utterance contains the information that

Angela Davis is a black militant, the elementary presupposition is not preserved. On the other hand, if it contains no information whether Angela Davis is a black militant, the elementary presupposition is preserved. As such, presuppositions raise questions not just about individual sentences and their truth or falsity but also about the uses of sentences in context.

Several pragmatic accounts of presupposition have been developed (e.g., [2],[5],[6],[7],[8],[9],[14],[17],[23],[24]). Though they take contextual factors into account, most of these theories run into problems as they require that presuppositions be entailed by the context, or that the presupposition be known by all participants prior to the utterance to avoid infelicity. In these frameworks, a tension emerges between the notion of contexts, which are essentially partial constructs, and the requirement of total information states invited by the definition of propositions as extensionally derived sets of total and consistent possible worlds.[3]

Our account avoids these problems. Like Gazdar ([5]), we attempt to explain presupposition behaviour in context in function of consistency. At the same time, we derive contexts from partial beliefs of agents who do not necessarily hold accurate or compatible views. We cast context as a consistent subset of agents' beliefs, namely, those propositions that are relevant to the situation. To achieve this, we use a two-valued notion of proposition taken from Property Theory ([20],[21],[22]). Whilst the behaviour of the partial belief states is governed by Obeid's K-T three-valued logic ([12],[13]) propositions remain classical. Our emphasis is not only on the behaviour of presuppositions in context, but also on the impact of agents' beliefs on all aspects of presupposition behaviour. In particular, we contend that only the beliefs of the agent can trigger the defeat, accommodation or failure of presuppositions. We consider the case where presupposition contributes new information (accommodation); where it confirms old information (satisfaction), and when it contains information that is inconsistent with the agent's belief state (failure/defeasibility). We present an account of the projection problem.

2 Context and Belief

Utterances are interpreted in contexts, and seem to receive different interpretations according to varying situations. We are aiming to state a pragmatic notion of presupposition relative to contexts, where a context is a "relevant" subset of an agent's beliefs.

[3] This tension underlies difficulties, for instance, in Heim ([6]), Beaver ([1], [2]) and Karttunen ([8]), who predict that *If the table is red, John's wife will be happy* presupposes *If the table is red, John has a wife*, as well as *Zorn's Lemma is consistent with the Axiom of Choice*.

2.1 The Model

It is our intuition that, when people communicate, they know different things, or there would be no point in communicating. This suggests that any realistic model of communication must allow for partiality in what agents know. Since agents retain inferential capabilities we assume their beliefs are consistent,[4] and the model represents agents as partial, consistent sets of propositions. This constrains the agent's reasoning capacity, which must now deal with partial information. Agents' beliefs may now also be subject to revision. An agent can only interpret an utterance with respect to what (s)he knows. Consequently, we cast contexts as a consistent subset of an agent's beliefs, namely those propositions which bear on the interpretation of the utterance on hand. Interpretation relies on maintaining consistency in the context whilst adding the utterance's information. Failure to complete the proof will point to those propositions which induce failure. This model, and an accompanying implementation, was first developed to deal with modal and hypothetical questions ([3]). It builds on the definition of proposition taken from Property Theory ([20],[21],[22]), a weak first order theory with fine grained intensionality, which allows a classical two-valued notion of proposition whilst maintaining partial information states governed by three-valued logic ([12],[13]). We use the framework to model the effects of context on presupposition behaviour in the interpretation process.

Property Theory vs Possible Worlds. In the semantic literature the notion of possible worlds is often introduced into the representation language in order to account for intensionality. In such approaches, a proposition is a function which associates with each world or circumstance a truth value. Semantic frameworks along these lines are not always easy to consolidate with the requirements of partial contexts. To begin with, propositions which are truthfunctionally equivalent (say, p and q) are indistinguishable and an account of knowledge and belief based in such frameworks forces us to conclude that if an agent knows p, (s)he must also know q. Secondly, where such frameworks are used to model a partial common ground, Beaver ([1]) points out that these are still defined in terms of total, consistent worlds. This means that common grounds cannot be flawed in some domains and consistent in others.[5] Finally, in such frameworks, inconsistency, once reached, is irrecoverable and, presumably, communicating agents cannot hold contradictory beliefs.
In order to avoid these complications, we require an intensional, fine grained notion of proposition, compatible with partial information states in which contradiction is recoverable and beliefs can be revised. A number of such theories

[4] This requirement is introduced for simplicity and can be weakened to apply only to contexts, not to the entire belief state of an agent.

[5] Beaver [1] points out this can be remedied by viewing propositions and not worlds as objects of common ground and dropping the assumption of completion under logical closure. This leads to a variety of technical difficulties with inference.

exist. In our case, we used Turner's Property Theory ([20], [21], [22]).[6]
In Turner's Property Theory propositions, properties and relations are basic, and are independent of truth conditions or sets. The theory builds in the first instance, a language of terms: essentially the untyped λ-calculus, with additional logical constants. Some of these terms will correspond to propositions. Complex propositions are defined axiomatically by introducing appropriate logical constants. Some propositions will be true propositions. The truth of complex proposition will depend on the truth of the constituent propositions. Properties are terms that form propositions when applied to another term. λ-application models the act of predication. The truth functional behaviour of terms is formalised in a meta language of well formed formulae (wff): a first order logic with two primitive predicates: P for "is a proposition", and T, for "is a true proposition". Axioms governing T are only significant for terms that are propositions. The result is a highly intensional theory as the notion of equality is that of the λ-calculus, and not based on the notion of logical equivalence. Two propositions can be logically equivalent without being the same proposition.

Formal Theory. The following is taken from Turner ([21]) and presents a formalization of the language of terms (the untyped λ-calculus), well-formed formulae (wff) and the axioms that provide the closure conditions for propositions (P) and true propositions (T).

The Language of Terms
Basic Vocabulary:

Individual variables	x,y,z,...
Individual constants	c,d,e,...
Logical constants	$\wedge$, $\vee$, $\neg$, $\Rightarrow$, $\Leftrightarrow$, Ξ, Θ, $\approx$

Inductive Definition of Terms:

(i) Every variable or constant is a term
(ii) If t is a term and x is a variable then $\lambda x.t$ is a term.
(iii) If t and t' are terms then (tt') is a term.

The Language of Wff
Inductive Definition of Wff:

(i) If t and s are terms then $s = t$, P(t), T(t) are atomic wff.
(ii) If ϕ and ϕ' are wff then $\phi \& \phi'$, $\phi \vee \phi'$, $\phi \rightarrow \phi'$, $\sim\phi$ are wff.
(iii) If ϕ is a wff and x a variable then $\exists x\phi$ and $\forall x\phi$ are wff.

The theory is governed by the following axioms:

[6] The decision was influenced by the fact that a number of NLP based implementations of Turner's Property Theory exist.

Axioms of the $\lambda\beta$-Calculus

$\lambda x.t = \lambda y.t[y/x]$ y not free in t
$(\lambda x.t)t' = t[t'/x]$

This defines the equivalence of terms.

Axioms of Propositions

(i) $P(t)$ & $P(s) \rightarrow P(t \wedge s)$
(ii) $P(t)$ & $P(s) \rightarrow P(t \vee s)$
(iii) $P(t)$ & $P(s) \rightarrow P(t \Rightarrow s)$
(iv) $P(t) \rightarrow P(\neg t)$
(v) $\forall x P(t) \rightarrow P(\Theta \lambda x.t)$
(vi) $\forall x P(t) \rightarrow P(\Xi \lambda x.t)$
(vii) $P(s \approx t)$

P characterises those terms that have the status of propositions.

Axioms of Truth

(i) $P(t)$ & $P(s) \rightarrow (T(t \wedge s) \leftrightarrow T(t)$ & $T(s))$
(ii) $P(t)$ & $P(s) \rightarrow (T(t \vee s) \leftrightarrow T(t) \text{ v } T(s))$
(iii) $P(t)$ & $P(s) \rightarrow (T(t \Rightarrow s) \leftrightarrow T(t) \rightarrow T(s))$
(iv) $P(t) \rightarrow (T(\neg t) \leftrightarrow \sim T(t))$
(v) $\forall x P(t) \rightarrow (T(\Theta \lambda x.t) \leftrightarrow \forall x T(t))$
(vi) $\forall x P(t) \rightarrow (T(\Xi \lambda x.t) \leftrightarrow \exists x T(t))$
(vii) $T(s \approx t) \leftrightarrow s = t$
(viii) $T(t) \rightarrow P(t)$

T characterises those terms that correspond to true propositions.

Relations are defined recursively:

(i) $\mathcal{R}el_0\, t \leftrightarrow P(t)$
(ii) $\mathcal{R}el_n(\lambda x.t) \leftrightarrow \mathcal{R}el_{n-1}(t)$

Properties and propositions are 1 and 0 place relations respectively.

Partial Information States. We are now in a position to model contexts as consistent collections of propositions and to determine the logical regimen governing them. K-T is a propositional, non-monotonic logic which employs Kleene's strong three-valued connectives ([10]), and which is extended with two modal operators (the language can be propositional as the knowledge base is assumed sorted and closed). The semantics of the logic is expressed in terms of states of partial information which allow an agent to be uncertain about the truth or falsity of her/his knowledge, and where possible, to make assumptions on the basis of what is not known to be false. Complete information is hard to obtain, even in the most manageable situations: in most cases, a reasoner does not know everything that is pertinent to the investigation at hand. There are propositions whose truth status cannot be decided. Traditionally, the issue of revision and partiality is addressed at the level of the proposition, where (non-monotonic) formalisms resort to adding intermediary truth values between truth and falsity. This, in fact, is one of the basic and most important features which distinguishes three-valued logics from the classical ones. Apart from the fact that this is intuitively unappealing (in the sense that propositions seem to be things that are true or false - but which one need not know whether they are true or false), this traditional approach has a further disadvantage in that it causes logical difficulties. In particular A→A is not an axiom of such logics. The model we propose - that of deploying partial collections of classical two-valued propositions in belief states governed by a three-valued logic (in this case K-T) - has none of these disadvantages.

The Logic K-T. In K-T ([3],[12],[13]) a proposition is either accepted as true, accepted as false or not known at all. The basic language L_{K-T} which we shall use is a propositional logic. Starting with primitive propositions True, False, p,q,r,... more complicated ones are formed via closure under negation ¬, conjunction &, disjunction ∨, implication → and epistemic possibility M. That is, if A and B are wff then so are ¬A, A&B, A∨B, A→B and MA. Let N be the dual of M, i.e. NA=¬M¬A. →, & and ∨ are Kleene's strong connectives ([10]). Given A, MA is false if A is false, otherwise MA is true. ¬, & and M may be taken as primitives. ∨ and → may be defined in terms of & and ¬ as follows:

Definition KT1. A ∨ B = ~(¬A & ¬B)

Definition KT2. (A → B) = ¬A ∨ B

Let A ↔ B stand for (A → B) & (B → A). Note that A → B is undefined if both A and B are undefined. We also define a truth functional implication ⊃ as follows:

Definition KT3. (A ⊃ B) = M(¬A & B) ∨ ¬A ∨ B.
⊃ is truth functional in the sense that the truth value of A ⊃ B is true if both A and B have the same truth value. Let A = B stand for (A ⊃ B) & (B ⊃ A).

Definition KT4. A model structure for L_{K-T} is K = ⟨B,R,g⟩ where B is a non-empty set, R is a binary relation on B and g is a truth assignment function g for atomic wffs. The interpretation of R may be thought of as "epistemically possible" extension between states. Given b, b_1 are members of B, we shall write b R b_1 to mean that the state b_1 is an "epistemically possible" extension of the state b.

We employ the notation K $\vdash_g$ A (resp. K $\dashv_g$) to mean that A is accepted as true (resp. false) in K with respect to g. For convenience, reference to g will be omitted except when a confusion may arise. Let A, B be wffs, then the truth $\vdash$ and the falsity $\dashv$ notions are recursively defined as follows:

Definition KT5.

(i)	K,b $\vdash$ True
(ii)	K,b $\vdash$ p iff g(b,p) = True for p atomic
(iii)	K,b $\vdash$ A & B iff K,b $\vdash$ A and K,b $\vdash$ B
(iv)	K,b $\vdash$ $\neg$A iff K,b $\dashv$ A
(v)	K,b $\vdash$ MA iff ($\exists$ $b_1 \in$ B) (b R b_1 and K,b_1 $\not\vdash$ $\neg$A)
(i')	K,b $\dashv$ False
(ii')	K,b $\dashv$ p iff g(b,p) = False for p atomic
(iii')	K,b $\dashv$ A & B iff K,b $\dashv$ A or K,b $\dashv$ B
(iv')	K,b $\dashv$ $\neg$A iff K,b $\vdash$ A
(v')	K,b $\dashv$ MA iff ($\forall$ $b_1 \in$ B) (if b R b_1 then K,b_1 $\vdash$ $\neg$A)

The logic K-T is the smallest set of L_{K-T} which is closed under the following axiom schemas and inference rules. We shall write $\vdash_{K-T}$ A to mean that A is a "theorem" of K-T.

Axiom Schemas:

(a1) A $\supset$ (B $\supset$ A & B)
(a2) A $\supset$ (B $\rightarrow$ A)
(a3) A & B $\supset$ A | A & B $\supset$ B
(a4) (A $\rightarrow$ B) $\supset$ ((B $\rightarrow$ C) $\supset$ (A $\rightarrow$ C))
(a5) $\neg\neg$ A $\equiv$ A
(a6) $\neg$(A & B) $\equiv$ ($\neg$A $\vee$ $\neg$B)
(a7) A $\rightarrow$ MA

Inference Rules:
Modus Ponens for $\supset$ together with (r1), (r2) and (r3).

(r1) From $\neg$A $\vee$ B infer $\neg$MA $\vee$ B
(r2) From A $\supset$ B infer MA $\rightarrow$ MB
(r3) If not($\vdash$ $\neg$A) then $\vdash$ MA

Note that (r3) states that from the inability to infer $\neg$A infer MA.

3 Pragmatic Presupposition for Simple Sentences

In this model, the utterance $\mathcal{U}$(S,$\mathcal{C}$,ϕ) of a sentence S with propositional content ϕ isolates a context $\mathcal{C}$, a subset of the hearer's beliefs. Note that lexically and syntactically ambiguous S may differ in propositional content and may isolate different contexts. The interpretation consists of a proof of ϕ within $\mathcal{C}$ under K-T. The context includes all and only those propositions necessary for such a

proof.[7] Failure to close the proof points to propositions which the agent may consider in a revision scenario.
In its application to presupposition, a number of elementary presuppositions are derived on the basis of lexical and syntactic clues.[8] Whether a particular elementary presupposition survives as a presupposition of the utterance depends on a number of conditions, embodied in a series of recursive definitions (Definition 1 to 8). Here, we start by exploring the base case for simple sentences. In the following section, we introduce the recursive rules for determining the presuppositions of complex sentences: conditionals, conjunctions and disjunctions.

3.1 Elementary Presupposition

Definition 1: Elementary Presuppositions (ϵ-presuppose)
A sentence S with propositional content ϕ ϵ-presupposes ρ if (i) S contains lexical items or syntactic constructs (called presuppositions triggers) that trigger ρ and (ii) $\{\phi\} \cup \{\rho\}$ is consistent.

Elementary presuppositions are candidate presuppositions which may or may not survive as presuppositions of the utterance. They are propositions which can be derived entirely on the basis of lexical and syntactic clues in the sentence, without any reference to context. Consider, for example, the sentences below. The (b) and (c) sentences (a.o) are elementary presuppositions of the (a) sentence.

(8) a. John does not regret lying to his parents.
......b. John has lied to his parents. (Factive)
......c. There is John. (Proper name)

(9) a. John's children are asleep.
......b. John has children. (Possessive)
......c. There is John. (Proper name)

(10) a. The King of France is bald.
.......b. There is a King of France. (Definite Description)
.......c. There is France. (Proper name)

Candidate presuppositions must, furthermore, be consistent with the propositional content of the sentence from which they derive. For example, *The King of France does not exist* has as an elementary presupposition *France exists*, but not *There is a King of France.*

[7] The decision as to which propositions to include in such a context is problematic, and is sensitive to the domain of discourse, but see [3] for some experimentation.
[8] This is common practise and we have implemented a parser which derives elementary presuppositions together with a semantic interpretation ϕ.

3.2 Presuppositional Effects

We intend to treat the following aspects of presupposition behaviour: presupposition as new information (accommodation), presupposition as the information taken for granted (satisfaction) and presupposition failure together with defeasibility.

The following definitions expand on the relationship a candidate presupposition may entertain with a context. Elementary presuppositions which do not meet the criteria laid out here will not survive, as they are undefined.

In the definitions below $\mathcal{U}$(S,$\mathcal{C}$,ϕ) is the utterance of sentence S with propositional content ϕ in context $\mathcal{C}$.

Definition 2: Accommodation (α-presuppose)
An utterance $\mathcal{U}(S,\mathcal{C},\phi)$ α-presupposes ρ in a context $\mathcal{C}$ iff (i) S ϵ-presupposes ρ; (ii) $\mathcal{C} \cup \{\rho\}$ is consistent and, (iii) $\mathcal{C} \not\vdash \rho$.

We define accommodation as the situation where an elementary presupposition contributes new information to the agent's belief state. Note that in the logic K-T, this will happen in all cases where the agent holds no prior beliefs which explicitly confirm or contradict the elementary presupposition in question. Consider, for example, the following exchange.

(11) a. Are you going to lunch?
.......b. No, I've got to pick up my sister. (Example from Stalnaker [18].)

A hearer who did not know whether I have a sister, can now do so by accommodating the new information.

Definition 3: Presupposition Satisfaction (σ-presuppose)
A presupposition ρ of an utterance $\mathcal{U}(S,\mathcal{C},\phi)$ is satisfied by the context of utterance $\mathcal{C}$ iff (i) S ϵ-presupposes ρ and (ii) $\mathcal{C} \vdash \rho$.

Satisfaction occurs when an agent already holds beliefs which confirm the information contained in an elementary presupposition. In the exchange

(12) a. Are you going for lunch?
.......b. I have a sister. I have to pick up my sister.

the presuppositon that I have a sister is already present in the context when interpreting the second sentence in (12b). It is then satisfied by the context of utterance. Similarly, suppose the exchange in (12) is initiated by my uncle. The presupposition that I have a sister is then part of the set of background beliefs. It is satisfied by the context of utterance.

Definition 4: Presupposition Failure
$\mathcal{U}(S,C,\phi)$ fails ρ iff (i) S ϵ-presupposes ρ and (ii) $C \vdash \neg\rho$.

Presupposition failure is the result of an elementary presupposition contradicting beliefs the agent already holds. Consider, the sentence *The King of France is bald* uttered in a context that contains the information that there is no King of France. In this context its presupposition *There is a King of France* fails.

Because we are working with partial belief states containing propositions which are not in grounded possible worlds, contradiction in a context is not irrecoverable. Indeed, it is possible to identify exactly which propositions give rise to the contradiction and devise a strategy for restoring consistency. Elementary presuppositions deriving from negative sentences are defeasible. Agents may defeat defeasible presuppositions to maintain consistency.

Definition 5: Defeasibility
$\forall\rho$ if $\tilde{S}$ ϵ-presupposes ρ then defeasible(ρ), where $\tilde{S}$ is a negative sentence.

If the elementary presupposition causing the contradiction is defeasible, consistency in the context can be restored by defeating it. For example, if the sentence *The King of France is not bald* is uttered in a context that contains the information that there is no King of France, it is possible for the hearer to interpret the sentence without being committed to the existence of the King of France, and to arrive at a reading where the King of France is not bald because there is no King of France, by defeating the presupposition.

If on the other hand, the candidate presupposition is not defeasible, the agent can restore consistency by either rejecting the utterance, or revising previously held beliefs. The decision as to which course of action to take rests with the agent and is beyond the scope of this work. If the sentence *John's children came to the party* is uttered in a context that contains the information that John has no children, its elementary presupposition *John has children* is not defeasible. It is difficult to accept this sentence in the set context. The agent will be in a situation of stalemate.

For our purposes, we equate pragmatic presupposition with accommodation.

Pragmatic Presupposition (Π-presuppose)
$\mathcal{U}(S,C,\phi)$ Π-presupposes ρ iff $\mathcal{U}(S,C,\phi)$ α-presupposes ρ.

3.3 The Model at Work - Examples

1. S = The King of France is bald, S ϵ-presupposes (a.o.) ρ = There is a King of France. (i) If in C nothing is known about the government system of France, ρ will be accommodated. (ii) If in C it is known that France has a king, then ρ will be satisfied. (iii) If in C it is known that France has no king, then ρ will fail.

Note that ρ is not defeasible.

2. S = The king of France is not bald. S ϵ-presupposes (a.o.) ρ = There is a King of France. If in $\mathcal{C}$ it is known that France has no king, ρ fails. Note however that ρ is defeasible (S is negative) and the agent may defeat ρ (leading to a reading where the King of France is not bald, because there is no King of France).

3. S = John's wife is away. ρ = John has a wife. (i) If in $\mathcal{C}$ it is not known whether John is married, then $\mathcal{U}$(S,$\mathcal{C}$,ϕ) α-presupposes ρ and thus Π-presupposes ρ. (ii) If in $\mathcal{C}$ it is known that John has a wife, then $\mathcal{U}$(S,$\mathcal{C}$,ϕ) σ-presupposes ρ. (iii) If in $\mathcal{C}$ it is known that John is not married, then $\mathcal{U}$(S,$\mathcal{C}$,ϕ) fails ρ.

4. S = John's wife is not away. ρ = John has a wife. If in $\mathcal{C}$ it is known that John is not married, then $\mathcal{U}$(S,$\mathcal{C}$,ϕ) fails ρ, but ρ is defeasible (S is negative) and the agent can choose to defeat ρ.

4 Complex Presuppositional Effects

Langendoen and Savin(1971) contended that presuppositions of a complex sentence should be derivable compositionally. Yet, in particular, conditionals have given rise to formulations of the projection problem where presuppositions of lower clauses are sometimes not inherited by the whole of the complex sentence. Truth conditional, entailment based accounts - such as [2],[6],[8] - tend to experience problems as the requirement that presuppositions are entailed by the context of utterance leads to incorrect predictions.[9] Most of these problems can be traced to the commitment such theories have to notion of truth (built in possible world foundations) rather than the simple requirement of consistency. Instead, our model of context, allows us to exploit the power of consistency in partial information states, regardless of the truth or falsity of the proposition involved.

Starting from the basic formulations given above, we propose a treatment which predicts correctly which presuppositions survive in complex sentences: conditionals, conjunctions and disjunctions. The definitions of pragmatic presupposition and defeasibility remain as they are.

Definition 6: Conditionals
Cond 1
An utterance $\mathcal{U}$(*if* S_1 *then* S_2, $\mathcal{C}$, $\psi \rightarrow \chi$), *where* S_1 ϵ-*presupposes* ρ_i *and* S_2 ϵ-*presupposes* $\gamma_{1...n}$, α-*presupposes* (σ-*presupposes,fails*) ρ_i *iff (i)* $\{\chi\} \cup \{\gamma_1, .., \gamma_n\} \cup \{\rho_i\}$ *is consistent or* ρ_i *is defeasible, and (ii)* $\mathcal{U}(S_1, \mathcal{C}, \psi)$ α-*presupposes* (σ-*presupposes,fails*) ρ_i.

[9] For instance, for Heim ([6]), Beaver ([2]) and Karttunen ([8]) the sentence *If John makes coffee, his wife will be happy* presupposes *If John makes coffee, he has a wife.*

Cond 2

An utterance $\mathcal{U}$(if S_1 then S_2, $\mathcal{C}$, $\psi \rightarrow \chi$), where S_1 ϵ-presupposes $\rho_{1...n}$, and S_2 ϵ-presupposes γ_i, α-presupposes (σ-presupposes, fails) γ_i iff (i) $\{\psi\} \cup \{\rho_1, ..., \rho_n\} \cup \{\gamma_i\}$ is consistent or γ_i is defeasible, and (ii) $\mathcal{U}(S_2, \mathcal{C}', \chi)$ α-presupposes (σ-presupposes,fails) γ_i, where $\mathcal{C}' = \mathcal{C} \otimes \{\psi\} \otimes \{ \rho_1, ..., \rho_n \}$.

$\mathcal{C}' = \mathcal{C} \otimes \{\beta\}$ is the consistent update of $\mathcal{C}$ with β by revising $\mathcal{C}$. Agents suspend prior beliefs when investigating the consequences of interpreting conditionals.

Examples:

5. S = If there is a King of France, then the Queen of France is bald. S_1 ϵ-presupposes ρ_1 = France exists. S_2 ϵ-presupposes γ_1 = France exists, γ_2 = There is a Queen of France. If $\mathcal{C}$ contains *France exists*, then $\mathcal{U}$(S, $\mathcal{C}$, $\psi \rightarrow \chi$) σ-presupposes ρ_1 and γ_1, and α-presupposes γ_2. $\mathcal{U}$(S,$\mathcal{C}$, $\psi \rightarrow \chi$) Π-presupposes γ_2.

6. S = If the King of France has a son, then the King of France's son is bald. S_1 ϵ-presupposes ρ_1 = France exists, ρ_2 = There is a King of France. S_2 ϵ-presupposes γ_1 = France exists, γ_2 = There is a King of France, γ_3 = The King of France has a son. If $\mathcal{C}$ contains *France exists* and *There is a King of France*, then $\mathcal{U}$(S, $\mathcal{C}$, $\psi \rightarrow \chi$) σ-presupposes ρ_1, ρ_2, γ_1, γ_2 and γ_3. $\mathcal{U}$(S, $\mathcal{C}$, $\psi \rightarrow \chi$) carries no pragmatic presuppositions. If $\mathcal{C}$ contains *There is no King of France*, then ρ_2 will fail as ρ_2 is not defeasible. $\mathcal{U}$(S, $\mathcal{C}$, $\psi \rightarrow \chi$) does not Π-presuppose.

7. S = *If there is no King of France, then the King of France is bald. S_1 ϵ-presupposes ρ_1 = France exists. S_2 ϵ-presupposes γ_1 = France exists, γ_2 = There is a King of France. Regardless of the content of $\mathcal{C}$, the utterance of S is unacceptable as γ_2 is not defeasible.

8. S = If the King of France does not exist, then the King of France is not bald. S_1 ϵ-presupposes ρ_1 = France exists. S_2 ϵ-presupposes γ_1 = France exists, γ_2 = There is a King of France. If in $\mathcal{C}$, it is not known that France exists, nor that France has a king, then $\mathcal{U}$(S, $\mathcal{C}$, $\psi \rightarrow \chi$) α-presupposes ρ_1, σ-presupposes γ_1 and γ_2 is canceled as it is defeasible. $\mathcal{U}$(S, $\mathcal{C}$, $\psi \rightarrow \chi$) pragmatically presupposes ρ_1.[10]

Definition 7: Conjunctions

Conj 1

An utterance $\mathcal{U}$(S_1 and S_2, $\mathcal{C}$, $\psi \wedge \chi$), where S_1 ϵ-presupposes ρ_i and S_2 ϵ-presupposes $\gamma_{1...n}$, α-presupposes (σ-presupposes, fails) ρ_i iff (i) $\{\chi\} \cup \{\gamma_1, .., \gamma_n\} \cup \{\rho_i\}$ is consistent or ρ_i is defeasible, and (ii) $\mathcal{U}(S_1, \mathcal{C}, \psi)$ α-presupposes (σ-presupposes,fails) ρ_i.

[10] Note that ρ_1 is also defeasible.

Conj 2

An utterance $\mathcal{U}(S_1$ *and* S_2, $\mathcal{C}$, $\psi \wedge \chi)$, *where* S_1 ϵ*-presupposes* $\rho_{1...n}$, *and* S_2 ϵ*-presupposes* γ_i, α*-presupposes (*σ*-presupposes,fails)* γ_i *iff (i)* $\{\psi\} \cup \{\rho_1, ..., \rho_n\} \cup \{\gamma_i\}$ *is consistent or* γ_i *is defeasible, and (ii)* $\mathcal{U}(S_2, \mathcal{C}', \chi)$ α*-presupposes (*σ*-presupposes,fails)* γ_i, *where* $\mathcal{C}' = \mathcal{C} \oplus \{\psi\} \oplus \{\rho_1, ..., \rho_n\}$.

$\mathcal{C}' = \mathcal{C} \oplus \{\beta\}$ is the consistent update of $\mathcal{C}$ with β by revising β. False conjunctions may carry presuppositions.

Example:

9. S = There is a King of France and the Queen of France is bald. S_1 ϵ-presupposes ρ_1 = France exists. S_2 ϵ-presupposes γ_1 = France exists, γ_2 = There is a Queen of France. If $\mathcal{C}$ contains *France exists*, then $\mathcal{U}$(S, $\mathcal{C}$, $\psi \wedge \chi$) σ-presupposes ρ_1 and γ_1, and α-presupposes γ_2. $\mathcal{U}$(S,$\mathcal{C}$, $\psi \wedge \chi$) Π-presupposes γ_2.

10. S = *There is no King of France and the King of France is bald. S_1 ϵ-presupposes ρ_1 = France exists. S_2 ϵ-presupposes γ_1 = France exists, γ_2 = There is a King of France. Regardless of the content of $\mathcal{C}$, the utterance of S is unacceptable as γ_2 is not defeasible.

11. S = There is no King of France and the King of France is not bald. ρ_1 = France exists, γ_1 = France exists, γ_2 = There is a King of France. If in $\mathcal{C}$, it is not known that France exists, nor that France has a king, then $\mathcal{U}$(S, $\mathcal{C}$, $\psi \wedge \chi$) α-presupposes ρ_1, σ-presupposes γ_1 and γ_2 is cancelled as it is defeasible.

12. S = If John is married and still living with his wife, then he will hate Peter's roommate. (If (S_1 and S_2) then S_3). S_1 ϵ-presupposes ρ_1 = John exists. S_2 ϵ-presupposes γ_1 = John exists, γ_2 = John has a wife. S_3 ϵ-presupposes δ_1 = John exists, δ_2 = Peter exists, δ_3 = Peter has a roommate. If in C it is known that *John exists* and *Peter exists* an utterance $\mathcal{U}$(S, $\mathcal{C}$, $\psi \rightarrow \chi$) σ-presupposes ρ_1, γ_1, δ_1, δ_2 and α-presupposes δ_3. $\mathcal{U}$(S, $\mathcal{C}$, $\psi \rightarrow \chi$) Π-presupposes δ_3.

Definition 8: Disjunctions

Disj 1

An utterance $\mathcal{U}(S_1$ *or* S_2, $\mathcal{C}$, $\psi \# \chi)$, *where* S_1 ϵ*-presupposes* ρ_i *and* S_2 ϵ*-presupposes* $\gamma_{1...n}$, α*-presupposes (*σ*-presupposes,fails)* ρ_i *iff (i)* $\{\psi\} \cup \{\rho_i\} \not\vdash \chi$, *and (ii)* $\{\chi\} \cup \{\gamma_1, ..., \gamma_n\} \cup \{\rho_i\}$ *is consistent, and (iii)* $\mathcal{U}(S_1, \mathcal{C}, \psi)$ α*-presupposes (*σ*-presupposes,fails)* ρ_i.

Disj 2

An utterance $\mathcal{U}(S_1$ *or* S_2, $\mathcal{C}$, $\psi \# \chi)$, *where* S_1 ϵ*-presupposes* $\rho_{1...n}$, *and* S_2 ϵ*-presupposes* γ_i, α*-presupposes (*σ*-presupposes,fails)* γ_i *iff (i)* $\{\chi\} \cup \{\gamma_i\} \not\vdash \psi$, *and (ii)* $\{\psi\} \cup \{\rho_1, ..., \rho_n\} \cup \{\gamma_i\}$ *is consistent, and (iii)* $\mathcal{U}(S_2, \mathcal{C}, \chi)$ α*-presupposes (*σ*-presupposes,fails)* γ_i.

Examples:
13. S = Either there is a King of France or the Queen of France is bald. S_1 ϵ-presupposes ρ_1 = France exists, S_2 ϵ-presupposes γ_1 = France exists, γ_2 = There is a Queen of France. If $\mathcal{C}$ contains *France exists*, then $\mathcal{U}$(S, $\mathcal{C}$, $\psi \vee \chi$) σ-presupposes ρ_1 and γ_1, and α-presupposes γ_2. $\mathcal{U}$(S,$\mathcal{C}$, $\psi \vee \chi$) Π-presupposes γ_2.

14. S = Either the King of France is in hiding or the King of France is wise. S_1 ϵ-presupposes ρ_1 = France exists, ρ_2 = There is a King of France, S_2 ϵ-presupposes γ_1 = France exists, γ_2 = There is a King of France. If $\mathcal{C}$ contains *France exists*, then $\mathcal{U}(S_1, \mathcal{C}, \psi)$ σ-presupposes ρ_1, and α-presupposes ρ_2. $\mathcal{U}(S_2, \mathcal{C}, \chi)$ σ-presupposes γ_1 and α-presupposes γ_2; $\mathcal{U}$(S, $\mathcal{C}$, $\psi \vee \chi$) Π-presupposes ρ_2 and γ_2.

15. S = *Either the King of France has a son or the King of France's son is bald. S_1 ϵ-presupposes ρ_1 = France exists, ρ_2 = There is a King of France. S_2 ϵ-presupposes γ_1 = France exists, γ_2 = There is a King of France, γ_3 = The King of France has a son. Regardless of the content of $\mathcal{C}$, S is unacceptable.

16. S = Either the King of France does not exist or the King of France is not bald. S_1 ϵ-presupposes ρ_1 = France exists. S_2 ϵ-presupposes γ_1 = France exists, γ_2 = There is a King of France. If in $\mathcal{C}$, it is not known that France exists, nor that France has a king, then $\mathcal{U}$(S, $\mathcal{C}$, $\psi \# \chi$) α-presupposes ρ_1, γ_1. γ_2 is canceled. $\mathcal{U}$(S, $\mathcal{C}$, $\psi \# \chi$) pragmatically presupposes ρ_1, γ_1.

5 Comparison with other work

Using our model, we successfully treat cases which are problematic for other approaches.

(a) *John does not realize that Zorn's Lemma is inconsistent with the Axiom of Choice.* (Gazdar([5]))[11]. Gazdar([5]) can never presuppose *Zorn's Lemma is inconsistent with the Axiom of Choice* because there are no worlds in which this is true. Our model predicts (a) Π-presupposes *Zorn's Lemma is inconsistent with the Axiom of Choice* in an empty context.

(b) *If France has an intelligent king, then the King of France is the only intelligent monarch in Europe.* (Soames([15])). Gazdar([5]) predicts (b) presupposes *There is a King of France.* In our model *There is a King of France* is satisfied, but not Π-presupposed.

(c) *If John has children, then Mary will not like his twins.* (Heim([6])). Gazdar([5]) predicts (c) presupposes nothing. Our model predicts (c) Π-presupposes

[11] For each case, the author who mentioned the problem is given in brackets

John has twins in contexts where nothing is known about John's children.

(d) *If John has twins, then Mary will not like his children.* (Heim([6])). Gazdar ([5]) predicts (d) presupposes *John has children.* Our model predicts this is not a pragmatic presupposition.

(e) *The King of France didn't come.* van der Sandt([24]) and Beaver([2]) predict inconsistency in contexts where there is no King of France. Our model specifies that the elementary presupposition *There is a King of France* is defeasible.

(f) *If John made coffee, then his wife will be happy.* (van der Sandt([24])). Heim ([6]) predicts (f) presupposes *If John made coffee, he has a wife* in contexts where it is not known whether John has a wife or not. In possible worlds accounts, like Heim's, presuppositions must be satisfied by the context of utterance (i.e., entailed by the context) in order for an utterance of S to be felicitous. Our model predicts (f) Π-presupposes *John has a wife.*

(g) *If the problem was difficult, then Morton isn't the one who solved it.* (Soames ([15])). Karttunen ([8]) and Karttunen and Peters([9]) filtering conditions predict wrongly that (g) presupposes *If the problem was difficult, then someone has solved it* and not, as in our model *Someone has solved the problem.* Beaver([2]) predicts as Karttunen ([8]) and Karttunen and Peters([9]). In his account presupposition is represented as a test of the context which is represented by sets of possible worlds: a presuppositional sentence is a valid utterance in a given context if its presupposition has no effect on that context, i.e., the presupposition must be entailed by the context of utterance.

(h) *Hilda used to beat her husband and she has stopped doing so.* (van der Sandt([23])). Gazdar([5]) predicts (h) presupposes *Hilda used to beat her husband.* Our model, correctly, predicts (h) presupposes nothing.

(i) *John has children and his sons are bald.* (Soames ([14])). Karttunen ([8]) and Karttunen and Peters ([9]) predict (i) presupposes *If John has children, then John has sons.* Our model predicts *John has sons.*

(j) *Either the King of France is one of the few intelligent monarchs in Europe or France does not have an intelligent king.* (Soames ([16])). Karttunen ([8]), Heim ([6]) and Beaver ([2]) predict that (j) presupposes *There is a King of France*, we predict that (j) presupposes nothing.

(k) *Either the King of France isn't wise or the French generals aren't under the King's control.* (Soames ([14])). Karttunen and Peters ([9]) predict that (k) presupposes nothing. Our model predicts that (k) presupposes *There is a King of France.*

(l) *If Haldeman is guilty, then Nixon is guilty, too.* (Gazdar ([5])). Gazdar predicts that (l) presupposes *Someone other then Nixon is guilty.* We predict that (l) presupposes nothing.

(m) *The King of France is not bald and France has no king.* (van der Sandt ([23])). Karttunen and Peters ([9]) cancel the elementary presupposition *France exists* by a special cancelling operator which neutralises all the elementary presuppositions in its scope. In our model only *There is a King of France* is defeated.

(n) *If all Smith brothers have children, then John Smith's children will probably inherit the family fortune.* ((Soames ([16])). Gazdar ([5]) presupposes *John Smith has children.* We presuppose nothing.

(o) *If John does not have children, then it wasn't his child who won the fellowship.* (Soames ([14])). Karttunen and Peters ([9]) predict that (o) presupposes *John has a child,* or nothing depending on whether negation is treated as a "hole" or a "plug". Our model predicts that (o) presupposes *Someone won the fellowship.*

(p) *Either all of John's children are bald, or baldness isn't hereditary.* (Soames ([14])). Karttunen and Peters ([9]) predict that (p) presupposes *Either baldness isn't hereditary or John has children.* Our model predicts that (p) presupposes *John has children.*

(q) *Either Bill met the King of Slobovia or Bill met the President of Slobovia.* (Soames ([14])). Karttunen and Peters([9]), Karttunen([8]), Soames([14]) predict that (q) presupposes *Bill met the King of Slobovia or Slobovia has a president* and *Bill met the President of Slobovia or Slobovia has a King,* in contexts in which is known that countries with kings do not have presidents. In our model (q) presupposes nothing in this context. In contexts where nothing is known about systems of government, (q) presupposes *Slobovia has a King* as well as *Slobovia has a President.*

6 Conclusions

We have presented a model of partial belief states which draw on a classical notion of presupposition, and we have shown its advantages in modelling presuppositional behaviour. We have presented a collection of recursive rules which predict accurately simple and complex presuppositional effects, including the projection problem. We have demonstrated, by means of extensive examples, how our approach solves problems encountered by traditional accounts of presupposition based on possible worlds and entailment.

7 References

1. D. I. Beaver. "The Kinematics of Presupposition". *Reader of the Fifth European Summer School in logic, language and information,* 1993.

2. D. I. Beaver. *What Comes First in Dynamic Semantics.* ILLC Prepublication Series LP-93-15, University of Amsterdam. Amsterdam, 1993.
3. A. de Roeck, R. Ball, K. Brown, C. Fox, M. Groefsema, N. Oeid and R. Turner. "Helpful Answers to Modal and Hypothetical Questions". *Procceedings of the 1991 ACL, European Chapter.* Berlin, 1991.
4. G. Frege. "On Sense and Reference". In P.T. Geach and M.Black editors, *Translations from the Philosophical Writings of Gottlob Frege.* Blackwell, Oxford, 1952.
5. G. Gazdar. *Pragmatics: Implicature, Presupposition, and Logical Form.* Academic Press, New York, London, 1979.
6. I. Heim. "On the Projection Problem for Presuppositions". *Proceedings of the West Coast Conference on Formal Linguistics,* 2:114-126. Stanford, 1983.
7. L. Karttunen. "Presuppositions and Compound Sentences". *Linguistic Inquiry* 4:169-193, 1973.
8. L. Karttunen. "Presupposition and Linguistic Context". *Theoretical Linguistics,* 1:181-194, 1974.
9. L. Karttunen and S. Peters. "Conventional Implicature". In C.-K. Oh and D. Dinneen editors, *Syntax and Semantics, Presupposition,* 11:1-56. Academic Press, New York, London, 1979.
10. S. Kleene. *Introduction of Metamathematics.* Van Nostrand, 1952.
11. D. T. Langendoen and H. B. Savin. "The Projection Problem for Presuppositions". In C. J. Fillmore and D. T. Langendoen, editors, *Studies in Linguistic Semantics,* pages 54-60. Holt, Reinhart and Winston, New York, 1971.
12. N. Obeid. "Partial Models Basis for Non-Monotonic Reasoning". Research Notes CSM-140. Department of Computer Science, University of Essex, U.K., 1990.
13. N. Obeid. "Three Valued Logic and Non-monotonic Reasoning". *Journal of Computers and Artificial Intelligence,* vol. 15, no. 6, 1996. (To appear)
14. S. Soames. "A Projection Problem for Speaker Presuppositions". *Linguistic Inquiry,* 10(4):623-666, Fall 1979.
15. S. Soames. "How Presuppositions are inherited: A Solution to the Projection Problem". *Linguistic Inquiry,* 13(3):483-545. Summer 1982.
16. S. Soames. "Presupposition", in D. Gabbay and F. Guenthner, editors, *Handbook of Philosophical Logic - Topics in the Philosophy of Language,* pages 553-617. D. Reidel Publishing Company, Dordrecht, 1989.
17. R. C. Stalnaker. "Presuppositions", *Journal of Philosophical Logic,* 2:447-457, 1973.
18. R. C. Stalnaker. "Pragmatic Presuppositions", In M.K. Munitz and P.K. Unger, editors, *Semantics and Philosophy,* pages 197-213. New York University Press, New York, 1974.
19. P.F. Strawson. "On Refering", *Mind* 59:320-344, 1950.
20. R. Turner. "A Theory of Properties", *Journal of Symbolic Logic,* 52(2):455-472, 1987.
21. R. Turner. "Properties, Propositions and Semantic Theory", *Proceedings of the Workshop on Computational Linguistics and Formal Semantics,* Lugano, 1988.
22. R. Turner. *Truth and Modality for Knowledge Representation,* Pitman Press, 1990.
23. R. A. van der Sandt. *Context and Presupposition,* Croom Helm, London, 1988.
24. R. A. van der Sandt. "Presupposition Projection as Anaphora Resolution", *Journal of Semantics,* 9:333-377, 1992.

Connected Sets of Types and Categorial Consequence

JACEK MARCINIEC

Adam Mickiewicz University
Poznań, Poland
jacmar@math.amu.edu.pl

Abstract. Being a complement to [9], which concerns mainly general properties of infinite, unifiable sets of arbitrary terms, this paper provides an analysis of some specific features of sets of types and their behaviour under the influence of substitutions, especially unifiers.

1 Introduction

Although it is a common linguistic strategy to create a description of a whole (infinite) language on the basis of its small (finite) fragment, there are not too many formal theories describing the very process. In the field of categorial grammar, a promising attempt to formalise the procedures being mentioned have been undertaken by Buszkowski [1,2] and van Benthem [10]. The methods they used incorporate the standard unification algorithm. Following Buszowski's approach several further modifications of his procedure have been proposed. Buszkowski and Penn [3] described a discovery procedure which, unlike the earlier one, generate a non rigid output whenever the input data do not admit a rigid one. They introduced the new notion of *optimal unification* serving as an engine for their learning algorithm. In [8] a discovery procedure sensitive to negative postulates has been elaborated. There *restricted optimal unification* makes the task to be completed.

A learning algorithm is supposed to provide a solution — a grammar — both *compatible* with initial data and possibly simple. By *compatibility* is usually meant an ordinary inclusion between an input set of sentences (or subset of type-assignment) and the language (or type-assignment) generated by the output grammar. There can be, however, quite a difference between the two (often as the cost of simplicity). Thus, it is important to establish the relation under consideration precisely. In order to do this a further investigation of the behaviour of unification discovery procedures is necessary. In this paper we focus on a *connectivity* of sets of types, which is a property related to that introduced by Kanazawa with respect to grammars, namely *having no useless type* (cf. [4,5]). We examine the effect of various substitutions (also unifiers) on sets of types from the point of view of preservation of connectivity. These considerations lead to the conclusion that connectivity is a common property for the grammars being obtained by unification procedures analysed so far.

The paper is organised as follows. In section 2 we introduce our notation and outline necessary facts concerning unification (both standard and related to infinite sets). Although we formulate the results for types they are also valid for arbitrary terms. Then some basics about classical categorial grammars are reminded. In section 3 we deal with sets of functor-argument structures over the set of types, reducibility and the effect of substitutions on sets of reducible expressions. Section 4 provides a generalisation of Buszkowski's unification discovery procedure to infinite sample case. Finally, in section 5, we define a compact consequence operator on the universe of functor-argument structures.

2 Preliminaries

By ω we denote the set of natural numbers.

Definition 1. The set of all *functor-argument structures* on the set of *atoms* V — $FS(V)$ — is defined as the smallest set satisfying the following conditions:

$$V \subseteq FS(V),$$
$$\text{if } A_1, \ldots, A_n \in FS(V) \text{ then } (A_1, \ldots, A_n)_i \in FS(V),$$
$$\text{for all } n \geqslant 2, 1 \leqslant i \leqslant n.$$

If $A = (A_1, \ldots, A_n)_i \in FS(V)$ then A_i is *the functor* whereas each A_j, for $j \neq i$, is *an argument* in structure A.

Definition 2. Let $A \in FS(V)$. A sequence $A_0, \ldots, A_k$ such that $A_0 = A$ and A_{j+1} is the functor of A_j, for all $j = 0, \ldots, k-1$, will be called an *f-path* in A. Elements of this f-path will be called *subfunctors* of A. We will write $B \angle^f A$ when B is a subfunctor of A. The only subfunktor of A which is an atom will be denoted $\uparrow_f(A)$ and referred to as *the main functor* of A.

Definition 3. For any $S \subseteq FS(V)$, $SUB(S)$ denotes the smallest set such that:

$$S \subseteq SUB(S),$$
$$\text{if } (A_1, \ldots, A_n)_i \in SUB(S) \text{ then } A_j \in SUB(S),$$
$$\text{for all } j = 1, \ldots, n.$$

$SUB(S)$ consists of all *substructures* of structures from S. For technical reasons we designate two subsets of the set $SUB(S)$: $Arg(S)$ — the set of all arguments of elements of $SUB(S)$ and $Fun(S)$ —the set of all functors of elements of $SUB(S)$. Observe that $Arg(S)$ and $Fun(S)$ do not need to be disjoint.

Definition 4. The *length* $l(A)$ of a functor-argument structure $A \in FS(V)$ is defined as follows:

$$l(A) = \begin{cases} 1 & \text{if } A \in V \\ \sum_{j=1}^{n} l(A_j) & \text{if } A = (A_1, \ldots, A_n)_i \end{cases}$$

The *height* $h(A)$ of functor-argument structure $A \in FS(V)$ we define:

$$h(A) = \begin{cases} 0 & \text{if } A \in V \\ max\{h(A_j) : j = 1, \ldots, n\} + 1 & \text{if } A = (A_1, \ldots, A_n)_i \end{cases}$$

We will write, that a set $T \subset FS(V)$ is bounded with respect to length (height) if $(\exists N \in \omega)(\forall t \in T)(l(t) \leqslant N)$ $((\exists N \in \omega)(\forall t \in T)(h(t) \leqslant N)$). $l(T)$ $(h(T))$ will denote $max\{l(t) : t \in T\}$ $(max\{h(t) : t \in T\})$ respectively. We admit the case $l(T) = \infty$ $(h(T) = \infty)$.

Definition 5. A mapping $\Phi : FS(P) \to FS(Q)$ is a *homomorphism* between sets of functor-argument structures if for all $(A_1, \ldots, A_n)_i \in FS(P)$ the following holds:

$$\Phi((A_1, \ldots, A_n)_i) = (\Phi(A_1), \ldots, \Phi(A_n))_i. \tag{1}$$

In what follows we assume that each mapping $\Phi : P \to FS(Q)$ expands to a homomorphism from $FS(P)$ to $FS(Q)$ according to (1).

For any mapping Φ and a subset S of its domain, $\Phi[S]$ will denote the image of S.

Definition 6. A set $Pr = Const \cup Var$, where $Const \cap Var = \emptyset$, is called a set of *primitive types*. Members of $Tp = FS(Pr)$ will be called *types*. For any $T \subseteq Tp$ we set: $Var(T) = SUB(T) \cap Var$, $Const(T) = SUB(T) \cap Const$, $Pr(T) = SUB(T) \cap Pr$.

Remark 7. In the case of types we will often use a standard notation, writing

$$x_1, \ldots, x_{i-1} \backslash x_i / x_{i+1}, \ldots, x_n$$

instead of

$$(x_1, \ldots, x_n)_i.$$

Definition 8. A *substitution* is any homomorphism $\alpha : Tp \to Tp$ fulfilling the condition $\alpha(c) = c$, for any $c \in Const$. By Σ we will denote the set of all substitutions. A substitution α is *atomic* with respect to a set of types T, if $(\forall x \in Var(T))(\alpha(x) \in Pr)$. A substitution α is *reversible* with respect to $T \subset Tp$, if there exists a substitution β, such that $(\beta \circ \alpha)[T] = T$. We say that a substitution σ *unifies* a set of types T if $\sigma[T]$ is a singleton. A set $T \subseteq Tp$ is said to be *unifiable* if there exists a unifier of T. A unifier η of T is called a *most general unifier* (mgu) of T if, for any unifier σ of T, there is a substitution α such that $\sigma = \alpha \circ \eta$.

Proposition 9. *For any unifiable and finite set of types T, there exists an mgu of T, and it can be effectively found (cf. [7]).*

Two types u and v are said to be *variants*, if there are substitutions α and β such that $v = \beta(u)$ and $u = \alpha(v)$. If η_1 and η_2 are mgu-s of some $T \subseteq Tp$ then $\eta_1[T]$ and $\eta_2[T]$ are variants.

Proposition 10. *For any substitution α and a type t:*

$$l(\alpha(t)) \geqslant l(t), \tag{2}$$
$$\uparrow_f(\alpha(t)) = \uparrow_f(\alpha(\uparrow_f(t))) \tag{3}$$
$$\uparrow_f(t) \in Const \Rightarrow \uparrow_f(\alpha(t)) = \uparrow_f(t), \tag{4}$$
$$(\forall u \in Tp)(u \angle^f t \Rightarrow \alpha(u) \angle^f \alpha(t)). \tag{5}$$

2.1 Infinite set unification

According to [9], there exists a most general unifier of any (even infinite) unifiable set of types (or terms). Moreover

Proposition 11. *Let T be an infinite and unifiable set of types. There exists an atomic substitution α such that*

- *$\alpha[T]$ is finite,*
- *for each substitution η, if η is an mgu of $\alpha[T]$ then $\eta \circ \alpha$ is an mgu of T.*

It is important for our further considerations to look at the shape of a most general unifier with some more detail.

Definition 12. Let T be a set of types. A substitution $\ulcorner x : t \urcorner$, where $t \in SUB(T)$ and $x \in Var(T) \setminus Var(t)$ will be referred to as an *inner* substitution (for T).

Theorem 13. *Let T be a unifiable, possibly infinite set of types. There exists a most general unifier η of T and*

$$\eta = \gamma \circ \beta_m \circ \cdots \circ \beta_1 \circ \alpha,$$

where

- *α is atomic with respect to T,*
- *γ is atomic with respect to $\beta_m \circ \cdots \circ \beta_1 \circ \alpha[T]$,*
- *β_j, for $j = 1, \ldots, m$, is an inner substitution for $\beta_{j-1} \circ \cdots \circ \beta_1 \circ \alpha[T]$.*

Proof. (sketch) Let T be a unifiable set of types and let α be the substitution announced by Proposition 11. Then an mgu η of T must have a form $\gamma \circ \beta \circ \alpha$, where β is the result of the unification algorithm on the (finite) input $\alpha[T]$, while γ is atomic. Analizing the standard unification algorithm, one can easily observe that its output is always a superposition of some number of inner substitutions (cf. [7]). □

Definition 14. Let $\mathcal{T} = \{T_1, \ldots, T_n\}$ be a finite family of (possibly infinite) nonempty sets of types. A substitution σ is a unifier of $\mathcal{T}$ if it is a unifier of each T_i, $i = 1, \ldots, n$. A unifier η of $\mathcal{T}$ is called an mgu of $\mathcal{T}$ if, for any unifier σ of $\mathcal{T}$, there is a substitution α such that $\sigma = \alpha \circ \eta$.

The problem of unifiability of $\mathcal{T}$ can easily be reduced to that of set of types.

Definition 15. Let $\mathcal{T} = \{T_1, \ldots, T_n\}$ be a family of countable sets of types. Assume $T_i = \{t_i^0, t_i^1, \ldots\}$, for all $i = 1, \ldots, n$. Let $M = \sup\{card(T_i) : i \in \{1, \ldots, n\}\}$ (we admit the case $M = \infty$). In case $card(T_i) < M$ we set $t_i^j = t_i^0$, for all $M \geqslant j > card(T_i)$. We define

$$\bigotimes \mathcal{T} = \{(t_1^j, \ldots, t_n^j)_1\}_{0 \leqslant j \leqslant M}.$$

Proposition 16. *Let $\mathcal{T} = \{T_1, \ldots, T_n\}$ be a family of countable sets of types. Then:*

- *σ is a unifier of $\mathcal{T}$ iff σ is a unifier of $\bigotimes \mathcal{T}$*
- *η is an mgu of $\mathcal{T}$ iff η is an mgu of $\bigotimes \mathcal{T}$*

Below we recapitulate the main results from [9].

Theorem 17. *Let $\mathcal{T} = \{T_1, \ldots, T_n\}$ be a unifiable family of nonempty, possibly infinite sets of types. There exist a family $\mathcal{U} = \{U_1, \ldots, U_n\}$, mgus η of $\mathcal{T}$ and σ of $\mathcal{U}$ such that, for all $i = 1, \ldots, n$, U_i is finite, $U_i \subseteq T_i$ and $\eta[T_i] = \sigma[U_i]$.*

Example 18. An infinite set of types need not be unifiable, even though each its finite subset is unifiable:

$$x_1$$

$$(x_2, x)_1$$

$$((x_3, x)_1, x)_1$$

$$(((x_4, x)_1, x)_1, x)_1$$

$$\vdots$$

Theorem 19. *Let $\mathcal{T} = \{T_1, \ldots, T_n\}$ be a not unifiable family of nonempty, possibly infinite sets of types such that, for all $i = 1, \ldots, n$, T_i is bounded with respect to height. There exists a not unifiable family $\mathcal{U} = \{U_1, \ldots, U_n\}$ such that, for all $i = 1, \ldots, n$, $U_i \subset T_i$ and U_i is finite.*

2.2 Classical categorial grammars

Definition 20. By a *classical categorial grammar* we mean a triple

$$G = (V_G, I_G, s_G)$$

where a finite set of atoms V_G is called *the lexicon* of G, a mapping $I_G : V_G \to 2^{Tp}$ is called *the initial type-assignment* of G, $s_G \in Pr_c$ is called *the principal type* of G.

The terminal type-assignment $T_G : FS(V_G) \to 2^{Tp}$ is defined as follows:

$$T_G(v) = I_G(v), \text{ for } v \in V_G,$$
$$T_G((A_1, \ldots, A_n)_i) =$$
$$\{a_i \in Tp : (\exists(a_1, \ldots, a_n)_i \in T_G(A_i))(\forall j \neq i)(a_j \in T_G(A_j))\}.$$

Throughout this paper we will use the expression ***grammar*** in the meaning of classical categorial grammar. For any grammar G and $t \in Tp$, we define a *category of type* t: $CAT_G(t) = \{A \in FS(V_G) : t \in T_G(A)\}$. $FL(G) = CAT_G(s_G)$ will be called *the F-language generated by* G. A grammar G is said to be finite (*rigid*) iff $card(I_G(v)) < \aleph_0$ ($card(I_G(v)) = 1$), for all $v \in V_G$. A set L is *rigid* (*rigidly describable*) if $L = FL(G)$ ($L \subseteq FL(G)$) for some rigid grammar G. A grammar G is *compatible* with $L \subseteq FS(V)$ if $L \subseteq FL(G)$. For any grammars G and H we write $G \subseteq H$ iff $V_G = V_H, s_G = s_H$ and $I_G(v) \subseteq I_H(v)$, for all $v \in V_G$.

3 Type reduction and unification

The properties of infinite, unifiable sets of types, sketched in the preceding section, are subject to general characteristics of infinite sets of terms — no type specific properties were taken into consideration. Types, however, can be combined into complex, reducible expressions related to each other. Substitutions usually affect these relationships between reducible structures. In this section we analise the connection between reducibility an unification. Since we consider functor-argument structures over the set of types (being structures as well), we use brackets [and $]_i$ to build such structures and we reserve symbols $\mathbb{A}, \mathbb{B}, \ldots$ for elements of $FS(Tp)$. According to (1) we expand substitutions to homomorphisms on $FS(Tp)$. We also introduce an auxiliary notation: we will write $x._a\!\measuredangle.y$, if x is a direct argument of some subfunctor of y, that is if there exists a structure $(z_1, \ldots, z_n)_i$ such that $(z_1, \ldots, z_n)_i \angle^f y$ and $x = z_j$ for some $j \in \{1, \ldots, n\} \setminus \{i\}$.

Definition 21. We define the relation $\rightarrowtail \subset FS(Tp) \times Tp$ as the smallest relation satisfying the following conditions:

$t \rightarrowtail t$ for all $t \in Tp$,
if $\mathbb{A}_i \rightarrowtail (t_1, \ldots, t_n)_i$ and $\mathbb{A}_j \rightarrowtail t_j$ for all $j \in \{1, \ldots, n\} \setminus \{i\}$,
then $[\mathbb{A}_1, \ldots, \mathbb{A}_n]_i \rightarrowtail t_i$.

We say that $\mathbb{A}$ reduces to t, if $\mathbb{A} \rightarrowtail t$. A structure $\mathbb{A} \in FS(Tp)$ is *reducible* if there exists $t \in Tp$ such that $\mathbb{A} \rightarrowtail t$.

Proposition 22. *For all* $\mathbb{A} \in FS(Tp)$ *there exists at most one type* $t \in Tp$, *such that* $\mathbb{A} \rightarrowtail t$.

Lemma 23. *Let* $\mathbb{A} \in FS(Tp)$ *be reducible. Denote*

$a = \uparrow_f(\mathbb{A})$.

Clearly $a \in Tp$. *let* $a_0, a_1, \ldots, a_m$ *be the maximal f-path in* a. *Then there exists* $k \in \{0, \ldots, m\}$, *such that:*

1° $\mathbb{A} \rightarrowtail a_k$,
2° *for all* $l < k$ *there exists* $\mathbb{A}_l \in SUB(\mathbb{A})$, *such that* $\mathbb{A}_l \rightarrowtail a_l$,
3° *for all* $l < k$ *and for each* b, *such that* $b._a\!\!\not<^f\!.a_l$, *there is* $\mathbb{B} \in SUB(\mathbb{A})$, *such that* $\mathbb{B} \rightarrowtail b$.

Proof. We prove the lemma by structural induction. If $\mathbb{A} \in Tp$ then $m = 0$ and $k = 0$.

Assume that $\mathbb{A} = [\mathbb{A}_1, \ldots, \mathbb{A}_n]_i$ is reducible and our thesis holds for all $\mathbb{A}_j$, $j \in \{1, \ldots, n\}$. Since $a = \uparrow_f(\mathbb{A})$ then also $a = \uparrow_f(\mathbb{A}_i)$. By induction there is some k, such that $\mathbb{A}_i \rightarrowtail a_k$. Consequently $a_k = (a_{k_1}, \ldots, a_{k_n})_i$ where $a_{k_i} = a_{k+1}$ and $\mathbb{A} \rightarrowtail a_{k+1}$. It remains to prove 2° and 3° in the case $l = k$. However, $\{a_{k_j} : j \in \{1, \ldots, n\} \setminus \{i\}\}$ constitute the set of all direct arguments of a_k and $\mathbb{A}_j \rightarrowtail a_{k_j}$ for all $j \in \{1, \ldots, n\} \setminus \{i\}$. □

Definition 24. A type t is *attainable* from the set of types T, if

$$(\exists \mathbb{A} \in FS(T))(\mathbb{A} \rightarrowtail t).$$

Proposition 25. *If a type* t *is attainable from the set of types* T, *then* t *is a subfunctor of some element of* T.

Corollary 26. *The total number of primitive types attainable from the set* $T \subset Tp$ *cannot be greater then the cardinality of* T.

Definition 27. The set of types T is *connected* if the following two conditions hold:

$$(\forall x \in Var(T))(\exists \mathbb{A} \in FS(T))(\mathbb{A} \rightarrowtail x) \tag{6}$$

$$(\forall x \in Var(T))(\exists t \in T)(x._a\!\!\not<^f\!.t). \tag{7}$$

Remark 28. As we have already mentioned, our notion of connectivity corresponds to the concept of a grammar with no useless type introduced by Kanazawa in [4,5]. We use different name since there are some differences between the two notions.

Proposition 29. *For any connected set of types* T:

$$card(Var(T)) \leqslant card(T).$$

Definition 30. Let $T \subset Tp$ and let t_1, t_2 be two types attainable from T. We say that type t_1 depends on t_2 with respect to T — $t_1 \underset{T}{\leftleftarrows} t_2$ — iff

$$(\forall \mathbb{A}_1 \in FS(T))(\mathbb{A}_1 \rightarrowtail t_1 \Rightarrow (\exists \mathbb{A}_2 \in SUB(\mathbb{A}_1))(\mathbb{A}_2 \neq \mathbb{A}_1 \wedge \mathbb{A}_2 \rightarrowtail t_2).$$

Proposition 31. *For any set of types* T, *the relation* $\underset{T}{\leftleftarrows}$ *is transitive and irreflexive.*

Lemma 32. *For all $t \in Tp$, $\alpha \in \Sigma$ and $y \in Var$ the following hold:*

$$y \cdot_a \sphericalangle^f . \alpha(t) \Rightarrow (\exists x \in Var)(y \cdot_a \sphericalangle^f . \alpha(x) \vee y = \alpha(x)).$$

Proof. We prove the lemma by structural induction on t. If $t \in Pr$ then either $t \in Const$ and then $\{y \in Var : y \cdot_a \sphericalangle^f . \alpha(t)\} = \emptyset$, or $t \in Var$ and then $x = t$. Assume now that $t = (t_1, \ldots, t_n)_i$ and our thesis holds for each $t_1, \ldots, t_n$. Then $\alpha(t) = (\alpha(T_1), \ldots, \alpha(t_n))_i$. Let $y \in Var$ be such that $y \cdot_a \sphericalangle^f \alpha(t)$. Then either $y \cdot_a \sphericalangle^f . \alpha(t_i)$ and our thesis holds by induction, or $y = \alpha(t_j)$, for some $j \neq i$ which is possible only if $t_j \in Var$. □

The following theorem is a generalization of Kanazawa's main lemma concerning learnability of categorial languages.

Theorem 33. *Let $T \subset Tp$ be finite and connected and let α be a substitution irreversible for T, such that $\alpha[T]$ is also connected. Then*

$$card(Var(\alpha[T])) < card(Var(T)). \tag{8}$$

Proof. Assume that $Var(T) = \{x_1, \ldots, x_N\}$. Denote $t_j = \alpha(x_j)$ and $y_j = \uparrow_f(t_j)$ for all $j \in \{1, \ldots, N\}$. First we show:

$$Var(\alpha[T]) \subset \{y_1, \ldots, y_N\}. \tag{9}$$

Let $y \in Var(\alpha[T])$. Since $\alpha[T]$ is connected, by (6), we get $y = \uparrow_f(t)$ for some $t \in \alpha[T]$. Then there exists $t' \in T$ such that $t = \alpha(t')$. Let $\uparrow_f(t') = x_j$. Then by Proposition 10 we get

$$y = \uparrow_f(t) = \uparrow_f(\alpha(\uparrow_f(t'))) = \uparrow_f(\alpha(x_j)) = \uparrow_f(t_j) = y_j.$$

Thus we have proven (9), which implies $card(Var(\alpha[T])) \leqslant card(Var(T))$. Suppose that $card(Var(\alpha[T])) = card(Var(T))$. Then $y_k \neq y_l$ whenever $k \neq l$. Using Proposition 10, one easily derives:

$$(\forall t \in T)(\forall j \in \{1, \ldots, N\})(\uparrow_f(t) = x_j \Leftrightarrow \uparrow_f(\alpha(t)) = y_j). \tag{10}$$

We prove now that for all $j \in \{1, \ldots, N\}$, the following hold:

$$(\forall t \in \alpha[T])(y_j = \uparrow_f(t) \Rightarrow t_j \angle^f t), \tag{11}$$

$$y_j \underset{\alpha[T]}{\leftleftarrows} t_j, \tag{12}$$

$$y_k \cdot_a \sphericalangle^f . t_j \Rightarrow y_j \underset{\alpha[T]}{\leftleftarrows} y_k. \tag{13}$$

Indeed, (11) easily follows from (10) and Proposition 10. To prove (12) let us assume that $\mathbb{A} \rightarrowtail y_j$ for some $\mathbb{A} \in FS(\alpha[T])$. Let $a = \uparrow_f(\mathbb{A})$ and let $a_0, \ldots, a_m$ be the longest f-path in a. From Lemma 23 and Proposition 22, it follows that $a_m = y_j$. Then, by (11), there is $l \in \{0, \ldots, m\}$, such that $t_j = a_l$. Consequently, by Lemma 23 again, $\mathbb{A}_l \rightarrowtail t_j$ for some $\mathbb{A}_l \in SUB(\mathbb{A})$, which yields (12). In addition, $y_k \cdot_a\!\measuredangle^f\!.t_j$ implies $\mathbb{B} \rightarrowtail y_k$ for some $\mathbb{B} \in SUB(\mathbb{A})$, which justifies (13).

From Lemma 32 we obtain:

$$y_j \neq t_j \Rightarrow (\exists k \in \{1, \ldots, N\})(y_j \cdot_a\!\measuredangle^f\!.t_k). \tag{14}$$

Observe that $y_j \cdot_a\!\measuredangle^f\!.t_k$ implies $y_k \neq t_k$. Thus, by (13) and (14) we get:

$$y_j \neq t_j \Rightarrow (\exists k \in \{1, \ldots, N\})(y_k \neq t_k \wedge y_k \underset{\alpha[T]}{\Leftarrow} y_j). \tag{15}$$

Since α is irreversible for T, there must be sume y_{j_0} such that $y_{j_0} \neq t_{j_0}$. Then, by (15), there exists an infinite sequence $y_{j_0}, y_{j_1}, \ldots$ of variables from $Var(\alpha[T])$ fullfiling the condition that $y_{j_{k+1}} \underset{\alpha[T]}{\Leftarrow} y_{j_k}$ for all $k = 0, 1, \ldots,$ which is impossible by the properties of the relation $\underset{\alpha[T]}{\Leftarrow}$ and the finiteness of $Var(\alpha[T])$. The above contradiction has been derived from the supposition that $card(Var(\alpha[T])) = card(Var(T))$. □

Proposition 34. *Let T be any connected set of types. If a substitution α fullfills the condition:*

$$SUB(\alpha[T]) \subset \alpha[SUB(T)], \tag{16}$$

then the set $\alpha[T]$ is also connected.

Proof. Fix $x' \in Var(\alpha[T])$. By (16) $x' = \alpha(x)$ for some $x \in Var(T)$. Since T is connected, there exist $\mathbb{A} \in FS(T)$ and $t \in T$, such that $\mathbb{A} \rightarrowtail x$ and $x._a\!\measuredangle^f\!.t$. Then $\alpha(\mathbb{A}) \rightarrowtail \alpha(x) = x'$ and $x'._a\!\measuredangle^f\!.\alpha(t)$, which justifies the connectivity of $\alpha[T]$ since x' has been chosen arbitrarily. □

Proposition 35. *Let T be a connected set of types and let α be an inner or atomic substitution. Then $\alpha[T]$ is also connected.*

Proof. According to Proposition 34 if suffices to show that both kinds of substitutions mentioned fulfill (16). We use depth induction on $t' \in SUB(\alpha[T])$. The case $t' \in \alpha[T]$ is trivial. Assume that for some $t' = (t'_1, \ldots, t'_n)_i \in SUB(\alpha[T])$ there exists $t \in SUB(T)$, such that $t' = \alpha(t)$. We aim to show that the same holds for each t'_j, $j \in \{1, \ldots, n\}$. Fix j. There are two cases possible:
CASE 1: $t = (t_1, \ldots, t_n)_i$ — then of course $t'_j = \alpha(t_j)$.
CASE 2: $t \in Var$. Then α must be an inner substitution and $\alpha = \ulcorner t : t' \urcorner$. Moreover, $t' \in SUB(T)$ and $t \notin SUB(t')$. Hence $\alpha(t') = t'$ and, consequently, $t'_j = \alpha(t'_j)$. □

Definition 36. A family $\mathcal{T} = \{T_1, \ldots, T_n\}$ is connected if the set $\bigcup \mathcal{T}$ is connected.

Lemma 37. *Let $\mathcal{T} = \{T_1, \ldots, T_n\}$ be a unifiable and connected family of sets of types and let η be an mgu of $\mathcal{T}$. Then the family*

$$\{\eta[T_1], \ldots, \eta[T_n]\}$$

is also connected.

Proof. By Proposition 16 and Theorem 13

$$\eta = \gamma \circ \beta_k \circ \cdots \circ \beta_0 \circ \alpha,$$

where α is an atomic substitution wrt $\bigotimes \mathcal{T}$, γ is atomic wrt $\beta_k \circ \cdots \circ \beta_1 \circ \alpha[\bigotimes \mathcal{T}]$, and b_j, for $j = 1, \ldots, k$ is an inner substitution for $\beta_{j-1} \circ \cdots \circ \beta_1 \circ \alpha[\bigotimes \mathcal{T}]$. Denote

$$\eta_j = \beta_j \circ \cdots \circ \beta_1 \circ \alpha,$$

for $j = 1, \ldots, k$. Since both atomic and inner substitutions preserve connectivity, it suffices to show that each β_j, for $j = 1, \ldots, k$, is an inner substitution for $\eta_{j-1}[\bigcup \mathcal{T}]$. Suppose not. Then, we find some $j \in \{1, \ldots, k\}$, such that β_j is not inner for $\eta_{j-1}[\bigcup \mathcal{T}]$. We know however, that

$$\beta_j = \ulcorner x_j : t_j \urcorner,$$

where

$$t_j \in SUB(\eta_{j-1}[\bigotimes \mathcal{T}])$$

and

$$x_j \in SUB(\eta_{j-1}[\bigotimes \mathcal{T}]) \setminus Var(t_j).$$

Consequently

$$t_j \notin SUB(\eta_{j-1}[\bigcup \mathcal{T}]).$$

But

$$SUB(\eta_{j-1}[\bigotimes \mathcal{T}]) = \eta_{j-1}[\bigotimes \mathcal{T}] \cup SUB(\eta_{j-1}[\bigcup \mathcal{T}]),$$

hence $t_j \in \eta_{j-1}[\bigotimes \mathcal{T}]$. Let $u \in \eta_{j-1}[\bigotimes \mathcal{T}]$ be such that $x_j \in Var(u)$. Then $\beta_j(x_j) = t_j \in SUB(\beta_j(u))$ but $t_j \neq \beta_j(u)$. Thus, the set $\{t_j, \beta_j(u)\}$ is not unifiable and so is $\eta_j[\bigotimes \mathcal{T}]$ since $\{t_j, \beta_j(u)\} \subset \eta_j[\bigotimes \mathcal{T}]$. This however contradicts the assumption that η unifies $\bigotimes \mathcal{T}$ — then also $\gamma \circ \beta_k \circ \cdots \circ \beta_{j+1}$ unifies $\eta_j[\bigotimes \mathcal{T}]$. □

4 A discovery procedure with infinite input

As the relation between an *infinite* language and a *finite* set of postulates is of our main interest, a generalisation of Buszkowski's procedure to the infinite sample case turned out to be particularly useful.

Definition 38. Designate a type $s \in \mathit{Const}$. Let $A \in FS(V)$. Let $\mathcal{V}_A$ be any one-to-one function from $\mathit{Arg}(A)$ to Var. We define a relation $\overset{A}{\mapsto} \subseteq SUB(A) \times Tp$:

$$A \overset{A}{\mapsto} s$$
$$B \overset{A}{\mapsto} \mathcal{V}_A(B) \text{ for } B \in \mathit{Arg}(A)$$
$$\text{if } (B_1, \ldots, B_n)_i \overset{A}{\mapsto} t_i \text{ and } (\forall j \neq i)(\mathcal{V}_A(B_j) = t_j) \text{ then } B_i \overset{A}{\mapsto} (t_1, \ldots, t_n)_i$$

Example 39. Consider the following set of atoms:

$$V = \{\text{John, climbing, likes, is, dangerous, although}\}$$

Let A denotes the structure:

$$((\text{John}, (\text{likes}, \text{climbing})_1)_2, \text{although}, (\text{climbing}, (\text{is}, \text{dangerous})_1)_2)_2. \tag{17}$$

We fix a function $\mathcal{V}_A$:

$$(\underbrace{(\underbrace{\text{John}}_{x_1}, (\text{likes}, \underbrace{\text{climbing})_1}_{x_2})_2}_{x_4}, \text{although}, \underbrace{(\underbrace{\text{climbing}}_{x_2}, (\text{is}, \underbrace{\text{dangerous})_1}_{x_3})_2}_{x_5})_2.$$

Then the relation $\overset{A}{\mapsto}$ consists of the following pairs:

$$((\text{John}, (\text{likes}, \text{climbing})_1)_2, \text{although}, (\text{climbing}, (\text{is}, \text{dangerous})_1)_2)_2 \overset{A}{\mapsto} s$$
$$(\text{John}, (\text{likes}, \text{climbing})_1)_2 \overset{A}{\mapsto} x_4$$
$$(\text{likes}, \text{climbing})_1 \overset{A}{\mapsto} x_1 \backslash x_4$$
$$(\text{climbing}, (\text{is}, \text{dangerous})_1)_2 \overset{A}{\mapsto} x_5$$
$$(\text{is}, \text{dangerous})_1 \overset{A}{\mapsto} x_2 \backslash x_5$$
$$\text{John} \overset{A}{\mapsto} x_1$$
$$\text{climbing} \overset{A}{\mapsto} x_2$$
$$\text{likes} \overset{A}{\mapsto} (x_1 \backslash x_4)/x_2$$
$$\text{is} \overset{A}{\mapsto} (x_2 \backslash x_5)/x_3$$
$$\text{dangerous} \overset{A}{\mapsto} x_3$$
$$\text{although} \overset{A}{\mapsto} x_4 \backslash s / x_5$$

Definition 40. Let $L \subseteq FS(V)$ be countable. We assume that $L = \{S_1, S_2, \ldots\}$. Also, for each $i \geqslant 1$ we fix a one-to-one function $\mathcal{V}_{S_i} : \mathit{Arg}(S_i) \to \mathit{Var}$, such that:

$$\mathit{Rng}(\mathcal{V}_{S_{n+1}}) \cap \bigcup_{i=1}^{n} \mathit{Rng}(\mathcal{V}_{S_i}) = \emptyset. \tag{18}$$

We define a relation $\overset{L}{\mapsto} \subseteq SUB(L) \times Tp$:

$$\overset{L}{\mapsto} = \bigcup_{i=1}^{\infty} \overset{S_i}{\mapsto} \tag{19}$$

Definition 41. Let $L \subseteq FS(V)$ be countable. Denote $V_L = V \cap SUB(L)$. *The general form* determined by L — $GF(L)$ — is the grammar defined as follows:

$$V_{GF(L)} = V_L,$$
$$s_{GF(L)} = s,$$
$$I_{GF(L)}(v) = \{t \in Tp : v \overset{L}{\mapsto} t\}$$

Example 42. The structure (17) from the Example 39 determines the following grammar:

$$\begin{array}{ll} \text{John} & \to x_1, \\ \text{likes} & \to (x_1\backslash x_4)/x_2, \\ \text{climbing} & \to x_2, \\ \text{although} & \to x_4\backslash s/x_5, \\ \text{is} & \to (x_2\backslash x_5)/x_3, \\ \text{dangerous} & \to x_3. \end{array}$$

Consider the set of structures L consisting of the structure (17) together with the following two structures:

$$((\text{brave}, \text{John})_1, (\text{likes}, (\text{dangerous}, \text{climbing})_1)_1)_2,$$

$$(\text{John}, (\text{is}, \text{brave})_1)_2.$$

We establish relevant relations:

$$\underbrace{(\underbrace{(\overbrace{\text{brave}}^{x_{13}/x_{11}}, \underbrace{\text{John}}_{x_{11}})_1}_{x_{13}}, \overbrace{(\overbrace{\text{likes}}^{(x_{13}\backslash s)/x_{14}}, \underbrace{(\overbrace{\text{dangerous}}^{x_{14}/x_{12}}, \underbrace{\text{climbing}}_{x_{12}})_1}_{x_{14}})_1}^{x_{13}\backslash s})_2}_{s}$$

$$\underbrace{(\underbrace{\text{John}}_{x_{21}}, \overbrace{(\overbrace{\text{is}}^{(x_{21}\backslash s)/x_{22}}, \underbrace{\text{brave}}_{x_{22}})_1}^{x_{21}\backslash s})_2}_{s}$$

As a result we get the following general form $GF(L)$:

$$\begin{array}{ll}\text{John} & \to x_1, x_{11}, x_{21},\\ \text{brave} & \to x_{13}/x_{11}, x_{22}\\ \text{likes} & \to (x_1\backslash x_5)/x_2, (x_{13}\backslash s)/x_{14},\\ \text{dangerous} & \to x_4, x_{14}/x_{12},\\ \text{climbing} & \to x_2, x_3, x_{12},\\ \text{although} & \to x_5\backslash s/x_6,\\ \text{is} & \to (x_3\backslash x_6)/x_4, (x_{21}\backslash s)/x_{22}.\end{array} \tag{20}$$

Lemma 43. *For all $A \in SUB(L)$ we have:*

$$T_{GF(L)}(A) = \{t \in Tp : A \overset{L}{\mapsto} t\}$$

Proof. We prove the lemma by structural induction. For $A \in V$ our thesis holds by the definition of $GF(L)$.

Suppose $t_i \in T_{GF(L)}((A_1, \ldots, A_n)_i)$. By the definition of terminal type assignment there exist $t_j, j \neq i$ such that $t_j \in T_{GF(L)}(A_j)$ and $(t_1, \ldots, t_n)_i \in T_{GF(L)}(A_i)$. By induction $A_j \overset{L}{\mapsto} t_j$ and $A_i \overset{L}{\mapsto} (t_1, \ldots, t_n)_i$. There exists $l \in \omega$ such that $A_i \overset{S_l}{\mapsto} (t_1, \ldots, t_n)_i$. It follows from the definition of $\mapsto$ that there are $B_1, \ldots, B_n$ such that $B_i = A_i$, $\mathcal{V}_{S_l}(B_j) = t_j$ for $j \neq i$ and $(B_1, \ldots, B_n)_i \overset{S_l}{\mapsto} t_i$. Also, for any $A \in FS(V)$ and $B \in SUB(A)$:

$$\text{if } \mathcal{V}_A(B) = t \text{ then } (\forall C \in SUB(L))(C \overset{L}{\mapsto} t \Rightarrow C = B).$$

Consequently, $B_j = A_j$, for $j = 1, \ldots n$

To finish the proof suppose that $(A_1, \ldots, A_n)_i \overset{L}{\mapsto} t_i$. Then $(A_1, \ldots, A_n)_i \overset{S_l}{\mapsto} t_i$ for some $S_l \in L$. Since $A_j \in Arg(S_l)$ for all $j \neq i$ there exist $t_j, j \neq i$ such that $\mathcal{V}_{S_l}(A_j) = t_j$ for $j \neq i$. By the definition of $\mapsto$ we get $A_i \overset{S_l}{\mapsto} (t_1, \ldots, t_n)_i$ and finally, by induction, $t_j \in T_{GF(L)}(A_j), j \neq i$ and $(t_1, \ldots, t_n)_i \in T_{GF(L)}(A_i)$ which entails $t_i \in T_{GF(L)}((A_1, \ldots, A_n)_i)$. □

Corollary 44. $FL(GF(L)) = L$

Remark 45. All the notions concerning families of sets of types (boundeness, connectivity, unifiability ect) when applied to a grammar G will refer to the set $\{I_G(v) : v \in V_G\}$. We also denote

$$Var(G) = \bigcup_{v \in V_G} Var(I_G(v)).$$

Proposition 46. *For any $L \subset FS(V)$, the grammar $GF(L)$ is connected.*

Proof. Denote

$$T = \bigcup_{v \in V_{GF(L)}} I_{GF(L)}(v).$$

Let $TYP : SUB(L) \to FS(Tp)$ be the homomorphizm obtained from $I_{GF(L)}$ by expansion. Clearly, if $B \in SUB(L)$ then $TYP(B) \in FS(T)$. It is also easy to prove by structural induction that, for any $B \in SUB(L)$ and $t \in Tp$:

$$TYP(B) \rightarrowtail t \Leftrightarrow B \overset{A}{\mapsto} t. \tag{21}$$

Now, let $x \in Var(T)$. By the definitions of GF and $\mapsto$, there exist $S_l \in L$ and $(B_1, \ldots, B_n)_i \in SUB(S_l)$ such that $\mathcal{V}_{S_l}(B_j) = x$ for some $j \neq i$. Then, there exist $t_1, \ldots, t_n$ such that $B_i \overset{A}{\mapsto} (t_1, \ldots, t_n)_i$ and $t_j = x$. From (21) we get $TYP(B_j) \rightarrowtail t_j = x$ and $TYP(B_i) \rightarrowtail (t_1, \ldots, t_n)_i$. Thus both x and $(t_1, \ldots, t_n)_i$ are attainable from T. Moreover, by Proposition 25, $(t_1, \ldots, t_n)_i$ is a subfunctor of some element of T and $x = t_j$ is its direct argument. □

Definition 47. For any grammar G and a substitution α we define the grammar $\alpha[G]$:

$$V_{\alpha[G]} = V_G,$$
$$s_{\alpha[G]} = s_G,$$
$$(\forall v \in V_G)(I_{\alpha[G]}(v) = \alpha(I_G(v)).$$

Proposition 48. *For any substitution α, grammar G and $A \in FS(V_G)$:*

$$\alpha(T_G(A)) \subseteq T_{\alpha[G]}(A).$$

Corollary 49. *For any grammar G and substitution α, $FL(G) \subseteq FL(\alpha[G])$*

Theorem 50. *Let $L \subseteq FS(V)$ be nonempty (possibly infinite). Then, for any grammar G, the following conditions are equivalent:*

(i) G is rigid and compatible with L,
(ii) $G = \sigma[GF(L)]$ for some unifier σ of $GF(L)$.

Proof. (ii)⇒(i) follows from Corollary 49.
We prove (i)⇒(ii). Recall definitions 38 and 40. We define a substitution:

$$\sigma(x) = \begin{cases} T_G(A) & \text{if } (\exists l \in \omega)(\mathcal{V}_{S_l}(A) = x) \\ x & \text{otherwise.} \end{cases}$$

Since G is rigid and $I_G(v) \neq \emptyset$ for all $v \in SUB(L)$, it is enough to show that $\sigma(I_{GF(L)}(v)) \subseteq I_G(v)$ for all $v \in V$. By structural induction on t we prove:

$$(\forall t \in Tp)(\forall A \in SUB(L))(A \overset{L}{\mapsto} t \Rightarrow \sigma(t) = T_G(A)) \tag{22}$$

If $t \in Var$ then $A \overset{L}{\mapsto} t$ implies $t = \mathcal{V}_{S_l}(A)$ for some $S_l \in L$. If $t = s$ then $A \overset{L}{\mapsto} t$ implies $A \in L$. Suppose now that (22) is true for all t_j, $j = 1, \ldots, n$. Let $A_i \overset{L}{\mapsto} (t_1, \ldots, t_n)_i$ for some $A_i \in SUB(L)$. There exists $l \in \omega$ such that

$A_i \overset{S_i}{\mapsto} (t_1, \dots, t_n)_i$. Denote $A_j = \mathcal{V}_{S_i}^{-1}(t_j)$, for $j \neq i$. Then $(A_1, \dots, A_n)_i \overset{L}{\mapsto} t_i$ and $A_j \overset{L}{\mapsto} t_j$ for $j \neq i$. By induction $\sigma(t_i) = T_G((A_1, \dots, A_n)_i)$ and $\sigma(t_j) = T_G(A_j)$ for $j \neq i$ which implies, by the definition of terminal type assignment, $\sigma((t_1, \dots, t_n)_i) = T_G(A_i)$. From (22) immediately follows $(\forall v \in V)(\forall t \in Tp)(t \in I_{GF(L)}(v) \Rightarrow \sigma(t) = I_G(v))$. □

Corollary 51. *For any nonempty $L \subseteq FS(V)$, L is rigidly describable if and only if $GF(L)$ is unifiable.*

Definition 52. Let L be rigidly describable. By Theorem 17 there exists an mgu of $GF(L)$. The grammar $RG(L) = \eta[GF(L)]$, where η is an mgu of $GF(L)$, will be called *the rigid grammar determined by L.*

Example 53. It is easy to show that the following substitution

$$\ulcorner x_2 : x_1, x_3 : x_1, x_4 : x_1/x_1, x_5 : s, x_6 : s, x_{11} : x_1, x_{12} : x_1, x_{13} : x_1,$$
$$x_{14} : x_1, x_{21} : x_1, x_{22} : x_1/x_1 \urcorner$$

is a most general unifier of the grammar (20). Hence, our initial set of structures generates the rigid grammar:

John	$\rightarrow x_1,$
brave	$\rightarrow x_1/x_1,$
likes	$\rightarrow (x_1\backslash s)/x_1,$
dangerous	$\rightarrow x_1/x_1,$
climbing	$\rightarrow x_1,$
although	$\rightarrow s\backslash s/s,$
is	$\rightarrow (x_1\backslash s)/(x_1/x_1).$

Proposition 54. *For any $L \subset FS(V)$, if the grammar $RG(L)$ exists, then it is connected.*

Proof. A direct consequence of Lemma 37 and Proposition 46. □

Lemma 55. *Let G_1 and G_2 be two unifiable grammars such that $G_1 \subseteq G_2$. Let η_1 and η_2 be mgus of G_1, G_2 respectively. Then there exists substitution α such that $\eta_2[G_2] = \alpha \circ \eta_1[G_1]$.*

Proof. Since η_2 is also a unifier of G_1, there must exist a substitution α such that $\eta_2 = \alpha \circ \eta_1$. Then $\eta_2[G_2] = \eta_2[G_1] = \alpha[\eta_1[G_1]]$. □

Corollary 56. *Let $L \subset FS(V)$ be rigidly describable and $L_1 \subseteq L$. Then there exists a substitution α such that $RG(L) = \alpha[RG(L_1)]$.*

Proof. Recall the construction of $GF(L)$. For each $S_i \in L_1$ we choose the same function $\mathcal{V}_{S_i}$ to define both $\overset{L_1}{\mapsto}$ and $\overset{L}{\mapsto}$. Then $GF(L_1) \subseteq GF(L)$, so our thesis follows from Lemma 55. □

Corollary 57. *Let L be rigidly describable. Then, for any grammar G the following conditions are equivalent:*

(i) G is rigid and compatible with L,
(ii) $G = \alpha[RG(L)]$, for some substitution α.

Proof. Let $RG(L) = \eta[GF(L)]$. Since η is an mgu of $GF(L)$, any unifier of $GF(L)$ has a form $\alpha \circ \eta$, so our thesis follows immediately from Theorem 50. □

Theorem 58. *Let L be rigidly describable and nonempty. Then:*

$$L \subseteq FL(RG(L)) \tag{23}$$
$$L_1 \subseteq L \Rightarrow FL(RG(L_1)) \subseteq FL(RG(L)) \tag{24}$$
$$FL(RG(FL(RG(L)))) = FL(RG(L)) \tag{25}$$
$$(\exists L' \subseteq L)(card(L') < \aleph_0 \wedge FL(RG(L')) = FL(RG(L))). \tag{26}$$

Proof. (23) is an immediate consequence of Corollaries 44, 49 and 57. (24) follows from Corollaries 49 and 56.

To justify (25) it suffices to prove that $FL(RG(FL(RG(L)))) \subseteq FL(RG(L))$. According to Corollary 57 there exists α such that $RG(L) = \alpha[RG(FL(RG(L)))]$ so our thesis holds by Corollarry 49.

Finally we will prove (26). By Theorem 17, there exists a finite grammar $G \subseteq GF(L)$ such that $RG(L) = \sigma[G]$ for some mgu σ of G. By the definition of $GF(L)$, $t \in I_G(v)$ implies $v \overset{L}{\mapsto} t$. For all $v \in V$ and $t \in I_G(v)$ we choose $S_{v,t} \in L$ such that $v \overset{S_{v,t}}{\mapsto} t$. Denote $L' = \{S_{v,t}\}_{v \in V, t \in I_G(v)}$. Clearly L' is finite and $G \subseteq GF(L') \subseteq GF(L)$. By Lemma 55 there are substitutions α and β such that $RG(L) = \alpha[RG(L')]$ and $RG(L') = \beta[\sigma[G]] = \beta[RG(L)]$. Our thesis holds by Corollary 49. □

5 Categorial consequence

Definition 59. Let $L \subseteq FS(V)$. *A categorial consequence* of L — $Cn(L)$ — is defined as follows:

$$Cn(L) = \begin{cases} FL(RG(L)) & \text{if } L \text{ is rigidly describable} \\ FS(V_L) & \text{otherwise} \end{cases}$$

Theorem 60. *Cn satisfies Tarski's conditions:*

$$(\forall L \subseteq FS(V))(L \subseteq Cn(L)) \tag{27}$$
$$(\forall L_1, L_2 \subseteq FS(V))(L_1 \subseteq L_2 \Rightarrow Cn(L_1) \subseteq Cn(L_2)) \tag{28}$$
$$(\forall L \subseteq FS(V))(Cn(Cn(L)) = Cn(L)) \tag{29}$$
$$(\forall L \subseteq FS(V))(\exists L' \subseteq L)(card(L') < \aleph_0 \wedge Cn(L') = Cn(L)) \tag{30}$$

Proof. Conditions (27), (28) and (29) easily follow from Theorem 58, since $FS(V)$ is not rigidly describable. We will prove (30) assuming L is not rigidly describable.

Let $L \subseteq FS(V)$ be an infinite, not rigidly describable set of structures. We aim to show that there exists a finite, not rigidly describable subset of L. We consider two cases.

CASE 1: for each $v \in V$, $I_{GF(L)}(v)$ is bounded with respect to height. By Theorem 19 there exists a finite, not unifiable grammar $G \subset GF(L)$. Employing the same reasoning as in the proof of Theorem 58 (26), one can easily justify the existence of a finite set $L' \subset L$, such that $G \subset GF(L') \subset GF(L)$. Clearly a grammar $GF(L')$ is not unifiable and so L' is not rigidly describable, which implies $Cn(L') = FS(V)$.

CASE 2: there exists $v_0 \in V$ such that $I_{GF(L)}(v_0)$ is not bounded with respect to height. Suppose that each finite subset of L is rigidly describable. Then there exists an infinite sequence $L_0 \subset L_1 \subset \ldots$ of finite subsets of L such that, for all $i \in \omega$,

$$h(I_{RG(L_i)}(v_0)) < h(I_{RG(L_{i+1})}(v_0)). \tag{31}$$

By Corollary 56, for every $i \in \omega$ there exists a substitution α_i such that $RG(L_{i+1}) = \alpha_i[RG(L_i)]$. Observe that a substitution α_i is irreversible for each $i \in \omega$ — the existence of β_i such that $RG(L_i) = \beta_i[RG(L_{i+1})]$ would contradict (31). By Proposition 54 and Theorem 33 we get

$$card(Var(RG(L_{i+1})) < card(Var(RG(L_i))),$$

for all $i \in \omega$. This however is impossible by Proposition 29. □

According to the definition of our consequence operator *inconsistent* should be understood as *non-rigidly describable*. As we have already mentioned, the algorithm worked out by Buszkowski and Penn in [3] can cope with such inconsistent data. However, it is hard to expect a straightforward generalisation of the material presented in this paper to the non-rigid case. Although some of our results may be adapted, there still remains the problem of interpretation of multiple solutions of non-rigid algorithm (when several non-equivalent grammars are compatible with initial data).

References

1. W. BUSZKOWSKI, *Solvable Problems for Classical Categorial Grammars*, Bull. Pol. Acad. Scie. Math. 35 (1987), pp. 373–382.
2. W. BUSZKOWSKI, *Discovery Procedures for Categorial Grammars*, in [6].
3. W. BUSZKOWSKI AND G. PENN, *Categorial Grammars Determined from Linguistic Data by Unification*, Studia Logica XLIX, 4 (1990), pp. 431–454.
4. M. KANAZAWA, *Identification in the Limit of Categorial Grammars*, Journal of Logic, Language and Information, Vol. 5 No. 2, (1996), pp. 115–155.

5. M. KANAZAWA, *Learnable Classes of Categorial Grammars*, Dissertation, Stanford University, 1994.
6. E. KLEIN AND J. VAN BENTHEM (eds), Categories, Polymorphism an Unification, Universiteit van Amsterdam, Amsterdam, 1987.
7. J. W. LLOYD, Foundations of Logic Programming, Springer-Verlag, Berlin, 1987.
8. J. MARCINIEC, *Learning Categorial Grammars by Uniffcation with Negative Constraints,* Journal of Applied Non-Classical Logics, 4 (1994), pp. 181-200.
9. J. MARCINIEC, *Infinite Set Unification with Application to Categorial Grammar,* Studia Logica LVIII, 3 (1997), to appear.
10. J. VAN BENTHEM, *Categorial Equations,* in [6].

Generation as Deduction on Labelled Proof Nets

Josep M. Merenciano* and Glyn Morrill**

Departament de Llenguatges i Sistemes Informàtics
Universitat Politècnica de Catalunya
Campus Nord
Jordi Girona Salgado, 1–3
E–08034 Barcelona

Abstract. In the framework of labelled proof nets the task of *parsing* in categorial grammar can be reduced to the problem of first-order matching under theory. Here we shall show how to use the same method of labelled proof nets to reduce the task of *generating* to the problem of higher-order matching.

1 Introduction

Categorial grammar provides a mechanism for the analysis of linguistic expressions on the basis of lexicalism and the parsing as deduction paradigm ([17]).[3] In accordance with *lexicalism* each lexical entry of the language encapsulates all the information needed to analyse the lexical item, and the grammar itself only needs to know how to manage these resources. In the particular case of categorial grammar, a lexical categorisation is a formula, or type, constructed over some basic types by logical connectives; and the grammar constitutes the connectives' syntactic behaviour (i.e. the laws governing the connectives). Within the *parsing as deduction* paradigm the problem of analysing some linguistic expression is rendered as the problem of proving (i.e. deducing) theorems in a deductive system. In categorial grammar this means that to analyse a linguistic expression we have to construct a sequent and prove its validity in the logic of categorial connectives: the linguistic expression is well-formed if and only if the sequent is valid in the logic. Thus, the language accepted is defined not by a set of grammar rules (as in context free grammar) but by the meaning of the categorial types assigned to the lexical items.

In practise it is not parsing itself which is useful so much as the fact that parsing is tantamount to performing the process of *interpretation*: computing the semantics associated with a given concrete syntax (we shall say: prosodics). The opposite process is *generation*: computing the prosodics associated with a given semantics. For present purposes prosodics is limited to word order, and the semantics is understood as a logical form expressed as a term of higher-order logic. We offer here a uniform framework for the computational tasks of interpretation and generation.

* E-mail: `meren@lsi.upc.es`.

** E-mail: `morrill@lsi.upc.es`, HTTP: `//www-lsi.upc.es/~glyn/`.

[3] The work we report was partially supported by project KOALA: DGICYT PB95–0787.

Methods for categorial interpretation based on proof nets ([5], [1], [18]) and labelling of deductive systems ([3]) have been developed in [12], [14], [15] and [11]. The formalism of *proof nets* provides a representation of the fundamental structure of proofs, in the same way that parse trees do for context free grammar derivations. Using proof nets we avoid "spurious ambiguity": it is always the case that two distinct (Cut-free) proof nets represent distinct associations of prosodics and semantics. In *labelled deductive systems* we use labels to formalise metalanguage of connectives in *labelled formulas* which are pairs ⟨label, formula⟩. In the categorial application the label is split into the two linguistic dimensions: ⟨⟨prosodics, semantics⟩, categorial type⟩.

Combining labelling and proof nets yields labelled proof nets for categorial grammar, a parsing framework that expresses the proof search restrictions in terms of (first-order) unifications. In fact, a clausal structuring of proof search allows one to deal with one-way unification, i.e. *matching*, in which one of the two terms to be unified contains no variables. Starting the search for proof nets with the prosodics of the goal instantiated to a ground term but its semantics expressed with a metavariable, the interpretation of a linguistic expression is computed by constructing a proof net: the prosodic labelling controls the proof search, and the semantic labelling allows us to retrieve the associated semantic form.

In this paper we invoke the same techniques used for parsing and interpreting linguistic expressions in order to generate from the logical form. The idea is that we can use labelled formulas in such a way that the semantic labelling controls the proof search while the prosodic labelling is used to retrieve the word order associated with the initial logical form. The main difficulty arises with the label unification: we must now unify typed λ-terms, for which even the second order problem is undecidable ([6]). In the special case of Second-Order Linear Unification (SOLU: where variables are first-order but constants may be first- or second-order, and each abstraction binds exactly one variable occurrence) unifiability is still undecidable. But if no free variable occurs more than twice, SOLU is decidable ([10]). Importantly, the labelled categorial proof nets adhere to this latter condition: each free variable appears exactly twice. Indeed, a clausal structuring again maintains a flow of information such that one term in each unification pair contains no free variables, i.e. we need only to deal with matching. In SOL matching there is a computable finite set of most general unifiers. Thus, we are able to present a terminating algorithm for categorial generation for the case of second order implicational categorial logic.[4]

Section 2 outlines proof nets for implicational linear logic; section 3 describes the methods involved in our categorial parsing as deduction on labelled proof nets; section 4 shows how to use these methods for the task of generation; finally, in the appendix we describe higher-order unification and the SOLU matching algorithm.

[4] It is a sufficient condition for termination of our method that every lexical logical form contain at least one constant. The method is complete for (second-order) logical forms without logical constants.

2 Calculus of linear implication

In this section we outline construction of proof nets for implicational linear logic. This serves two purposes. Firstly, the calculus of linear implication provides a point of reference for sublinear categorial calculi such as associative Lambek calculus to be used later. Secondly, and more importantly, the applications of the latter to linguistic processing will be seen as a refinement of the basic problem of linear implicational theorem proving considered here.

Let us assume sequents $\Gamma \Rightarrow A$ where Γ is a multiset (bag) of formulas, and A a single formula, built just out of the linear implication. The (intuitionistic) linear sequent calculus is as follows.

(1) a. $A \Rightarrow A$ id

b. $$\frac{\Gamma \Rightarrow A \qquad A, \Delta \Rightarrow B}{\Gamma, \Delta \Rightarrow B}\text{Cut}$$

c. $$\frac{\Gamma \Rightarrow A \qquad B, \Delta \Rightarrow C}{\Gamma, A \multimap B, \Delta \Rightarrow C}{\multimap}\text{L}$$

d. $$\frac{\Gamma, A \Rightarrow B}{\Gamma \Rightarrow A \multimap B}{\multimap}\text{R}$$

This calculus is also known in categorial contexts as Lambek-van Benthem calculus. It enjoys Cut-elimination, i.e. every sequent which is a theorem has a Cut-free proof, and is thus decidable since in the two logical rules the conclusion has one more connective than the premises. However, the sequent proofs copy contexts around in a cumbersome manner, and the partitionings required by binary rules are a costly form of non-determinism in proof search. A much deeper proof syntax is provided by proof nets.

Cut-elimination also entails the subformula property: all the formulas that can appear in a Cut-free proof already occur as subformulas of the sequent to be proved. In proof nets we work directly on the formation trees of formulas, in which all subformulas are already present as subtrees. We mark all subformulas with an explicit polarity, ^{a} or ^{s}, to indicate antecedent or succedent occurrences, rather than using positioning with respect to the sequent arrow; these polar formulas are unfolded recursively into formation trees with atomic leaves as follows:

(2) $$\frac{A^{\overline{p}} \qquad B^p}{A \multimap B^p}$$

The polarities p and $\overline{p}$ are complementary. Polarities are propagated in such a way that it is indicated whether subformulas would have antecedent or succedent occurrences in sequent proofs.

To try to construct a proof net for a sequent we first mark each formula in the sequent with a polarity marker ^{a} or ^{s}, to indicate antecedent or succedent occurrences, as shown in (3).

(3) $$\frac{A^{\mathrm{s}}\ A_1^{\mathrm{a}}\ \ldots\ A_n^{\mathrm{a}}}{A_1, \ldots, A_n \Rightarrow A}$$

The result is a bag of formulas with polarity. We then recursively unfold these polar formulas. The result of this is called a *proof frame*. A *proof structure* is the result of linking each literal to exactly one other, which must have the same atom with the opposite polarity. A proof structure is a *proof net*, i.e. is well-formed as a proof, if and only if it meets a global condition, the *long trip condition*, which can be expressed in various ways, and which ensures that the proof structure corresponds to a sequent proof. The links of proof nets are instances of the sequent axiom; but it must be assured that in $\multimap$R inferences the hypothetical A really is used in the proof of B and not in some other subproof.

Following on earlier work ([14], [15], [11]), we present the following linear clausal engine for the construction of proof nets, though without any proof of correctness here. It addresses the basic problem of partitioning for binary sequent rules by putting a list of goals in the consequent of a single sequent and using unary sequent rules together with checks that hypotheses have been used in the requisite subproofs. Formulas are labelled with constants and variables of an Associative and Commutative (AC) term algebra representing bags. A sequent $\Delta \Rightarrow \Sigma$ comprises a database Δ which is a bag of formulas labelled by distinct constants, and an agenda Σ which is a list of items each of which is either a formula labelled with a variable (all distinct), or an assignment := to a variable of an AC term formed by multiset addition $\oplus$ (a total operation), subtraction $\ominus$ (a partial operation) and the empty bag $\emptyset$. One attempts to prove a sequent $A_1, \ldots, A_n \Rightarrow A$ by proving $a_1\colon A_1, \ldots, a_n\colon A_n \Rightarrow [\alpha\colon A]$. The search terminates successfully with proof of the empty agenda from the empty database:

(4) $$\Rightarrow []$$

The variables labelling agenda formulas will in fact be assigned the labels of those database formulas which are used in their proof, i.e. in the overall case, α will be $a_1 \oplus \ldots \oplus a_n$. There are three rules. Reading from conclusion to premises, RES (resolution) states that to prove an atom A first on the agenda, choose a database clause with head A which through zero or more implications implies A; prove the antecedents of these implications, and the label for A is then the sum of those for the antecedent proofs plus that for the clause chosen (we now write the implications in the logic programming, right-to-left, direction):

(5) $$\frac{\Delta \Rightarrow [\alpha_1\colon A_1, \ldots, \alpha_n\colon A_n, \alpha := \alpha_1 \oplus \cdots \oplus \alpha_n \oplus k|\Sigma]}{\Delta, k\colon (\cdots(A \circ\!\!- A_n) \circ\!\!- \cdots) \circ\!\!- A_1 \Rightarrow [\alpha\colon A|\Sigma]}\text{RES, } \alpha_i \text{ new vars.}$$

The rule DT (deduction theorem) states that to prove $B \circ\!\!- A$ first on the agenda one assumes A and proves B, and then checks that A has been used to prove B:

(6)
$$\frac{\Delta, k\colon A \Rightarrow [\beta\colon B, \gamma := \beta \ominus k|\Sigma]}{\Delta \Rightarrow [\gamma\colon B \circ\!\!- A|\Sigma]}\text{DT, } k \text{ new constant, } \beta \text{ new variable}$$

When the assignment condition in (6) is checked by (7) the evaluation succeeds if the hypothesis has been used but fails otherwise (since $\ominus$ is a partial operation):

(7)
$$\frac{\Delta \Rightarrow \Sigma[\alpha \leftarrow EVAL(\alpha')]}{\Delta \Rightarrow [\alpha := \alpha'|\Sigma]}\text{Assig}$$

Let us consider the construction of the proof net for $C \circ\!\!- B, B \circ\!\!- A \Rightarrow C \circ\!\!- A$:

(8)

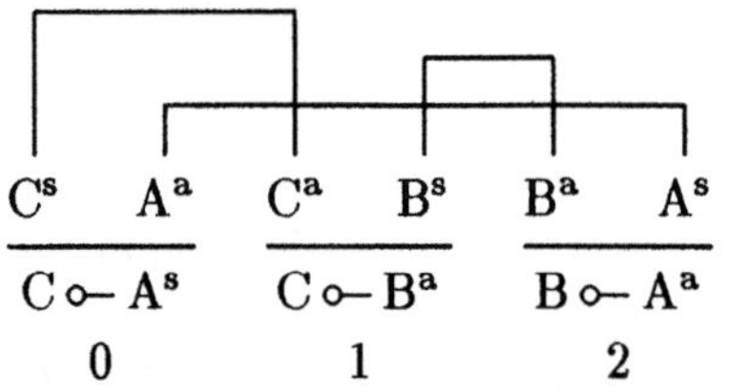

We shall reference subformulas by their tree, 0, 1, ... from left-to-right, and their node address within the tree given as a sequence of l(eft)s and r(ight)s starting at the root. Then, reading from the conclusion up to the axiom, the successive states in the construction of (8) are as follows.

(9)
$$\Rightarrow []$$
$$\overline{\Rightarrow [\alpha_0 := (\mathrm{a}_3 \oplus \mathrm{a}_2 \oplus \mathrm{a}_1) \ominus \mathrm{a}_3]}\text{Assig}$$
$$\overline{\Rightarrow [\alpha_1 := \mathrm{a}_3 \oplus \mathrm{a}_2 \oplus \mathrm{a}_1, \alpha_0 := \alpha_1 \ominus \mathrm{a}_3]}\text{Assig}$$
$$\overline{\Rightarrow [\alpha_2 := \mathrm{a}_3 \oplus \mathrm{a}_2, \alpha_1 := \alpha_2 \oplus \mathrm{a}_1, \alpha_0 := \alpha_1 \ominus \mathrm{a}_3]}\text{Assig}$$
$$\overline{\Rightarrow [\alpha_3 := \mathrm{a}_3, \alpha_2 := \alpha_3 \oplus \mathrm{a}_2, \alpha_1 := \alpha_2 \oplus \mathrm{a}_1, \alpha_0 := \alpha_1 \ominus \mathrm{a}_3]}\text{Assig}$$
$$\overline{\mathrm{a}_3\colon 0r \Rightarrow [\alpha_3\colon 2r, \alpha_2 := \alpha_3 \oplus \mathrm{a}_2, \alpha_1 := \alpha_2 \oplus \mathrm{a}_1, \alpha_0 := \alpha_1 \ominus \mathrm{a}_3]}\text{RES}$$
$$\overline{\mathrm{a}_2\colon 2, \mathrm{a}_3\colon 0r \Rightarrow [\alpha_2\colon 1r, \alpha_1 := \alpha_2 \oplus \mathrm{a}_1, \alpha_0 := \alpha_1 \ominus \mathrm{a}_3]}\text{RES}$$
$$\overline{\mathrm{a}_1\colon 1, \mathrm{a}_2\colon 2, \mathrm{a}_3\colon 0r \Rightarrow [\alpha_1\colon 0l, \alpha_0 := \alpha_1 \ominus \mathrm{a}_3]}\text{RES}$$
$$\overline{\mathrm{a}_1\colon 1, \mathrm{a}_2\colon 2 \Rightarrow [\alpha_0\colon 0]}\text{DT}$$

To begin, one is trying to prove 0 from 1 and 2. Since 0 is implicational, in the first step $0r$ is added to the database and $0l$ is put on the agenda. This goal is attempted by resolution with clause 1 (highest link in the proof net). The new goal issued is attempted by resolution with clause 2 (middle link in the proof net). The next goal issued is resolved with the unit clause $0r$ put into the database at the first step (lowest link in the proof net).

3 Categorial parsing as deduction on labelled proof nets

3.1 Lambek Calculus

We shall deal with an implicational version **L** of associative Lambek Calculus ([9]) with formulas or (categorial) types defined by the connectives \ ('under') and / ('over') on the basis of atomic types $\mathcal{A}$, as shown in (10).

(10) $\mathcal{F} = \mathcal{A} \mid \mathcal{F}\backslash\mathcal{F} \mid \mathcal{F}/\mathcal{F}$

The two connectives are directional implications. By way of illustration of the notation, let us assume atomic types such as S (sentence), N (nominal), CN (common noun) and PP (prepositional phrase); then intransitive verbs, requiring a subject nominal on the left to form a sentence, have type N\S; transitive verbs, combining with an object on the right to form an intransitive verb phrase, have type (N\S)/N.

The interpretation of the categorial connectives is made prosodically in the field of a semigroup, i.e. a set L closed under an associative operation +, and semantically in a frame of function spaces, i.e. an indexed family $\{D_\tau\}_{\tau\in\mathcal{T}}, \mathcal{T} = \mathcal{D} \mid \mathcal{T} \to \mathcal{T}$ where $\{D_\tau\}_{\tau\in\mathcal{D}}$ are basic domains, and $D_{\tau_1\to\tau_2}$ is the set of functions from D_{τ_1} to D_{τ_2}. A mapping T which associates a semantic function space with each categorial type is such that $T(A\backslash B) = T(B/A) = T(A) \to T(B)$. Each categorial type A is interpreted as a subset of $L \times T(A)$. The signs of type $A\backslash B$ (B/A) are those which concatenate prosodically with signs of type A on the left (right), and apply semantically as functions, to yield signs of type B:

(11) $D(A\backslash B) = \{\langle s, m\rangle \mid \forall\langle s', m'\rangle \in D(A), \langle s'+s, m(m')\rangle \in D(B)\}$
$D(B/A) = \{\langle s, m\rangle \mid \forall\langle s', m'\rangle \in D(A), \langle s+s', m(m')\rangle \in D(B)\}$

In order to present calculi for reasoning about categorial types we use labelling to codify information from the interpretation clauses. Prosodic labels are terms over variables and constants constructed by the operator +; semantic labels are typed λ-terms. We define a sequent calculus as follows.[5] A *type assignment statement* is of the form $\alpha - \phi$: A where α is a prosodic term, ϕ a semantic term and A a categorial type. A *configuration* is a multiset (bag) of type assignment statements in which the terms are all variables, and are all distinct. A *sequent* $\Gamma \Rightarrow X$ comprises an antecedent Γ which is a configuration and a succedent X which is a type assignment statement. We read a sequent as stating that (for all interpretations), if the objects referred to in the antecedent are in

[5] The prosodic labelling is not essential for Lambek sequent calculus: the prosodic information can be left implicit in antecedents structured as sequences (ordered sequent calculus). The semantic information can also be recovered from a sequent proof: the associated lambda term is a notation for the proof as natural deduction, according to the Curry-Howard correspondence. But labelled sequent calculus is more general than ordered sequent calculus; both the prosodic and the semantic labelling are used in the subsequent development of proof nets, and the methods we describe apply not just to Lambek calculus but to a wider class of categorial logics which can be expressed in the general labelled format.

the types indicated, then the object referred to in the succedent is in the type indicated. The theorems of the calculus are generated by the following sequent rules.

(12) a. $a - x\colon A \Rightarrow a - x\colon A$ id

b. $$\frac{\Gamma \Rightarrow \alpha - \phi\colon A \qquad a - x\colon A, \Delta \Rightarrow \beta[a] - \psi[x]\colon B}{\Gamma, \Delta \Rightarrow \beta[\alpha] - \psi[\phi]\colon B}\text{Cut}$$

c. $$\frac{\Gamma \Rightarrow \alpha - \phi\colon A \qquad b - y\colon B, \Delta \Rightarrow \gamma[b] - \chi[y]\colon C}{\Gamma, d - w\colon A\backslash B, \Delta \Rightarrow \gamma[\alpha{+}d] - \chi[(w\ \phi)]\colon C}\backslash\text{L}$$

d. $$\frac{\Gamma, a - x\colon A \Rightarrow a{+}\gamma - \psi\colon B}{\Gamma \Rightarrow \gamma - \lambda x\psi\colon A\backslash B}\backslash\text{R}$$

e. $$\frac{\Gamma \Rightarrow \alpha - \phi\colon A \qquad b - y\colon B, \Delta \Rightarrow \gamma[b] - \psi[y]\colon C}{\Gamma, d - w\colon B/A, \Delta \Rightarrow \gamma[d{+}\alpha] - \psi[(w\ \phi)]\colon C}/\text{L}$$

f. $$\frac{\Gamma, a - x\colon A \Rightarrow \gamma{+}a - \psi\colon B}{\Gamma \Rightarrow \gamma - \lambda x\psi\colon B/A}/\text{R}$$

The notation $[\cdot]$ indicates distinguished suboccurrences of terms. By way of example, there is the following derivation of a case of "subject type raising":

(13) $$\frac{\dfrac{a - x\colon \text{N} \Rightarrow a - x\colon \text{N} \qquad c - z\colon \text{S} \Rightarrow c - z\colon \text{S}}{a - x\colon \text{N},\ b - y\colon \text{N}\backslash\text{S} \Rightarrow a{+}b - (y\ x)\colon \text{S}}\backslash\text{L}}{a - x\colon \text{N} \Rightarrow a - \lambda y(y\ x)\colon \text{S}/(\text{N}\backslash\text{S})}/\text{R}$$

Each lexical entry is a type assignment statement $\alpha - \phi\colon A$ where α and ϕ are closed (contain no free variables). Examples of lexical assignments are given in figure 1.[6] Consider the following derivation:

(14) $$\frac{\dfrac{a - x\colon \text{CN} \Rightarrow a - x\colon \text{CN} \qquad b - y\colon \text{N} \Rightarrow b - y\colon \text{N}}{d - w\colon \text{N/CN},\ a - x\colon \text{CN} \Rightarrow d{+}a - (w\ x)\colon \text{N}}/\text{L} \qquad c - z\colon \text{S} \Rightarrow c - z\colon \text{S}}{d - w\colon \text{N/CN},\ a - x\colon \text{CN},\ e - v\colon \text{N}\backslash\text{S} \Rightarrow d{+}a{+}e - (v\ (w\ x))\colon \text{S}}\backslash\text{L}$$

Substituting the prosodics and semantics for 'the', 'dog' and 'runs' we derive that **the+dog+runs** with semantics (**run** (**the dog**)) is a sentence. Of course the lexical semantics can be elaborated and more complex examples may invite λ-reduction in computational implementations, but we see here the essential features of analysis. We can also see here the essential computational problem

[6] We omit here details of inflection and morphology; see e.g. chapter 6 of [13].

John	- **j**	:	N
Mary	- **m**	:	N
runs	- **run**	:	N\S
likes	- **like**	:	(N\S)/N
votes	- **vote**	:	(N\S)/PP
talks	- **talk**	:	(N\S)/PP
for	- **for**	:	PP/N
about	- **about**	:	PP/N
the	- **the**	:	N/CN
dog	- **dog**	:	CN
who	- $\lambda x \lambda y \lambda z[(y\ z) \wedge (x\ z)]$	:	(CN\CN)/(S/N)
seeks	- λx(**try** (x **find**))	:	(N\S)/(((N\S)/N)\(N\S))

Fig. 1. Lexical Assignments

with this proof syntax: although the Cut-elimination property renders decidability (since in the logical rules the conclusion has one more connective than the premises) distinct proofs may define the same analysis. For example (15), which is not the same proof as (14), nevertheless derives the same labelled conclusion.

(15)
$$\dfrac{a - x\colon \mathrm{CN} \Rightarrow a - x\colon \mathrm{CN} \qquad \dfrac{b - y\colon \mathrm{N} \Rightarrow b - y\colon \mathrm{N} \qquad c - z\colon \mathrm{S} \Rightarrow c - z\colon \mathrm{S}}{b - y\colon \mathrm{N},\ e - v\colon \mathrm{N}\backslash\mathrm{S} \Rightarrow b{+}e - (v\ y)\colon \mathrm{S}}\backslash L}{d - w\colon \mathrm{N/CN},\ a - x\colon \mathrm{CN},\ e - v\colon \mathrm{N}\backslash\mathrm{S} \Rightarrow d{+}a{+}e - (v\ (w\ x))\colon \mathrm{S}}/L$$

This "spurious ambiguity" of the sequent proof syntax is remedied in the syntax of proof nets, to which we now turn.

3.2 Labelled Proof Nets

As before, in the proof nets we work directly on the formation trees of formulas, but now they are labelled. Marking labelled subformulas for polarity ^{a} or ^{s}, polar type assignment statements are unfolded recursively into formation trees with atomic leaf types as follows:[7]

(16)
$$\dfrac{\alpha - \phi\colon A^{\overline{p}} \qquad \alpha{+}\gamma - (\chi\ \phi)\colon B^{p}}{\gamma - \chi\colon A\backslash B^{p}} \qquad \dfrac{\gamma{+}\alpha - (\chi\ \phi)\colon B^{p} \qquad \alpha - \phi\colon A^{\overline{p}}}{\gamma - \chi\colon B/A^{p}}$$

α and ϕ new variable/constant as $p = \mathrm{a/s}$

Metavariables and Skolem constants correspond to the quantifers of the inter-

[7] The unfolding is a little different than that in [12], which instantiates λ-abstraction in succedent unfolding in such a way that extraction of semantics in parsing is immediate. The current version will be used uniformly for parsing and generating, serving to maximise a symmetry that would otherwise be less apparent.

pretation clauses and are introduced into labels in accordance with the polarity of context.

The definitions of proof frame and proof structure are just as before, but now we have labels. Any sublinear calculus must satisfy the linear long trip condition on proof nets, to ensure linear validity. But we have a further condition in view of sublinear structure, which is that the unification problem comprising the linked prosodic terms be solvable. So far as we are aware, the prosodic and semantic labelling actually subsume the linear labelling of section 2, in that unifiability of either ensures the relevant use of hypotheses; however for consistency we continue to include the linear labelling.[8]

This means, then, that in order to check that a proof structure is a proof net we have to determine the solvability of a *first-order unification system*, i.e. the solvability (under associativity) of the set of prosodic equations induced by the linking. However, from a processing point of view we do not want to construct whole proof structures and then test if they are proof nets, but rather propagate constraints and prune search in the course of conjecturing linking. Indeed, we do not want to take a given proof frame as our point of departure, since that presupposes a selection of lexical assignments: for n words each k-ways lexically ambiguous there are k^n such choices and we do not want to have to enumerate them all, but select them only when they must be brought into, and are compatible with, the search and proof construction.

A suitable method is obtained by generalising the clausal engine of the previous section, which in fact allows us to practice a top-down backtracking parse search restricted to one-way unification (matching), i.e. unification in which one term has no free variables. The generalisation includes resolution with lexical clauses, with control of the label tokens being introduced into the proof. Sequents now have the form $\Delta \Rightarrow {}_{\delta}\Sigma$ where a control parameter δ is a multiset of constant tokens, the cardinalities which lexical insertion must meet as a necessary condition for successful proof construction. The lexical insertion resolution rule LRES requires the lexical assignment of type $(\cdots(A \multimap A_n) \multimap \cdots) \multimap A_1$ (ignoring directionality) to a sign ς and decrements $\delta \oplus \#(\varsigma)$ according to the count $\#(\varsigma)$ of the lexical sign ς on the label dimension controlling the proof search (prosodics for parsing; semantics for generation). The remaining rules are

[8] By retaining an appropriate ordering it is possible to restrict attention in **L** to *planar* linking in virtue of noncommutativity, which is certainly of crucial computational importance (though not enough to ensure the long trip condition). But our first concern here is with the generality of our methodology for generation, which does not need to rely on any noncommutativity and which extends to all manner of sublinear calculi through unification under theory as in [14]. Although introduced as long ago as [18], whether the prosodic unifiability alone assures the long trip condition has not been shown. Nor does it appear that unification under associativity (nondeterministic) is imperative for **L**: [15] and [16] propose formulations on the basis of just structural term unification (deterministic). Still, it seems unlikely that the present proposals would be irrelevant to such refinements as could be either necessary or advantageous. That the semantic unification is necessary but not sufficient is certain, since this checks validity as natural deduction, but does not check order.

unaltered except that they transmit the control parameter.

(17) $$\overline{\Rightarrow_{\emptyset}[\,]}$$

(18) $$\frac{\Delta \Rightarrow {}_{\delta}[\alpha_1\colon A_1, \ldots, \alpha_n\colon A_n, \alpha := \alpha_1 \oplus \cdots \oplus \alpha_n \oplus k|\Sigma]}{\Delta, k\colon (\cdots(A \circ\!- A_n) \circ\!- \cdots) \circ\!- A_1 \Rightarrow {}_{\delta}[\alpha\colon A|\Sigma]}\text{RES, } \alpha_i \text{ new vars.}$$

(19) $$\frac{\Delta \Rightarrow {}_{\delta}[\alpha_1\colon A_1, \ldots, \alpha_n\colon A_n, \alpha := \alpha_1 \oplus \cdots \oplus \alpha_n|\Sigma]}{\Delta \Rightarrow {}_{\delta\oplus\#(\varsigma)}[\alpha\colon A|\Sigma]}\text{LRES, } \alpha_i \text{ new vars.}$$

(20) $$\frac{\Delta, k\colon A \Rightarrow {}_{\delta}[\beta\colon B, \gamma := \beta \ominus k|\Sigma]}{\Delta \Rightarrow {}_{\delta}[\gamma\colon B \circ\!- A|\Sigma]}\text{DT, } k \text{ new constant, } \beta \text{ new variable}$$

(21) $$\frac{\Delta \Rightarrow {}_{\delta}\Sigma[\alpha \leftarrow EVAL(\alpha')]}{\Delta \Rightarrow {}_{\delta}[\alpha := \alpha'|\Sigma]}\text{Assig}$$

Let us consider first just parsing our example 'the dog runs' as S; see figure 2. The trace of search states is as follows:

(22) $$\cfrac{\cfrac{\cfrac{\cfrac{\cfrac{\cfrac{\Rightarrow_{\emptyset}[\,]}{\Rightarrow_{\emptyset}[\alpha_0 := \emptyset]}\text{Assig}}{\Rightarrow_{\emptyset}[\alpha_1 := \emptyset, \alpha_0 := \alpha_1]}\text{Assig}}{\Rightarrow_{\emptyset}[\alpha_2 := \emptyset, \alpha_1 := \alpha_2, \alpha_0 := \alpha_1]}\text{Assig}}{\Rightarrow_{\mathsf{dog}}[\alpha_2\colon 2r, \alpha_1 := \alpha_2, \alpha_0 := \alpha_1]}\text{LRES}}{\Rightarrow_{\mathsf{the}\oplus\mathsf{dog}}[\alpha_1\colon 1l, \alpha_0 := \alpha_1]}\text{LRES}}{\Rightarrow_{\mathsf{the}\oplus\mathsf{dog}\oplus\mathsf{runs}}[\alpha_0\colon 0]}\text{LRES}$$

Initially, the agenda comprises the type S unit clause at 0 with prosodic term **the+dog+runs**. There are no clauses in the database, so we must resolve by LRES with a lexical clause projecting a type S head. We do not need to attempt resolving with any lexical entry unless the prosodic constant(s) occurring in the entry are contained in the bag of tokens controlling the proof search.[9] Since 'the' and 'dog' do not project S, we can only resolve with the lexical clause for 'runs', the prosodic label of which must be unified with **the+dog+runs**. This instantiates a to **the+dog** (in this case there is no other unifier) and the new agenda comprises the type N unit clause at $1l$ with prosodic term **the+dog**. For the same reasons again, this must resolve with the lexical clause for 'the', in-

[9] In practice, we can precompute a *working set* of lexical entries, being those the constants of which are contained in the target assignment. Skolem constants and metavariables need to be refreshed on each invocation, but, the rest of the lexicon can be ignored.

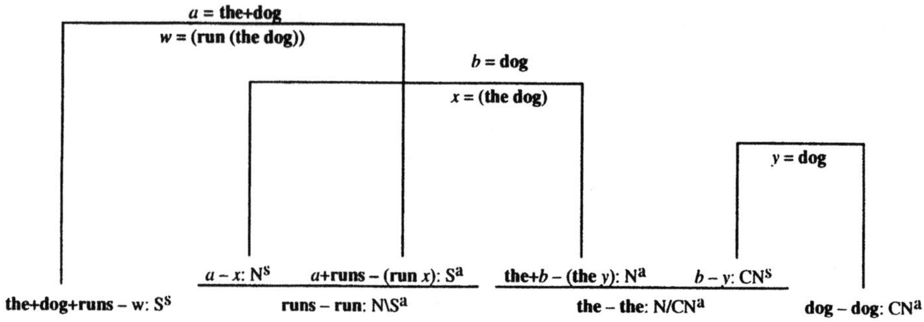

Fig. 2. Proof net for parsing of 'the dog runs'

stantiating b to **dog**, and the subgoal issued resolves with the unit lexical clause for 'dog'. Tracing back, the three successive steps yield semantically $y = \mathbf{dog}$, $x = (\mathbf{the\ dog})$ and $w = (\mathbf{run\ (the\ dog)})$, which last represents the semantic interpretation. Note that this is the only proof net for this (unambiguous) expression: the problem of spurious ambiguity that is encountered in the syntax of sequent calculus is not present in that of proof nets.

By way of a slightly more involved example we consider parsing 'John talks about' as S/N (as in the analysis of a relative clause 'who John talks about' given the second-order assignment to the relative pronoun); see figure 3. First, the unit N clause in the body of the initial agenda is put into the database and the S head is linked to the head of the lexical clause for 'talks' which projects an S. The prosodic unifier is $\{b = \mathbf{John}, a = \mathbf{about{+}d}\}$. The two (unit) clauses in the body of the lexical clause go into the agenda; the N is resolved with the unit lexical clause for 'John', and the PP with the lexical clause for 'about', when $c = \mathbf{d}$. Now the agenda comprises an N unit clause with prosodic label **d** and we terminate by resolving with the corresponding clause added to the database at the first step. Tracing back the semantics we end up with $(v\ \mathbf{w}) = ((\mathbf{talk\ (about\ w)})\ \mathbf{j})$ which clearly has solution $v = \lambda w((\mathbf{talk\ (about}\ w))\ \mathbf{j})$.

This last example shows that recovery of semantics can involve a mild degree of higher-order unification. In the continuation we address the task of generation and this will require a direct confrontation with higher-order unification.

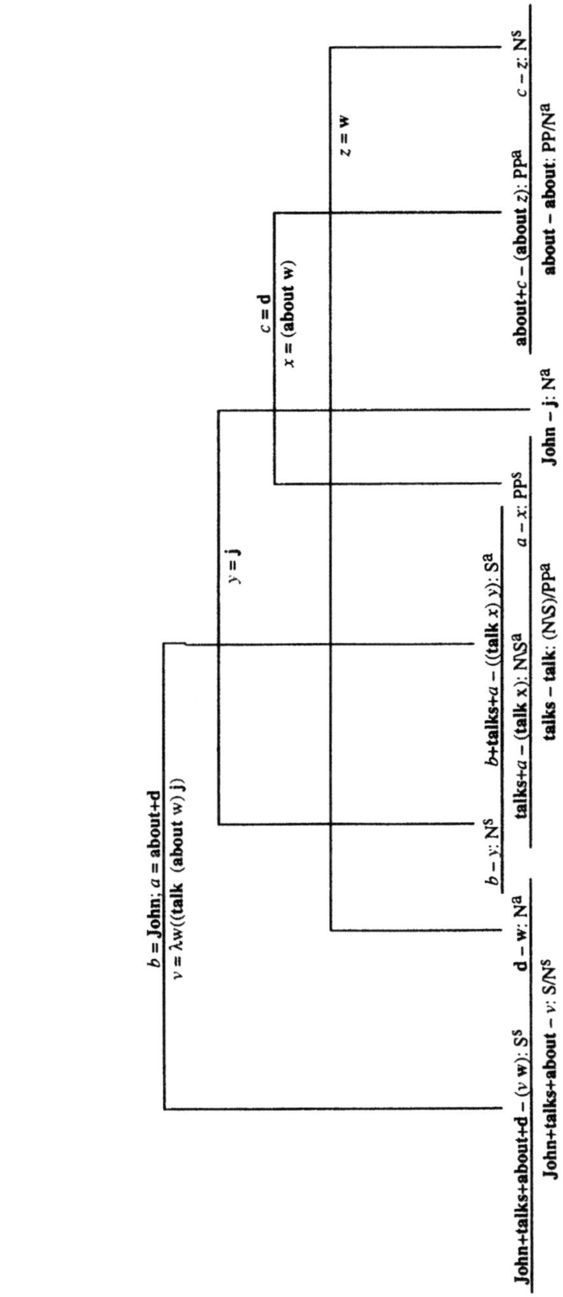

Fig. 3. Proof net for parsing of 'John talks about'

4 Categorial generation as deduction on labelled proof nets

Now we will use the same techniques to *generate* from the semantic form. The basic idea is that we can use bidimensional labelled formulas $\alpha - \phi$: A in such a way that the semantic labelling controls the proof search while the prosodic labelling is used to retrieve the word order associated with the semantic form. To do this it is enough to express in the semantic label of the goal a closed λ-term representing the source semantics, leave a metavariable in the prosodic label, determine solvability of the unification system expressed by (semantic) linking, and confirm solvability of the unification system induced over prosodic labels, recovering the prosodic unknown.

Using the goal-driven strategy for proof search above we have to resolve, for each linking, a higher-order matching problem. Like matching under associativity, higher-order matching is non-deterministic in that (already considering only normal forms) in general there is not a unique most general unifier. For example, the unification problem $\{(x\ \mathbf{f}) = (\mathbf{f}\ (\mathbf{f}\ \mathbf{a}))\}$ has solucions $x = \lambda z(z\ (\mathbf{f}\ \mathbf{a}))$ and $x = \lambda z(\mathbf{f}\ (z\ \mathbf{a}))$ neither of which is more general than the other. It's known that third-order matching is decidable; though it's not known whether the problem in general is decidable, the conjecture is that it is ([7]); see also [8], [6], [4] and [2].

Decidability is not enough however: in processing we are interested in effectively computing all possible unifiers, and in general this is not possible because with higher-order terms we can have an infinite number of unifiers for a given equation that cannot be expressed with a finite number of most general unifiers. If we restrict the linguistic fragment to expressions with a second-order semantic form the problem reduces to second-order linear matching because the semantic unfolding maintains linearity. This particular problem is semi-decidable, but if no free variable occurs more than twice we obtain decidability; furthermore, in this case we have a finite number of (second-order linear) most general unifiers and an algorithm to compute them ([10]). Critically, our semantic unfolding definition is such that we have exactly two occurrences of each free variable. Note that restriction to second-order types is not so bad: Montague's grammar is at most third order.

Once a proof net has been built we can confirm ordering well-formedness and retrieve the word order associated with the semantics by solving the equations on prosodic labels generated by the linking. Thus, if the matching problem for a given fragment of λ-calculus is computable, so also is the task, within that fragment, of generating linguistic expressions from their semantics, if each lexical semantics contains at least one constant. This last condition is not necessary to ensure a finite search space, but it is sufficient, since it bounds the number of LRES inferences that can be made. It is the analogue of an assumption that lexical items contain at least one prosodic constant (i.e. that no type is lexically assigned to the empty string) which is sufficient (though not necessary) to ensure termination of certain parsing methods.

Figure 4 shows generation of 'John talks about' from $\lambda w((\mathbf{talk}\ (\mathbf{about}\ w))\ \mathbf{j})$. As with the prosodic control of search in parsing, we do not need to attempt resolving with any lexical entry unless the bag of (semantic) constants occurring lexically is contained in the bag of such constants controlling the proof search.[10] The entries for 'about' and 'John' do not project S: after adding the conditionalised N to the database, the head of the literal initially on the agenda is matched to the head of the lexical clause for 'talks'. A unifier performing the matching is $\{x = (\mathbf{about\ w}), y = \mathbf{j}\}$. The N goal resolves with 'John', the PP goal with the clausal head for 'about' under $z = \mathbf{w}$, and the N goal issued is resolved at the last step with the N put into the database at the first step.

The structure is just like that for parsing, but with known and unknown information inverted. Since matching under associativity is non-deterministic one must in general be prepared to backtrack and try different unifiers in parsing (though this does not arise in our examples); likewise for higher-order matching in generation, where indeed the non-determinism of matching is more severe. The confirmation and recovery of prosodic form is also invoked by matching, as with parsing. Working backwards we have at the last step $c = \mathbf{d}$, then $a = \mathbf{about{+}d}$ and $b = \mathbf{John}$. Finally, we solve $e{+}\mathbf{d} = \mathbf{John{+}talks{+}about{+}d}$, generating the prosodic form **John+talks+about**.

One last example is given in figure 5.[11] The main interest is the semantic matching at the first step, which requires x to be mapped to a second-order λ-abstracted term. In the appendix we discuss an algorithm for the case of second-order matching. Although that is not enough for the current example, which is third-order, it does enable us to compute in the manner we have presented the task of generation not only for the associative Lambek calculus as elucidated, but also for a much wider range of sublinear labelled calculi. This is because the only adjustment necessary is accommodation of prosodic matching under the relevant theory. Until now no such general method has been available. The principle issues arising are: how to perform matching for a wider class of λ-terms, and how to extend treatment to include *logical* constants. We hope to be able to address these questions in future work.

---

[10] Again, we can in practice precompute a working set of lexical entries and ignore the rest of the lexicon.

[11] For explanation of the categorial assignment to 'seeks' see chapter 5 of [13].

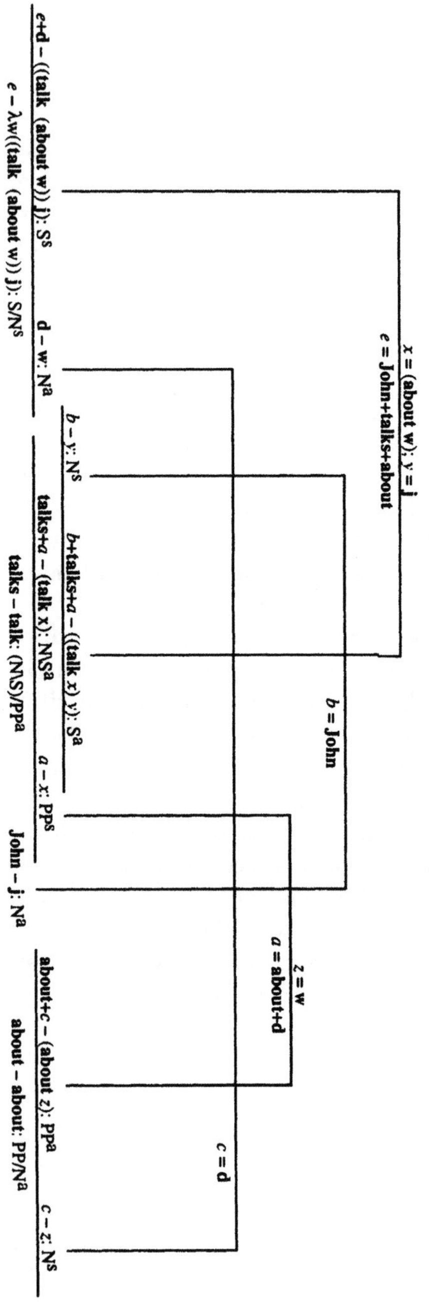

Fig. 4. Proof net for generation of 'John talks about'

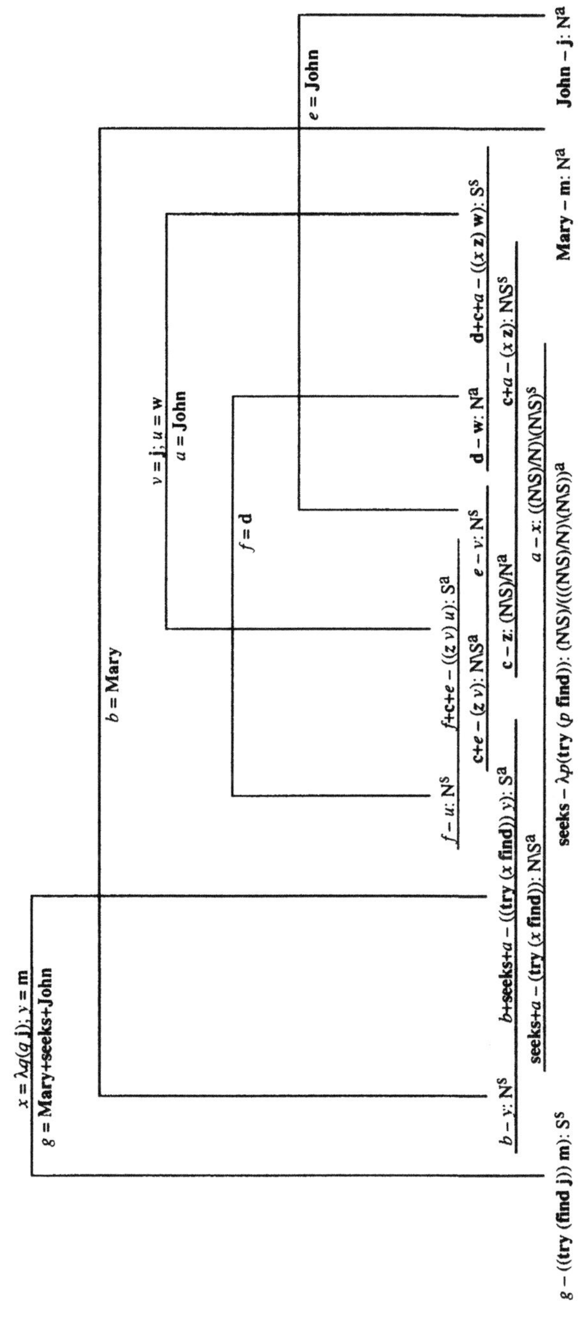

Fig. 5. Proof net for generation of 'Mary seeks John'

Appendix: Higher-order unification

Higher-order unification is the task of unifying typed λ-terms. We assume single-bind, i.e. linear, λ-terms. All λ-terms can be expressed in $\beta\eta$-long normal form as shown in (23a), where each ψ_i is in $\beta\eta$-long normal form; ϕ is a constant or a variable (free or bound), called the *head* of the term. In (23b) we show an abbreviated "flattened" form that we use for the nested functional application in (23a); and in (23c), vector-style notations for iterated functional application and λ-abstraction.

(23) a. $\lambda x_1 \lambda x_2 \ldots \lambda x_n (\ldots((\phi\ \psi_1)\ \psi_2)\ \ldots \psi_m)\ m, n \geq 0$
b. $\lambda x_1 \lambda x_2 \ldots \lambda x_n . \phi(\psi_1, \psi_2, \ldots, \psi_m)$
c. $\lambda \overline{x_n} \phi(\overline{\psi_{\{1,\ldots,m\}}})$

We say a term is *rigid* when its head is a constant or a bound variable, and *flexible* when its head is a free variable.

A higher-order unification equation is a pair of terms to be unified, $\phi = \psi$, and a Higher-Order Unification System (HOUS) is a set of such equations, that must be satisfied simultaneously. A common method for solution of a HOUS is that of transformations ([19], [4]): there are a set of transformation rules that transform a system S to a system S' with the same set of unifiers. The transformation rules we will use not only transform the HOUS but will also compute a unifier; any state of the process is represented by the unifier σ computed up to the current moment and the current unification system S (to which σ has been applied): $\langle S, \sigma \rangle$; the end of the process is marked by transformation into the empty system.

Application of transformation rules has the form (24): some (*active*) unification equation $\phi = \psi$ is removed and replaced by subproblems R, and a substitution ρ is applied to the system and composed with the substitution to date.

(24) $\langle S \cup \{\phi = \psi\}, \sigma \rangle \Longrightarrow \langle \rho(S \cup R), \rho \circ \sigma \rangle$

At each stage $\beta\eta$-long normal form is to be restored. There are three kinds of transformation depending on the nature of the terms in the active equation: flexible/flexible, flexible/rigid, and rigid/rigid. The algorithm for the particular case of linear second-order matching is adapted from the unification algorithm of [10] (in fact, we only have to drop from it the flexible/flexible case).

If two terms to be unified have different length lambda prefixes the unification fails (it means they are not of the same type). Otherwise, we assume α-conversion making the λ-prefixes identical. The rigid/rigid case checks the identity of the two heads and tries to unify the parameters:

(25) $\lambda \overline{x_n} . \phi(\overline{\psi_{\{1,\ldots,m\}}}) = \lambda \overline{x_n} . \phi(\overline{\chi_{\{1,\ldots,m\}}})$
$R = \{\lambda \overline{x_n} . \psi_1 = \lambda \overline{x_n} . \chi_1, \ldots, \lambda \overline{x_n} . \psi_m = \lambda \overline{x_n} . \chi_m\}$
$\rho = \{\}$

For the flexible/rigid case we choose in a don't know non-deterministic way to *project* or to *imitate*. The projection rule instantiates the head of the flexible term, a free variable x, with the identity function (it must, then, be of a first-order endocentric type $\tau \to \tau, \tau \in \mathcal{D}$):

$$\begin{aligned} &(26)\ \lambda\overline{x_n}.\phi(\overline{\psi_{\{1,\ldots,m\}}}) = \lambda\overline{x_n}.x(\chi) \\ &R = \{\lambda\overline{x_n}.\phi(\overline{\psi_{\{1,\ldots,m\}}}) = \lambda\overline{x_n}.\chi\} \\ &\rho = \{x = \lambda y.y\} \end{aligned}$$

The imitation rule decomposes (in a don't know non-deterministic way) the flexible term into a set of m new flexible terms, arranging a linear allocation of the arguments $\chi_1, \ldots, \chi_p$ as the arguments of m new variables $z_1, \ldots, z_m$ to be unified with the m terms $\psi_1, \ldots, \psi_m$ This allocation is given by a partition $R_1, \ldots, R_m$ of $1, \ldots, p$.

$$\begin{aligned} &(27)\ \lambda\overline{x_n}.\phi(\overline{\psi_{\{1,\ldots,m\}}}) = \lambda\overline{x_n}.x(\overline{\chi_{\{1,\ldots,p\}}}) \\ &R = \{\lambda\overline{x_n}.\psi_1 = \lambda\overline{x_n}.z_1(\overline{\chi_{R_1}}), \ldots, \lambda\overline{x_n}.\psi_m = \lambda\overline{x_n}.z_m(\overline{\chi_{R_m}})\} \\ &\rho = \{x = \lambda\overline{y_p}.\phi(z_1(\overline{y_{R_1}}), \ldots, z_m(\overline{y_{R_m}}))\} \end{aligned}$$

References

1. V. Danos and L. Regnier. The structure of multiplicatives. *Archive for mathematical logic*, (28):181–203, 1989.
2. Gilles Dowek. Third order matching is decidable. In *7th Annual IEEE Symposium of Logic in Computer Science*, pages 2–10, 1992.
3. Dov Gabbay. *Labelled Deductive Systems*. Oxford University Press, 1996.
4. Jean Gallier and Wayne Snyder. Designing unification procedures using transformations: a survey. In *Workshop Logic For Computer Science*. MSRI Berkeley, 1989.
5. Jean-Yves Girard. Linear logic. *Theoretical Computer Science*, 50(1):1–102, 1987.
6. W. Goldfard. The undecibility of the second-order unification problem. *Theoretical Computer Science*, 13(2):225–230, 1981.
7. G. Huet. *Constrained Resolution: A Complete Method for Higher-Order Logic*. PhD thesis, Case Western Reserve University, 1972.
8. G. Huet. A unification algorithm for typed λ-calculus. *Theoretical Computer Science*, 1(1):27–57, 1975.
9. J. Lambek. The mathematics of sentence structure. *American Mathematical Monthly*, (65):154–170, 1958.
10. Jordi Levy. Linear second-order unification. *Rewriting Techniques and Applications*, 1996.
11. Xavier Lloré and Glyn Morrill. Difference lists and difference bags for logic programming of categorial deduction. In *Proceedings of the Sociedad Española para el Procesamiento del Lenguaje Natural*, pages 115–129, 1995.
12. Michael Moortgat. Labelled deductive systems for categorial theorem proving. In *Proceedings Eight Amsterdam Colloquium*, pages 403–424, Amsterdam, 1992. Institute of Language, Logic and Information, Universiteit van Amsterdam.
13. Glyn Morrill. *Type Logical Grammar: Categorial Logic of Signs*. Kluwer Academic Publishers, 1994.
14. Glyn Morrill. Clausal proofs and discontinuity. *Bulletin of the Interest Group in Pure and Applied Logics*, 3(2–3):403–427, 1995.

15. Glyn Morrill. Higher-order linear logic programming of categorial deduction. In *Proceedings ACL*, pages 133–140, 1995.
16. Glyn Morrill. Memoisation of categorial proof nets: parallelism in categorial processing. In Michele Abrusci and Claudia Casadio, editors, *Proof and Linguistic Categories: Proceedings 1996 Roma Workshop*, pages 157–169. Università di Bologna, 1996. To appear in S. Manandhar, W. Nutt and G. Lopez (eds.), Springer-Verlag.
17. F. Pereira and D. Warren. Parsing as deduction. In *Proceedings ACL*, pages 132–144, 1983.
18. Dirk Roorda. *Resource Logics: Proof-theoretical Investigations*. PhD thesis, Universiteit van Amsterdam, 1991.
19. Wayne Snyder and Jean Gallier. Higher-order unification revisited: Complete sets of transformations. *Journal of Symbolic Computation*, (8):101–140, 1989.

Semilinearity as a Syntactic Invariant*

Jens Michaelis[1] and Marcus Kracht[2]

[1] Universität Potsdam, Institut für Linguistik/Innovationskolleg, Postfach 60 15 53, D – 14415 Potsdam
michael@ling.uni-potsdam.de
[2] Freie Universität Berlin, II. Mathematisches Institut, Arnimallee 3, D – 14195 Berlin
kracht@math.fu-berlin.de

Abstract. Mildly context sensitive grammar formalisms such as multi-component TAGs and linear context free rewrite systems have been introduced to capture the full complexity of natural languages. We show that, in a formal sense, Old Georgian can be taken to provide an example of a non-semilinear language. This implies that none of the aforementioned grammar formalisms is strong enough to generate this language.

Introduction

What we have in mind when we use the term *syntactic invariant* is, roughly speaking, a property, valid within some (formal) grammar theory, which remains "robust under slight modifications" of this theory. In the following we direct our particular attention to one such property: *Semilinearity (of a language)*.

Introducing the definition of semilinearity, Parikh proved that any context free language (CFL) is semilinear (see e.g. [10]). It has been shown that there is a need to go beyond the class of all CFLs, if we want to define a formal language in terms of phrase structure grammar or some related formalism to capture the *complexity of natural language* (see e.g. [6]). To cope with this problem, *mild context sensitivity* is intended to be one appropriate, but rather informally defined grammar type, determining a proper subclass of context sensitive grammars. Originally, a mildly context sensitive grammar (MCSG) was defined by three necessary properties (see e.g. [7]). *Constant growth* of the language produced by such a grammar is one of those, and a somewhat strengthened version of this property of a language is that of being *semilinear*. In fact, this latter property is common to all grammars within one of the "classical" formalism types where each of these types constitutes a subclass of all MCSGs. In particular if the grammar belongs to the class of all tree adjoining grammars (TAGs) or the class of

* This paper has been worked out at the University of Potsdam within the *Innovationskolleg 'Formale Modelle kognitiver Komplexität' (INK II/A 12)* funded by the Deutsche Forschungsgemeinschaft (DFG). We have benefitted largely from discussions with Annius Groenink. Many thanks also to Winfried Boeder for his help concerning Old Georgian, and to two anonymous referees for fixing up several of the "very non-English" formulations within the preceeding version of this paper.

all head grammars (HGs) as well as to their generalized extensions, to the class of all multicomponent TAGs (MCTAGs) or the class of all linear context free rewrite systems (LCFRSs), respectively. The class of TAGs is weakly equivalent to the one of HGs,[1] and the same holds for the class of MCTAGs and LCFRSs ([16]). See also [8] for a survey on MCSGs. Our special interest in the property of being semilinear is motivated by the question:

(Q) Is it reasonable to expect a grammar formalism to generate a semilinear language, if the formalism is intended to capture human language capacity?

We are going to argue that to answer (Q) is not a trivial matter. Not least, since due to the syntactic analysis of Boeder ([1]), the phenomenon of *Suffixaufnahme* of genitive suffixes in *Old Georgian* can be taken to provide a possible counterexample. But, before we consider this case (see Sect. 2), we want to give a formal definition of *semilinear sets* and *semilinear languages*, respectively. Then we state a (technical) proposition which will be used to show that, in a formal sense, Old Georgian is not semilinear. For these purposes we first mention some conventions applying to our notation. All these preliminaries are done in Sect. 1 of this paper, while a proof of the proposition is given in the Appendix. In Sect. 3 we consider two other languages, where each of them already has been introduced in the literature as an example of a language not derivable by any MCTAG. For each of these two languages we briefly check for the possibility of extending the corresponding result to the more general one that the language is non-semilinear at all. Section 4 is reserved for a discussion of our result presented in Sect. 2. In particular, our example is compared to the two examples mentioned in Sect. 3. Furthermore, we will show in outline how the technical tools we used in the Old Georgian case can be interpreted with regard to a general proof method within the framework of formal language theory. Some final remarks are given in Sect. 5.

1 Notations, Definitions, and a Proposition

We denote the set of real numbers and natural numbers (non negative integers) by $\mathbb{R}$ and $\mathbb{N}$, respectively. $\mathbb{N}_+$ is taken to be the set of all natural numbers $n > 0$. For any $n \in \mathbb{N}_+$ and any non-empty set M the set M^n is the set of all finite sequences of length n, or all n-tuples, $u = (u_0, \ldots, u_{n-1})$ in M, where $u_i \in M$ is the $(i+1)$–th component of u. In the case $M \subseteq \mathbb{R}$ and if $u_i = 1$ for some i while all other components of u are 0 we also write $e^{(i)}$ instead of u. $e^{(i)}$ is called the $(i+1)$–th unit tuple (unit vector). This is due to the fact that we will use $\mathbb{R}^n$ also as an abbrevation for the common n-dimensional (vector) space $(\mathbb{R}^n, +_{\mathbb{R}^n}, \cdot_{S_\mathbb{R}}, 0_{\mathbb{R}^n})$ over $\mathbb{R}$ defined in a canonical way. Here, $+_{\mathbb{R}^n}$ and $\cdot_{S_\mathbb{R}}$ denote the common addition and outer product (scalar product) on $\mathbb{R}^n$ defined

[1] More generally, these two classes fall into a broader range of weakly equivalent grammar types ([15]), where each of these has been proposed to capture natural language capacity in a formal way.

componentwise by means of the common addition $+_{\mathbb{R}}$ and multiplication $\cdot_{\mathbb{R}}$ on $\mathbb{R}$, respectively. Recall that $\cdot_{S_{\mathbb{R}}}$ is a function mapping $\mathbb{R} \times \mathbb{R}^n$ to $\mathbb{R}^n$.[2] $0_{\mathbb{R}^n}$ denotes the neutral element with respect to $+_{\mathbb{R}^n}$ (the null-vector). Then, $\mathbb{N}^n$ can be considered as the substructure $(\mathbb{N}^n, +_{\mathbb{N}^n}, \cdot_{S_{\mathbb{N}}}, 0_{\mathbb{N}^n})$ of $\mathbb{R}^n$, where $+_{\mathbb{N}^n}$ and $\cdot_{S_{\mathbb{N}}}$ are the restrictions of $+_{\mathbb{R}^n}$ and $\cdot_{S_{\mathbb{R}}}$ to the domains $\mathbb{N}^n \times \mathbb{N}^n$ and $\mathbb{N} \times \mathbb{N}^n$, respectively, both taking values in $\mathbb{N}^n$. $0_{\mathbb{N}^n}$, the neutral element with respect to $+_{\mathbb{N}^n}$, thus is identical with $0_{\mathbb{R}^n}$. Furthermore, we sometimes think of $\mathbb{N}^n$ just as the "simple" monoid $(\mathbb{N}^n, +_{\mathbb{N}^n}, 0_{\mathbb{N}^n})$.

For any finite non-empty set Σ (a set of terminals), Σ^* is not only taken to denote the set of all finite sequences (of all strings) in Σ including the empty string ϵ, but also the monoid $(\Sigma^*, \cdot_{\Sigma^*}, \epsilon)$, where $\cdot_{\Sigma^*}$ is the usual concatenation operation of strings in Σ^*.

We will drop the subscripts of the just introduced operation symbols in all cases when it does not lead to misunderstandings, and furthermore usually drop the remaining dot "$\cdot$" after doing so. If, for some non-empty set M, we simply refer to a set M^n we will (tacitly) assume n to be in $\mathbb{N}_+$.

Definition 1. Let $M \subseteq \mathbb{N}^n$. Then

(a) we call M **linear**, if for some $k \in \mathbb{N}$ there are some $u^{(0)}, u^{(1)}, \ldots, u^{(k)} \in \mathbb{N}^n$, such that $M = \{u^{(0)} + \sum_{i=1}^{k} n_i\, u^{(i)} \mid n_i \in \mathbb{N} \text{ for } 1 \leq i \leq k\}$.

(b) we call M **semilinear**, if for some $k \in \mathbb{N}$ there are some linear $M_1, \ldots, M_k \subseteq \mathbb{N}^n$, such that $M = \bigcup_{i=1}^{k} M_i$.

It can be shown ([4]),

Lemma 2. *Let $M, N \subseteq \mathbb{N}^n$ be semilinear. Then, $M \cap N \subseteq \mathbb{N}^n$ is semilinear.*

Definition 3. For some $n \in \mathbb{N}_+$ let $\{w_i \mid 0 \leq i < n\}$ be an enumeration of Σ, a finite set of terminal symbols with cardinality n. The **Parikh mapping** $p_\Sigma : \Sigma^* \to \mathbb{N}^n$ is then defined inductively by means of $\cdot_{\Sigma^*}$ and $+_{\mathbb{N}^n}$ in the following way:

$$\begin{aligned} \epsilon &\mapsto 0_{\mathbb{N}^n} \\ w_i &\mapsto e^{(i)} && \text{for } 0 \leq i < n \\ \alpha\beta &\mapsto p_\Sigma(\alpha) + p_\Sigma(\beta) && \text{for all } \alpha, \beta \in \Sigma^* \end{aligned}$$

The image $p_\Sigma[L] := \{p_\Sigma(\alpha) \mid \alpha \in L\} \subseteq \mathbb{N}^n$ of a language $L \subseteq \Sigma^*$ under p_Σ is called the **Parikh image** of L. If $p_\Sigma[L]$ is semilinear, L is called a **semilinear language**.

Due to its inductive definition, the aforementioned Parikh mapping p_Σ is a surjective homomorphism which maps the monoid $(\Sigma^*, \cdot_{\Sigma^*}, \epsilon)$ onto the monoid $(\mathbb{N}^n, +_{\mathbb{N}^n}, 0_{\mathbb{N}^n})$; and p_Σ is 1–1 (injective) iff Σ consists of exactly one element.

[2] For any two non-empty sets M_1 and M_2, $M_1 \times M_2$ denotes the set of all pairs, built up by the elements of M_1 and M_2.

For each string $\alpha \in \Sigma^*$ the $(i+1)$–th component of the Parikh image $p_\Sigma(\alpha)$ just provides the result of counting the number of appearances of the terminal symbol $w_i \in \Sigma$ within α. Thus, whether or not a language L is semilinear depends only on the strings belonging to L and not on the (derivational) structures (corresponding to a possibly underlying grammar) represented by those strings. Moreover, the order of the terminals that appear within those strings is disregarded.[3]

Definition 4. For any $m \in \mathbb{N}$ and any $\alpha = (a_0, \ldots, a_m) \in \mathbb{R}^{m+1}$ with $a_m \neq 0$, we take P_α to denote the function $f : \mathbb{R} \rightarrow \mathbb{R}$ defined by $x \mapsto \sum_{i=0}^{m} a_i x^i$ for every $x \in \mathbb{R}$. That is, P_α is the **(real) polynomial (of degree m) corresponding to α.**

We are now able to state the proposition which we actually are interested in.

Proposition 5. *For some natural numbers $m, n \geq 2$ let $\alpha = (a_0, \ldots, a_m)$ be a finite sequence in $\mathbb{R}^{m+1}$, where $a_m > 0$, and let a given $M \subseteq \mathbb{N}^n$ have the following properties:*

(i) For any $k \in \mathbb{N}_+$ there are some numbers $l_2^{(k)}, \ldots, l_{n-1}^{(k)} \in \mathbb{N}$ for which the n-tuple $(k, P_\alpha(k), l_2^{(k)}, \ldots, l_{n-1}^{(k)})$ belongs to M.
(ii) For any $k \in \mathbb{N}_+$ the value $P_\alpha(k)$ provides an upper (lower) bound for the second component l_1 of any n-tuple $(k, l_1, \ldots, l_{n-1}) \in M$ (that is $l_1 \leq P_\alpha(k)$ ($l_1 \geq P_\alpha(k)$) for any such n-tuple).

Then M is not semilinear.

A proof of this more general proposition is given in the Appendix. Here, with regard to our further considerations, we just want to state a corollary, which emphasizes a special case of the last proposition; namely the case $m = 2$, $\alpha = (1/2, -1/2, 0)$, and P_α an upper bound in the sense of condition (ii). This corollary also completes the part of the rather technical preliminaries.

Corollary 6. *Let M be a subset of $\mathbb{N}^n$, where $n \geq 2$, which has the properties:*

(i) For any $k \in \mathbb{N}_+$ there are some numbers $l_2^{(k)}, \ldots, l_{n-1}^{(k)} \in \mathbb{N}$ for which the n-tuple $(k, (k^2 - k)/2, l_2^{(k)}, \ldots, l_{n-1}^{(k)})$ belongs to M.
(ii) For any $k \in \mathbb{N}_+$ the value $P(k) := (k^2 - k)/2$ provides an upper bound for the second component l_1 of any n-tuple $(k, l_1, \ldots, l_{n-1}) \in M$ (that means $l_1 \leq P(k)$ for any such n-tuple).

Then M is not semilinear.

[3] Notice, that a mapping $p_\Sigma : \Sigma^* \rightarrow \mathbb{N}^n$ according to Definition 3 for some given set of terminals Σ depends on the enumeration chosen for Σ. But, independently of such a choice, the corresponding mapping is unique up to an isomorphism on $\mathbb{N}^n$, induced by a permutation π on $\{0, \ldots, n-1\}$. In this sense it is reasonable to speak of *the* Parikh mapping p_Σ with respect to a given set of terminals Σ.

2 Old Georgian

In this section, first we briefly introduce the phenomenon, shown by Old Georgian, to which our further argumention is related. Then, we are going to determine a sublanguage (fragment) L_M of Old Georgian of which the Parikh image $p_\Sigma[L_M]$ is a set $M \subseteq \mathbb{N}^n$ according to Corollary 6 above. This fragment is not only non-semilinear itself, but also prevents the entire Old Georgian language from being semilinear.

Old Georgian is one of those languages which show the phenomenon called *Suffixaufnahme* (literal: *taking up of suffixes*[4]). That is, the Old Georgian grammar allows for multiple case(-number)-marking of nouns by adding "extra" case suffixes to the "inner" case suffix, where the (possibly empty) inner case suffix is obligatory and signals case in the "usual" sense, that is to say, the case immediately assigned to the smallest NP to which a noun belongs (which is the only marked case, for example, in the Indo-European language family). Each additional case-marker is the result of some indirect case assignment, and in this sense an explicit "reference" to the syntactical function of a noun(phrase) as a part of some more comprehensive constituent. Taking the case-suffixes of a noun in their "left-to-right-order" they can be described as the reflex of a left recursive, increasing structural embedding of NPs. Such a description is possible at least with regard to an underlying basic structure as it is assumed in [1]. More concretely, in Old Georgian, complex NPs, including stacked genitive NPs, cannot only be of the following basic form.[5]

Davit-is	*galob-isa*	*muql-ta*	*ama-t*	(1)
$[[[[$David-Gen $]_{NP_4}$	singing-Gen $]_{NP_3}$	verse-Pl(Gen)	Art-Pl(Gen) $]_{NP_2}$	

ҫartkuma-j
recitation-Nom $]_{NP_1}$

'the recitation of the verses of the song of David'

The "sub–NPs" can also appear in reversed order. But then corresponding to the stacking of the NPs, a stacking of case suffixes appears as well.

tkuenda	*micemul*	*ars*	*cnob-ad*	*saidumlo-j*	*igi*	*sasupevel-isa*	(2)
to=you	given	is	knowing-Adv	mystery-Nom	Art=Nom	kingdom-Gen	

m-is *γmrt-isa-jsa-j*
Art-Gen god-Gen-Gen-Nom

'Unto You it is given to know the mystery of the kingdom of God'

[4] But, see [11] for the (non-)possibility of an appropriate translation of the term *Suffixaufnahme*.

[5] Actually, the structure of (1) is only nearly basic, since Boeder assumes nouns to be phrase-final within the basic structure, while an article shifts to the right of its noun by undergoing clitic-movement.

qovel-i igi sisxl-i saxl-isa-j m-is Saul-is-isa-j (3)
all-Nom Art=Nom blood-Nom house-Gen-Nom Art-Gen Saul-Gen-Gen-Nom

'all the blood of the house of Saul'

According to Boeder ([1]), the examples (2) and (3) are a result of ordinary agreement, instantiated by an optional application of some recursive (transformational) rules to the underlying basic structure as given with the example (1). If we apply Boeder's analysis to the general case, especially the analysis of constructions like (3), then (abstracting from determiners and other lexical categories) complex nominative NPs consisting of k stacked NPs, $k \in \mathbb{N}_+$, may have the form

$$\mathrm{N}_1\text{-}\mathrm{Nom}\ \ \mathrm{N}_2\text{-}\mathrm{Gen}\text{-}\mathrm{Nom}\ \ \mathrm{N}_3\text{-}\mathrm{Gen}^2\text{-}\mathrm{Nom}\ \ \ldots\ \ \mathrm{N}_k\text{-}\ \mathrm{Gen}^{k-1}\text{-}\mathrm{Nom} \qquad (4)$$

Here, for $1 \leq i \leq k$, N_i denotes some noun(stem). That is to say, for any such NP, $\sum_{i=0}^{k-1} i = k^2/2 - k/2$ is the number of genitive suffixes appearing in it. Moreover,

the number of all genitive suffixes of all nouns within a complex NP consisting of k stacked NPs, where $k \in \mathbb{N}_+$, is bounded by $k^2/2 - k/2$. (5)

This is due to the restrictions on the applicability of the rules, proposed by Boeder. These restrictions come up with the given basic structure

$$[[[\ldots[\mathrm{N}_k\text{-}\mathrm{Gen}]_{\mathrm{NP}_k} \ldots \mathrm{N}_3\text{-}\mathrm{Gen}]_{\mathrm{NP}_3}\ \ \mathrm{N}_2\text{-}\mathrm{Gen}]_{\mathrm{NP}_2}\ \ \mathrm{N}_1\text{-}\mathrm{Nom}]_{\mathrm{NP}_1} \qquad (6)$$

Roughly speaking, an indirect case assignment to N_i-Gen is only possible "upwards" with respect to the stacked NPs. That is to say, such an assignment to N_i-Gen is only possible with respect to the NPs in which NP_i is properly embedded, and possible only one time for each NP_j with $1 \leq j < i$. Thus, the maximal number of suffixes that can be taken up by N_i-Gen is $i - 1$.

Take the set Σ to be the Old Georgian lexicon, and $L_G \subseteq \Sigma^*$ to be the language of Old Georgian. Before we proceed, we just want to emphasize one observation which can be made so far. If we want to deal with a finite lexicon (a set of terminal symbols or atomic elements), (4) demands that at least some kind of "global" genitive suffix Gen has to be a lexical entry (terminal symbol) on its own. Notice, due to (4) there are uncountable many (pairwise distinct) possibilities of multiple-case marking of a noun: there is no upper bound on the number of genitive suffixes that "can be added" because of the fact that the number $k \in \mathbb{N}_+$ of instances of some nouns within a complex NP is not (finitely) limited.

As announced at the begining of this section, we now determine a non-semilinear fragment $L_M \subseteq L_G$. For any $k \in \mathbb{N}_+$ this fragment includes at least one sentence in which a complex NP corresponding to (4) can be found. But, in addition, we try to keep such a sentence "as simple as possible" with respect to its structural complexity. The idea is to fix an intransitive verb and to define the members of L_M in such a way that each member is a grammatical sentence which consists of exactly one instance of the fixed verb and an NP, which is therefore necessarily the subject. For some $n \in \mathbb{N}$ let us now take $\{w_i \mid 0 \leq i < n\}$ to be an enumeration of Σ. For simplicity, not effecting our considerations in general, we assume

$$\begin{array}{ll} w_0 & \text{to be some fixed noun(stem)} , \\ w_1 & \text{the genitive suffix Gen} , \\ w_2 & \text{a nominative suffix} , \\ w_3 & \text{a genitive article} , \\ w_4 & \text{a nominative article} , \\ w_5 & \text{a fixed intransitiv verb} . \end{array} \tag{7}$$

Now consider the linear, and hence semilinear, set

$$R = \left\{ e^{(4)} + e^{(5)} + \sum_{i=0}^{3} n_i e^{(i)} \mid n_i \in \mathbb{N} \right\} \subseteq \mathbb{N}^n \tag{8}$$

Then the full pre-image of R with respect to the Parikh mapping p_Σ is the language

$$L_R := p_\Sigma^{-1}[R] = \{\alpha \in \Sigma^* \mid \text{there is an } u \in R \text{ with } p_\Sigma(\alpha) = u\} \subseteq \Sigma^* \tag{9}$$

The language L_R includes all strings of Σ^* which consists of exactly one appearance of w_4 and w_5 and an arbitrary number of appearances of $w_0, \ldots, w_3$. We now define the language L_M as the set of all strings belonging not only to L_R but also to L_G, that is

$$L_M := L_G \cap L_R \subseteq \Sigma^* \tag{10}$$

Then, the Parikh image $p_\Sigma[L_M]$ of L_M clearly is a subset of the intersection of the Parikh images of L_G and L_R. But $p_\Sigma[L_M]$ even is identical with this intersection, since L_R is defined as the full pre-image of R with respect to p_Σ; that is

$$M := p_\Sigma[L_M] = p_\Sigma[L_G] \cap p_\Sigma[L_R] = p_\Sigma[L_G] \cap R \tag{11}$$

Recall that L_M only includes strings of $L_R \subseteq \Sigma^*$. But all strings within L_M are grammatical in the sense that they belong to L_G as well. Since we can assume that the intransitive verb needs to be combined with one nominative subject-NP to produce a well-formed sentence, it is reasonable to conclude that each string of L_M consists of one (possibly complex) nominative subject-NP besides the single instantiation of w_5, the fixed intransitive verb. Moreover, since an NP cannot assign nominative case to its complement but only the oblique case genitive, at least the underlying basic structure of this subject-NP can only be of the form (6). That is to say, the subject-NP itself can only consist of k stacked NPs, $k \in \mathbb{N}_+$, where each of these stacked NPs has genitive as its immediate case, except for the "highest" one which must have nominative case. But then, because of (4) and (5) the set M can not be semilinear according to the Corollary 6. Now, we recall that the set R is in particular semilinear, and that the intersection of two semilinear sets is semilinear itself (Lemma 2). Then, due to (11), we may finally conclude that $p_\Sigma[L_G]$ can not be semilinear, and thus Old Georgian is a non-semilinear language.

3 Semilinearity and MCTAGs

Although a "weak" property on its own,[6] semilinearity seems to be a "strong" property with respect to natural language formalisms, as we have just seen. Remember that (as is shown in [16]) semilinearity is a necessary property of e.g. any multicomponent TAL (MCTAL), that is, any language generated by an MCTAG. Due to other examples, it has already been doubted whether TAGs and/or even MCTAGs, and thus LCFRSs, are appropriate tools for natural language. E.g. Rambow ([14]) states the inadequacy of MCTAGs to capture the phenomenon of Scrambling as it appears in German. Nevertheless, also his proposal for a revised grammar formalism only gives rise to grammars that produce a semilinear language.

Manaster-Ramer ([9]) argues that Dutch is no tree adjoining language (TAL) referring to a certain subset of coordination phrases which is no TAL. He informally outlines that, on the basis of a generalized extension of this subset, the same kind of argumentation is even possible if the term *TAL* is replaced by *MCTAL*. A formal elaboration of this is given by Groenink ([5]). Radzinski ([13]) proves that the language of all Chinese number-names is no MCTAL. Like Groenink, Radzinski refers to a certain sublanguage which is a non-MCTAL, and he also uses a pumping lemma to show this. In both cases, Dutch and Chinese number-names, the corresponding sublanguage can be shown to be non-semilinear in general by means of Proposition 5, or at least a similar one in the Dutch case.

The final conclusion of Radzinski, as well as that of Groenink, is based on the argument that the considered sublanguage is the intersection of the entire language with a certain regular language, since both authors refer to the property that MCTALs are closed under intersection with regular sets. We implicitly used a similar, but strictly weaker property of semilinear languages in the Old Georgian case. It is related to the fact that a language is semilinear iff it is *letter equivalent* to a regular language (see Sect. 4 for more details). And, taking for granted Radzinski's general assumptions about the Chinese number-names, in a nearly identical way as in the Old Georgian case, the corresponding sublanguage can be used to show that the entire Chinese number-names system is non-semilinear as well, and thus not only a non–MCTAL.

3.1 Chinese Number-Names

The sublanguage of the Chinese number-names, considered by Radzinski ([13]), includes all well-formed strings composable only of instances of *wu (five)* and *zhao (*am. *trillion)* and consisting of at least one instance of each. This set is the following one:

$$L_M := \{wu\ zhao^{k_1} \ldots\ wu\ zhao^{k_m} \mid m, k_i \in \mathbb{N}_+\ ,\ k_1 > k_2 > \ldots > k_m\} \qquad (12)$$

[6] E.g., if Σ is a finite set with at least two elements there are uncountable many semilinear languages $L \subseteq \Sigma^*$.

Let $\{w_i \mid 0 \leq i < n\}$ be an enumeration of the Chinese number-names lexicon Σ, where $w_0 = \mathsf{wu}$ and $w_1 = \mathsf{zhao}$, and let $L_{CN} \subseteq \Sigma^*$ be the language of all such number names. Then, by Proposition 5, the Parikh image $M := p_\Sigma[L_M]$ is a non-semilinear subset of $\mathbb{N}^n$. The appropriate polynomial P_α, providing a lower bound in the sense of (ii) of Proposition 5, is of degree 2 and looks similar to that of the Old Georgian case, namely $P_\alpha(x) = x^2/2 + x/2$. Due to the definition of L_M and (12), we may conclude that

$$M = p_\Sigma[L_{CN}] \cap \{e^{(0)} + e^{(1)} + n_0 e^{(0)} + n_1 e^{(1)} \mid n_0, n_1 \in \mathbb{N}\} \tag{13}$$

Thus, if L_{CN} were semilinear, then M, as the intersection of two semilinear sets, would be as well. Hence, L_{CN} cannot be semilinear in general.

3.2 Dutch Coordination Phrases

Groenink ([5]) considers a fragment L_M of the language Dutch, which can be written as the infinite union $\bigcup_{k \in \mathbb{N}} L_k$, where for each $k \in \mathbb{N}$, L_k is the following sublanguage of Dutch

$$\begin{aligned} L_k \;=\; & \textit{dat Jan Piet Marie Fred}^k \\ & (\textit{hoorde leren}^k \textit{ uitnodigen})^+ \textit{ en } (\textit{zag leren}^k \textit{ omhelzen}) \end{aligned} \tag{14}$$

That is, e.g. for $k = 1$ the shortest string belonging to L_k is

dat	*Jan*	*Piet*	*Marie*	*Fred*	*hoorde*	*leren*	*uitnodigen*	*en*
that	Jan	Piet $_1$	Marie $_2$	Fred $_3$	hear-past $_1$	teach-inf $_2$	invite-inf $_3$	and

(14′)

zag	*leren*	*omhelzen*
saw-past $_1$	teach-inf $_2$	embrace-inf $_3$

'that Jan heard Piet teach Marie to invite Fred and saw him teach her to embrace him'

Now, let be $w_0 = \mathsf{Fred}$ and $w_1 = \mathsf{leren}$ in an enumeration $\{w_i \mid 0 \leq i < n\}$ of the Dutch lexicon Σ. Then the Parikh image $M := p_\Sigma[L_M]$ is of the form

$$M = \{(k, k \cdot m + k, l_2^{(k \cdot m)}, \ldots, l_{n-1}^{(k \cdot m)}) \mid k \in \mathbb{N}, m \in \mathbb{N}_+\} \subseteq \mathbb{N}^n \tag{15}$$

for some appropriate $l_i^{(k \cdot m)} \in \mathbb{N}$, $2 \leq i < n$, for each $k \in \mathbb{N}$ and $m \in \mathbb{N}_+$. The set M can be shown to be non-semilinear.[7] Then it is an immediate consequence that L_M must be a non-MCTAL, as is shown in [5].

4 Discussion

Radzinski is aware of the fact that it is not quite clear whether the Chinese number-names system can be considered as properly related to an I-language

[7] We omit a proof here, since it differs from that of Proposition 5 in certain details, though it can be done in a similar manner.

(in the sense of Chomsky) or rather as related to an interface between a natural language component of the human cognitive endowment and a "mathematical" one. Therefore, Radzinski admits that the consequences of his example for the natural language Chinese do not become obvious at once. But also, if the first possibility is supposed to be the right one, it does not immediately become decidable whether the Chinese language "in its entirety" is a non-semilinear language.[8]

In contrast to the case of Chinese number-names, it does not become clear as quickly that the entire Dutch language is non-semilinear. This is due to reasons we will not go into in detail here. They are related to the fact that coordination phenomena in general present rather problematic data for an appropriate linguistical analysis. This is already mentioned by Manaster-Ramer ([9]), when he discusses his argumentation. He notices that his observation strongly depends on what is assumed to belong to the Dutch language in general by means of a competence–performance distinction. Looking at some examples, Manaster-Ramer on the one hand points out the possibility of "dropping" some of the NPs explicitly appearing in coordination phrases like (14). On the other hand, he shows that to "pump in" some new NPs, without simultaneously pumping in new verbs, is possible as well. Roughly speaking, the latter possibility is to coordinate some of the NPs as a complex NP which itself is part of an NP coordination. As far as we see, both possibilities (dropping and pumping in) together, even make validity of the argumentation that Dutch is no (simple) TAL very uncertain, at least in terms of weak equivalence.

However, it is not our intention to judge the conclusions of Radzinski and Manaster-Ramer, respectively Groenink, rigorously. We just wanted to emphasize some possible objections raised by the authors themselves, since the Old Georgian example seems to avoid the corresponding difficulties. First of all, there should be no doubt that this example falls into the domain of natural language capacity. Secondly, compared to the Dutch coordination-phenomenon the complex NP constructions of Old Georgian, considered above, have the advantage that they represent a strict morpho-syntactic phenomenon. That is to say, with regard to the case suffixes the underlying (syntactic) structure is "directly visible"; which is not necessarily the case e.g. within a coordination of coordinated NPs in Dutch. This kind of "visibility" turns out to be possible at least in the case of Suffixaufnahme as it is given with (4). Recall that, in accordance with (5), (4) is the "most complex" case by means of the total number of genitive suffixes which may appear as suffixes of the nouns within a complex NP consisting of k stacked NPs for some $k \in \mathbb{N}_+$. And in fact, our argumention is in some sense strictly concentrated on this case. We do not have to take care of all possibilities of Suffixaufnahme coming up with the application of some (recursive) rules to

[8] Such a decision may be advanced, if, as proposed in [9], a certain kind of constraint on "classificatory capacity" is assumed to come up with an appropriate grammar for natural language. According to Radzinski, the validity of such a constraint at least implies that Chinese turns out to be a non-MCTAL in case of "proper inclusion" of the Chinese number-names within the Chinese language.

a given basic structure of a complex NP like (6) as long as the total number of "addable" genitive suffixes is bounded as stated in (5). The definition of the Old Georgian fragment L_M is only an implicit one, also allowing for complex NPs in which the "full range of possible suffixes" is only partially realized like in (2). Moreover, since L_M actually is defined by means of its Parikh image $p_\Sigma[L_M]$, a priori there is no restriction on the order in which the stacked NPs have to appear within the subject-NP of a member of L_M. This is reasonable since there are also examples of preposed genitive NPs showing agreement by Suffixaufnahme.

P̣avle-js-i tav-isa moḳueta-j (16)
Paul-Gen-Nom head-Gen cutting-Nom

'the decapitation of the head of Paul'

Although Boeder ([1]) argues that "leftward" Suffixaufnahme is non-recursive and even limited to the possibility of taking up one single suffix like in (16), the contrary would not effect our argumentation. This also holds if it turned out that sentences including NPs like (2.1) or (2.2) belong to Old Georgian. According to Boeder, such NPs are in all probability ungrammatical.

γmrt-isa-jsa sasupevel-isa saidumlo-j (2.1)

sasupevel-isa γmrt-isa-jsa saidumlo-j (2.2)

More generally, all our considerations are independent of the (generative) grammar formalism which we prefer to investigate the underlying structures of complex NPs in Old Georgian.[9] Our argumentation stays valid as long as, on the one hand, complex NPs are in general allowed to have a surface structure like (4), and on the other hand, a kind of "upper bound-restriction" on the appearing suffixes like (5) holds, as we assume to be the case due to the analysis of Boeder.

Besides the particular result concerning Old Georgian our approach offers a more general perspective on a formal approach to languages or on dealing with formal languages. Let us recall first the definition of *constant growth* as it is proposed in [7] as a necessary property of a mildly context sensitive language (MCSL), a language derivable by an MCSG. A language L has constant growth iff there is some constant $c_0 \in \mathbb{N}$ and some finite set of constants $C \subseteq \mathbb{N}$ such that for any $\alpha \in L$ with $|\alpha| \geq c_0$ there is some $\alpha' \in L$ and some $c \in C$ for which the equation $|\alpha| = |\alpha'| + c$ holds. Here, for any $\beta \in L$, $|\beta|$ denotes its length. Indeed, this definition can be thought of as a kind of a weak pumpability condition, which also is true for the somewhat strengthend version, the definition of semilinearity of a language. (It should be clear that each semilinear language a fortiori has the constant growth property.) And, in this sense our Proposition 5 provides a kind of weak pumping lemma. We already mentioned in Sect. 3 that our formal

[9] E.g., a grammar in terms of a GB- or minimalist framework in which we want (in particular and in contrast to Boeder's approach) some kind of Freezing principle (in the sense of [17]) to be valid, or at least descriptively adequate (see e.g. [2]).

argumentation applying to Old Georgian is similar to a standard proof method in the framework of formal languages: first, to figure out a fragment of a given language L, where the fragment does not fall into a class of formal languages $\mathcal{L}$ which is closed under intersection with regular languages. Second, to show that the fragment is the intersection of L and a regular language, that is to show that L cannot belong to $\mathcal{L}$. In our considerations we first fixed the non-semilinear fragment L_M of Old Georgian L_G, then we argued that the Parikh image $p_\Sigma[L_M]$ is the intersection of the Parikh images of L_G and of the semilinear language $L_R \subseteq \Sigma^*$. Finally, we concluded that $p_\Sigma[L_G]$ cannot be semilinear referring to the property that the set of semilinear subsets of $\mathbb{N}^n$ is closed under intersection.

Actually, we do not need the last mentioned property in this general form, since L_R is a context free language and we have $p_\Sigma[L_R] = R$. L_R even is a regular language. Assuming L_G to be semilinear there would be a regular language L'_G which is *letter equivalent* to L_G, since any language is semilinear iff it is letter equivalent to a regular language.[10] L_R is the full pre-image of R with respect to p_Σ, thus the following equation can be given.

$$p_\Sigma[L_G \cap L_R] = p_\Sigma[L_G] \cap p_\Sigma[L_R] = p_\Sigma[L'_G] \cap p_\Sigma[L_R] = p_\Sigma[L'_G \cap L_R] \quad (17)$$

But L_M is the intersection of L_G and L_R. According to (17), and because $L'_G \cap L_R$ is context free, even regular, the Parikh image $p_\Sigma[L_M]$ would be semilinear. This would contradict the result shown in Sect. 2.

5 Some Final Remarks

Old Georgian is only one of several languages which show the phenomenon of Suffixaufnahme.[11] But, as far as we know, there is no other such language which allows for an unbounded iteration of Suffixaufnahme as is possible in Old Georgian, at least with regard to genitive case suffixes. In most languages this process is strictly limited to the possibility of taking up just one additional case suffix. However, there are e.g. some Australian language families in which a limited stacking of up to four case suffixes can be found (see [3]). Thus Old Georgian does not only show a phenomenon which is not widespread among natural languages in general, it seems to be even a rather bizzare language among those which allow for multiple case-marking. And, it should be remarked here, that nowadays Suffixaufnahme in Modern Georgian is at best only marginally possible and in any case non recursive.

Nevertheless, according to our argumentation Old Georgian provides a natural languge which, in a formal sense, is not semilinear in general, and thus no MCTAL in particular. Now, the intention underlying the definition of *mild context sensitivity* is to add a sufficient amount to the capacity of the context

[10] Two languages L_1, $L_2 \subseteq \Sigma^*$ are said to be *letter equivalent* if $p_\Sigma[L_1] = p_\Sigma[L_2]$. Although not explicitly stated, the mentioned equivalence is already proven in [10]. The "only if" is even shown for context free languages.

[11] [12] provides a collection of papers on this topic.

free grammar-type, which is just the necessary amount to capture natural language complexity. Thus, the question arises which kind of mildly context sensitive grammar formalism could be appropriate to deal with Old Georgian. The Simple Literal Movement Grammars (simple LMGs) of Groenink ([5]) seem to provide such a searched for tool. They can be thought of as a generalization of LCFRSs where a restricted non-linear rewriting is allowed. However, the class of all simple LMLs, the class of all languages derivable by some simple LMG, is known to be identical with PTIME ([5]). Thus for example also the language $\{a^{(2^n)} \mid n \in \mathbb{N}\}$ is a simple LML. Therefore, the class of simple LMLs includes languages which do not have constant growth. Groenink gives the simple LMG-type definition to cope with languages like the Dutch fragment to which we referred in Sect. 3 and which is no MCTAL. To restrict the class of simple LMGs in a reasonable way with respect to natural languages, Groenink proposes a revised definition of mild context sensitivity. In particular this definition contains a strengthend version of the constant growth property which he calls *finite pumpability* and which allows for several non-semilinear languages like the Dutch fragment. Whether this finite pumpability property also is fullfilled by the Old Georgian fragment L_M, which we have taken into account, depends on what is "really" contained in it. That is to say, it depends on an explicit definition of L_M which has not been necessary to give within our argumentation. Without looking at further details we want to finish our considerations here, just by claiming that, as far as we see, at least along the lines of Boeder's paper there does not seem to be a reason to exclude the Old Georgian fragment to be finite pumpable in the sense of Groenink.

Appendix

In order to prove Proposition 5, we first recall a classical result in Analysis as

Lemma 7. *For some* $m \in \mathbb{N}$ *let* $\alpha = (a_0, \ldots, a_m) \in \mathbb{R}^{m+1}$ *be a finite sequence where* $a_m > 0$. *Then, there is some* $r_0 \in \mathbb{R}$ *such that* $P_\alpha(x) = \sum_{i=0}^{m} a_i x^i > 0$ *for all* $x \in \mathbb{R}$ *for which* $x > r_0$.

Proof of Proposition 5. First, we define a set $\overline{M}$ as a subset of M. For this purpose we choose fixed numbers $l_2^{(k)}, \ldots, l_{n-1}^{(k)} \in \mathbb{N}$ for any $k \in \mathbb{N}_+$ according to property (i) and set

$$\overline{M} := \left\{ \left(k, P_\alpha(k), l_2^{(k)}, \ldots, l_{n-1}^{(k)}\right) \mid k \in \mathbb{N}_+ \right\} \tag{18}$$

The proof will be done by contradiction. Assume M is semilinear and notice that M is not empty. Then there exists a $\mu \in \mathbb{N}_+$ and linear sets $N_1, \ldots, N_\mu \subseteq \mathbb{N}^n$ for which we have

$$M = \bigcup_{j=1}^{\mu} N_j \tag{19}$$

Since $\overline{M}$ is an infinite subset of M there must be an N_j, $1 \leq j \leq \mu$, which contains an infinite subset of $\overline{M}$. We take N to be such an N_j and choose $u^{(0)}, u^{(1)}, \ldots, u^{(\nu)} \in \mathbb{N}^n$ for some appropriate $\nu \in \mathbb{N}$ such that

$$N = \left\{ u^{(0)} + \sum_{j=1}^{\nu} n_j u^{(j)} \mid n_j \in \mathbb{N} \text{ for } 1 \leq j \leq \nu \right\} \tag{20}$$

For $0 \leq i < n$ and for $0 \leq j \leq \nu$ let $u_i^{(j)}$ be the $(i+1)$–th component of $u^{(j)}$. In the special case $j = 0$ we will simply write u instead of $u^{(0)}$, and u_i instead of $u_i^{(0)}$, to denote the corresponding n–tuple and its components. Notice, that $\nu \geq 1$ because N is infinite. In particular the set N contains an infinite subset of $\overline{M}$. Hence, there must be an unbounded (strongly) increasing (infinite) sequence $(k_i)_{i \in \mathbb{N}}$ in $\mathbb{N}_+$ for which we have

$$\left(k_i, P_\alpha(k_i), l_2^{(k_i)}, \ldots, l_{n-1}^{(k_i)}\right) \in N \tag{21}$$

Using (20) and (21) we now fix some $n_1^{(k_i)}, \ldots, n_\nu^{(k_i)} \in \mathbb{N}$ for every $i \in \mathbb{N}$, or every element of the sequence $(k_i)_{i \in \mathbb{N}}$, such that the following equation holds

$$u + \sum_{j=1}^{\nu} n_j^{(k_i)} u^{(j)} = \left(k_i, P_\alpha(k_i), l_2^{(k_i)}, \ldots, l_{n-1}^{(k_i)}\right) \tag{22}$$

That is to say, for all $i \in \mathbb{N}$ we have especially

$$u_0 + \sum_{j=1}^{\nu} n_j^{(k_i)} u_0^{(j)} = k_i \tag{22.1}$$

$$u_1 + \sum_{j=1}^{\nu} n_j^{(k_i)} u_1^{(j)} = P_\alpha(k_i) \tag{22.2}$$

Since not only N is infinite, but also the projection of N to the first component, there must be a natural number ω with $1 \leq \omega \leq \nu$ for which the first component $u_0^{(\omega)}$ of $u^{(\omega)}$ is different from zero. We may assume w.l.o.g. that $u_0^{(1)}, \ldots, u_0^{(\omega)}$ all are different from 0 and that $u_0^{(\omega+1)}, \ldots, u_0^{(\nu)}$ all are identical with 0. Then, for some fixed element K of the sequence $(k_i)_{i \in \mathbb{N}}$ we can distinguish two cases.

<u>1. case</u>: $n_j^{(K)} u_1^{(j)} = 0$ for any natural number j with $\omega < j \leq \nu$.

We first notice, because of (22.1) it follows immediately that

$$n_j^{(K)} \leq K \text{ for } 1 \leq j \leq \omega \text{ , since } u_0^{(j)} > 0 \text{ in such a case.} \tag{23}$$

Carrying on we define $m_1 := \max\{u_1^{(j)} \mid 1 \leq j \leq \omega\}$ and let β be the finite sequence $(a_0 - u_1, a_1 - \omega m_1, a_2, \ldots, a_m) \in \mathbb{R}^{m+1}$. Then, by Lemma 7 applied to the polynomial P_β and due to the fact, that $(k_i)_{i\in\mathbb{N}}$ is an unbounded increasing sequence, we may suppose K to be great enough to fulfill

$$0 < (a_0 - u_1) + (a_1 - \omega m_1)K + \sum_{i=2}^{m} a_i K^i = P_\beta(K) \tag{24}$$

Thus, the following inequality can be given

$$\begin{aligned}
& u_1 + \sum_{j=1}^{\nu} n_j^{(K)} u_1^{(j)} \\
= \quad & u_1 + \sum_{j=1}^{\omega} n_j^{(K)} u_1^{(j)} && \text{, since } n_j^{(K)} u_1^{(j)} = 0 \text{ for } \omega + 1 \leq j \leq \nu \\
\leq \quad & u_1 + \omega m_1 K && \text{, by (23) and according to the definition of } m_1 \\
< \quad & a_0 + a_1 K + \sum_{l=2}^{m} a_i K^i && \text{, by (24)} \\
= \quad & P_\alpha(K)
\end{aligned}$$

But, this provides a contradiction, since K is an element of the sequence $(k_i)_{i\in\mathbb{N}}$ and so (22.2) holds especially for K. (1. case)

<u>2. case</u>: $n_j^{(K)} u_1^{(j)} \neq 0$ for some natural number j with $\omega < j \leq \nu$.

We may assume w.l.o.g. that $j = \nu$. Then $n_\nu^{(K)} > 0$ as well as $u_1^{(\nu)} > 0$. And so, we can continue by concluding

$$(n_\nu^{(K)} - 1)\, u_1^{(\nu)} < n_\nu^{(K)}\, u_1^{(\nu)} < (n_\nu^{(K)} + 1)\, u_1^{(\nu)} \quad \text{, since } u_1^{(\nu)} > 0 \tag{25}$$

Hence, on the one hand we have

$$\left.\begin{aligned}
u_0 + \sum_{j=1}^{\nu-1} n_j^{(K)} u_0^{(j)} + (n_\nu^{(K)} + 1)\, u_0^{(\nu)} &= K \text{ , due to (22.1) since } u_0^{(\nu)} = 0 \\
u_1 + \sum_{j=1}^{\nu-1} n_j^{(K)} u_1^{(j)} + (n_\nu^{(K)} + 1)\, u_1^{(\nu)} &> P_\alpha(K) \qquad \text{, by (22.2) and (25)}
\end{aligned}\right. \tag{26.1}$$

and on the other hand we have

$$\left.\begin{aligned}
u_0 + \sum_{j=1}^{\nu} n_j^{(K)} u_0^{(j)} + (n_\nu^{(K)} - 1) u_0^{(\nu)} &= K \text{ , due to (22.1) since } u_0^{(\nu)} = 0 \\
u_1 + \sum_{j=1}^{\nu-1} n_j^{(K)} u_1^{(j)} + (n_\nu^{(K)} - 1) u_1^{(\nu)} &< P_\alpha(K) \qquad \text{, by (22.2) and (25)}
\end{aligned}\right. \tag{26.2}$$

Notice, that the elements

$$z^> := u + \sum_{j=1}^{\nu-1} n_j^{(K)} u^{(j)} + (n_\nu^{(K)} + 1) u^{(\nu)}$$

$$z^< := u + \sum_{j=1}^{\nu-1} n_j^{(K)} u^{(j)} + (n_\nu^{(K)} - 1) u^{(\nu)}$$

both belong to N since $n_\nu^{(K)} > 0$, and therefore both belong to M too. But (26.1) and (26.2) point out that this is a contradiction to the property (ii) of the set M in any case. Assuming $P_\alpha(K)$ to be the corresponding upper bound for the second component of any n-tuple which belongs to M and which first component is K, we can refer to $z^>$, providing a contradiction by (26.1). Assuming $P_\alpha(K)$ to be the corresponding lower bound presupposed by property (ii) we can refer to $z^<$ and (26.2). (2. case)

The two considered cases are the only ones that can appear. So, we have just shown that the set M cannot be semilinear, that is to have proven the proposition. □

References

1. Winfried Boeder. Suffixaufnahme in Kartvelian. In [12], pages 151–215.
2. M. A. Browning. Bounding conditions on representations. *Linguistic Inquiry* 22:541–562, 1991.
3. Nick Evans. Multiple-case in Kayardild: Anti-iconic suffix ordering and the diachronic filter. In [12], pages 396–428.
4. Seymour Ginsburg and Edwin H. Spanier. Bounded ALGOL-like languages. *Transactions of the American Mathematical Society*, 113:333–368, 1964.
5. Annius V. Groenink. Mild context-sensitivity and tuple-based generalizations of context-free grammar. In D. E. Johnson and L. S. Moss, editors, *Special Issue on the Mathematics of Language, Linguistics and Philosophy*, forthcoming. Also available as Report CS-R9634, Centrum voor Wiskunde en Informatica (CWI), Amsterdam, 1996.
6. Riny Huybregts. The weak inadequacy of context-free phrase structure grammars. In G. de Haan, M. Trommelen, and W. Zonneveld, editors, *Van Periferie naar Kern*, pages 81–99. Foris Publications, Dordrecht, 1984.
7. Aravind K. Joshi. Tree adjoinig grammars: How much context-sensitivity is required to provide reasonable structural descriptions? In D. Dowty, L. Karttunen, and A. Zwicky, editors, *Natural Language Parsing. Theoretical, Computational and Psychological Perspective*, pages 206–250. Cambridge University Press, New York, 1985.
8. Aravind K. Joshi, K. Vijay-Shanker, and David J. Weir. The convergence of mildly context-sensitive grammar formalisms. In P. Sells, S. Shieber, and T. Wasow, editors, *Foundational Issues in Natural Language Processing*, pages 31–81. MIT Press, Cambridge (Mass.), 1991.
9. Alexis Manaster-Ramer. Dutch as a formal language. *Linguistics and Philosophy*, 10:221–246, 1987.

10. Rohit J. Parikh. On context-free languages. *Journal of the Association for Computing Machinery*, 13:570–581, 1966.
11. Frans Plank. (Re-)introducing Suffixaufnahme. In [12], pages 3–110.
12. Frans Plank, editor. *Double Case. Agreement by Suffixaufnahme*. Oxford University Press, New York, 1995.
13. Daniel Radzinski. Chinese number-names, tree adjoining languages, and mild context-sensitivity. *Computational Linguistics*, 17:277–299, 1991.
14. Owen Rambow. *Formal and Computational Aspects of Natural Language Syntax*. PhD thesis, University of Pennsylvania, Philadelphia, PA, 1994.
15. K. Vijay-Shanker and David J. Weir. The equivalence of four extensions of context-free grammars. *Mathematical Systems Theory*, 27:511–546, 1994.
16. David J. Weir. *Characterizing Mildly Context-Sensitive Grammar Formalisms*. PhD thesis, University of Pennsylvania, Philadelphia, PA, 1988.
17. Kenneth Wexler and Peter W. Culicover. *Formal Principles of Language Aquisition*. MIT Press, Cambridge (Mass.), 1980.

Quantitative Constraint Logic Programming for Weighted Grammar Applications*

Stefan Riezler

Graduiertenkolleg ILS, Seminar für Sprachwissenschaft,
Universität Tübingen, Wilhelmstr. 113, 72074 Tübingen, Germany.
riezler@sfs.nphil.uni-tuebingen.de

Abstract. Constraint logic grammars provide a powerful formalism for expressing complex logical descriptions of natural language phenomena in exact terms. Describing some of these phenomena may, however, require some form of graded distinctions which are not provided by such grammars. Recent approaches to weighted constraint logic grammars attempt to address this issue by adding numerical calculation schemata to the deduction scheme of the underlying CLP framework.
Currently, these extralogical extensions are not related to the model-theoretic counterpart of the operational semantics of CLP, i.e., they do not come with a formal semantics at all.
The aim of this paper is to present a clear formal semantics for weighted constraint logic grammars, which abstracts away from specific interpretations of weights, but nevertheless gives insights into the parsing problem for such weighted grammars. Building on the formalization of constraint logic grammars in the CLP scheme of [11], this formal semantics will be given by a quantitative version of CLP. Such a quantitative CLP scheme can also be valuable for CLP tasks independent of grammars.

1 Introduction

Constraint logic grammars (CLGs) provide a powerful formalism for complex logical description and efficient processing of natural language phenomena. Linguistic description and computational practice may, however, often require some form of graded distinctions which are not provided by such grammars.

One such issue is the task of ambiguity resolution. This problem can be illustrated for formal grammars describing a nontrivial domain of natural language as follows: For such grammars every input of reasonable length may receive a large number of different analyses, many of which are not in accord with human perceptions. Clearly there is a need to distinguish more plausible analyses of an input from less plausible or even totally spurious ones.

This problem has successfully been addressed by the use of weighted grammars for disambiguation in regular and context-free grammars. Weighted grammars assign numerical values, or weights, to the structure-building components

* I am greatly indebted to Steven Abney, Thilo Götz and Paul King for their valuable comments on this paper. Furthermore, I would like to thank Graham Katz, Frank Morawietz and two anonymous LACL referees for their helpful suggestions.

of the grammars and calculate the weight of an analysis from the weights of the structural features that make it up. The correct analysis is chosen from among the in-principle possible analyses by assuming the analysis with the greatest weight to be the correct analysis. This approach also allows parsing to be speeded up by pruning low-weighted subanalyses.

The idea of weighted grammars recently has been transferred to highly expressive weighted CLGs by [8,9] and [7]. The approaches of Erbach and Eisele are based on the feature-based constraint formalism CUF ([5,4]), which can be seen as an instance of the constraint logic programming (CLP) scheme of [11]. These approaches extend the underlying formalism by assigning weights to program clauses, but differ with respect to an interpretation of weights in a preference-based versus probabilistic framework. Erbach calculates a preference value of analyses from the preference values of the clauses used in the analyses, whereas Eisele assigns application probabilities to clauses from which a probability distribution over analyses is calculated.

There is an obvious problem with these approaches, however. Even if the formal foundation of the underlying framework is clear enough, there is no well-defined semantics for the weighted extensions. This means that these extralogical extensions of the deduction scheme of the underlying constraint logic program are not related to the model-theoretic counterpart of this operational semantics, i.e., they do not come with a formal semantics at all. This is clearly an undesirable state of affairs. Rather, in the same way as CLGs allow for a clear model-theoretic characterization of linguistic objects coupled with the operational parsing system, one would prefer to base a quantitative deduction system on a clear quantitative model-theory in a sound and complete way.

The aim of this paper is to present a clear formal semantics for weighted CLGs, which abstracts away from specific interpretations of weights, but gives insight into the parsing problem for weighted CLGs. Building on the formalization of CLGs in the CLP scheme of [11], this formal semantics will be given by a quantitative version of CLP. Such a quantitative CLP scheme can also be valuable for CLP tasks independent of grammars.

Previous work on related topics has been confined to quantitative extensions of conventional logic programming. A quantitative deduction scheme based on a fixpoint semantics for sets of numerically annotated conventional definite clauses was first presented by van Emden in [26]. In this approach numerical weights are associated with definite clauses as a whole. The semantics of such quantitative rule sets is based upon concepts of fuzzy set algebra and crucially deals with the truth-functional "propagation" of weights across definite clauses. Van Emden's approach initialized research into a now extensively explored area of quantitative logic programming. For example, annotated logic programming as introduced by [25] extends the expressive power of quantitative rule sets by allowing variables and evaluable function terms as annotations. Such annotations can be attached to components of the language formula and come with more complex mappings as a foundation for a multivalued logical semantics. Such extended theories are interpreted in frameworks of lattice-based logics for generalized annotated logic programming ([15]), possibilistic logic for possibilistic logic programming ([6]) or logics of subjective probability for probabilistic logic programming ([20,21]) and probabilistic deductive databases ([17,18]).

Aiming at a formal foundation of weighted CLGs in a framework of quantitative CLP, we can start from the ideas developed in the simple and elegant framework of [26], but transfer them to the general CLP scheme of [11]. This means that the form of weighted CLGs under consideration allows us to restrict our attention to numerical weights associated with CLP clauses as a whole. Furthermore, the simple concepts of fuzzy set algebra can also provide a basis for an intuitive formal semantics for quantitative CLP. Such a formal semantics will be sufficiently general in that it is itself not restricted by a specific interpretation of weights. Further extensions should be straightforward, but have to be deferred to future work. Our scheme will straightforwardly transfer the nice properties of the CLP scheme of [11] into a quantitative version of CLP.

2 Constraint Logic Programming and Constraint Logic Grammars

Before discussing the details of our quantitative extension of CLP, some words on the underlying CLP scheme and grammars formulated by these means are necessary. In the following we will rely on the CLP scheme of [11], which generalizes conventional logic programming (see [19]) and also the CLP scheme of [12] to a scheme of definite clause specifications over arbitrary constraint languages. A very general characterization of the concept of constraint language can be given as follows.

Definition 1 ($\mathcal{L}$). A constraint language $\mathcal{L}$ consists of

1. an $\mathcal{L}$-signature, specifying the non-logical elements of the alphabet of the language,
2. a decidable infinite set VAR whose elements are called variables,
3. a decidable set CON of $\mathcal{L}$-constraints which are pieces of syntax with unknown internal structure,
4. a computable function V assigning to every constraint $\phi \in \mathsf{CON}$ a finite set $\mathsf{V}(\phi)$ of variables, the variables constrained by ϕ,
5. a nonempty set of $\mathcal{L}$-interpretations INT, where each $\mathcal{L}$-interpretation $\mathcal{I} \in \mathsf{INT}$ is defined w.r.t. a nonempty set $\mathcal{D}$, the domain of $\mathcal{I}$, and a set ASS of variable assignments $\mathsf{VAR} \to \mathcal{D}$,
6. a function $[\![\cdot]\!]^{\mathcal{I}}$ mapping every constraint $\phi \in \mathsf{CON}$ to a set $[\![\phi]\!]^{\mathcal{I}}$ of variable assignments, the solutions of ϕ in $\mathcal{I}$.
7. Furthermore, a constraint ϕ constrains only the variables in $\mathsf{V}(\phi)$, i.e., if $\alpha \in [\![\phi]\!]^{\mathcal{I}}$ and β is a variable assignment that agrees with α on $\mathsf{V}(\phi)$, then $\beta \in [\![\phi]\!]^{\mathcal{I}}$.

To obtain constraint logic programs, a given constraint language $\mathcal{L}$ has to be extended to a constraint language $\mathcal{R}(\mathcal{L})$ providing for the necessary relational atoms and propositional connectives.

Definition 2 ($\mathcal{R}(\mathcal{L})$). A constraint language $\mathcal{R}(\mathcal{L})$ extending a constraint language $\mathcal{L}$ is defined as follows:

1. The signature of $\mathcal{R}(\mathcal{L})$ is an extension of the signature of $\mathcal{L}$ with a decidable set $\mathcal{R}$ of relation symbols and an arity function $\mathsf{Ar} : \mathcal{R} \to \mathbb{N}$.
2. The variables of $\mathcal{R}(\mathcal{L})$ are the variables of $\mathcal{L}$.
3. The set of $\mathcal{R}(\mathcal{L})$-constraints is the smallest set s.t.
   - ϕ is an $\mathcal{R}(\mathcal{L})$-constraint if ϕ is an $\mathcal{L}$-constraint,
   - $r(\mathbf{x})$ is an $\mathcal{R}(\mathcal{L})$-constraint, called an **atom**, if $r \in \mathcal{R}$ is a relation symbol with arity n and $\mathbf{x}$ is an n-tuple of pairwise distinct variables,
   - $\emptyset$, F & G, $F \to G$ are $\mathcal{R}(\mathcal{L})$-constraints, if F and G are $\mathcal{R}(\mathcal{L})$-constraints,
   - $\phi \,\&\, B_1 \,\&\, \ldots \,\&\, B_n \to A$ is an $\mathcal{R}(\mathcal{L})$-constraint, called a **definite clause**, if $A, B_1, \ldots, B_n$ are atoms and ϕ is an $\mathcal{L}$-constraint. We may write a definite clause also as $A \leftarrow \phi \,\&\, B_1 \,\&\, \ldots \,\&\, B_n$.
4. The variables constrained by an $\mathcal{R}(\mathcal{L})$ -constraint are defined as follows: If ϕ is an $\mathcal{L}$ -constraint, then $\mathsf{V}(\phi)$ is defined as in $\mathcal{L}$; $\mathsf{V}(r(x_1, \ldots, x_n)) := \{x_1, \ldots, x_n\}$; $\mathsf{V}(\emptyset) := \emptyset$; $\mathsf{V}(F \,\&\, G) := \mathsf{V}(F) \cup \mathsf{V}(G)$; $\mathsf{V}(F \to G) := \mathsf{V}(F) \cup \mathsf{V}(G)$.
5. For each $\mathcal{L}$ -interpretation $\mathcal{I}$, an $\mathcal{R}(\mathcal{L})$-interpretation $\mathcal{A}$ is an extension of an $\mathcal{L}$-interpretation $\mathcal{I}$ with relations $r^{\mathcal{A}}$ on the domain $\mathcal{D}$ of $\mathcal{A}$ with appropriate arity for every $r \in \mathcal{R}$ and the domain of $\mathcal{A}$ is the domain of $\mathcal{I}$.
6. For each $\mathcal{R}(\mathcal{L})$ -interpretation $\mathcal{A}$, for each $\mathcal{L}$ -interpretation $\mathcal{I}$, $[\![\cdot]\!]^{\mathcal{A}}$ is a function mapping every $\mathcal{R}(\mathcal{L})$ -constraint to a set of variable assignments s.t.
   - $[\![\phi]\!]^{\mathcal{A}} = [\![\phi]\!]^{\mathcal{I}}$ if ϕ is an $\mathcal{L}$-constraint,
   - $[\![r(\mathbf{x})]\!]^{\mathcal{A}} = \{\alpha \in \mathsf{ASS} \mid \alpha(\mathbf{x}) \in r^{\mathcal{A}}\}$,
   - $[\![\emptyset]\!]^{\mathcal{A}} = \mathsf{ASS}$,
   - $[\![F \,\&\, G]\!]^{\mathcal{A}} = [\![F]\!]^{\mathcal{A}} \cap [\![G]\!]^{\mathcal{A}}$,
   - $[\![F \to G]\!]^{\mathcal{A}} = (\mathsf{ASS} \setminus [\![F]\!]^{\mathcal{A}}) \cup [\![G]\!]^{\mathcal{A}}$.

A constraint logic program then is defined as a definite clause specification over a constraint language.

Definition 3 (definite clause specification). A definite clause specification $\mathcal{P}$ over a constraint language $\mathcal{L}$ is a set of definite clauses from a constraint language $\mathcal{R}(\mathcal{L})$ extending $\mathcal{L}$.

Relying on terminology well-known for conventional logic programming, Höhfeld and Smolka's generalization of the key result of conventional logic programming can be stated as follows:[1] First, for every definite clause specification $\mathcal{P}$ in the extension of an arbitrary constraint language $\mathcal{L}$, every interpretation of $\mathcal{L}$ can be extended to a minimal model of $\mathcal{P}$. Second, the SLD-resolution method for conventional logic programming can be generalized to a sound and complete

[1] Further conditions for this generalization to hold are decidability of the satisfiability problem, closure under variable renaming and closure under intersection for the constraint languages under consideration.

operational semantics for definite clause specifications not restricted to Horn theories. In contrast to [12], in this scheme constraint languages are not required to be sublanguages of first order predicate logic and do not have to be interpreted in a single fixed domain. This makes this scheme usable for a wider range of applications. Instead, a constraint is satisfiable if there is at least one interpretation in which it has a solution. Moreover, such interpretations do not have to be solution compact. This was necessary in [12] to provide a sound and complete treatment of negation as failure, which is not addressed in [11].

The term constraint logic grammars expresses the connection between CLP and constraint-based grammars. Constraint-based grammars allow for a clear model-theoretic characterization of linguistic objects by stating grammars as sets of axioms of suitable logical languages. However, such approaches do not necessarily provide an operational interpretation of their purely declarative specifications. This may lead to problems with an operational treatment of declaratively well-defined problems such as parsing. CLP provides one possible approach to an operational treatment of various such declarative frameworks by an embedding of arbitrary logical languages into constraint logic programs. CLGs thus are grammars formulated by means of a suitable logical language which can be used as a constraint language in the sense of [11].[2]

For example, for feature based grammars such as HPSG ([23]), a quite direct embedding of a logical language close to that of [24] into the CLP scheme of [11] is done in the formalism CUF ([5,4]). This approach directly offers the operational properties of the CLP scheme by simply redefining grammars as constraint logic programs, but is questionable in losing the connection to the model-theoretic specifications of the underlying feature-based grammars. A different approach is given by [10] where a compilation of a logical language close to that of [16] into constraint logic programs is defined. This translation procedure preserves important model-theoretic properties by generating a constraint logic program $\mathcal{P}(\mathcal{G})$ from a feature-based grammar $\mathcal{G}$ in an explicit way.

The parsing/generation problem for CLGs then is as follows. Given a program $\mathcal{P}$ (encoding a grammar) and a definite goal G (encoding the string/logical form we want to parse/generate from), we ask if we can infer an answer φ of G (which is a satisfiable $\mathcal{L}$-constraint encoding an analysis) proving the implication $\varphi \rightarrow G$ to be a logical consequence of $\mathcal{P}$.

[2] Clearly, a direct definition of an operational semantics for specific constraint-based grammars is possible and may even better suit the particular frameworks. However, such approaches have to rely directly on the syntactic properties of the logical languages in question. Under the CLP approach, arbitrary constraint-based grammars can receive a unique operational semantics by an embedding into definite clause specifications. The main advantage of this approach is the possibility to put constraint-based grammar processing into the well-understood paradigm of logic programming. This allows the resulting programs to run on existing architectures and to use well-known optimization techniques worked out in this area.

3 Quantitative Constraint Logic Programming

3.1 Syntax and Declarative Semantics of Quantitative Definite Clause Specifications

Building upon the definitions in [11], we can define the syntax of a quantitative definite clause specification $\mathcal{P}_{\mathrm{F}}$ very quickly. A definite clause specification $\mathcal{P}$ in $\mathcal{R}(\mathcal{L})$ can be extended to a quantitative definite clause specification $\mathcal{P}_{\mathrm{F}}$ in $\mathcal{R}(\mathcal{L})$ simply by adding numerical factors to program clauses.

The following definitions are made with respect to implicit constraint languages $\mathcal{L}$ and $\mathcal{R}(\mathcal{L})$.

Definition 4 ($\mathcal{P}_{\mathrm{F}}$)**.** A quantitative definite clause specification $\mathcal{P}_{\mathrm{F}}$ in $\mathcal{R}(\mathcal{L})$ is a finite set of quantitative formulae, called quantitative definite clauses, of the form: $\phi \;\&\; B_1 \;\&\; \ldots \;\&\; B_n \;{}_f\!\rightarrow A$, where A, $B_1, \ldots, B_n$ are $\mathcal{R}(\mathcal{L})$-atoms, ϕ is an $\mathcal{L}$-constraint, $n \geq 0$, $f \in (0,1]$. We may write a quantitative formula also as $A \leftarrow_f \phi \;\&\; B_1 \;\&\; \ldots \;\&\; B_n$.

Such factors should be thought of as abstract weights which receive a concrete interpretation in specific instantiations of $\mathcal{P}_{\mathrm{F}}$ by weighted CLGs.

In the following the notation $\mathcal{R}(\mathcal{L})$ will be used more generally to denote relationally extended constraint languages which possibly include quantitative formulae of the above form.

To obtain a formal semantics for $\mathcal{P}_{\mathrm{F}}$, first we have to introduce an appropriate quantitative measure into the set-theoretic specification of $\mathcal{R}(\mathcal{L})$-interpretations. One possibility to obtain quantitative $\mathcal{R}(\mathcal{L})$-interpretations is to base the set algebra of $\mathcal{R}(\mathcal{L})$-interpretations on the simple and well-defined concepts of fuzzy set algebra (see [27]).

Relying on Höhfeld and Smolka's specification of base equivalent $\mathcal{R}(\mathcal{L})$-interpretations, i.e., $\mathcal{R}(\mathcal{L})$-interpretations extending the same $\mathcal{L}$-interpretation, in terms of the denotations of the relation symbols in these interpretations, we can "fuzzify" such interpretations by regarding the denotations of their relation symbols as fuzzy subsets of the set of tuples in the common domain.

Given constraint languages $\mathcal{L}$ and $\mathcal{R}(\mathcal{L})$, we interpret each n-ary relation symbol $r \in \mathcal{R}$ as a fuzzy subset of $\mathcal{D}^n$, for each $\mathcal{R}(\mathcal{L})$-interpretation $\mathcal{A}$ with domain $\mathcal{D}$. That is, we identify the denotation of r under $\mathcal{A}$ with a total function: $\mu(\_; r^{\mathcal{A}}) : \mathcal{D}^n \rightarrow [0,1]$, which can be thought of as an abstract membership function. Classical set membership is coded in this context by membership functions taking only 0 and 1 as values.

Next, we have to give a model-theoretic characterization of quantitative definite clauses. Clearly, any monotonous mapping could be used for the model-theoretic specification of the interaction of weights in quantitative definite clauses and accordingly for the calculation of weights in the proof-theory of quantitative CLP. For concreteness, we will instantiate such a mapping to the specific case of Definition 5 resembling [26]'s mode of rule application. This will allow us to state the proof-theory of quantitative CLP in terms of min/max trees which in turn enables strategies such as alpha/beta pruning to be used for efficient searching. However, this choice is not crucial for the substantial claims of this paper and generalizations of this particular combination mode to specific applications should be straightforward, but are beyond the scope of this paper.

The following definition of model corresponds to the definition of model in classical logic when considering only clauses with $f = 1$ and mappings $\mathcal{D}^n \rightarrow \{0,1\}$.

Definition 5 (model). An $\mathcal{R}(\mathcal{L})$ -interpretation $\mathcal{A}$ extending some $\mathcal{L}$ -interpretation $\mathcal{I}$ is a model of a quantitative definite clause specification $\mathcal{P}_{\mathrm{F}}$ iff for each $\alpha \in \mathsf{ASS}$, for each quantitative formula $r(\mathbf{x}) \leftarrow_f \phi \,\&\, q_1(\mathbf{x}_1) \,\&\, \ldots \,\&\, q_k(\mathbf{x}_k)$ in $\mathcal{P}_{\mathrm{F}}$: If $\alpha \in [\![\phi]\!]^{\mathcal{I}}$, then $\mu(\alpha(\mathbf{x}); r^{\mathcal{A}}) \geq f \times min\{\mu(\alpha(\mathbf{x}_j); q_j^{\mathcal{A}}) |\ 1 \leq j \leq k\}$.

Note that the notation of an $\mathcal{R}(\mathcal{L})$ -interpretation $\mathcal{A}$ will be used more generally to include interpretations of quantitative formulae. $\mathcal{R}(\mathcal{L})$ -solutions of a quantitative formula are defined as $[\![r(\mathbf{x}) \leftarrow_f \phi \,\&\, q_1(\mathbf{x}_1) \,\&\, \ldots \,\&\, q_k(\mathbf{x}_k)]\!]^{\mathcal{A}} = \{\alpha \in \mathsf{ASS} \mid \text{If } \alpha \in [\![\phi]\!]^{\mathcal{I}}, \text{ then } \mu(\alpha(\mathbf{x}); r^{\mathcal{A}}) \geq f \times min\{\mu(\alpha(\mathbf{x}_j); q_j^{\mathcal{A}}) |\ 1 \leq j \leq k\}\}$.

The concept of logical consequence is defined as usual.

Definition 6 (logical consequence). A quantitative formula $r(\mathbf{x}) \leftarrow_f \phi$ is a logical consequence of a quantitative definite clause specification $\mathcal{P}_{\mathrm{F}}$ iff for each $\mathcal{R}(\mathcal{L})$ -interpretation $\mathcal{A}$, $\mathcal{A}$ is a model of $\mathcal{P}_{\mathrm{F}}$ implies that $\mathcal{A}$ is a model of $\{r(\mathbf{x}) \leftarrow_f \phi\}$.

Furthermore, we have that $r(\mathbf{x}) \leftarrow_f \phi$ is a logical consequence of $\mathcal{P}_{\mathrm{F}}$ implies that $r(\mathbf{x}) \leftarrow_{f'} \phi$ is a logical consequence of $\mathcal{P}_{\mathrm{F}}$ for every $f' \leq f$.

A **goal** G is defined to be a (possibly empty) conjunction of $\mathcal{R}(\mathcal{L})$ -atoms and $\mathcal{L}$ -constraints. We can, without loss of generality, restrict goals to be of the form $r(\mathbf{x}) \,\&\, \phi$, i.e., a (possibly empty) conjunction of a single relational atom $r(\mathbf{x})$ and an $\mathcal{L}$ -constraint ϕ. This is possible as for each goal $G = r_1(\mathbf{x}_1) \,\&\, \ldots \,\&\, r_k(\mathbf{x}_k) \,\&\, \phi$ containing more than one relational atom, we can complete the program with a new clause $C = r(\mathbf{x}_1, \ldots, \mathbf{x}_k) \leftarrow_1 r_1(\mathbf{x}_1) \,\&\, \ldots \,\&\, r_k(\mathbf{x}_k) \,\&\, \phi$ with G as antecedent and a new predicate with all variables in G as arguments as consequent. Submitting the new predicate $r(\mathbf{x}_1, \ldots, \mathbf{x}_k)$ as query yields the same results as would be obtained when querying with the compound goal G.

Given some $\mathcal{P}_{\mathrm{F}}$ and some goal G, a $\mathcal{P}_{\mathrm{F}}$ **-answer** φ of G is defined to be a satisfiable $\mathcal{L}$ -constraint φ s.t. $\varphi\ {}_f\!\rightarrow G$ is a logical consequence of $\mathcal{P}_{\mathrm{F}}$. A quantitative formula $\varphi\ {}_f\!\rightarrow r(\mathbf{x}) \,\&\, \phi$ is defined to be a logical consequence of $\mathcal{P}_{\mathrm{F}}$ iff every model of $\mathcal{P}_{\mathrm{F}}$ is a model of $\{\varphi\ {}_f\!\rightarrow r(\mathbf{x}) \,\&\, \phi\}$. An $\mathcal{R}(\mathcal{L})$ -interpretation $\mathcal{A}$ is defined to be a a model of $\{\varphi\ {}_f\!\rightarrow r(\mathbf{x}) \,\&\, \phi\}$ iff $[\![\varphi]\!]^{\mathcal{A}} \subseteq [\![\phi]\!]^{\mathcal{A}}$ and $\mathcal{A}$ is a model of $\{r(\mathbf{x}) \leftarrow_f \varphi\}$.

Aiming to generalize the key result in the declarative semantics of CLP—the minimal model semantics of definite clause specifications over arbitrary constraint languages—to our quantitative CLP scheme, first we have to associate a complete lattice of interpretations with quantitative definite clause specifications.

Adopting Zadeh's definitions for set operations, we can define a partial ordering on the set of base equivalent $\mathcal{R}(\mathcal{L})$ -interpretations. This is done by defining set operations on these interpretations with reference to set operations on the denotations of relation symbols in these interpretations. We get for all base equivalent $\mathcal{R}(\mathcal{L})$ -interpretations $\mathcal{A}$, $\mathcal{A}'$:

- $\mathcal{A} \subseteq \mathcal{A}'$ iff for each n-ary relation symbol $r \in \mathcal{R}$, for each $\alpha \in \mathsf{ASS}$, for each $\mathbf{x} \in \mathsf{VAR}^n$: $\mu(\alpha(\mathbf{x}); r^{\mathcal{A}}) \leq \mu(\alpha(\mathbf{x}); r^{\mathcal{A}'})$,
- $\mathcal{A} = \bigcup X$ iff for each n-ary relation symbol $r \in \mathcal{R}$, for each $\alpha \in \mathsf{ASS}$, for each $\mathbf{x} \in \mathsf{VAR}^n$: $\mu(\alpha(\mathbf{x}); r^{\mathcal{A}}) = sup\{\mu(\alpha(\mathbf{x}); r^{\mathcal{A}'}) | \mathcal{A}' \in X\}$,
- $\mathcal{A} = \bigcap X$ iff for each n-ary relation symbol $r \in \mathcal{R}$, for each $\alpha \in \mathsf{ASS}$, for each $\mathbf{x} \in \mathsf{VAR}^n$: $\mu(\alpha(\mathbf{x}); r^{\mathcal{A}}) = inf\{\mu(\alpha(\mathbf{x}); r^{\mathcal{A}'}) | \mathcal{A}' \in X\}$,
- $sup\, \emptyset = 0$, $inf\, \emptyset = 1$.

Clearly, the set of all base equivalent $\mathcal{R}(\mathcal{L})$ -interpretations is a **complete lattice** under the partial ordering of set inclusion.

Next we have to apply the syntactic notions of renaming and variant to the quantitative case. A **renaming** is a bijection $\mathsf{VAR} \to \mathsf{VAR}$ which is the identity except for finitely many exceptions and VAR is a decidable infinite set of variables.

A quantitative formula κ' is a ρ**-variant** of a quantitative formula κ under a renaming ρ iff $\mathsf{V}(\kappa') = \rho(\mathsf{V}(\kappa))$, where V is a computable function assigning to every quantitative formula κ the set $\mathsf{V}(\kappa)$ of variables occurring in κ; $\kappa' = \kappa\rho$, i.e., κ' is the quantitative formula obtained from κ by simultaneously replacing each occurrence of a variable X in κ by $\rho(X)$ for all variables in $\mathsf{V}(\kappa)$; and $[\![\kappa]\!]^{\mathcal{A}} = [\![\kappa']\!]^{\mathcal{A}}\rho := \{\alpha \circ \rho | \alpha \in [\![\kappa']\!]^{\mathcal{A}}\}$ for each interpretation $\mathcal{A}$.

A quantitative formula κ' is a **variant** of a quantitative formula κ if there exists a renaming ρ s.t. κ' is a ρ-variant of κ.

Using these definitions, we can state the central equations which link the declarative and procedural semantics of $\mathcal{P}_\mathrm{F}$.

Definition 7. Let $\mathcal{P}_\mathrm{F}$ be a quantitative definite clause specification in $\mathcal{R}(\mathcal{L})$, $\mathcal{I}$ be an $\mathcal{L}$-interpretation. Then the countably infinite sequence $\langle \mathcal{A}_0, \mathcal{A}_1, \mathcal{A}_2, \ldots \rangle$ of $\mathcal{R}(\mathcal{L})$ -interpretations extending $\mathcal{I}$ is a $\mathcal{P}_\mathrm{F}$-chain iff for each n-ary relation symbol $r \in \mathcal{R}$, for each $\alpha \in \mathsf{ASS}$, for each $\mathbf{x} \in \mathsf{VAR}^n$:

$\mu(\alpha(\mathbf{x}); r^{\mathcal{A}_0}) := 0$,
$\mu(\alpha(\mathbf{x}); r^{\mathcal{A}_{i+1}}) := max\{f \times min\{\mu(\alpha(\mathbf{x}_j); q_j^{\mathcal{A}_i}) | \ 1 \leq j \leq n\} \mid$ there is a variant $r(\mathbf{x}) \leftarrow_f \phi \ \& \ q_1(\mathbf{x}_1) \ \& \ \ldots \ \& \ q_n(\mathbf{x}_n)$ of a clause in $\mathcal{P}_\mathrm{F}$ and $\alpha \in [\![\phi]\!]^{\mathcal{A}_i}\}$.

Before stating the central theorem concerning the declarative semantics of quantitative definite clause specifications, we have to prove the following useful lemma (cf. [26], Lemmata 2.10', 2.11'):

Lemma 8. *For each $\mathcal{P}_\mathrm{F}$, for each $\mathcal{P}_\mathrm{F}$-chain $\langle \mathcal{A}_0, \mathcal{A}_1, \mathcal{A}_2, \ldots \rangle$, for each n-ary relation symbol $r \in \mathcal{R}$, for each $\alpha \in \mathsf{ASS}$, for each $\mathbf{x} \in \mathsf{VAR}^n$, there exists some $n \in \mathbb{N}$ s.t. $\mu(\alpha(\mathbf{x}); r^{\bigcup_{i \geq 0} \mathcal{A}_i}) = \mu(\alpha(\mathbf{x}); r^{\mathcal{A}_n})$.*

Proof. We have to show that the supremum $v = sup\{\mu(\alpha(\mathbf{x}); r^{\mathcal{A}_i})|\ i \geq 0\}$ can be attained for some $n \in \mathbb{N}$.

$v = 0$: For $v = 0$, we have $n = 0$.

$v > 0$: For $v > 0$, we have to show for any real ϵ, $0 < \epsilon < v$: $\{\mu(\alpha(\mathbf{x}); r^{\mathcal{A}_i})|\ i \geq 0 \textit{ and } \mu(\alpha(\mathbf{x}); r^{\mathcal{A}_i}) \geq \epsilon\}$ is finite.
Let F be the finite set of real numbers of factors of clauses in $\mathcal{P}_\mathrm{F}$, m be the greatest element in F s.t. $m < 1$ and let q be the smallest integer s.t. $m^q < \epsilon$.
Then, since each real number $\mu(\alpha(\mathbf{x}); r^{\mathcal{A}_i})$ is a product of a sequence of elements of F, the number of different products $\geq \epsilon$ is not greater than $|F|^q$ (in combinatorics' talk, the permutation of $|F|$ different things taken q at a time with repetitions) and thus finite.
Hence, the supremum is the maximum attained for some $n \in \mathbb{N}$. □

Now we can obtain minimal model properties for quantitative definite clause specifications similar to those for the non-quantitative case of [11]. Theorem 9 states that we can construct a minimal model $\mathcal{A}$ of $\mathcal{P}_\mathrm{F}$ for each quantitative definite clause specification $\mathcal{P}_\mathrm{F}$ in the extension of an arbitrary constraint language $\mathcal{L}$ and for each $\mathcal{L}$-interpretation. This means that—due to the definiteness of $\mathcal{P}_\mathrm{F}$—we can restrict our attention to a minimal model semantics of $\mathcal{P}_\mathrm{F}$.

Theorem 9 (definiteness). *For each quantitative definite clause specification $\mathcal{P}_\mathrm{F}$ in $\mathcal{R}(\mathcal{L})$, for each $\mathcal{L}$-interpretation $\mathcal{I}$, for each $\mathcal{P}_\mathrm{F}$-chain $\langle \mathcal{A}_0, \mathcal{A}_1, \mathcal{A}_2, \ldots\rangle$ of $\mathcal{R}(\mathcal{L})$-interpretations extending some $\mathcal{L}$-interpretation $\mathcal{I}$:*

(i) $\mathcal{A}_0 \subseteq \mathcal{A}_1 \subseteq \ldots$,
(ii) *the union $\mathcal{A} := \bigcup_{i \geq 0} \mathcal{A}_i$ is a model of $\mathcal{P}_\mathrm{F}$ extending $\mathcal{I}$,*
(iii) *$\mathcal{A}$ is the minimal model of $\mathcal{P}_\mathrm{F}$ extending $\mathcal{I}$.*

Proof. **(i)** We have to show that $\mathcal{A}_i \subseteq \mathcal{A}_{i+1}$. We prove by induction on i showing for each constraint language $\mathcal{L}$, for each quantitative definite clause specification $\mathcal{P}_\mathrm{F}$ in $\mathcal{R}(\mathcal{L})$, for each $\mathcal{L}$-interpretation $\mathcal{I}$, for each $\mathcal{P}_\mathrm{F}$-chain $\langle \mathcal{A}_0, \mathcal{A}_1, \mathcal{A}_2, \ldots\rangle$ of $\mathcal{R}(\mathcal{L})$-interpretations extending some $\mathcal{L}$-interpretation $\mathcal{I}$, for each n-ary relation symbol $r \in \mathcal{R}$, for each $\alpha \in \mathsf{ASS}$, for each $\mathbf{x} \in \mathsf{VAR}^n$, for each $i \in \mathbb{N}$: $\mu(\alpha(\mathbf{x}); r^{\mathcal{A}_i}) \leq \mu(\alpha(\mathbf{x}); r^{\mathcal{A}_{i+1}})$.

Base: $\mu(\alpha(\mathbf{x}); r^{\mathcal{A}_0}) = 0 \leq \mu(\alpha(\mathbf{x}); r^{\mathcal{A}_1})$.

Hypothesis: Suppose $\mu(\alpha(\mathbf{x}); r^{\mathcal{A}_{n-1}}) \leq \mu(\alpha(\mathbf{x}); r^{\mathcal{A}_n})$.

Step: $\mu(\alpha(\mathbf{x}); r^{\mathcal{A}_n}) = v > 0$

$\Longrightarrow$ there exists a variant $r(\mathbf{x}) \leftarrow_f \phi \ \&\ q_1(\mathbf{x}_1) \ \&\ \ldots \ \&\ q_k(\mathbf{x}_k)$ of a clause in $\mathcal{P}_\mathrm{F}$ s.t. $v = f \times min\{\mu(\alpha(\mathbf{x}_1); {q_1}^{\mathcal{A}_{n-1}}), \ldots, \mu(\alpha(\mathbf{x}_k); {q_k}^{\mathcal{A}_{n-1}})\}$ and $\alpha \in [\![\phi]\!]^{\mathcal{A}_{n-1}}$, by Definition 7

$\Longrightarrow$ $\mu(\alpha(\mathbf{x}_1); {q_1}^{\mathcal{A}_n}) \geq \mu(\alpha(\mathbf{x}_1); {q_1}^{\mathcal{A}_{n-1}})$,
$\ldots, \mu(\alpha(\mathbf{x}_k); {q_k}^{\mathcal{A}_n}) \geq \mu(\alpha(\mathbf{x}_k); {q_k}^{\mathcal{A}_{n-1}})$ and $\alpha \in [\![\phi]\!]^{\mathcal{A}_n}$, by the hypothesis

$\Longrightarrow \mu(\alpha(\mathbf{x}); r^{\mathcal{A}_{n+1}}) \geq v$, by definition of $\mu(\alpha(\mathbf{x}); r^{\mathcal{A}_{i+1}})$

$\Longrightarrow \mu(\alpha(\mathbf{x}); r^{\mathcal{A}_n}) \leq \mu(\alpha(\mathbf{x}); r^{\mathcal{A}_{n+1}})$.

For $v = 0$ follows immediately $\mu(\alpha(\mathbf{x}); r^{\mathcal{A}_n}) \leq \mu(\alpha(\mathbf{x}); r^{\mathcal{A}_{n+1}})$.

Claim (i) follows by arithmetic induction.

(ii) We have to show that $\mathcal{A} := \bigcup_{i \geq 0} \mathcal{A}_i$ is a model of $\mathcal{P}_\mathrm{F}$ extending $\mathcal{I}$. We prove that for each clause $r(\mathbf{x}) \leftarrow_f \phi \mathbin{\&} q_1(\mathbf{x}_1) \mathbin{\&} \ldots \mathbin{\&} q_k(\mathbf{x}_k)$ in $\mathcal{P}_\mathrm{F}$, for each $\alpha \in \mathsf{ASS}$: If $\alpha \in [\![\phi]\!]^{\mathcal{A}}$, then $\mu(\alpha(\mathbf{x}); r^{\mathcal{A}}) \geq f \times min\{\mu(\alpha(\mathbf{x}_j); q_j{}^{\mathcal{A}}) | \; 1 \leq j \leq k\}$.

Note that since every $\mathcal{A}_i$ is an $\mathcal{R}(\mathcal{L})$ -interpretation extending $\mathcal{I}$, $\mathcal{A}$ is an $\mathcal{R}(\mathcal{L})$ - interpretation extending $\mathcal{I}$.

Now let $r(\mathbf{x}) \leftarrow_f \phi \mathbin{\&} q_1(\mathbf{x}_1) \mathbin{\&} \ldots \mathbin{\&} q_k(\mathbf{x}_k)$ be a clause in $\mathcal{P}_\mathrm{F}$ s.t. for some $\alpha \in \mathsf{ASS} : \alpha \in [\![\phi]\!]^{\mathcal{A}}$ and $\mu(\alpha(\mathbf{x}_i); q_i{}^{\mathcal{A}}) = min\{\mu(\alpha(\mathbf{x}_j); q_j{}^{\mathcal{A}}) | \; 1 \leq j \leq k\} = v$.

Then there exists some $n \in \mathbb{N}$ s.t. $v = \mu(\alpha(\mathbf{x}_i); q_i{}^{\mathcal{A}_n}) = min\{\mu(\alpha(\mathbf{x}_j); q_j{}^{\mathcal{A}_n}) | \; 1 \leq j \leq k\}$, by Lemma 8 and since for all j s.t. $1 \leq j \leq k : \mu(\alpha(\mathbf{x}_j); q_j{}^{\mathcal{A}}) = sup\{\mu(\alpha(\mathbf{x}_j); q_j{}^{\mathcal{A}_i}) | \; i \geq 0\}$

$\Longrightarrow \mu(\alpha(\mathbf{x}); r^{\mathcal{A}_{n+1}}) \geq f \times v$, by Definition 7

$\Longrightarrow \mu(\alpha(\mathbf{x}); r^{\mathcal{A}}) \geq \mu(\alpha(\mathbf{x}); r^{\mathcal{A}_{n+1}})$, since $\mu(\alpha(\mathbf{x}); r^{\mathcal{A}}) = sup\{\mu(\alpha(\mathbf{x}); r^{\mathcal{A}_i}) | \; i \geq 0\}$

$\Longrightarrow \mu(\alpha(\mathbf{x}); r^{\mathcal{A}}) \geq f \times min\{\mu(\alpha(\mathbf{x}_j); q_j{}^{\mathcal{A}}) | \; 1 \leq j \leq k\}$.

This completes the proof for claim (ii).

(iii) We have to show that $\mathcal{A}$ is the minimal model of $\mathcal{P}_\mathrm{F}$ extending $\mathcal{I}$. We prove for every base equivalent model $\mathcal{B}$ of $\mathcal{P}_\mathrm{F} : \mathcal{A}_i \subseteq \mathcal{B}$, which gives $\mathcal{A} \subseteq \mathcal{B}$, by induction on i showing for each constraint language $\mathcal{L}$, for each quantitative definite clause specification $\mathcal{P}_\mathrm{F}$ in $\mathcal{R}(\mathcal{L})$, for each $\mathcal{L}$ -interpretation $\mathcal{I}$, for each $\mathcal{P}_\mathrm{F}$ -chain $\langle \mathcal{A}_0, \mathcal{A}_1, \mathcal{A}_2, \ldots \rangle$ of $\mathcal{R}(\mathcal{L})$ -interpretations extending some $\mathcal{L}$ -interpretation $\mathcal{I}$, for each n-ary relation symbol $r \in \mathcal{R}$, for each $\alpha \in \mathsf{ASS}$, for each $\mathbf{x} \in \mathsf{VAR}^n$, for each $i \in \mathbb{N}$: $\mu(\alpha(\mathbf{x}); r^{\mathcal{A}_i}) \leq \mu(\alpha(\mathbf{x}); r^{\mathcal{B}})$.

Base: $\mu(\alpha(\mathbf{x}); r^{\mathcal{A}_0}) = 0 \leq \mu(\alpha(\mathbf{x}); r^{\mathcal{B}})$.

Hypothesis: Suppose $\mu(\alpha(\mathbf{x}); r^{\mathcal{A}_{n-1}}) \leq \mu(\alpha(\mathbf{x}); r^{\mathcal{B}})$.

Step: $\mu(\alpha(\mathbf{x}); r^{\mathcal{A}_n}) = v > 0$

$\Longrightarrow$ there exists a variant $r(\mathbf{x}) \leftarrow_f \phi \mathbin{\&} q_1(\mathbf{x}_1) \mathbin{\&} \ldots \mathbin{\&} q_k(\mathbf{x}_k)$ of a clause in $\mathcal{P}_\mathrm{F}$ s.t. $v = f \times min\{\mu(\alpha(\mathbf{x}_1); q_1{}^{\mathcal{A}_{n-1}}), \ldots, \mu(\alpha(\mathbf{x}_k); q_k{}^{\mathcal{A}_{n-1}})\}$ and $\alpha \in [\![\phi]\!]^{\mathcal{A}_{n-1}}$, by Definition 7

$\Longrightarrow \mu(\alpha(\mathbf{x}_1); q_1{}^{\mathcal{B}}) \geq \mu(\alpha(\mathbf{x}_1); q_1{}^{\mathcal{A}_{n-1}})$, $\ldots, \mu(\alpha(\mathbf{x}_k); q_k{}^{\mathcal{B}}) \geq \mu(\alpha(\mathbf{x}_k); q_k{}^{\mathcal{A}_{n-1}})$ and $\alpha \in [\![\phi]\!]^{\mathcal{B}}$, by the hypothesis

$\Longrightarrow \mu(\alpha(\mathbf{x}); r^{\mathcal{B}}) \geq v$, since $\mathcal{B}$ is a model of $\mathcal{P}_\mathrm{F}$

$\Longrightarrow \mu(\alpha(\mathbf{x}); r^{\mathcal{A}_n}) \leq \mu(\alpha(\mathbf{x}); r^{\mathcal{B}})$.

For $v = 0$ follows immediately $\mu(\alpha(\mathbf{x}); r^{\mathcal{A}_n}) \leq \mu(\alpha(\mathbf{x}); r^{\mathcal{B}})$.

Claim (iii) follows by arithmetic induction. □

Proposition 10 allows us to link the declarative description of the desired output from $\mathcal{P}_{\mathrm{F}}$ and a goal, i.e., a $\mathcal{P}_{\mathrm{F}}$ -answer, to the minimal model semantics of $\mathcal{P}_{\mathrm{F}}$. This is done by connecting the concept of logical consequence with the concept of minimal model.

Proposition 10. *Let $\mathcal{P}_{\mathrm{F}}$ be a quantitative definite clause specification in $\mathcal{R}(\mathcal{L})$, φ be an $\mathcal{L}$ -constraint and G be a goal. Then $\varphi \;_v\!\!\rightarrow G$ is a logical consequence of $\mathcal{P}_{\mathrm{F}}$ iff every minimal model $\mathcal{A}$ of $\mathcal{P}_{\mathrm{F}}$ is a model of $\{\varphi \;_v\!\!\rightarrow G\}$.*

Proof. if: For each minimal model $\mathcal{A}$ of $\mathcal{P}_{\mathrm{F}}$: $\mathcal{A}$ is a model of $\{\varphi \;_v\!\!\rightarrow G\}$

$\Longrightarrow$ for every base equivalent model $\mathcal{B}$ of $\mathcal{P}_{\mathrm{F}}$: $\mathcal{B}$ is a model of $\{\varphi \;_v\!\!\rightarrow G\}$, since $\mathcal{A} \subseteq \mathcal{B}$ by Theorem 9, (iii)

$\Longrightarrow$ $\varphi \;_v\!\!\rightarrow G$ is a logical consequence of $\mathcal{P}_{\mathrm{F}}$.

only if: $\varphi \;_v\!\!\rightarrow G$ is a logical consequence of $\mathcal{P}_{\mathrm{F}}$

$\Longrightarrow$ every model of $\mathcal{P}_{\mathrm{F}}$ is a model of $\{\varphi \;_v\!\!\rightarrow G\}$, by Definition 6

$\Longrightarrow$ $\mathcal{A}$ is a model of $\{\varphi \;_v\!\!\rightarrow G\}$. □

The following toy example will illustrate the basic concepts of the declarative semantics of quantitative definite clause specifications.

Example 11. Consider a simple program $\mathcal{P}_{\mathrm{F}}$ consisting of clauses 1, 2 and 3. Let for the sake of the example be $[\![X = \phi \;\&\; X = \psi]\!]^{\mathcal{I}} = \emptyset$ for each $\mathcal{L}$ -interpretation $\mathcal{I}$.

1 $p(X) \leftarrow_{.7} X = \phi$.
2 $p(X) \leftarrow_{.5} X = \phi$.
3 $p(X) \leftarrow_{.9} X = \psi$.

A $\mathcal{P}_{\mathrm{F}}$ -chain for predicate p and an object $\alpha(X)$ allowed by the $\mathcal{L}$ -constraint $X = \phi$ is constructed as follows.

$$\mu(\langle\alpha(X)\rangle\,; p^{\mathcal{A}_0}) = 0,$$
$$\mu(\langle\alpha(X)\rangle\,; p^{\mathcal{A}_1}) = max\{.7 \times min\ \emptyset, .5 \times min\ \emptyset\} = .7,$$
$$\mu(\langle\alpha(X)\rangle\,; p^{\mathcal{A}_2}) = max\{.7 \times min\ \emptyset, .5 \times min\ \emptyset\} = .7,$$
$$\vdots$$

The membership value of this object in the denotation of p under the minimal model $\mathcal{A}$ of $\mathcal{P}_{\mathrm{F}}$ is attained in step 1 and calculated as follows.

$$\mu(\langle\alpha(X)\rangle\,; p^{\bigcup_{i\geq 0}\mathcal{A}_i}) = sup\{0, .7, .7, \ldots\} = .7\ .$$

Clearly, $\mathcal{A}$ is a model of clauses 1 and 2. A similar calculation can be done for clause 3.

3.2 Operational Semantics of Quantitative Definite Clause Specifications

The proof procedure for quantitative CLP is a search of a tree, corresponding to the search of an SLD-and/or tree in conventional logic programming and CLP. Such a tree is defined with respect to the inference rules $\xrightarrow{r}$ and $\xrightarrow{c}$ of [11] and a specific calculation of node values. The structure of such a tree exactly reflects the construction of a minimal model and thus may be defined as a min/max tree. In the following we will assume implicit constraint languages $\mathcal{L}$ and $\mathcal{R}(\mathcal{L})$ and a given quantitative definite clause specification $\mathcal{P}_{\mathrm{F}}$ in $\mathcal{R}(\mathcal{L})$. Furthermore, V will denote the finite set of variables in the query and the V-solutions of a constraint ϕ in an interpretation $\mathcal{I}$ are defined as $[\![\phi]\!]^{\mathcal{I}}_{\mathsf{V}} := \{\alpha|_{\mathsf{V}} \mid \alpha \in [\![\phi]\!]^{\mathcal{I}}\}$ and $\alpha|_{\mathsf{V}}$ is the restriction of α to V.

The first inference rule is given by a binary relation $\xrightarrow{r}$, called goal reduction, on the set of goals.

$$A \;\&\; G \xrightarrow{r} F \;\&\; G \text{ if } A \leftarrow F \text{ is a variant of a clause in } \mathcal{P}$$
$$\text{s.t. } (\mathsf{V} \cup \mathsf{V}(G)) \cap \mathsf{V}(F) \subseteq \mathsf{V}(A).$$

A second rule takes care of constraint solving for the $\mathcal{L}$-constraints appearing in subsequent goals. The rule takes the conjunction of the $\mathcal{L}$-constraints from the reduced goal and the applied clause and gives, via the black box of a suitable $\mathcal{L}$- constraint solver, a satisfiable $\mathcal{L}$-constraint in solved form if the conjunction of $\mathcal{L}$-constraints is satisfiable. The constraint solving rule can then be defined as a total function $\xrightarrow{c}$ on the set of goals.

$$\phi \;\&\; \phi' \;\&\; G \xrightarrow{c} \phi'' \;\&\; G \text{ if } [\![\phi \;\&\; \phi']\!]^{\mathcal{I}}_{\mathsf{V} \cup \mathsf{V}(G)} = [\![\phi'']\!]^{\mathcal{I}}_{\mathsf{V} \cup \mathsf{V}(G)}$$
for each $\mathcal{L}$-interpretation $\mathcal{I}$ and for all $\mathcal{L}$ -constraints ϕ, ϕ' and ϕ''.

Definition 12 (min/max tree). A min/max tree determined by a query G_1 and a quantitative definite clause specification $\mathcal{P}_{\mathrm{F}}$ has to satisfy the following conditions:

1. Each max-node is labeled by a goal. The value of each nonterminal max-node is the maximum of the values of its descendants.
2. Each min-node is labeled by a clause from $\mathcal{P}_{\mathrm{F}}$ and a goal. The value of each nonterminal min-node is $f \times m$, where f is the factor of the clause and m is the minimum of the values of its descendants.
3. The descendants of every max-node are all min-nodes s.t. for every clause C with $\xrightarrow{r}$ -resolvent G' obtained by C from goal G in a max-node, there is a min-node descendant labeled by C and G'.
4. The descendants of every min-node are all max-nodes s.t. for every $\mathcal{R}(\mathcal{L})$ - atom $r(\mathbf{x})$ in goal $G \& \phi \& \phi'$ in a min-node with $\xrightarrow{c}$ -resolvent $G \& \phi''$, there is a max-node descendant labeled by $r(\mathbf{x}) \;\&\; \phi''$.
5. The root node is a max-node labeled by G_1.
6. A success node is a terminal max-node labeled by a satisfiable $\mathcal{L}$ -constraint. The value of a success node is 1.

7. A failure node is a terminal max-node which is not a success node. The value of a failure node is 0.

Definition 13 (proof tree). A proof tree for goal G_1 from $\mathcal{P}_F$ is a subtree of a min/max supertree determined by G_1 and $\mathcal{P}_F$ and is defined as follows:

1. The root node of the proof tree is the root node of the supertree.
2. A max-node of the proof tree is a max-node of the supertree and takes *one* of the descendants of the supertree max-node as its descendant.
3. A min-node of the proof tree is a min-node of the supertree and takes *all* of the descendants of the supertree max-node as its descendants.
4. All terminal nodes in the proof tree are success nodes ϕ, ϕ',... s.t. ϕ & ϕ' & $\ldots \xrightarrow{c} \varphi$ and φ is a satisfiable $\mathcal{L}$-constraint, called answer constraint.
5. Values are assigned to proof tree nodes in the same way as to min/max tree nodes.

To prove soundness and completeness of this generalized SLD-resolution proof procedure, some further concepts have to be introduced.

First, we have to take care of **renaming closure** of the generalized constraint language $\mathcal{R}(\mathcal{L})$. A constraint language is said to be closed under renaming iff every constraint has a ρ-variant for every renaming ρ. Clearly, $\mathcal{R}(\mathcal{L})$ is closed under renaming if the underlying constraint language $\mathcal{L}$ is closed under renaming. Furthermore, for each $\mathcal{R}(\mathcal{L})$ closed under renaming, for each $\mathcal{R}(\mathcal{L})$-interpretation $\mathcal{A}$: $\mathcal{A}$ is a model of an $\mathcal{R}(\mathcal{L})$-constraint iff $\mathcal{A}$ is a model of each of its variants.

Next, we have to redefine a **complexity measure** for goal reduction for the quantitative case. This measure is crucial in proving termination of goal reduction and works by keying steps of the minimal model construction to steps of the goal reduction process.

- The complexity of a variable assignment α for an atom $r(\mathbf{x})$ in the minimal model $\mathcal{A}$ s.t. $\mu(\alpha(\mathbf{x}); r^{\mathcal{A}}) > 0$ is defined as $comp(\alpha, r(\mathbf{x}), \mathcal{A}) := min\{i| \mu(\alpha(\mathbf{x}); r^{\mathcal{A}}) = \mu(\alpha(\mathbf{x}); r^{\mathcal{A}_i})\}$.
- The complexity of α for goal $G = r_1(\mathbf{x}_1)$ & ... & $r_k(\mathbf{x}_k)$ & ϕ in $\mathcal{A}$ s.t. $\alpha \in [\![\phi]\!]^{\mathcal{A}}$ and $\mu(\alpha(\mathbf{x}_i); {r_i}^{\mathcal{A}}) > 0$ for all $i : 1 \leq i \leq k$ is defined as $comp(\alpha, G, \mathcal{A}) := \{comp(\alpha, r_i(\mathbf{x}_i), \mathcal{A})| \ 1 \leq i \leq k\}$ where $\{\ldots\}$ is a multiset.
- The V-complexity of α for goal $G = r_1(\mathbf{x}_1)$ & ... & $r_k(\mathbf{x}_k)$ & ϕ in $\mathcal{A}$ s.t. $\alpha \in [\![\phi]\!]_V^{\mathcal{A}}$ and $\mu(\alpha(\mathbf{x}_i); {r_i}^{\mathcal{A}}) > 0$ for all $i : 1 \leq i \leq k$ is defined as $comp_V(\alpha, G, \mathcal{A}) := min\{comp(\beta, G, \mathcal{A})| \ \beta \in [\![\phi]\!]^{\mathcal{A}}, \ \mu(\beta(\mathbf{x}_i); {r_i}^{\mathcal{A}}) > 0$ for all $i : 1 \leq i \leq k$ and $\alpha = \beta|_V\}$ where the minimum is taken with respect to a total ordering on multisets s.t. $M \leq M'$ iff $\forall x \in M \setminus M', \exists x' \in M' \setminus M$ s.t. $x < x'$.

Clearly, the constraint solving part of the deduction scheme does not affect the denotation or complexity of subsequent goals.

The following proofs show that the quantitative proof procedure is sound and complete with respect to the above stated semantic concepts. Again, there is a close similarity to the corresponding statements for the non-quantitative case of [11].

Theorem 14 (soundness). *For each quantitative definite clause specification $\mathcal{P}_F$, for each goal G, for each $\mathcal{L}$-constraint φ: If there is a proof tree for G from $\mathcal{P}_F$ with answer constraint φ and root value v, then $\varphi \;_v\!\rightarrow G$ is a logical consequence of $\mathcal{P}_F$.*

Proof. The result is proved by induction on the depth d of the proof tree, where one unit of depth is from max-node to max-node.

Base: We know that proof trees of depth $d = 0$ have to take the form of a single max-node labeled by a satisfiable $\mathcal{L}$-constraint ψ with root value 1. Then $\psi \;_1\!\rightarrow \psi$ is a logical consequence of $\mathcal{P}_F$.

Hypothesis: Suppose the result holds for proof trees of depth $d < n$.

Step: Let $G_0 = r(\mathbf{x})\ \&\ \phi$ be a goal labeling a proof tree of depth $d = n$ with answer constraint ψ and root value h,
let $G_0' = q_1(\mathbf{x}_1)\ \&\ \ldots\ \&\ q_k(\mathbf{x}_k)\ \&\ \phi\ \&\ \phi'$ be a goal labeling the min-node obtained from G_0 via $\stackrel{r}{\longrightarrow}$ using the variant $C' = r(\mathbf{x}) \leftarrow_f \phi'\ \&\ q_1(\mathbf{x}_1)\ \&\ \ldots\ \&\ q_k(\mathbf{x}_k)$ of a clause C in $\mathcal{P}_F$,
and let $G_1 = q_1(\mathbf{x}_1)\ \&\ \phi'', \ldots, G_k = q_k(\mathbf{x}_k)\ \&\ \phi''$ be goals labeling max-nodes obtained from G_0' via $\stackrel{c}{\longrightarrow}$.

Then each goal $G_1, \ldots, G_k$ labels a proof tree of depth $d < n$ with respective answer constraint $\psi_1, \ldots, \psi_k$ and root value $g_1, \ldots, g_k$ s.t. $h = f \times min\{g_1, \ldots, g_k\}$ and for each model $\mathcal{A}$ of $\mathcal{P}_F$: $[\![\psi]\!]^{\mathcal{A}} = [\![\psi_1\ \&\ \ldots\ \&\ \psi_k]\!]^{\mathcal{A}}$, by definition min/max tree

$\Longrightarrow$ $\psi_1 \;_{g_1}\!\rightarrow G_1, \ldots, \psi_k \;_{g_k}\!\rightarrow G_k$ are logical consequences of $\mathcal{P}_F$, by the hypothesis

$\Longrightarrow$ for each model $\mathcal{A}$ of $\mathcal{P}_F$, for each $\alpha \in \mathsf{ASS}$: $[\![\psi]\!]^{\mathcal{A}} \subseteq [\![\phi'']\!]^{\mathcal{A}}$ and if $\alpha \in [\![\psi]\!]^{\mathcal{A}}$, then $\mu(\alpha(\mathbf{x}_1); q_1{}^{\mathcal{A}}) \geq g_1, \ldots, \mu(\alpha(\mathbf{x}_k); q_k{}^{\mathcal{A}}) \geq g_k$, by definition of logical consequence

$\Longrightarrow$ for each model $\mathcal{A}$ of $\mathcal{P}_F$, for each $\alpha \in \mathsf{ASS}$: $[\![\psi]\!]^{\mathcal{A}} \subseteq [\![\phi']\!]^{\mathcal{A}}$ and if $\alpha \in [\![\psi]\!]^{\mathcal{A}}$, then $\mu(\alpha(\mathbf{x}); r^{\mathcal{A}}) \geq f \times min\{\mu(\alpha(\mathbf{x}_1); q_1{}^{\mathcal{A}}), \ldots, \mu(\alpha(\mathbf{x}_k); q_k{}^{\mathcal{A}})\}$, since each model $\mathcal{A}$ of $\mathcal{P}_F$ is a model of C' iff $\mathcal{A}$ is a model of C

$\Longrightarrow$ for each model $\mathcal{A}$ of $\mathcal{P}_F$, for each $\alpha \in \mathsf{ASS}$: $[\![\psi]\!]^{\mathcal{A}} \subseteq [\![\phi]\!]^{\mathcal{A}}$ and if $\alpha \in [\![\psi]\!]^{\mathcal{A}}$, then $\mu(\alpha(\mathbf{x}); r^{\mathcal{A}}) \geq h$

$\Longrightarrow$ $\psi \;_h\!\rightarrow r(\mathbf{x})\ \&\ \phi$ is a logical consequence of $\mathcal{P}_F$.

The result follows by arithmetic induction. □

Theorem 15 (completeness). *Let $\mathcal{P}_F$ be a quantitative definite clause specification in $\mathcal{R}(\mathcal{L})$, $\mathcal{L}$ be closed under renaming, $\mathcal{A}$ be a minimal model of $\mathcal{P}_F$, G be a goal of the form $r(\mathbf{x})\ \&\ \phi$, $\alpha \in [\![\phi]\!]^{\mathcal{A}}_V$ and $\mu(\beta(\mathbf{x}); r^{\mathcal{A}}) = v$ s.t. $v > 0$ and $\alpha = \beta|_V$. Then there exists a proof tree for G from $\mathcal{P}_F$ with answer constraint φ and root value v and $\alpha \in [\![\varphi]\!]^{\mathcal{A}}_V$.*

Proof. The result is proved by induction on $c = comp_V(\alpha, G, \mathcal{A})$.

Base: We know that goals with complexity $c = \emptyset$ have to take the form of a satisfiable $\mathcal{L}$-constraint χ. Then there exists a proof tree for χ from $\mathcal{P}_F$ consisting of a single max-node labeled with χ and root value 1.

Hypothesis: Suppose the result holds for goals with complexity $c < N$.

Step: Let $G_0 = q(\mathbf{x})\ \&\ \psi$, $\alpha' \in [\![\psi]\!]_V^{\mathcal{A}}$, $\alpha'' \in [\![\psi]\!]^{\mathcal{A}}$, $\alpha' = \alpha''|_V$, $comp_V(\alpha', G_0, \mathcal{A}) = comp(\alpha'', G_0, \mathcal{A}) = N$, $comp(\alpha'', q(\mathbf{x}), \mathcal{A}) := i$, $\mu(\alpha''(\mathbf{x}); q^{\mathcal{A}}) = h$ and $h > 0$.

First we observe, that $\mu(\alpha''(\mathbf{x}); q^{\mathcal{A}_i}) = h$, since $comp(\alpha'', q(\mathbf{x}), \mathcal{A}) := i$

$\Longrightarrow$ there exists a variant $q(\mathbf{x}) \leftarrow_f \psi'\ \&\ q_1(\mathbf{x}_1)\ \&\ \dots\ \&\ q_k(\mathbf{x}_k)$ s.t. $h = f \times min\{\mu(\alpha(\mathbf{x}_1); q_1{}^{\mathcal{A}_{i-1}}), \dots, \mu(\alpha(\mathbf{x}_k); q_k{}^{\mathcal{A}_{i-1}})\}$ and $\alpha'' \in [\![\psi']\!]^{\mathcal{A}_{i-1}}$ and $(\mathsf{V} \cup \mathsf{V}(\psi)) \cap \mathsf{V}(\psi'\ \&\ q_1(\mathbf{x}_1)\ \&\ \dots\ \&\ q_k(\mathbf{x}_k)) \subseteq \mathsf{V}(q(\mathbf{x}))$, by definition 7 and renaming closure of $\mathcal{R}(\mathcal{L})$, finite V and infinitely many variables in VAR

$\Longrightarrow$ $G_0 \xrightarrow{r,c} G_0'$ s.t. $G_0' = q_1(\mathbf{x}_1)\ \&\ \dots\ \&\ q_k(\mathbf{x}_k)\ \&\ \psi''$ and $[\![\psi'']\!]_V^{\mathcal{A}} = [\![\psi\ \&\ \psi']\!]_V^{\mathcal{A}}$, by definition of the inference rules.

Next, $\alpha' \in [\![\psi'']\!]_V^{\mathcal{A}}$, since $\alpha'' \in [\![\psi]\!]^{\mathcal{A}}$, $\alpha'' \in [\![\psi']\!]^{\mathcal{A}_{i-1}} \subseteq [\![\psi']\!]^{\mathcal{A}}$, $\alpha'' \in [\![\psi\ \&\ \psi']\!]^{\mathcal{A}}$, $[\![\psi\ \&\ \psi']\!]_V^{\mathcal{A}} = [\![\psi'']\!]_V^{\mathcal{A}}$ and $\alpha' = \alpha''|_V$.

Finally, $comp_V(\alpha', G_0', \mathcal{A}) < N$, since $comp_V(\alpha', G_0', \mathcal{A}) \leq comp(\alpha'', G_0', \mathcal{A}) < \{i\} = \{comp(\alpha'', q(\mathbf{x}), \mathcal{A})\} = comp(\alpha'', G_0, \mathcal{A}) = comp_V(\alpha', G_0, \mathcal{A}) = N$.

Now we can obtain goals $G_1 = q_1(\mathbf{x}_1)\ \&\ \psi'', \dots, G_k = q_k(\mathbf{x}_k)\ \&\ \psi''$ from G_0' s.t. $\alpha' \in [\![\psi'']\!]_V^{\mathcal{A}}$, $\mu(\alpha''(\mathbf{x}_1); q_1{}^{\mathcal{A}}) = g_1 > 0, \dots, \mu(\alpha''(\mathbf{x}_k); q_k{}^{\mathcal{A}}) = g_k > 0$, $\alpha' = \alpha''|_V$ and $comp_V(\alpha', G_1, \mathcal{A}) < N, \dots, comp_V(\alpha', G_k, \mathcal{A}) < N$.

$\Longrightarrow$ for each goal $G_1, \dots, G_k$, there exists a proof tree from $\mathcal{P}_F$ with respective answer constraint $\chi_1, \dots, \chi_k$ and respective root value $g_1' = g_1, \dots, g_k' = g_k$ and $\alpha' \in [\![\chi_1\ \&\ \dots\ \&\ \chi_k]\!]_V^{\mathcal{A}} = [\![\chi]\!]_V^{\mathcal{A}}$, by the hypothesis

$\Longrightarrow$ there exists a proof tree for G_0 from $\mathcal{P}_F$ with answer constraint χ and root value $h' = f \times min\{g_1', \dots, g_k'\} = f \times min\{g_1, \dots, g_k\} = h$ and $\alpha' \in [\![\chi]\!]_V^{\mathcal{A}}$.

The result follows by arithmetic induction. □

Returning to our toy example, the proof procedure for quantitative definite clause specifications can be illustrated as follows.

Example 16. Starting from the simple program of Example 11, a min/max tree for query $p(X)\ \&\ X = \phi$ and $\mathcal{P}_F$ is constructed as follows.

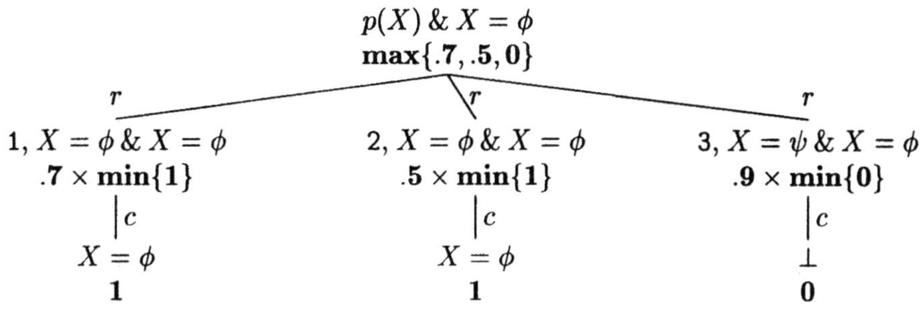

This tree contains two success branches and one failure branch (from left to right). The proof trees obtained from this min/max tree are as follows.

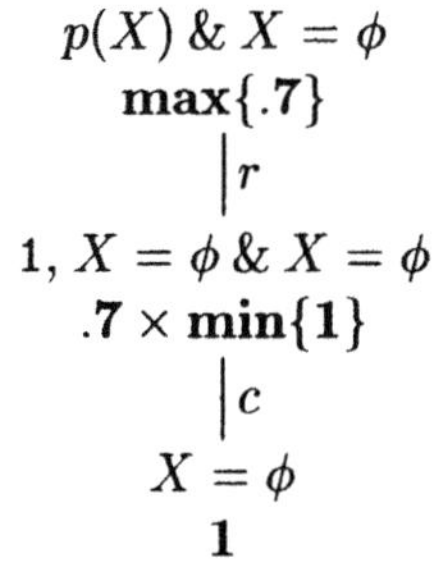

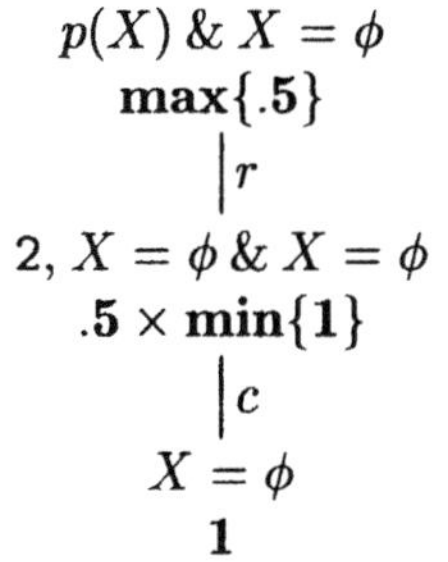

$$p(X) \mathbin{\&} X = \phi$$
$$\mathbf{max}\{.7\}$$
$$\Big|\, r$$
$$1,\ X = \phi \mathbin{\&} X = \phi$$
$$.7 \times \mathbf{min}\{1\}$$
$$\Big|\, c$$
$$X = \phi$$
$$1$$

$$p(X) \mathbin{\&} X = \phi$$
$$\mathbf{max}\{.5\}$$
$$\Big|\, r$$
$$2,\ X = \phi \mathbin{\&} X = \phi$$
$$.5 \times \mathbf{min}\{1\}$$
$$\Big|\, c$$
$$X = \phi$$
$$1$$

Clearly, $X = \phi \,_{.7} \to p(X) \mathbin{\&} X = \phi$ is a logical consequence of $\mathcal{P}_F$.

As proposed by [26], search strategies such as alpha-beta pruning (see [22]) can be used quite directly to define an interpreter for quantitative rule sets. The same techniques can be applied to a min/max proof procedure in quantitative CLP. In general, the amount of search needed to find the best proof for a goal, i.e., the maximal valued proof tree for a goal from a program, will be reduced remarkably by controlling the search by the alpha-beta algorithm.

4 Quantitative CLP and Weighted CLGs

To sum up, the quantitative CLP scheme presented above allows for a definition of the parsing problem (and similarly of the generation problem) for weighted

CLGs in the following way: Given a program $\mathcal{P}_F$ (coding some weighted CLG) and a query G (coding some input string), we ask if we can infer a $\mathcal{P}_\mathrm{F}$-answer φ of G (coding an analysis) at a value v (coding the weight of the analysis) proving $\varphi \ {}_v\!\!\rightarrow G$ to be a logical consequence of $\mathcal{P}_\mathrm{F}$. The concept of weighted logical consequence thus can be seen as a model-theoretic counterpart to the operational concept of weighted inference.

We showed soundness and completeness results for a general proof procedure for quantitative constraint logic programs with respect to a simple declarative semantics based on concepts of fuzzy set algebra. These terms in turn allow for a deeper characterization of the concept of weighted logical consequence: A $\mathcal{P}_\mathrm{F}$-answer to a query $G = r(\mathbf{x})\ \&\ \phi$ at value v is a satisfiable $\mathcal{L}$-constraint φ such that for each model $\mathcal{A}$ of $\mathcal{P}_\mathrm{F}$ holds: If φ is satisfiable, then ϕ is satisfiable and all objects assigned to $\mathbf{x}$ by a solution of φ are in the denotation of $r(\mathbf{x})$ at a membership value of at least v.

Considering concrete instantiations and applications of this formal scheme, the remaining question is how to give the concept of weight an intuitive interpretation. In the following we will briefly discuss two possible interpretations of weighted CLGs each of which is determined by the specific aims of a specific application.

One interpretation of weights is as a correlate to the degree of grammaticality of an analysis. In [8,9], Erbach attempts to calculate the degree of grammaticality of an analysis from the application probabilities of clauses used in the analysis and additional user-defined weights.[3] Regardless of the motivation for this specific determination of degrees of grammaticality, the choice to interpret weights in correspondence to degrees of grammaticality severely restricts the possible applications of such weighted CLGs.

Considering for example the problem of ambiguity resolution which is also addressed by Erbach, we think that the concepts of preference value and degree of grammaticality should be clearly differentiated. As discussed in [1], the problem of ambiguity resolution cannot be reduced to some few unrealistic examples. Instead, when describing a nontrivial part of natural language, grammars of the usual sort will produce massive artificial ambiguity where we can find grammatical readings even for the most abstruse analyses. Suppose for example a grammar which licenses, among many others, analyses such as ***1) John believes*** $[$***Peter saw Mary***$]_S$ and ***2) John believes*** $[New\ York_N\ taxi_N\ drivers_N]_{NP}$. Such a grammar would also license the analysis ***3) John believes*** $[Peter_N\ saw_N\ Mary_N]_{NP}$ (provided a noun entry for the noun reading of ***saw***), which is clearly less preferred than *1)*. Analysis ***3)*** otherwise is not less grammatical, as we can find an acceptable reading (where the NP refers to the $Mary$ associated with some kind of *saw* called a ***Peter saw***). Degrading the weight of the rule $NP \rightarrow N$

[3] Erbach sketches a calculation scheme which employs a restricted summation over clause weights instead of a minimization as is done in our quantitative CLP scheme. This calculation scheme could easily be captured by our quantitative CLP scheme by replacing *min* by a restricted sum in the relevant definitions of the declarative semantics and accordingly of the procedural semantics of our scheme.

N N (licensing multiple nominal modifications) would on the other hand also degrade the weight of *2)*, which prevents a disambiguation by an interpretation of weights in terms of degrees of grammaticality.

Considering the problem of graded grammaticality, it seems necessary to employ richer models for a determination of degrees of grammaticality. A first attempt to incorporate degrees of grammaticality investigated by psycholinguistic experiments into CLGs is presented in [13,14].[4] Weighted CLGs interpreted in a serious framework of graded grammaticality then could provide a valuable framework for a clear procedural and declarative treatment of graded grammaticality in CLGs.

Another interpretation of weighted CLGs is possible from the viewpoint of probabilistic grammars. This approach has been shown to be fruitful, e.g., for the problem of ambiguity resolution. The simple but useful approximation adopted here is to assume the most plausible analysis of a string to be the most probable analysis of that string.

An attempt to transfer the techniques of probabilistic context-free grammars (see [3]) to CLGs was presented in [7]. In this approach the derivation process of CLGs is defined as a stochastic process by the following stochastic model: Each program clause gets assigned an application probability and the probabilities of all clauses defining one predicate have to sum to 1. The probability of a proof tree is calculated as the product of the probabilities of the rules used in it.[5] In order to make the probabilities of proof trees as defined by the stochastic model constitute a proper probability distribution, an additional normalization with respect to the overall probability of proof trees has to be made.[6]

What is interesting about probabilistic language models is their ability to estimate the probabilistic parameters of the model in accord to empirical probability distributions. Eisele attempts to estimate the probability of clauses proportional to the expected frequency of clauses in derivations. Unfortunately, this approach to parameter estimation is incorrect when applied to the probabilistic CLG model of Eisele. This means that the probability distribution over proof trees as defined by a probabilistic CLG model estimated by the expected clause frequency method is not in accord with the frequency of the proof trees in the training corpus. Similarly, when dealing with unparsed corpora, the EM-algorithm used for parameter estimation optimizes the wrong function when applied to this model. The reason for this incorrectness is that the set of trees generated from such a probabilistic CLG model is constrained in a way which violates basic assumptions made in the applied parameter estimation method. In other words, the probabilistic CLG model defined by Eisele could be said to

[4] Keller concentrates on experimental investigation of degrees of grammaticality and sketches a model of graded grammaticality based on ranked constraints. Such a model should easily be given a formal basis in terms of our quantitative CLP scheme.

[5] This calculation scheme also could easily be captured by our quantitative CLP scheme by replacing min by a product accordingly in the relevant definitions of the declarative and procedural semantics of our scheme.

[6] [3] discuss further conditions on consistency of probabilistic grammars which would have to be satisfied also by a probabilistic CLG model.

be incorrect, in the sense that it makes an independency assumption for clause applications which is violated by the languages generated from such probabilistic CLGs.

Since the proposed parameter estimation method is only provably correct for the context-free case, the probabilistic language model of Eisele faces a severe restriction. The only approach we know of to present a correct parameter estimation algorithm for probabilistic grammars involving context-dependencies is the model of stochastic attribute-value grammars of [2], a discussion of which is beyond our present scope.

5 Conclusion

We presented a simple and general scheme for quantitative CLP. Our quantitative extension straightforwardly transferred the nice properties of the CLP scheme of [11] into close analogs holding for a quantitative version of CLP. With respect to related approaches to quantitative extensions of conventional logic programming, our extension raises ideas from this area to the general framework of CLP.

We showed soundness and completeness results with respect to a declarative semantics based on concepts of fuzzy set algebra. This approach to a declarative semantics was motivated by the aim to give a clear and simple formal semantics for weighted CLGs.

Clearly, more expressive quantitative extensions of CLP are possible and will be addressed in future work. Regarding the interest in computational linguistics problems such as ambiguity resolution, however, a necessary prerequisite for a more sophisticated semantics for probabilistically interpreted quantitative CLP is the development of a probabilistic model for CLP which allows for correct parameter estimation from empirical data.

References

1. Steven Abney. Statistical methods and linguistics. In Judith Klavans and Philip Resnik, editors, *The Balancing Act*. The MIT Press, Cambridge, Massachussetts, 1996.
2. Steven Abney. Stochastic attribute-value grammars. Unpublished manuscript, University of Tübingen, September 1996.
3. Taylor L. Booth and Richard A. Thompson. Applying probability measures to abstract languages. *IEEE Transactions on Computers*, C-22(5):442–450, 1973.
4. Jochen Dörre and Michael Dorna. CUF - a formalism for linguistic knowledge representation. In Jochen Dörre, editor, *Computational Aspects of Constraint-Based Linguistic Description I*, pages 3–22. DYANA-2 Deliverable R1.2.A, 1993.
5. Jochen Dörre and Andreas Eisele. A comprehensive unification-based grammar formalism. Technical report, DYANA Deliverable R3.1.B, 1991.
6. Didier Dubois, Jérôme Lang, and Henri Prade. Towards possibilistic logic programming. In *Proceedings of the 8th International Conference on Logic Programming (ICLP '91)*, pages 581–595, Paris, 1991.

7. Andreas Eisele. Towards probabilistic extensions of constraint-based grammars. In Jochen Dörre, editor, *Computational Aspects of Constraint-Based Linguistic Description II*, pages 3–21. DYANA-2 Deliverable R1.2.B, 1994.
8. Gregor Erbach. Towards a theory of degrees of grammaticality. CLAUS Report 34, Computational Linguistics at the Univerity of the Saarland, 1993.
9. Gregor Erbach. *Bottom-Up Earley Deduction for Preference-Driven Natural Language Processing*. PhD thesis, Computational Linguistics, Universität des Saarlandes, Saarbrücken, August 1995.
10. Thilo Götz. Compiling HPSG constraint grammars into logic programs. In *Workshop on Computational Logic and Natural Language Processing*, Edinburgh, 1995.
11. Markus Höhfeld and Gert Smolka. Definite relations over constraint languages. LILOG Report 53, IBM Deutschland, Stuttgart, 1988.
12. Joxan Jaffar and Jean-Louis Lassez. Constraint logic programming. Technical report 74, Department of Computer Science, Monash University, 1986.
13. Frank Keller. Extraction from complex noun phrases. A case study in graded grammaticality. Master's thesis, Institut für maschinelle Sprachverarbeitung, Universität Stuttgart, August 1996.
14. Frank Keller. How do humans deal with ungrammatical input? Experimental evidence and computational modelling. In Dafydd Gibbon, editor, *Natural Language Processing and Speech Technology. Results of the 3rd KONVENS Conference*, pages 27–34, Berlin, 1996. Mouton de Gruyter.
15. Michael Kifer and V. S. Subrahmanian. Theory of generalized annotated logic programming and its applications. *Journal of Logic Programming*, 12:335–367, 1992.
16. Paul J. King. An expanded logical formalism for head-driven phrase structure grammar. Arbeitspapiere des Sonderforschungsbereichs 340 59, University of Tübingen, 1994.
17. Laks V. S. Lakshmanan. An epistemic foundation for logic programming with uncertainty. In *Proceedings of the 14th Conference on Foundations of Software Technology and Theoretical Computer Science*, Madras, India, 1994.
18. Laks V. S. Lakshmanan and Fereidoon Sadri. Probabilistic deductive databases. In *Proceedings of the International Logic Programming Symposium (ILPS '94)*, Ithaca, NY, 1994.
19. J. W. Lloyd. *Foundations of Logic Programming*. Springer, Berlin, 1987.
20. Raymond Ng and V. S. Subrahmanian. Probabilistic logic programming. *Information and Computation*, 101:150–201, 1992.
21. Raymond Ng and V. S. Subrahmanian. A semantical framework for supporting subjective and conditional probabilities in deductive databases. *Journal of Automated Reasoning*, 10:191–235, 1993.
22. Nils J. Nilsson. *Principles of Artificial Intelligence*. Springer, Berlin, Heidelberg, New York, 1982.
23. Carl Pollard and Ivan A. Sag. *Head-Driven Phrase Structure Grammar*. University of Chicago Press, Chicago, 1994.
24. Gert Smolka. A feature logic with subsorts. LILOG Report 33, IBM Deutschland, Stuttgart, 1988.
25. V. S. Subrahmanian. On the semantics of quantitative logic programs. In *Proceedings of the 4th IEEE Symposium on Logic Programming*, pages 173–182, Washington D.C., 1987. Computer Society Press.
26. M. H. van Emden. Quantitative deduction and its fixpoint theory. *The Journal of Logic Programming*, 1:37–53, 1986.
27. L. A. Zadeh. Fuzzy sets. *Information and Control*, 8:338–353, 1965.

Strict LT_2 : Regular :: Local : Recognizable

James Rogers

University of Central Florida, Orlando FL 32816-2362, USA

Abstract. We provide a characterization of the local sets (sets of trees generated by CFGs) in terms of definability in a restricted logical language, which we contrast with a similar characterization of the recognizable sets (sets of trees accepted by finite-state tree automata). In a strong sense, the distinction between these two captures abstractly the distinction between ordinary CFGs and those in which labels are finitely extended with additional features (as in GPSG). In terms of descriptive complexity, the contrast is quite profound—while the recognizable sets are characterized by a monadic second-order language, the local sets are characterized by a severely restricted modal language. In the domain of strings, there is an analogous contrast between the regular languages and the strict 2-locally testable languages, a weak subclass of the star-free sets.

1 Introduction

In the early sixties, in the context of exploring decidability of properties of sequences, Büchi [3] and Elgot [6] established a *descriptive* characterization of the regular sets in terms of definability in the monadic second-order theory of the natural numbers with successor—the theory that is now known as S1S. The idea is that if we interpret an alphabet Σ as a set of monadic predicate variables, then we can interpret non-empty sequences drawn from Σ, i.e., possibly infinite non-empty strings in Σ, as assignments associating each variable $\sigma \in \Sigma$ with a subset of $\mathbb{N}$: namely, the set of positions in the string at which σ occurs. The regular sets are, under this interpretation, the sets of strings that are satisfying assignments for some formula $\varphi(\Sigma)$ in the language of S1S.

To be precise, let $\mathsf{N}_1 = \langle \mathbb{N}, 0, \leq, s \rangle$ the structure of the natural numbers with zero, the usual ordering, and successor.[1] The language of S1S includes the signature of N_1, a set of variables ranging over $\mathbb{N}$ and another ranging over arbitrary subsets of $\mathbb{N}$, quantification over both sorts of variables, and the usual logical connectives. S1S is the set of all sentences in this language that are true in N_1. The set of sequences defined by a formula $\varphi(\Sigma)$ with free-variables among those in Σ are just those generated by the assignments that make $\varphi(\Sigma)$ true in N_1.

Büchi and Elgot were concerned with infinite sequences for which Büchi introduced a class of finite automata over infinite strings that are now referred to

[1] The ordering is actually inessential since it is monadic second-order definable from successor.

as *Büchi automata*. Büchi's central result is that S1S is decidable. He establishes this by showing that, for any S1S formula, there is a Büchi automaton that accepts exactly the set of its satisfying assignments, and that it is decidable if the set accepted by such an automaton is empty. Then $(\exists \mathbf{X})[\varphi(\mathbf{X})] \in$ S1S iff the set accepted by the automaton for $\varphi(\mathbf{X})$ is non-empty.[2] As finiteness is definable in S1S, one can restrict to finite strings by restricting the sets assigned to the variables in Σ to be finite. There is an additional complication in that one must deal with the empty string, but this is inconsequential. Under these circumstances Büchi's automata become simple finite state automata. Thus any subset of Σ^* that is definable in S1S is regular and, since the converse is easy to show, definability in S1S characterizes the regular languages.

This result provides a powerful tool for establishing language-theoretic complexity results that is particularly attractive in the realm of constraint-based approaches to syntax: constraints or principles that are definable in S1S can define only regular languages. The utility of the result, of course, is limited by the weakness of the class it characterizes; the regular languages are not particularly interesting from a linguistic point of view. The obvious step, then, is to extend the result to larger language-theoretic complexity classes.

Intuitively, one can approach capturing the context-free languages in a manner similar to Büchi's characterization of the regular languages by noting that the characteristic operation in generating regular languages is concatenation of strings while the characteristic operation in generating CFLs is substitution in strings, and that substitution in strings is analogous to concatenation of trees in the following sense: substitution of γ for X in a sentential form $\alpha X \beta$ corresponds to concatenating the derivation tree for $\alpha X \beta$ with a local tree (a tree of depth one) at X expanding X to γ. Now, one can interpret trees as a generalization of the natural numbers with successor in which there are multiple successor functions, i.e., if we take $\mathsf{N}_1 = \langle \mathbb{N}, 0, \leq, s \rangle$ to be the complete unary branching tree, the complete n-branching tree is $\mathsf{N}_n = \langle T_n, \epsilon, \triangleleft^*, \trianglelefteq, r_i \rangle_{i<n}$ where:

- T_n is the complete n-branching tree domain (i.e., $\{0, \ldots, n-1\}^*$).
- ϵ is the root of T_n.
- r_i is the ith successor function: $r_i(w) = w \cdot i$.
- $\triangleleft^*$ is reflexive domination: $w \triangleleft^* w \cdot v$ for all $w, v \in T_n$.
- $\trianglelefteq$ is the lexicographic order on T_n: $w \trianglelefteq v$ iff $w \triangleleft^* v$ or there is some $u \in T_n$ and $i < j$ such that $u \cdot i \triangleleft^* w$ and $u \cdot j \triangleleft^* v$.[3]

Rabin [13] has explored SnS in a manner similar to Büchi's exploration of S1S, including defining a type of finite-state automaton over infinite trees, and a similar, but much more difficult, proof of decidability of SnS for all $n \leq \omega$. Again in this context, if we restrict our attention to the finite structures we find ourselves in more familiar territory. In the finite case, Rabin automata reduce to ordinary finite-state tree automata [8]. One gets, then, that sets of finite trees

[2] Or, more directly but less intuitively clear, a sentence φ is in S1S iff the automaton for φ accepts; since Σ is empty, acceptance is independent of the input.

[3] Again, $\triangleleft^*$ is definable except in N_ω—the ω-branching tree—as is $\trianglelefteq$. In N_1 $\triangleleft^* = \trianglelefteq = \leq$.

are definable in SnS, $n < \omega$ (or, equivalently, sets of finite trees with bounded branching are definable in SωS) iff they are *recognizable*.[4] The class of string languages that are the yields of recognizable sets are exactly the CFLs. Thus the move from strings (S1S) to trees (SnS) lifts the result from regular languages to CFLs: principles and constraints on trees that are definable in SnS for $n < \omega$ license only weakly context-free languages. (See [12] and [5].)

While SnS gives us a weak characterization of the CFLs—in terms of string sets—in most linguistic applications we are more interested in strong characterizations of classes of languages—in the way grammars analyze those strings, i.e., the set of structures they generate. From this point of view the result is not completely satisfactory; the recognizable sets are a strict superset of the *local sets*—the sets of derivation trees generated by CF grammars. A useful example of a set of trees separating the two is the set of binary branching trees in which at most one node is labeled 'B' while all others are labeled 'A'. The set is not local: if a CFG can rewrite any 'A' to 'AB', for instance, then it can rewrite every 'A' in this way. While the label of a node in a tree generated by a CFG depends only on the labels of its parent and siblings, tree automata assign each node a *state* (which depends only on the state and label of the parent and the states of the siblings) as well as a label. The example set is recognizable because a tree automaton can distinguish nodes that dominate 'B's from those that don't by assigning them distinct states—by storing a bounded amount of context in the state it can distinguish 'A's that may rewrite to 'B' from those that may not.

Note that if we refine the categories labeling the trees to distinguish 'A's that dominate 'B's (call them 'A/B') from those that don't (call them just 'A'), we get a set of binary branching trees in which at most one node is labeled 'B' while all others are labeled either 'A', if they do not dominate a 'B', or 'A/B', if they do, which *is* a local set. The original set, then, is a *projection* (a relabeling via a typically many-to-one mapping of categories to categories) of a local set. This approach works in general. A set of trees is a projection of a local set whenever it is possible to refine its categories into finitely many sub-categories in a way that distinguishes nodes that must expand in distinct ways. In the case of the recognizable sets this is always possible. Since the automaton can only distinguish nodes on the basis of their label and its state, if we divide each category into distinct sub-categories for each state we will be able to capture the behavior of the automaton with a CFG. Since there are only finitely many states, the refinement is finite. Thus the recognizable sets are projections of the local sets (the converse is easy to see as well) [14].

Sets of finite trees (with bounded branching), then, are definable in SnS, $n < \omega$ iff they are a projection of a local set. As the notation employed in the example is intended to imply, there is a close connection between this mechanism of refining categories on the basis of limited context and the slashed categories of GPSG and HPSG. Thus, at least in some domains, the recognizable sets are

[4] We distinguish the terms *recognizable* and *regular*, reserving them for sets of trees and sets of strings respectively.

essentially the strongly context-free sets. One can argue, on the other hand, a position requiring every category distinguished by a theory of syntax to have empirical justification. Under this assumption arbitrary refinement of categories is highly suspect. If the projection is necessary, then the ontology of the theory is defective. If the original set of categories is correct, then the projection should be impermissible. In any case it would be desirable to have a notion of exactly what the formal power of the projection is. Thus the question arises, how must one restrict SnS in order to characterize the local sets themselves? There is, of course, a trivial way of doing this. We could restrict ourselves to a class of formulae that are essentially direct translations of context-free rewrite rules. But we would like a more natural class of formulae, perhaps even a class that is maximal in the sense that all non-trivial extensions of the class permit definition of non-local sets. The larger class will not have increased descriptive power—we could take the trivial translations as a normal form for the formulae in the class—but we would hope that the larger class would offer better insight into the distinction between local and recognizable sets, as well as allowing more natural expression of constraints defining local sets.

In this paper we define a sub-language of SnS that characterizes the local sets. The key insight behind this result is the fact that the local sets are characterized by "subtree substitution closure": A recognizable set is local iff it is closed under substitution of sub-trees at similarly labeled nodes. As a corollary, we get that the local sets are closed under intersection but not under union. This, of course, is in contrast to the class of context-free string languages which is closed under union but not intersection, and is in contrast to the recognizable sets as well which are closed under all Boolean operations (since the language of SnS is closed wrt the Boolean connectives). The corollary implies that any language characterizing the local sets will not be closed wrt disjunction. On the other hand, the language must support some disjunction—the labels on nodes must be contingent on the labels of the nodes that occur in the same local trees. Similarly, the language will need some form of universal quantification since the productions of a CFG specify conditions that hold for every local tree occurring in the set. But unrestricted quantification, even just first-order universal quantification, allows definition of non-local sets. For instance $(\forall x, y)[(A(x) \vee B(x)) \wedge (B(x) \wedge B(y) \rightarrow x \approx y)]$ picks out our example non-local set. We need, then, a restricted form of quantification.

We are left with a language, Loc, employing restricted quantification in the form of what are, in essence, modal operators for parent, child and left- and right-sibling. Nesting of these operators and of disjunction is restricted in such a way that labels on nodes can only depend on the labels of its parent, its children, or its siblings. We show that a set of finite trees with bounded branching is definable in Loc iff it is local. While Loc is not all that far removed from the trivial translation of CF rewriting rules, it is not hard to show that it is close to being maximal—each syntactic form we rule out can be used to define a non-local set.

Perhaps the primary significance of this result is the way in which it demonstrates how profoundly weak CFGs are as generators of trees. This weakness is highlighted if we reverse the generalization that lifted us from regular to recognizable sets and consider the class of strings we can define as unary branching trees. In this case we are left with the language Loc_1 with operators only for immediate predecessor and immediate successor. The class of sets of strings definable in in this language is the class of ***strict 2-locally testable*** languages (strict LT_2), an extremely weak subclass of the star-free languages [11].

This accounts for the title of this paper. From the point of view of descriptive complexity, the natural generalization of the class of regular languages, in moving from strings to trees, is the class of recognizable sets. The class of languages corresponding analogously to the local sets is the class of strict LT_2 languages. This is confirmed by a number of other parallels in the relationships between these classes. It is not hard to show that the strict LT_2 languages are characterized by a suffix substitution closure condition that is the string equivalent of the subtree substitution closure condition of the local sets. Similarly, if we examine, in the realm of unary branching trees, the proof of the fact that the recognizable sets are projections of local sets we get that every regular set is the projection (more typically in the context of strings, the homomorphic image) of a strict LT_2 language—in essence, a result that was arrived at via a different route by Chomsky and Schützenberger in the early 60's [4].

In the following section we formalize the notions of local and recognizable sets, and establish the distinction between them. Next, we sketch existing descriptive characterizations of the regular and context-free string languages and the recognizable sets. Nearly all of the results of these sections are not new here, although the presentation is, perhaps, somewhat idiosyncratic. The exception is Lemma 11, which is a much simplified version of a result of Fine's [7]. In Section 4, we develop our main contribution, a descriptive characterization of the local sets. Finally, we close by exploring what the characterization tells us about the relationship between these classes of sets of trees and about the formal significance of allowing the syntactic properties of categories to depend on a bounded amount of their context.

2 Local and Recognizable Sets

We begin with a formal development of the classes of trees that yield context-free languages.

2.1 Trees

The foundation of our notion of trees is Gorn's [9] view of trees as collections of node addresses.

Definition 1 (Tree-domains). A *tree-domain*, T, is a subset of $\mathbb{N}^*$ that is both "downward" and "left" closed:

$$wv \in T \Rightarrow w \in T, \text{ for all } w, v \in T$$
$$wi \in T \Rightarrow wj \in T, \text{ for all } w \in T, j < i \in \mathbb{N}$$

The *complete, n-branching tree-domain*, T_n, is the tree-domain in which every node has exactly n successors, i.e., $\{i \mid i < n\}^*$.

Most relationships in trees that arise in linguistic theories can be resolved into relationships of (hereditary) constituency and of the left-to-right ordering of strings. These have natural definitions on tree-domains. They can be combined to provide a total order on the nodes of the tree-domain which coincides with the lexicographic ordering of their addresses.

Definition 2. If T is a tree-domain for all $w, v \in T$, then:

- **(Domination)** $w \triangleleft^* v \overset{\text{def}}{\Longleftrightarrow} (\exists u \in T)[wu = v]$.
- **(Precedence)** $w \prec v \overset{\text{def}}{\Longleftrightarrow} (\exists u \in T, i < j \in \mathbb{N})[ui \triangleleft^* w \text{ and } uj \triangleleft^* v]$.
- **(Lexicographic Order)** $w \trianglelefteq v \overset{\text{def}}{\Longleftrightarrow} w \triangleleft^* v$ or $w \prec v$.

Note that $\trianglelefteq$ is the ordinary lexicographic order on the strings in T.

Commonly, (but not universally) when trees are used to express syntactic analyses each node is labeled with the category of the phrase it spans. We will take the set of category labels to be an arbitrary finite alphabet Σ. Our primary objects of interest, then, are tree-domains with labels drawn from Σ.

Definition 3 (Σ-labeled trees). For Σ any finite set (an alphabet), a *Σ-labeled tree*, $\langle T, \tau \rangle$, is a tree-domain, T, along with a map $\tau : T \to \Sigma$, i.e., an assignment of Σ to the nodes of the tree-domain.

As usual, we extend τ to sequences of nodes by taking $\tau(\langle w_0, \ldots, w_n \rangle)$ to be $\langle \tau(w_0), \cdots, \tau(w_n) \rangle$.

The defining characteristic of the "context-freeness" of a syntactic theory is that it is (or can be) stated in terms of *local* relationships—relationships that hold between a category and its immediate constituents (i.e., between categories labeling a node and its children) or between phrase mates (categories labeling siblings). Such relationships can be expressed as local trees.

Definition 4 (Local trees). The *local tree* occurring at a node w in a Σ-labeled tree $\mathcal{T} = \langle T, \tau \rangle$ is the pair

$$L(\mathcal{T}, w) \overset{\text{def}}{=} \langle \tau(w), \tau(\langle wi \mid i \in \mathbb{N}, wi \in T \rangle) \rangle .$$

(That is, the pair consisting of the label of that node and the sequence of labels of its children.)

The set of local trees occurring in $\mathcal{T}$ is

$$L(\mathcal{T}) \overset{\text{def}}{=} \{L(\mathcal{T}, w) \mid w \in T\} .$$

Finally, there are specific sequences of the nodes or labels in a tree and, in particular, sets of such sequences (i.e., languages) that have distinguished roles in the theory.

Definition 5. Suppose $\mathcal{T} = \langle T, \tau \rangle$ is a Σ-labeled tree. Then:

- The set of *leaves* of $\mathcal{T}$ is the set of its atomic categories—those labeling nodes with no children:

$$l(\mathcal{T}) \stackrel{\text{def}}{=} \{\sigma \in \Sigma \mid \langle \sigma, \epsilon \rangle \in L(\mathcal{T})\}$$

- The *yield* of $\mathcal{T}$ is the sequence of labels of the leaves of $\mathcal{T}$ in left-to-right order:

$$\mathrm{Yd}(\mathcal{T}) \stackrel{\text{def}}{=} \tau(\langle w_i \mid w_i \in l(\mathcal{T}), i < j \Rightarrow w_i \prec w_j \rangle).$$

- A *path* in $\mathcal{T}$ is a set $p \subseteq T$ where:
  1. $\varepsilon \in p$
  2. $w \in p$ and $w0 \in T \Rightarrow (\exists i)[wi \in p]$
     (i.e., if w is in p and has children in T then some child of w is in p.)
  3. $w, v \in p \Rightarrow w \triangleleft^* v$ or $v \triangleleft^* w$
     (i.e., p is linearly ordered by $\triangleleft^*$.)
- The *path language* of $\mathcal{T}$ is the set of words in Σ^* that label paths in $\mathcal{T}$ (in order of domination):

$$\mathrm{PL}(\mathcal{T}) \stackrel{\text{def}}{=} \{\tau(\langle w_0, \ldots, w_n \rangle) \mid \{w_i \mid i \leq n\} \text{ a path in } \mathcal{T}, i < j \Rightarrow w_i \triangleleft^* w_j\}.$$

Again as usual, we extend these to a set of trees $\mathbb{T}$ by taking the union over each tree in the set, e.g.,

$$L(\mathbb{T}) \stackrel{\text{def}}{=} \bigcup_{\mathcal{T} \in \mathbb{T}} [L(\mathcal{T})].$$

In particular, the yield of a set of trees $\mathbb{T}$ is the string language associated with that set

$$\mathrm{Yd}(\mathbb{T}) \stackrel{\text{def}}{=} \{\mathrm{Yd}(\mathcal{T}) \mid \mathcal{T} \in \mathbb{T}\}.$$

2.2 Local Sets

While Context-free grammars are familiar objects, we present them in a somewhat unusual manner, one that is chosen to emphasize the relationships between CFGs and the local sets and between CFGs and tree automata.

Definition 6 (Context-free grammars). A (positive) *context-free grammar* (CFG) is a finite set of local trees over some alphabet Σ:

$$G \subseteq \Sigma \times \Sigma^*, \text{ finite}.$$

For any $\Sigma_0 \subseteq \Sigma$ the set of trees *admitted* by G wrt Σ_0 is the set of finite trees constructed from the local trees in G in which the root is labeled with some symbol in Σ_0:

$$G(\Sigma_0) \stackrel{\text{def}}{=} \{\mathcal{T} = \langle T, \tau \rangle \mid T \text{ finite}, \ \tau(\epsilon) \in \Sigma_0, \text{ and } L(\mathcal{T}) \subseteq G\}$$

The set of terminal symbols of G is:

$$\Lambda_G \stackrel{\text{def}}{=} \{\sigma \in \Sigma \mid \langle \sigma, \epsilon \rangle \in G\}.$$

This definition generalizes the standard notion of CFG in two ways: we allow a finite set of start symbols (rather than just one), and we allow productions for terminal symbols. Thus terminal symbols may label interior nodes of the tree, although, since leaves are local trees with empty sequences of children and must be licensed by G, only terminal symbols may label the leaves (i.e., $l(\mathcal{T}) \subseteq \Lambda(G)$). These generalizations are inconsequential for string languages, of course, but are significant when considering the set of trees admitted by a grammar, where the standard notion is unnaturally restrictive. Note that all grammars in this form are *positive*—they do not admit languages including the empty string. Since local trees with empty sequences of children are taken to be terminals, there is no way of erasing a non-terminal.

Definition 7 (Local sets). A set of trees is *local* iff it is the set of trees admitted by some CFG.

It should be clear that a tree is admitted by a CFG iff it is a derivation tree generated by that CFG in its more typical presentation. It follows that the local sets yield context-free languages.

Theorem 8 (Gécseg and Steinby [8]). *The* context-free (string) languages *are exactly the yields of the local sets.*

2.3 Properties of the Local Sets

In this section we establish a closure property that characterizes the local sets—they contain every tree that can be derived from the other trees in the set by substituting any subtree for another rooted at a similarly labeled node. This implies non-closure of local sets under union and complement, a property that will play a prominent role in developing their descriptive characterization.

Definition 9 (Subtrees). Suppose $\mathcal{T} = \langle T, \tau \rangle$ is a Σ-labeled tree for some Σ and $w \in T$. Then:

- $T{\downarrow_w} \stackrel{\text{def}}{=} \{v \mid wv \in T\}$, the *sub-domain* of T *rooted at* w.
- $T{\uparrow_w} \stackrel{\text{def}}{=} T \setminus \{wv \mid v \in \mathbb{N}^*\}$, the *sub-domain* of T *properly above* w.
- $\mathcal{T}{\downarrow_w} \stackrel{\text{def}}{=} \left\langle T{\downarrow_w}, \tau|_{T{\downarrow_w}} \right\rangle$, the *sub-tree* of $\mathcal{T}$ *rooted at* w.

Definition 10 (Tree substitution). Let $A = \langle T^A, \tau^A \rangle$ and $B = \langle T^B, \tau^B \rangle$ be labeled trees (not necessarily over the same alphabet) and $w \in T^A$. Let

- $T^A \stackrel{w}{\leftarrow} T^B \stackrel{\text{def}}{=} T^A{\uparrow_w} \cup \{wv \mid v \in T^B\}$ and
- $(\tau^A \stackrel{w}{\leftarrow} \tau^B)(v) \stackrel{\text{def}}{=} \begin{cases} \tau^B(u), & \text{if } v = wu \\ \tau^A(v), & \text{otherwise}. \end{cases}$

Then $A \stackrel{w}{\leftarrow} B \stackrel{\text{def}}{=} \left\langle T^A \stackrel{w}{\leftarrow} T^B, \tau^A \stackrel{w}{\leftarrow} \tau^B \right\rangle$.

Thus $A \overset{w}{\leftarrow} B$ is the result of substituting B for the sub-tree rooted at w in A.

Lemma 11 (Subtree substitution closure). *A set, $\mathbb{T}$, of finite trees with bounded branching is local iff for all $A = \langle T^A, \tau^A \rangle, B = \langle T^B, \tau^B \rangle \in \mathbb{T}$, all $w \in T^A$, and all $v \in T^B$ if $\tau^A w = \tau^B v$ then $A \overset{w}{\leftarrow} B{\downarrow_v} \in \mathbb{T}$.*

That is, $\mathbb{T}$ is a local set iff it is closed under substitution of subtrees rooted at similarly labeled nodes.[5]

Proof. Let

$$G^{\mathbb{T}} = L(\mathbb{T}), \quad \Sigma_0^{\mathbb{T}} = \{\sigma \mid (\exists \langle T, \tau \rangle \in \mathbb{T})[\tau(\varepsilon) = \sigma]\}.$$

$G^{\mathbb{T}}$ is the set of all local trees occurring in $\mathbb{T}$, $\Sigma_0^{\mathbb{T}}$ the set of all symbols labeling the root of some tree in $\mathbb{T}$. $L(\mathbb{T})$ is finite since Σ is finite and the branching is bounded.

It is easy to see that every $\mathcal{T}$ in $\mathbb{T}$ is also in $G^{\mathbb{T}}(\Sigma_0^{\mathbb{T}})$.

For the converse, suppose that $\mathcal{T} = \langle T, \tau \rangle \in G^{\mathbb{T}}(\Sigma_0^{\mathbb{T}})$. Choose $\mathcal{T}_\varepsilon = \langle T_\varepsilon, \tau_\varepsilon \rangle \in \mathbb{T}$ such that $\tau_\varepsilon(\varepsilon) = \tau(\varepsilon)$. Since $\tau(\varepsilon) \in \Sigma_0^{\mathbb{T}}$, such $\mathcal{T}_\varepsilon$ exists.

For each $w \in T$, in lexicographic order:

- Choose $\mathcal{T}' = \langle T', \tau' \rangle \in \mathbb{T}$ and $v \in T'$ such that $L(T', v) = L(T, w)$. Such $\mathcal{T}'$ and v exist because $L(T, w) \in L(\mathbb{T})$.
- Let $\mathcal{T}_{w'} = \mathcal{T}_w \overset{w}{\leftarrow} \mathcal{T}'{\downarrow_v}$ where w' is the successor of w (in the lexicographic order).

Then:

- $\mathcal{T}_{w'} \in \mathbb{T}$ for each $w \in T$, since $\mathcal{T}_\varepsilon$ is and $\mathbb{T}$ is closed under subtree substitution.
- For each $w \in T$, the substructure of $\mathcal{T}_{w'}$ restricted to nodes in local trees rooted at ε through w in lexicographic order is equal to the substructure of $\mathcal{T}$ similarly restricted.

It follows that, if w is the maximal node in T, then $\mathcal{T} = \mathcal{T}_{w'} \in \mathbb{T}$. ⊣

Corollary 12. *The class of local sets is closed under intersection, but not under complement or union.*

Note, in contrast, that the class of context-free string languages is closed under union, but not under intersection or complement.

2.4 Recognizable Sets

Tree automata can be thought of as CFGs with a set of auxiliary labels (states) that are employed in controlling the derivation but do not show up in the derived tree.

---

[5] This is a simplified version of a similar result, in a somewhat different setting, due to Kit Fine [7].

Definition 13 (Tree Automata). A *tree automaton* over an alphabet Σ and a finite set of states Q is a finite set of triples:

$$\mathcal{A} \subseteq \Sigma \times Q \times Q^*, \text{ finite} .$$

For any $Q_0 \subseteq Q$ the set of trees *recognized* by $\mathcal{A}$ (wrt Q_0) is

$$\begin{aligned} &\mathcal{A}(Q_0) \stackrel{\text{def}}{=} \\ &\quad \{\mathcal{T} = \langle T, \tau \rangle \mid T \text{ finite and} \\ &\qquad \exists r : T \to Q \text{ such that} \\ &\qquad\quad r(\epsilon) \in Q_0 \text{ and} \\ &\qquad\quad (\forall w \in T)[\langle \tau(w), r(w), r(\langle wi \in T \rangle) \rangle \in \mathcal{A}]\}. \end{aligned}$$

Which is to say, $\langle T, \tau \rangle$ is accepted by $\mathcal{A}$ wrt Q_0 iff it is possible to assign states in Q to the nodes in T, with the root being assigned a state in Q_0, that is consistent with $\mathcal{A}$ in the sense that if a node labeled σ is assigned state q and its children are assigned the sequence of states $\langle q_0, \ldots, q_n \rangle$ (ε if there are no children) then $\langle \sigma, q, \langle q_0, \ldots, q_n \rangle \rangle$ is in $\mathcal{A}$. The assignment r of states to nodes in the $\mathcal{T}$ is referred to a *run* of $\mathcal{A}$ (for Q_0) on $\mathcal{T}$.

A set of trees is *recognizable* iff it is $\mathcal{A}(Q_0)$ for some $\mathcal{A}$ and Q_0.

$$\begin{aligned} \mathcal{A}_{1B} = \{ &\langle A, S_0, \langle S_0, S_1 \rangle \rangle , \\ &\langle A, S_0, \langle S_1, S_0 \rangle \rangle , \\ &\langle A, S_1, \langle S_1, S_1 \rangle \rangle , \\ &\langle A, S_0, \epsilon \rangle , \\ &\langle A, S_1, \epsilon \rangle , \\ &\langle B, S_0, \langle S_1, S_1 \rangle \rangle , \\ &\langle B, S_0, \epsilon \rangle \quad \} \end{aligned}$$

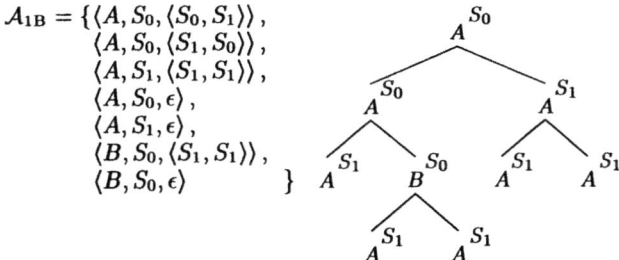

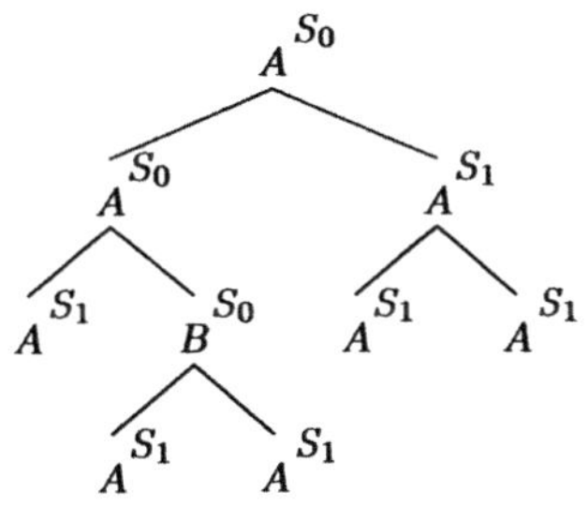

Fig. 1. Separating the recognizable and local sets.

Clearly every local set is recognizable—take Q to be Σ. The converse is not true, however, the inclusion is proper. For example, let $\mathcal{A}_{1B}$ be the tree automaton of Fig. 1. The set $\mathcal{A}_{1B}(\{S_0\})$ is the set of binary-branching trees in which at most one node is labeled B, all others are labeled A (a set we will refer to as "OneB"). To see that this is not a local set, note that if the local tree $\langle A, \langle A, B \rangle \rangle$, for instance, occurs in a tree accepted by a CFG then it must occur in that CFG. But then that CFG will license trees in which $\langle A, \langle A, B \rangle \rangle$ occurs any number of times.

The automaton of the example recognizes OneB by distinguishing nodes that may dominate a B from those that may not by assigning them distinct states (S_0 and S_1, respectively). If we make that state explicit by labeling the trees with pairs in $\Sigma \times Q$ then the set becomes a local set.

$$
\begin{array}{l}
G_{1B} = \\
\quad \{ \langle A, S_0 \rangle \to (\langle A, S_0 \rangle, \langle A, S_1 \rangle), \\
\quad\ \ \langle A, S_0 \rangle \to (\langle A, S_1 \rangle, \langle A, S_0 \rangle), \\
\quad\ \ \langle A, S_0 \rangle \to (\langle B, S_0 \rangle, \langle A, S_1 \rangle), \\
\quad\ \ \langle A, S_0 \rangle \to (\langle A, S_1 \rangle, \langle B, S_0 \rangle), \\
\quad\ \ \langle A, S_0 \rangle \to \quad \varepsilon, \\
\quad\ \ \langle A, S_1 \rangle \to (\langle A, S_1 \rangle, \langle A, S_1 \rangle), \\
\quad\ \ \langle A, S_1 \rangle \to \quad \varepsilon, \\
\quad\ \ \langle B, S_0 \rangle \to (\langle A, S_1 \rangle, \langle A, S_1 \rangle), \\
\quad\ \ \langle B, S_0 \rangle \to \quad \varepsilon \qquad \}
\end{array}
$$

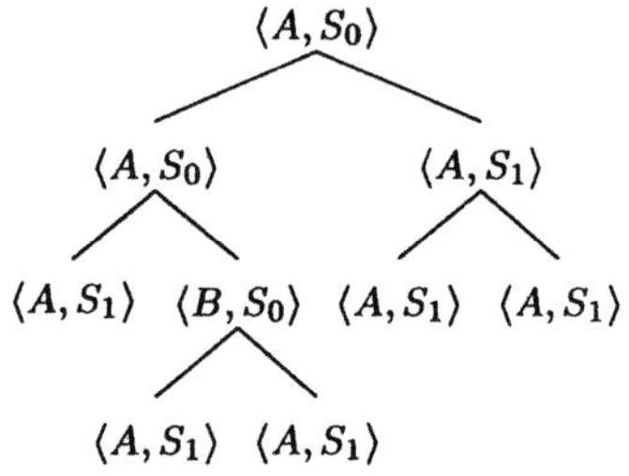

Fig. 2. Making the state explicit.

The CFG G_{1B} of Fig. 2 generates trees in which no more than one node is labeled $\langle B, S_0 \rangle$, all nodes that properly dominate such a node are labeled $\langle A, S_0 \rangle$, and those that don't are labeled $\langle A, S_1 \rangle$. In effect we are making OneB local by refining the original categories ($\{A, B\}$) into finitely many sub-categories ($\{\langle A, S_0 \rangle, \langle A, S_1 \rangle, \langle B, S_0 \rangle, \langle B, S_1 \rangle\}$) which distinguish those nodes that may dominate Bs from those that may not. Note that the original trees are recoverable from the "refined" trees by taking the first projection of their labels. This approach works in general—whenever it is possible to refine the categories labeling a set of trees into finitely many sub-categories in such a way that the ways in which a given category may be expanded is determined entirely by its sub-category then the equivalent set of trees labeled with the sub-categories will be a local. This is always the case for recognizable sets.

Definition 14. Suppose $\mathcal{T} = \langle T, \tau \rangle$ is a tree and the range of τ is a set of n-tuples. The ith*-projection* of $\mathcal{T}$, for $0 < i \leq n$ is $\langle T, \pi_i \circ \tau \rangle$—$T$ with nodes labeled with the ith component of their labels in $\mathcal{T}$.

Lemma 15 (Thatcher). *Every recognizable set is the projection of a local set.*

Proof. The proof simply carries out the idea of the example. Suppose $\mathbb{T} = \mathcal{A}(Q_0)$ for some tree automaton $\mathcal{A}$ over Σ and Q and set of initial states Q_0. Let $\hat{\mathcal{A}}(Q_0)$ be the set of $\Sigma \times Q$-labeled trees:

$$\hat{\mathcal{A}}(Q_0) = \{\langle T, \tau \rangle \mid \mathcal{T} = \langle T, \pi_1 \circ \tau \rangle \in \mathcal{A}(Q_0) \text{ and } \pi_2 \circ \tau \text{ is a run of } \mathcal{A} \text{ on } \mathcal{T}\}.$$

Which is to say that $\langle T, \tau \rangle \in \hat{\mathcal{A}}(Q_0)$ iff the first projection of $\mathcal{T}$ is a tree in $\mathcal{A}(Q_0)$ and the second projection of τ encodes a run of $\mathcal{A}(Q_0)$ on that tree.

Thus $\mathcal{A}(Q_0)$ is a projection of $\hat{\mathcal{A}}(Q_0)$. That $\hat{\mathcal{A}}(Q_0)$ is a local set follows from the fact that it is closed under subtree substitution, which follows easily from the definition of recognition. ⊣

Corollary 16. *A language is a CFL iff it is the yield of a recognizable set.*

This follows from the fact that we might as well the label the leaves in $\hat{\mathcal{A}}(Q_0)$ with Σ.

3 Descriptive Characterizations

We now turn to the characterization of these language-theoretic classes as classes of structures definable in certain restricted logical languages.

Definition 17 (SnS). Let $\mathsf{N}_n = \langle T_n, \epsilon, \triangleleft^*, \preceq, r_i \rangle_{i<n}$, where T_n is the complete n-branching tree-domain, ε is the root of T_n, $\triangleleft^*$ and $\preceq$ are domination and lexicographic order on T_n, respectively, and r_i takes elements of T_n to their i^{th} child.

SnS is the monadic second-order theory of N_n; *wSnS* is the *weak* monadic second-order theory of N_n, the theory in which second-order quantification is restricted to finite sets.

Finiteness is a definable property of subsets in SnS, therefore wSnS is a definable fragment of SnS.

Theorem 18 (Büchi [3]). *S1S is decidable.*

Theorem 19 (Rabin [13]). *SnS is decidable for all $n \leq \omega$.*

Büchi's result is a special case of Rabin's. Rabin first establishes this result for the $n = 2$ case. The proof is based on the idea that assignments making some formula $\varphi(\mathbf{X})$ over the signature of S2S true in N_2 are, in effect, $\mathcal{P}(\mathbf{X})$-labeled trees with domain T_2 (where $\mathcal{P}(\mathbf{X})$ is the powerset of the set of elements of $\mathbf{X}$). He gives an effective procedure for constructing, for any such $\varphi(\mathbf{X})$, a *Rabin tree-automaton*—an automaton over infinite trees which is, in essence, a tree automaton with an acceptance condition based on the sets of states that occur infinitely often along the paths of the tree—which accepts a $\mathcal{P}(\mathbf{X})$-labeled tree iff it encodes a satisfying assignment for $\varphi(\mathbf{X})$. It follows that $(\exists \mathbf{X})[\varphi(\mathbf{X})] \in S2S$ iff the set of trees accepted by this automaton is non-empty. He then shows that emptiness is decidable for sets of trees accepted by this class of automata and that the class of sets of labeled trees they accept (the class of *Rabin recognizable sets*) is closed under Boolean operations. Thus, the result extends to arbitrary formulae over the signature of S2S.

Rabin then generalizes this result to SnS for all $n \leq \omega$ by showing that N_n for any such n can be embedded in N_2 via the map $h : T_n \to (1^*0)^*$ where:

$$h(w) = \begin{cases} \varepsilon & \text{if } w = \varepsilon \\ h(u) \cdot 1^i \cdot 0 & \text{if } w = ui. \end{cases}$$

This map locates the ith child of w at the left child of the ith node on the right-most branch of the subtree rooted at w. This is pretty much the standard way of interpreting an arbitrarily branching tree as a binary branching tree. The contribution of the proof is the observation that the range of h and the relations and functions of N_n in terms of the range of h are all definable on N_2.

Definition 20. A set $\mathbf{T}$ of Σ-labeled trees, where $\Sigma = \{\sigma_1, \ldots, \sigma_m\}$, is *definable in* S$n$S iff there is a formula $\varphi(X_U, X_1, \ldots, X_m)$ such that

$$\mathsf{N}_n \models \varphi[X_U \mapsto T, X_i \mapsto \tau^{-1}(\sigma_i)] \Leftrightarrow \langle T, \tau \rangle \in \mathbf{T}.$$

In words, the trees in the set encode all and only the satisfying assignments for φ.

Lemma 21. *A set of finite trees is definable in* SnS *iff it is recognizable.*

This is a consequence of the fact that, if we restrict ourselves to sets of finite trees, Rabin's tree automata reduce to ordinary tree automata. Note that, since the language of SnS is closed wrt all Boolean connectives, this implies that recognizable sets are closed under all Boolean operations.

Theorem 22 (Büchi [3]). *A language is regular iff it is the path language of a set of finite (unary branching) trees definable in S1S.*

This follows from the fact that the path languages of recognizable sets are regular.

Theorem 23 (Doner [5]). *A language is context-free iff it is the yield of a set of finite trees definable in wSnS for some $n < \omega$.*

Since we are restricting ourselves to sets of finite trees and finiteness is definable in SnS, we need not restrict Doner's result to weak SnS. Similarly, when we are working with sets of trees with bounded branching we can assume that the bound is given explicitly and work in SωS.

Corollary 24. *A language is context-free iff it is the yield of a set of finite trees definable in SnS for some $n < \omega$; equivalently, if it is the yield of a set of finite trees with bounded branching that is definable in SωS.*

Thus definability in S1S and SωS characterize the regular and context-free languages in the *weak* sense—they characterize the string languages. But, in linguistic applications, we are generally more interested in the way in which a theory of syntax analyzes those strings, with the structures it assigns to them. While this makes no difference for Büchi's result, at the context free level it is significant—definability in SnS does not characterize the local sets but, rather, the recognizable sets. Whether the distinction is significant is open to debate. The mechanism of refining the categories of a recognizable set to resolve it into a local set is, in essence, the same mechanism as the slashed categories of GPSG and HPSG. In the OneB example we are distinguishing 'A's that dominate 'B's in very much the same way we might distinguish VPs that dominate an NP gap (i.e., a VP/NP) from those that do not (an ordinary VP). From one point of view, then, the distinction between local and recognizable sets is not linguistically significant.

On the other hand, to the extent that theories of syntax are intended to be accounts of naturally occurring phenomena, one would expect that the categories they distinguish should all be empirically justified—should be identifiable from observable regularities of language. Arbitrary refinement of those categories would then be highly suspect; the need for such refinement should suggest that the original ontology was incomplete, but its extension ought not be undertaken without similar justification. From this point of view the distinction between local and recognizable sets is quite significant. In any case it would be desirable to have a notion of exactly what the formal power of the projection mapping the recognizable sets into the local sets is.

4 Descriptive Characterization of the Local Sets

We would like to define a class of formulae that characterize the local sets in the same way that language of SωS characterizes the recognizable sets, i.e., sets of trees will be definable by formulae in the class iff they are local. We could do this minimally by restricting to formulae that are more or less direct translations of context-free productions, but, while this class suffices, it is overly restrictive. We would like to find a more natural class of formulae, certainly one that supports more natural expression of linguistically interesting constraints, perhaps even a class that is maximal in the sense that all non-trivial extensions of the class permit definition of non-local sets.

In this section we define such a class. As it turns out, the class is not that far removed from the minimal "direct translation of CFG rewriting rules", but it is, in fact, close to maximal—each syntactic form that we exclude can be used to license non-local sets.

The corollary to the subtree substitution closure lemma assures that there is no such class of formulae that is robust in the sense of being closed under Boolean connectives. The fact that the local sets are not closed under union implies that it cannot be characterized, for instance, by any class of formulae defined by quantifier prefix or by any other class of formulae closed under disjunction. On the other hand, the class of formulae must include some disjunction—the labels on nodes will be contingent on the labels of the nodes that occur in the same local trees. What we need then, is a class of formulae with limited disjunction.

Similarly, we will need some form of universal quantification since the productions of a CFG specify conditions that hold for every local tree occurring in the set. Unrestricted universal quantification, on the other hand, even only first-order, allows definition of non-local sets. For instance

$$(\forall x, y)[(A(x) \vee B(x)) \wedge (B(x) \wedge B(y) \rightarrow x \approx y)]$$

picks out the set *OneB*. We need, then, a restricted form of quantification as well.

The motivating idea is that we can ensure that subtree substitution closure will hold by limiting formulae in such a way that their truth at a node depends only on one or the other of the local trees that node is a member of. We start by restricting existential quantification to nodes that are immediately related by parent or sibling—to the form:

$$(\exists y)[x \mathrm{P} y \wedge \phi(y)],$$

where y is new and $\mathrm{P} \in \{\triangleleft, \triangleright, \prec, \succ\}$ which are interpreted as follows:

$$\mathsf{N}_n \models x \triangleleft y[x \mapsto w, y \mapsto v] \overset{\text{def}}{\Longleftrightarrow} v = wi, i < n \qquad \text{(Parent)}$$
$$\mathsf{N}_n \models x \triangleright y[x \mapsto w, y \mapsto v] \overset{\text{def}}{\Longleftrightarrow} w = vi, i < n \qquad \text{(Child)}$$
$$\mathsf{N}_n \models x \prec y[x \mapsto w, y \mapsto v] \overset{\text{def}}{\Longleftrightarrow} w = ui, v = u \cdot (i+1) \quad \text{(Left Sibling)}$$
$$\mathsf{N}_n \models x \succ y[x \mapsto w, y \mapsto v] \overset{\text{def}}{\Longleftrightarrow} w = u \cdot (i+1), v = ui \quad \text{(Right Sibling)}$$

Satisfaction of a formula employing such restricted quantification is relative to the interpretation of x. We will say that a formula of this form is made true in N_n (in general) by an assignment, s, iff it is made true by every assignment that extends s with $x \mapsto w$ for any $w \in \mathsf{N}_n$, i.e., if it is made true by s at every point in N_n. In effect, then, we limit ourselves to a single universal quantifier that takes scope over the entire formula.

This is the standard interpretation of diamond modalities from correspondence theory, where the relations underlying the modalities are parent, left sibling, and their inverses. Following this connection we will use modality-flavored abbreviations for the restricted quantifiers:

$$\triangleleft\, \varphi(x) \equiv (\exists y)[x \triangleleft y \wedge \varphi(y)]$$
$$\triangleright\, \varphi(x) \equiv (\exists y)[x \triangleright y \wedge \varphi(y)]$$
$$\prec\, \varphi(x) \equiv (\exists y)[x \prec y \wedge \varphi(y)]$$
$$\succ\, \varphi(x) \equiv (\exists y)[x \succ y \wedge \varphi(y)]$$

Furthermore we will use:

$$\bot \equiv (\exists x)[x \triangleleft x] \qquad\qquad \top \equiv \neg\bot.$$

Restricting quantification in this way leaves us with a perfectly normal modal language for trees (see [1,2,10]), albeit a very weak one. It is, in fact, too weak to axiomatize the theory of trees, but it is perfectly adequate to define local sets among the class of sets of of finite trees. The problem, of course, is that it is still too strong—it is disjunctively closed.

Consider the set of trees sketched schematically in Fig. 3. This includes all trees of the form on the left in which the portion between the 'A's is iterated zero or more times, but does not include the tree on the right. The set is non-local since substitution of the subtree rooted at the lower C in the tree on the left for that rooted at the upper C produces the excluded tree. This set of trees is not difficult to define in our restricted language:

$$A \vee B \vee C \vee a \vee b \vee c \tag{1}$$
$$\neg\triangleright\top \rightarrow A \tag{2}$$
$$\neg\triangleleft\top \leftrightarrow a \vee b \vee c \tag{3}$$
$$A \rightarrow \triangleleft(\neg\succ\top \wedge a \wedge \prec(C \wedge \neg\prec\top) \vee \neg\succ\top \wedge c \wedge \neg\prec\top) \tag{4}$$
$$B \rightarrow \triangleleft(\neg\succ\top \wedge C \wedge \prec(b \wedge \neg\prec\top)) \tag{5}$$
$$C \rightarrow \triangleleft(\neg\succ\top \wedge (A \vee B) \wedge \neg\prec\top) \tag{6}$$
$$C \rightarrow \prec b \vee \triangleleft B. \tag{7}$$

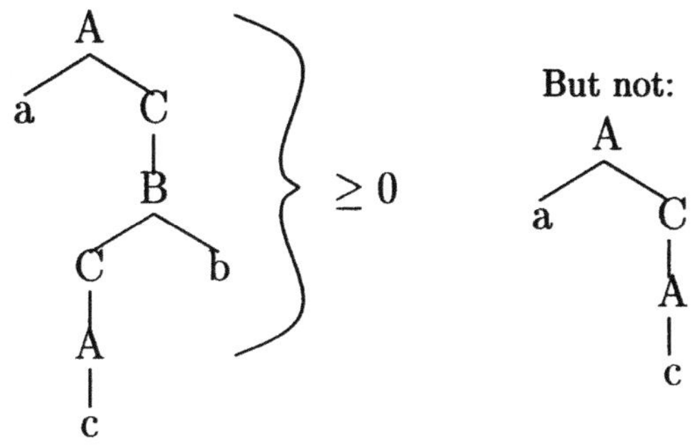

Fig. 3. A non-local set

The first portion of this is harmless. The problem is (7) which requires 'C's to either have a b on their right or a B as a child. This rules out the excluded tree. The problematic axiom is a constraint that relates the form of the dominating local tree to that of the dominated local tree. Thus it will not, in general, be preserved if we insert that dominated tree into a new context. The intuition here is that if we rule out such constraints by limiting disjunction to conditions that hold in the same local tree then we will get invariance with respect to subtree substitution.

To this end we define three sub-languages with the modal prefixes restricted in such a way that they can express only conditions that hold immediately at a node (Loc_P), in the dominated local tree (Loc_+), or in the dominating local tree (Loc_-).

- Loc_P — Modal-free formulae
- Loc_+ — formulae over $\{\wedge, \vee, \neg, \triangleleft, \triangleright, \prec, \succ\}$ and $X(x)$ such that
  - all $\{\prec, \succ, \triangleright\}$ are in the scope of exactly one more $\triangleleft$ than $\triangleright$, and
  - all $\triangleleft$ are in the scope of exactly as many $\triangleright$ as $\triangleleft$.
- Loc_- — formulae over $\{\wedge, \vee, \neg, \triangleleft, \triangleright, \prec, \succ\}$ and $X(x)$ such that
  - all $\{\prec, \succ, \triangleright\}$ are in the scope of exactly as many $\triangleleft$ as $\triangleright$, and
  - all $\triangleleft$ are in the scope of exactly one more $\triangleright$ than $\triangleleft$.

We then limit disjunction to formulae within Loc_+ or within Loc_-.

- Loc — conjunctions of
  - disjunctions of formulae in Loc_+, and
  - disjunctions of formulae in Loc_-.

Note that $\text{Loc}_P = \text{Loc}_+ \cap \text{Loc}_-$ and thus purely propositional formulae are unrestricted.

It is not hard to find examples of non-local sets that can be defined using disjunctions of formulae in any of the forms of Loc_+ with any of the forms of Loc_-. The form of (7) is one example, where $\prec b$ is in Loc_- and $\triangleleft B$ is in Loc_+. Another can be found by replacing it with

$$C \rightarrow \triangleleft B \vee \triangleright B$$

which also excludes the desired tree. The languages Loc_+ and Loc_- are not exhaustive. There are formulae in the full language that are in neither. These are all, in effect, of forms similar to:

$$\triangleleft\triangleleft\phi \quad \text{or} \quad \triangleright\{\prec,\succ,\triangleright\}\phi.$$

It is similarly easy to find examples of disjunctions of formulae in these forms and formulae in Loc_P that define non-local trees, for example,

$$A \rightarrow \neg\triangleright\triangleright A$$

serves just as well for (7). In this sense the language Loc is very nearly minimally restricted.

4.1 Definability in Loc Characterizes the Local Sets

Lemma 25. *Every local set is definable in* Loc.

Proof. Suppose G is a CFG over Σ and the local trees in G with root A are:

$$\langle A, \langle A_1\ A_2\ A_3\rangle\rangle\,,\ \langle A, \langle A_4\ A_5\rangle\rangle \text{ and } \langle A, \varepsilon\rangle\,.$$

We can capture the requirement that every local tree with root labeled A is one of these three with:

$$\begin{aligned} A(x) \rightarrow \triangleleft\, (&\succ \bot \wedge A_1(x) \wedge \prec (A_2(x) \wedge \prec (A_3(x) \wedge \prec \bot)) \ \vee \\ &\succ \bot \wedge A_4(x) \wedge \prec (A_5(x) \wedge \prec \bot) \ \vee \\ &\bot\ ). \end{aligned}$$

This is a disjunction in Loc_+. The conjunction of all such formulae for the local trees in G, then, is a Loc formula that enforces the condition that every local tree occurs in G. We can conjoin this with

$$\bigvee_{A\in\Sigma} [A(x)]$$

and, for some $\Sigma_0 \subseteq \Sigma$,

$$\neg\triangleright\top \rightarrow \bigvee_{A\in\Sigma_0} [A(x)]$$

which require all nodes to be labeled in Σ and the root to be labeled in Σ_0. These are disjunctions in Loc_P and Loc_-, respectively, and so the entire conjunction is in Loc. It is easy to verify that a set of finite trees satisfies this conjunction iff it is in $G(\Sigma_0)$. ⊣

For the converse, we begin by establishing normal forms for Loc_+ and Loc_-.

Lemma 26 (Loc_+-Normal Form). *Every* Loc_+ *formula is expressible as a disjunction of conjunctions of* Loc_+ *formulae in which:*

- *the* $\triangleright$*-depth is 0.*
- *the* $\triangleleft$*-depth is no more than 1.*
- *no* $\{\prec, \succ\}$ *occurs outside the scope of* $\triangleleft$.
- *no* $\triangleleft$ *occurs inside the scope of* $\{\prec, \succ\}$.

That is, disjunctions of conjunctions of formulae of the form

$$(\triangleleft \{\prec, \succ\}^*)^{\leq 1} \mathsf{Loc_P}.$$

Proof. The proof follows from some simple equivalences in Loc_+ (where the underlined material is the same on both sides of the equivalence):

$$\triangleleft \underline{\{\prec, \succ\}^*_i} \triangleright \varphi(x) \equiv \triangleleft \underline{\{\prec, \succ\}^*_i} \top \wedge \varphi(x).$$
$$\triangleleft \underline{\{\prec, \succ\}^*_i} \triangleright \neg\varphi(x) \equiv \triangleleft \underline{\{\prec, \succ\}^*_i} \top \wedge \neg\varphi(x).$$
$$(\text{since } \triangleleft \underline{\{\prec, \succ\}^*_i} \top \rightarrow \triangleleft\triangleright \top.)$$
$$\triangleleft \neg\underline{\{\prec, \succ\}^*_i} \triangleright \varphi(x) \equiv \triangleleft \neg\underline{\{\prec, \succ\}^*_i} \top \vee (\neg\varphi(x) \wedge \triangleleft \top).$$
$$\triangleleft \neg\underline{\{\prec, \succ\}^*_i} \neg \triangleright \varphi(x) \equiv \triangleleft \neg\underline{\{\prec, \succ\}^*_i} \top \vee (\varphi(x) \wedge \triangleleft \top).$$
$$(\text{since } \triangleleft \top \rightarrow \triangleleft\triangleright \top.)$$

⊣

Lemma 27 (Loc_--Normal Form). *Every* Loc_- *formula (if interpreted over trees with bounded branching) is expressible as a disjunction of conjunctions of* Loc_- *formulae in which:*

- *the* $\triangleleft$*-depth is 0.*
- *the* $\triangleright$*-depth is no more than 1.*
- *no* $\{\prec, \succ\}$ *occurs inside the scope of* $\triangleright$.

That is, disjunctions of conjunctions of formulae of the form

$$(\{\prec, \succ\}^* \triangleright)^{\leq 1} \mathsf{Loc_P}.$$

Proof. Again the proof follows from some simple equivalences in Loc_- (assuming that branching is bounded to be no more than n):

$$\triangleright\triangleleft \varphi(x) \equiv \triangleright \top \wedge \varphi(x) \vee \bigvee_{i<n} [\prec^i \varphi(x)] \vee \bigvee_{i<n} [\succ^i \varphi(x)].$$
$$\triangleright \neg \triangleleft \varphi(x) \equiv \triangleright \top \wedge \neg\varphi(x) \wedge \bigwedge_{i<n} [\neg \prec^i \varphi(x)] \wedge \bigwedge_{i<n} [\neg \succ^i \varphi(x)].$$

⊣

Lemma 28. *Every set of finite trees with bounded branching definable in* Loc *is local.*

Proof. This follows from the fact that every Loc formula is logically equivalent to a conjunction of formulae in either Loc_+-normal form or Loc_--normal form and is thus true at a point iff each of those conjuncts is true at that point. But the truth of a formula in Loc_+-normal form at some point w depends only on the local tree rooted at w while the truth of a formula in Loc_--normal form depends only on the local tree rooted at w's parent. It follows that this will be preserved by subtree substitution. ⊣

Theorem 29. *A set of finite trees with bounded branching is local iff it is definable in* Loc.

5 Consequences

Perhaps the main thing to be gotten from this characterization of the local sets is an appreciation of just how weak CFGs are as generators of trees, or, equivalently a realization that the refinement of categories on the basis of even bounded context has considerably stronger formal consequences than it might first appear. In terms of descriptive complexity, the projection that strips the contextual information lifts us from an extremely weak language, Loc, all the way to the monadic second-order language. In linguistic terms this suggests that the question of whether to admit slashed categories, i.e., whether to allow even limited refinement of the fundamental categories of the theory, is not a minor point but, in fact, has significant formal consequences.

One way to use this characterization to get an intuitive notion of the distinction between local and recognizable sets is to consider what happens when we reverse the process that lifted us from regular to context-free string languages. If we restrict our models to unary branching trees we are left with the a language in which one can talk only about immediate successor and immediate predecessor:

$$\mathsf{Loc}_1 \stackrel{\text{def}}{=} (\triangleleft\triangleright)^{\mathsf{i}}\triangleleft\mathsf{Loc}_{\mathsf{P}} \text{ or } (\triangleright\triangleleft)^{\mathsf{i}}\triangleright\mathsf{Loc}_{\mathsf{P}}.$$

Membership on sets of strings definable in this language depends only on relationships between adjacent positions in the string and can be tested by considering each such pair of positions independently. This places them within the class of ***strict 2-locally testable*** languages (strict LT_2) an extremely week subclass of the star-free languages [11] and, as every strict LT_2 language is definable in Loc_1, definability in Loc_1 characterizes strict LT_2. Thus our intuition that generalizing strings to trees should lift us from regular sets to local sets is, in fact, misleading. The tree analog of the class of regular sets is the class of recognizable sets, the string analog of the class of local sets is strict LT_2.

We can verify this analogy in a couple of ways. It is easy to see that strict LT_2 languages are closed under suffix substitution, the string analog of subtree substitution. Also, if we consider the string analog of Thatcher's proof that the recognizable sets are projections of local sets we get a construction in which we form sequences of pairs in which the first projections form a string in the language and the second form the sequence of states visited by a finite-state automaton in accepting that string. Such sequences form a strict LT_2 language. Thus the regular sets are projections of the strict 2-locally testable sets, a fact that turns out to be a minor variation of a result that appears in Chomsky and Schützenberger's 1963 paper on CFLs [4].

References

1. Patrick Blackburn, Claire Gardent, and Wilfried Meyer-Viol. Talking about trees. In *EACL 93*, pages 21–29. EACL, 1993.
2. Patrick Blackburn and Wilfried Meyer-Viol. Modal logic and model-theoretic syntax. In Martin de Rijke, editor, *Advances in Intensional Logic*, pages 27–58. Kluwer, 1996.
3. J. R. Büchi. Weak second-order arithmetic and finite automata. *Zeitschrift für mathematische Logik und Grundlagen der Mathematik*, 6:66–92, 1960.
4. N. Chomsky and M. P. Schüzenberger. The algebraic theory of context-free languages. In P. Braffort and D. Hirschberg, editors, *Computer Programming and Formal Systems*, Studies in Logic and the Foundations of Mathematics, pages 118–161. North-Holland, Amsterdam, 2nd (1967) edition, 1963.
5. John Doner. Tree acceptors and some of their applications. *Journal of Computer and System Sciences*, 4:406–451, 1970.
6. Calvin C. Elgot. Decision problems of finite automata design and related arithmetics. *Transactions of the American Mathematical Society*, 98:21–51, 1961.
7. Kit Fine. A new characterization of context-free languages. Manuscript, Sept. 1991.
8. Ferenc Gécseg and Magnus Steinby. *Tree Automata.* Akadémiai Kiadó, Budapest, 1984.
9. Saul Gorn. Explicit definitions and linguistic dominoes. In John F. Hart and Satoru Takasu, editors, *Systems and Computer Science, Proceedings of the Conference held at Univ. of Western Ontario, 1965.* Univ. of Toronto Press, 1967.
10. Marcus Kracht. Syntactic codes and grammar refinement. *Journal of Logic, Language, and Information*, 4:41–60, 1995.
11. Robert McNaughton and Seymour Papert. *Counter-Free Automata.* Number 65 in Research Monograph. MIT Press, Cambridge, MA, 1971.
12. J. Mezei and J. B. Wright. Algebraic automata and context-free sets. *Information and Control*, 11:3–29, 1967.
13. Michael O. Rabin. Decidability of second-order theories and automata on infinite trees. *Transactions of the American Mathematical Society*, 141:1–35, July 1969.
14. J. W. Thatcher. Characterizing derivation trees of context-free grammars through a generalization of finite automata theory. *Journal of Computer and System Sciences*, 1:317–322, 1967.

Pomset Logic and Variants in Natural Languages

Irene Schena

Dipartimento di Scienze dell'Informazione
Via di Mura Anteo Zamboni 7, 40127 Bologna, Italy
schena@cs.unibo.it

Abstract. We propose a uniform solution based on Pomset Logic to several different syntactic phenomena in Natural Languages, and in particular topicalization, relative clauses, interrogative clauses, extraposition, discontinuous constituents and cliticization. We show that Pomset Logic is expressive enough to describe all the linguistic transformations due to these phenomena, in the sense that all transformations can be expressed by provable statements of the logic, on suitable types. Obviously, the specific transformations of each language are part of its grammatical specification.

1 Variants in Natural Languages

A Natural Language is a finite or infinite set of sentences belonging to a spoken language, everyone of finite length, generated by concatenation from a finite set of words.

The Natural Languages flexibility, in particular of spoken languages, reveals itself especially through the different *variants* of a certain sentence.
These variants consist of movements of simple elements in a sentence comprising, with some abuse of terminology, discontinuous constituents.

In particular, among the linguistics phenomena, which characterize sentence variants, there are: topicalization (ex. (1)), direct interrogative principal (ex. (2)), direct interrogative subordinate (ex. (3)), indirect interrogative (ex. (4)), direct relative (ex. (5)) and indirect relative (ex. (6)), discontinuous constituents (ex. (7)), negation (ex. (8)) and cliticization (ex. (9)).

(1) a. "Piero ama Maria"
 b. "*Maria*, Piero ama"
(2) b. "Mario fa che cosa"
 b. "*Che cosa* fa *Mario*"
(3) a. "La radio dice che Mario fa che cosa"
 b. "*Che cosa* dice la radio che fa *Mario*?"
(4) a. "So Mario fa che cosa"
 b. "So *che cosa* fa *Mario*"
(5) a. "Il vaso Mario ha comprato che, è caduto"
 b. "Il vaso *che* Mario ha comprato , è caduto"

(6) a. "Il vaso Franco dice che Mario ha comprato che, è caduto"
b. "Il vaso *che* Franco dice che Mario ha comprato, è caduto"
(7) a. "Mario eats up the cabbage"
b. "Mario *eats* the cabbage *up*"
(8) a. "Marie regarde Pierre"
b. "Marie *ne* regarde *pas* Pierre"
(9) a. "Io vedo Mario"
b. "Io *lo* vedo"

In our paper, we shall analyse these phenomena of Natural Languages in the framework of Pomset Logic. Pomset Logic, that is a variation of Linear Logic [4], has been recently proposed by Lecomte and Retoré [8] as a new linguistic tool. We shall describe how to modify their approach in order to address the problem of variants.

2 Pomset Logic

This paragraph is a short introduction to Pomset Logic, largely borrowed from Lecomte and Retoré's presentation [8].
Pomset Logic is a particular logical calculus inspired by Linear Logic.

Definition 1. The *language* $\mathcal{L}_p$ of Pomset Logic consists of the following set of formulas:

$$\mathcal{L}_p = \mathcal{N} \mid \mathcal{L}_p \parr \mathcal{L}_p \mid \mathcal{L}_p \otimes \mathcal{L}_p \mid \mathcal{L}_p < \mathcal{L}_p$$

where:

- $\mathcal{A}$ is a set of atomic symbols;
- $()^{\perp}$ is the unary symbol of negation;
- $\otimes$ or *times* is the binary symbol of multiplicative conjunction;
- $\parr$ or *par* is the binary symbol of multiplicative disjunction;
- $<$ is the binary symbol of the multiplicative connective *before*;
- $\mathcal{N} = \mathcal{A} \cup \mathcal{A}^{\perp}$ is the set of atomic symbols and their duals;

Remark. The extension of *De Morgan laws* to the language $\mathcal{L}_p$ is the following: $((A^{\perp})^{\perp}) \equiv A$, $(A \parr B)^{\perp} \equiv B^{\perp} \otimes A^{\perp}$, $(A \otimes B)^{\perp} \equiv B^{\perp} \parr A^{\perp}$, $(A < B)^{\perp} \equiv A^{\perp} < B^{\perp}$.

Roughly, a *cut* is a proof conclusion of the form $A \otimes A^{\perp}$.
A conclusion of a proof is a partial ordered multi-set of formulas and cuts of the form[1]: $A_1, \ldots, A_n, \bullet_1, \ldots, \bullet_p[i]$
The main novelty of Pomset Logic with respect to Linear Logic is the connective *before*. The most important properties of this connective are the following [8, 12]:

[1] Where cuts are represented by the symbol "•".

Proposition 2.

- $<$ *is associative and non-commutative*
- *let* $A \multimap B \equiv A^{\perp} \mathbin{⅋} B$ *(linear implication); then:*
  $A \otimes B \multimap A < B$ *and* $A < B \multimap A \mathbin{⅋} B$
- $<$ *is* self-dual

Intuitively, the before connective corresponds to *sequential composition*, in the sense that it can be considered as a temporal precedence relation on formulas.

Proofs in this logic can be conveniently represented by means of graphs, called proof nets. Proof nets are a special kind of BR-graphs, defined below.

Definition 3. A *BR-graph* is an edge coloured graph: there are *B-edges* which are blue (bold, B) and *R-edges* which are red (regular, R).
The B-edges are undirect, they correspond to logic formulas and define a perfect matching of the graph.
The R-edges may be also direct (R-arcs) and they correspond to connections between formulas.

NAME	GRAPH	CONCLUSIONS	PREMISES
Axiom	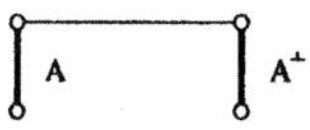	A and A⊥	none
Times	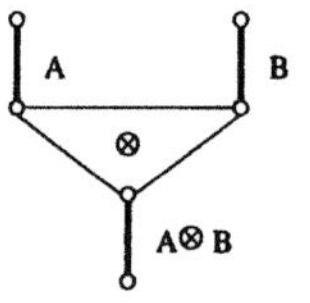	A⊗ B	A and B
Before	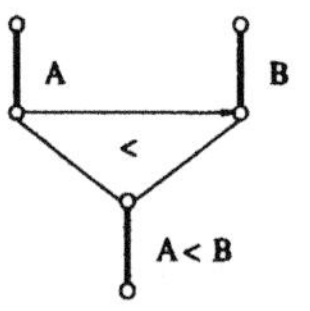	A< B	A and B
Par	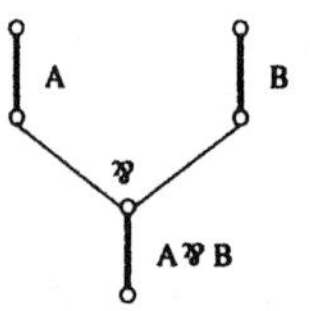	A⅋ B	A and B

Fig. 1. Links in a proof structure.

A *link* is one of the BR-graphs represented in figure 1.
Note that the par link has no connection between its two premises; the before

link has an unidirectional connection, while the times link has a bidirectional connection.

Definition 4. A *proof structure* is a BR-graph where:

- any B-edge is the conclusion of exactly one link and the premise of at most one link; the B-edges which are not premises of any link are the final conclusions of the proof structure;
- a set of R-arcs between the final conclusions defines a strict partial order;
- a subset of conclusions are cuts, marked with a "•".

Definition 5. An *Æ-circuit*[2] is a circuit in which the edges are alternatively B and R without passing through the same edge two times.

Definition 6. An *proof net* is a proof structure without Æ-circuits.

Cut elimination is a local graph rewriting, turning a proof net into a proof net [13]. We shall use cut elimination in section 6, but, for lack of space!, we cannot recall its definition in this paper.

Theorem 7. *The calculus of proof nets enjoys strong normalisation and confluence: every proof net with cuts can be reduced to a cut free proof net [8].*

3 Pomset Logic and Natural Languages

The order induced by "<" is temporal rather than spatial [13]. Having a spatial order, which is the word order in a sentence, the main idea of Lecomte and Retoré's model [8], is that incomplete proof nets, called modules, are associated with the categories corresponding to each word or expression. In order to build up sentences and phrases, we add together modules to other modules by the plugging operation. The proof net induces a partial order on its axioms, that is the expected spatial order on words.

Definition 8. Let α be an axiom link of a proof net. We write $\{\alpha^1, \alpha^2\}$ for its two B-edges or formulas; so $(\alpha^1)^\perp = \alpha^2$.
Let $i, j, k, l, \ldots$ be indices belonging to the set $\{1, 2\}$ (see figure 2). Given two axiom links α and β of an ordered proof net, we say that $\alpha \lhd \beta$ iff there exist $i, j \in \{1, 2\}$ and an R-arc from a formula $F(\alpha^i)$ to a formula $G(\beta^j)$ in the proof net, and this R-arc either belongs to a before link or to the order on conclusions and cuts.
We write $\overset{*}{\lhd}$ for the transitive closure of $\lhd$.

Proposition 9. *The relation* $\overset{*}{\lhd}$ *is a partial order on the axioms of a proof net.*

---

[2] *Æ = alternate elementary.*

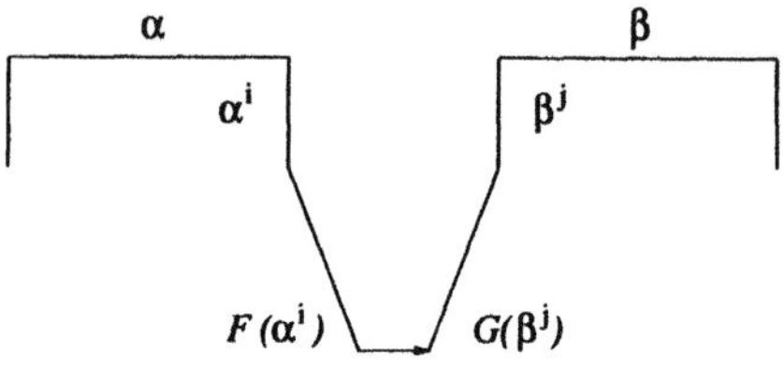

Fig. 2. Axiom links α e β such that $\alpha \lhd \beta$.

4 The Linguistic Model

Our aim is to define a linguistic model, based on Pomset Logic, which can be uniformly applied to most cases of discontinuities and movements in Natural Languages[3] and in particular a model which expresses correctly the word order in a sentence.
In the case of complex sentences, we must inherit the word order of the subordinate inside the principal sentence. To this aim, we introduce a classification of axioms and we extend the partial order relation between axioms.

Following the idea of Chomskian transformation and using the cut operation between proof nets, we propose a method for obtaining sentences with moved elements from sentences lacking the same. So, our model is rather different from the other syntactic theories of Categorial Grammars, like Lambek Calculus [6], which generate directly all the possible constituents orders.

Definition 10. A *module* is a proof net in which some formulas or B-edges are the conclusions of no link. These formulas are called the hypothesis of the module.

Definition 11. The *plugging* of two modules M_1 and M_2 is a module obtained by identifying pairs of B-edges (b_1, b_2), corresponding to the same type and with $b_1 \in M_1$ and $b_2 \in M_2$, which satisfy one of the two conditions:

- b_1 is a conclusion of M_1 and b_2 an hypothesis of M_2
- b_1 is an hypothesis of M_1 and b_2 a conclusion of M_2

Therefore, a module is associated with every word or expression. This module has the type of the word or expression corresponding to its category in the Lambek Calculus. In particular, we can say that words and expressions of the lexicon of a Natural Language, are the *labels* of the axiom links, which are of different type according to the same associated words and expressions.

Definition 12. Axiom links can be of the following type:

1. *premise axiom*: a module which can be:
   - *simple axiom* α: of the form represented in figure 3; where:

[3] Topicalization, relative clauses, interrogative clauses, extraposition, discontinuous constituents and cliticization [13].

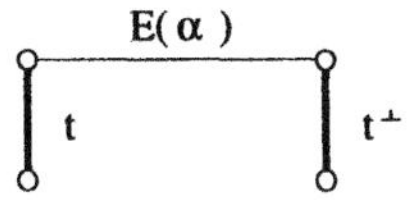

Fig. 3. Simple axiom α.

- $E(\alpha)$ represents the word which labels the axiom link α;
- t represents the type of the word $E(\alpha)$;
- $t^{\perp}$ represents the main formula of the axiom link α.

– *discontinuous axiom* δ: of the form represented in figure 4; where:

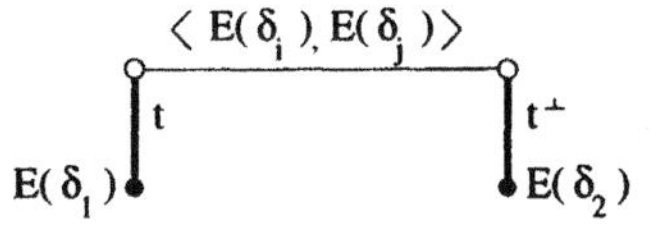

Fig. 4. Discontinuous axiom δ of extremities δ_1 and δ_2, where the pair of indices $(i, j) \in \{(1,2),(2,1)\}$.

- δ_1, δ_2 represent the extremities of the axiom link δ;
- $E(\delta_1)$, $E(\delta_2)$ represent the words which form a discontinuous constituent, and they label respectively δ_1 and δ_2;
- $\langle E(\delta_1), E(\delta_2)\rangle$ or $\langle E(\delta_2), E(\delta_1)\rangle$, represent the label of the axiom link δ;
- $t^{\perp}$ and t represent respectively the types of the words $E(\delta_1)$ and $E(\delta_2)$.

2. *conclusion axiom* γ: an axiom which identifies uniquely the module of which it is a conclusion[4]. The possible types of this axiom are marked in figure 5(a) and 5(b), and in figure 6(a) and 6(b)[5].
   A conclusion axiom is not labeled by any word or expression and its type t can be S (principal sentence), SS (subordinate sentence) or np (noun phrase), according to which result it represents, when the hypothesis of the module containing the conclusion axiom are identified with conclusions of other modules.

Now we define the different types of modules.
Given the definition of module at the beginning of this section, we have the following types of module:

Base module

It can be:

– *simple module*: represented by a premise axiom (see figure 3 and figure 4).

[4] In every module there is only one conclusion axiom.
[5] The conclusion axiom is marked.

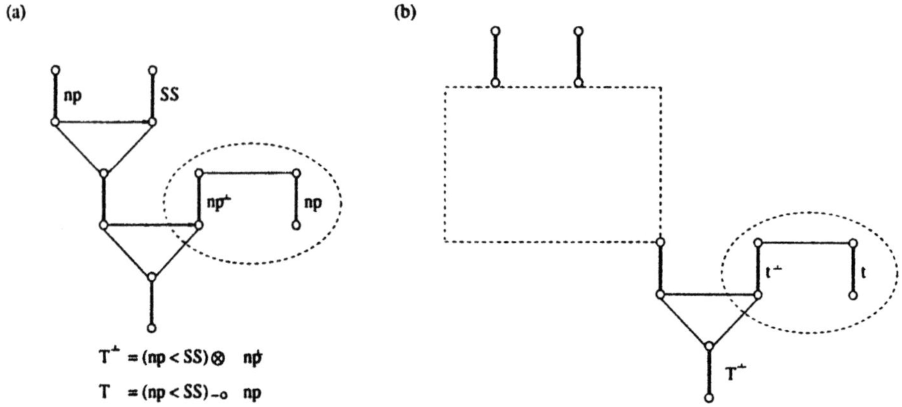

Fig. 5. (a) Example of structured base module. (b) Possible form of structured base module.

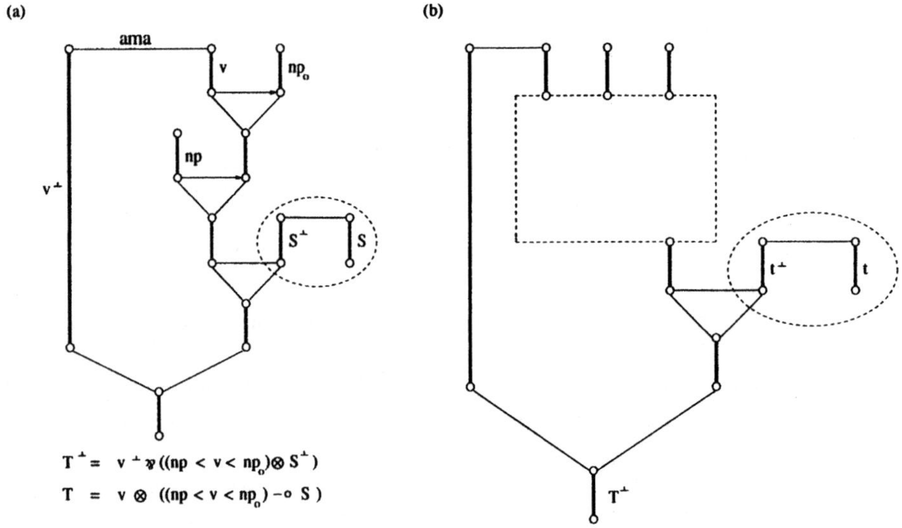

Fig. 6. (a) Example of structured base module associated with the verb *ama*. (b) Possible form of structured base module.

- *structured module*: identified by a conclusion axiom, marked in the figures, and it can be of two forms, respectively represented in figure 5 and 6. In figure 5(a) the conclusion axiom has type np, and in figure 6(a) it has type S. This kind of modules have a conclusion $T^{\perp}$, represented respectively by $(np < SS) \otimes np^{\perp}$ and $v^{\perp} ⅋ ((np < v < np_o) \otimes S^{\perp})$, which is the dual of a structural type T, respectively $(np < SS) \multimap np$ and $v \otimes ((np < v < np_o) \multimap S)$, corresponding to the complex category associated with the considered module (see section 6).
  For instance, in figure 6(a) we have a structured module associated with the

verb *ama*, identified by a conclusion axiom of type S. The types $\boldsymbol{np}$ and $\boldsymbol{np_o}$ are the hypothesis of the module and the conclusion $T^{\perp}$ is the dual of the type associated with the verb *ama*. Intuitively, the type T associated with the verb *ama*, corresponds to a complex category: in fact the central part, $\boldsymbol{np} < \boldsymbol{v} < \boldsymbol{np_o}$, represents the structural description of the functor arguments, while the final part, $-\mathrm{o}S$, represents the functor result. So, this formula tells us that, given a subject $\boldsymbol{np}$, which comes before the considered verb $\boldsymbol{v}$, which comes before a direct object $\boldsymbol{np_o}$, we obtain a sentence $\boldsymbol{S}$.

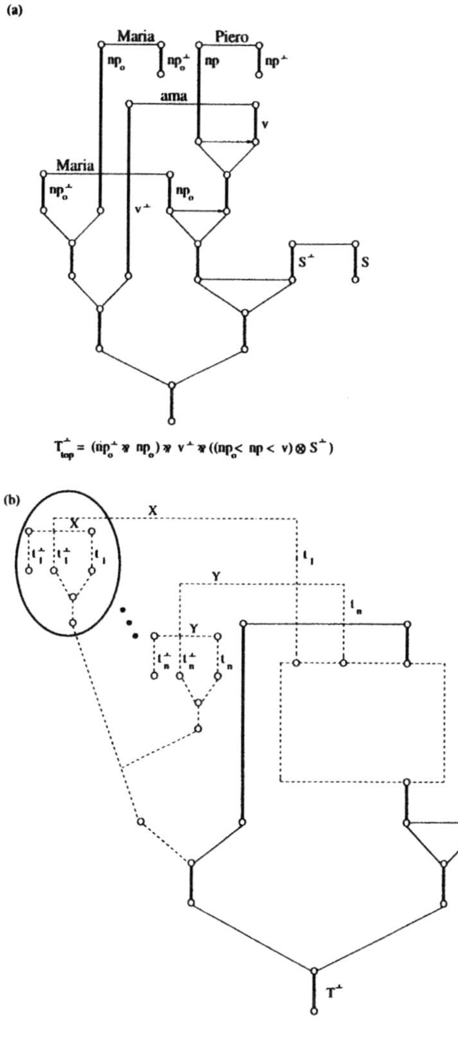

Fig. 7. (a) Example of transformed module: proof net associated with the topicalized sentence *Maria, Piero ama*. (b) Possible form of transformed module.

Transformed module

Here starts the original contribution of our work.
In figure 7 there is the result of a *transformation* on a structured base module. Formulas of the kind $(t_i{}^{\perp}\wp t_i)$ in these figures are called *displacers*, since they allow the movement of t_i in the sentence.
The example of figure 7(a), is the proof net associated with the topicalized sentence *Maria, Piero ama.* Compare it with the net of figure 6(a): in this net the word order is $np < v < np_o$. In order to get the new order $np_o < np < v$, np_o and v are connected to suitable displacers. The correct order of the topicalized sentence is inherited from the associated *transformation*, described below.
The general case is described in figure 7(b).
In particular, a displacer can be involved in a par link with an arbitrary number of other displacers. Each displacer (see the oval region in figure 7(b)) involves two axioms of the same type, which are labeled by a *same* word.

A *transformation* is a map $T_{transf} \multimap T \equiv T_{transf}{}^{\perp}\wp T$, or better a proof with conclusions $T_{transf}{}^{\perp}$ and T. T is the type corresponding to the module or proof net, associated with the sentence or phrase which we want to transform, T_{transf} is the type corresponding to the transformed module associated with the sentence or phrase transformed from the type T.
Performing a transformation consists of making a cut between the conclusion T of the transformation with conclusions $T_{transf}{}^{\perp}$ and T, and the conclusion $T^{\perp}$ of the structured module associated with the sentence or phrase to transform. After cut elimination, we obtain the transformed module.
This is probably quite obscure, but everything should become clear in section 6, where we shall make several examples to show how transformations are used in order to obtain sentences in which there have been movements of constituents (in general sentences different from affirmative declarative sentences).

5 Extending the order relation

Since we defined new axioms, that are discontinuous and conclusion axioms, we must also extend the order relation defined in section 3 on axioms of different modules. In this way the order induces a spatial order between words of the principal and the subordinate sentence, passing through the unique conclusion axiom of the subordinate.
This section is quite technical, and it can be skipped at a first reading of this paper.

Definition 13. Given the axiom links α and β of an ordered proof net, we say that $\alpha \lhd' \beta$ iff one of the following statements is true:

(1) $\alpha \lhd \beta$, where:
   - α and β are a simple axiom of the module M or a conclusion axiom of another module M' and internal to the considered module M because of a plugging;

(2) $\delta \lhd \beta$, where:

- α is an extremity of the discontinuous axiom δ of the module M, such that δ is never passed through by the Æ-path, containing a before link, from α to β;
- β is a simple axiom of the module M or a conclusion axiom of another module M' and internal to the considered module M because of a plugging.

Symmetrically:

$\alpha \lhd \delta$, where:

- α is a simple axiom of the module M or a conclusion axiom of another module M' and internal to the considered module M because of a plugging;
- β is an extremity of the discontinuous axiom δ of the module M, such that δ is never passed through by the Æ-path, containing a before link, from α to β.

(3) $\delta \lhd \delta'$, where:

- α and β are an extremity of the discontinuous axiom δ of the module M, such that δ is never passed through by the Æ-path, containing a before link, from α to β;

(4) $\alpha \lhd \gamma$, where:

- α is a simple axiom of the module M or a conclusion axiom of another module M' and internal to the considered module M because of a plugging;
- γ is the conclusion axiom of the module M' and internal to the module M because of a plugging;
- β is in M' and can be a simple axiom either an extremity of a discontinuous axiom or a conclusion axiom of another module and internal to the considered module M' because of a plugging.

Symmetrically:

$\gamma \lhd \beta$, where:

- γ is the conclusion axiom of the module M' and internal to the module M because of a plugging;
- α is in M' and can be a simple axiom either an extremity of a discontinuous axiom or a conclusion axiom of another module and internal to the considered module M' because of a plugging;
- β is in M and can be a simple axiom or a conclusion axiom of another module and internal to the considered module M because of a plugging.

(5) $\gamma \lhd \gamma'$, where:

- γ is the conclusion axiom of the module M' and internal to the module M because of a plugging;
- γ' is the conclusion axiom of the module M'' and internal to the module M because of a plugging;
- α is in M' and can be a simple axiom either an extremity of a discontinuous axiom or a conclusion axiom of another module and internal to the considered module M' because of a plugging;

- β is in M'' and can be a simple axiom either an extremity of a discontinuous axiom or a conclusion axiom of another module and internal to the considered module M'' because of a plugging.

Proposition 14. *The relation* $\overset{*}{\lhd}'$ *is a partial order on the axioms of a proof net.*

Proof. We can consider only cases (4) and (5) of definition 13, in which one or both axiom links involved by the relation $\lhd'$ are internal to a module different from the considered one. In fact in case (1) we have the relation $\lhd$, which is a partial order (see section 3); in cases (2) and (3), $\lhd'$ is partial order induced on extremities of axioms.
Let:

- α and α' simple axioms[6], be internal to the module M;
- γ be the conclusion axiom of the module M' and internal to the module M because of a plugging;
- γ be the conclusion axiom of the module M'' and internal to the module M because of a plugging;
- β and β' be axioms links of the module M';
- δ and δ' be axioms links of the module M''.

We have the following possible cases:

1. $\alpha \lhd' \beta$ *and* $\beta \lhd' \alpha' \Rightarrow \alpha \lhd \gamma$ *and* $\gamma \lhd \alpha' \Rightarrow \alpha \lhd \alpha' \Rightarrow \alpha \lhd' \alpha'$
2. $\alpha \lhd' \beta$ *and* $\beta \lhd' \alpha \Rightarrow \alpha \lhd \gamma$ *and* $\gamma \lhd \alpha \Rightarrow \alpha \lhd \alpha \Rightarrow$ Absurd!
3. $\alpha \lhd' \beta$ *and* $\beta \lhd' \delta \Rightarrow \alpha \lhd \gamma$ *and* $\gamma \lhd \gamma' \Rightarrow \alpha \lhd \gamma' \Rightarrow \alpha \lhd' \delta$
4. $\alpha \lhd' \beta$ *and* $\beta \lhd' \beta' \Rightarrow \alpha \lhd \gamma \Rightarrow \alpha \lhd' \beta'$
5. $\beta \lhd' \alpha$ *and* $\alpha \lhd' \alpha' \Rightarrow \gamma \lhd \alpha$ *and* $\alpha \lhd \alpha' \Rightarrow \gamma \lhd \alpha' \Rightarrow \beta \lhd' \alpha'$
6. $\beta \lhd' \alpha$ *and* $\alpha \lhd' \beta' \Rightarrow \gamma \lhd \alpha$ *and* $\alpha \lhd \gamma \Rightarrow \gamma \lhd \gamma \Rightarrow$ Absurd!
7. $\beta \lhd' \alpha$ *and* $\alpha \lhd' \delta \Rightarrow \gamma \lhd \alpha$ *and* $\alpha \lhd \gamma' \Rightarrow \gamma \lhd \gamma' \Rightarrow \beta \lhd' \delta$
8. $\beta \lhd' \beta'$ *and* $\beta' \lhd' \alpha \Rightarrow \gamma \lhd \alpha \Rightarrow \beta \lhd' \alpha$
9. $\beta \lhd' \beta'$ *and* $\beta' \lhd' \delta \Rightarrow \gamma \lhd \gamma' \Rightarrow \beta \lhd' \delta$
10. $\beta \lhd' \delta$ *and* $\delta \lhd' \alpha \Rightarrow \gamma \lhd \gamma'$ *and* $\gamma' \lhd \alpha \Rightarrow \gamma \lhd \alpha \Rightarrow \beta \lhd' \alpha$
11. $\beta \lhd' \delta$ *and* $\delta \lhd' \beta' \Rightarrow \gamma \lhd \gamma'$ *and* $\gamma' \lhd \gamma \Rightarrow$ Absurd!
12. $\beta \lhd' \delta$ *and* $\delta \lhd' \delta' \Rightarrow \gamma \lhd \gamma' \Rightarrow \beta \lhd' \delta''$

Now we make some remarks.

Remark. In transformed modules, we have two occurrences of an axiom, labeled in the same way, of the type marked in figure 7(b).
In particular, the two occurrences must be equal, because they correspond to the same word or expression, and this property must be inherited during cut elimination in the transformation process[7]. In this way it will be seen that the same word or expression has changed its position in the sentence.

[6] In the case of discontinuous axiom the proof is analogous.

[7] A more formal approach would probably consists in switching to first order logic, without quantifiers, but with the possibility of unification on a cut formula.

Remark. In transformed modules there are not inconsistency, with respect to the order relation on axioms, like:

$E(\alpha) <_s E(\beta)$ and $E(\beta) <_s E(\alpha)$, where:

- α is the axiom link involved by a displacer;
- β is an axiom link.

In fact, as we see in figure 7(b) only one of the two axiom links will be involved in before links. This means that only one of these axioms can be in order relation with other axioms and this is the axiom that should be considered when recovering the word order in the sentence.
Moreover, by definition of transformed module, all displacers are not involved in any before link, but only by other par links (see figure 7(b)). Therefore, in transformed modules there are no Æ-circuits, because only par links, the displacers, are added with respect to base modules.

Remark. The specific transformations (but not the transformed modules) of each language must be fixed a priori, as part of its grammatical specification, in the same way as modules are associated with words or expressions in the lexicon [13].

6 Examples

In this section we shall make a couple of examples of transformations on sentence structure: topicalization, phrase *wh-* movement and discontinuous constituent.

Fig. 8. Two simple axioms associated with the words *Piero* and *Maria*.

In figure 8 we have two simple modules, coinciding with two simple axioms, associated with the words *Piero* and *Maria*, of noun category $\boldsymbol{np}$.
Remember that in figure 6(a) we have a structured module associated with the verb *ama*, identified by a conclusion axiom of type $\boldsymbol{S}$.
Now we identify $\boldsymbol{np}$ of the module in figure 8 with $\boldsymbol{np}$ of the module in figure 6(a), and moreover $\boldsymbol{np_o}$ of the module in figure 8 and $\boldsymbol{np_o}$ of the module in figure 6(a). We have done the plugging operation twice. Because of these pluggings, we obtain the proof net associated with the declarative active affirmative sentence (see figure 9):

1. Piero ama Maria[8]

[8] Piero loves Maria.

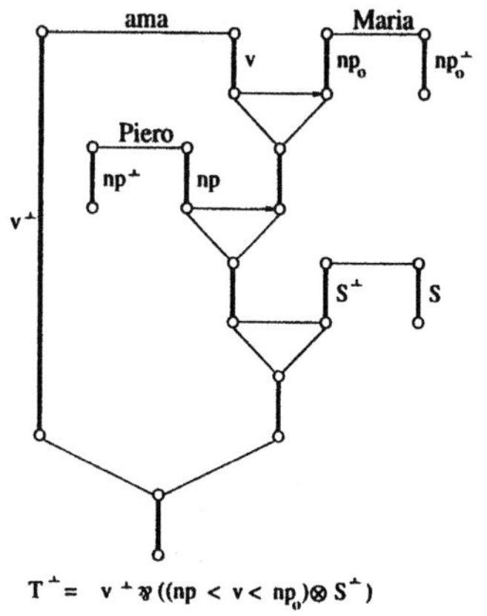

Fig. 9. Proof net associated with the sentence *Piero ama Maria.*

The type S of this sentence is the type of the conclusion axiom. Sentence 1. is correct, because this module is a proof net.
Moreover, it induces a spatial order on the words of the considered sentence, that is ***Piero*** $<_s$ ***ama*** and ***ama*** $<_s$ ***Maria***.

Now we consider the topicalization phenomena, which consists in this case of the movement of np_o to the initial position, obtaining the topicalized sentence:

2. *Maria* Piero ama[9]

In a proof net associated with a sentence, we can note that the verb plays a central role in the description of the sentence structure, so we shall *work* on the verb type, and in particular on the corresponding main formula.
In fact, we want a different spatial order of sentence 1., namely the order in the topicalized sentence 2. So we shall restructure sentence 1, working on its verb.

If the type of the verb *ama* is T, its main formula is:

$$T^\perp = v^\perp ⅋ ((np < v < np_o) \otimes S^\perp)$$

where np_o represents the noun phrase which shall be topicalized.
Let the (de)topicalization process be represented by the function:

$(*) T_{top} \multimap T \;\equiv\; {T_{top}}^\perp ⅋ T$
where:

- ${T_{top}}^\perp = (({np_o}^\perp ⅋ np_o) ⅋ v^\perp) ⅋ ((np_o < np < v) \otimes S^\perp)$
  is the type dual of the verb *ama* in sentence 2. At the beginning of the formula there is the displacer, $({np_o}^\perp ⅋ np_o)$, involving the axioms which will be labeled with the topicalized constituent *Maria*[10].

---

[9] *Mary* Piero loves.

[10] Initially the label, as we can see, is a variable X.

- $T = v \otimes ((np^{\perp} < v^{\perp} < np_o{}^{\perp}) \bindnasrepma S)$

is the type of the verb *ama* in sentence 1.

The correct transformation is described by the proof net in figure 10[11].

$$T_{top}^{\perp} = (np_o^{\perp} \bindnasrepma np_o) \bindnasrepma v^{\perp} \bindnasrepma ((np_o < np < v) \otimes S^{\perp}) \qquad T = v \otimes ((np^{\perp} < v^{\perp} < np_o^{\perp}) \bindnasrepma S)$$

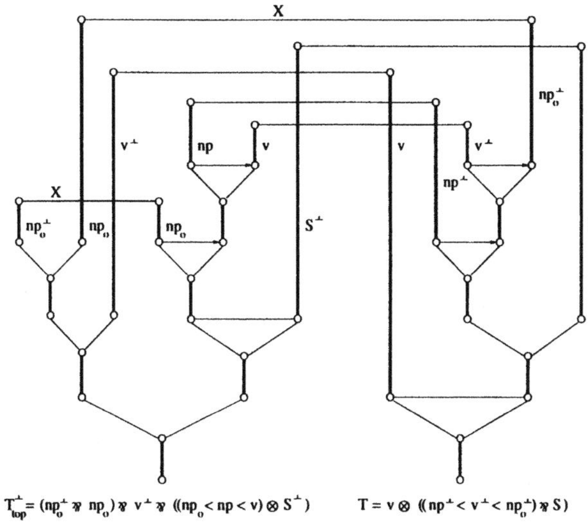

Fig. 10. Proof net with conclusions $T_{top}{}^{\perp}$ and T.

In this proof net, while in the net part corresponding to T, the direct object which we have to move, np_o, follows the verb v (like in sentence 1.), in the net part corresponding to $T_{top}{}^{\perp}$, the same np_o comes before the subject np (as in the topicalized sentence 2.) The displacer at the beginning of the proof net, allows the reposition of the phrase np_o.

Finally, in order to obtain the proof net associated to sentence 2., we make a cut between the conclusion T of the proof net with conclusions $T_{top}{}^{\perp}$ and T, and the conclusion $T^{\perp}$ of the proof net associated with sentence 1.

After cut elimination, we obtain the proof net associated with the topicalized sentence 2., represented in figure 7(a), where the verb *ama* has the type:

$$T_{top} = ((np_o{}^{\perp} \otimes np_o) \otimes v) \otimes ((np_o < np < v) \multimap S)$$

which describes exactly the topicalized sentence structure.

We can note that the variables X which labeled the two axioms of the displacer, after cut elimination are istantiated to the topicalized noun phrase *Maria*. The word spatial order in the proof net associated with sentence 2. is just the order we want, *Maria* $<_s$ *Piero* and *Piero* $<_s$ *ama*.

---

[11] It is trivial to check the absence of Æ-circuits. We used Asperti criterion [1] to prove that the proof structure in figure 10 is a proof net: we verified that this proof structure is deadlock free.

In the second example, we consider a direct interrogative subordinate sentence, in all its possible forms[12]:

3. *Che cosa* dice la radio che fa *Mario*?
4. *Che cosa* la radio dice che fa *Mario*?
5. *Che cosa* dice la radio che *Mario* fa?
6. *Che cosa* la radio dice che *Mario* fa?

It is an example of unlimited dependencies between the phrase *wh-*, *che cosa*, and its position of direct object in the interrogative sentence (see 5.), because the moved element is at a distance not definable a priori.

7. La radio dice che *Mario* fa *che cosa*[13]

The proof net for the corresponding declarative active affirmative sentence 7. is represented in figure 11.

$$T_p^\perp = v^\perp \, \mathcal{P} \, ((np< v< cons <SS) \otimes S^\perp)$$

$$T_x^\perp = v^\perp \, \mathcal{P} \, ((np< v< np_{wh}) \otimes SS^\perp)$$

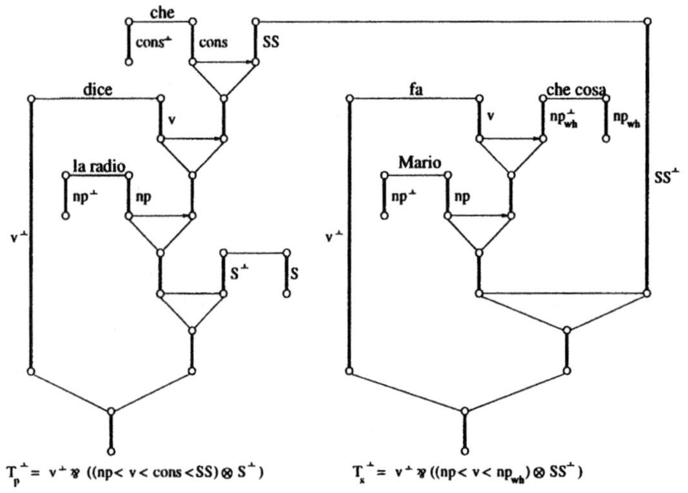

Fig. 11. Proof net associated with the sentence *La radio dice che Mario fa che cosa*.

Since we have to transform both the principal sentence, *la radio dice che*, and the subordinate sentence, *Mario fa che cosa*, the proof structure will have as conclusions:

– the dual type of the verb *dice* of the transformed principal sentence
– the dual type of the verb *fa* of the transformed subordinate sentence
– their types in the corresponding declarative active affirmative sentences.

---

[12] The first is normally used.
[13] The radio says that *Mario* does *what*.

So, we have the proof structure (see figure 12) with the conclusions[14]:

$T_{pint}{}^{\perp}, T_{sint}{}^{\perp}, T_p \otimes T_s$
where:

- $T_{pint}{}^{\perp} = ((np_{wh}{}^{\perp} \parr np_{wh}) \parr (np^{\perp} \parr np) \parr v^{\perp}) \parr ((np_{wh} < (np \otimes v) < cons < SS) \otimes S^{\perp})$
 is the dual type of the verb *dice* in sentence 3. We can note that at the beginning of the formula there are the displacers $(np_{wh}{}^{\perp} \parr np_{wh})$ and $(np^{\perp} \parr np)$ involving respectively the couples of axioms which will be labeled by the transformed phrases *che cosa* and *la radio*[15].
- $T_{sint}{}^{\perp} = ((np^{\perp} \parr np) \parr v^{\perp}) \parr ((np \otimes v) \otimes SS^{\perp})$
 is the dual type of the verb *fa* in sentence 3. We can note that at the beginning of the formula there is the displacer $(np^{\perp} \parr np)$ involving the couple of axioms which will be labeled by the transformed phrase *Mario*[16].
- $T_p = v \otimes ((np^{\perp} < v^{\perp} < cons^{\perp} < SS^{\perp}) \parr S)$
 is the type of the verb *dice* in sentence 7.
- $T_s = v \otimes ((np^{\perp} < v^{\perp} < np_{wh}{}^{\perp}) \parr SS)$
 is the type of the verb *fa* in sentence 7.

It is easy to prove [1] that the proof structure of conclusions $T_{pint}{}^{\perp}$, $T_{sint}{}^{\perp}$ and $T_p \otimes T_s$ is a proof net. Making a cut between the conclusion $T_p \otimes T_s$ of this proof net and the conclusions $T_p{}^{\perp}, T_s{}^{\perp}$ of the proof net associated with sentence 7., and normalising it, we obtain the proof net associated with the direct interrogative sentence, represented in figure 13, with conclusions:

$$T_{pint}{}^{\perp} = ((np_{wh}{}^{\perp} \parr np_{wh}) \parr (np^{\perp} \parr np) \parr v^{\perp}) \parr ((np_{wh} < (np \otimes v) < cons < SS) \otimes S^{\perp})$$

and

$$T_{sint}{}^{\perp} = ((np^{\perp} \parr np) \parr v^{\perp}) \parr ((np \otimes v) \otimes SS^{\perp}).$$

So, the type of the verb *dice* of sentence 3. will be:

$$T_{pint} = ((np_{wh}{}^{\perp} \otimes np_{wh}) \otimes (np^{\perp} \otimes np) \otimes v) \otimes ((np_{wh} < (np \otimes v) < cons < SS) \multimap S)$$

and the type of the verb *fa* of sentence 3. will be:

$$T_{sint} = ((np^{\perp} \otimes np) \otimes v) \otimes ((np \otimes v) \multimap SS)$$

which describe exactly the structure of the direct interrogative sentence and of its principal.

---

[14] Note that the comma on the right side of a sequent is equivalent to the par disjunction.

[15] Initially the labels are X and Y.

[16] Initially the label is Z.

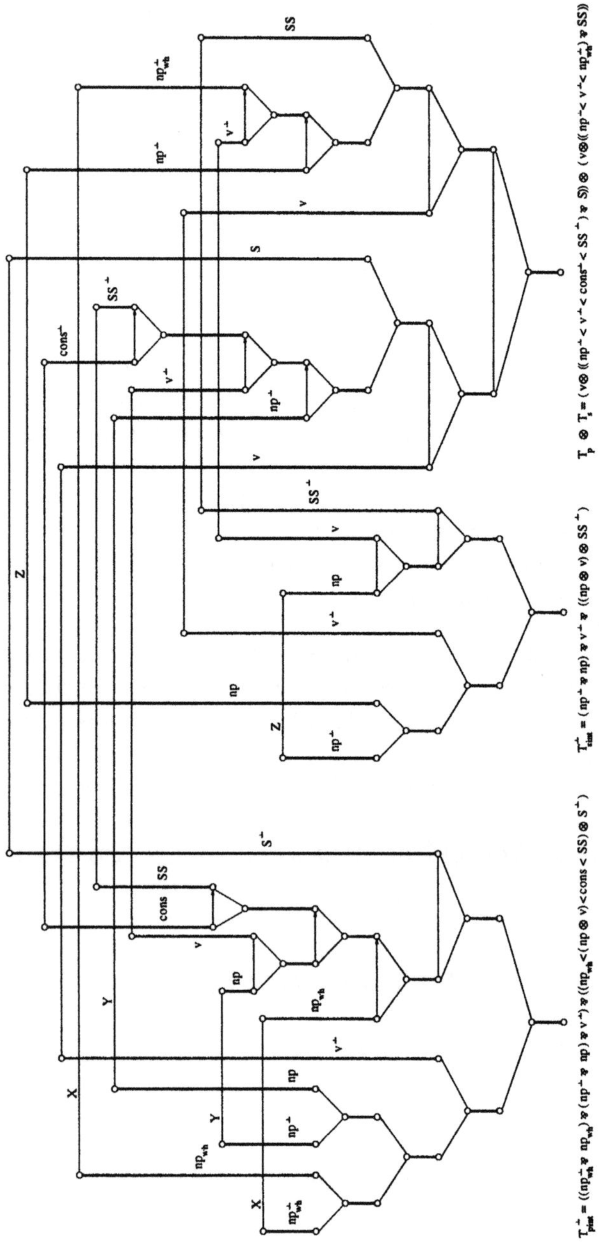

Fig. 12. Proof net with conclusions $T_{pint}{}^{\perp}$, $T_{sint}{}^{\perp}$ and $T_p \otimes T_s$.

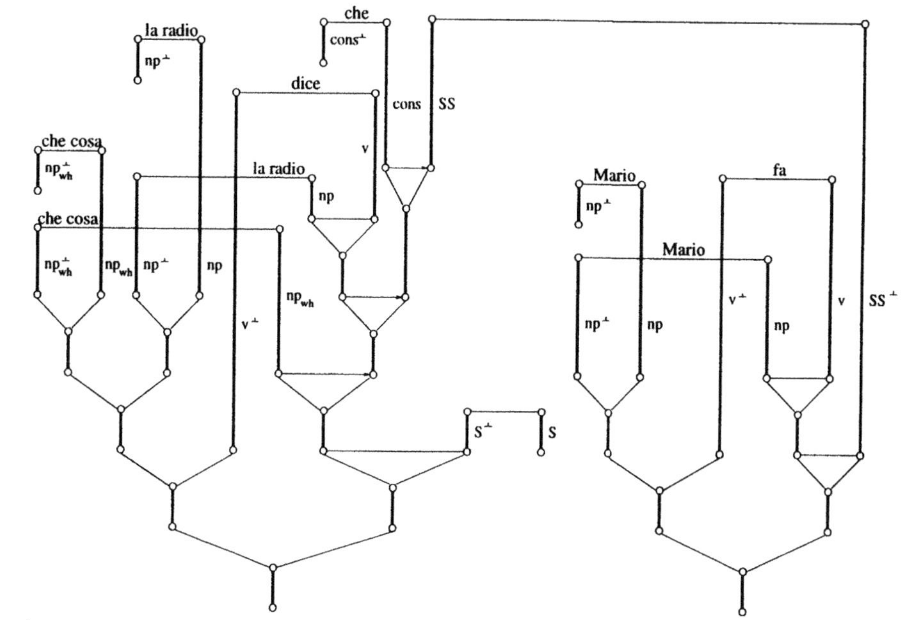

$T^{\perp}_{pint} = ((np^{\perp}_{wh} \wp np_{wh}) \wp (np^{\perp} \wp np) \wp v^{\perp}) \wp ((np_{wh} < (np \otimes v) < cons < SS) \otimes S^{\perp})$ $T^{\perp}_{sint} = (np^{\perp} \wp np) \wp v^{\perp} \wp ((np \otimes v) \otimes SS^{\perp})$

Fig. 13. Proof net associated with the sentence *Che cosa dice la radio che fa Mario?.*

In fact in the proof net associated with sentence 3., the word spatial order is the following: ***che cosa*** $<_s$ ***dice***, ***che cosa*** $<_s$ ***la radio***, ***dice*** $<_s$ ***che***, ***la radio*** $<_s$ ***che***, ***che*** $<_s$ ***fa*** and ***che*** $<_s$ ***Mario***.
Finally we note that there is no relative order between *dice* and *la radio*, and between *fa* and *Mario*. So, the proof net obtained, is the same for sentences 3., 4., 5. and 6., as we wished.

Finally, an example of discontinuous constituent:

8. Mario *eats up* the cabbage
9. Mario *eats* the cabbage *up*

The proof net associated to both sentences is represented in figure 14; in this proof net the word spatial order is ***Mario*** $<_s$ ***eats***, ***eats*** $<_s$ ***up*** and ***eats*** $<_s$ ***the cabbage***. So, there is no relative order between *up* and *the cabbage*: just the order we want.
The verb in this case is represented by a discontinuous axiom labeled $\langle \boldsymbol{eats}, \boldsymbol{up} \rangle$ and with type:

$$(v^{\perp} \otimes v) \otimes ((np < v^{\perp} < (np \otimes v)) \multimap S)$$

$$(v^{\perp} \mathbin{\rotatebox[origin=c]{180}{\&}} v) \mathbin{\rotatebox[origin=c]{180}{\&}} ((np< v^{\perp} < (np \otimes v)) \otimes S^{\perp})$$

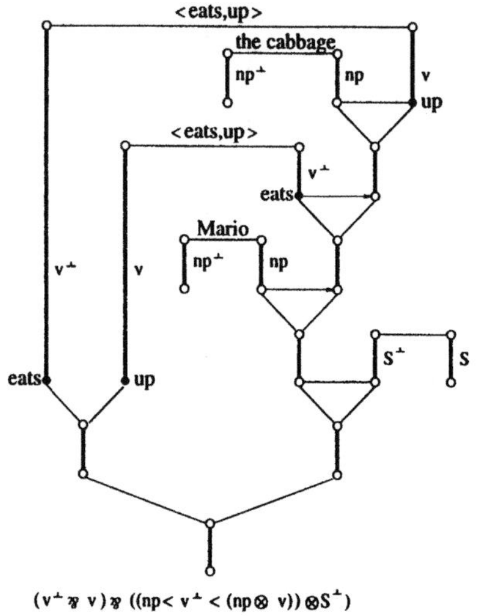

Fig. 14. Proof net associated with the sentence *Mario eats the cabbage up.*

7 Conclusions and Developments

In summary, we have defined a new Linguistic Model, based on Pomset Logic, to describe problems, like movements and discontinuos constituents, which characterize variants. In particular, we have introduced the transformation concept with respect to categorial theories (see [7, 3, 2]). This gives a more generative power to Lecomte and Retoré's model[17] without generating ungrammatical sentences.

The emphasis of the present work was just on the flexibility of Pomset Logic as a convenient tool for expressing different linguistic phenomena. The problem of defining a parsing algorithm and the study of its complexity, was outside of the scope of this work. Obviously, we can trivially generalize Retoré's algorithm: just try all the possible pluggings also considering all the transformed modules. However is completely unfeasible, in practice.
The practical implementation of our Model (and of Lecomte and Retoré's one!) is still an open problem.

Acknowledgements This work is part of my master thesis, carried out under the supervision of Prof. Andrea Asperti. I would like to thank him for all his suggestions.

---

[17] Obviously, as for modules, the set of transformations of a given language is part of its syntax and must be specified a priori.

References

1. A. Asperti. Causal Dependences in Multiplicative Linear Logic with MIX. In *Math. Struct. in Comp. Science*, vol. 5, pages: 351-380, 1995.
2. E. Bach. Categorial Grammars as Theories of Language. In *Categorial Grammars and Natural Language Structure*, R. T. Oehrle, E. Bach and D. Wheeler, vol. 32, pages: 17-34. Reidel Publishing Company, 1988.
3. C. Casadio. *Significato e Categorie*. CLUEB, 1987.
4. J.-Y. Girard Linear Logic. In *Theoretical Computer Science*, vol. 50, pages: 1-102, 1987.
5. G. Graffi. *Le Strutture del Linguaggio: Sintassi*. Il Mulino, 1994.
6. J. Lambek. The Mathematics of Sentence Structure. In *American Math. Monthly*, vol. 65, pages: 154-170. 1958
7. J. Lambek. Categorial and Categorical Grammars. In *Categorial Grammars and Natural Language Structure*, R. T. Oehrle, E. Bach and D. Wheeler, vol. 32, pages: 297-317. Reidel Publishing Company, 1988.
8. A. Lecomte, C. Retoré. Pomset Logic as an Alternative Categorial Grammar. In *Formal Grammar*, G. Morril and R. Oehrle. Foundation of Logic Language and Information, 1995.
9. A. Lecomte, C. Retoré. Words as Modules: a Lexicalised Grammar in the Framework of Linear Logic Proof nets. In *International Conference on Mathematical Linguistics, ICML'96*, edited C. Martin Vide. To be published in 1997 by John Benjamins.
10. C. Retoré. *Réseaux et Séquents Ordonnés*, Thèse de Doctorat, spécialité Mathématiques, Université Paris 7. Février 1993.
11. C. Retoré. *On the Relation between Coherence Semantics and Multiplicative Proof Nets*, Rapport de Recherche 2430, INRIA. December 1994.
12. C. Retoré. Pomset logic: A non-commutative extension of classical linear logic. In *Typed Lambda Calculus and Applications, TLCA'97*, R. Hindley and Ph. de Groote, vol. 1210, pages: 300-318, series LNCS. 1997
13. I. Schena. *Studio di un Calcolo Logico per la formalizzazione di Grammatiche Categoriali e sua applicazione al problema della Discontinuità nei Linguaggi Naturali*, Master Thesis, Corso in Scienze dell'Informazione, Università degli Studi di Bologna. July 1996.

Constraint Logic Programming for Computational Linguistics

Frieder Stolzenburg, stolzen@informatik.uni-koblenz.de[1]
Stephan Höhne, stephan@informatik.uni-frankfurt.de[2]
Ulrich Koch, koch@informatik.uni-koblenz.de[1]
Martin Volk, volk@ifi.unizh.ch[3]

[1] Universität Koblenz, Rheinau 1, D–56075 Koblenz, Germany
[2] Universität Frankfurt, Robert–Mayer–Str. 11–15, D–60325 Frankfurt, Germany
[3] Universität Zürich, Winterthurerstr. 190, CH–8057 Zürich, Switzerland

Abstract. In computational linguistics, we are often interested in developing grammar formalisms declaratively. However, tractability often becomes a problem then. Therefore, we want to argue for the use of constraint logic programming (CLP), and it is yet interesting to note that most logic based natural language systems have not attempted to employ CLP. Our framework and the prototype system UBS combines logic programming with constraint domains (e.g. typed feature structures and finite sets) and constraint techniques (e.g. coroutining).

[L'informatique linguistique souhaite souvent developper des formalismes grammaticaux de manière déclarative. Néanmoins cela conduit souvent a des problèmes d'efficacité. Nous voulons donc plaider pour l'utilisation de la programmation logique avec contraintes (CLP), et il est intéressant de remarquer qu'à ce jour les systèmes logiques de traitement des langues naturelles n'ont pas encore essayé d'utiliser la programmation logique avec contraintes. Notre méthode et le prototype UBS intègre à la programmation logique des domaines de contraintes (tels des structure de traits et des ensembles finis), et des techniques de contraintes (tel le coroutinage).]

1 Introduction

In computational linguistics, we are interested in developing grammar formalisms that are declarative and expressive enough to describe the linguistic information we need to represent. At the same time, grammar formalisms should be tractable by a computer program so that efficient natural language processing is possible. As far as the first aspect (declarativity) is concerned, logical formalisms or logic programming languages are a good means (see e.g. [14,15]). Nowadays they play an important role in computational linguistics. But the second aspect (tractability) is often a problem of computational linguistics systems.

Therefore, we want to argue for the use of logic programming plus constraints since it has been shown that the addition of constraint techniques leads to improved tractability in cases where constraints can be propagated through the search space. Such cases are frequent when working with grammar formalisms. We will show that one can easily build data structures such as feature structures and sets into declarative natural language processing systems. These data structures are widely used in constraint-based grammar formalisms, e.g. Lexical Functional Grammar (LFG) [16] and Head-Driven Phrase Structure Grammar HPSG [25,26]. Our framework combines positive disjunctive logic programming with constraint domains (i.e. typed feature structures and finite sets) and constraint techniques (e.g. coroutining and other techniques going beyond that).

1.1 Typed Feature Structures as a Basis

Many approaches in computational linguistics are based on feature structures and unification, where the unification operation is mostly explained in procedural terms. [5] gives a concise formalisation in this way. But there are phenomena that can hardly be expressed in such a pure unification framework. For example, unbounded dependency constructions can be more elegantly described with sets.

Numerous specialised and efficient algorithms for all aspects of such a grammar formalism have been proposed, e.g. for the treatment of disjunctive information. But the question remains: can all these procedures be safely combined in one system? In order to investigate this problem, it is a good idea to have a single declarative framework. One natural candidate is first-order predicate logic. However, in the subsequent discussion we will see that then efficiency may be lost.

1.2 A Formula-Based Approach

An excellent declarative approach to feature structures and some extensions is described in [14,15]. It uses Schönfinkel-Bernays' (SB) formulae to express feature structure constraints, sets, tree structures, etc. This class consists of closed formulae of the form

$$\exists x_1 \cdots \exists x_m \forall y_1 \cdots \forall y_n \alpha$$

where α contains neither quantifier nor function symbols. Since the satisfiability problem is decidable for this class—nevertheless, the problem is NP-complete provided that the number of universal quantifiers is fixed—, it appears to be a good choice as a grammar formalism. However, it is not enough to set up some constraints and then to hope that a general problem solver will take care of the rest. Instead, one needs dedicated constraint solving techniques, as will be shown below.

It seems that SB formulae are expressive enough for most linguistic purposes when the formulae are used as annotations on phrase structure rules. But simply reducing linguistic constraints to the SB class is not always helpful as a means for implementing grammars. [15] proposes a (minimal) model generation procedure for testing the satisfiability of a formula which, by the way, is very similar to the procedure in [21]. But it does not take into account any structural information that is present in the (linguistic) constraints. For example, unification in sort hierarchies can be done by table look-ups if the sort information is explicitly available. For each pair of sorts the table must then contain their unification, i.e. a sort plus the most general feature structure induced by this sort.

Furthermore, [15] needs disjunctive non-Horn rules to represent natural language grammar fragments. Thus, he goes beyond CLP [13], where only Horn clause logic is used. Logic programming can be extended such that both disjunctive rules and constraint solving techniques can be used simultaneously. A framework for this has been established in [4]. This can be seen as the theoretical basis of our implementation.

1.3 Constraint Logic Programming

We claim that we can have both declarativity and tractability if we use the CLP framework [13], possibly with disjunctive rules. Several suggestions on how to exploit CLP for natural language processing have been brought forth. For example, [29] introduces boolean constraints on feature values and finite domain constraints on feature value domains.

In this paper, we will introduce our system for implementing HPSG-style grammars, namely the constraint-based language UBS (UnifikationsBasierte Sprache) [32], which provides typed feature structures with unification, negation, disjunction, sets, and functionally dependent values. Rapid implementation of this system was possible by using the CLP language ECLiPSe Prolog [9].

1.4 Outline of the Paper

In Section 2, we illustrate how all the features just mentioned have been incorporated into our framework, referring to related work. Section 3 yields a more formal specification of our constraint theory which is well-suited for computational linguistics purposes. After that, we give a brief overview on the UBS system and related work in Section 4.

2 The Framework

In the sequel, we will introduce logic programs which are extended by a syntax for linguistically motivated structures. We allow the following items in argument positions of predicates for such programs: feature structures $[\cdot]$, sets $\{\cdot\}$, and arbitrary first-order terms, all of which can be combined by unification $\sqcap$, disjunction $\sqcup$, and negation $\neg$. A program can then be transformed into an equivalent constraint logic program as shown next. Certainly, the idea of transforming linguistic rules into Horn clauses plus constraints is already present in the literature, see e.g. [18,29]. But mostly only unification constraints are considered for feature structures.

A program with the extended syntax consists of finitely many rules of the form $p(\underline{s}) \leftarrow q_1(\underline{t}_1), \ldots, q_n(\underline{t}_n)$. Here the underlined arguments stand for lists of arguments in the extended syntax. They are transformed into

$$p(\underline{s}') \leftarrow c[\underline{s}', \underline{t}'_1, \ldots, \underline{t}'_n], q_1(\underline{t}'_1), \ldots, q_n(\underline{t}'_n)$$

where $c[\underline{s}, \underline{t}'_1, \ldots, \underline{t}'_n]$ denotes a sequence of calls to constraint predicates. Primes denote the transformed arguments. We will give examples of the transformation in Sections 2.3 and 4.1.

We may distinguish between two kinds of transformation steps: On the one hand, some operations can simply be reduced to logical connectives. This holds e.g. for feature structure unification and disjunction, which can be translated into logical conjunction and logical disjunction, respectively. On the other hand, some structures must be treated by dedicated constraint predicates. Examples of the latter are feature structures, sets, and—to a certain extent—negation. Since we argue for the use of CLP for natural language processing in this paper, let us discuss the constraint theories that are interesting in our context.

2.1 Typed Feature Structures

Different approaches for implementing feature structures in the CLP framework have been proposed. [31], for example, introduces untyped feature structures. In fact, the paper makes use of sorts but does not introduce sort hierarchies, and it claims that unification of feature structures can be done in quasi-linear time. But this complexity does not seem to be available for pure logic-based approaches.

For example, [15] represents the fact that a feature structure x has the value y for the feature f by the atom $arc(x, f, y)$. Unification then corresponds to logical conjunction $\wedge$. But in addition, the following axiom is required

$$\forall x, f, y_1, y_2 : arc(x, f, y_1) \wedge arc(x, f, y_2) \rightarrow y_1 = y_2$$

saying that features are functional. It is difficult for a general automated theorem prover to control search in such a way that we get quasi-linear complexity. As the following argument shows, there is also a problem with treating type information adequately.

Typed feature structures are becoming more and more important in computational linguistics theories. Type hierarchies—or better: sort hierarchies—can be expressed via logical implications, namely

$$\forall x : s(x) \rightarrow t(x)$$

iff s is a sub-sort of t. But again, this encoding leads to inefficiency, because usually the search space grows exponentially. But we can achieve quasi-constant time behaviour if we compile the type hierarchy into a unification table (see also [1] and Section 3.5). We can view this as a special constraint mechanism.

Another idea is to encode sort information into first-order terms, as done e.g. in [22,23,30]. Our implementation works similarly: both sort information and feature-value pairs are treated as constraint terms by using the so-called meta-terms of ECLiPSe [9]. These terms allow to define new data structures at Prolog level. Meta-terms behave like normal variables. However, when they are unified with another term, an event is raised and a user-defined handler must provide the result of the unification. Currently our implementation is limited to non-multiple inheritance sort hierarchies.

2.2 Sets

Sets can be used in the treatment of unbounded dependency constructions (such as relative clauses or wh-questions), but also for the treatment of linguistic quantifiers and anaphora resolution. The problem then arises how to unify these sets efficiently. [20] has proposed an attribute logic with set descriptions and respective operations. However, his set unification operation leads to a complex disjunction and hence to combinatorial explosion and inefficiency. This is because of the following constraint "multiplication" rule for sets (according to [20]):

$$\frac{z = [f : \{x_1, \ldots, x_m\}] \wedge z = [f : \{y_1, \ldots, y_n\}]}{\begin{array}{c} z = [f : \{x_1, \ldots, x_m\}] \wedge \\ x_1 = y_1 \sqcup \cdots \sqcup y_n \wedge \cdots \wedge x_m = y_1 \sqcup \cdots \sqcup y_n \wedge \\ y_1 = x_1 \sqcup \cdots \sqcup x_m \wedge \cdots \wedge y_n = x_1 \sqcup \cdots \sqcup x_m \end{array}}$$

We have developed a more efficient algorithm for set unification using CLP techniques [33]. The algorithm is based on delaying the non-deterministic choices as long as possible and other techniques going beyond that (see also Section 3.5). The basis is an efficient algorithm for treating membership-constraints, which are used in the implementation of the algorithm for unifying finite sets. Such a unification algorithm is not only useful for natural language applications but in any logic programming language that uses sets.

2.3 Negation

As in classical logics, a feature structure with negations can be rewritten in negation normal form if there are no variables in the scope of any negation. It then consists of negations of atomic values only. Let us give an example. Consider the following lexicon entry for the word *bark* given in abstract syntax:

$$\begin{array}{l} lexicon\_entry(bark, \\ \quad [agr : \boxed{1} \sqcap \neg_{index}[per : 3rd, num : sng]], \\ \quad [head : agr : \boxed{1}, subcat : \{\}] \\ ). \end{array}$$

This says that the word *bark* is any form but third person singular and that its agreement value is coreferenced with the agreement value of the *head* feature. Note that types (in this example: *index*) are written as subscripts left-adjacent to feature structures.

The negated complex feature structure which is unified with $\boxed{1}$ in our example can be removed. But then the variable $\boxed{1}$ has to be constrained by the condition

$$\boxed{1} \neq {}_{index}[\,] \vee \boxed{1} \neq [per : 3rd] \vee \boxed{1} \neq [num : sng]$$

where $\neq$ denotes disunification constraints. [8] yields the theoretical background for this kind of constraint.

3 A Constraint Theory for Computational Linguistics

Section 2 provided an informal overview on which constraint theories are useful in the context of computational linguistics. Now we are going to state formally how the three components mentioned so far—typed feature structures, finite sets, and negation—can be safely combined in one constraint system. Let us first define the notion of *constraint system* following the lines of [13]. In the sequel, we assume basic knowledge in the fields of logic programming and CLP. For this, the reader may consult [19] and [13], respectively.

Definition 1 (constraint system). A constraint system, often identified by its constraint theory $\mathcal{T}$—see below—consists of four components:

(1) D: a constraint domain, that is a non-empty set,
(2) Δ: an alphabet, containing at least the equality symbol $=$, which must be interpreted as the equality relation on D, and the constants $\perp$ and $\top$ with the meaning "false" and "true", respectively,
(3) $\mathcal{R}$: the set of all Δ-formulae, called constraints in this context, including all atomic Δ-formulae and closed at least under conjunction $\wedge$ and existential quantification $\exists$, and
(4) $\mathcal{T}$: the constraint theory, which can be identified by a Δ-interpretation $\Im$ over the domain D.

We want to elaborate a constraint theory $\mathcal{T}$ now which is well-suited for computational linguistics. As domain D, we consider hereditarily finite sets of typed feature structures. Thus, we start with introducing the concept of feature trees, and then we use them to build hereditarily finite sets.

3.1 Feature Trees and Sort Hierarchies

We model typed feature structures by finite feature trees. For this, we need a set $\mathcal{F}$ of features, and a set $\mathcal{S}$ of sorts. The definition of feature trees is given next. It follows the lines of [31].

Definition 2 (feature trees). A *path* p is a word over the set of all features. We use $\mathcal{F}^*$ to denote the set of all paths. A *tree domain* is a non-empty set $T \subseteq \mathcal{F}^*$ that is prefix-closed, i.e. $pq \in T$ implies $p \in T$. A *feature tree* is a partial function $\tau : \mathcal{F}^* \to \mathcal{S}$ whose domain must be a finite tree domain in this context.

Extending this work—and also the work in [14,15]—, we introduce a strong sort discipline which is similar to the one in [5]. This sort discipline is attractive because it sometimes makes sort inference possible. To this end, we first introduce a sort hierarchy. This is a partial ordering $\sqsubseteq$ on $\mathcal{S}$ that must be a lower semi-lattice at least with a bottom element. In addition, we need the concept of *appropriateness* for features and sorts [5].

Appropriateness conditions are meant to specify the features that are appropriate for each sort, and provide restrictions on their values in a way that respects the inheritance hierarchy. Appropriateness conditions are modelled by a partial function *Approp* mapping sorts and features to sorts. $Approp(s, f)$ specifies the most general sort that the feature f can have for an object of sort s.

Definition 3 (appropriateness). For each path $p = qf$ in the domain of a feature tree τ where $q \in \mathcal{F}^*$ and $f \in \mathcal{F}$, it must hold $\tau(p) \sqsubseteq Approp(\tau(q), f)$. If this condition does not hold for some path $p = qf$, then $\tau(p)$ has to be replaced by the greatest lower bound of $\tau(p)$ and $Approp(\tau(q), f)$. This means, we perform type inference at this point. $Approp : \mathcal{S} \times \mathcal{F} \rightharpoonup \mathcal{S}$ is a partial function satisfying the following conditions:

(1) For each feature $f \in \mathcal{F}$, there is a most general type $Intro(f) \in \mathcal{S}$ such that $Approp(Intro(f), f)$ is defined.
(2) If $Approp(s, f)$ is defined and $s \sqsubseteq s'$ where $s' \in \mathcal{S}$, then $Approp(s', f)$ is also defined, and $Approp(s, f) \sqsubseteq Approp(s', f)$.

Figure 1 shows an abstracted fragment of the sort hierarchy used in HPSG. The most general sort is an unspecified typed feature structure, because in HPSG everything is expressed by means of them, even phrase structure trees. In the left subtree of the hierarchy, the sort ***sign*** is introduced, which can be subdivided into phrases and words. In brackets, features are given together with a description of their domain. They are only mentioned at their $Intro(\cdot)$ point. Features are inherited by all sub-sorts. Value types can be specialised. For example, this is the case with the feature COMP-DTRS in ***head-adjunct-structure***.

3.2 Hereditarily Finite Sets of Typed Feature Structures

Now we build hereditarily finite sets of feature trees. A *hereditarily finite set* is a set of finite depth that is finite, whose members are finite, the members of whose members are finite, etc. We will now apply this schema to feature structures in the following definition.

Definition 4 (hereditarily finite sets). Let D_0 be the set of all feature trees. We define $D_{n+1} = D_n \cup \{\{t_1, \ldots, t_n\} \mid t_1, \ldots, t_n \in D_n\}$ for $n \geq 0$. Then, the set D' of all hereditarily finite sets of feature trees is defined as follows:

$$D' = \bigcup_{n=0}^{\infty} D_n$$

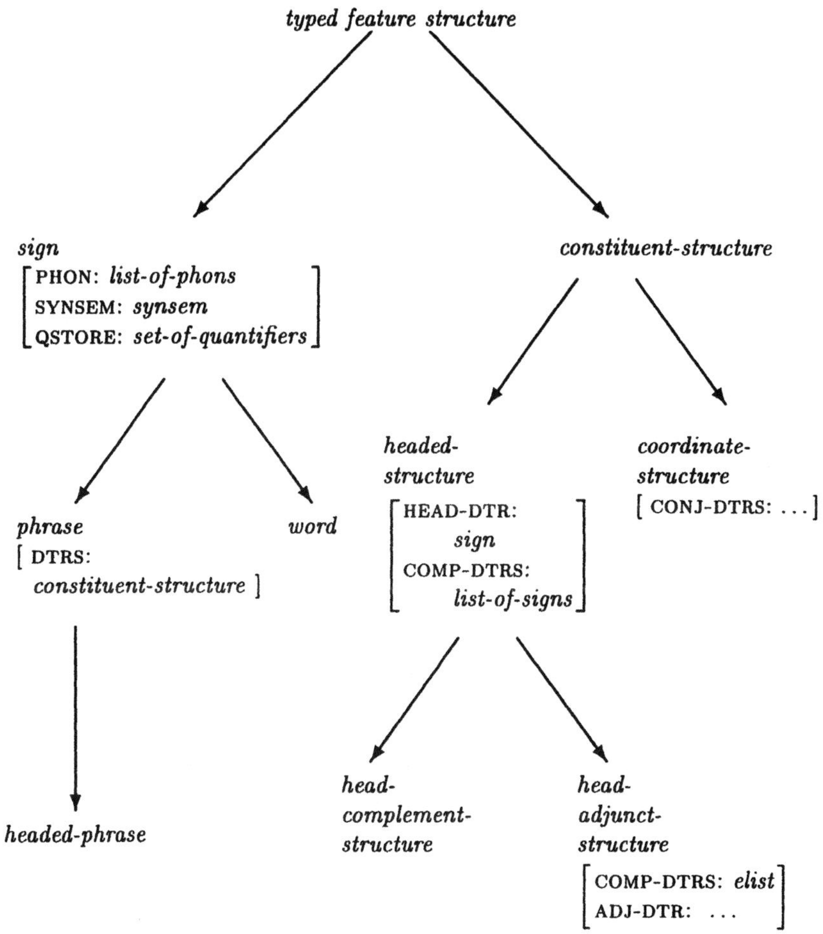

Fig. 1. Fragment of the HPSG sort hierarchy.

Since we will allow disjunction and a restricted form of negation in constraint formulae, we take as domain D in our context the power-set of D'. This means, we consider finitely nested sets of feature structures.

From a more general point of view, [3] investigates the combination of several constraint domains. For this, they introduce the concept of *amalgamated products*. In this context, our constraint domain may be seen as a combination of a domain of feature trees and a domain of nested, hereditarily finite sets. Both domains are "simply combinable structures" in the sense of [3].

3.3 Constraint Formulae and their Interpretation

After the definition of the domain D for our constraint theory, we will now determine the other components of our constraint system for computational linguistics according to Definition 1. We consider the alphabet Δ, which is the union of the following sets:

(1) $P_\Delta = \{=, \neq, \bot, \top\}$ (predicate symbols)
(2) $F_\Delta = \{s[\cdot], (f : \cdot), \sqcap, \sqcup, \neg, \emptyset, \{\cdot|\cdot\}\}$ where $f \in \mathcal{F}$, $s \in \mathcal{S}$ (function symbols)
(3) $V_\Delta = \{x, y, z, \ldots\}$ (countably infinite set of variables)
(4) $X_\Delta = \{\wedge, \vee, \exists\}$ (connectives and predicate symbols)

The set of constraints $\mathcal{R}$ now is a subset of the set of all formulae that can be built from the symbols in Δ. This means, the (possibly non-ground) terms and constraints come from a first-order language. Note that we do not allow all connectives and quantifiers in our language. Especially, we do not have full negation, and we have only existential quantification (with $\exists$). The use of the negation symbol $\neg$ is restricted due to efficiency considerations: there must not be any variables or sets in the scope of any negation symbol.

In [14], a similar restriction is set up, because otherwise the SB formulae class is not sufficient to express constraint-based grammars, and hence complexity is increased. On the one hand, it is observed in this paper that the general axioms for predicates describing set-values do not belong to the SB class. On the other hand, it is conjectured that in linguistic applications these predicates always appear positively. In this case, the axioms can be simplified such that they belong to the SB class.

The interpretation of most of the symbols in Δ is straightforward. For example, $\sqcap$ and $\sqcup$ can be reduced to set intersection and set union, respectively. Furthermore, this can be expressed by logical conjunction and disjunction. The following enumeration specifies how the symbols in Δ have to be interpreted.

Definition 5 (interpretation of symbols). The symbols in our constraint theory are interpreted as shown below. There, t denotes any term, and ϵ the empty path. $\Im$ is the interpretation function for our constraint theory $\mathcal{T}$. Finally, 0 and 1 denote the truth values "false" and "true", respectively.

(1) $s[t]^\Im$ is the set of all feature trees τ', for each feature tree $\tau \in t^\Im$, where $\tau'(\epsilon)$ is the greatest lower bound of s and $\tau(\epsilon)$, and $\tau'(p) = \tau(p)$ for all paths

$p \in \mathcal{F}^*$ with $p \neq \epsilon$. Note that the greatest lower bound of sorts can be precomputed in a table. If t is missing, then we define $s[]^{\Im} = \{\tau\}$, where τ is undefined everywhere except that $\tau(\epsilon) = s$.

(2) $(f : t)^{\Im}$ is the set of all feature trees τ', for each feature tree $\tau \in t^{\Im}$, where $\tau'(\epsilon) = \mathit{Intro}(f)$ and $\tau'(fp) = \tau(p)$ for all p that are in the domain of τ. Note that we do some sort inference at the root ϵ of τ'.

(3) Set symbols are interpreted as follows:
$\emptyset^{\Im} = \{\emptyset\}$ (empty set)
$\{t|t'\}^{\Im} = \{\{\tau\} \cup \tau' \mid \tau \in t^{\Im}, \tau' \in t'^{\Im}\}$ (finite set with tail)

(4) For the logical operators (function symbols), we define:
$(t \sqcap t')^{\Im} = t^{\Im} \cap t'^{\Im}$ (unification)
$(t \sqcup t')^{\Im} = t^{\Im} \cup t'^{\Im}$ (disjunction)
$(\neg t)^{\Im} = D \setminus t^{\Im}$ (negation)

(5) It remains to define the meaning of the predicate symbols:
$\bot^{\Im} = 0$ and $\top^{\Im} = 1$ (truth constants)
$(=^{\Im}) = \{(x, x) \mid x \in D\}$ (equality)
$(\neq^{\Im})$ is defined by: $t_1 \neq t_2$ iff $t_1 = \neg t_2$ or equivalently $\neg t_1 = t_2$ (inequality)
[Remember that the use of the negation symbol $\neg$ is syntactically restricted, as mentioned earlier.]

(6) The connectives and quantifiers in X_Δ are interpreted as expected, namely just classically.

3.4 Conventional Logic Programming versus CLP

The power of CLP stems from its ability of general and flexible constraint solving in a dedicated constraint domain instead of plain syntactic term unification.

Prolog—the most prominent logic programming language—allows to express programs, e.g. for natural language analysis, in a completely declarative manner. However, the plain Prolog language has some disadvantages, because e.g. a naïve implementation of sets and negation may introduce several additional parameters for each predicate in order to handle them correctly. This has been done in an earlier version of UBS [34].

This can be seen as a meta-programming approach. Meta-programs treat other programs as data. They analyse, transform and interpret other programs. The writing of meta-programs is easy in Prolog, but interpretation usually slows down computation. In order to overcome this problem, some CLP languages, e.g. ECLiPSe [9], provide meta-terms. We have implemented typed feature structures and sets partly by meta-terms.

Another problem of plain logic programming is that the ordering of subgoals may cause a lot of backtracking. A partial solution to this problem is the use of a delay mechanism. Roughly, the idea here is that invocation of a predicate is delayed until its arguments are sufficiently instantiated. This concept is related to *coroutining*, which means that the standard left-to-right computation rule of Prolog is modified by delaying (suspending) the execution of a goal [9]. [29] uses the term "active constraints" in this context. We used coroutining for the implementation of negation and linear precedence constraints.

The most general CLP technique is *constraint simplification.* This means, constraints are replaced by equivalent but "simpler" constraints. This concept is applied to finite domain constraints [35]. Furthermore, [10] introduces constraint handling rules (CHRs) which allow user-defined constraint simplification. CHRs define determinate conditional rewrite systems that express how conjunctions of constraints propagate and simplify. General constraint simplification is applied to finite domain constraints and, in our experimental implementation, to sets.

3.5 Constraint Simplification

The main result of this paper is that feature structures [31] with a strong sort discipline according to [5] and sets [24,20] can be safely combined in the CLP framework. By means of a dedicated constraint simplification algorithm—sketched below and stated in [32,33] in greater detail—we can improve processing efficiency in computational linguistics applications. The constraint simplification algorithms implement the intended semantics in a sound and complete manner. In the rest of this section, we discuss some aspects of constraint simplification in our constraint domain D.

Constraint simplification is denoted by $\Rightarrow$ but, for ease of notation, we only state the relevant part of the constraint store and omit the context if possible. We only list the most important constraint simplification rules of our implementation. The first rule detects type clashes: if s and t are terms of different types, i.e. s is a typed feature structure—with main functor $s[\cdot]$ or $(f : \cdot)$—and t is a set—with main functor $\emptyset$ or $\{\cdot|\cdot\}$—or vice versa, then a constraint store containing $s = t$ as a conjunct reduces to $\bot$ ($s = t \Rightarrow \bot$).

For typed feature structures, we apply the rule $x = s_1[t_1] \wedge x = s_2[t_2] \Rightarrow x = s[t]$, where s is the greatest lower bound wrt. $\sqsubseteq$ of s_1 and s_2 and t is obtained from t_1 and t_2 by the following unification procedure: t has the form $f_1 : u_1 \sqcap \cdots \sqcap f_n : u_n$, where the f_k with $1 \leq k \leq n$ are exactly the features such that *Approp*(s, f) is defined. For the value u_k of the feature f_k, it holds $u_k = \mathit{Approp}(s, f)[v_1 \sqcap v_2]$—this is added to the constraint store—, where v_1 and v_2 are the values of the feature f in t_1 and t_2, respectively. The values v_1 and v_2 may be omitted, if they are not defined in the respective feature structure.

In the implementation, a typed feature structure can be realised by a meta-term which is also called an *attributed variable*, i.e. x (from above) is a variable with attribute $s[t]$. The unification can be pre-computed in a table. In our experimental UBS system, we used several tables: `forward` and `backward` for type inference—this is not possible with [31]—and `unific` for the actual unification. Therefore, the HPSG sort hierarchy fragment from Figure 1 is internally presented within UBS by three tables whose contents are stated in Figure 2.

We have two rules for treating unification and disjunction, namely (a) $x = y \sqcap z \Rightarrow x = y \wedge y = z$ and (b) $x = y \sqcup z \Rightarrow x = y \vee x = z$. Rule (a) is not applied within typed feature structures. Disjunction, i.e. rule (b), is simply implemented by backtracking. This means, unification and disjunction can be reduced to logical conjunction and disjunction, respectively.

(1) *Intro*(·) points of attributes:

Sort	*Intro*(·) point
COMP-DTRS	*headed-structure*
DTRS	*phrase*
HEAD-DTR	*headed-structure*
PHON	*sign*
QSTORE	*sign*
SYNSEM	*sign*

(2) minimal feature structure for each sort:

Sort	Structure
constituent-structure	[]
coordinate-structure	[]
head-adjunct-structure	[COMP-DTRS : *empty-list*, HEAD-DTR : *sign*]
head-complement-structure	[COMP-DTRS : *list-of-signs*, HEAD-DTR : *sign*]
headed-phrase	[DTRS : *constituent-structure*, PHON : *list-of-phons*, QSTORE : *set-of-quantifiers*, SYNSEM : *synsem*]
headed-structure	[COMP-DTRS : *list-of-signs*, HEAD-DTR : *sign*]
phrase	[DTRS : *constituent-structure*, PHON : *list-of-phons*, QSTORE : *set-of-quantifiers*, SYNSEM : *synsem*]
sign	[PHON : *list-of-phons*, QSTORE : *set-of-quantifiers*, SYNSEM : *synsem*]
word	[PHON : *list-of-phons*, QSTORE : *set-of-quantifiers*, SYNSEM : *synsem*]

(3) unification table for given sort hierarchy:

Sort 1	Sort 2	Unification
constituent-structure	*coordinate-structure*	*coordinate-structure*
constituent-structure	*head-adjunct-structure*	*head-adjunct-structure*
constituent-structure	*head-complement-structure*	*head-complement-structure*
constituent-structure	*headed-structure*	*headed-structure*
empty-list	*list-of-signs*	*empty-list*
head-adjunct-structure	*headed-structure*	*head-adjunct-structure*
head-complement-structure	*headed-structure*	*head-complement-structure*
headed-phrase	*phrase*	*headed-phrase*
headed-phrase	*sign*	*headed-phrase*
phrase	*sign*	*phrase*
sign	*word*	*word*

Fig. 2. Tables representing the HPSG sort hierarchy.

Complex negations can be reduced to simple cases. For this, we make use of De Morgan's laws and eliminate double negation, i.e. $\neg(t \sqcap t') \Rightarrow \neg t \sqcup \neg t'$, $\neg(t \sqcup t') \Rightarrow \neg t \sqcap \neg t'$, and $\neg\neg t \Rightarrow t$. Since we forbid negation of sets, we only have to consider the case of a negated feature structure: $\neg s[f_1 : t_1 \sqcap \cdots \sqcap f_n : t_n] \Rightarrow x$, where x is a new variable which is constrained by $x \neq s[] \vee x = s[f_1 : \neg t_1] \vee \cdots \vee x = s[f_n : \neg t_n]$.

Note that $\neq$ denotes a non-unifiability constraint, which can be reduced to the disunification constraint of Prolog II [8]. Because of the restricted use of negation in our context, we must only be able to treat inequations of the form $x \neq s[]$. Such constraints are simply delayed until there is another (positive) constraint $x = s'[\cdot]$. Then, $x \neq s[] \Rightarrow \bot$ if $s' \sqsubseteq s$, or $x \neq s[] \Rightarrow \top$ if s and s' are definitely not unifiable, i.e. their greatest lower bound is the bottom element in $\mathcal{S}$. Otherwise, the constraint is delayed again, i.e. we make use of coroutining.

For solving constraints with sets, we use an internal constraint predicate $\in$, i.e. membership-constraints. Let us agree on the following notation: $\{s|t\}$ stands for $\{s\} \cup t$ in the usual notation. Here, t is a set (variable). $\{s_1, s_2|t\}$ is an abbreviation of $\{s_1|\{s_2|t\}\}$, and $\{s\}$ of $\{s|\emptyset\}$. Now, we have the constraint rule $\{x_1, \ldots, x_m\} = \{y_1, \ldots, y_n\} \Rightarrow x_1 \in \{y_1, \ldots, y_n\} \wedge \cdots \wedge x_m \in \{y_1, \ldots, y_n\} \wedge y_1 \in \{x_1, \ldots, x_m\} \wedge \cdots \wedge y_n \in \{x_1, \ldots, x_m\}$. This is simplified further by general constraint simplification techniques:

The most effective idea for simplifying set constraints is the following: a membership-constraint $x \in \{y_1, \ldots, y_n\}$ can be understood as the disjunction $x = y_1 \sqcup \cdots \sqcup y_n$. This is equivalent to $x = y_1 \vee (x \neq y_1 \wedge x = y_2) \vee \cdots \vee (x \neq y_1 \wedge \cdots \wedge x \neq y_{n-1} \wedge x = y_n)$. Thus, we employ disunification constraints $\neq$ once again. In addition, constraint techniques such as delayed execution and the first-fail principle [35], i.e. membership-constraints with the fewest remaining choices are solved first, lead to even more improvements in this context. The advantages of this procedure over other approaches (e.g. the one in [2]) is demonstrated in [33].

4 CLP Systems for Computational Linguistics

In this section, we introduce our system UBS in greater detail. Firstly, we discuss some details of our implementation. Secondly, we give an overview on the whole work done in the UBS project. Finally, we discuss related work.

4.1 Implementation

We have built a prototype system: UBS, a language for the implementation of constraint-based grammars. A UBS program differs from an ordinary Prolog program in that special terms (feature structures, sets, negated or disjunctive terms) are allowed in argument positions. The implemented system includes an interactive output module which prints out UBS terms to the screen in an indented fashion.

It is interactive in that the user can navigate through the term structure with the help of a special purpose command language. Furthermore, it is possible to specify arbitrary paths within feature structures or sorts whose values should be excluded from the output. Coreferent terms are printed only once preceded by a number. Further occurrences are identified by the same number.

The first part of every UBS program is the definition of the sort hierarchy. There the grammar writer has to specify the feature structure sorts. Then UBS rules are written using the operators for unification, disjunction, negation, and implication as introduced in Section 2. Even functional dependencies can be represented: a function call $p(x_1, \ldots, x_n)$ is performed by a call to an $(n+1)$-place predicate p that instantiates its last argument to a value that depends on the first n arguments.

UBS was recently used to write an HPSG-style grammar that covers German relative clauses such as Example 1 [17]. The underlying linguistic theory partly makes use of the results in [28].

Example 1.	*Der*	*Junge,*	*der*	*die*	*Frau*	*sieht,*	*lacht.*
			NOM				
	the	boy	who	the	woman	sees	laughs

"The boy who sees the woman is laughing."

The grammar uses negation of sorts. These negated sorts are interpreted by UBS with the help of CLP. The declaratively stated HPSG principles such as the Head Feature Principle (HFP) were implemented straightforwardly. Also, the lexicon entries look like those in the HPSG literature [25]. However, to increase efficiency, the linear precedence (LP) rules of HPSG are not stated explicitly. Instead, they are implicit in the predicate `order_consts/2`, which is called by the Constituent Order Principle. Furthermore, immediate dominance (ID) rules have been added in order to decrease the number of choices during parsing. However, parsing is still too slow for real-life applications.

Let us recall the idea behind ID/LP rules mentioned in the last paragraph. A context-free grammar—with a set V_T of terminals, a set V_N of non-terminals, a special start symbol S, and production rules like $\alpha \rightarrow \beta_1 \ldots \beta_n$, where $\alpha \in V_N$ and $\beta_i \in V_T \cup V_N$—includes two types of information: (a) giving the immediate constituents of phrase symbols, and (b) defining the order in which the constituents must occur. Therefore, new grammar formalisms divide these components into ID and LP rules. In HPSG, ID schemata are a small set of constraints on the immediate constituency of phrases.

In our implementation, coroutining is used for delaying the LP constraints in order to avoid setting up too many useless tests. The execution of a goal can be delayed by explicitly stating the delay conditions. For this purpose, the programmer writes `delay` clauses, for instance:

```
delay order_consts(PHRASE, PHONS) if var(PHRASE), var(PHONS).
```

The effect of this declaration is that the execution of a goal of the form `order_consts(PHRASE,PHONS)` is delayed if the arguments `PHRASE` and `PHONS` are uninstantiated variables. The goal is "rewoken" as soon as one of these variables is instantiated.

As was mentioned above, `order_consts/2` is called by the Constituent Order Principle. It enforces the LP rules that are relevant to the syntactic phenomena covered by the grammar. The following UBS clause implements the LP rule [HEAD ¬V] $\prec$ [COMPLEMENT]:

```
order_consts(
    $h_comp_ph &
    head_dtr:node:(phon:HEAD_PHON..
                   synsem:loc:cat:head:(@head & ^ @verb))..
    comp_dtrs:(COMPS & ([] # [_])),
    $conc(HEAD_PHON, $extract_phons(COMPS))).
```

This rule states that a non-verbal head must be realised before all of its complements. `$h_comp_ph` is a call to the predicate `h_comp_ph/1`, which enforces some constraints common to all head-complement phrases, i.e. phrases that consist of a head and zero or more complements. `&`, `#` and `^` are the unification, disjunction and negation operators, respectively. `@` is the sort operator: for each sort `t`, `@t` denotes a term of sort `t` that is not further specified. In the above clause, `@verb` has to be negated.

`COMPS` is unified with a list that contains at most one element, to ensure that the head-complement phrase has at most one complement daughter. Finally, `$extract_phons(COMPS)` extracts the phonological values of `COMPS`, yielding a list, and the call to `conc/3` concatenates the phonological value of the head daughter with this list. Remember that n-ary functions are implemented as $(n+1)$-place predicates.

4.2 Linear Precedence Constraints

In another project UBS is being used to implement a grammar with ID rules and LP constraints. In the same project we also investigate how to use CLP to handle word order variation, a problem that often arises in the analysis of German. It has been observed that LP constraints can be realized via negative constraints. Given the LP constraint $A \prec B$ and a phrase containing the constituents X and Y (in this order), we set up the constraint $\langle X, Y\rangle = \neg\langle B, A\rangle$. That means if X unifies with B then Y must not unify with A, or vice versa.

[27] has introduced so-called word order domains (WODs) represented as sets of words. A WOD defines a mapping from syntactic and semantic functor-argument-structure to phonology. This is achieved by the Domain Principle (DP), the feature *dom*, the binary feature *union*, and the operation of domain union. The DP states that the functor (i.e. the head of the phrase) is an element of the current domain and that every argument is either an element of this domain, if *union* $= -$, or that its domain is unioned with the current domain, if *union* $= +$.

Only verbal constituents can have *union* = +. For all non-verbal constituents, *union* = − holds. Domain union is the essential operation here. For example, the following two German phrases permit domain union, because the functors *zu_lesen*, *geraten* and *hat* have the feature *union* = +.

Example 2.	*(weil)*	*jemand*	*ihm*	*geraten*	*hat,*	*es*	*zu_lesen*
	(because)	somebody	him	advised	has	it	to_read

"(because) somebody advised him to read it"

If we do not take any LP constraints into consideration, 6! = 720 permutations are generated. Note that we consider *zu_lesen* as one item. With LP constraints, domain union (intuitively a shuffling operation) results in 10 possible sentence orderings, among them:

Example 3. (weil) jemand es ihm zu_lesen geraten hat
Example 4. (weil) jemand es ihm geraten hat zu_lesen

As UBS allows negation, the LP constraints can be directly implemented. With the Prolog built-in predicates `subset/2` and `findall/3` all tuples of the domain are generated. The LP rules act as active constraints on the domains. They are called directly with the domain principle, exploiting the delay mechanism of CLP languages.

Hence, the constraint technique of coroutining helps us to make the the treatment of WOD constraints more efficient [12]. As soon as enough data is available, the LP rules are evaluated and, if necessary, grammatically incorrect sentences are rejected. Thus, the LP rules work as a constraint on the domain. The implementation follows the constrain-and-generate paradigm.

4.3 Finite Domain Constraints

Finite Domain Constraints (FDCs) [35] can be used if there is a finite set of solutions out of which we can eliminate elements which are no longer valid step by step. FDCs are not used in UBS, but they are potentially useful for computational linguistics. In principle, it is no problem to make use of the FDC solver that is built into ECLiPSe for UBS.

[29] gives three examples for using FDCs in natural language processing. The first involves subcategorisation frames. Such a frame describes the necessary complements of a verb. Most verbs have more than one frame. For example, a verb may have a transitive and an intransitive reading. If we find an accusative object during parsing, we can eliminate the intransitive reading by removing the corresponding subcategorisation frame from the set of possible solutions.

The second example deals with set intersection. It models the problem of whether there is a non-empty set in the intersection of the set of all semantic restrictions of a verb and the set of the semantic properties of its complements. The third example concerns the construction of a complex tree from local trees. For every daughter in a local tree there is a finite set of local trees where each tree has this node as mother node. Therefore the construction of complex trees can be seen as a finite domain constraint. [29] also mentions that FDCs are useful for typed feature structures. Typing enforces that only a specified set of features may be used within a given feature structure.

4.4 Another Constraint-Based Approach

In [6,7], another constraint-based approach for computational linguistics is developed: the DF constraint system. DF terms can express typed feature structures with set-valued features. This approach attempts to express the object-oriented programming paradigm in logic. According to [7], $s : t$ states that s is either an object of type t, or a subtype of t. In addition, $s[u@w_1, \ldots, w_n \rightarrow v]$ states that feature u of object (or class) s has value v, where w_i are the arguments of u, i.e. features may have arguments here.

The object-oriented approach permits the construction of parametrised types. [7] contains the following example involving the *append* method for arbitrary lists:

$$\begin{aligned}&nil[append@L : list \rightarrow L]\\&L' : list[head \rightarrow H; tail \rightarrow T[append@L : list \rightarrow Z];\\&\qquad append@L \rightarrow Y[head \rightarrow H; tail \rightarrow Z]]\end{aligned}$$

$s[u@w_1, \ldots, w_n \twoheadrightarrow v]$ means that u is a set-valued feature, one of whose elements is v. $s[u@w_1, \ldots, w_n \Rightarrow t]$ and $s[u@w_1, \ldots, w_n \Rrightarrow t]$ restrict the type of (one element of) u to be t. Multiple methods (features) can be collapsed into a single structure, as in $s[u@w_1, \ldots, w_n \rightarrow v; x@y_1, \ldots, y_m \Rightarrow z]$. @ is omitted for features that take no arguments. As can be seen from this discussion, sorts (types) are first-class citizens, i.e. they can occur in every position where constant values can occur.

The above mentioned membership tests appear to be the only operations on set-valued features, whereas UBS allows sets as values. See also [11], which compares different notions of sets in unification-based approaches to grammar. However, UBS is not object-oriented. In this respect, the introduction of parametrised types in [7] is very interesting. [7] gives the constraint solving procedure for DF formulae, which relies on several axioms. One of these is the functionality of single-valued features. The others state the properties of admissible sort hierarchies.

[7] does not deal with the question of complexity, other than saying that the satisfiability problem for DF clauses is NP-hard. According to [7], an implementation is intended, but not carried out. Our approach is implemented and allows to use any constraint solver from the CLP field.

5 Conclusion

We have shown that CLP can be used to implement typed feature structures, sets, and negation. Our language UBS uses the constraint handling facilities of ECLiPSe to provide these devices. They help in formulating concise grammatical descriptions for natural language phenomena and make processing more efficient. UBS employs the following constraint techniques: it uses meta-terms for sets, delaying techniques (coroutining) for LP constraints and also for negation. Our system contains a novel algorithm for unifying finite sets which applies general constraint simplification techniques, and a new method of treating LP constraints by negation.

We have also presented a theoretical framework for feature structures with a strong sort discipline as required for HPSG-style grammars. Using CLP techniques for natural language processing definitely offers an advantage over pure logic programming. There, the above described problems have to be treated via meta-programming and thus lose efficiency. It is yet interesting to note that most logic-based natural language systems have not attempted at all to employ CLP.

We have stated that declarativity and tractability of logical formalisms for computational linguistics can be achieved by means of CLP techniques. But it remains an open research question how big an efficiency improvement we get by using CLP for large applications. It is only when this question has been answered that CLP can be employed in large size natural language engineering.

Acknowledgements

We would like to thank Peter Baumgartner, Sven Hartrumpf, some anonymous referees and the participants of the Conference on *Logical Aspects of Computational Linguistics* for comments on this paper and helpful discussion.

References

1. Hassan Aït-Kaci, Robert Boyer, Patrick Lincoln, and Robert Nasr. Efficient implementation of lattice operations. *ACM Transactions on Programming Languages and Systems*, 11(1):115–146, 1989.
2. Puri Arenas-Sánchez and Agostino Dovier. Minimal set unification. In Manuel Hermenegildo and S. Doaitse Swierstra, editors, *Proceedings of the 7th International Symposium on Programming Language Implementation and Logic Programming*, pages 397–414. Springer, Berlin, Heidelberg, New York, 1995. In LNCS 982.
3. Franz Baader and Klaus U. Schulz. On the combination of symbolic constraints, solution domains, and constraint solvers. In Ugo Montanari and Francesca Rossi, editors, *Proceedings of the 1st International Conference on Principles and Practice of Constraint Programming, Cassis, France*, pages 380–397. Springer, Berlin, Heidelberg, New York, 1995. In LNCS 976.
4. Peter Baumgartner and Frieder Stolzenburg. Constraint model elimination and a PTTP-implementation. In Peter Baumgartner, Reiner Hähnle, and Joachim Posegga, editors, *Proceedings of the 4th Workshop on Theorem Proving with Analytic Tableaux and Related Methods*, pages 201–216. Springer, Berlin, Heidelberg, New York, 1995. In LNAI 918.
5. Bob Carpenter. *The Logic of Typed Feature Structures. With Applications to Unification Grammars, Logic Programs and Constraint Resolution.* Cambridge University Press, Cambridge, New York, Melbourne, 1992.

6. Liviu-Virgil Ciortuz. Object-oriented inferences in a logical framework for feature grammars. In Rafael C. Carrasco and Jose Oncina, editors, *Proceedings of the 2nd International Colloquium on Grammatical Inference and Applications*, pages 45–56. Springer, Berlin, Heidelberg, New York, 1994. In LNCS 862.
7. Liviu-Virgil Ciortuz. DF constraint system. Technical Report IT-95-280, Université de Lille I, 1995.
8. Alain Colmerauer. Theoretical model of Prolog II. In Michel van Canegham and David H. D. Warren, editors, *Logic programming and its applications*, pages 3–31. Ablex Publishing Corporation, Norwood, NJ, 1986.
9. ECRC GmbH, München. *ECLiPSe 3.5: User Manual – Extensions User Manual*, 1995.
10. Thom Frühwirth. Constraint handling rules. In Andreas Podelski, editor, *Constraints: Basics and Trends*, pages 90–107. Springer, Berlin, Heidelberg, New York, 1995. In LNCS 910.
11. Peter Gerstl. Mengenkonzepte in Unifikationsgrammatiken. IWBS Report 223, IBM Deutschland, Stuttgart, 1992.
12. Stephan Höhne. Wortstellung bei deutschen Infinitiven: Konzeption eines Parsers auf der Basis typisierter Merkmalstrukturen und HPSG und Implementierung in einer constraint-basierten logischen Programmiersprache. Diplomarbeit, Johann-Wolfgang-Goethe-Universität, Frankfurt, 1996.
13. Joxan Jaffar and Michael J. Maher. Constraint logic programming: a survey. *Journal of Logic Programming*, 19,20:503–581, 1994.
14. Mark Johnson. Features and formulae. *Computational Linguistics*, 17(2):131–151, 1991.
15. Mark Johnson. Computing with features as formulae. *Computational Linguistics*, 20(1):1–25, 1994.
16. Ronald Kaplan and Joan Bresnan. Lexical functional grammar: A formal system for grammatical representation. In Joan Bresnan, editor, *The Mental Representation of Grammatical Relations*, pages 173–281. MIT Press, Cambridge, MA, London, England, 1982.
17. Ulrich Koch. Deutsche Relativsätze in HPSG. Studienarbeit S 437, Universität Koblenz, 1996.
18. Christoph Lehner. *Grammatikentwicklung mit Constraint-Logikprogrammierung.* DISKI 29. infix, Sankt Augustin, 1993.
19. John Wylie Lloyd. *Foundations of Logic Programming.* Springer, Berlin, Heidelberg, New York, 1987.
20. Suresh Manandhar. An attributive logic of set descriptions and set operations. In *Proceedings of the 32nd Annual Meeting of the Association for Computational Linguistics*, 1994.
21. Rainer Manthey and François Bry. SATCHMO: a theorem prover implemented in Prolog. In Ewing Lusk and Ross Overbeek, editors, *Proceedings of the 9th International Conference on Automated Deduction, Argonne, Illinois, USA, 1988*, pages 415–434. Springer, Berlin, Heidelberg, New York, 1988. In LNCS 310.
22. Chris S. Mellish. Implementing systemic classification by unification. *Computational Linguistics*, 14(1):40–51, 1988.
23. Chris S. Mellish. Term-encodable description spaces. In D. R. Brough, editor, *Logic Programming, New Frontiers*, pages 189–207. Intellect Books, 1992. Proceedings of the *Conference in Bristol, UK, 1990.*
24. Carl J. Pollard and M. Drew Moshier. Unifying partial description of sets. In Philip Hanson, editor, *Information, Language, and Cognition*, pages 285–322. University of British Columbia Press, Vancouver, BC, 1990.

25. Carl J. Pollard and Ivan A. Sag. *Information-Based Syntax and Semantics. Volume 1: Fundamentals.* CSLI, Leland Stanford Junior University, 1987. CSLI Lecture Notes 13.
26. Carl J. Pollard and Ivan A. Sag. *Head-Driven Phrase Structure Grammar.* University of Chicago Press, Chicago, London, 1994. CSLI publication.
27. Mike Reape. Domain union and word order variation in German. In John Nerbonne, Klaus Netter, and Carl Pollard, editors, *German in Head-Driven Phrase Structure Grammar*, chapter 5, pages 151–197. CSLI, Leland Stanford Junior University, 1994. CSLI Lecture Notes 46.
28. Ivan A. Sag. English relative clause constructions. *Journal of Linguistics*, 1997. To appear.
29. Patrick Saint-Dizier. *Advanced Logic Programming for Language Processing.* Academic Press, London, 1994.
30. Peter H. Schmitt and Wolfgang Wernecke. Tableau calculus for order-sorted logic. In Karl Hans Bläsius, Ulrich Hedtstück, and Claus-Rainer Rollinger, editors, *Sorts and Types in Artificial Intelligence*, pages 49–60, Berlin, Heidelberg, New York, 1989. Workshop, Eringerfeld, Springer. In LNAI 418.
31. Gert Smolka and Ralf Treinen. Records for logic programming. *Journal of Logic Programming*, 18:229–258, 1994.
32. Frieder Stolzenburg. Typisierte Merkmalstrukturen und HPSG. Eine Erweiterung von UBS in SEPIA. Diplomarbeit D 192, Universität Koblenz, 1992.
33. Frieder Stolzenburg. Membership-constraints and complexity in logic programming with sets. In Franz Baader and Klaus U. Schulz, editors, *Frontiers in Combining Systems*, pages 285–302. Kluwer Academic, Dordrecht, The Netherlands, 1996.
34. Frieder Stolzenburg and Martin Volk. UBS – Eine unifikationsbasierte Sprache zur Implementation von HPSG. *LDV-Forum*, 9(1):10–13, 1992.
35. Pascal Van Hentenryck. *Constraint Satisfaction in Logic Programming.* MIT Press, Cambridge, MA, London, England, 1989.

Representation Theorems for Residuated Groupoids

Marek Szczerba

Adam Mickiewicz University,
Faculty of Mathematics and Computer Science,
ul. Matejki 48/49, 60-769 Poznań, Poland

Abstract. In this paper we will prove two representation theorems for residuated groupoids with respect to two kinds of powerset frames: powerset residuated groupoids [4] and relativized relational frames [1]. They yield the strong completeness of the Non Associative Lambek Calculus with respect to these frames.

1 Introduction

In 1986 Buszkowski [3] established a completeness result for Lambek Calculus (LC) with respect to so-called generalized standard semantics i.e. powerset residuated semigroups over arbitrary semigroups. In this paper we will prove that every residuated groupoid is isomorphically embeddable into a powerset residuated groupoid. Whereas Buszkowski [3] and Kołowska [5] prove analogous results (for residuated semigroups and residuated algebras) by means of proof theoretic methods, which employ some special Labeled Deductive Systems, our proof is based on a direct, step by step, construction in the style of [1]. As a consequence, we obtain a completeness theorem for Non Associative Lambek Calculus (NLC).

Around 1988 van Benthem suggested a relational semantics for LC. In [2] he proves that LC is sound w.r.t. that kind of semantics. In [1], Andréka & Mikulás, prove that LC is complete w.r.t. relativized relational semantics. In fact they show that every residuated semigroup is isomorphically embeddable into a so-called representable relational structure. Here we define a notion of relativized relational residuated groupoid which is appropriate for NLC. We will show that every residuated groupoid is isomorphically embeddable into a relativized relational residuated groupoid, which yields the strong completeness of NLC with respect to the appropriate semantics.

Residuated groupoids considered in this paper are an essentially more general class of algebras than all kinds of implication algebraic structures discussed in Rasiowa [10], and the representation theorems proven there, although closely related to representation theorems for positive implication algebras and implication algebras from [10], require another treatment.

Powerset residuated groupoids are natural algebraic frames for minimal logics of types, recently studied in e.e. Moortgart [9] and Kurtonina [6] in the context of categorial grammar.

We start from the definition of a residuated groupoid.

Definition 1. An algebra $\mathcal{A} = \langle A, \cdot, \rightarrow, \leftarrow, \leqslant \rangle$ is called a ***residuated groupoid*** if $\langle A, \cdot \rangle$ is a groupoid, $\leqslant$ is a partial ordering and binary operations $\leftarrow$, $\rightarrow$ satisfy the equivalences:

$$(*) \qquad x \leqslant z \leftarrow y \ \text{ iff } \ x \cdot y \leqslant z \ \text{ iff } \ y \leqslant x \rightarrow z,$$

where $x, y, z \in A$.

Remark. For every residuated groupoid $\mathcal{A} = \langle A, \cdot, \rightarrow, \leftarrow, \leqslant \rangle$, $\leqslant$ satisfies the monotonicity condition:

$$\text{if } x \leqslant y \ \text{ then } \ x \cdot z \leqslant y \cdot z \text{ and } z \cdot x \leqslant z \cdot y,$$

where $x, y, z \in A$.

Proof. Assume $x \leqslant y$. Of course $y \cdot z \leqslant y \cdot z$, and by $(*)$, we have $y \leqslant (y \cdot z) \leftarrow z$. Since $\leqslant$ is partial ordering we obtain $x \leqslant (y \cdot z) \leftarrow z$. Again by $(*)$, we have $x \cdot z \leqslant y \cdot z$. The proof of the second inequality is similar. □

We recall the axiomatization of NLC. Formulas are built from atomic formulas (propositional variables) by means of three binary operation symbols: $\leftarrow, \rightarrow, \cdot$. Sequents are of the form $A \Rightarrow B$ where A, B are formulas. The axioms and rules of NLC are as follows [8]:

Axiom scheme: $A \Rightarrow A$.

Rules of inference:

$$\frac{A \cdot B \Rightarrow C}{A \Rightarrow C \leftarrow B} \qquad \frac{A \cdot B \Rightarrow C}{B \Rightarrow A \rightarrow C}$$

$$\frac{A \Rightarrow C \leftarrow B}{A \cdot B \Rightarrow C} \qquad \frac{B \Rightarrow A \rightarrow C}{A \cdot B \Rightarrow C}$$

$$\frac{A \Rightarrow B \quad B \Rightarrow C}{A \Rightarrow C}.$$

See also [8] for Gentzen-style version of NLC.

By standard methods of Lindenbaum algebras one proves the strong completeness of NLC with respect to residuated groupoids. Accordingly, our representation theorems immediatly imply the afore mentioned completeness theorems for NLC.

2 Relativized Relational Residuated Groupoids

Let U denote a nonempty set, and E a binary relation on it. We will consider three binary operations on $\mathcal{P}(E)$ defined as follows:

$$\begin{aligned} X \circ Y &= \{\langle x,y\rangle \in E \mid \exists z\,(\langle x,z\rangle \in X \;\&\; \langle z,y\rangle \in Y)\},\\ X \Rightarrow Y &= \{\langle x,y\rangle \in E \mid \forall u\,(\langle u,x\rangle \in X \;\&\; \langle u,y\rangle \in E \textit{ entail } \langle u,y\rangle \in Y)\},\\ Y \Leftarrow X &= \{\langle x,y\rangle \in E \mid \forall v\,(\langle y,v\rangle \in X \;\&\; \langle x,v\rangle \in E \textit{ entail } \langle x,v\rangle \in Y)\},\end{aligned}$$

where $X, Y \subseteq E$.

Lemma 2. *For every nonempty relation E the algebra $\langle \mathcal{P}(E), \circ, \Rightarrow, \Leftarrow, \subseteq\rangle$ is a residuated groupoid.*

Proof. For $X, Y, Z \subseteq E$ we show the equivalences:

$$X \subseteq Z \Leftarrow Y \text{ iff } X \circ Y \subseteq Z \text{ iff } Y \subseteq X \Rightarrow Z.$$

For the implication from left to right of the first equivalence, let us assume $X \subseteq Z \Leftarrow Y$ and $\langle x,y\rangle \in X \circ Y$. Hence there is z such that $\langle x,z\rangle \in X$ and $\langle z,y\rangle \in Y$. By assumption, $\langle x,y\rangle \in E$, and $\langle x,z\rangle \in Z \Leftarrow Y$, then we have $\langle x,y\rangle \in Z$. For the other direction, let $X \circ Y \subseteq Z$, $\langle x,y\rangle \in X$, $\langle y,z\rangle \in Y$ and $\langle x,z\rangle \in E$. Therefore $\langle x,z\rangle \in X \circ Y \subseteq Z$, and consequently $\langle x,y\rangle \in Z \Leftarrow Y$.

The same reasoning applies to the second equivalence. □

Definition 3. The algebra $\langle \mathcal{P}(E), \circ, \Leftarrow, \Rightarrow, \subseteq\rangle$, where E is a nonempty binary relation, will be called a *relativized relational residuated groupoid.*

Theorem 4. *Every residuated groupoid is isomorphically embeddable into a relativized relational residuated groupoid.*

Proof. Let $\mathcal{A} = \langle A, \cdot, \rightarrow, \leftarrow, \leqslant\rangle$ be a residuated groupoid. We build, step by step, a directed labelled graph $\mathbb{G} = \langle \mathbb{U}, \mathbb{E}, \mathbb{L}\rangle$ where $\mathbb{U}$ is the set of nodes, $\mathbb{E} \subseteq \mathbb{U} \times \mathbb{U}$ is the set of edges and $\mathbb{L} : \mathbb{E} \mapsto A$ is the labelling function. Function $\mathbb{L}$ of this graph will be used for defining a map:

$$h : \langle A, \cdot, \rightarrow, \leftarrow, \leqslant\rangle \mapsto \langle \mathcal{P}(\mathbb{E}), \circ, \Rightarrow, \Leftarrow, \subseteq\rangle,$$

$$h(a) = \{\langle x,y\rangle \in \mathbb{E} \mid \mathbb{L}(\langle x,y\rangle) \leqslant a\},$$

which will be an isomorphism. This graph we build in ω steps.

oth step We start from a graph $G = \langle U, E, L\rangle$, where

$$\begin{aligned} U &= \{u_a, v_a \mid a \in A\},\\ E &= \{\langle u_a, v_a\rangle \mid a \in A\},\\ L &= \{\langle\langle u_a, v_a\rangle, a\rangle \mid a \in A\}.\end{aligned}$$

$n+1$st step In this step we have graph $G_n = \langle U_n, E_n, L_n\rangle$ and, for every ordered triple $\langle\langle x,y\rangle,a,b\rangle \in (E_n \setminus E_{n-1}) \times A \times A$, we add two new elements: $u(x,y,a,b) = \langle\langle x,y\rangle,a,b,1\rangle$, $v(x,y,a,b) = \langle\langle x,y\rangle,a,b,2\rangle$, and if inequality $L_n(\langle x,y\rangle) \leqslant a\cdot b$ holds then we add one more element $z(x,y,a,b) = \langle\langle x,y\rangle,a,b,3\rangle$. To simplify the notation we write $L_n(x,y)$ instead of $L_n(\langle x,y\rangle)$ and u,v,z instead of $u(x,y,a,b), v(x,y,a,b), z(x,y,a,b)$ (see Fig. 1).

$$\begin{aligned}
U_{n+1} = {} & U_n \cup \{u,v \mid \langle\langle x,y\rangle,a,b\rangle \in (E_n \setminus E_{n-1}) \times A \times A\} \cup \\
& \cup \{z \mid \langle\langle x,y\rangle,a,b\rangle \in (E_n \setminus E_{n-1}) \times A \times A \,\&\, L_n(x,y) \leqslant a\cdot b\}, \\
E_{n+1} = {} & E_n \cup \{\langle u,x\rangle, \langle u,y\rangle, \langle x,v\rangle, \langle y,v\rangle \mid \langle\langle x,y\rangle,a,b\rangle \in (E_n \setminus E_{n-1}) \times A \times A\} \cup \\
& \cup \{\langle x,z\rangle, \langle z,y\rangle \mid \langle\langle x,y\rangle,a,b\rangle \in (E_n \setminus E_{n-1}) \times A \times A \,\&\, L_n(x,y) \leqslant a\cdot b\}, \\
L_{n+1} = {} & L_n \cup \{\langle\langle u,x\rangle,a\rangle, \langle\langle u,y\rangle, a\cdot L_n(x,y)\rangle, \langle\langle x,v\rangle, L_n(x,y)\cdot b\rangle, \langle\langle y,v\rangle,b\rangle \mid \\
& \quad \mid \langle\langle x,y\rangle,a,b\rangle \in (E_n \setminus E_{n-1}) \times A \times A\} \cup \\
& \cup \{\langle\langle x,z\rangle,a\rangle, \langle\langle z,y\rangle,b\rangle \mid \langle\langle x,y\rangle,a,b\rangle \in (E_n \setminus E_{n-1}) \times A \times A \,\& \\
& \quad L_n(x,y) \leqslant a\cdot b\}.
\end{aligned}$$

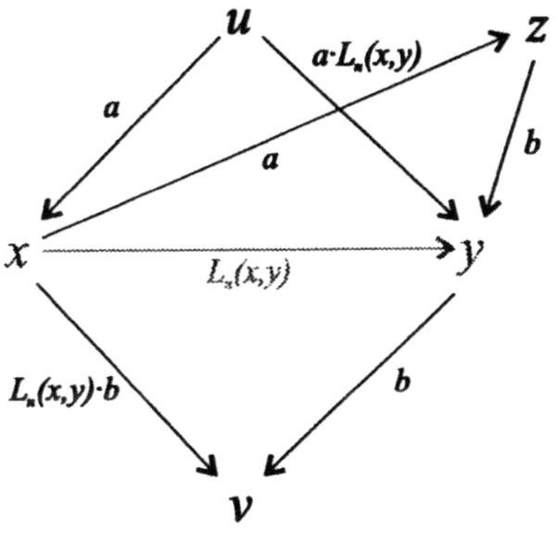

Fig. 1.

Let:

$$\mathbb{G} = \bigcup_{n\in\omega} G_n, \quad i.e.\ \mathbb{U} = \bigcup_{n\in\omega} U_n,\ \mathbb{E} = \bigcup_{n\in\omega} E_n,\ \mathbb{L} = \bigcup_{n\in\omega} L_n.$$

Lemma 5. *For every triangle in $\mathbb{E}$, i.e. $\langle x,y\rangle, \langle x,z\rangle, \langle z,y\rangle \in \mathbb{E}$, we have:*

$$\mathbb{L}(x,y) \leqslant \mathbb{L}(x,z)\cdot\mathbb{L}(z,y).$$

Proof. (induction by n). Since there are no triangles in G_0, the lemma holds for $n=0$. Assume the lamma holds for G_n, we will prove it for G_{n+1}. Let $\langle x,y\rangle, \langle x,z\rangle, \langle z,y\rangle$ be a triangle in G_{n+1} and not in G_n i.e. at least one pair belongs to E_{n+1}. Consider nodes of the triangle. Becouse in every pair, we add in $n+1$st step, one element is from U_n and the other from $U_{n+1} \setminus U_n$, there is no possibility that all of them are from U_n. For the same reason we have to exclude case that one of them belongs to U_n and the other two to $U_{n+1} \setminus U_n$. The only possibility is that two elements, out of the three one, are from U_n and the other is from U_{n+1}. Then, according to the ways of adding new elements to our graph, we have three subcases:

1. $x, y \in U_n, \langle x, y\rangle \in E_n$ and there are $a, b \in A$ such that $\mathbb{L}(x,y) \leqslant a \cdot b$. So we add element $z = \langle\langle x,y\rangle, a, b, 3\rangle$, and pairs $\langle x,z\rangle, \langle z,y\rangle$, and put $\mathbb{L}(x,z) = a, \mathbb{L}(z,y) = b$. Hence $\mathbb{L}(x,y) \leqslant \mathbb{L}(x,z) \cdot \mathbb{L}(z,y)$.
2. $x, z \in U_n, \langle x, z\rangle \in E_n$. Then for triple $\langle\langle x,z\rangle, a, b\rangle$ we add element $y = \langle\langle x,z\rangle, a, b, 2\rangle$, and pairs $\langle x,y\rangle, \langle z,y\rangle$, and put $\mathbb{L}(x,y) = \mathbb{L}(x,z) \cdot b, \mathbb{L}(z,y) = b$. Hence $\mathbb{L}(x,y) \leqslant \mathbb{L}(x,z) \cdot \mathbb{L}(z,y)$.
3. $z, y \in U_n, \langle z, y\rangle \in E_n$. Then for triple $\langle\langle z,y\rangle, a, b\rangle$ we add element $x = \langle\langle z,y\rangle, a, b, 1\rangle$, and pairs $\langle x,z\rangle, \langle x,y\rangle$, and put $\mathbb{L}(x,z) = a, \mathbb{L}(x,y) = a \cdot \mathbb{L}(z,y)$. Hence $\mathbb{L}(x,y) \leqslant \mathbb{L}(x,z) \cdot \mathbb{L}(z,y)$.

Now we have to show that h is a monomorphism.

1. We prove that h is an isomorphism w.r.t. $\leqslant$, i.e. $a \leqslant b$ iff $h(a) \subseteq h(b)$. Let $a \leqslant b$ and $\langle x,y\rangle \in h(a)$ i.e. $\mathbb{L}(x,y) \leqslant a$ but transitivity of $\leqslant$ gives us $\mathbb{L}(x,y) \leqslant b$, so $\langle x,y\rangle \in h(b)$. The other direction is easy since in 0th step we add: elements u_a, v_a, a pair $\langle u_a, v_a\rangle$ and put $L(u_a, v_a) = a$, now from assumption $\mathbb{L}(u_a, v_a) \leqslant b$.
2. From 1 and antisymmetry of $\subseteq$ we have that h is one-one.

   We check that h preserves the operations:
3. Checking: $h(a \cdot b) = h(a) \circ h(b)$.
   Inclusion from left to right implies from our construction: let $\langle x,y\rangle \in h(a \cdot b)$ then there is $n_0 = \min\{n \mid \langle x,y\rangle \in E_n\}$. In the $n_0 + 1$st step we add element $z = \langle\langle x,y\rangle, a, b, 3\rangle$ and pairs $\langle x,z\rangle, \langle z,y\rangle$ such that $L_{n_0+1}(x,z) = a, L_{n_0+1}(z,y) = b$, therefore $\langle x,y\rangle \in h(a) \circ h(b)$.
   For the other direction let us assume that $\langle x,y\rangle \in h(a) \circ h(b)$. Then there is z such that $\langle x,z\rangle \in h(a), \langle z,y\rangle \in h(b)$. From Lemma 5 we have $\mathbb{L}(x,y) \leqslant a \cdot b$.
4. Checking the operation $\rightarrow$: $h(a \rightarrow b) = h(a) \Rightarrow h(b)$.
   For inclusion from left to right let us assume that $\langle x,y\rangle \in h(a \rightarrow b)$ i.e. $\mathbb{L}(x,y) \leqslant a \rightarrow b$ and from (*) we have $a \cdot \mathbb{L}(x,y) \leqslant b$. Let $u \in \mathbb{U}$ and $\langle u,x\rangle, \langle u,y\rangle \in \mathbb{E}$ and $\mathbb{L}(u,x) \leqslant a$. Then from Lemma 5 we have $\mathbb{L}(u,y) \leqslant \mathbb{L}(u,x) \cdot \mathbb{L}(x,y) \leqslant a \cdot \mathbb{L}(x,y) \leqslant b$, so $\langle x,y\rangle \in h(a) \Rightarrow h(b)$.
   For the other direction let $\langle x,y\rangle \in h(a) \Rightarrow h(b)$ and $n_0 = \min\{n \mid \langle x,y\rangle \in E_n\}$. Then in the $n_0 + 1$st step we add element $u = \langle\langle x,y\rangle, a, b, 1\rangle$, and pairs $\langle u,x\rangle, \langle u,y\rangle$, and put $L_{n_0+1}(u,x) = a, L_{n_0+1}(u,y) = a \cdot L_{n_0}(x,y)$. Of course $\langle u,x\rangle \in h(a)$ and $\langle u,y\rangle \in \mathbb{E}$ then $\langle u,y\rangle \in h(b)$, so $a \cdot L_{n_0}(x,y) \leqslant b$ and from (*) we have $L_{n_0}(x,y) \leqslant a \rightarrow b$.
5. Checking the operation $\leftarrow$: $h(b \leftarrow a) = h(b) \Leftarrow h(a)$.
   This case is similar to the previous one.

□

3 Powerset Residuated Groupoids

Let $\mathcal{B} = \langle B, \bullet \rangle$ be a groupoid. We define three binary operations on $\mathcal{P}(B)$ as follows:

$$X \circ Y = \{x \bullet y \mid x \in X,\ y \in Y\},$$
$$X \Rightarrow Y = \{z \in B \mid \forall x (x \in X \textit{ entail } x \bullet z \in Y\},$$
$$Y \Leftarrow X = \{z \in B \mid \forall x (x \in X \textit{ entail } z \bullet x \in Y\},$$

where $X, Y \subseteq B$.

In [4] the algebra $\langle \mathcal{P}(B), \circ, \Leftarrow, \Rightarrow, \subseteq \rangle$ is called *the powerset residuated groupoid over* $\langle B, \bullet \rangle$. It is easy to show that every powerset residuated groupoid is a residuated groupoid.

Theorem 6. *Every residuated groupoid is isomorphically embeddable into a powerset residuated groupoid.*

Proof. Let $\mathcal{A} = \langle A, \cdot, \leftarrow, \rightarrow, \leqslant \rangle$ be a residuated groupoid. For the proof of this theorem we build a partially ordered groupoid $\mathcal{B} = \langle B, \bullet, \preccurlyeq \rangle$ which is a superstructure of $\langle A, \cdot\ \leqslant \rangle$ and we will show that mapping $h : \mathcal{A} \longmapsto \mathcal{P}(B)$, defined as:

$$h(a) = \{c \in B \mid c \preccurlyeq a\},$$

is a monomorphism. This groupoid we build in ω steps.

oth step $B_0 = A,\ \ \cdot_0 = \cdot,\ \ \leqslant_0 = \leqslant .$

$n + 1$st step In this step we have the groupoid $\mathcal{B}_n = \langle B_n, \cdot_n, \leqslant_n \rangle$ and for every ordered triple $\langle c, a, b \rangle \in (B_n \setminus B_{n-1}) \times A \times A$, such that inequality $c \leqslant_n a \cdot b$ holds, we add two new elements c^1_{ab}, c^2_{ab} and for them we define $\leqslant_{n+1}, \cdot_{n+1}$ as follows:

1. for $x \in A$:
   $c^1_{ab} \leqslant_{n+1} x$ iff $a \leqslant x$,
   $c^2_{ab} \leqslant_{n+1} x$ iff $b \leqslant x$,
2. $c^1_{ab} \cdot_{n+1} c^1_{ab} = a \cdot a$,
   $c^1_{ab} \cdot_{n+1} c^2_{ab} = c$,
   $c^2_{ab} \cdot_{n+1} c^1_{ab} = b \cdot a$,
   $c^2_{ab} \cdot_{n+1} c^2_{ab} = b \cdot b$,
3. for $x \in A$:
   $c^1_{ab} \cdot_{n+1} x = a \cdot x$,
   $c^2_{ab} \cdot_{n+1} x = b \cdot x$,
   $x \cdot_{n+1} c^1_{ab} = x \cdot a$,
   $x \cdot_{n+1} c^2_{ab} = x \cdot b$,

4. for $x \in B_{n+1} \setminus \{c^1_{ab}, c^2_{ab}\}$:
   $c^1_{ab} \cdot_{n+1} x = a \cdot_{n+1} x,$
   $c^2_{ab} \cdot_{n+1} x = b \cdot_{n+1} x,$
   $x \cdot_{n+1} c^1_{ab} = x \cdot_{n+1} a,$
   $x \cdot_{n+1} c^2_{ab} = x \cdot_{n+1} b.$

Let us notice that definition (iv) is correct e.g. for $x = c^1_{ab}, y = f^2_{de}$ we have:

$$x \cdot_{n+1} y = c^1_{ab} \cdot_{n+1} f^2_{de} = \begin{cases} a \cdot_{n+1} f^2_{de} = a \cdot e \\ c^1_{ab} \cdot_{n+1} e = a \cdot e \end{cases}$$

Let $\mathcal{B} = \langle B, \bullet, \preccurlyeq \rangle = \langle \bigcup_{n \in \omega} B_n, \bigcup_{n \in \omega} \cdot_n, \bigcup_{n \in \omega} \leqslant_n \rangle$.

Lemma 7. *For every $x, y \in B$ and $u, v \in A$ if $x \preccurlyeq u, y \preccurlyeq v$ then $x \bullet y \preccurlyeq u \cdot v$.*

Proof. (by induction). Case $n = 0$ is easy. Let us assume the lemma is true for B_{n-1}. We have two cases:

1. $x \in B_n, y \in B_{n-1}$, (for the case $x \in B_{n-1}, y \in B_n$ we procced in a similar way).
   Then, x was added in the nth step, so there are $c \in B_{n-1}$ and $a, b \in A$ such that $c \leqslant_{n-1} a \cdot b$ and we have two subcases:
   (a) $x = c^1_{ab}$, then by (i) we have $a \leqslant u$, so $c^1_{ab} \cdot_n y \overset{(iv)}{=} a \cdot_n y = a \cdot_{n-1} y$ and by induction $a \cdot_{n-1} y \leqslant_{n-1} a \cdot v$, but $a \cdot v \leqslant u \cdot v$ hence, $c^1_{ab} \cdot_n y \leqslant_n u \cdot v$.
   (b) $x = c^2_{ab}$, then by (i) we have $b \leqslant u$, so $c^2_{ab} \cdot_n y \overset{(iv)}{=} b \cdot_n y = b \cdot_{n-1} y$ and by induction $b \cdot_{n-1} y \leqslant_{n-1} b \cdot v$, but $b \cdot v \leqslant u \cdot v$ hence, $c^2_{ab} \cdot_n y \leqslant_n u \cdot v$.
2. $x, y \in B_n$. We have two subcases:
   (a) x, y were not formed out of the same triple. For this case we have four possibilities: $x = c^1_{ab}, y = f^1_{de}; x = c^1_{ab}, y = f^2_{de}; x = c^2_{ab}, y = f^1_{de}; x = c^2_{ab}, y = f^2_{de}$. We will show only one case, the other are similar: $x \cdot_n y = c^1_{ab} \cdot_n f^2_{de} \overset{(iv)}{=} a \cdot e \overset{(i)}{\leqslant} u \cdot v$.
   (b) x, y were formed out of the same triple. For this case we have four posibillities:
   $x = c^1_{ab}, y = c^1_{ab}$ then by (i) $a \leqslant u, a \leqslant v$ so $x \cdot_n y \overset{(ii)}{=} a \cdot a \leqslant u \cdot v,$
   $x = c^1_{ab}, y = c^2_{ab}$ then by (i) $a \leqslant u, b \leqslant v$ so $x \cdot_n y \overset{(ii)}{=} c \leqslant_n a \cdot b \leqslant u \cdot v,$
   $x = c^2_{ab}, y = c^1_{ab}$ then by (i) $a \leqslant v, b \leqslant u$ so $x \cdot_n y \overset{(ii)}{=} b \cdot a \leqslant u \cdot v,$
   $x = c^2_{ab}, y = c^2_{ab}$ then by (i) $b \leqslant u, b \leqslant v$ so $x \cdot_n y \overset{(ii)}{=} b \cdot b \leqslant u \cdot v.$

□

Since $\preccurlyeq \subseteq B \times A$ Lemma 7 shows us that $\langle B, \bullet, \preccurlyeq \rangle$ is a partially ordered groupoid.

Lemma 8. *For every $x \in B$ and $u, v \in A$ if $u \bullet x \preccurlyeq v$ then $x \preccurlyeq u \to v$.*

Proof. Since $A \subseteq B$ we have two casses $x \in A$ and $x \in B \setminus A$. The first case is easy becouse in A we have $(*)$. For the second case there are $n, \langle c, a, b \rangle \in (B_{n-1} \setminus B_{n-2}) \times A \times A$ such that $c \leqslant_{n-1} a \cdot b$ and we have two subcases:

1. $x = c^1_{ab}$, then $u \cdot_n c^1_{ab} \overset{(iii)}{=} u \cdot a \leqslant v$ and from $(*)$ $a \leqslant u \to v$, then by (i) $c^1_{ab} \leqslant u \to v$,
2. $x = c^2_{ab}$, then $u \cdot_n c^2_{ab} \overset{(iii)}{=} u \cdot b \leqslant v$ and from $(*)$ $b \leqslant u \to v$, then by (i) $c^2_{ab} \leqslant u \to v$.

□

Lemma 9. *For every $x \in B; u, v \in A$ if $x \bullet u \preccurlyeq v$ then $x \preccurlyeq v \leftarrow u$.*

Proof. Like in the previous lemma. □

Lemma 10. *For every $x \in B; u, v \in A$ if $x \preccurlyeq u \cdot v$ then there are elements $s, t \in B$ such that $s \preccurlyeq u$, $t \preccurlyeq v$ and $x = s \bullet t$.*

Proof. If $x \in B$ then there is n such that x was added in the nth step. But from assumption $x \leqslant_n u \cdot v$ then in the $n+1$st step we add elements x^1_{uv}, x^2_{uv} and put $x^1_{uv} \leqslant_{n+1} u, x^2_{uv} \leqslant_{n+1} v, x^1_{uv} \cdot_{n+1} x^2_{uv} = x$. □

Now we have to show that h is a monomorphism.

1. We prove that h is an isomorphism w.r.t. $\leqslant$ i.e. $u \leqslant v$ iff $h(u) \subseteq h(v)$. From (i) and transitivity of $\leqslant$ in A we have inclusion from left to right. The other direction is easy.
2. From 1 and antisymmetry of $\subseteq$ we have that h is one-one.
3. Checking: $h(u \cdot v) = h(u) \circ h(v)$. From Lemma 10 we have inclusion from left to right, whereas the other inclusion from Lemma 7.
4. Checking the operation $\to$: $h(u \to v) = h(u) \Rightarrow h(v)$. For inclusion from left to right let $x \preccurlyeq u \to v$ and take $y \in B$ such that $y \leqslant u$. From Lemma 7 we have $y \bullet x \preccurlyeq u \cdot (u \to v)$ and from $(*)$ we know that $u \cdot (u \to v) \leqslant v$ hence $y \bullet x \leqslant v$. For the other direction let $x \in h(u) \Rightarrow h(v)$. Then $u \bullet x \preccurlyeq v$, since $u \in h(u)$. From Lemma 8 we have $x \preccurlyeq u \to v$.
5. Checking the operation $\leftarrow$: $h(v \leftarrow u) = h(v) \Leftarrow h(u)$. Proof of this case is like the proof of the previous case but instead Lemma 8 we use Lemma 9.

□

References

1. Andréka, H., Mikulás, Sz., "Lambek Calculus and its Relational Semantics: Completeness and Incompleteness", *Journal of Logic, Language and Information*, 3(1), 1994.
2. van Benthem, J., *Language in action*, North-Holland, Amsterdam, 1991.
3. Buszkowski, W., "Completeness results for Lambek Syntactic Calculus", *Zeitschr. f. math. Logik und Grundlagen d. Math.*, 32, 13-28, 1986

4. Buszkowski, W., "Mathematical Linguistics and Proof Theory", in J. van Benthem and A. ter Menlen (eds.), *Handbook of Logic and Language*, North Holland, Amsterdam, to appear.
5. Kołowska-Gawiejnowicz, M., "Powerset Residuated Algebras and Generalized Lambek Calculus", *Mathematical Logic Quarterly*, to appear.
6. Kurtonina, N., Frames and Labels. A Model Analysis of Categorial Inference, Ph.D. Thesis, University of Utrecht, 1995.
7. Lambek, J., "The mathematics of sentence structure", *American Mathematical Monthly*, 65, 154-170, 1958.
8. Lambek, J. "On the calculus of syntactic types", in R. Jacobson (ed.), *Structure of Language and Its Mathematical Aspects*, AMS, Providence, 1961.
9. Moortgat, "Categorial Gramar", in: J. van Benthem and A. ter Menlen (eds.), *Handbook of Logic and Language*, North Holland, Amsterdam, to appear.
10. Rasiowa, H., An algebraic approach to non-classical logics, Polish Scientific Publishers and North Holland, Amsterdam, 1974.

Author Index

Springer and the environment

At Springer we firmly believe that an international science publisher has a special obligation to the environment, and our corporate policies consistently reflect this conviction.
We also expect our business partners – paper mills, printers, packaging manufacturers, etc. – to commit themselves to using materials and production processes that do not harm the environment. The paper in this book is made from low- or no-chlorine pulp and is acid free, in conformance with international standards for paper permanency.

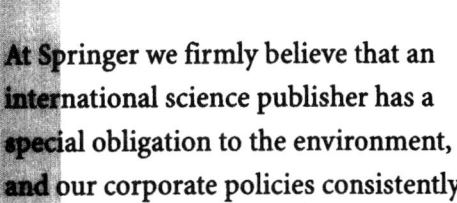

Lecture Notes in Artificial Intelligence (LNAI)

Vol. 1187: K. Schlechta, Nonmonotonic Logics. IX, 243 pages. 1997.

Vol. 1188: T.P. Martin, A.L. Ralescu (Eds.), Fuzzy Logic in Artificial Intelligence. Proceedings, 1995. VIII, 272 pages. 1997.

Vol. 1193: J.P. Müller, M.J. Wooldridge, N.R. Jennings (Eds.), Intelligent Agents III. XV, 401 pages. 1997.

Vol. 1195: R. Trappl, P. Petta (Eds.), Creating Personalities for Synthetic Actors. VII, 251 pages. 1997.

Vol. 1198: H. S. Nwana, N. Azarmi (Eds.), Software Agents and Soft Computing: Towards Enhancing Machine Intelligents. XIV, 298 pages. 1997.

Vol. 1202: P. Kandzia, M. Klusch (Eds.), Cooperative Information Agents. Proceedings, 1997. IX, 287 pages. 1997.

Vol. 1208: S. Ben-David (Ed.), Computational Learning Theory. Proceedings, 1997. VIII, 331 pages. 1997.

Vol. 1209: L. Cavedon, A. Rao, W. Wobcke (Eds.), Intelligent Agent Systems. Proceedings, 1996. IX, 188 pages. 1997.

Vol. 1211: E. Keravnou, C. Garbay, R. Baud, J. Wyatt (Eds.), Artificial Intelligence in Medicine. Proceedings, 1997. XIII, 526 pages. 1997.

Vol. 1216: J. Dix, L. Moniz Pereira, T.C. Przymusinski (Eds.), Non-Monotonic Extensions of Logic Programming. Proceedings, 1996. XI, 224 pages. 1997.

Vol. 1221: G. Weiß (Ed.), Distributed Artificial Intelligence Meets Machine Learning. Proceedings, 1996. X, 294 pages. 1997.

Vol. 1224: M. van Someren, G. Widmer (Eds.), Machine Learning: ECML-97. Proceedings, 1997. XI, 361 pages. 1997.

Vol. 1227: D. Galmiche (Ed.), Automated Reasoning with Analytic Tableaux and Related Methods. Proceedings, 1997. XI, 373 pages. 1997.

Vol. 1228: S.-H. Nienhuys-Cheng, R. de Wolf, Foundations of Inductive Logic Programming. XVII, 404 pages. 1997.

Vol. 1229: G. Kraetzschmar, Distributed Reason Maintenance for Multiagent Systems. XIV, 296 pages. 1997.

Vol. 1236: E. Maier, M. Mast, S. LuperFoy (Eds.), Dialogue Processing in Spoken Language Systems. Proceedings, 1996. VIII, 220 pages. 1997.

Vol. 1237: M. Boman, W. Van de Velde (Eds.), Multi-Agent Rationality. Proceedings, 1997. XII, 254 pages. 1997.

Vol. 1244: D. M. Gabbay, R. Kruse, A. Nonnengart, H.J. Ohlbach (Eds.), Qualitative and Quantitative Practical Reasoning. Proceedings, 1997. X, 621 pages. 1997.

Vol. 1249: W. McCune (Ed.), Automated Deduction – CADE-14. Proceedings, 1997. XIV, 462 pages. 1997.

Vol. 1257: D. Lukose, H. Delugach, M. Keeler, L. Searle, J. Sowa (Eds.), Conceptual Structures: Fulfilling Peirce's Dream. Proceedings, 1997. XII, 621 pages. 1997.

Vol. 1263: J. Komorowski, J. Zytkow (Eds.), Principles of Data Mining and Knowledge Discovery. Proceedings, 1997. IX, 397 pages. 1997.

Vol. 1266: D.B. Leake, E. Plaza (Eds.), Case-Based Reasoning Research and Development. Proceedings, 1997. XIII, 648 pages. 1997.

Vol. 1265: J. Dix, U. Furbach, A. Nerode (Eds.), Logic Programming and Nonmonotonic Reasoning. Proceedings, 1997. X, 453 pages. 1997.

Vol. 1285: X. Jao, J.-H. Kim, T. Furuhashi (Eds.), Simulated Evolution and Learning. Proceedings, 1996. VIII, 231 pages. 1997.

Vol. 1286: C. Zhang, D. Lukose (Eds.), Multi-Agent Systems. Proceedings, 1996. VII, 195 pages. 1997.

Vol. 1297: N. Lavrač, S. Džeroski (Eds.), Inductive Logic Programming. Proceedings, 1997. VIII, 309 pages. 1997.

Vol. 1299: M.T. Pazienza (Ed.), Information Extraction. Proceedings, 1997. IX, 213 pages. 1997.

Vol. 1303: G. Brewka, C. Habel, B. Nebel (Eds.), KI-97: Advances in Artificial Intelligence. Proceedings, 1997. XI, 413 pages. 1997.

Vol. 1307: R. Kompe, Prosody in Speech Understanding Systems. XIX, 357 pages. 1997.

Vol. 1314: S. Muggleton (Ed.), Inductive Logic Programming. Proceedings, 1996. VIII, 397 pages. 1997.

Vol. 1316: M.Li, A. Maruoka (Eds.), Algorithmic Learning Theory. Proceedings, 1997. XI, 461 pages. 1997.

Vol. 1317: M. Leman (Ed.), Music, Gestalt, and Computing. IX, 524 pages. 1997.

Vol. 1319: E. Plaza, R. Benjamins (Eds.), Knowledge Acquisition, Modelling and Management. Proceedings, 1997. XI, 389 pages. 1997.

Vol. 1321: M. Lenzerini (Ed.), AI*IA 97: Advances in Artificial Intelligence. Proceedings, 1997. XII, 459 pages. 1997.

Vol. 1323: E. Costa, A. Cardoso (Eds.), Progress in Artificial Intelligence. Proceedings, 1997. XIV, 393 pages. 1997.

Vol. 1325: Z.W. Raś, A. Skowron (Eds.), Foundations of Intelligent Systems. Proceedings, 1997. XI, 630 pages. 1997

Vol. 1328: C. Retoré (Ed.), Logical Aspects of Computational Linguistics. Proceedings, 1996. VIII, 435 pages. 1997.

Lecture Notes in Computer Science

Vol. 1297: N. Lavrač, S. Džeroski (Eds.), Inductive Logic Programming. Proceedings, 1997. VIII, 309 pages. 1997. (Subseries LNAI).

Vol. 1298: M. Hanus, J. Heering, K. Meinke (Eds.), Algebraic and Logic Programming. Proceedings, 1997. X, 286 pages. 1997.

Vol. 1299: M.T. Pazienza (Ed.), Information Extraction. Proceedings, 1997. IX, 213 pages. 1997. (Subseries LNAI).

Vol. 1300: C. Lengauer, M. Griebl, S. Gorlatch (Eds.), Euro-Par'97 Parallel Processing. Proceedings, 1997. XXX, 1379 pages. 1997.

Vol. 1301: M. Jazayeri, H. Schauer (Eds.), Software Engineering - ESEC/FSE'97. Proceedings, 1997. XIII, 532 pages. 1997.

Vol. 1302: P. Van Hentenryck (Ed.), Static Analysis. Proceedings, 1997. X, 413 pages. 1997.

Vol. 1303: G. Brewka, C. Habel, B. Nebel (Eds.), KI-97: Advances in Artificial Intelligence. Proceedings, 1997. XI, 413 pages. 1997. (Subseries LNAI).

Vol. 1304: W. Luk, P.Y.K. Cheung, M. Glesner (Eds.), Field-Programmable Logic and Applications. Proceedings, 1997. XI, 503 pages. 1997.

Vol. 1305: D. Corne, J.L. Shapiro (Eds.), Evolutionary Computing. Proceedings, 1997. X, 313 pages. 1997.

Vol. 1307: R. Kompe, Prosody in Speech Understanding Systems. XIX, 357 pages. 1997. (Subseries LNAI).

Vol. 1308: A. Hameurlain, A M. Tjoa (Eds.), Database and Expert Systems Applications. Proceedings, 1997. XVII, 688 pages. 1997.

Vol. 1309: R. Steinmetz, L.C. Wolf (Eds.), Interactive Distributed Multimedia Systems and Telecommunication Services. Proceedings, 1997. XIII, 466 pages. 1997.

Vol. 1310: A. Del Bimbo (Ed.), Image Analysis and Processing. Proceedings, 1997. Volume I. XXII, 722 pages. 1997.

Vol. 1311: A. Del Bimbo (Ed.), Image Analysis and Processing. Proceedings, 1997. Volume II. XXII, 794 pages. 1997.

Vol. 1312: A. Geppert, M. Berndtsson (Eds.), Rules in Database Systems. Proceedings, 1997. VII, 214 pages. 1997.

Vol. 1313: J. Fitzgerald, C.B. Jones, P. Lucas (Eds.), FME '97: Industrial Applications and Strengthened Foundations of Formal Methods. Proceedings, 1997. XIII, 685 pages. 1997.

Vol. 1314: S. Muggleton (Ed.), Inductive Logic Programming. Proceedings, 1996. VIII, 397 pages. 1997. (Subseries LNAI).

Vol. 1315: G. Sommer, J.J. Koenderink (Eds.), Algebraic Frames for the Perception-Action Cycle. Proceedings, 1997. VIII, 395 pages. 1997.

Vol. 1316: M. Li, A. Maruoka (Eds.), Algorithmic Learning Theory. Proceedings, 1997. XI, 461 pages. 1997. (Subseries LNAI).

Vol. 1317: M. Leman (Ed.), Music, Gestalt, and Computing. IX, 524 pages. 1997. (Subseries LNAI).

Vol. 1318: R. Hirschfeld (Ed.), Financial Cryptography. Proceedings, 1997. XI, 409 pages. 1997.

Vol. 1319: E. Plaza, R. Benjamins (Eds.), Knowledge Acquisition, Modeling and Management. Proceedings, 1997. XI, 389 pages. 1997. (Subseries LNAI).

Vol. 1320: M. Mavronicolas, P. Tsigas (Eds.), Distributed Algorithms. Proceedings, 1997. X, 333 pages. 1997.

Vol. 1321: M. Lenzerini (Ed.), AI*IA 97: Advances in Artificial Intelligence. Proceedings, 1997. XII, 459 pages. 1997. (Subseries LNAI).

Vol. 1322: H. Hußmann, Formal Foundations for Software Engineering Methods. X, 286 pages. 1997.

Vol. 1323: E. Costa, A. Cardoso (Eds.), Progress in Artificial Intelligence. Proceedings, 1997. XIV, 393 pages. 1997. (Subseries LNAI).

Vol. 1324: C. Peters, C. Thanos (Ed.), Research and Advanced Technology for Digital Libraries. Proceedings, 1997. X, 423 pages. 1997.

Vol. 1325: Z.W. Raś, A. Skowron (Eds.), Foundations of Intelligent Systems. Proceedings, 1997. XI, 630 pages. 1997. (Subseries LNAI).

Vol. 1326: C. Nicholas, J. Mayfield (Eds.), Intelligent Hypertext. XIV, 182 pages. 1997.

Vol. 1327: W. Gerstner, A. Germond, M. Hasler, J.-D. Nicoud (Eds.), Artificial Neural Networks – ICANN '97. Proceedings, 1997. XIX, 1274 pages. 1997.

Vol. 1328: C. Retoré (Ed.), Logical Aspects of Computational Linguistics. Proceedings, 1996. VIII, 435 pages. 1997. (Subseries LNAI).

Vol. 1329: S.C. Hirtle, A.U. Frank (Eds.), Spatial Information Theory. Proceedings, 1997. XIV, 511 pages. 1997.

Vol. 1330: G. Smolka (Ed.), Principles and Practice of Constraint Programming – CP 97. Proceedings, 1997. XII, 563 pages. 1997.

Vol. 1331: D. Embley, R. Goldstein (Eds.), Conceptual Modeling – ER '97. Proceedings, 1997. XV, 479 pages. 1997.

Vol. 1332: M. Bubak, J. Dongarra, J. Waśniewski (Eds.), Recent Advances in Parallel Virtual Machine and Message Passing Interface. Proceedings, 1997. XV, 518 pages. 1997.

GPSR Compliance

The European Union's (EU) General Product Safety Regulation (GPSR) is a set of rules that requires consumer products to be safe and our obligations to ensure this.

If you have any concerns about our products, you can contact us on ProductSafety@springernature.com

In case Publisher is established outside the EU, the EU authorized representative is:

Springer Nature Customer Service Center GmbH
Europaplatz 3
69115 Heidelberg, Germany

Batch number: 09624486

Printed by Printforce, the Netherlands